A HISTORY OF MODERN BURMA

Burma

A HISTORY OF MODERN BURMA

By *John F. Cady*

PROFESSOR OF HISTORY

OHIO UNIVERSITY

❖

CORNELL UNIVERSITY PRESS

ITHACA, NEW YORK

This work has been brought to publication with the assistance of a grant from the Ford Foundation.

PRINTED IN THE UNITED STATES OF AMERICA BY THE
VAIL-BALLOU PRESS, INC., BINGHAMTON, NEW YORK

Preface

EVENTS of World War II and of the years following thereafter have rendered obsolete virtually all earlier interpretations of the modern history of Burma. The new situation has completely invalidated the older perspective, which usually called for describing the quaint life and folkways of the Burmese people or for portraying the somewhat painful progress of economic and governmental modernization of the country under British rule. Several prewar British students of Burma, notably John S. Furnivall and Maurice Collis, sensed the importance of ascertaining what colonial "advancement" was doing to Burmese society and of counteracting, if possible, the causes of growing social demoralization and political unrest. But Collis was a literary man who dealt in episodes, and Furnivall wrote as an economic analyst and a critic of contemporaneous British policy. Neither attempted to present a systematic account of political developments. Even the American author, John L. Christian, refused to take seriously Burmese aspirations for self-rule and political independence. World War II and succeeding events have forced the acceptance of a new perspective of renaissant Burmese nationalism and have resulted in the re-emergence of independent Burma among the free nations of the world. Perhaps the required reorientation may be somewhat easier for an American student to achieve than for Britons who may have been too closely identified with the prewar point of view.

The purpose of this book is to set forth in a systematic way what happened politically to Burma and to the Burmese people during the last century and a half. In this context, the period of British rule becomes simply another episode, although a very memorable one, in an older national existence which has now reappeared as the tides of European imperialism have receded. Twentieth-century Burma can never return to the pattern of the eighteenth century, for both the country itself and its world relationships, political, economic, and cultural, have unalterably changed. But the inscrutable images of the Buddha and the imposing spire of the Shwe Dagon pagoda which saw the foreign armies come to Rangoon in 1824 have now witnessed their departure, and the new chapter of Burma's history must perforce have some relevance to the older one. The book will therefore describe at the outset the traditional institutions of old Burma, political, social, and cultural, and indicate how these were altered by British rule. The central theme will be the revival of the Burmese national spirit, beginning directly prior to and during World War I and coming into full discordant expression in the two decades following 1920. The concluding chapters will describe the effects of World War II and the circumstances under which Burma's political freedom was reestablished. Enough attention will be given to peripheral factors, economic, social, and religious, to provide a meaningful context for the narrative of political events.

A major difficulty, as well as an advantage, arises from the circumstance that the sources available for the history of Burma since 1800 are almost entirely in English. The historical chronicles prepared under the direction of the Burmese kings of this period are either nonexistent or else woefully inaccurate. The English sources include an enormous mass of undigested manuscript and printed material deposited in the Library Archives of the India Office in London and available at present only to 1901. More easily accessible are the published *Debates* and *Sessional Papers* of the British Parliament, plus the special studies and minutes of hearings developed in connection with successive British reform programs. To these must be added the English versions of numerous special investigations authorized from time to time by the Rangoon authorities plus the voluminous annual departmental reports and legislative proceedings of the Burma Government. Finally must be considered the scores of private memoirs, monographs, and travel accounts, both official and nonofficial in origin, extending over the century and a half under consideration.

The principal problem in interpreting Burma's history since 1800 arises from the one-sided character of these English-language sources, which inevitably portray the foreigners' version of events and reflect basic assumptions often at variance with the Burmese point of view. Both detachment and imagination are required in dealing with them. One is reminded of the dilemma of Plato's man in the cave who was capable of observing only shadows cast on the interior wall by passers-by. Clearly Burmese attitudes and motivation constitute the essential context for any account of basic political developments within the country. It is also difficult to attempt to explain and understand without seeming to justify or condemn.

Under the circumstances, any current historical interpretation can be regarded at best as only approximately correct and at present manifestly far from complete. A definitive account, even from the viewpoint of the English sources alone, will have to await the accessibility of the London archives since 1901 and the assimilation in a series of monographs of an immense mass of archival data going back to 1885. To this would have to be added in time the contributions of trained Burmese scholars dealing with their own sources and points of view. But a start has to be made in utilizing the sources which are at hand. A pioneer work, if carefully documented, can afford a valuable working base from which others later can fill in gaps and make necessary adjustments and reinterpretations.

My interest in the history of Burma dates from a short-term appointment, from 1935 to 1938, as Lecturer in History at Judson College, then part of Rangoon University. Subsequent assignments in Washington from 1943 to 1949 in the Office of Strategic Services and the Department of State made me keenly aware of the urgent need for a systematic political history of Burma. This study was begun in serious fashion in 1952, when I was serving as Visiting Professor of History in connection with Cornell's Southeast Asia Program. Materials available at the Library of Congress and in the archives of the American Baptist Foreign Mission Society at New York were examined with the assistance of a summer's grant-in-aid from the Social Science Research Council. The completion of the study was made possible through a 1955–1956 Fulbright Research grant in Burma, coupled with a Guggenheim Foundation award. The latter made possible a month's additional study in London en route home from Rangoon.

The voluntary undertaking of so arduous an assignment cannot be explained on the basis of sheer scholarly enthusiasm or personal curiosity. It stems in some measure at least from an interest developed in

Burma's varied peoples during the course of two decades and from a kind of vicarious concern for the political future of that country now free to work out its destiny. Burma needs to appraise itself quite as much as outsiders need to understand Burma. The country casts a kind of spell over its friends which they cannot break if they would. An insistent inner compulsion obliged me to undertake the task. The Burmese might say that the *nat* spirits drove me to it.

I have tried to present a detached and understanding account with a minimum of partisanship. Readers will recognize, I am sure, that the actors in the drama, both British and Burmese, frequently faced limited alternative choices; they were caught in the maelstrom of circumstances. Not all the admirable characters were included among the "nationalist patriots," and not all the selfish exploiters and demagogues were within the ranks of the "imperialist" foreigners. In any case, the picture of what happened is now far clearer to me than it was when I embarked upon the undertaking.

The author tenders his thanks to Longmans, Green & Co. for permission to quote from *A Civil Servant in Burma* by Sir Herbert Thirkell White, to Routledge & Kegan Paul, Ltd., for a quotation from *The Loyal Karens of Burma* by Donald Mackenzie Smeaton, and to U Thant of Burma for a quotation from an article by him in *New Burma* (1939).

A special word of thanks is due to a number of Burmese scholar friends at Rangoon University who read virtually the entire manuscript, especially to Professor U Kyaw Thet of the History Department and to the late U Kaung of the Historical Commission of the Union of Burma. Responsibility is mine for all factual data and for their interpretation as well. Finally, my thanks are due to a fellow Fulbrighter, Mrs. Johnanna Gibson, for her loyal co-operation in preparing the typed manuscript.

JOHN F. CADY

Athens, Ohio
May 1957

Social Developments under British Rule, 94. The Reign of Mindon Min, 1852–1878, 99. Foreign Relations of Burma under
Mindon Min, 1852–1878, 104. The Reign of King Thibaw, 1878–
1885, 111. The Deposition of King Thibaw, 116.

Contents

Illustrations

Part One

OLD BURMA AND
ITS DISAPPEARANCE

I

The Government of
Old Burma

KINGSHIP and governmental authority in eighteenth-century Burma stemmed from basic political and religious sanctions originating centuries earlier in ancient India. The standard India pattern of royalty had been borrowed by Burma's Pagan dynasty (eleventh to thirteenth centuries) either directly from India or from the conquered Mon Court at its Thaton capital in Lower Burma. The system was reproduced successively by Upper Burma's Thai rulers during the fourteenth and fifteenth centuries and again by the revived Burman Toungoo dynasty in the latter half of the 1500's. When the country was unified by the Burmans for the third time in the mid-eighteenth century by King Alaungpaya, himself a mere township headman of Moksobo (Shwebo), a labored effort was apparently made to revive all the traditional regalia of the court as well as other customary means of authenticating royal power. This traditional basis of divine kingship on the Indian model was finally destroyed in 1885 when the British Government erased the Burma Kingdom from the map. It is doubtful that it can ever be revived. But one of the reasons for the impaired authority of the newly resurrected Union of Burma republican government is that the visible trappings and the religious sanctions traditionally associated in Burma with royal authority are not currently in evidence.

An awareness of the political institutions of old Burma is important in its own right and also as contributing to the understanding of the

3

new Burma which has re-emerged since 1948 as an independent state. Generally speaking, the structure of governmental administration in newly independent Burma follows closely the improved patterns developed in British times, but the spirit of the exercise of authority owes much to pre-British custom as popularly recognized. Whether governmental authority can become effective apart from the revival of the traditional sanctions of royalty is not a subject with which history can be concerned, but it is relevant to point out that the vitality of cultural and political traditions are, in Burma as elsewhere, important conditioning factors in the historical process.

Part I of this study includes a description of the indigenous governmental and social institutions of old Burma and the story of their eventual disintegration under the relentless impact of the outside world. Chapter I in particular will explain the character and functioning of Burma's government in pre-British times, giving special emphasis to the various moral and religious sanctions which operated in support of royal authority.

Kingship in Burma: Indian Origins

Traditional governmental authority in Burma was sustained at the center by three important buttressing sanctions. The first was the direct borrowing from India of the concept of royalty associated with the venerable Code of Manu. This placed considerable emphasis on the magical properties of the court regalia and on the perennial need for the ministrations of Brahman priests at the palace. A second religious sanction was associated with an even more venerable principle derived from Hindu cosmology, which attributed divine status to the king by virtue of his occupancy of the hallowed precincts of the capital itself. The royal palace symbolized the very center of the universe, the abode of the gods, around which the sun, moon, and stars revolved. A third important support of royal power in Burma was derived from the popular regard for the king as the patron and supporter of the Buddhist faith. These three sanctions will be considered in turn.

According to the Indian tradition Manu was a kind of mythical first king and father of the race.[1] Manu's venerable code, which apparently dated in its completed form from the second century B.C., was regarded in India, and to some extent in Burma also, as a prime legal

[1] D. Mackenzie Brown, *The White Umbrella: Indian Political Thought from Manu to Gandhi* (Berkeley, 1953), p. 26.

4

authority, the arbiter between conflicting legal systems and principles.[2] Indian tradition conceived the king as a divinity in human form, usually the earthly embodiment of the god Indra. The coronation ceremony called for the utilization of a variety of regalia possessing magical properties, but it was climaxed when Brahman priests held over the head of the ruler, as he took his place on the throne, the White Umbrella, the symbol of divine sovereignty.[3]

Kingship arose in theory from the concern of the people to escape social chaos. The king's primary duty was to protect his people by punishing the unjust and the predatory strong. The ruler was supposed to be truthful and wise, considerate before acting, and capable of curbing his personal desire for wealth and pleasure. In order to achieve wisdom and self-control, the king was required to maintain at court several pure and aged Brahman advisers capable of instructing him in personal modesty and in the principles of the *Dharma* (*Dhamma*), or the firmament of the law.[4] Burma's kings were allegedly descendants of Manu.

The role of the Brahmans as chief advisers of the king did not, for several reasons, make the Hindu-type state a theocracy, and this was particularly true in Burma. The court Brahmans enjoyed the backing of no ecclesiastical organization contending for political power, and they were completely dependent on the favor of the king for their

[2] *Ibid.*, pp. 26–29. Warren Hastings in the eighteenth century had the Manu code translated into English for official use by the East India Company government. British officials coming to Tenasserim in the 1820's discovered it in Burma also. The code included provisions governing marriage relations, inheritance, debts, and so on, as well as the principles of government and kingship. King Alaungpaya, founder of Burma's Konbaung dynasty, authorized the compilation of a new Burmese-language version of the *Manu Kye Dhammathat,* including a summary of basic principles of customary law. See Maung Maung, *Burma in the Family of Nations* (Amsterdam, 1956), pp. 13–15.

[3] Robert Heine-Geldern, "Conceptions of State and Kingship in Southeast Asia" (Cornell University Southeast Asia Program Data Paper, no. 18, 1956), pp. 1–2; D. M. Brown, pp. 15–20. The six-foot canopy of the royal White Umbrella was usually decorated with golden leaves, and it had a bejeweled handle. For a full description of Burmese Court regalia, including umbrellas, barges, architectural characteristics, down to betel boxes and spittoons, see the Burmese treatise entitled *Shweponidan* (Rangoon, 1931).

[4] D. M. Brown, pp. 21–34. Brahman advisers warned the king against eighteen vices, ten of them arising from love of pleasure and eight from wrath and envy. In a letter of 1787, King Bodawpaya wrote to the governor of Bengal as follows: "In my service are ten Pandits learned in the *Shastra* and 104 priests whose wisdom is not to be equalled—agreeable to whose learning and intelligence I execute and distribute justice among my people." See India Office Archives, *Bengal Political Proceedings,* MSS. EUR., E63, no. 155, "Deputation to Ava," p. 2.

5

office and authority.[5] Learned Mon and Burman Theravada Buddhist scholars, working together at Pagan, repudiated the Hindu Tantric practices of the previous era and developed by 1274 the Burmese version of the book of the law, called the *Dhammavilasa*.[6] It was a Buddhist-style *Dhammathat* which repudiated caste and omitted references to Brahmanic sacerdotal functions except as they related to the authentication of royal authority.[7]

The functions of the Brahman priests at the Burmese Court were maintained down to the very end of the dynasty in 1885. They were prominently active at coronations, at royal weddings, and at royal audiences. They intoned benedictions as the king took his seat on the throne. They helped select auspicious locations for the capital and lucky dates for the initiation of important enterprises; they prophesied the future of both governments and individuals.[8] Brahman priests residing at the eighteenth-century Burmese Court frequently originated from neighboring Manipur, but more learned priests from Benares who were able to translate Sanskrit words into Burmese were much preferred.[9]

At the Burmese Court, the White Umbrella was reserved for the exclusive use of the king and his chief queen. For any other person to carry such an umbrella was an act of high treason. Only the chief queen, as the divine equal of the king, could address the monarch without prostrating herself.[10] Indian influence was also in evidence at the court in the exaggerated veneration paid to elephants in general (all were the property of the king) and to the sacred albino elephants in particular.[11]

[5] D. M. Brown, pp. 17–18, 31–34; Maung Ba Han, *A Legal History of India and Burma* (Rangoon, 1952), pp. 57, 68–70. In 1795, the Brahman advisers at the Burmese Court actually knew only Bengali. King Bodawpaya at the time was much concerned to obtain better-qualified Brahman attendants. See K. R. H. Mackenzie, *Burma and the Burmese* (London, 1853), p. 79.

[6] Tantric cults were designed to afford sensual gratification through drinking and sex orgies. They were also associated with the acquisition of such boons as longevity, invisibility, and invulnerability, as well as magical deliverance from evil influences.

[7] Ba Han, pp. 68–70; D. G. E. Hall, *Michael Symes: Journal of His Second Embassy to the Court of Ava in 1802* (London, 1955), p. 253.

[8] D. M. Brown, pp. 72–73. All European visitors to the Burma Court in modern times reported the conspicuous participation of Brahman priests at royal audiences.

[9] G. E. Harvey, *Outline of Burmese History* (Bombay, 1954), pp. 133, 136.

[10] *Ibid.*, pp. 189–192. The crown prince was entitled to use eight golden umbrellas. High officials and the Shan chiefs used fewer golden umbrellas, while lesser officials were permitted only red ones.

[11] Vincentius Sangermano, *A Description of the Burmese Empire* (London, 1833), pp. 76–79; Albert Fytche, *Burma Past and Present* (London, 1878), I, 145.

Occupancy of the Sacred Palace Precincts

Indian cosmology affirmed that at the very center of the universe (*Jambudvipa*) was located the sacred Mt. Meru, flanked by formidable mountain chains and forbidding seas, around which revolved the sun, moon, and stars. At the very summit of Mt. Meru was the city of the gods with its eight guardian spirits. The abodes of men were in the four world islands located at the cardinal points of the compass around the central Mt. Meru. In the Burmese adaptation of the Indian legend, *Zambudipa* became the great south island abode of mankind, and the royal palace area was a symbolic replica of the central cosmological island of Mt. Meru itself.[12]

The proper location and construction of the palace of the Burmese kings commanded all the learning of the Brahman advisers of the court joined to the wisdom of the soothsayers, numerologists, and astrologers. The king's residence must occupy the exact center of the selected square enclosure, the several sides of which ran perpendicular to the cardinal points of the compass. The gateways to the palace area were in multiples of four and were protected in the Burmese version by military units comparable to the eight guardian spirits of the mythical Mt. Meru. It was thus by virtue of the king's occupancy of the theoretical center of the universe, Mt. Meru, the city of the gods, that the Burmese king gained the status of divinity. At the time of the coronation, the newly crowned king was surrounded by eight Brahmans, representing the guardian spirits of Mt. Meru. In keeping with the symbolism of the four-walled capital city was the requirement that the king have four principal queens, four chief ministers, and four privy (interior) councilors.[13]

Since the royal palace was the symbolic center of the universe and the abode of the gods, firm possession of the capital city by the ruling monarch became a matter of overriding political importance. Its seizure by some rival prince was tantamount to dethronement of the incumbent ruler; such action by an outright charlatan usurper might produce a similar result. The ceremonial circling of the capital by the

---

Buddhist reverence for white albino elephants arose from the Indian legend that Gautama's last incarnation prior to his Buddhahood was as a white elephant. Sometimes Burmese women at the court and in the provinces, as an act of piety to obtain merit, volunteered to suckle infant elephants.

[12] Mackenzie, pp. 47–48. The Burmese word for Meru is here reported as *Meimmo* or *Meinmó*.

[13] Heine-Geldern, pp. 2–7. One of King Thibaw's alleged mistakes after 1878 was that he failed to acquire the requisite number of four queens.

newly crowned monarch signified his control over the entire empire. Because of the sacred character of the palace precincts, every person visiting it must, without exception, dismount when approaching the spire, lower his parasol, bow reverently at appropriate intervals, and eventually remove his footwear upon actual entry within the palace itself. These basic requirements of protocol were frequently resented by official British visitors as deliberate attempts to humiliate and degrade them. Such procedures were, for the Burmese, not subject to compromise because they stemmed from basic political and religious considerations connected with the exercise of sovereign authority.[14] The word "golden," a symbol of excellence, was reserved exclusively for reference to the royal palace and to its kingly occupant. It was not pure hyperbole when, in 1787, King Bodawpaya informed the governor of Bengal that "my palace, as the Heaven studded with gold and precious stones, is revered more than any other palace in the universe." [15]

Patronage of Buddhism as a Basis for Loyalty to the King

The most important positive basis on which popular allegiance to the king was acknowledged by the leading ethnic peoples of Burma (the Burmans, Mons, Shans, and Arakanese) was that royalty functioned as the promoter and defender of the Buddhist faith. Buddhism provided its devotees with uniform attitudes and social values and operated as a cohesive force uniting the territorial and national fragments of the Burma state. The basic Buddhist doctrine of karma (that deeds in a previous existence determined one's present status) was itself an important factor in rationalizing kingly authority, and no merit to be acquired under karma exceeded that derived from a service to the Buddha himself. For this reason, Burma's kings bestowed lavish patronage on Buddhist shrines and on the *Sangha* or monastic community. A ruler's proudest title related to his role as a promoter of the Buddhist faith, a function which was regarded by Burmans as the very *raison d'être* of the state. Despite the manifold abuses of power arising from royal despotism, which led Burmans traditionally to identify the government itself with such basic scourges as fire, flood, famine, and evil enemies, kingship merited popular appreciation be-

[14] *Ibid.,* pp. 7–8.
[15] Henry J. Ball, *An Account of the Burman Empire* (Calcutta, 1852), p. 23; India Office Archives, *Bengal Political Correspondence,* MSS. EUR., E63, no. 155, p. 2. News allegedly reached the "golden ears" and perfumed the "golden nose." To enter the royal presence was to sit at the "golden feet."

cause of its dedication to religious ends. Princely aspirants invariably stressed their capabilities as promoters of the faith.[16]

British authority, of course, failed to qualify as a promoter of Buddhism. The repeated outbreak of rebellions in the British-governed Arakan and Tenasserim coastal divisions in the 1830's arose less from economic or governmental grievances than from convictions that an indigenous ruler was required to foster the Buddhist faith. Subsequent rebellions following British annexation of Lower Burma in 1852 and the destruction of the royal influence in 1886 were led by pretenders and even by monks who solicited popular support as devoted adherents of the Buddhist faith and as restorers of kingship needed for its protection. The last important expression of the traditional type of Burmese nationalism was the attempt made by an ex-*pongyi* charlatan named Saya San in 1930–1931 to throw out alien British rule and to re-establish a Buddhist-oriented court. British efforts to mollify Burman-Buddhist unrest and to enlist popular support by developing efficient administration and by dispensing impartial justice failed largely because they were more or less beside the point. The cry of "Buddhism in danger" was one of the perennial appeals which political agitators could employ to enlist popular support.[17]

The Exercise of Royal Power

The exercise of the king's authority in old Burma depended also on the physical sanctions of political despotism and military predominance. The deferential allegiance of the nation was granted to the royal incumbent, securely installed in the palace fortress, protected by selected contingents of the army, and capable of wielding despotic authority. Unless a person was prepared to risk being classed as a traitorous rebel, no Burman dared question the theoretical right of the divine monarch to control the lives, the property, and the personal services of his subjects.[18] A prince or top government official who

---

[16] Heine-Geldern, p. 8. There is no apparent evidence in Burma of the "Mandate of Heaven" concept characteristic of the Chinese imperial system. Burma's king did participate in primitive animist ceremonies relating to planting and fertility.

[17] The foregoing section is based on data furnished by U Kaung of the Burma Historical Commission and by a recorded lecture of Professor U Kyaw Thet at the Rangoon-Hopkins Center of the University of Rangoon.

[18] Ma Mya Sein, *Administration of Burma* (Rangoon, 1938), p. 18. According to Heine-Geldern (p. 9), royal ownership of the soil of the country stemmed from the king's alleged descent from Naga serpent demons, the original masters of the soil.

happened to absent himself from the capital for any unusual period of time might also expect to face arrest on suspicion of treason.

The royal family stood apart from the population as a whole, for Burmese society included no hereditary nobility outside the circle of royalty.[19] The marked disparity of social status among Burmans, which will be described later, was in part a differentiation of their obligations to the king and in part an emanation of royal favor which could be withdrawn with the same caprice by which it was granted. For various reasons, including the qualitative superiority of royalty, the kings often selected their chief queens from the palace circle itself. All the children born to legitimate wives (customarily four in number) of the king enjoyed places of honor and importance in public affairs.

The crown prince (or *Einshemin*) maintained a pretentious court of his own including ranking officials and an armed bodyguard. He frequently presided over the Great Council and otherwise exercised a considerable influence on governmental affairs. The brothers of the king usually possessed standing somewhat ahead of the younger princes and inferior only to that of the heir to the throne. Royal princes and high officials of the bureaucracy were assigned, as *myosas* ("town eaters"), the enjoyment of the government's share of the revenues collectible from designated towns or village districts scattered throughout the kingdom.[20]

The reflected glory of royalty was such that the people were obliged to fall to their knees when the king's officials passed by. The highest honor to which a Burmese subject could attain was to qualify as the "King's First Slave." [21] The title *Wun* given to the high officials of the king meant "burden-bearer" and was approximately equivalent to the term "public servant." It was in theory the privilege of the *Wuns* to bear on their heads the burden of the golden feet of the king.[22] Crimi-

[19] C. J. F. S. Smith-Forbes, *British Burma and Its People* (London, 1878), p. 48; Htin Aung, "Customary Law in Burma," in Philip W. Thayer, ed., *Southeast Asia in the Coming World* (Baltimore, 1953), pp. 203–206.

[20] Michael Symes, *An Account of an Embassy to the Kingdom of Ava* (London, 1800), pp. 90, 372, 427. The king's title was *Mingyi* (great prince), that of the princes *Min* or *Thakin* (lord).

[21] John Pinkerton, *Voyages and Travels in All Parts of the World* (London, 1811), VIII, 422–424; taken from the Duke of Hamilton's *A New Account of the East Indies . . . 1688 to 1723* (1727). Hamilton visited Burma in 1709.

[22] Hall, *Symes*, p. 253. A formal communication from the chief ministers to Symes in 1802 contained the following preamble: "The Sovereign Prince of the golden city of Ummerpoora to whom the sovereigns of all states . . . owe homage and respect . . . ; We, the said chiefs ministers of the Great God observer of the law, who ever placing our heads under the golden soles of the royal feet."

nal law was reaffirmed personally by each successive ruler and was enforceable by the *Wuns* as an explicit emanation of the royal will.[23] The dethronement or death of the reigning monarch ordinarily meant the remission of fines and the summary pardon of all criminal offenders who had been convicted under the terminating regime.[24] In the abeyance of royal authority semianarchy prevailed until such time as a new ruler was firmly installed in the palace. The *Wuns* exercised no authority in their own right.[25]

The absolute character of royal authority in old Burma did not encourage the development of socially motivated governmental institutions. The influence of the Brahman priests at court was completely divorced from social or institutional improvement. Royal support of the Buddhist faith frequently meant the squandering of public revenues on fabulously expensive pagodas and monastic shrines, seemingly superfluous.[26] Old Burma was a shut-in state which maintained no windows open to the outside world capable of providing a broader perspective and a more progressive outlook. Its eventual adjustment to outside influences was, therefore, necessarily painful and slow. With the exception of King Mindon's enlightened rule in the third quarter of the nineteenth century, Burma's kings were too absorbed in crushing potential rivals, in waging predatory warfare on neighboring peoples, in collecting white elephants and building pagodas to concern themselves with governmental reforms.

[23] Pinkerton, IX, 418–419, from *The Voyage of Mr. Ralph Fitch, Merchant of London, to Ormuz and So to Goa in the East Indies, 1583 to 1591.*

[24] Htin Aung, pp. 205–210; Pinkerton, VIII, 422–423; Shway Yoe, *The Burman: His Life and Notions* (London, 1910), p. 13.

[25] One of the best contemporary statements of the royal status is the following, given by Father Sangermano (p. 73), who lived at Rangoon from 1783 to 1806: "The Burmese Emperor . . . is considered by himself and others absolute lord of the lives, properties, and personal services of his subjects; he exalts and depresses, confers and takes away honor and rank. . . . Every subject is the Emperor's born slave; and when he calls any one his slave he thinks to do him honor. . . . The possessions of all who die without heirs belong to the king. . . . To the king it belongs to declare war or to conclude peace; and he may in any moment call upon the whole population of his empire to enlist themselves in his army, and can impose upon them at his pleasure any labour or service."

[26] See Hall, *Symes*, pp. 137, 191–192, 205. Symes attributed the marked decline of well-being within Amarapura and its environs as far away as Pagan (cultivation neglected, villages abandoned), between the occasion of his first mission in 1795 and his second in 1802, to King Bodawpaya's neglect of government and his increasing absorption in the construction of a very large and expensive pagoda structure at nearby Mingun, which was eventually abandoned before completion. The project began prior to Symes's first mission.

11

The Palace Administration

Within the fortified palace area the king was unassailable. The formidable wall was flanked by a wide moat, and the fortified gateways were guarded by picked troops commanded by trusted military henchmen (*Win-hmus*). No unauthorized person, whatever his rank or dignity, was permitted to bring a weapon into the palace precincts. The king's unquestioned personal domination of the inner palace enclosure was capable of challenge, if at all, not by outsiders, but by the intrigues of his several score wives, each one intent on promoting her own influence or that of her particular son or daughter. Periodically a favorite queen might achieve complete ascendancy over her royal husband, a situation which was usually freighted with tragic consequences.[27] The chief queen maintained a considerable official establishment including a pretentious audience hall with a dais throne located at the end of the palace area opposite the king's throne room. She had her own ministers and a gilded royal barge for ceremonial occasions.

The elaborate court protocol required those seeking audience before the "golden feet" of the king to remove their shoes and to sit on the floor below the royal throne in order to avoid projecting the soles of their feet toward the king. Foreign dignitaries in the eighteenth century were usually spared the (to them) indignity of the requirement incumbent upon all indigenous visitors to prostrate themselves face downward before the royal presence.[28] Dire political consequences could attend any prolonged absence from the capital on the part of

[27] Thus from 1820 to 1836, and especially after 1831, King Bagyidaw's low-born chief queen in co-operation with her unprincipled brother gained complete ascendancy over the ill and moody king. The scheming pair accumulated such power and wealth as to completely submerge the legitimate heir apparent, whose mother had died, and also to challenge the brothers of the king. This situation led to Prince Tharrawaddy's successful rebellion of 1837. (See W. S. Desai, "The Rebellion of Prince Tharrawaddy," *Journal of the Burma Research Society* [hereafter cited as *JBRS*], XXV [1935], 109–110.) A similar sinister dominance over King Thibaw by his chief queen, Supayalat, following his succession in 1878, contributed to the final downfall of the dynasty in 1885.

[28] Symes, pp. 357–359; Hiram Cox, *Journal of a Residence in the Burmahn Empire* . . . (London, 1821), pp. 224–225, 264–268. Burmese court etiquette was allegedly copied from Pegu. Balbi's audience before the Burmese king of Pegu in 1583 (Pinkerton, IX, 402–403) required his making an obeissance on his knees as if kissing the ground three times upon entering the courtyard and three more times near the palace itself.

12

the ruler.[29] Weak kings, like Thibaw, never left the palace at all, and no important prince could enter the palace area while the king was absent.[30] Calamitous events invariably suggested that the palace site was ill-chosen.[31] In the troubled times from the third to the sixth decades of the nineteenth century, four separate capital sites were successively occupied. Such frequent shifts of capital sites were made despite the enormous expense and hardship involved.[32]

The administration of the palace proper was vested in the *Atwin-wuns* ("interior burden-bearers"), from four to eight in number, who presided over the *Byedaik* or palace secretariat. The *Atwinwuns* exercised direct control over a specialized group of royal retainers, the *atwintha* (*tha* = people), who were part of an elaborate regimental system of *ahmudan*-class persons liable for personal service at the capital.[33] Under the supervision of the *Atwinwuns*, the service corps at the palace performed a great variety of functions. Ceremonial attendants of the king and chief queen were drawn from men of royal blood. Responsible officials performed disciplinary functions relating to all residents of the palace including the numerous queens.[34] Lower ranks of the *atwintha* performed minor duties as the officers of the White Umbrella, as masons, carpenters, and gardeners assigned to care for buildings and grounds, as the palace cooks, barbers, and table

[29] Hall, *Symes*, pp. 139–140. In 1802, Symes found that King Bodawpaya's continued absence from his capital had resulted in the virtual abolition of the authority of the supreme *Hlutdaw* council and in the serious deterioration of of the governmental operations generally.

[30] Howard Malcom, *Travels in Southeast Asia* . . . (Boston, 1839), I, 106. The tradition dating from the sixteenth century under which rival kings actually led their troops in battle and waged armed duels from atop elephant mounts in a kind of token warfare (see Balbi's account of his 1583 visit to Pegu in Pinkerton, IX, 403–405) was nowhere in evidence under Alaungpaya's Konbaung dynasty of the eighteenth and nineteenth centuries.

[31] In point of fact the location of successive capitals in the vicinity of Ava, Amarapura, and Mandalay was dictated by the strategic necessity of controlling the Irrawaddy River route and the Myitnge River entrance to the Kyaukse granary area to the south.

[32] W. S. Desai, *History of the British Residency in Burma, 1826–1840* (Rangoon, 1939), pp. 328–330; Mya Sein, p. 16. This habit of shifting capitals was apparently a peculiar characteristic of the Konbaung dynasty, six of whose ten kings built new capitals.

[33] The vassal obligations of the *ahmudan* class of the population derived in part from their hereditary status and in part from their occupancy of royal lands.

[34] A *Daing-daw* handled rigorous disciplinary actions while the *Hpaw-hpet-kyaw* managed the milder cases. The *Anaukwun* was in charge of the formal court (*anaukyon*) for women residents.

attendants, the keepers of the betel-chewing apparatus, the drummers, and the bird shooers perched atop every building.[35] The particular *atwintha* who happened to be called to the palace for duty at a given time received no wages. The support of their families, who resided outside the walls, was provided by the other four or five families included in their service unit back home.

In the eighteenth and nineteenth centuries, the *Atwinwuns* also functioned as privy councilors to the king. Two members of the group were in perpetual attendance and available alternately day and night at the *Byedaik*, which was located adjacent to the king's private quarters. The privy councilors could advise the king on administrative matters as requested at regularly scheduled daily sessions.[36] Deputy representatives of the provincial governors (*Myowuns*) resident at the capital could be required to attend the morning sessions of the privy council to answer questions concerning developments in their several jurisdictional areas.[37] The influence of the *Atwinwuns* on policy varied widely from reign to reign according to the character of the particular king and from time to time according to his changing moods.[38] Under exceptional circumstances the *Atwinwuns* might dominate a weak ruler,[39] but they were subordinate in both rank and power to the *Wungyis* (great *Wuns*) of the *Hlutdaw*.

The palace staff also included under normal circumstances as a special adviser to the king a kind of chief censor appointed on permanent tenure, whose prerogative it was to criticize the actions of any

[35] *Ahmudan* groups of menial status were called *aso;* nonmenials were *asu* or *athin.* This exposition is based largely on manuscript notes taken by John S. Furnivall from a formal document compiled around 1762 entitled *Sambudipa U-Hsaung: Kyam,* or "The Garland of Zambudipa," pp. 1–16, 29, 38–40, 44–46. It was compiled from older Burman records and traditions describing the governmental institutions of Burma and was intended for the practical guidance of Alaungpaya's royal successors. It will be cited hereafter simply as "Furnivall, 'Notes.' "

[36] Each *Atwinwun* was attended by a secretary or *thandawsin* (royal writer), who could record any order which the king might wish to transmit via a royal reader (*nakandaw*) to the supreme council, or *Hlutdaw.* The palace *thandawsins* numbered around thirty, the *nakandaws* only four or five. The latter carried gilded notebooks as their insignia of office. See Mya Sein, p. 24; John Nisbet, *Burmah under British Rule and Before* (London, 1901), I, 151; H. Yule, *A Narrative of the Mission . . . to . . . Ava in 1855* (London, 1858), pp. 136–137.

[37] Pinkerton, VIII, 422. From Hamilton's *Account* of 1709.

[38] Sangermano, pp. 81–84.

[39] Symes, p. 90; Shway Yoe, pp. 511–512. Under King Thibaw (1878–1885) the *Atwinwuns* backed by the chief queen took over much of the work of the *Hlutdaw.*

official of the realm.[40] The other high officials of the palace supervised the granary, the elephants, the sword-bearing guards, and the palace guard. The royal treasury (*Shwedaik* = gold house) was also the depository for the sworn evidence (*sittans*) of the periodic revenue inquests on which taxation and headman appointments were based.[41]

Variations of official rank were strictly maintained, and dire punishment awaited anyone who pretended to any dignity for which he was not qualified. Rank at the court was indicated by the wearing of a golden chain (*salwé*), made up of multiple strands which fastened together over the left shoulder, hung across the breast and underneath the right arm. The king wore a *salwé* of twenty-four twisted strands, the crown prince one of eighteen, and lesser princes chains of twelve. A *Wungyi* merited nine strands, and subordinate *Wuns* six or three.[42] Rank also determined the number of stages permitted in the roof of the house of a prince or a high official, the type of dress and ornaments worn, the size, shape, or composition of the betel box, spittoon, pipe, or drinking cup to be used, the accouterments of one's horses, or the number and color of the umbrellas allowed in one's entourage. Elephants were the exclusive property of the king and could be ridden only by his express authorization.[43]

Sumptuary regulations also included special modes of speech and vocabulary to be used in addressing the king, high officials, and *pongyi* monks. The king was addressed as a form of deity, and he alone could use the peacock emblem. It was a treasonable offense for anyone to presume to trespass on royal prerogatives. Anklets, brocaded silk, velvet sandals, and precious jewels were reserved for use by royalty. Officials alone wore Indian-style long-tailed coats.[44] Strict conformity to propriety and the absence of unseemly strutting about were the rule in Upper Burma, especially in the vicinity of the capital. Rank and status outside the circle of royalty attached only to the office held and not to the person of the holder. Wealth per se could contribute little to one's status, since there was no social incentive for its ac-

[40] The title of the censor, literally translated was "person to whom king gave long life."

[41] See Nisbet, I, 157–161; Mya Sein, p. xlii.

[42] Mya Sein, pp. 20, 68, 81, 148; Shway Yoe, p. 490. The British resident in 1830 was given a *salwé* of nine strands as a mark of royal favor. Mr. Gladstone, in the early 1870's, was awarded a knightly *salwé* of fifteen strands; Britain's crown prince later received twenty-one strands. The *salwé* had a counterpart in the rank-denoting sashes of mandarin Chinese. It may also have been an adaptation of the sacred Brahmanical thread.

[43] Symes, pp. 244, 277, 310, 359.   [44] Shway Yoe, pp. 406–412.

cumulation. People generally preferred leisure to hard work and found gaming, daring adventure, or openhanded generosity much more fun than grubbing thriftiness.[45]

The Central System of Administration

Subordinate in rank only to the royal family were the *Wungyis*, the "great burden-bearers" who headed the central administration. Four of them were in regular attendance at the Royal Council Hall, where the executive council (*Hlutdaw*) [46] held daily public sessions extending from noon to three or four o'clock. During wartime emergencies or when important responsibilities were laid upon the governors of such strategic frontier posts as Rangoon or Arakan, the number of *Wungyis* might be increased temporarily to six or seven.[47]

The *Hlutdaw* in eighteenth-century Burma was competent to decide all matters of state, whether legislative, executive, or judicial, subject to the king's approval in matters of great moment. Decisions of the *Hlutdaw* council were based on free discussion within the group and were arrived at by majority vote, but the entire council assumed collective responsibility for all important actions submitted for royal approval. The crown prince sometimes presided over the council's deliberations and when he did so occupied the royal dais provided in the chamber. The king himself could also preside if he chose, or the council could request the personal presence of the king at important sessions.[48]

Royal edicts invariably bore the formal stamp of the *Hlutdaw*, and they were officially issued in its name rather than in the king's.[49] Rarely

[45] Sangermano, pp. 151–153. In return for presents of emeralds, Balbi in 1583 received from the Burmese king at Pegu a cup of gold and five pieces of China damask. See Pinkerton, IX, 403.

[46] The *Hlutdaw* (literally "place of release") may have had its origin in the early 1200's, when the Burman king relegated many of his powers to his four princely brothers to act as a kind of regency council. Eventually other eminent men of the realm were assigned to the *Hlutdaw* in preference to the princes, who were too often rivals for the throne. During the declining years of the Toungoo dynasty (1600's), one king became a virtual puppet of the *Hlutdaw;* its role at any time depended on the royal will. See Mya Sein, pp. 6, 14; Fytche, I, 240.

[47] John Crawfurd, *Journal of an Embassy . . . to the Court of Ava* (London, 1834), I, 28–30. In 1826, the governor of Pegu enjoyed *Wungyi* rank while acting as generalissimo to suppress rebellion in Lower Burma. He also served as the authorized negotiator with the British mission.

[48] The *Hlutdaw* throne from Thibaw's time is still displayed in the president's mansion at Rangoon.

[49] Crawfurd, II, 136–138; Symes, pp. 308–309; Yule, pp. 243–244. The crown prince in 1855 was ex officio a *Wungyi*. In 1802 when the *Wun* of the crown

did the king in practice reverse a considered decision of the *Hlutdaw,* although the king had authority to remove or even jail *Wungyis* who dared oppose his wishes. The record of the decisions reached by the *Hlutdaw* were presented daily to the king for review.[50]

The *Wungyis* accepted individual responsibility for administering various functional duties of government which fell within their respective fields of competence, such as military ordinance, army administration, river control, foreign relations, legal matters, or taxation. But the government was not departmentalized, and the council as a whole reviewed all the important administrative decisions of its several members. By custom the *Hlutdaw* was exempt from royal interference in its management of the public treasury (as distinct from the palace *Shwedaik*), the "presents" (or tribute) treasury, one of the three royal arsenals, and the depository of state supplies and equipment.

The whole *Hlutdaw* also functioned as a court of law hearing public petitions of grievance in the first instance and also acting as the supreme arbiter for appeals from provincial courts in both civil and criminal cases. Individual *Wungyis,* and their assistants, were also competent to settle at their private residences judicial business of a nonpublic nature.[51] In appealed criminal cases, the *Hlutdaw* was empowered to punish an inept or corrupt judge whose decision it might see fit to reverse. Virtually all foreign visitors to the Burman capital in modern times reported that the *Wungyis* were men of intelligence and administrative competence.

Each *Wungyi* was assisted by a *Wundauk* (*dauk* meant "prop" or "support"), usually a younger man of ability and promise appointed with the approval of the *Hlutdaw* as a whole. The *Wundauks* supervised the daily agenda of the *Hlutdaw,* participated actively in its discussions, and submitted opinions for consideration by the *Wungyis;* but they did not participate in the formal decisions of the *Hlutdaw.*[52] *Wundauks* might also be sent on important diplomatic assignments or be entrusted with administrative matters of moment. A score of more

---

prince and the prince himself had virtually usurped the *Hlutdaw*'s power, the royal statement to Michael Symes was still issued formally in the name of the *Hlutdaw.* See Appendix no. 9 in Hall, *Symes,* pp. 253–257.

[50] Cox, pp. 322, 342–344; Mya Sein, pp. 18–26.

[51] Yule, pp. 136–137, 243–246; Mya Sein, pp. 24–26; Hall, *Symes,* p. 182. The oath administered to witnesses was especially terrifying to any population believing in *Karma* and in *nat* spirits. Civil cases sent up to the *Hlutdaw* were screened by a special court called the *tayayon.*

[52] Crawfurd, II, 134; Mya Sein, p. 25.

17

expert secretaries (*seridawgyis*) handled administrative details both in preliminary stages of consideration and in the final implementation of decisions or policies once determined.[53] The *Hlutdaw* secretariat acted in a dual capacity, first to communicate with the throne and second as a link with territorial and departmental officials.[54]

The Burmese governmental system resembled that of China in making no provision at the capital for the reception of diplomatic emissaries from abroad or for their permanent residence near the court. The basic responsibility for diplomatic correspondence and for conducting important foreign visitors to the capital was customarily borne by the *Myowuns* located at the frontier points of contact, usually at Pegu, Bhamo, and, to some degree, Akyab. Thus in 1794 and in 1802 Britain's Michael Symes was accompanied to the capital by the *Myowun* of Pegu, who provided boats and crews for his journeys to Amarapura. A Chinese delegation, accompanied in like fashion by the Bhamo *Myowun*, was present at the capital at the time of Symes's first visit. Negotiations could proceed smoothly if the emissary was co-operative and conciliatory, as in the case of Symes,[55] or they could become maddeningly frustrating if the emissary became difficult, as in the case of Hiram Cox in 1798.[56]

Following the Anglo-Burman War of 1824–1825, the Burma Government assigned the post at Rangoon to a person with *Wungyi* status, who was instructed to negotiate all questions arising out of the execution of the peace treaty. The subsequent presence of a British Resident (Burney) at the capital during the 1830's, in accordance with the terms of the Yandabo treaty of 1826, was deeply resented by the court, which regarded him as a foreign spy and as a symbol of dynastic humiliation and national degradation.[57] An important defect

[53] Crawfurd, II, 139; Nisbet, I, 157–159.

[54] Symes, pp. 266–284; Furnivall, "Notes," pp. 27–28. Symes was conducted northward by the *Myowun* of Pegu and was met below Amarapura by a *Wundauk* and by two *Myowun* governors from provinces near the China border.

[55] Symes, pp. 266–284, 348.

[56] Cox, pp. 61–65, 74, 120–122, 133–139, 361, 382–390. Cox delivered, at the request of the court, a specially made horse-drawn royal carriage, dies for coinmaking, and some 5,000 minted rupees. When he insisted on being accorded the privileged status of a *Wungyi*, he was faced with the impossible demand that he take the same oath of allegiance to the king required of a *Wungyi*.

[57] Crawfurd, II, 335–336, 512–513; Desai, *History*, pp. 34–39; Mya Sein, pp. 13–15; Hall, *Symes*, pp. 93–96, 182. The peculiar importance attaching to the *Myowun* governships at Pegu, Syriam, and later Rangoon was due to their being the points of contact with foreigners. Under the Toungoo dynasty (sixteenth

in the Burmese system of foreign relations was the lack of continuity of obligation, extending from one king to his successors, to honor agreements entered into with foreigners. This was invariably the case if an earlier treaty agreement was repugnant to royal dignity or national interest.[58] The concept of the state as a continuing political personality from reign to reign was lacking.

Minor Officials and Revenue Sources

Governmental administration both at the center and in the provinces afforded careers for scholars learned in both Burmese and in Pali, the language of the Buddhist scriptures. The leading monasteries also employed expert secretaries and copyists to transcribe sacred manuscripts and to record the dictation of the learned *pongyis* (presiding monks). Burmans of learning and ability who aspired to a public career could entertain some assurance of recognition on the basis of their expert knowledge and general usefulness, although political connections were obviously important. The widespread literacy achieved through the agency of Burma's monastic schools contributed to secretarial competence at all levels of government.[59]

Local governmental affairs at the capital city, including both administration and courts, were handled by four *Myowuns* (city *Wuns* or governors), each of whom exercised jurisdiction over a separate district of the city and adjacent areas extending outward over a ten-mile radius. Except in their handling of serious criminal offenses and in their immediate subservience to any express orders from the *Hlut-daw*, the capital *Myowuns* acted on their own responsibility.[60] The capital city and its immediate riverine environs were by far the most

---

and seventeenth centuries) a brother of the king was in charge of Syriam. (See Pinkerton, VIII, 418.) The Pegu *Myowun* was acting as viceroy for much of Lower Burma in 1802, and he enjoyed *Wungyi* status after 1826. At the time of Symes's second mission to Amarapura in 1802, Governor-General Wellesley professed to believe that the Burmese viceroy of Arakan rather than the court itself was the author of the threatening letter which had occasioned sending the mission.

[58] Hall, *Symes*, p. 105.

[59] Shway Yoe, p. 35; Max and Bertha Ferrars, *Burma* (London, 1900), pp. 166–167. Court secretaries prepared routine royal orders (covering appointments, revenue collections, and general business) and public works specifications, while royal "notice writers" digested and answered communications from afar. Clerks listed the presents for the king and also administered the terrifying oaths at trials.

[60] The capital *myoyon* courts, like those in the provinces, included an official in charge of court fees called a *Konbodaing*. *Daing* means "person in charge"; *konbo* referred to civil court fees. Furnivall, "Notes," p. 56.

populous area of old Burma and were ordinarily the best-governed part of the kingdom.[61]

Regular sources of royal revenue varied in character. The king claimed all ivory and the produce of all mines of silver, amber, rubies, and sapphires. Provincial revenues were transmitted by regular officials, and annual tribute in silver and horses came from the vassal Shan princes. Special presents always accompanied particular requests. The king in 1800 claimed the proceeds of the 10 per cent tariff on imports and, subsequently, a 5 per cent levy on exports. The Rangoon port intendant transported his annal cargo of customs to the court regularly in December.[62] Most of the score or more eighteenth-century riverine *chauki,* or customs posts scattered along the Irrawaddy, which assessed duties on boats going upstream, were adjuncts of the royal treasury; other such posts provided royal personages with sources of private income.[63] The king subjected wealthy merchants, who were all duly registered under royal edict as "rich men" (*thutés*), to periodic extortion in the form of presents payable to the king at festival times.[64]

Only officials at the capital were paid in bullion. In provinces or districts, where the normal royal revenues were not already assigned to a princely "eater" (*myosa*) or were not utilized for the maintenance of military regiments, the governors normally forwarded in silver and in kind some 60 to 80 per cent of their authorized exactions under the basic household tax. Actual tax collections were invariably larger than the published amount, the difference being held back by the agents concerned. The basic household tax was apportioned roughly according to ability to pay, but it was not a levy on property or on income as such; it was rather a locally apportioned application of the king's claim to the personal services of all his people.[65] The actual assessment usually amounted to 10 or 15 per cent of the annual crop output. Minor royal taxes were levied on fruit trees, fishing and timber opera-

[61] Symes, pp. 98, 307; Henry Gouger, *Personal Narrative of Two Years' Imprisonment in Burmah* (London, 1860), pp. 50–51; Malcom, I, 214. Crawfurd (II, 174) reported as of 1826: "The seat of government and its neighborhood are in all respects owing to a more regular administration of law and greater facility of appeal, by far the best-governed portion of the kingdom." Symes, in 1802, reported the adverse effects on the capital area of misrule by the moody half-mad King Bodawpaya.

[62] Hall, *Symes,* p. 208. [63] Sangermano, pp. 91–96.

[64] Crawfurd, II, 131–132. The *thuté* title was hereditary and, once acquired, it continued as a burden even after one lost his wealth.

[65] Legally, all Burmans belonged bodily to the king. For this reason all were forbidden to leave the country, even women married to foreigners.

tions, resin oils, brokerage, ferries, and landing stages. One half of regular court fees and fines (*konbo*) also went to the palace treasuries.[66]

Despotism and the Problem of Succession

Many of the defects of the royal government of old Burma stemmed from its despotic character. Too much depended on the character and judgment of the king, frequently on his unpredictable mood or caprice. When the *Hlutdaw* was ably manned and was supported by the king in exercising its best judgment, the system worked with considerable effectiveness. But, even under optimum circumstances, poor communications between the capital and outlying areas left open the possibility of considerable abuse of authority on the part of provincial governors (*Myowuns*) and the parasitic overlords called *myosas*. Complaints against such abuses usually got sidetracked en route to the capital.[67] An irresponsible ruler could cancel the power of the *Hlutdaw Wungyis* and could make them little more than the automatic executors of the king's commands.[68] Burmans generally were not given to servility and flattery, but within the hierarchy of officialdom obsequious subservience accompanied by payment of appropriate gratuities was inflexibly demanded from above and yielded from below.[69]

An equally serious defect of royal despotism derived from the uncertainty of succession to the throne. The ruler's frequent elimination of rival kinsmen was regarded as necessary for governmental stability.[70] The only guarantee to orderly succession was for the reigning monarch to designate his heir (*Einshemin,* or "Lord of the Eastern

[66] Shway Yoe, 523–530. The collection and incidence of these royal taxes will be discussed again in the section on provincial government. The striking similarities between the Burmese and Siamese systems of government force the conclusion that they copied the same pattern and also borrowed from each other.

[67] Crawfurd, II, 157.

[68] Father Sangermano (pp. 81–82) and Symes (Hall, pp. 139–140, 149) so described the position of the *Hlutdaw* around 1800. King Bodawpaya, obsessed by his pagoda-construction project, virtually abdicated authority in favor of the crown prince and the latter's *Wun.*

[69] Gouger, p. 11. Cox ran afoul of this official system of interminable exactions in 1797. See Cox, pp. 382–411.

[70] Symes, pp. 58–66. The turbulent history of Burma from the death of King Alaungpaya in 1760 until 1782 witnessed princely rivalry and purges on an extreme scale. King Bodawpaya (1782–1819) was obliged to execute two rival nephews at the time of his accession, and he kept the able and enterprising Toungoo prince a virtual prisoner during most of his reign. One of the first acts of King Bagyidaw in 1819 was to execute the rival Toungoo prince.

House") well in advance and to see to it that he was securely installed and his acceptance widely acknowledged. The crown prince maintained a considerable establishment, frequently participating in government as presiding officer of the *Hlutdaw*. The designated heir was invariably a son or brother of the king, but he need not be the eldest son or any particular brother.[71]

The succession seldom occurred without untoward incident. Sometimes a ruler's premature designation of a successor, as in the case of King Mindon's action in 1866, was tantamount to serving the nominee with a death warrant.[72] Tragic consequences ensued when Mindon delayed naming another heir until he was on his deathbed in 1878. The situation led to the coup which placed the inexperienced and weak King Thibaw on the throne and was a preliminary step to the downfall of the dynasty.[73]

Even when the succession occurred without serious challenge, all major governmental posts at the capital and in provincial centers and also the *myosa* fief assignments were up for redistribution, so that a considerable measure of political confusion invariably ensued. A crisis would precipitate a period of general anarchy, during which only the residual authority of the hereditary township headmen was available to hold the villagers under control.

The overthrow of King Bagyidaw by his younger brother, Prince Tharrawaddy, in 1837, an event witnessed and fully reported by foreign observers, demonstrated clearly the traditional pattern of revolt.[74] King Bagyidaw's prestige and royal authority had been seriously undermined by his defeat in 1825 at the hands of the British and by his signing in 1826 of the Yandabo treaty, which surrendered extensive coastal portions of Burma (Arakan and Tenasserim). His power-hungry chief queen and her unscrupulous brother usurped control after 1831, when the king began his series of periodic lapses into deep melancholia bordering on insanity.[75] As the king's authority ebbed

[71] Shway Yoe, p. 60; H. T. White, *Burma* (London, 1923), p. 103. Succession by sons and brothers was equally divided under Burma's Konbaung dynasty (1755–1885) with five each.

[72] In this instance, King Mindon's ambitious sons engineered the assassination of an uncle who had been named *Einshemin*.

[73] Mya Sein, p. 18.

[74] Another and similar account of the pattern of rebellion, dating from around 1800, is given in Sangermano's *Burmese Empire* (pp. 61–72).

[75] Desai, *British Residency*, pp. 114–115, 124–125. The queen and her brother were reported to be the only wealthy persons in Burma by 1826. Four-fifths of the first indemnity installment of 25 lakhs of rupees (2.5 million) due the British were borrowed from the queen's hoard.

GOVERNMENT OF OLD BURMA

away, banditry spread throughout the countryside. A showdown crisis developed in 1837 when Prince Tharrawaddy defied a hostile move by the palace clique and withdrew from the capital. Accompanied by a motley crew of followers, he crossed the Irrawaddy River and proceeded northward toward the ancestral home of the dynasty at Moksobo (Shwebo).[76]

The subsequent steps in the pattern of rebellion followed in order: (1) Tharrawaddy established at Shwebo a countercenter of strength capable of repelling the halfhearted attacks of the royal troops sent to disperse his band; (2) the forces of rebellion including all enemies of the court party plus irregular troops and bandit elements flocked to his standard; (3) Tharrawaddy's agents exploited popular superstitions through the hired services of Brahman priests and other astrologers; (4) maximum confusion and anarchy were deliberately fomented in order to discredit and undermine governmental authority; (5) eventually the rebel army advanced against the dispirited forces at the capital, while endeavoring to foment disaffection and espionage among the defending troops; (6) then came the final collapse of the government and the surrender of the sacred palace fortress itself to the prince pretender. The old officials and *myosas* were quickly replaced by men drawn in large measure from partisans of the new king and including a number of outright bandit chieftains.[77] Moderating British influence prevented the traditional execution of all royal relatives capable of contesting the new king's pre-eminence. After Tharrawaddy's usurpation, the site of the capital was immediately shifted from Ava to nearby Amarapura. The new ruler subsequently refused to honor the Yandabo treaty of 1826 and, by studied ill-treatment, eventually forced the British Residency to vacate the Burman capital in 1840.[78]

[76] *Ibid.*, pp. 217–218, 230–233. Gouger (pp. 45–46) says that Prince Tharrawaddy in 1824 had "surrounded himself with bands of ruffians, bandits, pugilists . . . who lived near his palace, formed a kind of body-guard, and were ready at a moment's notice for any desperate undertaking."

[77] Desai, *British Residency*, pp. 70–76, 162–163, 251–270, and "The Rebellion of Prince Tharrawaddy," *JBRS*, XXV (1935), 109–120. The British Resident, Burney, reported in 1830 that Bagyidaw was a "spoilt child" and that his regular ministers were afraid of his ungovernable arrogance, pride, and violent temper. The queen and her brother, who did not lack ability, wielded more influence than all the ministers combined; the *Atwinwuns* were more subservient to them than were the *Wungyis*. The twenty-five-year-old heir apparent was a complete cipher, ignored by both factions.

[78] Desai, *British Residency*, pp. 410–412, 420–430. Henry Burney's rather officious intervention as British Resident during the course of the 1837 rebellion was in line with instructions given to Symes in 1802 (Hall, *Symes*, pp. 114–117) di-

Another forbidding aspect of the traditional pattern of succession was illustrated in 1845, when the Pagan prince (Pagan Min), one of the sons of the now-insane Tharrawaddy, put his father under restraint within the palace and took over the crown in a successful palace coup.[79] Pagan Min's seven-year reign, during which several ruffian *Myowuns* had free run of the capital, came to an abrupt end during the second Anglo-Burman War in 1852. In this instance the Mindon prince, a younger son of Tharrawaddy by an inferior wife, came out of his monastery sanctuary near the capital and then withdrew with personal followers—in the traditional pattern—northward to Shwebo, where he was quickly joined by supporters from all sides just as Tharrawaddy had been in 1837. The capital fell to the new incumbent when one of the *Wungyi* leaders within the walls led a mutiny of the defenders. The same *Wungyi* became a member of the new *Hlutdaw*, along with other reputable friends of King Mindon.[80] The new king flatly refused to acknowledge by formal treaty the loss of Lower Burma to the British, although he dealt with his unwelcome neighbor in responsible fashion and brought peace and improved government to his entire kingdom. The capital was again rebuilt at Mandalay in 1857.

Provincial Government

The several score constituent provinces of Burma were named after the cities which were the administrative seats of the governors, or *Myowuns*.[81] These governors functioned as an extension of the arbitrary authority of the king and the *Hlutdaw*, and they enjoyed no claim to local allegiance apart from their wielding of royal power. They exercised both military and civil jurisdiction, the latter comprehending fiscal, police, and judicial authority. The *Myowun* was regularly assisted by a tax collector and granary supervisor (*Akunwun*) and by a police and military officer (*Sitke*), who also supervised at times the administration of religious affairs. Assigned to an important

---

recting that Symes take advantage of any opening caused by rebellion to enhance British influence.

[79] The rebellion staged by a boon companion of Tharrawaddy in 1845 contributed to the king's final lapse into mental derangement. See R. R. Langham-Carter, "U Htaung Bo's Rebellion," *JBRS*, XXVI (1936), 33–34.

[80] Yule, pp. 236–242.

[81] Furnivall, "Notes," pp. 17–22. The provinces (*taings*) were grouped into eight *taing-gyis* (big *taings*). The principal cities were called *Myo-ma*. Rangoon *Myo-ma* had some 20,000 population in King Mindon's time; others were smaller.

frontier port city like Rangoon were a number of deputy *Wuns:* the *Yewun* in charge of war boats, the *Akaukwun* or shipping inspector and customs officer, and the *Shahbundar* or port intendant, ordinarily a foreigner who dealt directly with overseas traders.[82]

The major officials at any given provincial capital collectively constituted the public court, or *myoyon,* which acted as a kind of local *Hlutdaw* exercising wide administrative and judicial authority.[83] The *myoyon,* like the *Hlutdaw,* transacted its business in public sessions, held five days in every seven, in a large open hall elevated three feet above the ground and fitted with benches around the edges for the use of spectators. A record was kept of the evidence before the court, but no lawyers were used.[84] All judicial or administrative actions by the *yon* were subject to the review of the *Myowun,* who might or might not participate personally in court procedures.[85] Viceregal authority was frequently exercised by important *Myowuns* such as the one at Pegu. In extraordinary situations a *Wungyi* could be appointed to serve at Rangoon, in which case he exercised sweeping authority, both military and diplomatic, throughout Lower Burma.[86]

The police and judicial responsibilities of the royal administration in the provinces included the keeping of a population census and other local records, a function which required the co-operation of the local headmen. Persons who lacked occupational status or were otherwise suspected of evil designs could be required to give surety guarantees before the *myoyon* for their proper behavior. Minor policing func-

---

[82] *Shahbundar* meant "lord of the haven." Samuel White of seventeenth-century Mergui, made famous by Maurice Collis, was *Shahbundar* of that port. See Pinkerton, VIII, 430.

[83] Crawfurd, II, 140–142; Symes, pp. 142–147, 156, 161–164. The *myoyon* at Rangoon in 1800 included the *Yewun,* the *Akaukwun,* the *Shahbundar,* and the principal *seridawgyi.* It reported to the *Myowun* just as the *Hlutdaw* did to the king. The provincial *nakandaw,* who transmitted royal orders (written on pointed palm leaves) to the *Myowun,* acted as a kind of royal censor or spy and did not as a rule participate in the Rangoon *myoyon.*

[84] Individual members of the Rangoon *yon* heard cases of minor importance at their homes, just as the *Wungyis* did at the capital.

[85] Shway Yoe, pp. 52–513; Pinkerton, VIII, 424, by Hamilton in 1709. At the time of Symes's mission in 1802, the Rangoon *Yewun* and the Pegu *Myowun* were political rivals, each with a local following and with different connections at court. See Hall, *Symes,* pp. 121–122.

[86] G. D. E. Hall, *Early English Intercourse with Burma* (London, 1928), pp. 168–184; J. S. Furnivall, "Notes on the History of the Hanthawaddy," *JBRS,* IV (1914), 209–210; Symes, pp. 15–17, 470; Desai, *British Residency,* pp. 365–370. In 1826 a *Wungyi* was assigned to Rangoon, and in 1836 he was replaced by a governor of *Wundauk* rank.

tions were usually handled by the headmen, but all important criminal cases, especially those involving men from different townships, had to be tried by the *Myowun* himself.[87] Penalties usually took the form of fines remunerative to both *Myowun* and the court, or prisoners were placed in the stocks. The latter practice was partly dictated by security reasons, for the jails were notoriously insecure. Punishments imposed by the *Myowuns* could include death, enslavement, or mutilation. Incorrigible thieves unable to pay their fines were branded with gunpowder on their cheeks and tattooed on their breasts with symbols revealing to all their criminal status; some were deprived of all civil rights and consigned to the degrading status of executioners. Torture could be applied both to the accused and to hesitant witnesses.[88]

The jurisdiction of the *Myowun* was not compulsory in disputes of a civil character, for these could usually be settled more cheaply and equitably through the services of private arbiters.[89] Only the stubborn or foolhardy person ever allowed a civil dispute to reach the provincial *tayayon* (civil court), for court fees were ruinously high, and the review of important cases by the high civil court at the capital, or by the *Hlutdaw* itself, added greatly to the cost. Witnesses testifying before the *myo* court, as before the *Hlutdaw*, took a costly and terrifying oath invoking the vengeance of devouring spirits, the fate of endless rebirths, loss of speech and hearing, consignment to numerous hells and diseases, loss of family and home, and death by thunderbolt or wild animals, if they swore falsely.[90]

Customary law rather than the formal Code of Manu of Indian origin was actually applied in judicial procedures at all levels, but the objective was always to arrive at a common-sense settlement satisfactory to both parties rather than to apply any principle of law per se. The severest punishments were reserved for treason and improper

[87] Mya Sein, pp. 43–44; Sangermano, pp. 86–87.

[88] Crawfurd, II, 145–146; Malcom, I, 215–220; Symes, pp. 305–307. Harvey's account of the barbarities of Burman administration (*History of Burma* [London, 1925], pp. 358–360) delineates potential weaknesses and abuses; it can hardly be regarded as a balanced assessment.

[89] The standing orders given to provincial officials directed that they should "make important difficulties to become trivial and the trivial to disappear" (Furnivall, "Notes," pp. 29–30).

[90] Shway Yoe, p. 512; Sangermano, pp. 87–90; Malcom, I, 215–216; Mackenzie, pp. 24–25. Because civil court actions were remunerative to the judges, the *Hlutdaw* by the nineteenth century tended to encroach on the *Tayathugyi's* jurisdiction at the capital.

assumption of status or power.[91] Trials by ordeal were associated with magical rites. These sometimes involved contests between rival accusers to determine which one could remain longest submerged in water adjacent to grounded poles or which contestant could hold longest a burning candle.[92]

Local Government: The Myothugyi

In both Upper and Lower Burma, the Indian-type royal administration, including the authority of the *Myowuns* and his assistants, was superimposed over older traditional governmental institutions of a quasi-feudal character. The key personality to whom the population generally acknowledged direct personal allegiance was the hereditary township chief or *myothugyi*. An important difference between Upper and Lower Burma derived from the differentiation of status between the majority groups in the two areas. In Upper Burma, most of the pure Burman inhabitants of the irrigated royal lands in the so-called "home provinces," located near the capital and the adjacent Kyaukse region, in the Minbu-Magwe district, and in the Shwebo area, belonged to the hereditary *ahmudan* class, who owed personal service in lieu of taxes to the royal court. There were no royal lands in Lower Burma and, therefore, no persons of *ahmudan* status except chance migrants. The *ahmudan* population belonged to a number of specialized service units (*asu* or *athin*), which defined the nature of their services. In areas peripheral to the "home provinces" as well as throughout Lower Burma lived the taxpaying "non-Burman" *athi* population, including descendants of the earlier Pyu and Mon inhabitants as well as the Arakanese and the backward hill tribesmen.

In Upper Burma the *myothugyi* was normally the head of a regimental *asu* and functioned as a government official directly under the royal *Myowun*.[93] He took responsibility for settling disputes among

[91] Symes, p. 307. Shway Yoe (p. 522) comments: "The laws were really very mildly administered. . . . Capital sentences were on the whole rare, except where political considerations came in. Then there was no mercy. Cattle stealing was very severely punished, but murder could almost always be purged by a bloodbote."

[92] Symes, p. 468; Cox, p. 14; Nisbet, I, 177–178. Insertion of a finger in molten metal was an alternative form of ordeal. Ralph Fitch reported the water-submerging ordeal as practiced at Pegu in 1586. See Pinkerton, VIII, 422, 428–429.

[93] The word *athin* appeared again in the nationalist (*Wunthanu*) *athins* of the 1920's, although identity of meaning is doubtful. *Athintha* was a term used interchangeably with *ahmudan*. See Furnivall, "Notes," pp. 38–40.

his followers and ensured the performance of their duties, whether civilian or military, in the several types of regimental *asu*. In warfare the *myothugyi* normally commanded his own unit. He accepted and exercised no responsibility over the nonservice population who happened to live in his particular area. These latter, along with the majority *athi* population in *salut* (nonroyal) areas, were the concern of officials operating under the supervision of the *Athiwun* at the royal court. Individuals of *ahmudan* status who migrated to regions remote from their original homes did not thereby escape their traditional *asu* obligations or forfeit their personal allegiance to their respective *myothugyi* chiefs.[94] Apart from their enjoyment of access to royal lands and their substitution of personal services for payment of direct taxes, the *ahmudan* were not socially homogeneous and constituted in no sense a feudal aristocracy. They were simply obligated in special ways through their *myothugyi* chiefs to the support of the Burman king.[95]

Many of the *athi* communities of Lower Burma, living, as did the Mons, in established homogeneous groups, acknowledged in similar fashion their personal allegiance to hereditary *myothugyis*, who fully identified themselves with the interests of their own people. There were thirty Mon township units (*hkaing*) in Pegu province (*taing*) and thirty-two in Bassein.[96] In areas of Lower Burma where, because of displacement or decimation of populations such as occurred during the warfare of the latter half of the eighteenth century, many of the traditional *myothugyi*-led groups had disintegrated, a kind of artificial circle or regional headman (*taikthugyi*) was interposed between the *Myowun* and the surviving township units. The *taikthugyi* was common in areas where the population was more or less alien and imperfectly assimilated. He could acquire genuine authority locally by reason of his election by the villagers and the authentication of his selection by the local *Myowun* and the *Hlutdaw*.

The *taikthugyis* kept census records and helped enforce the obligation of the *athi* population to pay taxes and to fill army quotas in time of war. The "circle" administrative units appear to have been peculiar to nineteenth-century Lower Burma. When the British took over the

[94] *Ibid.*, pp. 23–25, 31–35, 38–40, 42–43.

[95] The *ahmudan* class paid a form of taxation in the obligation of the several home families of a particular unit to support the member called to duty at the capital. All such served at the capital without pay.

[96] The traditional "home" districts (*taings*) for the Mon population were Pegu, Moulmein, and Bassein (Furnivall, "Notes," pp. 17–22).

area in 1852, the *taikthugyis*, where found, numbered only three to seven to a province.[97]

The governing authority of the *myothugyi* whether in Upper or Lower Burma differed in extent and in kind from that of the royally appointed officials. As locally resident hereditary leaders of the people of their respective *hkaing* township units, the *myothugyis* normally held office for life. The *myothugyi*, in tending to identify himself with the interests of his own people, contrasted with the essentially arbitrary and often predatory authority of the royal officials. He was basically the protecting police officer, the local judge-arbiter of disputes, the apportioner and collector of taxes (in Lower Burma), the assigner of service obligations (in Upper Burma), and the recruiter of local quota-contingents for the armed forces in time of war. He thus constituted an indispensable bridge between the arbitrary authority of the king and the subject people.[98] The *athi* population like the *ahmudan* enjoyed cultivator rights in return for the acceptance of certain, although differing, political obligations. A customary disciplinary procedure throughout Burma was to deprive a troublemaker of his access to land.

The *myothugyi* also played a prominent role socially. He helped stage local festivals, boat races, and religious celebrations. He witnessed marriages and divorces, laid out irrigation channels, and conciliated controversies among his people.[99] He reported to the *Myowun* the presence of stranger arrivals in his particular *hkaing*, indicating name and status. The *athi myothugyi* or *taikthugyi* exercised general police authority over the people of his township or circle including stray *ahmudan* residents, but the latter were not obliged to pay the general household tax or to report for general army duty.[100]

A deceased headman was usually succeeded by his ablest son, but sometimes by a brother or even a brother-in-law. Legal authentication of the authority of successive incumbents in all cases had to be obtained from the *Hlutdaw*. The candidate presented his application in person

[97] *Ibid.*, pp. 23–25, 35–36, 41–42. Professor Luce has suggested that the term *athi* may have referred to a mere "worker," as distinct from servants of the king. The term *taing-dan* was sometimes used in place of *athi*. Alien groups were called *Kappas*.

[98] *Ibid.*, pp. 42–43.

[99] *Ibid.*; Ferrars, pp. 163–165; Mya Sein, pp. 48–56. The founder of the Konbaung dynasty, King Alaungpaya, gained his initial following as *myothugyi* of Moksobo (Shwebo).

[100] Mya Sein, pp. 48–63.

at the capital and submitted evidence in the form of sworn testimonials (*sittans*) as to his personal eligibility. These data were checked against official census records and previous revenue inventories taken in the district, all of which were kept in the *Shwedaik* (treasury) archives at the royal palace.[101] If the hereditary line pinched out, a new *myothugyi* could be designated by the *Hlutdaw* after local opinion and the archives were carefully consulted. *De facto* headmen who undertook to reconstitute dead township units by attracting settlers to their jurisdictions might subsequently obtain confirmation from the *Hlutdaw* on the presentation of evidence of their acknowledged leadership supported by formal recommendations from the *Myowun* or *myosa* of the area. The absence of authenticated *myothugyi* incumbents in disorganized areas of Lower Burma as of 1800 [102] apparently gave rise to the *taikthugyi* system. Only in Upper Burma were the villages all permanently organized communities, often differentiated along craft lines or for specialized forms of service to the court. Karen villages in Lower Burma were often migrant and not integrated with any regular governmental system.[103]

In all instances of formal confirmation of *myothugyi* appointments, the records of the action were duly filed with the *Shwedaik*, with the *Athiwun* at the capital, and also with the court of the provincial *Myowun*. The incumbent himself retained as tangible evidence of his authority an official palm-leaf document, signed and sealed, which recorded his confirmation and explained his duties.[104] The superior social status of the *myothugyi* was indicated locally by the type of house he was permitted to own, by the ten to fifteen armed retainers who might accompany his caparisoned horse or oxcart on tour, and by his privilege of using silver utensils and a red umbrella.[105]

Within his own immediate jurisdiction, the *myothugyi* took care of the collection of the household tax apportioned according to the

---

[101] *Ibid.*, pp. 34–35, 58–63.

[102] Yule, p. 253; Crawfurd, I, 23–24; Symes, pp. 16–17. In the 1770's, the *myothugyis* of Henzada, Danubyu, and Padaung fought the mutinous Talaings; in 1825 the Henzada *myothugyi*, possibly a Talaing, aided the British invaders.

[103] Hugh Tinker, *The Foundations of Local Self-Government in India, Pakistan, and Burma* (London, 1954), pp. 22–23.

[104] Mya Sein, pp. 44–47, 49–52, 56–57. Nineteenth-century records from Upper Burma reveal occasional instances of independent village administrations smaller than the township, under *ywathugyis* (*ywa* = village).

[105] *Ibid.*, p. 78. *Myothugyis* on journey customarily rode in carts and were preceded by outriders.

productivity of the region.[106] In areas distant from the township headquarters, he was assisted by a collector (*myetaing*) or possibly by a
ywagaung (village constable), both of whom received a 10 per cent
fee for tax collections made.[107] Neither the *myothugyi* nor his relatives
paid taxes personally. He customarily collected taxes from more households than he reported existing within his jurisdiction and pocketed
the difference. He usually undertook to shield his own people from
the exorbitant demands of court officials,[108] utilizing the assistance
of locally selected assessors in distributing the burden. Most of the
local tax was paid in kind.[109]

Newly developed agricultural land became the property of the person who cleared it and was not taxed as such. But since increased
productivity beyond one's family needs only invited accretions to the
household levies, there was little incentive to accumulate property in
land. Other revenues came from market dues, from the operation of
ferries and landing stages, from saltworks, brokerage services, and
timber concessions and fisheries.[110]

A heavy flat-rate capitation tax and other exactions were levied on
migrant and backward Karen peoples and on other peoples of Lower
Burma who were not assimilated into the regular system of government. Such peoples were assigned to the jurisdiction of a special
Wun.[111] The capitation tax was resented as a mark of subjection as

[106] Furnivall, "Notes," pp. 48–52. The *athi* alone paid special forest taxes in fiber,
bark, syrup, charcoal, palm-fruit rind for writing, tamarinds, tree cotton, and also
earth oil. The *tawkegaung* was the forestry officer.

[107] The *myetaings* and *ywagaungs* customarily gave "presents" of cloth and
produce to the *myothugyi* at the time of their appointments (Mya Sein, pp. 64–67,
71–73).

[108] *Ibid.*, pp. 68–76. High officials collected taxes on cattle sales, as well as a
pound fee for collecting stray cattle, and claimed presents of the ribs or flanks
of dead cattle. See Furnivall, "Notes," pp. 48–52.

[109] Yule, pp. 253–255; Tinker, p. 23. Wealthy persons paid 10 to 12 ticals, several
times the average household tax. Crops were assessed 5 to 15 per cent of output.

[110] Burmese customary law stressed the right of all agricultural laborers to compensation in the form of food and a change of clothing at the end of both planting
and harvest seasons. It also protected from encroachment that portion of the
peasant's crop required for his living and for food (*wunsa*). The river duties on
shipments of fish paste and rice upstream to the capital were substantial. See Htin
Aung, pp. 211–212; Mya Sein, pp. 66, 183–186; Crawfurd, II, 176; Yule, pp. 253–
255; Furnivall, "Notes," pp. 52–53.

[111] Malcom, I, 222–223; Furnivall, *JBRS*, IV (1914), 210–211; Mya Sein, p.
186. The Karens paid taxes in beeswax and elephant tusks and on numerous forest
products. The Karen poll tax in 1803 was calculated at 9 or 10 kyats (ticals) of
silver per head, which was probably twice as heavy as the tax levied on the average

well as for economic reasons. To a considerable degree, the indigenous system of local government in Lower Burma was submerged even prior to 1825 by the arbitrarily superimposed Burman system of royal officials, the *taikthugyis*, and the special *Wuns* for unassimilated peoples. British administrators in Lower Burma prior to 1886 apparently never made contact with a genuine Burman-type *myothugyi*-centered local government and hence imperfectly understood it.[112]

Unsalaried village and ward constables (*azat gaungs*) and subordinate ten-house *gaungs* (one for each ten-house group) acted as local police under authority of the *myothugyi*. Each village was palisaded, and itself assumed responsibility for posting a standing night watch to guard against marauding bandits. The well to do could escape watch duty by paying a fee. The *myothugyi* could arrest suspects, hold preliminary investigations, require surety guarantees by dubious characters, and sometimes flog minor offenders with the rattan. But real criminal cases, as already indicated, had to be handed over to the *Myowun* for trial.[113] Individual villagers were required to assist the headman in tracing the whereabouts of thieves on pain of being exiled from their community. Villages which harbored robbers or stolen goods were punishable collectively by the *myothugyi*. The latter was himself in turn held liable by the *Myowun* to make good the loss of unfound stolen goods and to pay a substantial fine in addition.[114]

Minor civil disputes were settled as far as possible locally by voluntary submission to an arbiter, as was customary in the villages of China. The arbiter's task was to arrive at an agreed solution out of court but in accordance with the generally recognized principles from customary law. Such agreements as well as formal court decisions were sealed by the participation of the disputants in a ceremonial "eating" of pickled tea. Failure to accept proffered tea was equivalent to appealing the case.[115] If a compromise settlement could not be reached

---

Burman family. Hill-cultivating (*taungya*) Karens and Chins paid only 1 kyat per household. Shan taxes were in the form of tribute from vassal rulers.

[112] See Tinker, pp. 23–24.   [113] Crawfurd, II, 144; Malcom, I, 100–101.

[114] Half of the criminal-case fines (*konbo*) was divided evenly between the *Myowun* and the king; the *Myowun* also shared equally with the queen's *Wun* another tenth portion; one-quarter was allocated to the writer-secretaries of the *myoyon* and one-eighth to messengers (*nakans*). The customary 30-tical fines for assault and the 15-tical fines for abusive language were similarly distributed. See Crawfurd, II, 151–155.

[115] Htin Aung, pp. 206–210. Civil court fees were called *taya-konbo*. Part of the assessed fines went to purchase the ingredients for the "pickled tea" ceremony.

locally, the dispute would have to go to the *myoyon* for adjudication. Thereafter, every approach to a judicial official called for payment by the complainant of fees, or presents (bribes), without which success in court was impossible. Most of the population kept as far away as possible from the courts.[116]

A final aspect of local government in Lower Burma, and in the Shan States as well, was the king's practice of assigning to the chief queens, to the great princes, and to *Wungyis* and other top officials the revenues from particular *taings* or *hkaings* which were normally due the ruler. These *myosas* or town "eaters" normally received half of the collected revenues, but they were usually in a position to exact additional goods and services. When the royal family was overnumerous, the *myosas* might control much of the cultivated countryside.[117] A *myosa* whose presence was not required at the capital usually resided in his "fief" or *jaghire*. If absentee, he collected his dues through a steward who took over in the name of the *myosa* the responsibility of governing the area. The great princes with the exception of the *Einshemin* took their titles from the regions assigned to them; thus, the sons of the king were frequently entitled the princes of Toungoo, Bassein, Pagan, Prome, or Tharrawaddy.[118] *Myosa* areas were usually badly governed, and the harried inhabitants frequently had no means of redress except to abandon their lands and seek residence elsewhere. The *myosa's* exactions, furthermore, did not exempt the people from extraordinary additional levies imposed by the court itself.[119] During the later decades of Mindon's rule (1852–1878), he tried to abolish the *myosa* system and to substitute in its place a graduated household tax (*thathameda*), from which revenue regular salaries could be paid to *Wungyis*, *Atwinwuns* and *Wundauks*, and other officials. He was only partly successful.[120]

[116] Crawfurd, II, 143–144; Nisbet, I, 19, 192–193; Mya Sein, pp. 68–76. Crawfurd (II, 149) comments cynically as follows on the character of the regular governmental courts as of 1826: "The Judges take bribes from both sides, and the decree . . . will [usually] be in favour of him who pays the highest. Both the judges and ministerial offices . . . gain a principal part of their emolument from litigation and therefore do all in their power to promote it. No prudent person . . . enters into a law suit." According to Maung Maung (*Burma in the Family of Nations*, pp. 15–18), royally appointed arbiters (*kundaws*) tried to work out an agreed settlement in civil cases prior to their coming before the *myoyon* court in a formal way.

[117] Sangermano, pp. 79, 86–88.

[118] Mya Sein, p. 33; Yule, pp. 243–244. The term *Thakin* (lord) was used interchangeably with *Min* (prince).

[119] Crawfurd, II, 162, 165–166.   [120] Fytche, I, 243.

The Burmese Army

Warfare was a traditional preoccupation of the Burman state and especially so in modern times. It was frequently waged as an exhibition of dynastic vigor and also as a means of affording adventurous excitement and opportunity for loot in slaves and goods. During the first half century of the Konbaung dynasty, established by King Alaungpaya in the 1750's, warfare was almost incessant. Following the conquest of his Mon rivals in 1755, Alaungpaya raided Manipur. Burman armies almost depopulated that country—astrologers, silversmiths, and cavalry units for the army were brought back to the capital as elite prisoner slaves. Then followed a series of exhausting and destructive wars waged against the Siamese state, from 1760 to 1767, resulting in the total destruction of the Thai capital city of Ayuthia. Upon the return of the Burmese armies from Siam, they were obliged to undertake in 1768–1769 the major task of repelling a substantial invasion of the Northern Shan States by the Chinese armies. Affairs in Siam went badly as a result of increasing local resistance and the insubordination of Burmese officials. Control over Siam was lost beyond recovery by 1776. Conquests began again under King Bodawpaya (1782–1819). Arakan was incorporated into the Burma state in 1784, and victorious Burman armies subsequently invaded Assam. Burma attained impressive geographical dimensions as a result of these conquests, but the costs were high.[121]

The military campaigns against Siam bore very heavily on the peoples of Lower Burma, which was in the path of contending armies. The number of general-levy draftees might run as high as one man for every three to six houses, with a minimum of one recruit for each supporting unit of eight to ten houses. The families of conscripts of doubtful loyalty were often held as hostages and made liable to execution in case of treachery, desertion, or cowardice.[122] The recruitment power of the *myothugyi* or the *taikthugyi* was often abused. Since he could demand army service of all, he usually began by drafting mem-

---

[121] Harvey, *Outline*, pp. 137–142, 145–146; Hall, *Symes*, p. 211. The handsome Mahamuni image together with 125 slave families to serve its new shrine were transported from Arakan to Amarapura in 1785 and housed in the impressive Arakan pagoda.

[122] Symes, pp. 318–320; Mya Sein, pp. 4–5; Yule, pp. 248–250. Symes (1794) referred to levies running as high as one recruit for 2 to 4 houses; Scott (Shway Yoe, pp. 505–508) mentions one for each group of 6, 12, or 20 houses; Yule mentions 2 soldiers for each group of 16 houses.

bers of well-to-do families, who were able and willing to pay generously to be excused. Pursuing these tactics down the economic scale, the *myothugyi* could realize from the operation a considerable profit, of which he kept a major share. He eventually recruited the required contingent from those unable or unwilling to pay for being excused.[123] Households not furnishing men had to share in the support of those sent up. The royal arsenals furnished only munitions and weapons, mainly antique firelocks of English and French make. Poorly supplied armies en route to and from Siam in the late eighteenth century were a scourge to the inhabitants of Lower Burma, sparing neither crops, houses, fruit trees, nor even monastic property.[124] Karen villagers usually fled to the mountains to escape labor service, while thousands of Mons prior to 1800 fled to Siam, where they augmented the anti-Burman forces.

The *athi* conscript or nonprofessional army served in township units led by *myothugyis* with the rank of sergeant (*thwethaukgyi*).[125] Above them came two ranks of professional officers, the *tathmus* (lieutenants commanding 100 men) and the *thenatsayes* (captains commanding 250 men). Many of the colonels (*Bos*) were civilian political appointees, who were qualified to ride elephants, to carry gold umbrellas and appropriately decorated dahs and bowls, and to be escorted by retainers. The appointment of a *Bo* was a special royal action authenticated by the *Hlutdaw;* each appointee was bound by a special oath of loyalty to the king. The post of commanding general (*Thenat Wun*) of the infantry was usually held by one of the four *Wungyis* or by a special appointee of *Wungyi* rank.[126]

The professional standing army, in contradistinction to the mass-

---

[123] The cost of avoiding service might run as high as 300 ticals, worth approximately 850 shillings in 1800.

[124] Malcom, I, 71–72, 222–223; Mya Sein, pp. 67–68; Symes, pp. 319–321; Shway Yoe, pp. 499–508; Yule, pp. 248–250; Sangermano, pp. 97–99; Hall, *Symes,* p. 211. Burmese soldiers carried their own sleeping mats, cooking pots, and wallets of rice and hot chillies. If supplementary food did not arrive from home, they took what they needed from the vicinity of the camp or route of march.

[125] Furnivall, "Notes," p. 57; Harvey, *History of Burma,* p. 340, and *British Rule* (London, 1946), pp. 24–25. Harvey states that brotherhood (*thwethauk*) bonds were sealed either by drinking each other's blood or by group drinking of a blood-water admixture using blood drawn from an animal sacrificed to the *nat* spirits. *Thwethaukgyis* as well as leaders of cavalry (*myingaungs*) and of war canoes (*penins*) sometimes acted as recruiting agents.

[126] R. R. Langham-Carter, "The Burmese Army," *JBRS,* XXVII (1937), 268–270. The title *Bo* was widely misappropriated during and after World War II.

levy service required of the *athi* population, was drawn from families of *ahmudan* status who owed personal allegiance to some regimental *myothugyi* or chief. They could be assigned to infantry, artillery, cavalry, archery, boatmen, or elephant units. *Daing* (service) units, consisting of three or four *ahmudan* families, contributed one member each to the armed forces assigned to guard the palace in peacetime and also assumed responsibility for supporting him and his family while resident at the capital. Some regular *ahmudan* military regiments came from as far south as Pyinmana and Minbu, but apparently none were drawn from Lower Burma. Infantry *asu* came from some localities, cavalry and artillery groups from others, while riverine towns furnished the war boats and marines.[127] The royal artillery regiments were recruited in large measure from descendants of Christian Portuguese and French captives taken at Rangoon, who by 1800 were Burmese in everything but religion. The cavalry units included many Shan and Manipuri horsemen (*Cassayers*). The elephantmen, exclusively Burman, moved the heavy guns.[128]

Ahmudan elements of the army were assigned access to varying amounts of royal land according to rank.[129] Regimental leaders gained social distinction by assuming titled appellations in place of their previous names. Holders of service land dressed according to status and also staged ceremonial functions, such as funerals, according to rank. Because *asu* membership was hereditary, the regimental groups had to be self-sustaining in providing new recruits. But as in Lower Burma, active service could be avoided by extra payments of support.[130] The full enrollment of an *ahmudan* recruit in the army was signalized by

[127] Symes, pp. 320–321; Hall, *Symes*, pp. 174–175; India Office Archives, *Bengal Political Proceedings*, MSS. EUR., D106, pp. 54–55. Symes, in 1802, witnessed a fairly impressive parade of scores of war boats mounting small cannon and carrying an estimated 10,000 to 20,000 men. War boats in 1795 had numbered around 500. River marines were respected as a fighting force by foreign observers. After steamboats were introduced on the Irrawaddy River by the British in 1852, the war boats came to perform only ceremonial functions.

[128] Mya Sein, pp. 4–5, 14–15; Langham-Carter, *JBRS*, XXVII (1937), 273–276. The Shwebo area was the home of a Burman cavalry regiment. The Portuguese had been captured at the port and taken upcountry after 1600, while the French were acquired during the 1750's. See Pinkerton, VIII, 418–421, IX, 403.

[129] A private got 5 pés (one pé equaled 1¾ acres), a corporal 7½ pés, a sergeant 10 pés of royal land. The higher officers received income in addition to their land allotments.

[130] Mya Sein, pp. 74–76; Langham-Carter, *JBRS*, XXVII (1937), 254–267. *Ahmudan* lands carrying royal-service obligations were inherited and family owned. Such land claims could be leased or sold, but blood relations always had the first claim. Ancestral lands were divided among heirs, with daughters sharing with the sons equally. A daughter's share ceased to be *ahmudan* land if she married one not

the ceremonial placing of appropriate indelible tattooed insignia on the back of his neck indicating his obligation for royal service (the insignia for this was usually a royal dragon) in a particular *asu*.[131]

The Inner Household Brigade responsible for guarding the royal palace was composed in 1800 of six picked regiments, numbering at full strength some 3,000 to 4,000 men all told. Their commanders (*Windaw Hmus*) were important personages. Smaller units guarded the *Hlutdaw*. The Inner Brigade was seldom used in active campaigning. An Outer Brigade of similar size, also drawn from selected *ahmu-dan* areas, guarded the several gates of the walls of the capital itself and formed the nucleus of the regular army.[132] The actual size of the peacetime Burmese army at the capital, as reported by European observers, was considerably less than the theoretical twelve infantry regiments plus auxiliary and specialized units.[133] Long before King Thibaw's time (1878–1885) the Burmese army, rendered largely inactive by the near proximity of the British, had lost its once-acclaimed *élan*. An increasing number of *ahmudan* army retainers, after 1826, evaded their service duties.[134]

The traditional pride in one's *ahmudan* status and in tattooed service markings as an evidence of masculinity survived into the British period of the late nineteenth century. Even the youth of Lower Burma developed a kind of mania for patronizing the tattooing "*Sayas*," who displayed sample books of favorite designs. Virtually all upcountry Burmans were reported in the 1880's to be decorated with the blue

---

regularly liable to military or other royal service. A *daing-gaung* was frequently made responsible for the upkeep of the family-group land.

[131] Both Fitch (in the late 1500's) and Hamilton (in 1709) reported that the practice of tattooing prevailed only in Upper Burma. See Pinkerton, VIII, 424, IX, 422.

[132] Langham-Carter, *JBRS*, XXVII (1937), 264–273; Shway Yoe, p. 508. Rough braves (*asu gyun*) who were not tattooed performed sentry duty outside the capital.

[133] Symes (pp. 317–321), in 1795, reported only 2,000 saber and musket-armed infantrymen plus 300 cavalry, of which 700 only were in constant residence within the city. He estimated that some 2,000 additional troops divided up into small detachments were on duty outside the vicinity of the capital.

[134] Malcom, in 1835 (vol. II, Appendix, p. 109), reported that whereas the Burman army traditionally went "dancing to Siam," the payment of 150 ticals would not buy a soldier to attack the "white kulas" after 1825. Shway Yoe (pp. 497 ff.) gives a most unflattering picture of the flower of King Thibaw's army on parade, with the elephant-borne commanders flanked by personal guards and umbrella-bearers; artillery incapable of being fired; and a chattering, betel-chewing infantry column breaking ranks to converse with onlookers, grabbing proffered cheroots and a light, then scurrying to catch up, with their uniforms seemingly about to fall off.

tracery of a variety of animal forms (cats, elephants, monkeys, lizards, birds, as well as the traditional royal dragons). The practice did not decline until the second decade of the twentieth century. It was revived during the 1920's among the *Wunthanu* (nationalist) *athins* led by *pongyi* politicians, whose leaders revived hoary folk tales, widely believed, concerning the extraordinary powers of tattooing and other kinds of charms to bring good luck and even invulnerability to the wearers.[135]

Conclusion

The political fabric of pre-British Burma was obviously weak at many points. Governmental institutions and procedures were rudimentary outside the immediate environs of the capital, and even there the despotism of the king and the unsolved problem of succession contributed to instability. Poor communications with areas distant from the capital, the disruptive intrusion of the *myosa* fief system, and the primary allegiance of the population generally to hereditary local chiefs were all marks of governmental immaturity. To these were added the lack of a common basis of citizenship among Burmans and the incomplete assimilation of the Mons, the Arakanese, the Shans, and the numerous tribal groups living within Burma's natural boundaries.[136] Many of these elements of weakness, but by no means all of them, were measurably corrected during the period of British rule, but the latter was debilitating in other respects. The traditional integrating factors of widespread male literacy in Burmese, general effectiveness of Buddhist religious sanctions with regard to moral conduct, and popular allegiance to the sovereign authority as divine king and patron of the Buddhist faith were severely impaired after 1885. The simultaneous destruction of the vital institution of the *myothugyi* and the decay of discipline within the Buddhist monastic order contributed greatly to political and social demoralization so clearly in evidence after World War I. Later chapters will provide additional data bearing on many of these problems.

[135] Shway Yoe, pp. 508, 509. The author recorded that, as of 1881, "the belief of every Burman in the efficacy of these tattooed charms is practically irradicable." British administrators in the twentieth century discovered that one of the first evidences of planned insurrection was a marked increase of tattooing activity. The tattooing has been universally practiced among Shans down to the 1950's.

[136] Furnivall, "Burma Past and Present," *Far Eastern Survey*, XXII (Feb. 25, 1953), 21–24.

II

Social and Economic Aspects of Old Burma

THIS chapter does not purport to present a comprehensive description of social and economic life in old Burma,[1] but merely a clarification of important aspects of traditional Burmese society which eventually had a direct bearing on political developments in the twentieth century. These include a description of the several minority peoples, the Buddhist religion and its relation to the state, education, the position of women, and a summary estimate of the society as a whole.

The Minority Peoples

With the exception of the Shans, who inhabited the valley areas of the Upper Irrawaddy basin and the plateau country to the east of the central valley of Upper Burma, the political situation of the minority peoples was an unenviable one. Shan princes had themselves ruled Upper Burma for several centuries prior to the rise of the Burman Toungoo dynasty in the mid-sixteenth century. The surviving nineteenth-century *Sawbwa* princelings of the Shan States acknowledged tributary relationship to the Burmese Court in return for Burmese noninterference in Shan affairs. Except for the fact that daughters of the *Sawbwas* often found their way to the king's harem, Shan in-

---

[1] For good detailed treatments of Burmese society, see Shway Yoe, *The Burman: His Life and Notions* (London, 1882, 1896, 1910); Harold Fielding-Hall, *The Soul of a People* (London, 1899) and *A People at School* (London, 1906); H. T. White, *Burma* (Cambridge, 1923).

fluence in the Burman-inhabited valley regions was nil except in the upper reaches of the Irrawaddy basin. After the British eliminated the Burmese Court in 1885, the Shan States retained their autonomous tributary status to British Burma. The numerous non-Shan tribal peoples who inhabited the plateau were politically unimportant.

The second important minority group, the Talaings, or Mons,[2] who inhabited the northern Tenasserim coastal area and the lower Sittang and Irrawaddy valleys, had contributed much to Burma's historic culture but were traditional enemies of the Burmans. The Talaings made a final desperate effort to re-establish their supremacy in the mid-eighteenth century and actually captured Ava, only to suffer conclusive and ignominious defeat from the aroused Burmans under the leadership of the newly emergent Konbaung dynasty. This civil war and its accompanying depredations turned much of Lower Burma back into a jungle country infested with tigers, wild elephants, pigs, and deer. Symes, who journeyed to Pegu in 1795, observed on the shores of the river leading to the ancient Talaing capital carcasses of deer half eaten by tigers. He noted only an occasional hut standing amid vestiges of once-populous towns. In many areas abandoned cultivated areas were overgrown with tall grass. The formerly extensive Mon capital of Pegu turned out to be a city of only a few thousand people surrounded by a desolate jungle. The Pegu *Myowun*'s nondescript guard of 500 to 600 men in 1795 was officered by Christian descendants of Portuguese captives, and the provincial court was entertained by expertly trained captive Siamese dancers.[3] During the concluding years of the eighteenth century, thousands of Mon refugees found their way to Siam. Other visitors to Burma in 1820 and 1826 reported the river banks along the delta route from Rangoon to Henzada in precisely the same mosquito-infested and uncultivated state in which Symes had reported it in 1795. Only clusters of pagodas and palmyra palms remained to indicate abandoned river towns.[4]

British arrival in 1824 brought no immediate respite to Lower Burma. The remnant of the Talaing population in the delta area actively as-

[2] For the story of the Mon entry into Burma via Siam, see C. M. Enriquez, "Story of the Migrations," *JBRS*, XIII (1923), 77–81.

[3] Michael Symes, *An Account of an Embassy to the Kingdom of Ava*, pp. 165–168, 174, 182, 193, 201–205. Symes was favorably impressed by the complete absence of any evidence of drunkenness or debauchery at a major festival he attended at Pegu. He observed that such decorum could not be matched in Britain.

[4] Symes, p. 454; Crawfurd, II, 20; India Office Archives, *Bengal Political Correspondence*, MSS. EUR., D106, "A Description of Hindustan and Adjacent Countries by Walter Hamilton" (1820).

sisted the British invaders in the 1824–1825 campaign and accordingly suffered further repression at Burman hands following the withdrawal of the British from Rangoon in 1826. More than 10,000 of them fled subsequently to British-annexed Tenasserim.[5] None better than the Talaings, except possibly the Siamese, knew the fury of which the aroused Burman army was capable. The following explanation attributed by Crawfurd to Adoniram Judson is relevant:

The conduct of the Burmans in their predatory excursions is cruel and ferocious to the last degree. . . . "You see us here," said some of the chiefs to Mr. Judson, "a mild people living under regular laws. Such is not the case when we invade foreign countries. We are then under no restraints— we give way to all our passions—we plunder and murder without compunction or control. Foreigners should beware how they provoke us when they know these things." [6]

The Talaing population of the Tenasserim region suffered particularly from the fact that this coastal corridor was fiercely contested by the Burmese and Siamese during the last decades of the eighteenth century following the fall of Mon Pegu. Mergui and Tavoy changed hands several times during fighting which raged from 1785 to the final Burmese victory in 1793.

The people of the coastal kingdom of Arakan had long enjoyed political independence. Relations with nearby Bengal were usually unhappy, and conditions for several decades after 1690 were anarchic, because of chronic rebellion.[7] After Arakan fell to the invading Burman army in 1784, many Arakanese took to the hills and jungles, formed tribal robber bands, and carried on vexatious depredations against Burman authorities and into neighboring Chittagong for many years thereafter.[8] Following the suppression of a prolonged Arakanese rebellion in 1797, the Arakan area also became relatively deserted with jungles taking over where towns had once flourished. Some 50,000 refugees fled to Chittagong, where they became the cause of chronic difficulty between Burma and the East India Company.[9] A feeling of

[5] Crawfurd, II, 20–25.

[6] *Ibid.*, I, 422. An accompanying deposition dated 1826 from an Indian prisoner describes barbarities which had accompanied the Burmese capture of 6,000 Indians in Manipur and Assam during the wars of the previous year.

[7] Pinkerton, VIII, 416–418. Hamilton's account.

[8] Symes, pp. 104–110, 112–117.

[9] Shearman Bird, the company collector in Chittagong, reported in 1787 that Burmese forces pursuing Arakanese rebels across the border behaved well compared with the atrocious conduct of the rebel bands. The second Symes mission

separate national identity survived among the Arakanese into the mid-twentieth century.

Another sizable minority group in Lower Burma alien in both language and culture to the Burmans were the Karens. They were divided into three principal linguistic groups. The Sgaws, or Burmese Karens, lived mainly in the Irrawaddy delta and areas peripheral to it. The Pwos, or Talaing Karens, were concentrated near the coast around Bassein, Thaton, and Moulmein. A subdivision of the Pwos, the Pa-O or Toungthu people, lived in the Southern Shan States. Sgaw and Pwo languages were quite different, and the two groups had relatively little in common. The third group, or Bwe Karens, were more closely akin to the Sgaws than to the Pwos. They inhabited the rugged hill terrain between the Sittang and the lower Salween rivers.

The Karens generally were unimportant politically, for they were a backward animistic folk caught helplessly between the upper and nether millstones of the unterminable Talaing-Burman feud. They were too cowed to resist, and most of them tried to keep out of harm's way by hiding in the swamps or hills. No Karens were found north of the Prome-Toungoo line except for the Taungthus and Bwes in the Shan plateau area. They learned in time to endure heavy taxation and oppression with a kind of dull indifference.[10] The hill Karens developed only rudimentary political institutions and were even worse off than their cousins in Burma proper, mainly because of their interminable feuding habits and their shortage of good arable land.

The Karens were inveterately rural. During the early 1800's they carried on a major part of the agriculture of Lower Burma, maintaining a kind of wandering existence in semipermanent villages in the midst of the jungle waste. They were governed locally by their own chiefs and traditions and, as already explained, owed no public services to the Burma king as did the Burmans. They were not even a part of the *athi* population. They paid to the *Myowun* fixed annual imposts estimated at 18 ticals per family (twice the rate customary for *athi*

---

to Ava in 1802 was occasioned by an intemperate demand on the part of the Burmese viceroy of Arakan for the surrender of alleged criminals who had fled to Chittagong. This issue had been raised earlier in 1787. See India Office Archives, MSS. EUR., E63, no. 155, "Deputation to Ava."

[10] Shway Yoe, p. 445. The so-called Red Karens (related to the Bwes) inhabited the vassal Karenni state. The Padaungs living in the Shan States area were also kinsmen of the Karens. Many Karens fled to the Arakan Yoma in 1826–1827, but others were cut off from escape routes.

Burmans) plus various contributions in kind.[11] The Karen peoples cherished their own peculiar social and religious traditions and seldom intermingled with their Talaing or Burman neighbors. The friendly Father Sangermano in 1795 described them as "timorous, honest, mild-mannered, exceedingly hospitable to strangers." Very few Karens at the time knew how to read and write Burmese even imperfectly, and they possessed no written literature of their own.[12] Their most serious vice was their heavy addiction to strong drink, a practice abandoned subsequently only by the Christianized group.[13] Under the leadership of the highly respected Reverend Adoniram Judson, the American Baptist Mission began its pioneering work among the Karens after the first British war.

There is no conclusive proof that the Karens were systematically enslaved by the Burmans, as is often alleged, but they were forced to perform onerous services from time to time. It was to escape such burdensome duties that the valley Karens periodically sought refuge in the fastnesses of the Irrawaddy delta or in the mountains along the Siam or Arakan borders. Social as well as political cohesion among the Karens was lacking.[14] Karen affairs were handled by specially appointed *Wuns*, operating outside the regular administrative system. The dominant Burman element regarded them in unconcealed contempt as an inferior breed, the "wild cattle of the hills." The Karens were eventually rescued from this precarious status by British rule and by American missionary activity.

The primitive Chin peoples who inhabited the hill areas between Upper Burma and India north of Arakan also had reason to fear their

[11] Crawfurd, II, 170–171. The depressed spirit of the Karens is reflected in such proverbs as: "We are the eggs, other races are rock; the egg fell on the rock and was broken; the rock fell on the egg, and it was broken." See Harry I. Marshall, *The Karen People of Burma* (Columbus, 1922), p. 306.

[12] Symes, p. 207. The Pwo Karens were picking up spoken Burmese from the Mons during the early decades of the nineteenth century, but the Sgaws knew little Burmese. The Mon tongue was outlawed after 1755.

[13] Malcom, I, 44.

[14] D. M. Smeaton, *The Loyal Karens of Burma* (London, 1887), pp. 153–157. In an address to the viceroy of India in 1826, the Karen spokesmen complained that the Burmans forced them to pull their boats and logs, to cut rattan, to collect beeswax, to strip bark for cordage, to clear away ruins of cities, to build fortifications, and to weave large mats. Such duties, it was affirmed, sometimes took men away from their families weeks at a time. Other required services included providing vegetables, guarding of forts, and acting as guides in time of war.

Burman overlords. They were frequently robbed of their animals, land, and even womenfolk by Burman neighbors. As a measure of self-protection they allegedly adopted the practice of tattooing the faces of their women to make them less attractive to outsiders.

The wild Jingpaw or Kachin tribesmen, who lived in the hill country on both sides of the upper Irrawaddy Valley and across the China border, were alone among the minority races in offering strenuous resistance to Burmese control. The vigorous Kachins for generations defied the efforts of both the Burmese and the Chinese to tame them. They infested the hill areas and lived mainly by robbery and extortion, except in scattered areas where a *modus vivendi* was arranged with Shan neighbors.[15]

Trade and Land Ownership

The capital area of old Burma was the focal point of a considerable volume of trade coming in from a number of directions. From Lower Burma during the rainy season came hundreds of cargo boats laden with rough-milled rice, fish paste (*ngapi*), dried fish, salt, and European manufactured wares. The cargo boats were propelled by oars, by ropes from shore, by poles, and also by sails which caught the steady south wind of the summer monsoon.[16] The river journey from the delta to the capital might require three or four months. In a hurried three weeks' journey from Rangoon to Ava in 1835, an American visitor passed scores and even hundreds of such boats daily, the largest of them laden with an estimated 10,000 to 12,000 bushels of rice. He also commented admiringly on the hardihood, skill, energy, and unfailing good humor of the multitude of river boatmen engaged in the traffic. In the area of Pegu and throughout the delta, boats were the only means of travel, while the Irrawaddy River was the great upcountry artery of trade and communication. In nonriverine areas of Upper

[15] Shway Yoe, p. 452. Colonel Browne's account of the ill-fated Margary expedition's attempt to return to China in February, 1875, contains a realistic description of the Kachins with whom he had to deal. His party was actually rescued by Kachins following Margary's death. See H. A. Browne, *Reminiscences of the Court of Mandalay* (Woking, 1907), pp. 64–65, 67, 75. A recent study of the Kachins by E. R. Leach (*Political Systems of Highland Burma,* London, 1954) discovered practices of combating evil spirits allegedly responsible for sickness by staging a feast for the devil to sniff, a ceremony which is identical with practices described by Fitch for roughly the same area in 1586. See Pinkerton, IX, 421–422.

[16] Symes, p. 324.

Burma oxcart roads were used.[17] The traffic downstream carried sugar, cooking oils, and cotton, some of the cotton being destined for shipment via Prome overland to Arakan and thence to Bengal.[18] Considerable quantities of petroleum drawn from open-pit Yenangyaung wells [19] also went downstream, to be used for lamps and torches and for preserving wood, mats, and palm-leaf manuscripts.

From the plateau country east of the central valley numerous Shan bullock and horse caravans arrived during the winter dry season, bringing to the capital markets stick-lac, groundnuts, lead, sugar, manufactured umbrellas, cotton cloth, black cloth jackets, and lacquered boxes. The better animals from the caravans sometimes provided tribute to the Burma Court or were sold in the valley. A large suburb of the Burman capital was set aside for the accommodation of the Shan traders.[20] The Shans carried back salt, *ngapi*, dried fish, and betel nuts. The precious metal (gold and silver) produced at the Bawdwin mines site in the northern Shan area was the exclusive property of the king.

The China trade with Ava and Amarapura in the early nineteenth century was also surprisingly active. Most of the Chinese imports came by caravan to Bhamo and thence down the river to the boat terminal at Sagaing, opposite the capital. But mule caravans of enormous size also came to the capital area overland, presumably down the modern Lashio-Maymyo route to a market fair located some thirteen miles distant from Amarapura at the base of the plateau. Smaller caravans of around 50 men and 400 oxen each reached the fair as early as December, and larger ones estimated in size up to 1,000 men and 2,000

[17] Malcom, I, 89–90, 95, 225–226; Symes, p. 55.

[18] Malcom in 1835 (I, 223), estimated that 4 million pounds of Burma cotton per year were being sent to Arakan and 2 million to Dacca in Bengal.

[19] Numerous descriptions of these primitive oil wells can be found (Symes, pp. 442–443; Cox, pp. 34–45; Malcom, I, 91 ff.). They operated from shafts, some cut as deep as 220 feet, driven into the soil and rock strata by hand. A malodorous mixture of dingy green oil and water was drawn to the surface in covered wicker or metal receptacles by ropes passing over a revolving wooden cylinder. Two men holding the end of the rope ran down a declivity in the hoisting operation. Their partners at the well emptied the receptacle into an outside cistern or pool; from this the water drained away, leaving the oil at the top to be ladled off into huge earthen jars for the three-mile cart journey to the riverside. The oil wells numbered several hundred and were scattered over a twelve-mile-square area. Their daily output approximated 500 vis (1,750 pounds) each. The government leased the sites to private operators and collected a 5 per cent tax on the output.

[20] Malcom, I, 223.

ponies arrived in February. The Chinese traders brought gold leaf, paper, raw silk and floss, woven satins, velvets, cordage, arsenic, tea, spirits, honey, dried fruits, walnuts, preserves. The staple item of export to China was seeded raw cotton, grown extensively in Upper Burma. The Chinese also carried back amber, ivory, precious stones, betel nuts, edible birds' nests, and, by 1835, quantities of Bengal opium.[21]

The considerable colony of Chinese residing at the capital and at Sagaing, as reported in 1835, consisted mostly of traders, craftsmen, and producers of sugar. A later visitor in 1855, after rebellion in China had disrupted the trade, estimated the Chinese living near the capital at 2,000 families plus an additional 500 families at Bhamo.[22] In 1850 the Burmese king was operating a royal monopoly over the cotton trade, under which the Chinese were permitted to acquire cotton only on royal license at approximately twice the price paid by the king to the cultivator. The China trade, although declining as a result of Muslim rebellion in Yunnan, was still potentially profitable. By the 1860's the British in Lower Burma were becoming interested in the possible revival of the Burma-China trade.[23]

Burma's lack of interest in sea-borne trade stemmed from Ava's interior position and its apparent unconcern for the welfare of the Talaing, Arakanese, and Karen peoples who inhabited coastal Burma. This attitude was historically a perennial cause of Burman friction with the commercially sensitive government of Talaing Pegu. During the 1580's, Lower Burma had possessed three important ports of entry. Cosmin (Bassein) on the western edge of the delta received ships from India bringing cotton cloth, yarn, and opium. Syriam on the opposite side of the delta was visited by Arab ships bringing woolen cloth, scarlet and velvet fabrics, and opium. To Martaban at the mouth of the Salween River came ships from Malacca with sandalwood, Chinese porcelains, Borneo camphor, and pepper from Sumatran Achin. Eight selected brokers at Pegu handled the sale of all imports on a commission basis, and a large section of the city was set aside for for-

[21] *Ibid.*, pp. 114–115, 223–225; Symes, pp. 325, 432; Harvey, *Outline*, pp. 142, 154. At least three Burmese missions reached Peking after 1769.

[22] Yule, pp. 144–145; Malcom, I, 114–115, 223–225. Malcom, who came as the agent of the American Baptist Mission, recommended the stationing of a Chinese-language missionary at Amarapura or Sagaing.

[23] Yule, pp. 144–145. The French Lagrée-Garnier mission of 1867–1868 penetrated Yunnan via the Mekong Valley. The ill-fated Margary expedition of 1874–1875 was a counter British attempt to explore the possibilities of trade with China via Burma and Yunnan.

eign traders. Pegu's overseas exports at the time included gold and silver, precious stones, ivory, tin, lead, copper, stick-lac, rice wine, and sugar. Travelers making the ten-day journey from Cosmin to Dalla by boat across the Irrawaddy delta in the 1580's passed large riverine market towns and reported a fairly dense population.[24]

The commercial situation in Pegu in the eighteenth century was far different. By 1700, the capital of Pegu was reduced to 5 per cent of its former population as a result of recurrent and alternative Siamese and Burmese invasions. Syriam in 1709 still exported silver, rubies, timber, stick-lac, earth oil, and beeswax, but the hinterland was desolate.[25] Pegu staged a temporary political recovery during the 1740's, only to be crushed militarily by Burma during the 1750's, as already explained. After 1760 it was overrun repeatedly by armies en route to Siam. The once-prosperous overseas trade was completely wrecked.[26]

The principal export item from the ports of Rangoon and Syriam during the late eighteenth and early nineteenth centuries was teakwood, a timber widely used for construction and for shipbuilding purposes, especially in Calcutta. Teak exports as of 1795 were valued at £200,000 annually. The Burma Government forbade the export of rice from Rangoon in order to ensure an ample supply of cheap grain for the capital area. British imports at Rangoon in 1794–1795 included some £135,000 worth of hardware, coarse cloth, glassware, and broadcloth annually. In 1835, Rangoon, although a steadily growing city of 50,000 people, still lacked a wharf and a quay.[27]

The economic interests of Lower Burma were severely hampered by the prohibition on the export of rice in particular. There was also

[24] Pinkerton, IX, 398–401. One city called Coilan reportedly extended for a league on both sides of the stream. Other unidentified cities named were Silvansedi, Moggio, and Medon.

[25] A wild deer could be purchased at Syriam in 1709 for 3 or 4 English pence.

[26] Pinkerton, VIII, 418–422, 429, IX, 398–405. Pegu in the 1580's was surrounded by walls in the form of a square, with a crocodile-filled moat outside. Each of the four walls was pierced by five gates with broad through streets connecting gateways opposite each other. A new city was arising outside the walls to accommodate the surplus population (reported by Fitch and Balbi). Balbi was an eyewitness in 1583 of a burning orgy at Pegu, when several thousand rebels allegedly perished on a vast funeral pyre.

[27] Symes, pp. 455, 458–459; Malcom, I, 74–75. The Burma Government collected a 5 per cent duty on all exports and a 10 per cent duty on imports. Ships could be built in Burma for one-third less cost than at Calcutta, but British policy in the 1790's opposed shipbuilding operations at Rangoon for fear that their French enemies might be enabled to augment their navy. A major objective of Symes's mission to Ava in 1802 was to influence Burmans to deny French access to Burma's ports.

47

a shortage of labor in the south. Rice prices at Rangoon from 1795 to 1820, a time of low production, were only one-fifth to one-fourth those at Amarapura; in 1835 they were approximately half the prices prevailing at the capital.[28] Wages for laborers at Rangoon in 1835 were 12 ticals per month compared with only 5 ticals at Ava. Most of the skilled craftsmanship seems to have congregated in Upper Burma.[29] Any change of trading policy permitting the free export by sea of surplus rice from Rangoon, such as the British introduced after 1852, would inevitably transform the trade outlook of the entire country. The consequent development of Lower Burma agriculture would attract large numbers of agriculturalists and laborers from relatively crowded Upper Burma.

The Burmese monetary unit, the tical or kyat, was the one-hundredth part of a vis (three and one-half pounds) of silver. But coined silver was distrusted and was therefore sparingly used. Silver used in commerce had to be assayed for fineness by silversmith-bankers (*pymons*), who were usually hired by businessmen on a 1 per cent commission. The assayers often charged for their services only the silver which adhered to the utensil used. The export of silver was strictly forbidden. The tical in Lower Burma in 1835 was worth approximately the same as a Madras rupee, or around 50 American cents; it had been worth 60 cents at Ava in 1795. Money for hire was available in Lower Burma in 1835 at interest rates of 2 to 3 per cent per month with security and 4 to 5 per cent without it. The customary legal regulation that the amount of interest paid must never exceed the original value of the loan could usually be avoided by creditors, who exacted new notes from debtors every few months in order to keep their loans alive.[30]

Mortgage loans on houses or lands under Burman law were really conditional sales. They were usually redeemable by the first owner within a period of three years, during which time the lender had full

[28] The Rangoon price for rice in 1795 was 1 tical for 4 or 5 baskets compared with 1 tical per basket at the capital; the price ratio in 1820 was still four to one while 1 tical in 1835 would buy 20 baskets of rice at Rangoon and 10 at the capital. Fowls at Rangoon cost 2 rupees a dozen as compared with 3 rupees per dozen at Ava. Eggs at Rangoon were only 1 rupee per 100 in 1835. See Symes, p. 320; Malcom, I, 74–75; India Office Archives, *Bengal Political Correspondence,* MSS, EUR., D106, "A Description of Hindustan . . . by Walter Hamilton," II, 768.

[29] Malcom, I, 74–75.

[30] Symes, pp. 287–288, 320; Malcom, I, 228. Fractional units of the tical or kyat were the *mat* or quarter-tical, the *moo* or one-eighth, and the *to-bé* or one-sixteenth. The *to-bé* corresponded to the anna of India.

use of the property in lieu of interest payments. Undeveloped land especially in Lower Burma was so plentiful that it was valueless. Family estates usually began in the redemption of an area from the jungle. Continuous cultivation for ten years gave the developing family full title to such land. Family estates were kept intact and were shared equally by men and women heirs. The owners kept their claims alive by taking turns cultivating the estate. Even males who migrated elsewhere, as relaxed family ties permitted them to do, maintained theoretical titles to their shares of the family estate.[31] The sale of such an estate, like the customary mortgage arrangement, was always conditioned on the right of the original owner or owners to redeem it by paying back the purchase price. Family holdings in Lower Burma were frequently broken up, sometimes by warfare, by forced removal of population, or by simply abandoning sites for health or other reasons. Residents of Upper Burma, on the other hand, clung to their family land with the tenacity of religious fervor.[32] The powerful sanction employed in local communities of Upper Burma against troublemakers by denying them access to the family estate was correspondingly less effective in Lower Burma.

Government and Religion in Old Burma

The most important nonpolitical segment of the society in old Burma was the Buddhist *Sangha*, or sacred order of monks. The monks were influential because they touched virtually all elements of the population and because they were reverenced by the people. Pagoda shrines built for purposes of acquiring merit dotted the countryside everywhere, and each village had a monastery school, or *kyaung*, adjacent to it. The number of monks and neophytes resident at the capital alone in the early nineteenth century was estimated at no less than 20,000 or around one-fifth of the entire population of the city. Important regional shrines allegedly containing sacred relics of the Buddha, such as the Shwe Dagon at Rangoon, housed up to 1,000 or 1,500 occupants.[33]

[31] Htin Aung, "Customary Law in Burma," in Thayer, ed., *Southeast Asia in the Coming World*, pp. 203–213.

[32] Shway Yoe, pp. 532–533. Sangermano (p. 203) tells how the area of Pegu and Rangoon in 1800 was scourged by gnats, horseflies, mosquitoes, and leeches to add to its unattractiveness.

[33] Crawfurd, II, 128–131; Malcom, I, 264; Symes, pp. 210–213. Crawfurd's and Malcom's Ava reports were dated 1826 and 1836 respectively; Symes's report on Rangoon was in 1795.

Several nonreligious reasons for the vogue of monasticism in Burma have been advanced. The desire to escape onerous service demands which were levied on the population generally may have contributed something to the popularity of the life of the monk, as did, no doubt, disinclination to undertake the responsibilities for supporting a family. The absence in Burmese social tradition of any sacramental ideas of marriage or any religious motivation to re-enforce the natural urge to leave descendants for carrying on the family line has also been cited as a negative factor contributing to the tradition of celibacy in Burma.[34] Religious reasons and social prestige were also important factors. The monks constituted for Burman Buddhists the very embodiment of the moral order. They were the educators of youth and the custodians of sacred literature and learning. To preserve the treasure of Buddhism constituted traditionally the very *raison d'être* of the Burman state, the rationale of its historic mission. To acquire Pali scriptures, images of the Buddha, or allegedly sacred relics from India or Siam were frequently the objectives of warlike raids and major diplomatic missions.[35]

The Buddhist monks were recluses who withdrew from mundane affairs. The Trinity of the Buddha, the *Dhamma* (law), and the *Sangha* (order of monks) afforded under the faith the sole means of escape from the vanities and sufferings of life. The Buddhist faith equated life with suffering and affirmed that suffering was rooted in desire. Release from the endless and painful succession of reincarnations could therefore be found only by conquering desire and by following the eightfold path to purity.[36] The religious objective of monastic holiness was essentially individual rather than social.[37] The monks were in no sense ministers of religion engaged in preaching, exhorting, and comforting the needy. A sympathetic foreign observer in 1709 praised the monks for their open-minded tolerance, involving few polemics and no persecutions, and for their embodiment of principles of morality

[34] See J. Stuart, "Why Is Burma Sparsely Peopled?" *JBRS*, IV (1914), 1–6.

[35] G. E. Harvey, *British Rule in Burma, 1824–1942* (London, 1946), 25–26, 265.

[36] The eightfold path included right belief, feelings, speech, actions, means of livelihood, endeavor, remembrance, and meditation.

[37] The Buddhist decalogue set forth five universally applicable commands against taking life, stealing, adultery, lying, and drinking intoxicants; the five others, which were incumbent only on the monks (on holydays for the laity), forbade eating after midday, participation in dancing and music, use of cosmetics, occupation of elevated platforms inappropriate to one's status, and the handling of gold and silver.

and charity.[38] The *Sangha* normally did not rebuke transgressors except to deny to impostors who might attempt to enter the order the benefit and protection of the sacred robe while disgracing it by unworthy conduct. The monks afforded opportunity for the laity to acquire merit (*kutho*) by contributing to their needs as they made their daily rounds, for no monk solicited aid directly. Sometimes an evil community could be disciplined effectively by imposing a kind of interdict, during which the monks inverted their begging bowls and thus denied the laity opportunity to obtain merit. People accorded profound veneration to the genuinely holy monks, especially to the *pongyi* ("great glory") heads of monasteries. Local communities, on their part, could on occasion refuse alms and thus force careless monasteries (*kyaungs*) to exclude impostors.[39] No wearer of the yellow robe was subject to control by secular authorities at any level save that of the court itself acting usually on the advice and through the instrumentality of the designated hierarchy of the *Sangha*.[40]

Religious functions pertaining to government were performed, as indicated in Chapter I, not by the Buddhist monks, but by Brahman priests from India. These were allegedly men of pure caste, learned in astrology and numerology, competent to act as the custodians of the sacred ritual designed to buttress kingly authority.[41] Brahman magic played an essential role in determining the proper location of new capital sites, in regulating the calendar, and in selecting auspicious days for inaugurating important undertakings. Princes and *Myowuns* as well as court officials consulted Indian astrologers and soothsayers to obtain needed guidance. Brahman priests also allegedly counteracted the machinations of evil spirits (*nats*) and otherwise exploited the credulity and superstitions of the populace.[42] The importance attaching at court to such priestly services was indicated by the king's request in 1795 that Symes obtain sacred religious books from India and also a priestly Brahman of pure caste, well versed in astrology and accompanied by his wife.[43]

---

[38] Pinkerton, VIII, 426–429, by Hamilton, who here reflected European preferences.

[39] Nesbit, II, 144–148.   [40] *Ibid.*

[41] Symes (pp. 362–363) reported listening to a fifteen-minute recitative by several Brahman priests during his audience in 1795.

[42] *Ibid.*, p. 220. In 1795, the *Myowun* of Pegu selected the auspicious date for starting his journey with Symes to the capital after consulting his astrologer.

[43] *Ibid.*, p. 426.

51

In comparison with the excessive deference paid by the Burma Government to the alleged Indian wisdom of the Brahman priests, Chinese cultural influence was relatively faint and ineffective. Harvey records that it was customary at court to make images representing deceased kings and that these were worshiped or reverenced as ancestors of the ruling prince.[44] On the occasion of the entry of Prince Tharrawaddy into Ava as the new king in 1837, he performed a perfunctory obeisance before the gilded images of his dynastic ancestors.[45] Burman tradition contained no cult of the family, however, and such copying of Chinese patterns apparently carried little political vitality. At lower levels of Burmese culture, reverence for magical Hindu lore merged with various amoral indigenous cults concerned with ensuring the success of any kind of venture or with warding off malevolent spirits.[46]

Burmese history reveals numerous exceptions to the general rule that the Buddhist monks took no interest in politics and performed no governmental functions. On many occasions the government utilized the services of highly respected monks in connection with peace negotiations relating to civil strife, a practice designed to add an aura of sincerity to the proposals advanced.[47] On one historic occasion a monk dared to berate a king for employing trickery in such a diplomatic

---

[44] G. E. Harvey, *History of Burma*, p. 333.   [45] Desai, *History*, p. 327.

[46] See U Hla Baw, "Superstitions of Burmese Criminals," *JBRS*, XXX (1940), 376–383. Armed gangs (dacoits) following a religious ritual, selected a lucky day for adventure, avoiding any combination of day and month adding to thirteen and also boat travel on Fridays. They followed the direction from the tail to the head of the assumed position of the Naga serpent on the day selected. The gang always included an odd number of persons who must never walk past a cemetery. The screech of an owl, the howling of a dog, the meeting of a snake were bad omens. Charmed amulets were worn on the arm or around the waist (a boar's tusk, a deer's horn, an animal's skull bone), and such protective devices were re-enforced by frequent recitations of Pali stanzas over these charms. Victims could allegedly be induced to sleep by scattering ashes taken from the funeral pyre, burned on Saturday, of a person dying on Saturday. The aid of the *nats* could also be invoked by 1,000 repetitions of charmed phrases over human skull fragments strung on threads, if done in a graveyard on Saturday night while biting a dried piece of human flesh. The *nats* of the house of the victim could be placated by use of such charms and by appropriate accompanying rituals. Tattooing was also important, as was the display of flags and candles. Harvey (*History*, pp. 317–321) tells of even more gruesome practices, dating from primitive times, such as the eating of the roasted flesh of great magicians or princes as a means of partaking of their powers and the execution of human victims (*myosade*) to provide protective spirits for newly built palace foundations, city walls, or gates.

[47] Harvey, *History*, pp. 88, 233, 251, 255. This pattern of using monks as peace intermediaries was followed in the rebellion of 1837. See W. S. Desai, "The Rebellion of Prince Tharrawaddy," *JBRS*, XXV (1935), 118.

move involving the monk's aid.[48] On other occasions monks urged the deposition of unworthy monarchs; they sometimes led revolts, once aided royal personages to escape, and several times acted as interim regents.[49] The monks could also usually be counted on to challenge presumptuous royal pretensions to Buddhahood or to *pongyi* status.[50] Presiding monks at pagoda shrines, located both in the capital and in the provinces, protested at times to the court or to local *Wuns* against oppression or to obtain reprieve from death of a condemned person. Persons so rescued became pagoda slaves for life, however.[51] Monkish participation in rebellion was almost invariably on an unauthorized and individual basis.[52] Politically minded monks played prominent roles in arousing popular opposition to King Bagyidaw in 1831 and, subsequently, to British conquest in 1852 and 1886.[53] In 1852, King Mindon Min emerged from a monastery to take over the throne from his discredited brother Pagan Min. The new king summoned another *pongyi* from his cell to become one of his *Atwinwuns,* subsequently one of his *Wungyis.*[54]

The potential political influence of the Buddhist monks stemmed from popular reverence for wearers of the yellow robe and the assumed responsibility of the government to support the faith. It was destined to become a matter of importance in the rising tide of national feeling following World War I. In the time of the Burma kings, the government was far more concerned to keep the *Sangha* under effective royal control than were the monks to interfere in political affairs.

The Thathanabaing *and the Royal Commissions*

The principal agency by which the king exerted control over the Buddhist *Sangha* was the office of the *thathanabaing* (the accent is on *baing*), a kind of archbishop of the monastic hierarchy.[55] The incumbent was customarily the chief *pongyi* of an important monastery

[48] Harvey, *History*, pp. 62, 199. On this occasion the overbold monk discreetly departed immediately on a pilgrimage to Ceylon.

[49] *Ibid.*, pp. 97, 107, 177–188, 215, 235.

[50] Sangermano (pp. 74–75) tells of the monks' rejection in the late 1790's of King Bodawpaya's pretensions to being a *Bodhisattva,* or emergent Buddha.

[51] Fielding-Hall, *The Soul of a People,* pp. 86–87.

[52] Symes, pp. 95–97. In 1781–1782, for example, several monks, acting in alliance with a *Wungyi* and an *Atwinwun,* were involved in an abortive plot to overthrow a disreputable king. On this occasion the pretender prince, an ex-monk, took over rule for only eleven days.

[53] J. S. Furnivall, *Colonial Policy and Practice* (New York, 1948), pp. 199–200.

[54] Yule, pp. 99–100.

[55] Nisbet, II, 124. *Thathanabaing* meant "possessor of discipline and instruction."

kyaung at the capital and frequently the head of the monastery which the king himself, as a youth, had attended for an indeterminate period. The *thathanabaing* was selected by the king and retained office at his pleasure. The nominee of a deposed or deceased king automatically reverted to the status of mere *pongyi* on the accession of a new king. The primate was assisted by a commission consisting of eight other monks named by the court but presumably chosen to represent various sectarian divisions of the *Sangha*.[56] The *thathanabaing* exercised religious authority under royal mandate and served also as the channel for making royal authority effective throughout the monastic community.[57]

The *thathanabaing* and his associates at court were assisted by district "bishops" called *gainggyoks*. This system did not constitute a genuine ecclesiastical hierarchy, however, for the clergy over whom it presided was an aggregation of individual ascetics rather than an organized church community. The principal function performed by the organization was disciplinary. It exercised legal jurisdiction under the *Vinaya* rules governing monastic disputes, settled controversies involving pagoda lands, and ruled concerning flagrant personal offenses or theological deviations of the clergy. The *thathanabaing* and his local emissaries also supervised the holding of the official annual examinations (*batamabyan*) in the Pali scriptures, supervised monastic training at the higher levels, and recommended qualified monks for appointment as *pongyi Sayadaws* at important pagoda centers.[58]

Local monasteries were required to report the names and dates of reception of new resident monks plus data on withdrawals and disciplinary cases. They also kept records of visiting monks and took custody and responsibility for disseminating governmental proclamations and statutes. Routine discipline within a monastery was ordinarily maintained locally, but royal authority lay behind the power of the *thathanabaing* and the district *gainggyoks* to settle disputes, to expel offending members of the *Sangha*, and to enforce obedience to instructions transmitted from the capital. The only occasion when the king

[56] Because the leader of any given sect had no authority over monks of a different order, all important sects were represented at the office of *thathanabaing*. See Furnivall, *Colonial Policy*, p. 13.

[57] Nisbet, II, 124–127; Harvey, *History*, p. 326. Scott (Shway Yoe, pp. 108–110) asserts that all members of the commission were classified as *Sadaws* (*Sayadaws*), or royal teachers, and were therefore technically *thathanabaings*.

[58] Harvey, *History*, p. 326; Symes, pp. 210–213. The *Sayadaw* at Rangoon in 1795 displayed to Symes the engraved sacerdotal titles which had been given him by the existing king and by his predecessor.

accorded temporary deference to the *thathanabaing* was when the primate visited the court to recite from the temporarily vacated royal dais the ten laws incumbent on kingship.[59]

The *thathanabaing* was highly respected personally because of his religious eminence and as one of the great men of the kingdom.[60] The *kyaung* over which he presided was patronized directly by the king and was invariably one of the magnificent structures in the capital area. Symes in 1795 was at a loss for words to describe the primate's richly carved and gilded structure, with its five-tier roof supported by magnificent sixty-foot pillars. He reported the acting *thathanabaing* to be a man of only forty years, of lively demeanor, fat and jocular.[61] The American visitor, Malcom, in 1835, was equally impressed by the quarters of the then *thathanabaing*, who was a much older man and also much less cordial than the one Symes described.[62]

Working in close conjunction with the *thathanabaing* and his assistants were two high officials of the government appointed by and directly responsible to the king. One was the *Wutmye-wun*, or commissioner of ecclesiastical lands, while the other was the *Mahadan-wun*, or ecclesiastical censor. The first maintained authentic records of pagoda properties in both lands and slaves. He also supervised the utilization of royal revenue available for the maintenance of monasteries and pagodas. Periodic royal inventories guarded against possible overextension of religious property claims.[63] The *Mahadan-wun* and his staff of eight secretaries prepared annually, at the beginning of each Buddhist lent, an official list of the ordained clergy by districts, their ages, and the dates of their formal induction. The government also maintained in the important monastic training centers crown-appointed clerks (*Kyaung-serai*), who co-operated with the local *Sayadaws* in collecting the data needed for the operations of the two commissions in the capital, including conduct records.[64] Serious disciplinary actions

[59] Nisbet, II, 124–125. The king was on such occasions exhorted to eschew anger, dishonesty, oppression, and impatience and to cultivate piety, generosity, gentleness, and self-denial.

[60] Malcom, I, 264.

[61] Symes, pp. 387, 390–392. The palace tutor, or *Saya-Wungyi*, in 1826 and ordinarily, was not a monk at all but a man with a family. See Crawfurd, I, 496–497.

[62] Malcom, I, 98–99. Malcom's status as a missionary may have influenced the primate adversely; another factor was the American's apparent failure to display proper deference.

[63] Harvey, *History*, p. 326. Two comprehensive general inventories of pagoda properties were taken in 1784 and 1803.

[64] Malcom, I, 269–270.

against disorderly clergy were undertaken by the *Mahadan-wun* under the guidance of the *thathanabaing*. Some offenders were unfrocked; others were made to wear the white robe of the pagoda slave; the most serious offenders were turned over to the secular arm for punishment.[65] The *Mahadan-wun* also acted to suppress agitation by lay schismatics which might be productive of political disorder.[66]

Buddhist Monasticism at Provincial Levels

The monastic order outside the capital included a number of gradations of rank below the level of the district *gainggyoks*. Many of the *pongyi* heads of monasteries assumed in time the title of *Sayadaw* (royal teacher) by virtue of such designation by the *thathanabaing* and the court. To attain full *pongyi* rank, a monk was required technically to have proved his steadfastness by unflinching self-denial over a minimum period of ten years beyond his formal initiation as a full-fledged monk or *rahan* (Pali for "holy man"). Those who fulfilled twenty years of loyalty to their vows were eligible to be heads of monasteries and were greatly venerated by the people. Full *rahan* members of the order below the rank of *pongyi* were called the *Pyit-shins* (or *upesins*), a title earned by the passing of formal examinations in the scriptures at the age of twenty or above.

The younger novitiates, or *ko-yins*, who ranged as a rule between fourteen and twenty years, had all been subjected to the formal "shin-pyu" ceremony. This was usually an elaborate and costly affair involving both family and monk participation and signifying the youth's symbolic rejection of worldly desires and temptations. The *ko-yins* were only probationers and not really monks at all. Their residence within the monastery was of uncertain duration. Still younger than the *ko-yins* were the *kyaungtha* scholars, who attended the village *pongyi kyaung* school.[67]

The principal problem of monastic discipline developed in connection with the youthful *ko-yins*. Misbehaving *kyaungtha* scholars and younger *ko-yins* were kept under control by being soundly beaten

[65] Harvey, *History*, p. 326.

[66] Crawfurd, II, 124–126. For example, in the early nineteenth century a *Kolan* sect was suppressed by the court for criticizing the laxity of the clergy and for ridiculing the extravagant practice of building overnumerous pagodas as means of acquiring personal merit.

[67] *Pongyi* schools will be described below under the education heading. See Shway Yoe, pp. 108–110, 116.

across bare backs with bamboo flails by monastic disciplinarians,[68] but the older *ko-yins* sometimes defied control. One of the attractions of the yellow robe was the privileged and highly respected status enjoyed by its wearers, in contrast with the usually burdensome life incumbent on the laity.[69] The older *ko-yin* ranks included many loafers, divorce seekers, and avoiders of family and public duties, who used the robe for ulterior designs.[70] Even in pre-British times monasteries which were deficient in their discipline tended to become the refuge of malcontents and the nurseries of conspiracies against the reigning sovereign.[71] Since, under lax control, one might remain indefinitely in the status of *ko-yin* without taking the *upesin* qualifying examinations at all, this group did much to swell the number of the clergy to excessive size and measurably to discredit its standing. Whereas the real monks were universally respected and were reported by foreigners to be tolerant, humble, and friendly, frequently possessing a genuine scholarly interest, the unruly novitiates were often guilty of bigotry, folly, and offensive personal conduct.[72]

The four cardinal sins for which wearers of the yellow robe could be severely punished were carnal pleasure, stealing or coveting, taking of life, and presumptuous arrogance regarding one's status as a holy man. Willful offenders were living lies and were liable to public disgrace, social ostracism to the level of outcasts,[73] and sometimes to violent stoning. If a novitiate or a *rahan* found himself unable to live in continence and to forego ambition for power and wealth, the honorable thing to do was to leave the order. This could be done at any time without prejudice to one's personal standing in the community, the usual explanation being that one's *kan* or *karma* was not sufficient for the arduous test. The offense committed by a monk in pretending to a status for which he was not qualified was aggravated by the fact that religious preferment was open to all and that all laymen including the

---

[68] *Ibid.*, p. 29.   [69] Nesbit, II, 149.   [70] Malcom, I, 98–99, 264–270.

[71] C. J. F. S. Smith-Forbes, *British Burma and Its People* (London, 1878), p. 336.

[72] Malcom, I, 264–270.

[73] Shway Yoe, pp. 108, 116–122. In addition to pagoda slaves, the outcasts included jailers, executioners, and prostitutes. The status of pagoda slave persisted by social convention down to Burma's independence in 1948. As outcasts, they were denied normal economic opportunity and were obliged to continue to beg for a living. An "All-Burma Beggars Conference" which met at Minbu in July, 1955, was addressed by U Ba Swe, who denounced the persistence of the pagoda-slave status.

king were obligated to do reverence to the *rahans* and *pongyis*. Veneration was universally accorded to the really austere monks. A village
kyaung presided over by an intelligent and respected *pongyi* invited
there by the villagers was often a kind of village council chamber
where the cleric's advice was solicited regarding various local affairs.[74]

The national civilization of old Burma was held together in large
measure by the Buddhist *Sangha*.[75] It was the one cultural and political
bond which linked the Burmans with the Arakanese, the Talaings, and
the Shan population. Court opposition to the work of Christian missionaries among Burmese Buddhists as of 1826 and later was based primarily on the allegation that attempts to convert Buddhist Burmans
was equivalent to challenging their allegiance to the king. It was partly
due to the absence of such political considerations that no serious
governmental objection was raised to missionary work among plains
Karens, the Chinese, or the minority hill groups. The leading *Sayadaws*
of the monasteries were, as a rule, far more tolerant and open-minded
toward the Christian scriptures and toward Western learning generally
than were governmental officials and politically minded nationalists.[76]

Popular regard for the Buddhist faith was deeply ingrained. Sixteenth-
century European visitors to the Shwe Dagon pagoda shrine were much
impressed by the mile-long, tree-bordered avenue, fifty paces broad,
extending from the river's edge to pagoda hill, jammed on feast days
with pilgrims of all ranks including royalty.[77] In the Talaing-inhabited
Tenasserim coastal area following its acquisition by the British in 1826,
Buddhism seemed to be cherished by the people all the more jealously
out of popular concern to resist the impact of Western civilization and
control. The *kyaungs* and pagodas continued to be well supported, and
the rulings of the *thathanabaing* were respected even without the support of the Burman Court. The powerful inertia behind religious tradition was also demonstrated in the persistence of veneration of monks
long after growing laxity of discipline, especially in British-held areas,
had adulterated the purity of the *Sangha*.[78] Social life centered around
pagoda festivals, colorful light celebrations at the end of lent, and

[74] Smith-Forbes, pp. 335–336; Furnivall, *Colonial Policy*, p. 13. Smith-Forbes
wrote in 1878 that "although great laxity has . . . crept into the order of late
years in minor details, yet the chief and distinctive rules are strictly observed."

[75] Furnivall, *Colonial Policy*, p. 17.   [76] Crawfurd, II, 124–126.

[77] Pinkerton, IX, 400–401, 418. Balbi described the Shwe Dagon pagoda platform as larger than St. Mark's Square in Venice. Fitch declared that Dagon was
"the fairest place, as I suppose, that is in the world."

[78] Shway Yoe, p. 124. Scott, in 1881, noted increased laxity in Buddhism, but
he perceived no loss of popular strength for religion.

shin-pyu ceremonies. Until the end of the first decade of the twentieth century, the *kyaungs* continued to serve as the principal means of education.[79]

Education in Old Burma

At the age of around eight years, Burmese youth were sent to the monastery for schooling. Indulgent parents who up to that time had exacted little discipline from the lads now gave full authorization to the *rahans* to punish them for mischief or frivolity. The student *kyaung-thas* waited on the *upesins* and *pongyis* at meals, accompanied them on their morning alms-receiving rounds, drew water as needed, and cared for the monastic quarters generally. They also learned to read, write, and cipher, to memorize the Buddhist commandments and the Pali formulas used in pagoda worship. Although no loud or boisterous games were allowed at the monastery schools, life in the monasteries was enlivened by much storytelling and by the visits of traveling *sayas* and poets. The boys let off energy by shouting their lessons at the top of their lungs as they lay on their stomachs and kicked up their heels. Whether the students boarded at the *kyaung* or went home for their meals, they were uniformly subject to penance or punishment for misconduct. They had no choice but to attend school, because parents and relatives would usually send them back if they tried to run away. Students were supposed to continue in the *kyaung* school until initiated by the *shin-pyu* ceremony at the age of twelve to fifteen into *ko-yin* status. The *shin-pyu* afforded them the priceless opportunity to elevate themselves in future existences to the level of man, above the hell of mere animal existence.[80]

An initiated *ko-yin* turned his back on the attractions of carnal pleasures, wealth, personal adornment, family comforts, and other worldly desires during a longer or shorter period of residence at the monastery. The minimum acceptable period of residence for a novitiate was throughout one entire lenten season, extending from early summer into the autumn. Life as a *ko-yin* followed a memorable routine involv-

[79] Shway Yoe, pp. 211–223. In ch. ix, Shway Yoe gives a full description of a harvest and pagoda feast held in February at one of the famous Talaing shrines near Rangoon. It included feasting, bullock-cart racing, gossip with friends, flirting, puppet plays, *pwés* (dramatic entertainments), as well as offerings to the *rahans* and sermons on the law. With all of the merriment the participants nevertheless gained merit from the pilgrimage. Pagoda worship came regularly four times a month.

[80] Mi Mi Khaing, *The Burmese Family* (Bombay, 1946), pp. 1–7; Shway Yoe, pp. 14–20.

ing staying in after dark, sleeping at the monastery, rising at five-thirty in the morning for prayers and devotions, participation in the morning alms-receiving rounds, and fasting after noon of each day. Meanwhile they, like the *kyaungthas*, must act as servants to the *upesins* and *pongyis;* they must sweep, get water, bring food, wash bowls. The novice took a new Pali name, which he kept as long as he continued membership in the order. Especially rigid was the requirement to pay no attention to womenkind. Those who continued in the novitiate and carried on their Pali studies until the age of twenty could qualify as *rahans*. But barring disciplinary action, the novitiate might continue residence for a longer period even though failing to maintain progress scholastically.

In addition to the education of the *kyaungtha* and the *ko-yins*, the leading monastic centers afforded advanced training in higher Pali studies and in the Burmese classics. Such centers also provided instruction on a variety of nonreligious subjects, such as court protocol, engineering, construction, and manufacturing operations. Court pages and the numerous secretaries and readers used at the various higher levels of government frequently received their advanced training from the *pongyis*. Literary education for girls was provided under lay auspices, frequently within private families, but it was never as widespread as that provided for the boys.

Most Burman youth, of course, abandoned the life of a *ko-yin* and were married before the age of twenty. If they lacked a home of their own, they often went to live with the girl's parents for two or three years and were thereby absorbed into her family.[81] Life in the villages was arduous at seasonal intervals during the year. Unmarried youth who left the monastery were liable to be enlisted by *myothugyis* to serve in levies sent against dacoit bands or in the army during time of war. Sometimes work levies were required to dig tanks, repair canals, or build *zayats* (resthouses) or pagodas. Social mores put a premium on generosity and almsgiving rather than on acquisition of wealth, and there was little incentive to gain property. In the off season there was much loitering about, punctuated by boat trips to the rice mill, pagoda feasts, river races between crews of rival towns, cock and buffalo fights, sometimes by dacoity escapades. It was the native joviality and the laughter-loving gaiety of the Burmese, which a pessimistic religious

---

[81] Pinkerton, VIII, 425, from 1709. The marriage feast was invariably held at the bride's home.

outlook could not dampen, that made the people attractive.[82] Religion nevertheless contributed to the educational discipline, the standards of moral conduct, and the social values by which the people lived.

The monastic system in old Burma was also socially important as a democratic leveling agency. The sons of princes and of fishermen enjoyed the same status at the monastery, for entrance was open to all alike and all were subjected to the same discipline. The system undoubtedly helped translate ethical precepts into social mores. It inculcated reverence for piety and holiness along with Buddhism's realistic if gloomy assessment of life as consisting mainly of evil and suffering. Buddhism provided a logical relationship between goodness and personal destiny and offered to the pious a pathway of refuge and escape through *Buddha, Dhamma,* and *Sangha.* It is against these background considerations that one must assess the effects of the subsequent serious decline of the monastic system under British rule.[83]

The Status of Women

An old Burmese proverb listed among things not to be trusted a thief, the bough of a tree, a ruler, and a woman.[84] Many early European visitors nevertheless attested the remarkable degree of social freedom enjoyed by Burmese women, their dominant position in the home, and their status of economic equality with husbands and brothers. They were allowed to circulate socially and to marry foreigners, although as the wards of the king neither foreigners' wives nor their female children were permitted to leave the country. A departing husband must make provision for care of his family. Theoretically under Buddhist principles women were not regarded as belonging to the same scale of creation as men. Their evidence was worth less in court than a man's and, in fact, had to be taken outside the regular court premises. Among the lower classes women were sometimes sold into slavery because of unfaithfulness or merely to defray family debts, often for purposes of prostitution.[85] The wife always walked behind her husband and must never be elevated above him physically. Women always served the menfolk first at the table, spoiled and pampered their sons, and allegedly prayed that they might themselves be born as men next time.

[82] Shway Yoe, pp. 59–65; Nisbet, II, 232.
[83] Furnivall, *Colonial Policy,* pp. 199–200.   [84] Nisbet, II, 228.
[85] Symes, pp. 328–329; Pinkerton, VIII, 425.

But the wife's subordination was more theoretical than actual. She kept her own property and her maiden name. When provoked, she could belabor her husband with a sharp tongue. She assumed her full share of the burden and the profits of planting and reaping. She could also act for her husband-official in various capacities.[86] It was the universal custom to give wives the custody of the family cash and responsibility for all buying and selling. The groom brought his dowry to the home of the bride and often did not set up a separate household until some three or four years had elapsed. The property that husband and wife brought into the marriage union and an equitable portion of their joint earnings reverted to each in case of a divorce, which was fairly easy to obtain. Girls received from their mothers education in matters relating to their efficiency in home duties, at the bazaar, and in other business activities.[87] Polygamy was sometimes practiced, especially in situations where the first wife was childless, but in that case on conditions set by the first wife, who retained her priority of status.[88]

A woman in some respects was the foil of the masculine ideal of Buddhist perfection. As the very essence of male desire, she was, in theory, the fountainhead of life's evil and suffering, which the monastic system sought to surmount.[89] Her overt role as temptress was sometimes reflected in her dress, the tightly fitting skirt of which was described by numerous visitors as "open in the front so that in walking the right leg and part of the thigh were exposed." She wore an extra outer garment when going abroad or to the pagoda.[90] The female Burmese was earthly and mundane, practical and thrifty, sometimes to the point of greediness, and also attracted by foreigners. She was satisfied with the substance of equality, if not dominance, in the sphere of the home while conceding the theoretical superiority of man.

In contrast to pampered Burman youth, who eventually had to endure artificial discipline at the monastic school, their sisters learned

---

[86] Nisbet, II, 228 ff. Female headmen were by no means unknown.

[87] Malcom, I, 193; Sangermano, p. 165.

[88] Harvey, *British Rule*, pp. 24–25. Divorces, usually obtained by consent, were ratified in the presence of elders and registered with the *myothugyi* for a fee; but they were accorded only after tempers had cooled. Even concubines enjoyed a kind of legal status.

[89] Monastic rules forbade the *ko-yin* or the *rahan* to look at a woman, to be present in the same room with her, or to accept anything from her hand. See Nisbet, II, 201–203; also Pinkerton, IX, 421 (in 1586).

[90] This style of skirt, although clearly violating the high conventional Burmese standards of modesty, was widely reported. See Sangermano, pp. 157–165; Nisbet, II, 206; Pinkerton, VIII, 424–425, and IX, 421, in 1586 and 1709 respectively.

at an early age under the mother's care to do the marketing, to sew, spin, weave, to sweep, husk, winnow, and pound rice, to carry water and prepare food. A painful ear-boring ceremony for girls at the age of twelve or thirteen was the social equivalent of the more glamorous *shin-pyu* for boys. At seventeen or eighteen years of age, the average girl began working in the bazaar stall, self-confident and apparently adjusted to her life role. She could pursue directly and without apology her desire to make herself attractive to men, hampered by no such psychological conflict as her eventual spouse might experience from being too weak-willed or too handicapped by inadequate *karma* to pursue the ideal life of the *rahan*.

The conduct of the young man, by comparison, lacked steadiness. It tended to oscillate between extremes of leisurely monastic negation and participation in the violent daring of the dacoit gang. The first role was venerated on religious grounds and the second admired on grounds of masculinity, but each of them was in a sense an expression of his sense of frustration.[91] The failure of the Burman male to achieve a degree of social and psychological adjustment commensurate with that of his womenfolk apparently contributed to the subsequent development under British rule of male criminality and to the close correlation especially after 1920 between lawlessness and political unrest.

Summary Conclusions on Old Burma

One of the most sympathetic estimates of old Burma is the following statement by Michael Symes, who first visited the country in 1795–1796:

The Burmans . . . are certainly rising fast in the scale of Oriental nations. . . . They . . . have an undeniable claim to the character of a civilized and well instructed people. Their laws are wise and pregnant with sound morality; their police is better regulated than in most European countries; their natural disposition is . . . hospitable to strangers; their manners are rather expressive of manly candour, than [of] courteous dissimulation; the gradations of rank and the respect due to station are maintained with a scrupulousness which never relaxes. A knowledge of letters is so widely diffused that there are no mechanics, few of the peasants, or even of the common waterman . . . who cannot read and write. . . . The feudal system . . . still weakens as their acquaintance with the customs and manners of other nations extends; and unless the rage of civil discord be again excited, or some foreign power impose an alien yoke, the Burmans bid fair to be a prosperous . . . and enlightened people.[92]

[91] Nisbet, II, 181–183, 201–206.   [92] Symes, pp. 122–123.

Symes's flattering appraisal of old Burma was accorded qualified support by an American missionary visitor of 1835–1836 in the following statement which reflected that gentleman's more puritanical norms:

Temperance [in old Burma] is universal. The use of wine, spirits, opium, etc., is not only strictly forbidden both by religion and civil law, but is entirely against public opinion. I have seen thousands [of Burmans] together for hours on public occasions, rejoicing in all ardor, without observing an act of violence or a case of intoxication. . . . During my whole [period] of residence in the country, I never saw an immodest act or gesture in man or woman. . . .

Old people are always treated with marked reverence. . . . Gravity and reserve are habitual among all classes. . . . Men are seldom betrayed into anger, and still less seldom come to blows. . . . Thieving and pilfering are common, but perhaps not more so than in other countries. . . . These crimes . . . are for the most part perpetuated by a few of the basest sort. . . . The inadequacy of the government to the protection of the people makes it surprising that criminal offences are not more common. . . . Lying . . . prevails among all classes. . . . They never place confidence in the word of each other, and all dealings are done with chicanery and much disputing. Even when detected in a lie, no shame is manifested. . . . Never was a people more offensively proud, from the monarch . . . to the pettiest officer. . . . The meanest citizen seems to feel himself superior to the Peguans, Karens, Tongthoos, etc., around him. Gradations of rank are most minutely and tenaciously maintained.[93]

The picture of traditional Burmese society which emerges was attractive in many of its features. The men were inclined to be openhanded, economically unacquisitive, and even lackadaisical in business matters; the women were conversely industrious and thrifty. Both sexes possessed a good sense of humor; they were keen judges of character and particularly apt at mimicry and in coining nicknames, although their jesting sometimes tended toward the coarse and vulgar by puritanical standards. Burmans were nevertheless courteous toward women, never demonstrative of affection in public, tolerant rather than dogmatic in religion, and withal a moral nation by their accepted standards. They demanded sincerity on the part of the *Sangha,* and Buddhism was a cohesive and democratically leveling force. Except in confused times of political disturbances and rebellion, organized Burmese village communities were disciplined and law-abiding.

[93] Malcom, I, 189–191. Malcom here reflects the sympathetic observations of Judson and other American missionaries resident in Burma during the previous twenty years.

Local political authority centered in the hereditary *myothugyi*, whether of *ahmundan* or *athi* status, and every citizen knew to what headman, and on what terms, he was responsible personally. Age was respected; the elders were obeyed; the penalty of exclusion of malcontents from the village was ordinarily an effective sanction. King and *Hlutdaw* provided the ultimate basis of both political and religious authority, but central government played little role in the actual functioning of local institutions and day-to-day affairs. The people possessed capacity for daring and courage, not only in war but also in their ability to endure unavoidable adversity. Social status was prized above wealth, and Burmans put great store in personal dignity and in enjoyment of freedom from arbitrary restraint.[94]

On the negative side was the population's alleged lack of regard for truth as such, which perhaps accounted for personal hesitation to trust each other. A Burman commonly employed falsehood to counter the known deceit of his enemy. Popular superstitions were frequently exploited by the clever for ulterior ends, and the admiration for personal daring contributed not a little to the vogue of dacoity, especially so in times of rebellion. In positions of authority, the Burman was frequently domineering and boastful; power was feared and weakness despised. Political authority was generally abused by *myosas* and often by royal *Myowuns* operating at a distance from the capital and beyond the restraining arm of the *Hlutdaw*. Hence came the popular classification of government—along with fire, water, thieves, and malevolent persons—as a scourge to be avoided at all costs. Burmans were capable of reacting with impulsive violence and complete lack of restraint under circumstances of personal or national provocation.

Talaing enemies in Lower Burma could be assimilated because they were culturally on a par with the Burmans, but this was much less true of the timid Karens, who entertained profound distrust of their disdainful Burman masters. The impulse to generosity among the Burmans was frequently limited to works of merit for the benefit of one's own karma, while gratitude was sometimes listed as a rare virtue.[95]

Such generalizations concerning a nation of several million persons [96] can be regarded, of course, as only approximately accurate, but even

[94] This summary estimate owes much to L. N. Hanks, "The Quest for Individual Autonomy in Burmese Personality," *Psychiatry*, XII (1949), 285 ff.

[95] Nisbet, II, 222–227.

[96] Harvey, *Outline*, p. 149. The revenue inquest of 1803 reported the population of the country, exclusive of wild tribes, as 1,831,467. The total population of Burma proper probably did not exceed 3 million.

so they will provide a useful background against which to judge the effects of the proximity and the eventual control by British India during the three-quarters of the nineteenth century after 1825. Consideration of the initial changes which took place in consequence of British proximity will be taken up in the following chapter.

III

A Century of
British Relations, 1784-1886

FRICTION between the Burma Kingdom and British India developed after 1784, when a common frontier was established between Burma's newly acquired Arakan province and British-administered Chittagong. During approximately a quarter century, border difficulties were settled amicably, but relations worsened after 1811 and eventually reached the breaking point in the mid-twenties. In the first Anglo-Burman War of 1824–1825, a British expeditionary force, transported by sea to Rangoon, advanced on the Burman capital and imposed the punitive peace of Yandabo. Burma had to pay an indemnity of 10 million rupees, to abandon its claims to border states of India and its right to make war on Siam, and also to cede to the British the coastal provinces of Arakan and Tenasserim. The material sacrifices entailed were apparently somewhat less onerous from the point of view of the Burma Court than was the devastating loss of dynastic prestige. King Bagyidaw never recovered from the humiliating experience, and his successors were also seriously embarrassed by loss of face.

The downfall of Burma followed inevitably on the British annexation of the lower Irrawaddy Valley in 1852. British administration in areas adjacent to Burma from 1852 to 1885 transformed the traditional patterns of production and trade in a fashion which the well-intentioned but handicapped King Mindon (1852–1878) could not counter or equal. Burma's collapse came during the palsied reign of King Thibaw. Friction developed not only over British economic activities along the frontier but also over Mandalay's indiscrete dealings with French imperialist agents. The third and final Anglo-Burman War of 1885–1886 witnessed the deposition of the king and the final snuffing out of Burma's independence. The impact of the outside world thus proved to be too formidable for traditionalist and landlocked Burma to withstand.

Burma-British Relations, 1784–1824

The reign of King Bodawpaya (1728–1819) constituted a watershed separating Burma's eighteenth-century traditionalism from its unavoidable orientation toward the outside world in the nineteenth. Although Bodawpaya was perhaps the ablest of the several sons of Alaungpaya, founder of the Konbaung dynasty, the extravagances of the first two decades of his regime brought his country to the verge of economic ruin and political disaster.[1] His first move was to shift his capital from the supposedly ill-omened Ava to nearby Amarapura, a seemingly gratuitous and burdensome undertaking. The new tax registers compiled from the potentially useful general revenue inquest which he instituted in 1783 were used as a basis for extraordinary exactions to finance the adornment of the royal pagodas and the new capital.

In 1784, King Bodawpaya took advantage of faction-ridden conditions prevailing within the kingdom of Arakan to overrun that country. The victorious Burmese forces carried away to Amarapura some 20,000 Arakanese captives including King Thamada. To house the magnificent Arakanese Mahamuni image of the Buddha, which the conquerors transported as booty to Amarapura, King Bodawpaya erected as the first of his many imposing religious edifices the famous Arakan pagoda. The conquest of Arakan brought Burma for the first time into direct contact with the Chittagong coastal district of British-administered Bengal, for it was in this area that the harried Arakanese rebel bands took refuge. The troublesome problem of British-Burma border relations, which was destined to bring the two countries to war some forty years later, did not become immediately critical for several reasons. The Calcutta authorities tended at first to share Burmese repugnance against the turbulent refugees, and Bodawpaya's military ambitions

---

[1] The best brief accounts of Bodawpaya's regime are found in D. G. E. Hall's *History of South-East Asia* (London, 1955), pp. 502–514, and in the introductory chapter of his *Michael Symes: Journal* (London, 1956).

during the first two decades of his reign lay in the direction of Siam rather than India.

King Bodawpaya's series of abortive and sometimes disastrous wars with Siam, the first two of which occurred in 1783 and 1786, were closely integrated with repeated Mon risings in Lower Burma.[2] Resistance to wartime exactions and fear of Burmese vengeance led many of the Mon rebels to seek refuge in Siam, just as the Arakanese fled to Chittagong. Subsequent Burmese military forays into Siam, especially those of 1794 and 1798, entailed the levying of onerous burdens upon the entire population of Lower Burma. Whenever able to do so, the Arakanese, Mons, and Karens resisted the court's exactions; the alternatives were to flee the country or to hide away in the jungles and hills. Except for the prolonged Burmese occupation of the Chiengmai region of northwestern Siam, which the Thai eventually recovered in 1802, the exhausting wars with Siam and the attendant Lower Burma rebellions yielded completely negative results. Many previously cultivated areas of Lower Burma and Arakan reverted to jungle, and former cities and towns were devoid of population. Bodawpaya had indeed created a desert in lieu of peace.

A final factor contributing to the dismal outcome of the first two decades of the reign of Bodawpaya was the king's neglect of governmental duties. This was attributable in part to his religious obsessions (the white-elephant cult and pretensions to prospective Buddhahood) and to his mania for costly pagoda construction. Especially noteworthy was his abortive undertaking to build an enormous 500-foot spire at Mingun, a site several miles upstream and across the river from the capital. On his first visit to Burma in 1795, the observing Michael Symes noted the devastation of Pegu and the delta area; when he came a second time, in 1802, he reported that Upper Burma as well was impoverished because of malgovernment and excessive royal demands for taxes and labor services. Widespread lawlessness prevailed consequent to the king's neglect of his responsibilities.[3]

In spite of recurring difficulties along the Arakan frontier, relations between Amarapura and the Calcutta authorities were at first reason-

[2] Hall, *Symes*, pp. xxvi–xxix, xxxv.

[3] Michael Symes, *An Account of an Embassy to the Kingdom of Ava* (London, 1800), pp. 165–166, 201–205; Hall, *Symes*, pp. 140, 148, 191. Some of Bodawpaya's labor exactions were for constructive ends, such as the repair of the reservoir embankments of Upper Burma, but most of them were intended to promote the king's political ambitions or to satisfy his personal vanity.

ably friendly and co-operative. The Burmese forces which entered Chittagong in 1787 in pursuit of Arakanese rebels were well behaved, and they withdrew promptly on receipt of British assurances of aid in apprehending the disorderly bands and in expelling them from Bengal.[4] Border relations became more difficult during the middle 1790's, when the Arakanese staged futile rebellions in protest against the heavy war requisitions levied by the Burmese Court. As in the previous decade, neighboring Chittagong was entered by large bands of Arakanese refugees, numbering up to an estimated 50,000 in 1794 and an additional 10,000 in 1798.[5] British authorities were obliged to undertake, at considerable cost and trouble, to settle the newcomers on the land. They eventually closed the border to refugees in 1800. Conditions became more serious when Burmese forces invaded Chittagong to enforce the peremptory demand of Burma's Arakan viceroy for the return of all refugees.

Peaceful settlement of such frontier disputes was possible because the Amarapura government at the time entertained no territorial ambitions in the direction of India, and neither party wanted war. The two missions to Burma undertaken by Michael Symes in 1795 and 1802, as the official representative of the governor-general of India, achieved reasonably satisfactory settlements. Symes conceded in 1795 that Burma had the right to solicit the extradition of criminal fugitives hiding in Chittagong. In 1802, the Burmese Court promised to refrain from making further unreasonable demands regarding the frontier, while the Bengal authorities undertook to police the boundary more effectively.[6] Both parties kept their promises, and little difficulty was encountered for almost a decade thereafter. The death in 1803 of the principal Arakanese rebel leader, Nga Than De, helped to quiet the situation. Another factor was the near exhaustion of Burma as a result

[4] India Office Archives, *Bengal Political Correspondence*, MSS. EUR., E63, no. 155, "Deputation to Ava," pp. 17–22. British Chittagong spokesmen in May and June of 1787 admitted that the infamous conduct of the Arakanese bands had forfeited for them any claim to East India Company protection.

[5] Hall, *Symes*, pp. xxvi–xxix, xxxv.

[6] Hall, *Symes*, p. 192, and *South-East Asia*, pp. 505–507. Three Arakanese rebel leaders were actually turned over to Burma in 1794. In 1802, Bengal took the position that undue Burman severity within Arakan was responsible for much of the trouble. They demanded, therefore, verifiable evidence of criminal actions before they would surrender wanted refugees. Calcutta also professed to believe in 1802 that the Arakanese viceroy's ultimatum had not been authorized by the Burmese Court.

of King Bodawpaya's prolonged but futile warfare against Siam and the debilitating effects of his domestic policies.

The British authorities in India, meanwhile, had become greatly concerned, gratuitously so as events proved, about preventing the utilization of Burma's ports by enemy French war vessels bent on destroying Britain's Indian Ocean commerce. The prevention of possible Burman-French co-operation was the primary concern of both of the missions headed by Michael Symes and of two subsequent missions to Ava in 1803 and 1809 on the part of Lieutenant John Canning, acting as the agent of Symes.[7] Another potential cause of friction was the firm determination of most British agents not to shut their eyes to any gesture on the part of Burmese officials which might be considered derogatory to British dignity. But except in the case of the importunate Hiram Cox, who served as British Resident in Burma from late 1796 to early 1798, the emissaries of the Government of India usually subordinated their personal resentments to the substantive objectives of their respective missions.[8]

British-Burman relations began to deteriorate in 1811, when the son of Nga Than De, one Chan Byan (otherwise known as King Bering), took advantage of relaxed frontier control and renewed the civil war by invading Arakan from Chittagong. In his initial move, Chan Byan succeeded in overrunning the entire province, even to the point of capturing the capital of Mrogaung. He then offered without success to accept British suzerainty over Arakan in return for British aid in defending his gains.

Acting on the assumption that British authorities were implicated in the Chan Byan affair, the court ordered Burma troops in 1811 and 1812 following recovery of control in Arakan to invade Chittagong in pursuit of the defeated rebel forces. Canning (now captain) was accordingly sent on his third mission to Burma to protest the invasions and to challenge the Burmese allegation that Chan Byan's raids had been

[7] Symes, *Embassy to . . . Ava;* Hall, *Symes,* pp. xxix–xxxiii, and *South-East Asia,* pp. 509–511; G. T. Bayfield, *Historical Review of the Political Relations between the British Government in India and the Empire of Ava* (Calcutta, 1835), pp. 5–6, 10–13, 29–32. The Burma Court was understandably loath to concede that Anglo-French difficulties justified impairment of Burmese trade, even though French contacts were tenuous and unimportant. Bayfield's account, long considered standard, is marred by falsification of incidents in order to bolster the demands of prideful Britons for aggressive action.

[8] Hiram Cox, *Journal of a Residence in the Burmahn Empire* (London, 1821). Professor Hall (*Symes,* pp. xii–xiv, xlii) sums up the Cox story admirably.

instigated by the British. In this he was only partly successful, for he was confronted at Amarapura by evidence that indicated serious negligence on the part of the Bengal frontier authorities. Relations were not improved by the fact that the defeated Chan Byan easily found refuge in Chittagong despite Canning's pledge to prevent such re-entry. Later British efforts to curb Chan Byan's activities were not effective, and the situation continued tense until January, 1815, when the rebel leader's death ended the crisis. Most of the rebel groups surrendered to the British authorities by May, 1815, but Calcutta refused to surrender the prisoners in the absence of evidence of nonpolitical criminal activity.[9]

The outcome of the 1811–1814 episode was that the Burma Court adopted a warlike posture, this time directed toward India. In 1816–1817, Burma began a program of aggressive intervention in Manipur and to a lesser degree in the neighboring states of Assam and Chahar by elevating to power local princes friendly to presumed Burman overlordship. In June, 1818, the Burmese governor of Ramree directly challenged the British East India Company's control of parts of eastern Bengal and demanded that tax collections within the area be turned over to the Burmese king.

When the aged Bodawpaya was succeeded in 1819 by his popular, but ambitious and pampered grandson, King Bagyidaw, the stage was set for a clash between the rival imperialisms. The able Burmese military leader, Maha Bandula, occupied Assam in the early 1820's. He repelled the attacks of several Assamese pretenders, chased them westward into British Bengal, and then demanded, as in the previous case of Chittagong, that the Calcutta authorities apprehend and surrender all such refugees to his custody. At the same time, Burmese forces expelled the rajah of Manipur, proceeded to devastate that state, and then threatened neighboring Chahar, whither the Manipuri refugees had fled. British India, in early 1824, took both Chahar and Jaintia under its protection.[10] Chittagong was also threatened by mobilized Burmese forces, so that Calcutta became genuinely concerned about the security of the city of Dacca and all of eastern Bengal.

The immediate occasion of the outbreak of war was the disputed

[9] Hall, *South-East Asia,* pp. 512–513.
[10] Hall, *South-East Asia,* pp. 514–515, and *Symes,* pp. xiv–xxxv, lii, lxiii–lxxxiii; Bayfield, pp. 33–42; Maung Maung, *Burma in the Family of Nations,* pp. 30–31. The *Journal* of Hiram Cox, published in 1821, was an extremely anti-Burmese book, and its appearance seems to have aggravated British intransigence.

possession of a border island in the River Naaf, coupled with a minor clash of British and Burmese military units in Chahar state. Fort William at Calcutta declared war on March 5, 1824. A British expeditionary force based on the Andaman Islands landed at Rangoon unopposed on May 10.[11]

The First Anglo-Burman War and Its Aftermath

Although the British capture of Rangoon in May, 1824, had the immediate anticipated effect of forcing the withdrawal of all Burmese forces from the borders of India, the European invaders were unable to follow up their initial advantage. The onset of the summer monsoon in June and the woeful lack of needed supplies and transportation facilities obliged the British-Indian forces to remain confined to Rangoon until after the rainy season had subsided. During the interim, the military effectiveness of the garrison was sadly reduced by epidemics of fever and dysentery. Many deaths occurred, and only some 4,000 of the original 11,000-man expeditionary force were available for the defense of the city when a Burmese army of 60,000 men under General Bandula laid siege to it in the fall. The aid which the British had expected to receive from the dissident Mons of Lower Burma did not at first materialize, so that the situation became critical for a time. The Rangoon garrison nevertheless threw back repeated Burmese attacks and finally, in December, 1824, after re-enforcements had arrived from India, managed to break the siege and defeat the Burmese forces in the field.

The superior arms and discipline of the British-Indian forces spelled the difference. Maha Bandula was himself killed in April, 1825, while defending Danubyu. The turn of the tide encouraged the Mon and Karen enemies of the Burmans to offer active assistance to the invaders in food supplies, labor, and guide services. Even so, the still disease-ridden British forces were obliged to spend a second rainy season in garrison, this time at Prome. During the final stages of the campaign, the expeditionary forces were assisted by a river steamer sent over from Calcutta, a move which virtually canceled out the strong marine contingent of the Burmese army.[12] Meanwhile, the coastal areas of Burma, Tenasserim and Arakan particularly, were occupied by British forces, and pro-British rajahs were installed in Assam and Manipur.

[11] Hall, *South-East Asia*, p. 515.
[12] Hall, *South-East Asia*, p. 515, and *Europe and Burma* (London, 1945), pp. 113–120.

The relentless advance of the British-Indian forces upon the Burma capital during the dry season of 1825–1826 obliged the government to sue for peace. The treaty of Yandabo was signed on February 24, 1826. It levied upon Burma a staggering 10-million-rupee indemnity (£1 million) and specified the cession to Britain of the border areas of Tenasserim, Arakan, Manipur, and Assam. Burma also agreed to make no war on Siam, to accept a British Resident at the capital, and to negotiate a supplementary commercial treaty.[13] British forces retired to Rangoon upon payment of the first installment of the indemnity and then withdrew from the delta entirely, according to agreement, when the second installment was met [14] in late 1826. This rather precipitate withdrawal, dictated no doubt from concern for the health of the troops (most of the 15,000 British-Indian fatalities of the campaign were from illness), made it virtually impossible for the learned but ineffective British negotiator, John Crawfurd, to obtain a satisfactory commercial treaty in the fall of 1826.[15] British withdrawal also exposed their Mon and Karen collaborators, now in full-scale rebellion, to the vengeance of the returning Burmese authorities.

The principal concern of the Burmese Government following the humiliating defeat suffered in 1824–1825 was to undo as far as possible by peaceful means the consequences of the war. One of the most urgent tasks was to re-establish military control over the Mon and Karen-inhabited areas of Lower Burma. By the end of 1826, the rebel groups had established their control over virtually the entire delta area except for such palisaded garrison cities as Rangoon and Bassein. When John Crawfurd returned from Ava to Rangoon in late 1826, following his negotiation of the commercial treaty, he was obliged to negotiate locally for safe passage down the Rangoon River from the point where it branched off from the main channel of the Irrawaddy, for Karens controlled the passage. He reported at the time that the Mons were in complete control of the port area of Rangoon on both sides of the river, except for the Burmese-controlled city itself and the fortified environs of the nearby Shwe Dagon eminence, which had just been turned over to them by the departing British. A Karen force was reported at the time to be pushing across the delta to attack Bassein, which was apparently to have been its reward. Under the leadership of a ranking

---

[13] Hall, *South-East Asia*, pp. 516–517. [14] Bayfield, p. 44.
[15] Hall, *South-East Asia*, p. 520; John Crawfurd, *Journal of an Embassy . . . to the Court of Ava in the Year 1827* (London, 1834).

Wungyi and *Wundauk* entrusted by the court with military operations at Rangoon, the Rangoon garrison managed to beat off a Mon assault. The Burmans then sallied forth to take terrible vengeance on its local enemies.[16] Many Mon and Karen villages were utterly destroyed, and the captured inhabitants were either killed or carried away. The Mon language was thereafter prohibited throughout the Pegu province. *Myothugyis* at Prome, Henzada, and Padaung were executed for having aided the British forces.[17]

The consequences for the local inhabitants of the civil strife of 1826–1827 were dire. Famine conditions prevailed for a time throughout this normal Lower Burma granary, and the situation had to be relieved by rice shipments from India. Tigers invaded the vicinity of Rangoon carrying away both oxen and men.[18] Part of the difficulty developed from the efforts of the Burman Government to extract money from the Mon population to pay off the British indemnity, an attempt which eventually had to be abandoned. The harassed Karen tribesmen fled to the jungles and the hills. For a number of years thereafter, the villagers from Rangoon to Henzada, as observed by foreigners, were uniformly poor and miserable. Royal agents who were wringing money from the people of Prome in 1830 were keeping one-fourth of the take and the chief queen around three-eighths.[19] Such extortionate practices continued under emergency regulations which accorded to all of the *Myowuns* of Lower Burma the military rank of colonel (*Bo*). In the absence of regular *myothugyis*, these *Bo* officials were in a position to extort bribes and fines from all inhabitants able to purchase exemption from military and other royal services. A final abortive and desperate Mon rebellion began in 1838.[20] By 1844, the delta Karens were assidu-

---

[16] Crawfurd, I, 23–24, and II, ch. ii and p. 36; Henry Gouger, *Personal Narrative of Two Years' Imprisonment in Burmah* (London, 1860), pp. 255–260.

[17] W. S. Desai, *History of the British Residency in Burma, 1826–1840* (Rangoon, 1939), pp. 134, 188–190, 217–223, 233–235. The evidences of the devastation of Lower Burma were still visible in 1830 and 1833, when Major Burney traversed the area.

[18] Gouger, pp. 310–311, 313–316; *British Burma Gazetteer* (Rangoon, 1880), I, 483. Gouger described the decapitation of unarmed Mon rivermen at the hands of Burman dispatch bearers from Ava. Some 10,000 Peguan Mons found refuge across the Salween boundary into Tenasserim in 1826–1827.

[19] Desai, *British Residency*, pp. 64, 217–235. It was indicative of the dishonesty of the Burmese Court clique that the successive installments of the indemnity were met only by borrowing from the personal hoards of the chief queen and her brother.

[20] *Ibid.*, pp. 180–181; Hall, *South-East Asia*, pp. 525.

75

ously seeking aid from Moulmein, so much so that Calcutta felt obliged to warn British agents in Tenasserim not to get involved in any plans for a Karen rising.[21]

From Bagyidaw to Tharrawaddy and Pagan

Except for a brief period from 1830 to 1832, Bagyidaw's relations with the British were never cordial. His *Wungyis* in 1826 resisted successfully the efforts of John Crawfurd to obtain permission to export rice and silver from Rangoon. By an inordinate exhibition of suspicion and jealousy, the court forestalled the presence at the capital of a British Resident until 1830. Prior to 1830, the king attempted to regulate all matters relating to Arakan and Tenasserim through the *Wungyi* assigned to Rangoon, and he flatly refused the British invitation to establish a resident embassy in Calcutta.[22] The court also tried persistently but in vain to obtain cancellation of the final installments of the indemnity. It negotiated more successfully for the rectification of the Manipur-Burma boundary and presented so convincing a case of long-term Burman occupancy of the disputed Kubo Valley west of the Chindwin River that the area was formally restored to Burma in 1833.[23] For a time the Burmese entertained a lively hope that Tenasserim might also be recovered, especially after it became evident that it was both an economic and strategic liability for the East India Company. Tenasserim, of course, had never been a source of friction between Britain and Burma.[24]

The initial flattery and favors bestowed by the court in 1830–1832 upon Major Burney as British Resident at the capital, coupled with the decision to pay the final installment of the indemnity in October, 1832, were apparently intended to prepare the way for the expected gratis return of Tenasserim. Major Burney in 1830 had made a tentative but unacceptable offer to exchange Tenasserim for the former British holding of Negrais Island at the mouth of the Bassein River. The court was even more annoyed when the British agent undertook subsequently to expedite the exchange by suggesting that Burma's enemies, the Siamese, might accept the Tenasserim area in exchange for Kedah in

[21] India Office Archives, *India Secret Proceedings,* vol. 114 (1844), no. 165 of Oct. 18, 1944.
[22] Crawfurd, II, 422. From time to time, Bagyidaw sent special missions to Calcutta and Moulmein.
[23] Bayfield, pp. 60–62.
[24] Desai, *British Residency,* pp. 96–97; Hall, *South-East Asia,* pp. 520–522.

northern Malaya.[25] When the hope of retrocession of the southern coast was finally dashed, relations between the court and the Residency degenerated in an atmosphere of mutual recrimination. The Residency was regarded as a spying agency, and everything was done to discourage the continued presence of Major Burney and his staff at the capital. Residency spokesmen in their turn denounced the "benighted and half-savage" court as "a compound of arrogance and ignorance." [26]

The situation at the court worsened after 1831, when the king's chronic affliction of melancholia developed into a serious illness involving periodic lapses into insanity. This development enabled the unprincipled and avaricious Menthagyi, brother of the chief queen, to assume the top post in the regency commission. Because almost any change might possibly be for the better and since the scheming Menthagyi was little affected by the crushing sense of humiliation which had overwhelmed King Bagyidaw, spokesmen for the British Residency were not entirely displeased with the turn of events at the court. Prospects seemed further improved because the popular brother of the king, Prince Tharrawaddy, who was the sole alternative to the Menthagyi, was also allegedly pro-English.[27] The situation was described in 1835 by Dr. Bayfield, a member of Major Burney's Residency staff, as follows:

The King is deranged, alternately gloomy and melancholy, seldom violent. He is utterly incapable of attending to the ordinary affairs of state, which have consequently fallen into the hands of the Queen and her brother Men-tha-gyee, whose avaricious and grasping natures are involving the country in disaffection and ruin. Previous to his illness, His Majesty was much beloved by his people. . . . Their loyalty is not yet shaken.[28]

The interest of British authorities in the approaching crisis was indicated by the inauguration of espionage operations at the court, directed

[25] Desai, *British Residency*, pp. 13–15, 34–39, 45–46, 131–135.

[26] Bayfield, pp. 22, 35. Maung Maung (*Burma in the Family of Nations*, p. 34) cites the face-saving entry in the royal chronicle of the 1824–1825 campaign to the effect that after the white invaders had been permitted to advance as far as Yandabo and had exhausted their resources, the king from motives of generosity and piety sent them a large sum of money and ordered them out of the country.

[27] Bayfield, pp. 73–74. The chief queen was a clever, unscrupulous, unforgiving person, the daughter of a former governor of the jails. Her teen-age daughter was betrothed to the heir apparent, a callow young man of twenty years, who had not yet been elevated to the rank of *Einshemin*.

[28] *Ibid.*, p. 73.

mainly from Arakan, and by Major Burney's avowed determination to neglect no opportunity to extend and increase his personal influence over the court.[29]

The rivalry between the Menthagyi and Prince Tharrawaddy left the king almost out of account and the designated prince-heir entirely so. Tharrawaddy's numerous but disreputable personal following included military adventurers and bandit leaders. As the crisis developed in 1836–1837, gang robbery became endemic throughout Burma, in part as a result of instigation by Tharrawaddy's men. Police agencies were entirely unable to cope with the situation. A foreign visitor in 1836 reported that the main river route was infested by robber bands and that the people were huddled together in palisaded villages for mutual protection.[30]

During the course of the Tharrawaddy rebellion of 1837, already described in Chapter I, anarchy ensued, with every village for itself. In many areas, the inhabitants threw off all restraint and began attacking neighboring villages and plundering all traders and travelers, since to remain quiescent was to invite victimization. The rebel forces at Sagaing, opposite Ava, were commanded by a son and a younger brother of the great Bandula, but the bulk of the antigovernment forces was an accumulation of independent bandit groups.[31]

Once installed in the capital, Prince Tharrawaddy proved to be more popular than the displaced Menthagyi had been, but it may be doubted that the new regime was any real improvement. The prince himself was described, perhaps too discouragingly, as a demoralized, bloodthirsty person, and his followers as bold reckless spirits, interested more in power and loot than in governing.[32]

King Tharrawaddy's relations with Major Burney rapidly deteriorated, partly because the new ruler resented the Resident's officious political meddling and his attempts to halt the traditional purge of royal rivals.[33] The new king flatly refused to recognize as legally binding the Yandabo treaty which his predecessor had signed, although he stopped short of overt violation of its terms. By studied neglect and

[29] India Office Archives, *India Secret Proceedings, Index for 1837*, no. 5 from the Ava Residency, Sept. 10, 1837, and no. 9 of Nov. 29, 1837.

[30] Malcom, I, 115–117; Desai, *British Residency*, pp. 251–260.

[31] Desai, *British Residency*, pp. 261–270.

[32] R. R. Langham-Carter, "U Htaung Bo's Rebellion," *JBRS*, XXVI (1936), 33–34; Desai, "The Rebellion of Prince Tharrawaddy," *JBRS*, XXV (1935), 115–119.

[33] Hall, *South-East Asia*, p. 524.

ill-treatment he influenced the discouraged British Resident to abandon the capital in 1837—to the annoyance of Calcutta. Burney's two British successors were similarly forced out by mid-1839. The British were obliged thereafter to address official communications via the Burmese governor at Rangoon.[34]

Relations became critical around 1840. Tharrawaddy was strong enough militarily to crush the formidable Lower Burma Mon rebellion in 1838–1840. Because British-Indian military forces were heavily engaged at the time both in China and in Afghanistan, it appeared not unlikely that the Burmese army would attack Tenasserim and perhaps northern Siam. Tharrawaddy's three sons were assigned army commands at Rangoon, Bassein, and Toungoo respectively, where they enjoyed uninhibited opportunity to exhibit their military enthusiasm. In 1840, the Burmese Government charged the British with failure to prevent Siamese incursions into the Shan States area, in violation of Article 10 of the Yandabo treaty.[35] At this juncture the sensible and peaceful-minded *Wundauk* previously in charge at Rangoon was replaced by a reckless, unprincipled *Myowun* lacking diplomatic powers. For a time diplomatic relations were broken off. A Burmese army numbering 40,000 men massed at Rangoon in 1842.[36]

War did not come at this juncture for various reasons. The war party was undoubtedly restrained by the fact that the king, reflecting his brother's affliction, lapsed into insanity in 1842. The Burmans also realized that they could put no dependence in case of trouble on the disaffected population of Lower Burma. As previously indicated, Karen agents in 1843–1844 were actively soliciting British aid from Moulmein.[37] There was, furthermore, considerably more enthusiasm for defiant gestures aimed to bolster morale than for actually measuring strength with the disciplined British Indian army. The Burmese army was much less formidable than in 1824.

[34] H. A. Browne, *Reminiscences of the Court of Mandalay* (Woking, 1907), pp. 18–20; Desai, *British Residency*, pp. 292–302; Maung Maung, *Burma in the Family of Nations*, pp. 41–42. King Tharrawaddy felt that it was beneath his dignity as a ruler to respect papers such as merchants used, especially when such documents could be the basis for embarrassing demands.

[35] India Office Archives, *India Secret Proceedings*, vol. XIV (1838), Feb. 23, 1838. The commissioner of Tenasserim here transmitted a letter from the court of Siam demonstrating "that the Siamese Court is willing to join the British Government should matters eventually oblige it to have recourse to hostilities with Ava."

[36] Desai, *British Residency*, pp. 410–412, 423–430, 442–455; *The Cambridge History of India* (Cambridge, 1929), V, 566.

[37] Hall, *South-East Asia*, p. 525.

Tharrawaddy's mental instability, which was aggravated in 1844 by the development of internal rebellion in Upper Burma, afforded opportunity for one of his sons, the Pagan Min, to take over the reins of government in 1845. Pagan Min was even more vengeful and avaricious than his father had been, so that government in Burma went from bad to worse during the seven years of his misrule. He neglected the business of government and failed to control his royal officials. He killed off all relatives thought capable of challenging his control and otherwise thoroughly debauched his court at Amarapura. It required the shock of the second Anglo-Burmese War in 1852 to afford opportunity for responsible Burmese political leaders to bring a half brother of the king, one Mindon Min, from his monastery retreat to end the quarter century of frustrated misrule which had followed Burma's initial defeat at British hands.[38]

British Rule in Tenasserim, 1826–1852

The most important boon which British East India Company rule brought to the people of the Tenasserim coastal division (east and south of the mouth of the Salween) was the denial of its use as a corridor for armed controversy between Burma and Siam. Both parties had exploited the area by carrying away slaves, prisoners, and hostages, including at times unlucky foreign residents. Marching armies on many occasions had subjected the resident population to uncompensated requisition of labor, stores, money, boats, and cattle. These were in addition to the customary exactions by local Burmese officials charged with raising quotas for general military levies. Even a petty conflict could involve such dire penalties locally that the distressed population had no recourse but to flee to the jungle.[39] British rule brought this unhappy state of affairs to a welcome end.

A second contribution of British-Indian rule to Tenasserim was the establishment of orderly judicial processes and the consequent guarantee of security of life and property. The first resident British commissioner, N. D. Maingy, was an amiable and tactful person who came from Penang to set up headquarters at Amherst in 1826. At the outset, he worked out a successful application of justice along simple Burmese lines. Maingy established magistrate's courts at Amherst and Tavoy, before which any citizen or a selected friend could plead a grievance and receive redress. An informed Burman official was as-

---

[38] Browne, p. 20; Hall, *South-East Asia*, p. 526.
[39] Ma Mya Sein, pp. 13–14; Malcom, I, 71–72.

sociated with each court to explain to the magistrate the customary law applicable in each case. The presence of lawyers in court was not permitted; the magistrate himself made a brief abstract of the case and shortened the trials by charging one rupee for a court summons and a half-rupee fee for each witness called. Court costs in civil suits were fixed at 10 per cent of the amount involved, and these were remitted in case of hardship or if the parties effected a compromise settlement out of court sometimes on a basis suggested by the court itself. Jury trial was introduced in 1829 to the entertainment of both participants and onlookers. These practices proved to be very effective initially in keeping offenses under control, even though some of the punishments imposed were, from the viewpoint of Calcutta, decidedly unconventional. Court panels were kept clear, and most of the penalties were in the nature of fines or required labor.[40] Maingy succeeded in establishing order, in ending slavery (outlawed generally by London in 1833), in curbing divorce, thievery, and rape. At the time that he was recalled in the mid-thirties, he was engaged in the important task of formulating an elementary legal code based on Burmese custom and British modifications.[41]

Maingy also developed an administrative system based in large measure on the Burmese pattern. He made the old police officer, the *sitké*, a judge to try minor criminal and civil cases and gave him a generous 300-rupee monthly salary. The old *Akunwun*, or granary collector and supervisor, became the principal revenue clerk at 200 rupees a month. Former township headmen were variously employed for stipends ranging from 25 to 100 rupees per month. Circle headmen were appointed to act as local collectors under the supervision of British assistant district officers; they were paid on a commission basis. Police stations were confined to the towns; villages wanting protection had to set up their own nightly patrols. Indigenous leadership was thus fully utilized, and the system at first worked admirably. The inhabitants objected to paying regular taxes in money, which they now had to save against the date of payment, but they liked the introduction of coined money.[42]

Serious difficulty was encountered by Maingy in connection with

[40] Malcom, I, 72, 220; John S. Furnivall, "The Fashioning of Leviathan," *JBRS,* XXIX (1939), 18–35.

[41] Furnivall, *JBRS,* XXIX (1939), 43.

[42] *Ibid.,* pp. 44–45, 58–65; *The Cambridge History of India,* V, 566; Malcom, I, 71–72. When the British first permitted free sale of rice for export, the cultivators sold for cash far more than their allowable surpluses.

his ambitious road-building project for Tenasserim. Since hired labor, especially during the busy agricultural seasons, might cost as high as 2 rupees (4 shillings or $1) per day, Maingy hit upon the idea of requiring forced labor for short periods of seven to ten days' duration. Such services were assessed by rotation on individuals selected by circle groups for a nominal wage of 5 annas a day (15 cents). This measure was in presumed imitation of the Burma king's traditional right to exact personal services from his subjects. In some cases road construction required from an individual two months of enforced service per year. The inhabitants much preferred to travel by boat and resisted the road-building program so strenuously that Maingy eventually brought over convict labor from India to work on the roads. The results for law and order were distressing; jails had to be built to house the lawless, and the road-construction program was eventually abandoned.

British efforts at Moulmein to encourage labor emigration from independent Burma eventually ran aground on the unpopularity of the taxation system and road-building programs. Added to this was the absolute interdiction of departures by the Burmese Government. A number of the Talaings who had fled to Tenasserim in 1826–1827 eventually recrossed the Salween into Burma.[43] Other trouble developed because integrated groups migrating to Tenasserim insisted on maintaining their allegiance and paying their dues to their personal chiefs, no matter how widely they might be scattered in their new homes. They became restive when British pressure forced them to acknowledge the territorial jurisdiction of the salaried officials in their respective districts of residence.[44]

British attempts to bring in laborers from Malaya were also unsuccessful, and recourse was finally had to recruiting contract labor from India. The most useful newcomers were the several hundred Chinese who migrated north from Penang. Loyalty to their secret-society (*hui*) affiliations did not prevent the Chinese from taking Talaing wives and settling down, especially at Tavoy and Moulmein. Everywhere the Chinese demonstrated their striking adaptability and intelligence, and by 1835 they had made themselves virtually indispensable to the resident Europeans by reason of their abilities as craftsmen and as merchants. Some Chinese venders of opium and liquor corrupted the natives.[45]

[43] Furnivall, *JBRS*, XXIX (1939), 253–258.
[44] *British Burma Gazetteer*, I, 483–484.
[45] Malcom, I, 49, 66. Approximately 500 Chinese were living in Moulmein in 1835 compared to 2,000 Indian residents.

Maingy was superseded as commissioner in 1835 largely as a result of the complaint of European business interests who opposed his imaginative application of traditional Burmese legal standards. The judges of the Calcutta courts, who reviewed the legal records of Tenasserim, sympathized with the European demand that formal court procedures should utilize Indian law and that use of legal counsel be permitted, as well as access to regular justices of the peace. With Maingy's departure disappeared all sense of humor in the courts and all possibility of enlisting willing popular participation in jury duty and in other problems connected with police control and administration of justice.

Following the importation of inferior types of contract labor from Madras, which began in 1836, the situation in Moulmein became increasingly disorderly. Social homogeneity disappeared along with the weakening of local institutions. The task of policing became particularly difficult in the urban centers.[46] Government business generally multiplied and became evermore burdensome in the face of a shortage of East India Company staff sometimes careless in their duties. In 1842, Commissioner Blundell, grown irritable and ill-tempered, got involved in quarrels not only with the Government of Bengal, but also with local English merchants (teak and rice) at Moulmein and with the Burma Government. Administrative irregularities multiplied after 1842, and by the end of the decade poor accounts and misappropriation of revenues were widely prevalent.[47]

Blundell and other European observers realized that indigenous governmental institutions which did not fit into the British-Indian system were decaying and that the foundations of the traditional ties of village and family life were also giving way. But business demands invariably took precedence. From Calcutta's perspective, economic production needs were more important than accommodation to popular desires. Little attention was accordingly given Blundell's insistence that Talaings recently freed from Burmese misrule could not be handled by Bengali methods, especially if the attempt were made in accordance with the presumptuous pattern of personal privilege set up by the British mercantile community.[48]

The most encouraging aspect of British rule in Tenasserim from 1826 to 1852 was the steady economic development and population

[46] Furnivall, *JBRS*, XXIX (1939), 35–51.
[47] *The Cambridge History of India*, V, 569.
[48] Furnivall, *JBRS*, XXIX (1939), 70–75, 131–137. Business groups asked Blundell to fix wages for labor and to revive imprisonment for debt.

growth within the area. The population increased 50 per cent from 1835 to 1845 and another 50 per cent over the 1845 level by 1852. Rice acreage likewise increased almost 50 per cent from 1845 to 1852. The licensed cutting of the teak logs of Amherst District began in 1829, and the timber industry became for a time the most profitable source of wealth. Shipbuilding at Moulmein developed into a sizable industry, especially after the British Admiralty became interested in 1847. But the valuable timber was exploited wastefully; no new plantings were made, and an estimated three-fourths of the logs extracted escaped payment of assessed taxes. When the exasperated commissioner canceled the timber leases of the unco-operative timber merchants in 1846, the latter obtained Blundell's dismissal by Calcutta. Subsequently timid Karen jungle folk, who had been forced to work for Burman timber agents at little compensation, completed the ruin of the timber resources by burning several of the remaining forests. By 1850 the valuable forests of the Amherst District were gone,[49] and timber merchants began to eye the virtually untouched teak forests of Burma's Sittang Valley and the lower Irrawaddy Valley.

The quarter-century record of British rule in Tenasserim clearly demonstrated what could be accomplished in economic progress by a stable government geared to enhancing production for export and to utilizing outside capital, labor, and business experience. It also demonstrated how quickly indigenous political and social vitality could ebb away under alien rule, even when no politically motivated opposition was present.

Arakan to 1852

British administrative policy in Arakan paid little deference to traditional Burmese institutions, for it reflected more strongly than Tenasserim the influence of neighboring Bengal. At the outset the claims of wide personal jurisdiction advanced by the local *myothugyis* were admitted as valid, but their domains were regarded, in practice, as were the privately owned (*zamandari*) estates in Bengal. When the anomalous character of this policy became apparent, the administrative unit for taxation was sharply narrowed to circles of adjacent villages, and collections in each circle were made the responsibility of an appointive *taikthugyi*, who frequently could establish no hereditary claim to the allegiance of the taxpayers. The tendency of these tax farmers to exact undefined and unauthorized collections was checked in theory by the

[49] *The Cambridge History of India*, V, 566–567.

district authorities.[50] This policy destroyed immediately any identification between headmen and people on the traditional Burmese pattern.
The situation in Arakan was further demoralized in 1829, when the
commissioner explicitly canceled the hereditary basis of the office of
myothugyi and began to subdivide jurisdictions arbitrarily on a territorial unit basis as in India. The former *myothugyi* could become a
salaried clerk on the staff of a European district assistant. The appointed circle headmen, not the hereditary ex-*myothugyi*, assisted in
apprehending criminals and tried petty civil cases. Criminal jurisdiction was reserved for European handling.

Many of the Arakanese, especially those with some Indian admixture, were not unhappy at first to exchange Burmese for British rule.
But they developed no love for the alien administrative and judicial
system, while natural leaders resented the reduction of the entire population to the dead level of peasant cultivators. Disaffection centered
in men of property and social standing under the traditional order who
were being denied influence under the new regime.[51] Unrest increased
after 1829, and in 1836 a serious rebel uprising attempted to expel the
British. Indian Sepoys promptly drove the poorly armed malcontents
into the hills, where famine and the weather took their toll. An American visitor to Akyab city later in the same year reported many Bengali
Mussulmans among the city's 8,000 population, which included at the
time only 20 to 30 Buddhist monks. Hindustani was the lingua franca
for all inhabitants of Akyab including the Europeans.

The tense political situation in Arakan was gradually relieved by an
improvement in economic conditions. In contrast to Moulmein, food
and labor in Arakan were cheap, largely because of the presence
of Indians. Some 300,000 rupees' worth of cleaned rice was exported
from Akyab in 1836, and large numbers of Burmese and Chittagong
coasting vessels were then calling regularly at the port.[52] The expansion

[50] Each candidate *taikthugyi* submitted formal tenders explaining the extent
to which he would tax the people—the amounts he would remit to the government and those he would keep for himself. The commission was customarily
limited to 15 per cent. The possibility of private "arrangements" or bribery were
many.

[51] *British Burma Gazetteer*, I, 479–482; *The Cambridge History of India*, V,
563–565. Indians called the native Arakanese of all races by the deprecatory
name of "Mugs." Visitors in 1836 reported "Mugs" and half-caste Burmans to be
in the majority over the pure Burman population.

[52] Malcom, I, 121–128. The author reported in 1836 that fowls at Akyab were
1 rupee per dozen, ducks 1 rupee for 8, cleaned rice 1 rupee per basket, eggs 3
annas a dozen, and milk 1 rupee for 15 pints. A servant's wage was 6 rupees
per month without board. A few Chinese were living at Akyab.

of Arakanese rice acreage from 1830 to 1852, amounting to four and a half times, drew cultivators from Burma and gave full employment to the local population. Akyab in 1852 was the foremost rice-exporting city in the world. As early as 1836 the East India Company was realizing an annual profit of 6 lakhs of rupees (600,000) from Arakan. Revenues increased steadily thereafter. The land tax per acre was reduced by three-fourths to encourage expansion of cultivation, but increased acreage and the levying of multifarious other taxes more than made up the loss. Akyab District in particular, which contained 40 per cent of the population of Arakan, was in many respects a bona fide extension of East India Company rule from Bengal.[53]

The Second Anglo-Burman War, 1852

The second Anglo-Burman War contrasted sharply in its inception from the war of 1824–1825. The first one was provoked by military threats on the part of a proud and boastful Burmese Government at a number of points along the Indian border. The occasion of the second was resentment in British circles over the exaction in late 1851 of a trifling sum of 1,000 rupees by the *Myowun* of Pegu and Rangoon from the captains and crews of two British vessels for alleged violation of port rules. Both in Burma and Calcutta the British community chose to regard the incident as an intolerable and deliberate gesture on the part of the Burman authorities to demean Britishers. Thus the trifling nature of the incident and also its merits were from the outset overshadowed by considerations of prestige.[54]

Although it is clear from the records in the India Office Library that Governor Dalhousie, in December, 1851, deprecated for reasons of financial stringency any renewal of war with Burma, he did not rule out that contingency. He even went so far as to specify what immediate precautions should be taken against the possibility of strife. His method of protesting the exactions was to dispatch two vessels of the Royal Navy to Rangoon to deliver an ultimatum demanding that the Burman Court give immediate redress and remove the offending *Myowun*.[55] The alarmed Burmese Government, entirely unprepared for war, ac-

---

[53] *The Cambridge History of India*, V, 563–565; Malcom, I, 126–128. Opium and salt for export were company monopolies. Other taxes were levied on fruit trees, fishing nets, boats, toddy trees, buffaloes and plows, traders, honey and wax collectors, physicians and timber cutters.

[54] Hall, *South-East Asia*, pp. 526–527.

[55] India Office Archives, *India Secret Proceedings*, vol. 180 (1852), minute of Dec. 19, 1851.

cepted the terms of the ultimatum, replaced the offending *Myowun,* and offered to permit a British Resident to locate at Rangoon to facili- tate negotiations. But the new *Myowun* belonged to the anti-British party at court and tended to assume a somewhat unbending attitude. Alleged rudeness on his part precipitated a blockade of the Burma coast line by the British war vessels in early January, 1852. The break- down of relations came on January 22, 1852, following a brief naval action on the part of the volatile Commodore Lambert, commander of the British war vessels. Thereafter preparations for war proceeded apace.

Although Governor Dalhousie reprimanded Commodore Lambert for his unnecessarily abrupt conduct at Rangoon, he nevertheless ex- onerated him for having caused the war by insisting that it was in- evitable in any case. Granted continued border friction and British sensitivity, he was probably right. In February a new ultimatum was delivered to Burma, due to expire on April 1, which included a demand for an indemnity of 1 million rupees to cover the expenses of British preparations for war. In an explanatory minute sent to London at the time, Dalhousie dilated on the "enhanced conditions on which alone war can now be averted." [56]

In most respects it was Dalhousie's war. The complete lack of hesitation on his part and the thoroughgoing preparations for the campaign, including provisions for housing, medical care, and the uti- lization of units of the Royal Navy, were in sharp contrast to the fumbling ineptitude of the effort of 1824–1825.[57] In April, 1852, British forces captured Martaban (opposite Moulmein) and Rangoon; in May they took Bassein. These moves were supposedly merely punitive ges- tures to force Burmese acquiescence in the February ultimatum. But King Pagan stubbornly refused to treat with the British on such terms. On June 30, Governor Dalhousie proposed to London that the three occupied points be not surrendered, in view of the substantial advan- tages to be derived from British possession of the entire province of Pegu. He then proceeded from Calcutta to Rangoon, where he pre- pared in early August a definitive recommendation that Lower Burma be annexed by unilateral proclamation without bothering to attack the capital. This proposal received the complete approval of Lord Aber- deen's Liberal Party government at London, which included also Lord

---

[56] *Ibid.,* documents dated Jan. 2 and 22, Feb. 13 and 17, 1852; Hall, *South- East Asia,* p. 527.

[57] Hall, *South-East Asia,* p. 527.

Clarendon and the belligerent Lord Palmerston.[58] Prome was captured on October 10 and Pegu on November 22. The latter city withstood a strong counterattack by the Burmese in mid-December. On December 20 came the governor-general's proclamation adding Pegu as a third province of British Burma.

Meanwhile a serious refugee problem developed in Rangoon and Bassein, where large numbers of Karens, with their families and goods, crowded into the British-held areas for protection. Many of the Karen men took to the jungle to escape forced service at the behest of the Burmese authorities; others renewed the civil war. General Godwin, the British officer in command, at first refused to accept responsibility for protecting the minority peoples of Pegu province without specific sanction of Calcutta, which had theretofore warned against any such involvement.[59] Relief activities for the Karens in the Kemmendine quarter of Rangoon and to a lesser degree at Bassein were initiated and directed by American Baptist missionaries, who were afforded some assistance in supplies from the British army.[60] By early September, the British were considering the advisability of using irregular forces of "Malays" (Karens) to aid in establishing control. The governor-general himself in late 1852 stressed the necessity of "adopting severe measures against the bands of Burmese plunderers who have infested Lower Burma." The countryside was obviously in complete turmoil.[61]

The puzzling problem of how to bring the conflict to an end without proceeding with plans for a costly expedition against the capital of Burma was solved in early 1853 by the overthrow of Pagan Min. Disaffection developed first in the army, where the safety of the son of the great Bandula, together with his family, was threatened by the king because of the general's failure to defend Prome. He was joined in his conspiracy by a member of the *Hlutdaw* within the capital. In early December, British intelligence agencies in Arakan learned that the Royal Treasury and Arsenal had been taken over by the dissident

[58] *Ibid.*, pp. 527–528; India Office Archives, *India Secret Proceedings*, vol. 180 (1852), April 28, June 30, Aug. 13, 1852.

[59] India Office Archives, *India Secret Proceedings*, vol. 180 (1852), reported by H. Godwin, May 24, June 9 and 22, and Aug. 23, 1852.

[60] Calista Vinton Luther, *The Vintons and the Karens* (Boston, 1880), pp. 89–106.

[61] India Office Archives, *India Secret Proceedings*, vol. 180 (1852), Sept. 3 and Dec. 1, 1852.

faction. The pretender, as previously indicated, was a half brother of Pagan, one Mindon Min, who had spent most of his life in a monastery and who now opposed continuation of the war. In mid-December, he fled to the ancestral city of Shwebo, whither his partisans repaired. He entered the capital in February, 1853, when the Magwe *Mingyi*, chief minister of Pagan, declared in Mindon's favor. The impossible Pagan was deposed amid popular rejoicing. His life was spared by the new king, who was a man of humane instincts.[62]

This political revolution at Amarapura ended the official prosecution of the war on the part of the Burmese. All officials and regular army forces retired northward, while the continuing opposition in Lower Burma degenerated into sheer banditry. Political diversions at the capital enabled the British forces at Prome to advance some fifty miles northward to Myédé, so as to include within the unilaterally annexed domain some valuable teak forests. It was more than three years thereafter before a semblance of order was established in Lower Burma. The boundaries of the older Tenasserim province were extended northward to include the largely Karen-inhabited areas between the lower Salween and Sittang rivers. The remainder of the new acquisition was organized into the province of Pegu.

British Administration in Lower Burma, 1852–1870

British policy in the Pegu division, following the easy conquest and unilateral annexation of the area in 1852, reflected the experience gained in Arakan during the previous quarter century. Commissioner Arthur Phayre made no attempt to coerce the peacefully inclined King Mindon Min into acknowledging by formal treaty the British annexation. *De facto* British control was extended northward to an east-west line running about fifty miles above Prome on the west and above Toungoo on the east, into areas of predominantly Burman rather than Mon or Karen occupancy. The difficulty of establishing order within Lower Burma was aggravated by the withdrawal, at the time of Mindon's accession, of all government officers of *Wun* rank and many of the Burmese *myothugyis*. The indigenous Mon leaders of the delta area co-operated loyally with the British, but they were too few to man the vacated administrative posts and were unsuitable to use in Burman-inhabited areas. Resistance developed particularly among the royally designated *myothugyis* from Upper Burma who did not retire north-

[62] *Ibid.*, minute of Dec. 4, 1852; Hall, *South-East Asia*, p. 529.

ward. The authority of many of them prior to 1852 had rested on the support of armed retainers, often numbering as many as 300 to 600 men, rather than on any traditional hereditary grounds or their indentification with the people's interests. Like the relations between the feudal barons of Europe's Middle Ages, their feuding prior to 1852 was the curse of the countryside. Many of them became, after 1852, heads of marauding dacoit bands, whose persistent depredations were extremely difficult to counter.[63]

It was not until 1857 that Burmese political disaffection disappeared, and not until after 1870 that dacoit activities were effectively curbed. In 1858, a variant problem developed over a Karen rebellion in which an animist leader, one Meng-Loung, undertook to drive the English out of Burma in order to set up a Karen dynasty at Pegu. The Burmans took no part in the affair, but it was not suppressed without serious trouble. Police authorities in the Pegu division also had perennial difficulty enlisting good men and keeping the force up to strength.[64] Surrendered dacoits, who were sometimes reorganized into military police units for use against other outlaw bands, tended to become bullying and arrogant. The more responsible ex-*myothugyis* were eventually offered posts as salaried *myook* (township) officials in the British administration, as had been done earlier with selected Mon leaders. Thus the hereditary office of the *myothugyi*, who acted as a kind of tribal leader traditionally indentified with the interests of his people, virtually disappeared from Lower Burma.[65]

The administrative system as developed in Lower Burma below the posts held by Europeans operated at four levels. At the top were the *myooks* of the townships, usually men of social influence and character, appointed at first solely on the recommendation of the commissioners themselves or other high officials. Around 1870 a proportion of these *myook* appointments was opened to younger men by competitive examination based in part on knowledge of land surveying and of English. Few of the examination recruits could match the effectiveness of the more responsible Burmese-educated *myooks*. The *myooks* supervised tax collections and adjudicated petty civil and

---

[63] Albert Fytche, *Burma, Past and Present* (London, 1878), I, 126–132. Prior to 1852, eleven nonlocal Burman *myothugyis* functioned in Bassein District.

[64] *The Cambridge History of India*, VI, 446; Mya Sein, pp. 101–102; Fytche, I, 170–171.

[65] Fytche, I, 128–132, 140–141. Fytche describes these developments from his vantage point as British official at Bassein after 1852. In 1853, he enlisted 1,500 native volunteers in his pacification forces.

criminal cases, but took little responsibility for police affairs. They continued in office under more or less permanent tenure.[66]

At the second level were the circle headmen, or *taikthugyis*, local persons of influence selected by the deputy commissioners of the various administrative districts. The *taikthugyis* after 1861 became almost exclusively revenue officials. They were responsible under the *myook* not only for tax collections, but also for maintaining land surveys and records of land occupancy for tax purposes.[67] The *taikthugyis* were held strictly accountable for their conduct in office on pain of fine or dismissal. The turnover in personnel was fairly heavy.[68] After 1879, knowledge of land surveying became an essential qualification of the *taikthugyi*, who must also pass a simple test on revenue law. Under such rigorous survelliance from above, the circle headmen tended to lose the capacity to accept individual responsibility. They collected the taxes, but contributed very little else to public welfare and order.[69] As the tool of an alien government, which was exacting in its demands and punitive in its sanctions, the *taikthugyi* lost face and popular prestige. The traditional link between government and people represented by the traditional *myothugyi* was clearly not re-established through the artificially substituted circle headman set up under British rule.

At the third level of local administration were circle *gaungs*, strictly police officers, who, after 1861, were paid meager salaries from land revenue funds and who reported to the district superintendent of police. A particular *gaung* was responsible for trying petty cases and for enforcing order within an area averaging some nine miles square. The system was artificial because the traditional Burmese *ywagaung* had acted only as the village-level agent (often as a relative) of the *myothugyi*, not as a bona fide village official in his own right. Under

[66] *British Burma Gazetteer*, I, 485–501; H. T. White, *Burma* (Cambridge, 1923), pp. 95–96.

[67] The *taikthugyis* received a 10 per cent commission on collections up to 6,000 rupees and 5 per cent additional on collections above that figure. See Mya Sein, pp. 81–82, 108–109.

[68] Professional surveyors of landholdings were used for the first time in 1858 to supplement headman surveys; systematic field-by-field surveys for entire circle areas (up to 500 square miles) began in 1877, while the system of periodic cadastral surveys of Lower Burma district units began in 1880. It was extended to Upper Burma in 1890. See Burma, *Report of the Committee Appointed to Examine the Land Revenue System of Burma* (Rangoon, 1922), pp. 12–14. The author, J. S. Furnivall, explains that this type of systematic survey was not found elsewhere in India.

[69] Mya Sein, pp. 81–85, 109–112; *The Cambridge History of India*, VI, 442.

the less direct but authoritative direction of an alien superintendent of police, the *gaungs* could scarcely avoid making themselves personally offensive to the villagers and sacrificing the confidence of the people. They enjoyed correspondingly little popular co-operation.[70] The traditional practice of submitting local disputes to the *gaung* elders for the sifting of evidence and for mediatory settlement on a customary basis was gradually abandoned. The *gaung* became merely an arm of the police, while the *taikthugyi* washed his hands of all policing responsibilities. By 1875 the *gaungs* were losing standing among the people, and the policing situation in rural areas was noticeably deteriorating. Bad manners and insulting talk at the village level were no longer subject to traditional penalties, such as forced water-drawing, road making, the stocks, or actual expulsion, because the hands of the elders were tied. A favorite pastime of young men seeking adventure or a reputation for daring was to join a dacoit gang and bait the local *gaung*. Modulation into overt criminality frequently followed.[71] It was not due exclusively to the notorious pessimism of the older generation that many elders of Lower Burma lamented, in the 1870's, that the younger generation was losing good native qualities and was developing a feebler constitution (from indulgence in spirits and opium), greater arrogance, disrespect for parents and elders, and disregard of religion.[72]

At the fourth and final level was the almost pathetic village factotum, or *kyedangyi* (largest taxpayer), an office created by acts passed in 1876 and 1881. The *kyedangyi* was a man of all work. He was required to act as police informer, to assist executive officers and collectors, to gather vital statistics, to provide food, transportation, and forced labor as needed by district officers on tour, all for very meager remuneration. The incumbents enjoyed little or no authority in their own right and were accordingly obliged to submit to bullying indignities at the hands of both criminal elements and constable *gaungs*. British authorities expended much effort after 1880 lecturing the village *kyedangyis* about the nature and importance of their responsibilities, in the forlorn hope that the posts might serve as a training agency for selection of *myook* candidates. In 1884, the post of *kyedangyi* was made elective, although

---

[70] Mya Sein, pp. 88–92.
[71] Fielding-Hall, *The Soul of a People*, pp. 87–88; Mya Sein, p. 88.
[72] C. J. F. S. Smith-Forbes, *British Burma and Its People* (London, 1878), p. 45.

many village leaders were not particularly enthusiastic about accepting the thankless job. The conviction was growing among British administrators with Indian experience that development of the office of village headman was the primary essential for improvement of local government. The difficulties were that the village unit was too small and that the *kyedangyi* usually wielded no authority or influence.[73] The outcome of subsequent efforts to strengthen the role of the village *kyedangyi*, or *thugyi*, will be described in Chapter IV.

The four-level Burmese official hierarchy under British rule was artificial; it clearly lacked the vitality found in the indigenous governmental and social structure. Burmese society tended to level out because the government was alien and social stratifications, theretofore so rigidly maintained under indigenous Burmese custom, disappeared. The situation was not improved by the southward movement into British territory, especially after 1870, of uprooted Burman immigrants, who as newcomers lacked assimilation to their new villages of residence and were otherwise largely removed from the control of hereditary *myothugyis*, as well as from religious sanctions and customary law.[74] It was often not easy to distinguish between bona fide Burmese immigrant agriculturists and participants in the long-continued lawless raids southward across the border of old Burma. The same persons often assumed alternate roles.[75]

At the upper level of the administration, the three parts of British Burma were amalgamated in 1862, to become the equivalent of a governor's province of India, enjoying a large measure of administrative autonomy. Burma's top-ranking commissioners, serving under a chief commissioner, were invariably drawn from the India civil service. Provincial legislative autonomy was denied Burma until 1897.[76] At the District level a British deputy commissioner, substituting for the Burmese provincial *Myowun*, was the key official. The usually active and conscientious deputy commissioners exercised both executive and judicial authority. Working through the *myooks* and headmen, investigating disputes over revenue, trying cases promptly and economically, checking tax returns, inspecting areas where remission of

---

[73] Mya Sein, pp. 85, 113–115, 117–124.

[74] Harold Fielding-Hall, *A People at School*, pp. 5–7.

[75] *The Cambridge History of India*, V, 562, VI, 445.

[76] Harvey, *British Rule*, p. 77. The hill state of Karenni to the east of Toungoo was not annexed to British Burma, but was treated as a former tributary to Burma now in subordinate alliance with the British Government.

revenue was claimed because of crop failure, they could and did contribute much to the peace and growing prosperity of Lower Burma.[77]

Six leading municipalities were permitted after 1874 to govern themselves through commissioner-appointed committees, two-fifths nonofficial in personnel. The committees met monthly. They assessed and collected local taxes; they kept up the streets and the markets; they supervised the police, vital statistics, and, after 1879, hospitals and schools. In practice, municipal governments functioned well only under European direction.[78]

Economic and Social Developments under British Rule

The economic development of Lower Burma after 1852, handicapped as the area was by sparse population and disorder, was at first rather slow. An important advance was made toward preserving Burma's valuable timber resources by the establishment in 1856 of a forestry department to supervise the exportation of teakwood in particular. All teak trees became the exclusive property of the government, and timber operations conducted largely by British firms were authorized by lease arrangements, subject to cancellation in cases of abuse.[79] Rice acreage multiplied three times between 1852 and 1872, but at the latter date the cultivated area was still quite limited in extent. Lower Burma's trade both overseas and with Upper Burma increased steadily in volume, however, so that the Pegu province paid its way almost from the very start. Lower Burma's population doubled from 1852 to 1861. The use of steamboats on the Irrawaddy augmented the volume of British trade with the Burma Kingdom, although it disrupted the livelihood of thousands of persons previously employed in river traffic.[80] Funds for both railway construction and river transport were provided by the government on the basis of strategic and administrative needs. River transport was eventually turned over to the

[77] H. T. White, *A Civil Servant in Burma*, pp. 24–25.

[78] *British Burma Gazetteer*, I, 493–494.

[79] *The Cambridge History of India*, VI, 444; W. F. B. Laurie, *General Albert Fytche's Administration of British Burma* (London, 1873), pp. 10–11. The revenues, trade, and population of British Burma all nearly doubled from 1855 to 1865.

[80] Harvey, *Outline*, pp. 177–180, and *British Rule*, p. 64. The British-Burma treaty of 1862 permitted unrestricted trade between Upper and Lower Burma with no tariff impositions by the British. In 1867, British steam vessels were permitted to ply the Irrawaddy as far upstream as Bhamo, where a British commercial agent was allowed to reside. British subjects in Upper Burma enjoyed extraterritorial jurisdiction under the British Resident at Mandalay. Commissioner Fytche failed to persuade King Mindon to cancel all customs dues.

privately owned Irrawaddy Flotilla Company. The government railway running up the main river route was extended to Prome and up
the Sittang Valley to Toungoo. Construction of trunk roads and of
large river embankments were also financed by the government.[81]

The free export of rice from Rangoon to foreign markets tended to
raise the price of this staple food in Upper Burma. It also established
the possibility of marketing overseas the rice output from Lower Burma's expanding paddy acreage, a boon which had never before been
permitted to the delta area. The incentive afforded to cultivators was
not that land ownership could be acquired for those who cared to
develop virgin areas (this had long been the practice in Burma) but
rather that a receipt for a nominal tax assessment on newly developed
land, after three to five years of occupancy, was accepted as evidence
of the pioneer's claim and became immediately salable or acceptable
as collateral for a loan. Money obtainable from sale of paddy or from
loans based on land security in Lower Burma could then be spent
without social or legal restraint for new dresses, fine houses, elaborate
funerals or *shin pyu* ceremonies, and other external evidences of rising
social status. Such practices had previously been jealously proscribed
except among the higher levels of the social structure in old Burma.
Burmans with official connections, especially those who learned the
working of the new legal system, could also take up moneylending at
exorbitant rates of interest. This acquisitive type of businessman had
been virtually unknown in old Burma except among foreign residents.
Until the 1870's the rapacious Burman moneylenders had the field
pretty much to themselves.[82]

It was the combination of new-found individualism fostered by British rule, the ending of the sumptuary laws based on social status, the
disappearance of *myothugyis,* and the development of wage labor and
a money economy that completed the disintegration of Burma's traditional social structure. The decay of religious sanctions and community
mores were perhaps more symptoms than causes of the deteriorating
situation. It was during the agricultural boom of the 1870's following
the opening of the Suez Canal that crime again developed as a serious
problem in Lower Burma.[83] Other factors contributing to social-
economic change during the 1870's and early 1880's will be analyzed
later in this chapter.

[81] Albert D. Moscotti, "British Policy in Burma, 1917–1937" (Yale University
dissertation, 1950), pp. 5, 8–9, 11–12.
[82] Harvey, *British Rule,* pp. 49–50.   [83] *Ibid.,* pp. 38–40.

The developing British-Indian court system was in many respects constructive, but it added to the estrangement between people and government. The alien aspect of the new court was aggravated by the fact that the operative civil law, which had been enacted in India to cope with a more complex economic situation than existed in Burma, constituted a legal system so intricate and technical that it was unintelligible except as a means of remunerative dispute among professional lawyers. The overriding concern of British jurisprudence, namely to guard against the possibility of punishing the innocent, blunted the harsh effectiveness of Burmese justice in dealing with recognized swindlers and bullies. Scoundrels too often went scot free in lower-level courts, when perjury and bribery of magistrates were not uncommon. Courts of appellate jurisdiction wandered even farther away than did lower courts from the facts of a given case and from intelligible customary law. This chasm between indigenous standards of justice and the outcome of formal court proceedings tended inevitably to grow wider with the passage of time.[84] Publication of the laws in English left them unintelligible even to the educated Burmese public.

In the educational field, British authorities in Lower Burma endeavored from the late 1860's onward to integrate the better monastic schools of the area into a general program of secular education. Manuals covering geography and arithmetic were prepared in Burmese, and some English books covering literature and science were translated. Under a director of public instruction, appointed in 1866, examinations in Pali, Burmese, and arithmetic were standardized and money prizes and awards were advanced as incentives. Schoolmasters trained in the government normal school were attached to selected monastery schools, and public money was advanced for needed buildings and equipment.[85] But few of the *pongyis* were willing to cooperate, and the government could not possibly control thousands of small village *kyaungs* without the assistance of a Buddhist primate for Lower Burma, whom the authorities in India would not appoint. The initial effort was abandoned in the early 1870's, but integration continued as an objective down to 1910. Buddhist schools pretty well held their own in popular esteem until the end of the century, but at the higher levels of education, in particular, they had become irrelevant to economic and governmental needs.

[84] *Ibid.*, pp. 34–36.
[85] Fytche, II, 206–209. Albert Fytche, who succeeded Sir Arthur Phayre as chief commissioner in 1867, lacked Phayre's interest in the educational problem.

Lay government schools were few and poorly attended; some of the best middle and high schools were operated by the Christian missionaries.[86] The system of instruction was much the same as in the monasteries, but the lay schools were more strictly run. A fairly successful innovation in British Burma was the establishment of a limited number of so-called "house schools," which taught girls as well as boys. Special English-language schools were also started in the larger towns.[87] In the 1890's private lay Buddhist schools were begun at a number of towns, with a modernized curriculum patterned on that of the mission schools.

Buddhism in Lower Burma demonstrated remarkable survival power and vitality despite its separation from the fountainhead of disciplinary authority at the Burman capital. All Burmese Buddhists continued to look to the spiritual functionaries at Mandalay as the directing center of their religion even though functions of the royal commissions relative to definition of property holdings, discipline, and the registry of ordained monks in Lower Burma fell into abeyance. The effect of British refusal to recognize the authority of the Buddhist ecclesiastical code in Lower Burma aggravated traditional differences of an administrative character affecting both monastic and lay elements of the population in all of Burma.[88] The "high church" party (*Sulagandi*) demanded strict observance of monastic austerity, but conceded that the motive behind a particular action and the factor of free will in the acceptance of knowledge from the external world had a bearing on one's karma. The "low church" party (*Mahagandi*), with whom King Mindon sided, was less insistent on ritual observances, but held rigidly to the doctrine of karma, which denied that the intention or motive behind any given deed could modify its automatic effect on a person's destiny. The *thathanabaings* favored *Sulagandi* austerity, but they were usually in no position to act decisively, especially in Lower Burma. King Mindon disapproved the action of the *thathanabaing* in sending out several ecclesiastical emissaries on disciplinary and educational missions.[89]

The *Mahagandi* movement combined with the availability of foreign luxuries contributed to the marked trend in the direction of the "low church" standards in British Burma. The more puritanical *Sula-*

[86] Harvey, *British Rule,* p. 46. Perhaps the greatest contribution of the American Baptist Mission was in education.

[87] Fytche, II, 205–206.

[88] Smith-Forbes, pp. 325–326; Harvey, *British Rule,* pp. 26–27.

[89] Nisbet, II, 116–118, 124, 127.

gandi party, very much on the defensive, protested the growing tendency of monks to wear silken robes, to eat prepared meals in preference to the assorted contents of their alms bowls, to sell pagoda offerings for money, to use sandals and umbrellas on morning rounds, to receive gifts in coin, to attend *pwés* or popular entertainments, and to utilize balloons and fireworks at the light festivals celebrating the end of lent. Partisan religious friction reached the point of violence at Moulmein, Henzada, and Pegu, and the consequent visit of a *Sayadaw* from Mandalay in 1880 accomplished nothing to quiet the dissension. In some areas, rival abbots forbade the laity to give alms to opposing groups and recommended their excommunication, but neither side could impose its will. The smallest village still had its *pongyi kyaung* and pagoda shrine in 1880, but all was not religious serenity and peace.[90] Dissension and indiscipline within the *Sangha*, especially in Lower Burma, was destined to become progressively worse during the concluding decades of the century.[91] Nevertheless, few observers in 1900 suspected that monastic indiscipline would eventually find expression in overt political activity, as was the case after 1920.[92]

British rule in Tenasserim and Lower Burma liberated the Karen population from handicaps they had suffered under Burmese domination. Concurrently the persistent efforts of the American Baptist Mission in both evangelism and education accomplished an amazing transformation in a considerable part of the Karen population. Adoniram Judson's arrival in Burma in 1813 had antedated the first Anglo-Burmese War by more than a decade, but he and his associates accomplished their initial successes among the Tenasserim Karens after the British arrived. Lower Burma Karens had welcomed the British invaders in 1825–26, hoping that their long-prophesied deliverance, to come supposedly by sea, was at hand.[93] As already indicated, they suffered dire vengeance at Burmese hands after 1826, but a quarter

[90] Shway Yoe, pp. 149–152. The Mandalay *Sayadaw* refused to adjudicate a Lower Burma monastic dispute in 1880 when he learned that the parties concerned were gambling on the prospective outcome of his visit.

[91] Nisbet commented pessimistically as of 1900 (II, 154): "Slowly but surely the fabric of Buddhism . . . is being broken down and is crumbling away like so many pagodas. . . . Nothing is likely to intervene to stop the decay which has already begun."

[92] Fielding-Hall (*The Soul of a People*, p. 91) declared that "no one can imagine even in the far future any monk . . . desiring temporal power or interfering in any way with the government."

[93] D. M. Smeaton, *The Loyal Karens of Burma* (London, 1920), pp. 153–157. Judson's English-Burmese dictionary is still in many respects unexcelled.

century later they saw their dreams of deliverance come true. The arrival of British war vessels at Rangoon in 1852 was regarded by persecuted Christian Karens in Lower Burma as an answer to their prayers.

The missionary's bringing the Bible fitted into an old Karen tradition to the effect that a younger white brother would some day return to the Karens their long-lost sacred book.[94] American missionaries early reduced to writing in Burmese script the two most important Karen dialects and actually started a Karen newspaper at Tavoy in 1841. Mission schools began the laborious task of establishing a tradition of literacy among the Christianized Karens, and annual associational gatherings of the Karen Baptist churches contributed to the development of national consciousness. Christianity was attractive to the Karens politically because it constituted a cultural link with their British deliverers. Religiously, it afforded opportunity for cultural advancement and emancipated its adherents from the ever-present fear of evil spirits which had traditionally infested the minds of Karen jungle folk. Thus, especially among the Sgaw Karens, Christianity and pro-British Karen nationalism developed hand in hand. In 1881, a Karen National Association was formed to promote a broader sense of unity among all Karen peoples and to provide spokesmen for them in political matters. Karen leadership was largely Sgaw and Christian because the Christians constituted the educated minority, but the aims of the National Association were primarily political and encompassed all Karen groups.[95]

The Reign of Mindon Min, 1852–1878

The accession of King Mindon Min, as already indicated, occurred during the political crises following the British occupation of Lower Burma in 1852. The necessity of establishing the authority of the new regime in Upper Burma precluded any possibility of resisting the British occupation to the south, even if King Mindon had been so minded, which was not the case.[96] The new king was devoutly religious, a man of high character, well mannered and well intentioned,

[94] A. R. McMahon, *The Karens of the Golden Chersonese* (London, 1827), pp. 140–141. This *Ywa* tradition of the Karens contained many parallels to Old Testament tradition.

[95] Smeaton, pp. 213–218. The other principal Karen group in Lower Burma, the Pwo Karens, remained largely animist or Buddhist. The Bwe Karens living in the Sittang-Salween watershed were animist cousins of the Sgaw.

[96] Hall, *Europe and Burma*, pp. 146–147.

opposed to bloodshed, incapable of trickery. He was also informed on historical and economic matters, although lacking any adequate appreciation of the outside world. Without assuming a posture of either subservience or defiance, King Mindon won the respect of the neighboring British authorities as a man of integrity and progressive capabilities.[97]

The new king's domestic policies were heavily conditioned by the proximity of British rule and by the obvious need to strengthen and modernize his state. With respect to the loss of Lower Burma, he firmly refused to legalize the *de facto* British occupation by treaty recognition of its cession. Nor did he conceal his expectation that British India, without being threatened, would see fit in time to return the lost provinces to his government.[98] His hopes in this respect were apparently stimulated during the first decade of his reign by recurring crises affecting the British position in Asia. These were connected with the Crimean War (1854–1856),[99] the Sepoy Rebellion in India (1857–1858), and the Anglo-French War with China (1858–1860). But in no crisis incident did he raise his hand to force the issue.[100] During the very heat of the Russian War in 1855, King Mindon received Major Arthur Phayre at the capital in a generous and friendly fashion, providing for him an elaborate river escort and a reception committee including members of the *Hlutdaw*. Neither party on this occasion won a diplomatic victory, and no one suffered indignity; the gains were in the cultivation of mutual respect.[101] The king's lack of capability for intrigue was no doubt re-enforced by his awareness that his outmoded and dispirited army was no match for the British-Indian forces and that a reckless move might easily sacrifice all.

In an effort to strengthen his state, King Mindon sent missions abroad and fashioned a number of administrative reforms on recommendations brought back. His principal objectives were to eliminate

[97] Harvey, *Outline*, pp. 173–174.

[98] Henry Yule, *Narrative of the Mission to the Court of Ava in 1855* (London, 1858), pp. 76–78.

[99] "Phayre's Private Journal of His Mission to Ava," *JBRS*, XXII (1932), 78. During the Crimean conflict, Armenians, Muslim Indians, and Persians resident at Ava predicted freely that Russia would conquer India and force the British to abandon Pegu.

[100] Harvey, *British Rule*, pp. 20–21. During the 1857 rebellion in India, Mindon resisted Anglophobe court advice to strike at British defenses in Pegu by remarking, "We do not strike a friend when he is in distress."

[101] "Phayre's Private Journal," *JBRS*, XXII (1932), 77–81; Yule, pp. 60–87. Yule's tone is ultrasensitive and deprecatory of Burmese customs, but he reported without condescension that King Mindon had a good, intelligent face.

feudal vestiges and to strengthen the authority of the central government. Now that Lower Burma was no longer available for *myosa* assignment, he undertook in 1861 to abolish that system and the normal peculations of royal officials by paying to all princes and officials regular salaries and stipends from revenue resources.[102] To finance the salary system, Mindon introduced in 1862 the *thathameda* household income tax throughout all of Upper Burma, except apparently within Mandalay itself. The tax was assessed annually on a flexible pattern in April or May, following the harvesting of the crops and according to the observed prosperity of particular geographical units. The average per household assessment in such units varied from a low of 3 ticals in 1862 to a high of 10 ticals by 1885, the total demand for a given unit being calculated by multiplying the prosperity index by the number of households.[103] An important innovation under the *thathameda* tax system was that *ahmudan* members of service units who had moved from their original homes paid tax dues to the local *myothugyi,* not to their original regimental heads. Only the collectors, the *myothugyis,* and the indigent were exempt from paying this tax. Approximately 20 per cent of the total demand was usually withheld as compensation by collecting units at various levels. The most serious abuses developed from failure to report correctly the actual number of households.[104]

King Mindon's salary-payment scheme was never carried through in thoroughgoing fashion because revenues were never quite sufficient, and the *Myowuns* in the provinces continued to enjoy the customary fees and perquisites of their positions. The *thathameda* tax provided almost two-thirds of the royal revenue during the 1860's and 1870's. Other sources were the royal monopolies established on teak trees, earth oil, and precious stones, plus imposts, customs, and transit dues. Tribute collections from Shan princes continued as did rental payments on royal lands. The treasury was also overburdened by the heavy demands for building the new capital of Mandalay and for

[102] Harvey, *British Rule,* p. 21; Fytche, I, 243.

[103] Max and Bertha Ferrars, *Burma* (London, 1900), p. 170. Recommendations regarding tax unit classifications were made through the *myothugyis* and *Myowuns* and submitted for final approval by the *Hlutdaw* itself. Temporary modification of the demand could be made in case of crop failure. Apportionment of taxes to cover the demand from a given unit was made roughly according to income of particular households by the *myothugyi* and his assistants, in consultation with village elders.

[104] Mya Sein, p. 186; Nisbet, I, 162–165. Irrigated areas and those adjacent to rivers were assessed heavily, and these were often royal-service lands.

adorning it with pagodas.[105] The *thathameda* tax collections fell apart under Mindon's weak successor in conjunction with the spread of dacoity and the resumption of assessment of customary local exactions.[106]

Another administrative innovation of King Mindon was the establishment of some ten new posts of *Kayaingwun* each of whom supervised the work of a number of provincial *Myowuns*. The *Kayaingwuns* were charged with inspecting each *myoyon* court three times a year and with transmitting information, complaints, and petitions to the *Hlutdaw* on a bimonthly basis covering matters of administration. The *Kayaingwuns* exercised no original court jurisdiction, but they reviewed criminal decisions by the *Myowun* and referred to the *Hlutdaw* cases involving extreme punishment.[107]

In the economic field the king introduced coined money in 1861. He also purchased several river steamers and undertook with meager success to start factories and to develop the mining of coal and iron. He encouraged trade with Lower Burma but refused to cancel his own customs duties along the river route partly because the revenue was needed and partly out of fear that revived China trade down the river might pass Mandalay by in favor of Rangoon. In any case Rangoon, which the British developed extensively, inevitably displaced Mandalay as a commercial center. The volume of trade between the two Burmas increased rapidly after an agreement of 1867 which permitted British steamers to proceed upstream as far north as Bhamo. But the price of rice was high in Upper Burma, and neither production nor population kept pace with the rapid development of British Burma. When King Mindon died in 1878, the reforming faction at the court was still in the ascendancy, although their attempts to carry on under King Thibaw sadly miscarried.[108]

In 1866, the Kingdom of Burma was shocked by a brief but serious rebellion originating within the court itself. Two disaffected sons of King Mindon broke into a session of the *Hlutdaw* and killed the king's brother who, as *Einshemin*, was presiding over the council at the summer palace. The rebels also murdered supporters of the slain man, but they failed to capture Mindon. The latter hurried back to the

[105] Nisbet, I, 162–163; E. C. V. Foucar, *They Reigned in Mandalay* (London, 1946), pp. 27–28.

[106] Mya Sein, pp. 17–18; Nisbet, I, 165.

[107] Mya Sein, pp. 42–43. *Kayaingwuns* also were responsible for keeping census figures and accurate maps of the area and in general for supervising provincial government.

[108] *Ibid.*, pp. 17–18; Harvey, *Outline*, pp. 173–174.

capital palace, where he was able to withstand an all-night siege. The ruler was badly shaken. On this occasion, however, the army remained firmly loyal to the king, and the rebels fled aboard the royal steamer to British Burma, where they were promptly interned. The sequel was an abortive rising by the son of the murdered *Einshemin*, half-heartedly prosecuted from Shwebo. Other sons of the king successfully defended the capital.[109] One unfortunate aspect of the 1866–1867 episode was that King Mindon hesitated to risk again the consequences of naming and installing another *Einshemin*, as he should have done, well in advance of his death. The results of royal inaction proved tragic for the dynasty following Mindon's death in 1878.

Another major interest of Mindon Min was religious. In 1871, he convened at Mandalay the Fifth Great Buddhist Synod or Council. Its major accomplishment was the recitation of the corrected Pali texts of the Buddhist Tripitaka scriptures. At the king's orders, these texts were duly inscribed on 729 marble slabs which were accommodated in the veritable forest of sheltering pagodas (the *Kuthodaw*) located at the base of Mandalay hill. In the same year, 1871, the king prepared a bejeweled *hti* (umbrella tip) replacement for the Shwe Dagon pagoda at Rangoon and, with British consent, saw it put in place. Another of King Mindon's noteworthy adornments of Mandalay was the beautiful *Atumashi* pagoda, which was finally destroyed in World War II. The king also made his court the center of Burmese literary activity. Mandalay was known as *Shwemyo* or Golden City.[110]

King Mindon's attempts to bolster the discipline and morale of the army were largely ineffective. For this purpose he obtained the aid of an able military man, named De Facieu, who had fought with the British army in India during the 1850's.[111] But it was to no avail. An inactive army had no opportunity to recover its confidence and morale. The privileged status of the *ahmudan*-service population was being undermined by the king's *thathameda* taxation policy and by the steady exodus of such *ahmudan* persons toward Lower Burma, where employment opportunities were more easily available. The decline of Burma's military tradition tended to blur the once rigidly maintained distinction between *ahmudan* and *athi* subjects of the king. Attrition in the *ahmudan* ranks was signalized by their shift of habitation away from the now heavily taxed royal lands, by their intermar-

---

[109] Foucar, pp. 41–47; Hall, *South-East Asia*, p. 541.
[110] Harvey, *Outline*, pp. 173–180; Hall, *South-East Asia*, pp. 536, 543.
[111] Foucar, pp. 48–49.

riage with *athi* elements, and by the tendency of the vocational elements of the service *athins* to grow at the expense of the fighting regiments. Certainly by 1880 the Burma army was a mere shadow in spirit and discipline as well as in numbers of that force which under the great Bandula had started out in 1824 to conquer Assam and Bengal.[112]

Foreign Relations of Burma under Mindon Min, 1852–1878

King Mindon's relations with neighboring British authorities were always correctly friendly, but never cordial. The lost provinces were the barrier, and traditionalists at court gave him little leeway on this point. The king refused at first for prestige reasons to permit the residence at his capital of a British diplomatic agent. He was nevertheless willing to utilize the presence of foreigners at Mandalay, some of them known to be in British pay, in order to keep both himself and the Rangoon authorities informed on current happenings.[113] Relations improved for a time after the negotiation in 1862 of a commercial treaty with British Burma, which permitted the presence of a British Resident (Colonel Sladen) at Mandalay and accorded freer use of the river facilities to British steamboats. With British assistance, the king obtained for himself several river steamers. Following Lower Burma's welcome co-operation in interning the rebel princes in 1867, new negotiations were undertaken and extraterritorial jurisdiction over British subjects was accorded to the Resident at Mandalay. The court was also friendly at Mandalay in the 1860's to the Catholic vicar apostolic, Bishop Bigandet, and to the Anglican missionary, Dr. Marks.[114]

Friction developed mainly over the king's efforts to maintain Burma's status as an independent nation in opposition to the British presumption that it was already some sort of a dependency of British India. Particularly resented by the British were King Mindon's efforts to establish direct diplomatic relations with other powers. One of his

[112] Harvey, *British Rule*, p. 41; Mya Sein, pp. 17–18. Migrations from Upper Burma helped to double the population of Pegu from 1852 to 1861, and the influx increased after 1870. In theory only, all these immigrants to Lower Burma continued to be subjects (chattels) of the king.

[113] D. G. E. Hall, "New Light upon British Relations with King Mindon," *JBRS*, XVIII (1928), 1–11. Mindon used Father Abbona and a British merchant at Mandalay named Spears to exchange intelligence and even to negotiate with Governor-General Dalhousie and Commissioner Arthur Phayre. Spears departed from Mandalay in 1862.

[114] Hall, *South-East Asia*, pp. 539–542.

abortive efforts was the sending of a letter to President Pierce of the United States through an American Baptist missionary, the Reverend Mr. Kinkaird, asking that a treaty be concluded between the United States and Burma.[115] Early in his reign King Mindon sent a mission headed by the ranking member of the *Hlutdaw* to London and Paris, by-passing India entirely.[116] In 1856, to the great annoyance of the British, a French mission to Amarapura, proceeding via Rangoon, returned the Burmese visit, carrying presents to the Burmese Court.[117]

One of the apparent results of King Mindon's direct contacts with the French was his permission for the Paris Société des Missions Etrangères to establish at Bhamo a Catholic mission to act as a way station for the projected French missionary penetration of Tibet. A French missionary was first stationed at Bhamo in 1856. Previously Catholic missionaries resident in Burma had limited their concern for the most part to the descendants of French and Portuguese captives living either at Pegu or in the vicinity of the capital.[118] In the late 1850's, the long-time Italian missionary at Mandalay, Father Abbona, was replaced by the French Society's representative, Monsignor Bigandet. The latter held the papal title of vicar apostolic to Pegu and Ava.[119]

Mindon also encouraged Frenchmen and Italians to assist his government in various capacities.[120] Thus in 1859, one General M. d'Orgoni, acting under authorization from Mindon's court, passed through Rangoon en route to Mandalay accompanied by a number of skilled French artisans and engineers selected for service in Burma. He also brought with him a French-built river steamer, christened Alon Phra (Alaungpaya), which he hoped to sell to Burma. British observers at Rangoon alleged that D'Orgoni was also encouraging the king to stand up to the English in the eventual hope of recovering Burma's lost prov-

[115] This letter, written in Burmese, was identified and translated at Washington in 1924. It is undated except for the notation that it was delivered to President Pierce by the Reverend Mr. Kinkaird. It is in the National Archives at Washington.

[116] The mission was headed by the Kinwun Mingyi, an ex-monk friend of Mindon, whose printed diaries in Burmese are available in the Library of Congress collection.

[117] In response to London's inquiries regarding the objectives of the French mission, Paris replied that it was intended only to deliver presents to the Burma capital and that it carried no political significance.

[118] *Archives de Ministère des Affaires Etrangères, Chine,* XVII (1855), 90–91. In 1855, Father Libois of the Paris Society discussed the matter with Chargé de Courcy and he in turn with Foreign Minister Walewski.

[119] Browne, pp. 21–22.   [120] White, *A Civil Servant in Burma,* p. 29.

inces.[121] But official French political interest in Southeast Asia declined in 1860 following the discouraging outcome of the naval attacks on the Annamite ports of Tourane and Saigon.

During the late 1860's and the early 1870's, Burma's continuance as an independent state was sharply challenged by its falling within the scope of Anglo-French imperialistic rivalry in Eastern Asia. The question involved competition for preferred access to China's Yunnan province as a potential center of trade and political influence. The French approach to the area was via the Mekong and Red River valleys, while the British access must perforce be up the Irrawaddy Valley through Burma. British interest in the possibility of establishing overland trade contact between India and China was not new, for that topic had been indicated as a subordinate concern of the Symes mission of 1795.[122] This interest had been sustained by the fact that the China trade with Burma during the first half of the nineteenth century had continued in considerable volume, both by river and by the caravan route. China's raw silk, silk cloth, velvets, gold-leaf bullion, and tea were exchanged for Burma's cotton and salt. It was believed that if the predatory activity of Kachin tribesmen inhabiting the border region could be curbed, this trade might be capable of indefinite expansion.[123]

Unfortunately, Burma's trade with China came to a complete halt after 1855, when a small Sunni Moslem sect in Yunnan province, called the Panthays, rebelled against the oppressive and faltering control of the Manchu Chinese. Peking was challenged at the time by the Taiping Rebellion and was destined to face shortly thereafter the Anglo-French War of 1858–1860. Peking's countermove in Yunnan was to encourage freebooters, mainly Chinese and Shans, to harass the fledgling Panthay state. One of the casualties of the ensuing confusion was the exchange of goods between China and Burma. Only

[121] Browne, pp. 28–29; India Office Archives, *India Secret Proceedings,* vol. 226 (1859), items dated April 7, May 10, and Sept. 1, 1859.

[122] John F. Cady, *The Roots of French Imperialism in Eastern Asia* (Ithaca, N.Y., 1954), pp. 210–223, 282–286; Hall, *Symes,* pp. xxix–xxxv. From the time of Fytche's negotiation of 1867, it was a settled policy of British India to seek control over Burma's foreign relations. The matter was not pressed by Fytche. Burma undertook to avoid such status by sending the second diplomatic mission to Europe in 1872–1873. See Maung Maung, *Burma in the Family of Nations,* pp. 47–53.

[123] India Office Archives, *Bengal Political Correspondence,* MSS. EUR., E63, no. 155, p. 70, instructions to Symes, dated Feb. 6, 1795; see also a study entitled "Sketch of the Sinphos or the Kakhyens of Burma," in India Office Archives, *Tracts,* vol. 266 (Calcutta, 1847), pp. 30–41, 57–65.

to the extent that Chinese merchants at Bhamo or Mandalay were able to bribe the freebooters sufficiently did a trickle of trade continue to come through. One of the principal sufferers from the cessation of trade were the border Kachin hill tribesmen, whose traditional levying of blackmail on the transit trade, short of penalizing it to the point of discontinuance, had been an important source of tribal income.[124] A British explorer-investigator in 1863 discovered that both the Panthays and Kachins wanted to revive the trade, but that the hostile Shans and Chinese were blocking the move. The apparent possibility of obtaining Burmese co-operation in reopening the trade with China was a major concern of the Rangoon authorities in obtaining as part of the treaty of 1867 the right of British steamers to navigate the entire course of the Irrawaddy River up to Bhamo and the privilege of posting a British consul at that city.

Immediately following the conclusion of the 1867 treaty and prior to the assignment of a British consul at Bhamo, Rangoon authorities launched ambitious plans to survey southwestern China. Colonel Sladen, the British Resident at Mandalay, acting with Burmese consent and with liberal financial backing from the Rangoon Chamber of Commerce, succeeded in 1868 in making contact with the Panthay authorities. At the same time, one T. T. Cooper was sent by British consular agencies at Shanghai to proceed westward across China to the Burma border.[125] Colonel Sladen obtained Panthay assistance in clearing a path for him to the center of the Moslem state, where his proposal to reopen the trade with Burma was received with enthusiasm. But he encountered difficulties on his return journey. He ran out of money, and two members of his Panthay escort were killed.[126] Mr. Cooper, on his side, found the route to Bhamo so difficult and dangerous that he finally had to exit to India via Tibet and Katmandu in Nepal, which city he reached in July, 1868.[127] These extensive but largely abortive British explorations were undertaken in direct competition with those of the French Lagrée-Garnier mission, which pro-

---

[124] E. R. Leach, *Political Systems of Highland Burma* (London, 1954), p. 242. The Yunnan rebellion adversely affected the interests of Kachin tribesmen of north Burma. A formidable Kachin rising against the Burmans began in 1883, centering at Mogaung. By 1884, it had carried halfway to Mandalay.

[125] Fytche, II, 96–98; Clement Williams, *Through Burma to Western China . . . in 1863* (London, 1868), pp. 8–9.

[126] India Office Archives, Foreign Dept., *Political Proceedings*, vol. 483 (1868), nos. 33–37 of Jan. 7, 1868, nos. 54–71 of Feb., 1868, nos. 86–91 of March, 1868.

[127] *Ibid.*, March to Sept., 1868. The India Government paid 1,000 rupees in compensation to the families of the several Panthay victims.

ceeded up the Mekong River Valley into Yunnan and thence to Shanghai in 1867–1868.[128]

Colonel Sladen's report of his journey aroused great interest in Rangoon, in spite of its many discouraging aspects. Some local British officials began to advocate taking over immediate control of Burma's foreign relations. The authorities in India were less favorably impressed. They were conscious of other problems more pressing than that of French rivalry in Yunnan, and they considered the commercial prospects of the Burma-China border too dubious to warrant adventurous action.[129] The situation changed in 1873 when the feeble Panthay state collapsed. One indication of the continuing British interest in the affairs of Yunnan was the India Government's provision for a number of years thereafter of asylum, housing, and living allowances (totaling 550 rupees monthly in 1878) to a refugee Panthay leader, Prince Hassan.[130]

The French exploration headed by Lagrée and Garnier discovered that the Mekong Valley was unsuited for trade but that the Red River Valley leading directly into Yunnan via Tongking was eminently usable. The situation clearly indicated the desirability of French acquisition of Tongking, but nothing could be done at the time. During the declining years of the Second French Empire, Louis Napoleon was heavily involved elsewhere (in Mexico and Europe) and was not interested in Indochina. A brief flurry of local French imperialistic activity at Hanoi in 1873, in the interest of opening the route to Yunnan, even though abortive, served once more to revive Anglo-French rivalry. Burma was caught firmly in the squeeze between rival European imperialisms. The situation for Mandalay was ominous.[131]

In 1872, King Mindon sent a second diplomatic mission to Europe, headed as before by the Kinwun Mingyi. The objective was to developed diplomatic contacts apart from India and, if possible, to obtain arms. The mission concluded an innocuous commercial treaty

[128] *Ibid.*, nos. 123–127 of May, 1868; nos. 112–114 and 203–206 of July, 1868.

[129] *Ibid.*, May to Sept., 1868, nos. 143, 112–114, 163–165. Not only is the Lagrée mission here fully discussed, but other India Office records (nos. 174 and 264–267 for April, 1868) indicate that British intelligence was also keeping a close watch on the activities of French missionaries in Tibet and the vicinity of Upper Burma.

[130] Laurie, p. 11; Fytche, II, 100–107; Hall, *South-East Asia*, p. 542; India Office Archives, Foreign Dept., *Political Proceedings* for 1878, vol. 1218, p. 41, nos. 89 and 90. Prince Hassan's marriage in 1878 cost the India Government 8,000 rupees.

[131] Cady, pp. 282–286; Nisbet, I, 170–173; Foucar, pp. 60–83.

with Italy and another with France. In London, the Kinwun Mingyi was rebuffed by the Foreign Office. He was referred instead to the Government of India as the appropriate negotiating agent for Burma. Entertainment in England was largely by various Chambers of Commerce. The Burman visitors could do nothing to break the diplomatic boycott, but they did formulate plans to send Burman youth abroad for study and conceived an ambitious program for constitutional reform. When a French emissary presented himself at Mandalay in 1873 to exchange ratifications, King Mindon tried without success to obtain a firm promise of assistance. France was still under Prussian occupation, and Foreign Minister de Broglie was strongly anti-imperialist. Two secret proposals tentatively considered at Mandalay, namely that France proffer its good offices in any third-party dispute involving Burma and also provide officers to train the Burma army, were both repudiated by Paris.[132] British policy toward Burma during the remainder of the 1870's became increasingly aggressive.

The Hanoi incident of 1873 and the collapse of the Panthay rebellion in the same year afforded another occasion for the British to explore the feasibility of reviving the China trade.[133] With strong backing from Rangoon and from the British Associated Chambers of Commerce, the Secretary of State for India, Lord Salisbury, authorized a new survey of the trade route from Bhamo to China. Because Burma also had a positive interest in the China trade, King Mindon afforded generous assistance to the small but well-supplied British-Sikh contingent led by Colonel Horace A. Browne, which was assigned to this task. Colonel Browne proceeded from Rangoon to Bhamo in late 1874 to effect a junction with Consul A. R. Margary who was traveling overland to Bhamo from Shanghai and was to act as Browne's interpreter on the return journey. Colonel Browne was welcomed en route at Mandalay and was offered the use of the royal steamer in his journey to Bhamo. The *Myowun* at Bhamo later levied a two-rupee household contribution on the city to pay the cost of providing a 250-man Burmese armed escort to accompany Browne and Margary during the initial stages of their journey to the China border.[134]

The affair ended tragically. Consul Margary and a few companions, who ventured out ahead of the armed escort, were murdered by armed

[132] Hall, *South-East Asia*, pp. 544–545, Maung Maung, *Burma in the Family of Nations*, pp. 50–53. The Burmese diary of the Kinwun Mingyi told the account of his experiences in England.

[133] Browne, pp. 58–60, 83; Hall, *South-East Asia*, p. 543.

[134] Browne, pp. 65–95.

Chinese on February 21, 1875, in Kachin country short of the Yunnan border. The attempted annihilation by several thousand Chinese troops of Browne's own force of sixteen Sikh troopers and the few score accompanying Burmese soldiers occurred on the following day. It was only through the help of well-paid Kachin tribesmen that Browne's party was able to extricate itself from the ambuscade and return to Bhamo.[135] The loyal co-operation of the Bhamo *Myowun* and the Mandalay government throughout the affair left the British no basis for complaint.[136]

In spite of Mandalay's co-operation in the Browne-Margary episode but in agreement with increasing British presumption, British-Burman relations took a distinct turn for the worse later in 1875. On express orders from India, the British Resident at Mandalay, Shaw, abruptly discontinued compliance with the traditional requirement that shoes be removed in the king's presence. This had the effect of ending all royal audiences for the Resident and amounted in effect to the severance of diplomatic relations without ostensible cause. The action reflected increasing British concern over frustrated trading relations with Burma and over the presence of a colony of French and Italian adventurers at Mandalay. Rumors were rampant. Colonel Browne reported that a Frenchman commanding the royal steamer had picked up a rumor that the French Catholic Father Lecompte had mistranslated a clause of Burma's French commercial treaty to suggest that, in case Burma were again attacked, France would make Mandalay's cause its own. At the time of Browne's stay in Bhamo, he expressed concern over the fact that Father Lecompte and a companion were preparing to enter Yunnan en route to Tibet on what was apparently a nonpolitical mission.[137] Relations became much worse after 1878, when King Thibaw's intrigues with French agents were coupled with the revival of aggressive French imperialist activity in Tongking in 1881.

---

[135] Browne reveals (pp. 96–104) that Margary in the first instance had managed to pass westward through Yunnan only because Chinese officials en route, all of whom were in receipt of orders to stop him, had successively passed the responsibility on to others. Each official got Margary off his own hands as quickly as possible. The final plot was to kill the entire British Indian-Burman force on the Burma side of the Yunnan border in order to pin responsibility for the crime on the Burma Government if possible.

[136] Browne, pp. 58, 61–62, 68, 160–161; Hall, *South-East Asia*, p. 547. The British consul at Bhamo was withdrawn in 1878, when fuller knowledge of the difficult terrain discouraged the hope of any sizable trade with China.

[137] Hall, *Europe and Burma*, pp. 166–167.

The Reign of King Thibaw, 1878–1885

The unfortunate accession, already mentioned, of the weak and inexperienced King Thibaw, upon the death of King Mindon in September, 1878, was made possible in large measure by the previous king's fatal delay in nominating and installing an *Einshemin*. King Mindon's apparent preference as successor in 1878 was the Nyaungyan prince, the son of a favorite queen but not one of the blood royal and therefore of inferior rank at court. An opposing palace clique headed by the chief queen, Sinpyumashin, who had borne the king two daughters but no sons, seized control of the palace area during the final days of the king's illness. The eligible Nyaungyan and the Nyaung Ok princes very prudently refrained from responding to the royal summons to appear at the palace and thus escaped imprisonment by the guards.[138] Both princes took temporary refuge in the British Residency at Mandalay, whence they were eventually smuggled aboard an armed British steamer journeying to Rangoon, in November, 1878. Because their lives were subsequently endangered by would-be assassins sent from Upper Burma, the princes were transported to Calcutta for safety in early December.[139]

The selection of the youthful Prince Thibaw as the new king and as husband of Sinpyumashin's second daughter, Supayalat, was determined in part by the fact that the prince, unlike several of his older brothers, was personally a cipher and had no political following within the country. The Kinwun Mingyi hoped that a weak king would leave the *Hlutdaw* free to introduce constitutional reforms, but events proved otherwise. Prince Thibaw's mother, a Shan princess, had been divorced by the king for moral irregularities and had sought refuge from her disgrace by becoming a nun. Thibaw himself had spent all his life since the age of seven in a monastery, where he had earned a reputation of being kindhearted, well educated, and possessing some promise as a scholar. The disgraced mother had been befriended at various times by Sinpyumashin, and the young Thibaw, following his own amazing transition from monastery to the palace and marriage to Supayalat, was completely beholden to his mother-

[138] Browne, pp. 145–149. Mindon had forty-eight sons all told.

[139] *Ibid.*, pp. 175–176; White, *A Civil Servant in Burma*, p. 28; Foucar, pp. 54–63; Grattan Geary, *Burma after the Conquest* (London, 1886), pp. 126–128, 174. King Mindon planned to set up three regencies for various parts of his kingdom, one of them being for the Nyaungyan prince.

in-law for his sudden elevation. He was, in any case, quite incapable of resisting the domineering influence of both mother and daughter.[140]

Once the palace conspiracy got under way, it was the unscrupulous and power-hungry Supayalat and her henchman Taingda, one of the *Atwinwuns* and chief of the palace guard, who made the decisions.[141] The Kinwun Mingyi was quickly relegated to the background; he did manage to keep himself in office and continued to exercise a moderating influence until the fatal crisis of 1885. The actual control of governmental affairs passed to Taingda and to Queen Supayalat.[142]

The insecurity of the palace conspirators prompted their arrest at the outset of several hundred royal relatives. On February 18, 1879, occurred the royally sanctioned execution of thirty-two of the prisoners, including eight prince-brothers of the king. This action was not authorized by the *Hlutdaw,* but the Kinwun Mingyi apologetically explained to the British that it was taken to avoid civil war. The execution of other victims, up to the number of fourscore or more, came later. These included officials friendly to the British and even a few of Thibaw's own boyhood companions, who had been so bold as to warn the king of the dangers of petticoat rule. Thibaw found temporary escape from his depression and remorse in alcohol, leaving the direction of affairs to more vigorous hands.[143]

British authorities in Lower Burma, horrified over the orgy of executions at Mandalay but also in a mood to welcome any excuse for intervention, suggested privately to Viceroy Lord Lytton that if three fresh regiments could be brought over from Calcutta in ostensible support of the candidacy of the Nyaungyan prince, Burmese opinion would probably rally to his cause. Rangoon argued that the installation of an Anglophile ruler in Burma would also eliminate the hostile influences exerted at Mandalay by French and Italian adventurers, who were currently directing Burma's military preparations. The British business community at Rangoon in March, 1879, sent a memorial to the Secretary of State for India urging that settlement of pending differences and grievances with Mandalay be undertaken. London replied in April that procedure by ultimatum was inadvisable. The Nyaungyan

---

[140] Geary, pp. 174–175.

[141] Associated with Supayalat and Taingda was the Hlethin *Atwinwun,* an ex-guardsman who had previously achieved the rank of *Hpaungwun* (governor of the royal barges) and *Myowun* of Mandalay. Hlethin was married to Taingda's daughter. See Shway Yoe, pp. 490–496.

[142] *Ibid.,* pp. 494–496.   [143] Geary, p. 174.

prince on his own initiative returned to Rangoon from Calcutta in April, 1879, in anticipation of British intervention in his behalf.

But Viceroy Lytton had already been forced to embark on a war with Afghanistan in 1878 following Kabul's refusal of his demand that a British mission be received to balance the presence of Russians at the Afghan capital. Furthermore, the London Cabinet, immediately following the crucial Congress of Berlin, was much concerned to avoid a war in Asia.[144] The general situation counseled taking no gratuitous risks of trouble with Burma. Nothing overt could be done in any case as long as the members of the British Residency at Mandalay were devoid of the means of protection and therefore exposed to the wrath of the court party. The Nyaungyan prince was therefore required to return to Calcutta. The other candidate, the Nyaung Ok prince, eventually took up his residence at Pondicherry at the invitation of the French.[145] When Mandalay attempted in 1879 to communicate with the viceroy, British-Burma frontier officials refused the emissary transit privileges after he declined in advance to grant their treaty demands.[146]

A second opportunity for British intervention in the Burma Kingdom developed during the summer of 1879. Colonel Horace A. Browne, an avowed enemy of French influence in Burma, was sent to Mandalay as new British Resident in June, 1879, following the death of the previous incumbent, Shaw. Browne reported that the Kinwun Mingyi, fearful of war with Britain, was completely disillusioned with Thibaw and would gladly declare for the Nyaungyan prince if he could do so with safety. Even the queen mother herself was allegedly talking about marrying her other daughter, the elder sister of Supayalat, to Nyaungyan, doubtless to have a foot in both camps. Apparently only fear of the consequences of failure was preventing a coalescence of various political elements who were threatened by the palace clique. After some two months' residence at Mandalay during which time

---

[144] Maung Maung, *Burma in the Family of Nations,* pp. 56–60; Keith Feiling, *A History of England* (London, 1949), p. 950. Minor river incidents in 1879 were magnified by Rangoon business and government circles as affording excuses for punitive demands upon the Burma Court. London and New Delhi refused to go along with Rangoon.

[145] Browne, pp. 150–154. Browne, writing from Rangoon, was very caustic in his criticism of Lord Lytton's policy. See also Hall, *South-East Asia,* pp. 549–550.

[146] Geary, p. 128.

Browne's relations with the court steadily worsened, the Resident, in late August, abruptly withdrew to Rangoon with a portion of his staff, preparatory to a complete break in relations.[147]

Impending developments outside of Burma vetoed any plans which the British might have entertained in 1879 to set aside Thibaw's regime. On September 7, news reached Rangoon about the massacre at Kabul of the recently installed British Resident Cavagnari and his entire staff, an event which reopened the contest with the Russians for control of the buffer state of Afghanistan. Here the Russian threat was immediate, and the issue was clearly joined; in Burma, as of 1879, the French threat was still remote and no prior British military commitment had been made. The obvious unwisdom of overextending India's military resources by becoming involved in simultaneous wars at the eastern and western extremities of the Empire of India was reinforced by political considerations in England. There Mr. Gladstone's Liberal Opposition was already belaboring the Disraeli Ministry for embarking on allegedly gratuitous imperialistic adventures in both South Africa and Afghanistan.[148] The British Residency at Mandalay was accordingly ordered closed on September 21, 1879, not as a prelude to intervention but as a measure of precautionary security. The entire Residency staff was evacuated in early October, and relations between Rangoon and Mandalay remained seriously strained for months thereafter. Lord Lytton's *laissez faire* policy and the moderating influence of the Kinwun Mingyi at Mandalay were credited with keeping the peace.[149]

Under Thibaw's palsied rule the political situation in Burma grew steadily worse. Royal weakness and corrupt influences at court permitted the worst type of men to come to power. Honest collection of revenues received no support at court. Official appointees of Taingda (now a *Wungyi*) were particularly rapacious and susceptible to bribery. Not infrequently Taingda himself was allegedly allied with armed bandits operating throughout the countryside. Whereas Mindon's problems of political unrest had been associated mainly with Kachin disaffection in hilly northern Burma, under Thibaw armed bandits became increasingly active in the plains as well. At their

[147] Browne, pp. 182–187, 191.

[148] Feiling, p. 250. Disraeli's Ministry fell in 1880, and Gladstone brought both wars to an end shortly after he took office.

[149] Browne, pp. 165, 191. Browne complained that Lytton was more concerned about Russian infiltration of Britain's Central Asian sphere than about French actions at Mandalay.

optimum best, the local bandit *Bos* who took over *de facto* power in many localities were Burmese Robin Hood's, capable of responsible dealings if properly recompensed. At their worst they simply killed the *Myowuns*, burned unco-operative villages, and promoted chaos generally.[150] In Burma's Ningyan area (Pyinmana), located above British-held Toungoo, all offices were for sale: the post of *Kayaing* for 10,000 rupees, that of *Myowun* for 5,000 rupees, subordinate *Wun*-ships for 2,000 to 3,000 rupees, down to the *myothugyi*-ship for 1,200 rupees and the post of *ywathugyi* for 500 rupees. It was apparently Thibaw's *Myowun* at Ningyan who accepted bribes from the Bombay-Burmah Trading Corporation in compensation for his connivance at the more or less irregular export of teakwood timber obtained from the Burma side of the border. The *Lewun* of Ningyan was one of Thibaw's brothers-in-law.[151]

The Kinwun Mingyi nevertheless made a fairly serious attempt to reform the central administration during Thibaw's reign. He proposed to distribute governmental responsibilities between fourteen functional departmental heads, who would operate as a kind of cabinet in the European fashion. He assigned control of tax revenues and expenditures (key powers) plus the operation of royal monopolies to the four *Atwinwuns*, while three *Wungyis* took over departments covering royal lands, waterways, elephants, the arsenals, and the army. The other departments covering judicial appeals, foreign diplomatic and commercial relations, police, and civil administration were assigned to men of *Wundauk* rank.[152] One effect of the proposed reform would be to enhance the power of the *Atwinwuns* and to emasculate the traditional plenary authority of the *Hlutdaw*. The new system lacked the leadership of a strong prime minister backed by the king, which alone would have enabled such a cabinet to operate as a unified whole. The reform proposal had no chance of adoption.

On the eve of Thibaw's final quarrel with British Burma, in 1884–1885, the Burma administration was in a sad state of confusion, with lawless bands in actual control of much of the area. Rebels holding Sagaing, almost directly across the river from Mandalay, were defying

[150] Nisbet, I, 170–173; Foucar, pp. 60–83.
[151] See R. R. Langham-Carter, "Burmese Rule on the Toungoo Frontier," *JBRS*, XXVII (1937), 16–24. Furnivall (*Colonial Policy and Practice*, p. 21) concedes that there was more than mere blackmail behind the 1885 exaction of the fine of 23 lakhs of rupees (2.3 million) levied by Mandalay on the Bombay-Burmah Trading Corporation.
[152] Mya Sein, pp. 17–18, 27–31.

the government.[153] The renewal of the slaughter of followers of one of the exiled princes in 1884 stimulated demands at Rangoon for intervention or annexation. A formidable Shan rebellion began in June, 1883, and the Kachins invaded Upper Burma in force in 1884–1885.[154] Concurrently, Chinese freebooters, in 1884, helped Burmese authorities repel a Kachin attack upon Bhamo and the Chinese then themselves burned and sacked the city.[155]

The Deposition of King Thibaw

The ostensible cause of the third Anglo-Burman War, which resulted in the British annexation of the Burma Kingdom, was the *Hlutdaw*'s levying, in August, 1885, of an exorbitant fine of 2,300,000 rupees (23 lakhs) on the Bombay-Burmah Trading Corporation for allegedly illegal extraction of teak logs from Burma territory above Toungoo. The fine was calculated by the *Hlutdaw* on the basis of the corporation's own records of extractions, assuming that all of the logs were full-sized and dutiable at the established rate set in 1880. The corporation insisted that many logs were defective and cited supplementary local agreements of 1882 and 1883 covering lump-sum payments for such logs. On September 20, Burman authorities detained log rafts on the Burma side until an initial installment was paid on the assessed fines. Border friction in the area had been minimal, and the facts were subject to verification. The matter was clearly one capable of negotiation if firmly handled.[156] The Kinwun Mingyi subsequently tried to reduce Burma's claim to a not unreasonable 100,000 to 200,000 rupees albeit too late to effect a settlement.[157] The attempt to collect the extortionate fine was strictly speaking not the cause but rather the occasion for sending a British ultimatum in late October. The basic problem was stated succinctly by a one-time British governor of Burma, as follows: "The ultimate cause of intervention was the apprehension lest France or some other European Power should establish a preponderant influence

[153] Sir Charles Crosthwaite, *The Pacification of Burma* (London, 1912), p. 6; Foucar, pp. 181–187.

[154] Hall, *South-East Asia*, pp. 550, 556. An effort to negotiate a settlement of the disputed Manipur-Burma boundary was broken off in September, 1882, by action of Mandalay. See India Office Archives, Foreign Dept., *Political Proceedings* for 1882, vol. 1924, minutes of Sept. and Oct., 1882. Border friction in both Manipur and Karenni were minor irritants.

[155] Nisbet, I, 170–173.

[156] Langham-Carter, *JBRS*, XXVII (1937), 30; Hall, *Europe and Burma*, p. 177; Foucar, pp. 117–121.

[157] Geary, p. 134.

in Upper Burma and create a situation which would render our position in Lower Burma intolerable.[158]

Imperialistic rivalry between Britain and France in Southeast Asia had intensified following 1881, as a result of the aggressive policies pursued by successive French ministries after that date. Starting from the original French colony of Cochin-China, French control was extended progressively to Annam and Tongking and then westward to Laos, to the left bank of the Mekong River. This river also marked the easternmost boundary of Shan states tributary to Burma. Domination of Tongking's Red River Valley also afforded the French at long last easy commercial access to Yunnan province in China, an area of intense Anglo-French rivalry.[159] According to the rules by which imperialism operated, Britain was "entitled" to seek compensatory advantage in the same general area.[160] From 1883 to 1885 French intrigue actually extended to an alarming degree into the Kingdom of Burma as well. But as long as the anti-imperialist Gladstone Ministry of 1880–1885 continued in London, very little could be done. The temporary displacement of Gladstone from June to December, 1885, by Salisbury's Conservative Cabinet afforded the imperialist-minded British faction a golden opportunity in Burma to halt the (to them) disquieting succession of reversals of British imperialist policy.[161]

In response to French encouragement, the Burma Government, in the spring of 1883, had sent a mission composed of six high officials to Paris for the purpose of concluding a new treaty. The mission was

[158] White, A Civil Servant in Burma, pp. 102–103. From Nisbet (II, 1) comes the following estimate of the potential importance of British commercial activity in Yunnan: "The only counterpoise to this ceaseless French activity in Yunnan inaugurated by Roman Catholic Missionaries and energetically supported by the French Government, is the encouragement of British pioneers of commerce in Western China."

[159] The Margary affair of 1874–1875 and Garnier's attempted coup at Hanoi in 1874 had reflected the same rivalry.

[160] India Office Archives, Foreign Dept., Political Proceedings for 1884, vol. 2345, no. 548, pp. 319–320. British officials at Hongkong here urged that negotiators of the Chefoo Convention (in settlement of the Margary affair) exact from China the same provision for free trade via Burma that France obtained for Tongking in 1884.

[161] Ibid., p. 245, Oct. 27, 1884. Here is cited the prospective visit of a French scientist en route to Rangoon to study the resources of Burma, his party being financed by private and public funds. General Gordon had died at Khartoum in the African Sudan on January 26, 1885; in March of 1885 the Russians attacked Penjdeh in Afghanistan. The wars in South Africa and in Afghanistan had previously been liquidated by the Gladstone Ministry in 1881–1882 at the expense of British prestige.

not officially accredited, and many delays ensued. It was not until January 18, 1885, that the treaty was signed, ostensibly a purely commercial one. During the interim, the French Government was pressed by Britain's ambassador at Paris, Lord Lyons, to explain what was happening. Foreign Minister Ferry eventually gave assurances that only commercial topics were being discussed and that no French arms would be furnished Burma via Tongking, as London had feared would happen. The Burmese mission subsequently visited Italy, but did not this time go to England.[162]

Matters became more alarming from the British point of view after French Consul Haas, commissioned by Ferry's successor Freyçinet, reached Mandalay on June 1, 1885. Haas was an aggressive man, ambitious to achieve spectacular ends, and unwilling to be inhibited in his activities by his instructions. Within little more than a month, the French consul negotiated a railway concession stipulating that France would provide some £2.5 million (7½ per cent interest and a seventy-year lease) for construction of a line from Mandalay to Toungoo, to connect with the nearly completed British railway from Rangoon, and also an agreement to set up a currency-issuing state bank for Burma, capitalized also at some £2.5 million. These French loans were to be serviced from river customs receipts and royalties from oil. A Burmese Wun left for Paris before the end of July to exchange ratifications.

These facts plus additional rumors touching alleged French interest in the Bombay-Burmah Trading Corporation teak concessions and also river-steamer navigation were promptly communicated to the Rangoon authorities by the Italian consul at Mandalay, Andreino, who was apparently jealous of Haas. Reports of August, 1885, alleged that in accordance with a guarded promise secretly given to the Burmese envoys by Paris, the French consul had offered to provide arms and munitions to Burma via Tongking as soon as peace was restored, all in return for a French share in the profits of the ruby mines and a monopoly interest in Burma tea.[163] Both London and Rangoon were also much concerned over reported French advice to Mandalay to improve relations with Britain in order to gain time to obtain neutrality treaties with other states of Europe. If such advice were proffered,

---

[162] Geary, p. 154; Joseph Dautremer, *Burma under British Rule* (no date), pp. 70–71; Foucar, pp. 104–106.

[163] Geary, pp. 35–140; Dautremer, pp. 22, 70–73; Foucar, pp. 112–115; Langham-Carter, "Burmese Rule on the Toungoo Frontier," *JBRS*, XXVII (1937), 30–31.

it was not followed, for almost immediately thereafter, in August, 1885, the fine against the Bombay-Burmah Corporation was levied.[164]

Commissioner Bernard and other responsible Rangoon officials discounted much of the alarmist talk concerning French intentions to take over northern Burma. They were inclined to favor the mere displacement of King Thibaw by an Anglophile prince. Unfortunately for Bernard's plans, the eligible Nyaungyan prince had died at Calcutta in early 1885, leaving as virtually the only alternative to Thibaw the Nyaung Ok prince, who was living in style at Pondicherry at the time as protégé of the French. Actually official French policy regarding Burma was in retreat during 1885, for Consul Haas had overreached his instructions, and such aggressive tactics were under serious criticism within France itself. Open strife with China over Tongking broke out in February, 1885. Ferry's government fell in March, 1885, and a revulsion of popular French sentiment developed regarding such costly adventures as the war in Indochina. The French Chamber actually voted by a bare majority of one to retain control over Tongking. Under these circumstances, Lord Salisbury in the early autumn of 1885 was able to obtain from Prime Minister Freyçinet a repudiation of the diplomacy of Consul Haas and a disclaimer of any anti-British intentions on the part of France in the Burma Kingdom. Haas was recalled by Paris in October, 1885, for having acted without authorization.[165]

There was no disagreement at Rangoon that some advantage must be taken of the provocative action of the *Hlutdaw* in regard to the Bombay-Burmah Trading Corporation, as a means of establishing more satisfactory relations with Mandalay. There was a sharp difference of opinion, however, concerning precisely what ought to be done. Commissioner Bernard and many others of the civil service personnel with long experience in Burma envisaged serious difficulties in reconciling national-minded Upper Burma to the acceptance of alien rule and foresaw no prospect of commercial or revenue profits to compensate for the cost of pacifying and governing the vast areas involved. They argued that Thibaw should be replaced by another more acceptable ruler, even if it were the Myingun prince, Nyaung Ok, pro-French leanings and all. Others, including ex-Resident Colonel Sladen, argued

---

[164] Hall, *South-East Asia*, pp. 550–552.

[165] Geary, pp. 134–144, 154–156; Foucar, pp. 115–117. According to Hall (*South-East Asia*, p. 852), Paris was confronted with a copy of the secret letter containing Ferry's promise of military aid to Burma.

that French interference must be stopped and that the Burmese would never concede full allegiance to Britain if royal claimants were not eliminated entirely.[166] This latter view was supported by inquiries previously made at Pondicherry in October, 1884, which discovered that the Myingun prince was not only beholden to the French for his lush surroundings but also sanguine about his chances of returning to Burma via Bangkok or Saigon and the Shan States, presumably as a French protégé.[167]

The strategically sensitive and commercially minded members of the British community in Burma made much of the doubtful status of Myingun Min and urged outright annexation of Upper Burma. Such action, they argued, would rid Burma of French influence once for all, obtain unimpeded commercial access to timber, oil, and mineral resources of Upper Burma, and also afford opportunity to examine the possibility of reviving Burma's once-lucrative trade with Yunnan in competition with the French from Tongking. All in all the presumption was weighted heavily in favor of annexation. London's consent to the proposed demands was cabled to Rangoon on October 17.[168]

The British ultimatum of October 22, 1885, gave Burma less than twenty days, until November 10, to agree to arbitrate the Bombay-Burmah fine, to install a British Resident at Mandalay replete with guard, a steamer, and direct access (beshod) to the king, and to agree also to submit all questions of external relations to the control of the Government of India. The Kinwun Mingyi, who alone in the *Hlutdaw* took the demand seriously, proposed a conciliatory reply and made belated efforts to reduce the Bombay-Burmah fine to reasonable limits. But he was overruled by the Taingda *Wungyi* and Queen Supayalat. Mandalay replied on November 5 that the fine itself was not subject to negotiation although the corporation could petition relative to the amount specified. The court agreed to accept a British Resident "as in former times" but proposed to refer to the joint decision of France, Germany, and Italy the British demand for control over Burma's for-

---

[166] Geary, p. 150; Foucar, pp. 124–125.

[167] Geary, pp. 195–196; Hall, *South-East Asia,* pp. 174–175. Apparently one abortive attempt had been made earlier by Prince Myingun to proceed to Burma via Indochina. On this occasion he became seasick and accordingly returned to Pondicherry.

[168] Harvey, *British Rule,* p. 164; Maung Maung, *Burma in the Family of Nations,* pp. 64–66. The Chambers of Commerce of London and of Glasgow petitioned Randolph Churchill to annex Burma outright.

eign policy.[169] On November 7, King Thibaw appealed to his people to rally to resist the enemies of the Burma race, religion, and customs. The *Hlutdaw*'s negative reply reached Rangoon on November 9. British mobilization had actually started on October 19, three days before the date of the ultimatum. Armed steamers crossed the Burma border on November 14 towing barges carrying three infantry brigades plus naval and cavalry contingents. Myingyan fell on November 25, Ava and Sagaing on November 26 and 27, and Mandalay itself on November 28. Thibaw and his two principal queens, accompanied by an official escort, were taken immediately to Rangoon and thence to Madras.[170] Thus suddenly did the Konbaung dynasty cease to be.

In December, 1885, the Myingun prince offered to drop his French connections if he were allowed to assume the throne of Burma, but he received no encouragement from the Government of India. Two months later in Colombo a French vessel refused the request of the prince to transport him to Saigon; Myingun dared not take passage on an available British vessel en route to China.[171]

The elimination of King Thibaw was an accomplished fact by the time Gladstone returned to power in London in January, 1886, following the Liberal victory in the British general elections of December, 1885. The determination of the future political status of Burma was left in large measure to the decision of the Indian viceroy, who visited Burma in person early in 1886.

[169] Foucar, pp. 132–134.

[170] White, *Burma*, pp. 104–107; Geary, pp. 140–144; Dautremer, pp. 69–70; Foucar, pp. 135–139.

[171] Geary, p. 199.

Part Two

BRITISH COLONIAL RULE

IV

British Administration, 1886-1914

THE period from the annexation of Upper Burma in 1886 to World War I witnessed the high tide of British commerical and agricultural expansion in Burma and the fashioning of an administrative policy and program to serve growing economic needs. It was a period of seeming tacit recognition by Burmans generally of the advantages inherent in stable government and in the country's vigorously expanding economy. The traditional type of resistance by a royal pretender was dead. Positive adjustment to alien cultural influences was nevertheless slow. An educated Burman elite emerged to qualify for desirable posts in the bureaucratic structure, but their action left incipient nationalist sentiment inarticulate and without leadership. The unfamiliar administrative and legal system attuned not to Burman expectations but to the promotion of economic interests and foreign concepts of justice, British and Indian, failed to command the allegiance of the people. As the program unfolded, a large proportion of the population of Lower Burma became landless and transient, while traditional social, educational, and religious standards steadily eroded away. A disturbing measure of social demoralization was the inevitable outcome.

Social deterioration combined with increasing lack of respect for police and court authority contributed to an ever-growing problem of lawlessness. Desultory reforming efforts by well-meaning officials were ineffectual. Popular anxiety regarding cultural disintegration, an emerging sense of national humiliation, and nationalist resentment against

125

alien rule were eventually added to popular disrespect for police authority. The generation following 1886 constituted the prelude to the
political revival of Burma which occurred after 1917. Chapter IV will
discuss the political and administrative aspects of the prewar period.
Chapter V will cover the contemporaneous economic and social developments.

The Annexation of Upper Burma, 1886

The inflated expectations of the British business community in Burma
relative to the commercial advantages to be derived from unimpeded
economic access to Upper Burma including the possibility of commercial penetration of South China and Siam provided one of the important
reasons for the outright annexation of the Burma Kingdom in 1886.
This decision found support in the absence of any satisfactory princely
candidate to install as puppet ruler in place of King Thibaw and in
wishful thinking on the part of the British that the Burmans themselves
would welcome escape from royal misgovernment.[1]

Most of the civil servants who were conversant with the problems
to be encountered in controlling the area agreed with Commissioner
Charles Bernard in the view that a British protectorate over Upper
Burma could accomplish all that was required and would cost far less
in both money and effort than would direct rule.[2] Bernard pointed out
that Upper Burma's political background would render difficult British
administration along the lines employed in Lower Burma. Upper Burma
lacked a supply of cheap labor for public works, while its paucity of
rainfall limited the cultivable land area and contributed to its chronic
rice deficit. The cost of maintaining a military garrison plus the basic
cadre of British administrative agencies would exceed the average
annual revenues collected by King Thibaw's government (105 lakhs of
rupees), to say nothing of the expense of operating a regular Burmese
civil administration. Abolition of kingship, would, Bernard insisted,
entail difficulties and expenses far in excess of any profits to be realized
from the abolition of royal monopolies, from cancellation of customs
duties, or from the dubious possibility of extending British trade into
China.[3]

The practical difficulties of government encountered at Mandalay
immediately following the British occupation of the capital in late
November, 1885, forced the temporary utilization of the royal *Hlutdaw*

[1] Grattan Geary, *Burma after the Conquest* (London, 1886), pp. 5–9, 334.
[2] *Ibid.*, pp. 299–307, 311.   [3] *Ibid.*, pp. 299–307, 334.

as the symbol of authority. The commanding officer, Colonel Sladen, found to his chagrin that the progressive and co-operative Kinwun Mingyi, whom he had expected to use, had departed with King Thibaw. He was forced to the unwelcome decision of exploiting the influence of the disreputable Taingda Mingyi to keep alive some semblance of traditional authority.[4] With the aid of Taingda, Colonel Sladen induced the bulk of the *Wuns* and *myothugyis* in areas not occupied directly by the British officers to carry on as officials of the new regime or to yield their places to successors appointed from Mandalay.

But despite the willingness of the remnant of the *Hlutdaw* to cooperate and Taingda's demonstrated force of personality and genius for affairs, the latter's evil reputation made him a broken reed incapable of supporting authority. He was a villain to the British of Lower Burma and a traitor to many of the Burmese. Despite Colonel Sladen's insistence that Taingda's very substantial assistance should be acknowledged, the ex-minister, on December 27, was arrested publicly before the *Hlutdaw* itself and deported to Calcutta on Commissioner Bernard's orders. This action ended any possibility of further effective utilization of the traditional authority of the *Hlutdaw*. Other members, thrown into consternation, insisted that Taingda was no more responsible than they for what had happened and refused to credit British assurances concerning their own personal safety. The viceroy attempted to bolster the situation by reinstating the Kinwum Mingyi as a member of the *Hlutdaw,* but Delhi refused to reconsider the deportation of Taingda. The net outcome was to destroy the authority of the older government at its very heart and to precipitate a rapid transition from endemic disorder to outright rebellion.[5]

In view of the inevitable drift toward anarchy following the deposition of King Thibaw, the dismissal of Taingda can be regarded as only one contributing incident among many. Even before Thibaw's fall much of the countryside had been in a state of semidisorder, with armed brigands allied in many areas with officials in preying on the villagers.[6] The first reports of organized rebellion, as of mid-December, concerned remote areas of Bhamo, the Chindwin Valley, and the Shan plateau borders of the Sittang Valley. In the vicinity of Mandalay, disbanded soldiers, lacking rations and pay, eventually turned to law-

---

[4] *Ibid.*, pp. 202–219.

[5] *Ibid.*, pp. 220–229. By the end of December, dacoit bands for the first time began firing on British garrisons and detachments.

[6] Sir Charles Crosthwaite, *The Pacification of Burma* (London, 1912), pp. 6–9.

lessness. Friction developed easily between Burmese rowdies and British soldiers, who had been denied a good fight and were easily irritated.[7]

Since Burman villagers who obeyed the orders of the British-directed *Hlutdaw* to surrender their arms would become in the spreading anarchy only the easy victims of wandering dacoit bands, the situation degenerated quickly into "every community for itself." Village bands deliberately organized as foraging parties were sent out to grab what they could of grain, money, clothing, and other necessities before their own communities should suffer similarly. Such groups ordinarily used violence only when resisted or panicked; participation was a mark of public spirit and valor since it involved taking risks in behalf of family and community needs. It required only two or three weeks in December and early January for this nonpolitical (often "noncriminal") type of violence to take on an anti-British political character, usually in response to harsh repressive measures employed by British-Indian troops directed against all forms of armed violence and dacoity.

The policy adopted by the occupying army was to shoot all persons engaged in pillage or found in possession of arms. Armed repression was coupled with floggings and with the burning of villages wherever resistance was encountered. The relatively docile acceptance of British control at the outset proved deceptive. Instead of village bands fighting each other as rival foragers, the dacoit bands expanded their size for launching attacks on the military posts. Thus was initiated a spontaneous guerrilla warfare of formidable dimensions. By the end of January, 1886, when civil administration in Upper Burma collapsed, guerrillas became everywhere active, impetuous, and unafraid. Burmese advisers insisted that the remedy for such anarchy must begin with the proclamation of a new king, but the few prince pretenders who raised their heads aroused no general enthusiasm, and the British had no acceptable candidate of their own.[8] The most serious immediate threat to Mandalay came from a Shan rising in support of a *Sawbwa* candidate for the throne. Resistance was also formidable in the Shwebo area, original home of the Alaungpaya dynasty.[9]

On January 1, 1886, came the formal announcement from the viceroy, Lord Dufferin, that King Thibaw's territories had become part of

[7] Geary, pp. 45–55.

[8] *Ibid.*, pp. 45–55, 70–79, 83. One pretender in the Chindwin Valley was reported to have assembled 7,000 men behind him.

[9] *Ibid.*, pp. 270–272.

Her Majesty's dominions and would "during Her Majesty's pleasure, be administered by such officers as the Viceroy of India may from time to time appoint." London apparently did not intend by this proclamation to preclude the reconstitution of a Burmese Kingdom, and British proponents of direct rule living in Rangoon vented their dissatisfaction by deleting temporarily from the announcement the phrase "during Her Majesty's pleasure." The viceroy was nevertheless authorized by London to visit Burma in order to come to a final decision on the spot.

Upon Lord Dufferin's arrival at Mandalay on February 12, he completely abolished the *Hlutdaw*.[10] On February 17, he announced that the control of Upper Burma would remain in British hands under direct administrative control. British officers were ordered to suppress dacoity and to give effect to the proclamation of annexation. The character of the advice reaching Lord Dufferin was reflected in the optimistic declaration that he saw in Upper Burma no sign of anything approaching partisan warfare against the British. On February 26, Burma became formally a province of British India.[11]

Military activities were carried out with vigor. The ten original British military stations were eventually increased to twenty-five. Active patrolling by substantial detachments between adjacent stations carried the fight to the larger dacoit bands, forcing them to break up into smaller units. Repressive measures were accompanied by absorption of many unemployed in public works projects, such as roads and railway construction. It was early discovered that small limited-objective raids did no good at all and that harsh punitive measures including the burning of villages only made the dacoits fight more desperately.[12] As early as February, 1886, the disorder spread to Lower Burma as well. By mid-1886, a truly formidable rebellion had enveloped the

[10] Among the seven or eight of the principal ministers of Thibaw's government who were invited to become salaried advisers of the British were U Hlwa, U Po Si (both ex-*Myowuns*), and the Kinwun Mingyi. Men of learning and ability among the royal clerks, or *Sayedawgyis*, were also utilized as township and subdivisional officers, along with ex-*myothugyis* and sons of princes who might otherwise get into political mischief. In October, 1886, nine ex-ministers of Burma were on pension by the Government of India. See H. T. White, *A Civil Servant in Burma*, pp. 123–124, 145–151; India Office Archives, *Home Department (Upper Burma) Series*, vol. 2720, nos. 4 and 5, Oct., 1886.

[11] White, *A Civil Servant in Burma*, pp. 340–344; Crosthwaite, p. 9.

[12] White, *A Civil Servant in Burma*, pp. 257–265. White (p. 131) commented from personal experience in 1886 that burning villages was reserved for extreme cases, but he added: "It is very interesting to put a match to a thatched roof and see it blaze to the sky."

entire country, requiring the sending of considerable reinforcements from India led by the commander in chief of the Indian army.[13] It was four years before order was restored. Robed monks in many parts of Lower Burma violated all historic precedent by participating in the fighting, and the local Burmese police proved to be no match for spirited dacoit leaders.[14]

Lord Dufferin's announcement of the annexation of Burma on January 1, 1886, had been authorized by the Conservative Secretary of State for India, Lord Randolph Churchill.[15] It had preceded the actual advent of Mr. Gladstone's new Liberal Party government at London by only a few weeks and was therefore something in the nature of a Conservative *fait accompli*. The only question on which the new Parliament was asked to vote was whether or not the expenses of the Burma war (estimated at a modest £300,000 only) were to be charged to Indian or to British revenues. Gladstone's Undersecretary of State for India took the view that since the action had been taken not primarily for trade but for the protection of India's frontiers it should therefore be financed by India.[16] Government spokesmen argued that Lord Dufferin had been forced to go to war by French intrigue at Mandalay, active since 1882, and that the principle of India's paying the costs of wars waged east of Suez in which no European state was involved had long been established.[17]

Parliamentary opponents of annexation were handicapped by the fact that all parties were faced by a seemingly successful *fait accompli*. Lord Randolph Churchill had successfully forestalled debate on the Burma war itself when the queen's opening address to the Parliament was being considered. Conservatives generally supported the annexation in any case, and there was no compelling reason why an action taken on India's initiative should not be charged to Indian funds.

Anti-imperialists in Parliament, on February 22, 1886, argued, nevertheless, that it was not the Indians but the British Chamber of Commerce at Rangoon that favored the annexation, that Paris had expressly

[13] *The Cambridge History of India*, VI, 436–439.

[14] Donald Mackenzie Smeaton, *The Loyal Karens of Burma* (London, 1887), pp. 13–16. Smeaton's book is biased in favor of the Karens, but it contains correct factual data.

[15] Great Britain, *Parliament Debates*, 3d ser., vol. 302 (Feb. 22, 1886), pp. 161–162. These are hereafter cited *PD,C*.

[16] The debate revealed that during the twenty-one years from 1862 to 1883 British Burma's revenues had increased threefold (£1 to £3), its trade over five fold (£2 to £10.5), and its population by 50 per cent (2.5 to 3.7 million).

[17] *PD,C*, vol. 302 (Feb. 22, 1886), pp. 939–942, 953–956.

disavowed any intention to dominate Burma, and that the Bombay-Burmah Trading Corporation fine was a question which could have been settled by compromise.[18] They denounced the annexation as "high-handed violence" (akin to the Biblical seizure of Naboth's vineyard), which had been proposed in vain on numerous previous instances by interested parties. Burmans did not want their country stolen, and why should impoverished India be asked to pay for it in any case? [19] Most of the arguments presented in the official blue book on the affair, opponents argued, concerned trivial matters such as shoe wearing on pagoda premises and trade difficulties, both of which could have been negotiated or arbitrated. It was arrant nonsense, the argument continued, to insist that French concession hunters at Mandalay actually imperiled the safety of Lower Burma and India in view of firm British control over the only means of effective commerical access to Upper Burma. Would not the alleged threat to India's security next require Britain to annex Siam simply to keep the French out? [20]

One informed opponent (Mr. McIver) of the Burma annexation ridiculed particularly the alleged "general desire" of the Burmese to come under British rule. He called attention to the press accounts of numerous executions taking place and to the deployment of 16,000 troops. The violation of Burmese nationalist sentiment, which centered around the Buddhist religion and their semidivine king, he insisted, had set the people of both Upper and Lower Burma against their British conquerors. The establishment of a protectorate, he declared, would have left religious and nationalist sensibilities unaffected. The Liberal Party was being saddled with another imperialist legacy just as it had been in Egypt.[21]

Winding up the debate, Mr. Gladstone complimented Mr. McIver on his "thoughtful irrelevancies," but insisted that the merits of the Burma campaign were not the topic under discussion. He declared that under the "urgent and unforeseen necessity" clause of the law of 1858, the Government of India was not required to obtain prior consent of Parliament for such actions as the Burma campaign, since strategic interests rather than trade had been the alleged cause. Sentiments of nationality were, of course, worthy of respect, but they could not serve as an absolute rule to guide governmental action. Even if the evidence should indicate that the war was wanton and needless, Gladstone declared, it would not necessarily follow that a reversal of

[18] By Mr. Hunter, *ibid.*, pp. 942–947.　[19] By Mr. Richard, *ibid.*, pp. 948–953.
[20] By Dr. Clark, *ibid.*, pp. 973–980.　[21] *Ibid.*, pp. 956–963.

the annexation should occur, since such action now might do more harm than good. Accepting Lord Dufferin's appraisal of the local situation, Mr. Gladstone ruled that the war had been waged in good faith to protect the security, happiness, and prosperity of India, that it was "in reality, and certainly in intention a defensive war" and as such chargeable to Indian revenues.[22] The vote on the motion to charge the expenses of the Burma campaign to Indian revenues carried 297 to 82.[23] Burma was legally for the first time in its history a part of India.

The Pacification of Burma, 1886–1890

There existed in 1886 very little correspondence between British and Burmese points of view regarding the annexation of the kingdom. At the bottom of the difficulty was Rangoon's fallacious assumption that, because the Burmese people shared in some measure the British lack of regard for King Thibaw, they would therefore welcome a more humane and efficient government even though alien. The Burmese attributed misgovernment to the palace clique more than to King Thibaw, for whom several good things could be said. He had not exacted exorbitant revenues from the people; he had also treated captured dacoits with leniency and understanding, branding them with tattoo markings and sending them home rather than torturing or executing them, as the British were doing. If necessities of state and the need to forestall a general civil war had exacted under Thibaw the toll of the lives of several princes, what was that compared to the British policy of depriving the kingly symbol of all authority, thus unleashing the wholesale bloodshed of general anarchy, with the result that lawlessness and rebellion were hopelessly intermingled? British Indian troops were killing far more persons than Thibaw's government had ever been guilty of doing. Finally, Burmans pointed out that Thibaw's intrigues with the French, to which the British had objected, had not affected adversely the interests of the Burmese people themselves.[24]

The British grasped with difficulty the Burmese view that reverence for kingship was necessary to the religious as well as to the secular welfare of the nation. Far from resenting the necessity of groveling before a king, as Westerners assumed that the Burmese should do, the people recognized, as the British did not, that a king was a sorely

[22] *Ibid.*, pp. 963–970. Said Gladstone: "It was not to extend trade, to gratify passion or ambition, but because a door was threatened to be opened through which would have been brought into India danger, insecurity, loss of happiness and prosperity."

[23] *Ibid.*, p. 986.   [24] Geary, pp. 325–328.

needed symbol of authority in any case. This was true even if he had to be shorn of some of the plenary attributes of sovereignty and be forced to do what the English wanted him to do. A king, for example, was far more important to the Burmese people in his function of protecting and promoting religion than in his exercise of untrammeled control over the government's foreign policy. A final and irreducible demand on British policy made by a number of co-operating Burmans both at Mandalay and at Rangoon, but unfortunately rejected, was that the new government honor and protect religion by supporting the authority of the *thathanabaing*.[25]

By June, 1886, Upper Burma and much of Lower Burma were convulsed in a passion of insurrection. Local leaders usually struck out for themselves in unco-ordinated fashion. Dacoits were joined by military levies; freebooters were able to pose as patriots; and the most daring leaders became heroes of story and song. The rebellion eventually attained the proportions of a national rising. It was based not on any clearly defined patriotic purpose but rather drew its power from instinctive and traditional rootage. In the absence of a strong royal claimant, local disunity weakened the resistance effort to the point that no serious losses could be inflicted on the British-Indian forces; petty leaders also exerted limited popular appeal.[26]

In many plains villages of Burma practically every household had some male member fighting with a rebel gang. Friendly villages were protected, and unco-operative communities, including particularly those who dared to aid the British, were subjected to systematic intimidation and violence.[27] Self-seeking Burmans who offered their talents to the new regime, whether for administrative duties or as informer-constables to aid the military, were the least representative of the national will. Enlistment of Burmans in the British army was abruptly discontinued in 1887.[28]

It was apparently the initial application of coercive measures by the

[25] Geary (pp. 105–109, 114–115) reported an interview held with the Mandalay *thathanabaing* in December, 1885, in which the primate expressed little sorrow that Thibaw was gone but insisted that a good prince must be elevated to the throne to protect religion and to give essential security and comfort to the people. British officials refused to accept responsibility for enforcing the decisions of the *thathanabaing* because it would allegedly constitute interference with religion. See Hall, *South-East Asia*, pp. 622–623.

[26] Mya Sein, pp. 125–130.   [27] Nisbet, I, 113.

[28] Fielding-Hall, *The Soul of a People*, p. 81; Burma, Police Department, *Report of the Police Administration* for 1889, pp. 2–3 (published annually; cited hereafter as *RPA*); Crosthwaite, pp. 48–50, 53–55, 96–99.

British army indiscriminately against all armed bands, often in disregard of Burmese susceptibilities and of the ameliorative circumstances to be found in particular cases, that aroused such intense Burmese hostility. The facile assumption of some British army leaders that "wholesome severity" would have a "soothing effect on the villagers" was completely disproved as early as February, 1886.[29] At that time, General Prendergast ended the initial policy of executing all men captured and in possession of arms. Thereafter only criminals sentenced by civil officers were to be executed. But the chance of reconciliation had already been lost.[30]

Throughout 1886 and into 1887, every district of Upper Burma was in a ferment of revolt. Military posts and convoys were attacked, and virtually every male villager was ready to fight. The population accepted the hardships of war and enveloped all rebel movements in a conspiracy of silence. The rebellion lacked co-ordination and a unified political objective. Most of the leaders enjoyed no more than a local following; a few were former *Wuns,* some were *myothugyis;* others were mere outlaw bandits. The most serious threat developed in the vicinity of Mandalay, where three *Bos* acted somewhat independently but all allegedly in behalf of the Myingun prince. The Shwebo District also had its royal pretender.[31] For a time it seemed that Burma might never quiet down, but more troops and Indian police were brought in (up to the number of 40,500 by February, 1887) to man the numerous armed posts distributed ten to fifteen miles apart.

By March, 1887, when Commissioner Bernard retired in favor of Sir Charles Crosthwaite, the tide had begun to turn. The situation thereafter gradually improved. The trading classes were the first to come over to the British side. A group of genuinely pious *pongyis* of Upper Burma also worked for the restoration of peace.[32] The construction of the Toungoo-Mandalay railway from 1886 to 1889 afforded employment to many Burmans in a project which many approved.[33] The

---

[29] Geary, pp. 230–233.

[30] Geary (pp. 244–248) includes the following eyewitness judgment: "The promiscuous shooting of so-called dacoits was . . . a great, if it was not the sole, cause of the rapid spread of the movement of resistance . . . in Upper Burma. . . . Reckless resort to wholesale executions . . . worked disastrously. . . . No trumpet of sedition has such an infuriating effect on a population as the shrieks of the women in the villages . . . lamenting brothers and husbands slain not in battle, but as examples of the power and sternness of the conqueror."

[31] Nisbet, I, 113.

[32] Fielding-Hall, *The Soul of a People,* pp. 81–83, 133–137; Nisbet, I, 113.

[33] White, *A Civil Servant in Burma,* pp. 167–168.

most formidable bands were dispersed by early 1888, and all pretender *Bos* driven into hiding. As late as 1890 some 30,000 troops and Indian police were still being maintained in the peripheral areas of Upper Burma, with an additional 5,300 assigned to Lower Burma. The cost of the war had increased meanwhile from the original estimate of £300,000 to £635,600 in 1885–1886, to more than twice that sum in both 1887 and 1888, declining then to some £650,000 in 1889 and £865,000 in 1890. After 1890, the cost of the military police was absorbed by the Burma civil government.[34] Since the entire cost was assignable to Indian revenues in any case, Parliament had no occasion to review its optimistic estimate of the ease of pacification as presented in the debate of February 22, 1886.

The pacification of the extensive border areas peripheral to Upper Burma was accomplished expeditiously on the basis of indirect rule. The most serious difficulty was faced in the Southern Shan States area where a Shan pretender to the throne at Mandalay, the Limbin prince, had been in rebellion since Thibaw's time. The uprising had reduced most of the area to a condition of anarchy and desolation. A British political officer supported by a small but effective military force penetrated to the Yaunghwe-Inlé Lake area in early 1887. By posing as peacemakers between rivals rather than as conquerors, the expedition accomplished the collapse of the Limbin Confederacy and obtained the general acceptance of British suzerainty before the onset of the next rainy season in May.[35] During the succeeding dry season, November, 1887, to May, 1888, the newly appointed British superintendent of the Shan States accompanied by a military escort toured the Northern Shan States also. He settled local quarrels, confirmed the positions of those *Sawbwas* and *myosas* who submitted to British authority, and fixed for a five-year period the level of annual tribute payments. The Northern Shan States were placed under a separate political officer subordinate to the superintendent in August, 1888.[36]

The *de facto* control of the superintendent was regularized by the Shan States Act of 1888. This act accorded to the governor of Burma authority to appoint political officers for the area, to define and regulate

[34] Nisbet, I, 135–140. The total final cost of pacification was more than ten times the original estimate.

[35] J. G. Scott and J. P. Hardiman, *Gazetteer of Upper Burma and the Shan States* (Rangoon, 1901), I, 294–296; Crosthwaite, p. 143.

[36] Scott and Hardiman, *Gazetteer of Upper Burma,* I, 298, 300; India Office Archives, *Home Department (Upper Burma) Series,* vol. 3203 (Sept., 1888), pp. 63–64.

their powers, to designate laws applicable to one or more of the Shan States, and to permit modification of the customary law in accordance with justice, equity, and good conscience.[37] In January, 1889, the several Shan chiefs were issued restrictive agreements called *sanads*, fixing the limits of their respective jurisdictions and reserving to the British Burma Government power to qualify as became necessary the otherwise plenary jurisdiction of the *Sawbwas* over civil, criminal, and revenue matters. The British asserted their proprietary rights over all forests, mines, and mineral resources of the area. The chiefs were required to pay specified annual tribute, to maintain order and protect trade, to grant railway concessions as desired, to submit to settlement by the superintendent all interstate disputes, and to forego jurisdiction over European British residents.[38] Although the system of indirect rule worked very satisfactorily on the whole, the inevitable tendency was for resident British officials to expand the scope of their discretionary authority and gradually to take over specialized governmental functions.

The large trans-Salween Kengtung state was brought into subordinate alliance with Burma in 1890, and the Siam boundary was settled in 1892.[39] The Mekong River was eventually designated as the boundary between Kengtung and French Laos. A tentative boundary line between North Hsenwi state and Yunnan, agreed to in March, 1894, was reconsidered in 1897.[40] A 200-mile border stretch of Wa-Lahu country along the Yunnan border was never demarcated.[41]

The British encountered considerable trouble in the Kachin country of the Northern Shan States, where the warlike hillmen were encroaching on their Shan neighbors in Hsipaw and Hsenwi states. British military intervention was required in 1892, before the Kachins agreed to submit their grievances for settlement by the British superintendent. A special political officer to look after Kachin interests and to handle Kachin-Shan relations was appointed in November, 1893.[42] Chin

---

[37] *Burma Gazette*, pt. III (Nov. 17, 1888), p. 115.

[38] Scott and Hardiman, *Gazetteer of Upper Burma*, I, 313–316. In the smaller *Myelat* Shan States bordering Burma proper, the rulers became in effect the direct agents of the superintendent. See C. U. Aitchison, *Collection of Treaties, Engagements, and Sanads*, 5th ed. (Calcutta, 1931), XII, 221.

[39] Scott and Hardiman, *Gazetter of Upper Burma*, I, 307.

[40] *British Foreign and State Papers*, LXXXVII (1898), 1311–1319; Clarence Hendershot, "The Shan States—South of Yunnan," *Amerasia*, VII (July, 1943), 239–248.

[41] G. E. Mitton, *Scott of the Shan Hills* (London, 1936), pp. 205 ff.

[42] Clarence Hendershot, "The Conquest, Pacification, and Administration of

tribesmen to the west of the Chindwin River resisted British authority stubbornly and were not subdued until 1895.[43]

With the exception of the lead, zinc, and silver extracted from the
mines at Bawdwin, which found outlet through Burma, the major portion of the trade of the Northern Shan States was with China. But
Burma's trade with the Southern States, mainly in food, increased
steadily until, by 1910, it amounted annually to nearly 18 million
rupees. The Mandalay-Lashio railway in the Northern Shan States was
begun in 1895, and the Thazi-Yaunghwe branch railway into the Southern Shan States was begun in 1910 and completed during World War
I.[44]

Rebellion in Lower Burma and the Emergence of Karen Nationalism

The sympathetic insurrection which occurred in Lower Burma in
1886–1887 developed as a kind of political aggravation of an epidemic
of lawlessness dating from 1880. The situation was more disturbed than
in 1852, for resentment centered on the abolition of the crown as a
national and religious symbol.[45] The Burmese police were completely
ineffective in combating spirited rebel-dacoit leaders, who were especially active along the old Burma frontier and in the borders of the
Shan plateau near Toungoo. The rebels took vengeance on unco-
operative villages, especially Karen villages. The former were assisted
by politically minded monks, who, contrary to all historic precedent,
undertook an active role in the fighting. Although village administration was demoralized for a time, the upper structure of the government in most areas remained intact, so that anarchy was far less
universal than in Upper Burma. Only 5,000 troops were needed to
restore order in Lower Burma as compared to six times that number
for Upper Burma. Lawlessness persisted longest (into 1888–1889)
along the old Thayetmyo border area of the Irrawaddy Valley.[46]

One reason for the most prompt suppression of rebel operations in
Lower Burma was that the Karen population, especially the Christian

---

the Shan States by the British, 1886–1897" (University of Chicago thesis, 1937),
pp. 218–224. Some trouble was also encountered with Kachin chiefs west of
the Shan States area.

[43] Burma, *Report of the Frontier Areas Committee of Enquiry* (Rangoon, 1947),
pp. 9–10.

[44] Dautremer, pp. 330 ff.   [45] Mya Sein, pp. 133–135.

[46] Nisbet, I, 135.

Karens at Toungoo acting under missionary leadership, stood up to the attacking bands in stalwart fashion. Commissioner Bernard furnished some guns, but all Karen groups in the area participated. This phenomenon was in part an expression of the growing tide of Karen national sentiment, which already, in 1881, had prompted the organization of the Karen National Association. The association was a political organization designed to utilize the pervading clannish spirit of the Karens in order to bridge the gap between Christian and non-Christian Karens as well as between the various Karen language groups. Its announced objectives were to facilitate understanding and co-operation with the British rulers, to promote through education and self-help the social and economic advancement of the emerging nation, and to protect all Karen groups against any future threat of the restoration of Burman domination.[47]

The Christian Karens provided educated leadership for the Karen Association and otherwise contributed to its program. Christianity was popular among Karens as an alternative to Burmese Buddhism and also as the religion of Burma's new rulers. Christianity also freed its adherents from the all-pervading animist Karens' fear of evil spirits.[48] An educated Karen pastor usually enjoyed the confidence of his people and was in a position to uphold moral standards and curb drunkenness. He frequently kept records of rental contracts and sales, sold the community's paddy, hired oxen and coolies, retired moneylender debts, executed estates, and acted as umpire in local disputes.[49]

It was natural that American Baptist missionaries, who for two generations had identified themselves with Karen advancement, should regard the notable receptivity of that people as an opportunity to demonstrate what the gospel could do for an oppressed and degraded race. The local Karen churches promoted missionary activity among fellow Karens and sent messengers to annual Baptist associational gatherings and, after 1865, to the inclusive Burma Baptist Convention. It was only one additional step to project a political association under exclusive Karen control which would relieve the American missionaries from any responsibility for dealing with agencies of government. The missionaries still provided the Karen National Association with

[47] Smeaton, pp. 210–219.

[48] James Lee Lewis, "Self-supporting Karen Churches in Burma" (Central Baptist Seminary thesis, 1946), pp. 16–17.

[49] Smeaton, pp. 220–227. Smeaton declared: "The [Karen] pastor decides more suits, settles more disputes, and does more real business than a half dozen myookes and local judges."

such guidance and counsel as was compatible with their religious labors.[50]

In 1886, when anti-British Burmese dacoit bands, some of them led by monks, went on the loose, both religious and national sentiment among the Karens bolstered their will to oppose the rebel bands. Behind their readiness to volunteer to fight on the side of the government were the Old Testament-based assumptions that God's wrath was finally aroused against the idolatrous Buddhists and that the struggle would contribute to the triumph of Christianity and also to the security and well-being of the Karen nation.[51] The following excerpts from a letter written by an American missionary, Dr. Vinton, of Rangoon, dated February 28, 1886, will illustrate. He wrote:

One false step will put the torch to all of Burma. . . . I am warning Karens everywhere that the fight has not yet begun. Mr. Bernard told me he would arm the Karens in any threatened district if they would volunteer. I can put any number of Karens in the field.

The utter collapse of the [Burmese] police is indescribable. They are afraid for their lives, and dare not arrest bad characters or answer the openly treasonable talk of these blackguards. . . . The strangest of all is the presence of poongyees on the battlefield. This is unheard of in history.

The Karens universally interpret this as God's sign that Buddhism is to be destroyed forever. They say the challenge of Thebaw could be answered by the British government, but the challenge of the fighting poongyees can *only* be taken up fitly by Karens under their own missionaries. . . . I have never seen the Karens so anxious for a fight. This is . . . welding the Karens into a nation. . . . The heathen Karens to a man are brigading themselves under the Christians. This whole thing is doing good for the Karen. This will put virility into our Christianity.[52]

A subsequent letter from Vinton dated May 15, 1886, ran in part as follows:

I have been dacoit hunting literally all the time, and paying my own expenses. . . . I have succeeded in protecting my villages. . . . The cowardly and disloyal Burmese police have not pulled a trigger, but they do their best to discourage the only loyal and brave men in the province.

Two separate insurrections burst on us at once. The one at Shway Gyin was purely Shan. It was headed by the Mayankhyoung and Kyoukkalat Poongyees. The Buddhist priests have headed [rebels] everywhere, and actually fought themselves. . . . [Karens] brought several poongyee heads . . . and all of course claimed . . . the five thousand rupee [reward for the]

---

[50] *Ibid.*, pp. 215–217.   [51] Crosthwaite, p. 80.   [52] Smeaton, pp. 13–14.

Mayankhyoung poongyee. . . . I advised that the [wanted] pongyee be captured alive, for I knew that unless we had . . . convincing proof the government would never give the reward to the Karens.

The rebels burst like a torrent on our poor Christian villages. . . . The Karens had few guns in their hands, but mostly used spears, shields, and bows. . . . After a lot of trouble I got fifty smoothbores from Mr. Bernard [which] were handed over to the Karens [near Toungoo]. . . . The fighting was heavy and bloody. . . . Hunger made [the dacoits] desperate. . . . The Mayankhyoung *pongyi* was captured by a woman. . . . Every Karen clan except the Pghos [Pwos] were in arms that day. . . . Tribes that once were constantly fighting each other now stood side by side. From a loose aggregation of clans, we shall weld them into a nation yet. . . .

When the danger is over, the Karen will be as soundly hated as ever by the officials. [But] the Karen will not *shiko* if he can help it, and will not . . . [accept] those who enforce servility.[53]

Under British government, following the pacification, Karen and Burman villages learned to live peacefully side by side. But the Karens never lost their distrust of the Burmans, and Burmese officials in particular did not conceal their contempt for the Karens.[54] The Karens developed and maintained their own schools and churches, in many areas quite free of missionary assistance. They moved into the plains on both sides of the delta area and also developed fairly extensive riceland holdings in the very heart of the delta. Although the Christian Karens (largely Sgaws) were greatly in the minority, they provided the educated leadership for the entire group. Some of the Karens, but by no means in proportion to their numbers, attained minor posts in the government. A picked Karen levy of 100 men was used effectively in Upper Burma in 1887–1888. They were thereafter recruited in large numbers into the military police and the army, although not without considerable problems of discipline in their initial periods of training.[55] Since Burmans were not drawn into the army after 1887, ostensibly because they were not amenable to discipline, the Karens together

[53] *Ibid.,* pp. 14–16.

[54] San C. Po, *Burma and the Karens* (London, 1928), pp. 26–27.

[55] J. S. Furnivall, *Colonial Policy and Practice* (New York, 1948), pp. 178–184; India Office Archives, *Home Department (Upper Burma) Series,* vol. 3203 (1888), p. 163. An early-recruited Arakanese levy and one from Pegu were converted into civil police in 1861. Karens made up three-quarters of the indigenous military forces by 1890, but their recruitment to 1900 was slow because of problems of discipline. A Burman contingent of miners and sappers was used in Mesopotamia during World War I, but the body was later disbanded. No Burman units appeared thereafter until 1937.

with recruits from the Kachin and Chin hill tribes eventually made up virtually all of the effective indigenous security force.[56] The first noteworthy political recognition accorded the Karens was the appointment of Dr. San C. Po, an American-educated physician, to a seat in the Burma legislative council in 1916.[57]

After World War II, the Karens were destined to pay a dear price for their exaggerated nationalist ambitions, which had their origins during the pacification of 1886.

Revamping Administrative Machinery: The Village Headman

The annexation of Upper Burma and the difficulties encountered during the course of the pacification made inevitable some reorganization of the administrative machinery of the province. To the destruction of the authority of the court, the *Hlutdaw,* and the various grades of *Wuns,* consequent on annexation, was added the abrupt cancellation of the authority of the Upper Burma *myothugyis,* both *ahmudan* and *athi.* Many of the latter were disqualified because they had led rebel bands against the British Indian troops during the course of the disorder. The demonstrated failure of the indigenous police agencies of Lower Burma to cope with lawless bands as well as other growing evidences of weakness in the older governmental system negated any easy decision simply to extend to the newly occupied territory the already deficient administrative system developed in Lower Burma.

One recognized weakness of local administration in Lower Burma prior to 1885 was that it had put too much drudgery work on the village *kyedangyi* (as police informer, tax-collector aid, keeper of vital statistics, and minor executive officer) for little or no remuneration in return. The result was that the office was ordinarily filled by men of no local influence, who, because they lacked real authority, were forced to accept bullying by police constables and by bad hats as well. Much effort had been expended, with little effect, in the early 1880's to strengthen the futile *kyedangyi.* The introduction of rural self-government boards in India in 1882 had not been applied to

[56] Financial Commissioner Smeaton's urgent recommendation (*The Loyal Karens of Burma,* pp. 220–227) that the government actively encourage the Christianization and education of the Karens in co-operation with American Baptist missionaries was never carried out. He was one of the first British observers who recognized that the Karens could be developed into a political, social, and economic asset to Burma. Karens made up a majority of the indigenous military forces down to 1940.

[57] Great Britain, Parliament, H of C, *Sessional Papers,* (hereafter cited *PP,C.*), vol. XXXV for 1920 (Cmd. 746), pp. 5–6.

Burma because of the apparent difficulty of obtaining suitable men to serve on them. There was even some talk in 1883–1884 of making the office elective and of using it as a recruiting agency for *myooks*. Local administration in Lower Burma became so thoroughly demoralized by events of 1886–1887 that substantial changes were inevitable.[58]

The decision regarding administrative reforms fell to Sir Charles Crosthwaite, a man familiar with India but not with Burma, who took over the task of pacification from Commissioner Bernard in 1887. Following a hurried examination of the Burma situation, Crosthwaite concluded, on the basis of his India experience, that the basic difficulty stemmed from British Burma's denial of policing authority to the *mythogyis* and *taikthugyis* in 1861–1862. This decision, in turn, had allegedly left village *ywagaung* and *kyedangyi* assistants, acting as mere police informers and collectors, without authority in their own right. The professional police constables recruited after 1862 by the district superintendent of police and acting subsequently under the direction of an inspector general of police were far from satisfactory. They needed to be supplemented, according to Crosthwaite, by the designation of locally oriented village headmen vested with real authority.[59] In his concern to find historial precedent for his new village policy, Crosthwaite argued, quite fallaciously, that the old-type *myothugyi* as found in Upper Burma actually had usurped the power of the village *gaungs* and *kyedangyis,* whom he proposed now to restore to their rightful authority. Issuance of the emergency Upper Burma Regulation Act of 1887 started the reform.

The final decision, made in early 1888, was to designate a headman (*thugyi*) for each of Burma's 17,000 to 18,000 village tracts, to vest him with powers of collector, police officer, and petty magistrate, and to make the village unit the pivot on which the entire local administration would turn. The new village headmen would be held accountable for their conduct. All other potential Burman political leadership would be eliminated by leveling, in effect, the older stratified nonofficial social

[58] Mya Sein, pp. 117–124; Hugh Tinker, *Foundations of Local Self-Government in India, Pakistan, and Burma* (London, 1954), pp. 56–57; India Office Archives, *India Public Proceedings* for 1882, vol. 1848, pp. 1545–1547.

[59] Donnison, pp. 20–23, 28; Tinker, p. 49; Mya Sein, pp. 88–92, 101–102. Police superintendents encountered perennial difficulty enlisting good men and keeping the police force up to strength. Crosthwaite's proposals were a substitute for plans prepared by Lord Ripon as viceroy of India for establishing district and subdivisional councils after 1882.

order.[60] The *thugyis* were supposed to be influential citizens in their communities (not the old *kyedangyis*), enjoying either hereditary or electoral preference among their neighbors. But they were to be designated by and responsible to the several district deputy commissioners. In December, 1888, it was further resolved that the new *thugyi* should be entitled to carry a silver or gild-mounted dah and to use a red umbrella with gilt flaps, in imitation of the perquisites of the traditional *myothugyi*. In 1889, under the Burma Village Act, the village headman in Lower Burma took over tax-collector functions from the *taikthugyis*.[61]

Many of the Lower Burma police officials who were faced with villager-dacoit collusion favored Crosthwaite's drastic change, for in Lower Burma the old tribal structure had already been destroyed. In Upper Burma, the general policy after 1887 was to keep a cooperative *myothugyi* in place, but to enforce joint responsibility within village communities and to cancel any surviving remnants of the *myothugyi's ahmudan* personal control outside his immediate limited territorial jurisdiction. Some *myo* and *taikthugyis* were taken over into government service as *myooks*. The complete breakup of the old township or circle units was in some cases deferred until the death of the incumbent headmen, which in some instances did not occur until the second decade of the twentieth century.[62]

The official responsibilities of the new village headman were onerous and varied. He was basically police officer, petty magistrate, and tax collector, receiving in compensation a 10 per cent commission on collections made, plus exemption from taxes himself and the use of a small acreage grant of land. He was also responsible for village defense, for maintaining intervillage paths and roads, for keeping vital statistics and enforcing sanitary regulations, for agricultural functions including prevention of cattle disease, and for taking care of the needs of traveling officials.[63] In such matters as village defense, the clearing of paths, and the care of wells and burial grounds, the *thugyi* was empowered by law to require the assistance of any resident of his village tract on pain of legal punishment. Local governmental funds were obtainable from market rentals, sale of ferry and other licenses, plus a

[60] Mya Sein, pp. 158–159. [61] Tinker, pp. 56–57.

[62] Mya Sein, pp. 166–171. The initial excessive subdivision of village tracts was reversed in 1909–1910 in favor of creating somewhat larger units by amalgamation.

[63] *RPA* for 1889, p. 3. Minimum annual compensation for headmen was first set at 100 rupees, later at 180 rupees.

percentage allocated from land taxes, all such funds to be administered by the deputy commissioners.[64]

The duties of maintaining land survey records and of assessing the tax demand, formerly falling to township or circle headmen, were taken over entirely, in 1894–1895, by the Land Records Department, which had already been functioning for several decades. The headman system was eventually consolidated throughout the province under a new Burma Village Act of 1907.[65]

It is noteworthy that most of the British officials with long experience in Burma opposed Crosthwaite's reforms. They argued that the village unit was too small, that local residents capable of performing duties so greatly in excess of those of the traditional *ywagaung* or *kyedangyi* could not be found in many villages. They insisted also that the sweeping away of all the intermediate aspects of the traditional governmental structure, involving the substitution of impersonal law for the principle of personal jurisdiction, left a gap between government and people which no artificially improvised village-headman system could bridge.

The new headmen, like the old *kyedangyi*, was still at the beck and call of touring officials, subject to summons by overbearing *myooks*, and liable to official reprimand, fine, or dismissal for dereliction of duty. Few could be expected under such circumstances to generate the needed face and authority to function acceptably and simultaneously as head of the local militia, police officer, magistrate, work requisitioner, and tax collector. However feasible the system might have appeared on paper, experienced officials doubted the wisdom of staking so much in the local government field on so dubious a gamble.[66]

The Court System

Designating the village headman as a petty magistrate introduced him to a new function which he was usually not qualified to discharge. The only laws familiar to village elders were the customary rules applicable by arbitral procedure. An unbridgeable gap existed between

[64] Donnison, pp. 34–38; Great Britain, India Office, *Report of the India Statutory Commission* [hereafter cited as *ISCR*] XI (London, 1930), 423, 433.

[65] Mya Sein, p. 172.

[66] G. E. R. G. Brown, *Burma as I Saw It, 1889–1917* (New York, 1925), pp. 202–204; White, *A Civil Servant in Burma*, pp. 219–220. In 1897, for example, 697 headmen were fined, 341 village tracts were examined for dereliction of duty, and 171 collective fines were imposed. This situation was not destined to improve.

this type of personal jurisdiction and the official courts operating either under the direct control of the deputy commissioners or under the special judicial branch of the civil service.

The legal code applicable by Burma courts was an adapted amalgamation of English law principles and customary law, as developed in India prior to 1862. The India Central Legislature in 1863 set up six grades of courts in Burma and extended the Code of Civil Procedure to Burma. This code did not affect customary rules of succession, inheritance, marriage, or religious usage, however. The deputy commissioner acting as district magistrate handled at the outset most police cases, while the divisional commissioners acting as judge magistrates took over civil cases and important criminal cases. The appointment in 1872 of a special judicial commissioner for Burma marked the beginning of the separation of the executive and judicial functions. Within a few years' time the professional bench of the judicial commissioner was hearing more than 250 appeals from "amateur" lower-court rulings. It was also altering the sentences, usually in the direction of clemency, of several hundred additional cases called up for review. This practice of reviewing lower-level decisions spread later to the central administrative and revenue departments. A subordinate judicial commissioner for Upper Burma was appointed in 1890.[67]

The next administrative move was to introduce into the busiest districts full-time judicial officers for both civil and criminal cases at the *myook* and subdivisional levels of the governmental service. As late as 1883, government courts regularly ratified orders issued by the *taik* and *myothugyis*. The negation of a *myothugyi's* ruling by an official court in 1891 marked the end of his authority under customary law.[68] In 1900 the bench of the judicial commissioner became the Chief Court of Lower Burma, consisting of four judges. In 1905 all the full-time district judges were transferred from the executive to the newly created judicial branch of the civil service.[69] Only in certain sections of Upper Burma and in peripheral districts did the executive officers of government continue to function as magistrates. It was thus on the most unequal of terms that the village-headmen magistrates and the

[67] Donnison, p. 31; Ba Han, *A Legal History of India and Burma* (Rangoon, 1952), pp. 80–108. Dr. Ba Han testifies to the enormous debt which Burmese law owes to British experience and practices.

[68] J. S. Furnivall, "Reconstruction in Burma" (MS., 1943), pp. 21–23.

[69] Donnison, pp. 5–7, 31, 35–36, 40. Burma's separate High Court of Judicature, which was based on letters patent from the crown, was eventually established in 1922.

145

increasingly professionalized court system were supposed to collaborate.

Probably at no point did the British-type government wander into more bewildering paths from the Burman point of view than did the court system. Law as executed by the courts ceased to have much relevance to Burmese ideas of justice; it became instead a game of technicalities and rules which only the not-too-scrupulous legal profession seemed to understand and to profit from. For the personally administered justice based on familiar customary law and dispensed in *coram rege* by the old *myoyon* courts or *Hlutdaw* under the scrutiny of interested onlookers was now substituted an impersonal law alien in content and complex beyond comprehension in its professional ramifications. The seemingly worthy objective to accord unhurried professional attention to important court cases succeeded only in protracting litigious proceedings for the benefit of the legal profession. The Burman could understand the plenary authority of the deputy commissioner, acting as the British counterpart of the old *Myowun,* but the seemingly capricious fragmentation of his authority tended to confuse the observer and therefore to weaken somewhat the respect with which he had come to regard the key officer of the district administration.[70]

Another difficulty in coping with the rapidly expanding volume of court business, especially in criminal proceedings after 1900, was the increasingly unreliable character of the sworn evidence presented before the courts. People would lie to the judge whereas they would tell the truth to the executive officer, partly because the court was too remote, too formal, too abstract for them to trust. The type of oath administered to witnesses by a British court carried no religious or moral sanction to the Burman Buddhist and could hardly be administered with dignity by a non-Christian judge. It was at best an anemic substitute for the formidable imprecations contained in the terrifying traditional Burmese counterpart. For witnesses as for lawyers, trials became a game testing the wits rather than the veracity of participants. Witnesses were bribed, and so were many of the magistrates at the lower levels of justice. It proved impossible to enforce punishment for

---

[70] *Ibid.,* p. 41. Governor White, writing in 1913 (*A Civil Servant in Burma,* pp. 24–25) bemoaned the passing of the all-competent deputy commissioner, which he characterized as the "best [administrative] system ever devised or practiced for Burma." He predicted that the divorcement of the executive and judicial powers and curbing of the discretion of deputy commissioner by supervision and review of his decisions would act as "solvents which will gradually destroy the vitality of the administration."

libel even where directly contradictory evidence was obtained. When the records of such evidence taken in the lower courts was reviewed at higher levels, where the human element could not be taken into account and where the presumption was to give the accused the benefit of any doubt of his guilt, the final decision frequently had little relevance to objective fact and hence none to justice itself.[71]

The Burmese tradition as compared with the British put a higher value on infringements of personal dignity and a relatively lower one on violations of property rights. Personal assault aggravated by use of insulting words was a grave offense in the eyes of a Burman judge, whereas theft and misappropriation of funds were more lightly regarded. Such differences in standards were deeply ingrained. This did not mean, however, that certain basic principles of English common law were not valued in Burma.[72]

Generally speaking, the incidence of crime paralleled the increase of civil court litigation over land titles, for both were related to the rapid turnover of newly developed agricultural land in Lower Burma. It was a fairly simple matter in Upper Burma to apply the traditional Burmese rules concerning marriage, divorce, and inheritance. In a stable village community where the facts of a marriage were known, where the wife could easily establish her property rights, and where all of the children-heirs to a family estate were present to claim their equal share, it was easy enough for the elders who knew the facts to enforce the customary law. But when children moved away, were married to women or men from afar, and established no permanent residence and where no elder-magistrates knew the facts, one's status in the family and rights pertaining to it were hard to prove in court. Whereas the customary law relating to inheritance of personal property might be adjusted to changing conditions, the Burman would not consent to altering time-honored rules for inheritance of land. Thus

---

[71] G. E. Harvey, *British Rule in Burma*, pp. 34–37. Fielding-Hall (*The Soul of a People*, p. 101) tells that the willingness of madcap youth to confess and atone for crimes in 1890 had entirely disappeared by 1902 amid universal perjury.

[72] Harold Fielding-Hall, *A People at School* (London, 1906), pp. 216–222. Fielding-Hall discounts somewhat allegations of court corruption, on the grounds that the loser in any lawsuit would usually raise such a charge without any supporting evidence whatever. The counterevidence is nevertheless convincing. Dr. Ba Han (*A Legal History*, pp. 80–108) indicates four highly valued principles which Burmese law acquired from British precedent: (1) the principle of liberty conferred and controlled by law, (2) the sacredness of the guarantee of freedom within the law, covered by writ safeguards, (3) independence of the judicature from political interference, and (4) the principle of a person's right to impartial justice.

the restless buying and selling of land in Lower Burma played havoc with the social order dependent upon the land. When lawsuits occurred usually the lawyers got most of the money in the end.[73]

Increase of Functional Administrative Agencies

The rapid development of other functional aspects of governmental administration, especially after 1890, all centering in the growing secretariat at Rangoon, was a further departure from personalized authority in the traditional pattern. One of the most important contributions to the destruction of the authority of the *myothugyi* had been the introduction of the settlement officer in 1872. He was charged with demarcating and mapping landholdings according to the pattern of the cadastral surveys employed in less thoroughgoing form in India and to fix for a number of years, depending on soil, crop, and market facilities, equitable rates of taxation on an acreage basis. He acted at first in co-operation with general executive officers of the area. This new agency was necessitated in part by the casualness of the traditional system of land assessment, but also by the rapid expansion of agricultural cultivation in Lower Burma beginning in the 1870's. A special Land Records Department was set up in 1900 under the commissioner of settlements. A regular system of periodic settlement surveys was initiated covering all parts of administered Burma. Completed settlements were to remain in force up to twenty or thirty years.[74] Land taxes as fixed by the surveys were collected in cash by village headmen and by township and district officers, disregarding the traditional practice of payment in kind and the time-honored traditional identification of the *myothugyi* assessor-collector with his people's interests.[75]

The rapid expansion of the central secretariat at Rangoon during the

[73] Fielding-Hall, *A People at School,* pp. 225–235.

[74] Dautremer (pp. 184–186) describes in detail the cadastral survey as of 1910. Large polygons were surveyed and then subdivided into smaller classifications and finally into *Kwins* each averaging from one to four square miles in area. The cultivated land within each *Kwin* was then classified for purposes of taxes. The sum of the areas of all subdivisions must equal the area of the total unit. Remission of taxes was permissible under the rules when one-third or more of the crop was lost. As a rule, some five or six settlement parties were operating simultaneously after 1910 in diverse areas of Burma. The completed surveys usually enhanced the tax demand from a given district from 25 per cent to 30 per cent, except during depressed conditions of World War I, when the average increment was under 15 per cent. See Burma, *Report on the Administration of Burma* for 1914–1915, p. 14, for 1915–1916, p. v, for 1916–1917, pp. 14–16. Hereafter cited as *RAB.*

[75] Donnison, pp. 48–50.

quarter century between the pacification and the outbreak of World War I insulated the government more and more from personal contact with the people of the country.[76] In 1897, when the chief commissioner became a lieutenant governor and Burma for the first time was granted legislative autonomy, an appointive legislative council of 9 members was added. The new council included 4 nonofficial members, 2 Europeans, one Burman, and one Shan. When the legislative council was increased to 17 members in 1909, 2 elective members were included, one chosen by the Burma Chamber of Commerce and the other by the Rangoon Trades Association, both British organizations. The legislative council was increased to 30 members in 1915, all the additional members being appointed by the governor. The advisory executive council was, of course, entirely a projection of the governor's own personality, and he was likewise fully capable of curbing any sign of undue independence on the part of the largely appointive legislative council. To the governor's veto of legislation was added that of the Government of India and of the Secretary of State for India at London. Since Parliament very rarely debated a question relating to Burma, the entire line of command had almost as little relevance to the people of England as to the people of Burma.[77]

Working in conjunction with the governor's personal secretariat at Rangoon were approximately a score of specialized functional agencies each of which tended in accordance with the laws of the bureaucratic tradition to expand into separate departments of government. Several of these relating to the basic functions of police, magistracy, land survey, and general administration, including tax collection, have already been mentioned. The most important of the others were the Public Works Department under a chief engineer (dating from the 1870's) with representatives in the districts, the Department of Agriculture under a director (1906), and Departments of Public Health and Veterinary Medicine (1906).[78]

Every one of these functional agencies made tangible contributions to real needs, but almost without exception they failed dismally to

[76] The secretariat of the chief commissioner began, in 1862, with the addition to his staff of a general administrative secretary and three assistant secretaries. This group developed eventually into the executive council. A chief secretary for Upper Burma was added in 1886.

[77] Donnison, pp. 27–31, 38–39.

[78] Ibid., pp. 27–31, 38–44; Hall, *South-East Asia*, pp. 624–625. There were also departments for jails, medical services, the chaplaincy, marine and customs, fisheries, education, postal service, and co-operative credit.

enlist, in pursuit of their worthy objectives, the interest and active support of the people of the country. Officials too often made little attempt to understand the people, being content to apply Western methods for Western ends. The irrigation section of the Public Works Department has been adjudged virtually the only specialized agency that was fully appreciated by the Burmans and largely manned by them. Irrigation was for the Burman nothing strange and new. The medical and sanitation service, on the other hand, was largely Indian-manned and very meagerly appreciated by the Burman. The new education was largely alien in its content and unrelated to Burma's needs, except for the incidental advantage afforded successful students in getting a government job.[79]

Perhaps the most unappreciated of all British governmental innovations were the activities of the municipal corporations, which had been first authorized in 1874. There were at first seven self-governing municipalities plus a score or more of "town funds," administered by local officers with the aid of local advisory committees. Although a proportion of the membership of the municipal committees became elective after 1882, Burman participation in the administration was virtually nil. Paved streets, sidewalks, street lights, medical services, water supply, and other urban amenities served to meet essentially European rather than Burman standards. They called for the collection of additional taxes above the usual local income from market-stall rentals and assorted fees and licenses. Town populations as a rule resisted bitterly incorporation as municipalities, and whatever work was accomplished by municipal corporations was usually done by European residents.[80] The divisional commissioners kept municipal expenditures within budgetary limits, and the government could dissolve any town committee for cause.[81]

Inclusion of Burmese Personnel in the Administration

The inclusion of Burmese persons in the governmental administration after 1862 appears to have followed for many decades an opportunistic policy. At the outset, in both Lower and Upper Burma, posts were given to ex-princes, ex-*Wuns,* and ex-*myothugyis* who had administrative ability or social influence which could be utilized by the

[79] Donnison, pp. 44–50.
[80] *Ibid.,* pp. 9–10, 34. Rangoon, in later years, was an exception.
[81] *ISCR,* XI, 457–460.

government. The holding of preliminary qualifying tests developed in time into a full-fledged civil service examination system, covering command of English, knowledge of the elements of surveying and administrative procedures, and other relevant matters. At first the pay was low and prospects for advancement poor. Applicants usually qualified at the township officer (*myook*) level, and the abler ones rose later to the level of subdivisional officers or extra assistant commissioners.[82] Few of the younger officials could match in personality those taken over earlier from the Burman regime, but the standards of the Class II service tended gradually to improve.[83] The first Burman deputy commissioner was appointed in 1908, and the first Burman judge of the High Court in 1917.[84]

The emerging Burmese bureaucracy constituted a new middle class (called *a-so-ya-min* or simply *min*), affiliated neither with the people generally nor with the British ruling group. The official group comprised a definite social stratum with its own perquisites and types of snobbery. They moved about freely from post to post, mingling with others similarly on the move, rooted in no locality. They lived in large urban households which often included servant girls, sometimes distantly related, and they employed Indian servants to do the menial labor. Denied social intercourse with most Europeans, this group at the turn of the century still found its social pleasures in religious observances and pagoda feasts. The semi-Westernized Burman bureaucrat served the government and his family group and tended to look down on the village *thugyi* as an ignorant bumpkin. Many of them, but not all, became alienated from the interests or the viewpoint of the people as a whole,[85] especially so after the virus of nationalism emerged following World War I. The British administrative system permitted no scope or outlet for natives of capacity in political leadership.[86]

The first deliberate attempt to utilize nonofficial representation in the government was made largely in deference to the wishes of the European business community. The authorization of municipal corpo-

[82] Donnison, pp. 36–37.
[83] Former Governor White (*A Civil Servant in Burma,* pp. 262–263) affirmed that "many Burmese officers have been perfectly honest and have . . . justified the trust reposed in them. . . . They have now [1913] fair wages and many roads to dignity and honour. . . . A sounder tradition is gradually being crystallized and year by year the standard of morality is being raised."
[84] *The Cambridge History of India,* VI, 447.
[85] See Mi Mi Khaing, *The Burmese Family* (Bombay, 1946), pp. 18–21, 35, 46.
[86] Harvey, *British Rule,* p. 77.

rations and town committees has already been mentioned. Two non-official Europeans were included in the nominated legislative council of 1897. In 1909, following the Minto-Morley reforms, the British Burma Chamber of Commerce was permitted to elect a single representative to the 15-member council, of which only 6 were officials. Four Burmese, one Chinese, and one Indian, all appointed, were also included. European business representation was increased in 1915 by the election of a representative of the British Trades Association. By 1920, the council included 10 natives of Burma, plus 2 Indians and one Chinese, or 13 all told, in the total membership of 30. Business elements constituted a major fraction of the British and the non-British representation.

The legislative council, of course, was mainly an advisory body. It could initiate legislation only with the governor's consent and could only discuss the annual financial statement and other matters of general interest. It could not pass on the budget, nor could it question government officials on the conduct of the administration.[87]

Bureaucratic Standards in Burma's Administration

Official opposition within Burma to any proposal of popular self-government for the country, even in the very tentative form embodied in the Minto-Morley reforms,[88] was clearly reflected at the time in the views of the able governor, Sir Herbert Thirkell White. White insisted that the Minto-Morley reforms were unsuited to Burma and were gratuitously introduced because they were supported by no popular demand. He believed that the basic governmental objective must be to encourage efficiency within the services by improving the position and prospects of worthy officials, especially in departments manned by Burmans. His deprecatory comment on the reforms ran as follows:

I am thankful to say that, for the time being at least, the Province was saved from popular elections. In a country where after thirty years, it is rare to find Europeans or Burmans . . . willing to take an interest even in municipal elections, that would have been the last straw. But the Council had to be enlarged, a non-official majority secured, and the elective system introduced at least to the extent of enabling . . . the Burma Chamber of Commerce to elect its member and all the detailed rules of procedure, of budget discussions, of interpolations . . . framed for other Provinces, had to be

[87] David G. Hinners, "British Policy and the Development of Self-Government in Burma, 1935–1948" (University of Chicago thesis, 1951), pp. 13, 16, 19–20.

[88] Donnison (p. 39) quotes Lord Morley as follows: "If it could be said that this chapter of reforms led directly or indirectly to the establishment of a parliamentary system, I for one would have nothing to do with it."

applied to Burma. . . . No one in Burma is a penny the better, and . . . the net result is some waste of time and money. . . . The situation would be ludicrous if it were not pathetic.[89]

An alternative point of view was expressed in a perceptive assessment of British administrative policy made by Financial Commissioner Donald Smeaton, in 1887:

The highest excellence in any administration . . . consist in the perception of . . . capacity [for self-rule] and in leading it into those channels for which it is best suited. . . . We have dealt with all alike, neglecting distinctive national characteristics. . . . Both in method and in scope we are wrong. . . . We melt down all the subject races into one huge mass and then cast them ruthlessly in our Western World. . . . We have no art in our government. . . . The result . . . is . . . that the reforms which we endeavor to introduce strike no real root; the soil and climate are not congenial. . . . We have nowhere fostered the growth of real national life. . . .

Our thirty years' rule in the lower country [of Burma] has been, on the whole, less successful than in any other province of the Indian Empire. . . . We go about the business of civilizing subject peoples . . . with very little knowledge or appreciation of the human natures . . . with which we are dealing. This is why we remain aliens wherever we go. This is why our cut and dried civilization goes only skin deep. This is why our schemes of self-government find no genuine support among the populations of the East. Our heads are hot and busy, but our hearts are cold as stone. Our administration lacks . . . sympathy.[90]

Another understanding British observer, writing in 1906, commented that the officials who contributed to the strength, efficiency, and order of the British regime, operating almost as if interchangeable cogs in a vast machine, were often respected but seldom liked by the people. The officials of old Burma by contrast may have been less just and more demanding than the new civil service but they had been social leaders, participants in community affairs, creators of manners and fashions, patrons of literary talent and art. Gone were Burma's social leadership, its court functions, its best craftsmanship, its gold umbrellas

---

[89] White, *A Civil Servant in Burma* (New York: Longmans, Green & Co., 1913), pp. 293–296; reprinted by permission. In another connection Governor White insisted that Britain must "avoid the pernicious cant of thinking that our mission in Burma is the political education of the masses. Our mission," he added, "is . . . to preserve the best elements of their national life [and] by the maintenance of peace and order to advance the well-being of the Burman people."

[90] Smeaton, *The Loyal Karens of Burma* (London: Routledge & Kegan Paul, 1920), pp. 216–220, 236; reprinted by permission.

and its best Mandalay silks, its meaningful gradations of status. Such elimination had impaired public taste and therefore the fiber of national character itself. The Burman, in other words, had lost his pride of being a Burman; he resented being lectured about the West, being told to learn new things and to forget his traditional ways.[91]

A good deputy commissioner, serving as the key official in any district, must be able to work hard and fast, to use common sense and be friendly, but his administration increasingly lacked flexibility and capacity for adjustment within the manifold rules of government. He had to be concerned mainly, in his roles as policeman, collector, and censor, with troublemakers; too little time was available for positive accomplishment. The people accordingly wanted to see as little of him as possible. It was the exceptional British official who learned the language well and shared in the life of the people. He was more likely to regard their festivals and plays as frightfully noisy and over-long, and he almost certainly disliked their music. He thus found little community of taste with them whether in work or pleasure. In any case he was usually shifted to another post before he could get well acquainted locally. The most frequent popular contact with officials occurred when the Burman asked for some favor. In such cases the official must automatically resist being influenced. An overconscientious officer was often more offensive than one who was apathetic, because the latter could be more easily avoided. Each party bored the other, and both were aware of the fact.[92]

Fielding-Hall's oversimplified assessment of British-Burman relations, as given above, was naturally subject to exceptions, but it was probably accurate in the main.

[91] Fielding-Hall, *A People at School,* pp. 170–176.
[92] *Ibid.,* pp. 160–169.

V

Economic and Social
Developments, 1870-1914

OF equal importance with British administrative innovations in affecting the lives of the people of Burma prior to World War I was the economic and social transformation which accompanied British rule. The various areas of change were in many respects, of course, interrelated. Burma was a country with great potential resources to be exploited, and governmental policy was designed primarily to further economic development. The social by-products of the dual impact of rapid economic expansion and related administrative policies were incidental rather than planned, but they conditioned in large measure the attitude of the people toward alien rule and therefore contributed to the development of the political consciousness of the nation.

Political Implications of Burma's Economic Development

During the forty years prior to the outbreak of World War I, Burma was caught up in a maelstrom of world-wide commercial and industrial activity far in excess of anything the country had ever before experienced. The original European imperialist urge in Eastern Asia had been primarily commercial, interested in stimulating both inter-Asian trade and the marketing of European products, in return for specialty export products of Asia (pepper, spices, tea, silks, ceramics). This system had been largely displaced by the end of the nineteenth century, when the investment of outside capital had become the principal concern. The

155

objective was to accelerate colonial production of basic commodities demanded by the economies of the West, such as food products, rubber, minerals, timber, fibers.

In Burma this meant heavy outside investment in riceland development, railway and river transportation, grain and timber mills, rubber plantations, oil extraction and refineries, cement plants, and zinc, lead, silver, tin, and wolfram mining operations. The investment attractions held out by Burma were obvious: a cheap and abundant labor supply supplemented from India, a vast productive potential, hungry outside markets, expanding transport facilities, plus the protection and encouragement afforded to business by a friendly, stable, and reasonably efficient government. Under the convenient and widely accepted assumption that *laissez faire* principles of political economy were both beneficial and capable of general application, ideals of social justice and humanitarianism which were becoming operative in England as norms for economic and governmental policy found belated and ineffective transfer to colonial areas. Burmans, prior to World War I, lacked the means of understanding what was happening to their country. They were in no position to participate profitably in the economic transformation and could not hope to make effective any ideas that might be generated relative to improving Burmese prospects for participation. The country became increasingly prosperous as an addendum to the economy of the West, utilizing Western markets and enterprise, while the people remained relatively poor and quite incapable of controlling the vast economic forces playing on them.[1]

Expansion of Rice Production

The economic development which affected most intimately the life of the Burmese people was the rapid expansion of rice production. Prior to the opening of the Suez Canal in late 1869, Burma's rice exports amounted to some 400,000 tons annually. This sizable surplus reflected an increase in rice acreage in Lower Burma over the preceding fifteen years of some 740,000 acres.[2] In the twenty-five years from 1875 to 1900, the increase in Lower Burma's rice acreage reached the enormous total of 4.1 million acres, most of it in the Irrawaddy delta or in the lower valleys of the Sittang and Salween rivers. The five-year

[1] J. S. Furnivall, *Colonial Policy and Practice* (New York, 1948), pp. 2–7; Rupert Emerson, *Government and Nationalism in Southeast Asia* (New York, 1942), pp. 12–13.

[2] J. R. Andrus, *Burmese Economic Life* (Stanford, 1948), pp. 14, 43.

period from 1895 to 1900 alone accounted for an increase of more than 1.5 million acres.

The opening of the Suez Canal made possible not only a direct market in Europe for Burma's rice (one-half of the total export), but also a profitable triangular trade under which India was able to take more of Burma's rice by expanding its own markets in Europe, while Burma bought more capital and consumer goods from Europe. As a result, Lower Burma's traditional subsistence agriculture was rapidly displaced by commercial production of a single cash crop for export. This development occurred under a system of impersonal law designed to encourage free enterprise and freedom of contract and of land alienation. The traditional social and economic system was submerged so quickly and so completely that little opportunity was afforded to adjust to the new order of things. Imported items tended to replace goods of traditional Burman manufacture whether in small-scale industry or in household production. Skilled artisans and groups, like the river boatmen, saw their vocations vanish.[3]

The phenomenal expansion of rice production was accomplished under a triple stimulus: (1) the steady immigration of experienced agriculturalists from Upper Burma skilled in the art of wet rice cultivation; (2) abundant cash credits based on land security and provided, especially after 1880, by the Chettyar moneylender caste of South India; and (3) the importation of transient coolie laborers from India to cover peak seasonal demands for planting, harvesting, and milling the rice crop. Other Indian immigrants manned wharves, railways, and large river craft. Governmental policy facilitated the agricultural development by constructing bunds to protect large areas from threat of river floods, by developing railway and water systems of transportation for Lower Burma, and, for a time, by subsidizing the steamship companies which were transporting the Indian laborers from Indian ports to Rangoon.[4]

An important contributing factor to the expansion of agricultural

---

[3] *Ibid.,* pp. 14–16.

[4] J. S. Furnivall, *Introduction to the Political Economy of Burma* (Rangoon, 1938), pp. 66, 85–87; Burma, Home Dept., *Interim Report of the Riot Inquiry Committee* (hereafter cited as *IRRIC*), pp. 14–17. Private traffic in coolies began in 1870. The Burma Government started to recruit laborers in Bengal in 1874, when some 7,000 prospective cultivators were brought over at a cost of 100,000 rupees. The Laborer Act of 1876 set up a recruiting agency in Cocanada, Madras, and the Rangoon government began subsidizing the steamship companies at so much per head brought over. As many as 83,000 Indian laborers entered Burma in 1883 at a cost to the government of 300,000 rupees.

credit was the Land Revenue Act of 1876. This law required the payment of taxes continuously for twelve years before the holder could gain clear title to a newly developed piece of land. But it also provided that an "occupancy right" obtained by payment of nominal land revenue for a single year could be used as security for loans to cover the purchase of such things as food, the cost of clearing and drainage, cattle, and seed, and the planting of a crop. The lender (Indian or Burman) or the trader (usually Chinese) almost invariably moved in to take over the "occupancy right" before full heritable permanent ownership could be acquired. The squatter-occupant thereupon had to move on to another virgin area and repeat the process. Fever, cattle disease, conflicting claims, and flood damage took heavy toll of the struggling cultivators. Persons of wealth, aided by the connivance of officials, would sometimes stake out claims without improving them, pay the annual taxes for twelve years, while waiting for adjacent areas to be developed, and then sell their full title at a substantial profit.[5]

Usury was also a major problem for cultivators. The hazards of developing new land were so great that few operations could sustain, over a series of years, interest rates on secured loans ranging from 15 per cent to 36 per cent per annum and much higher rates on unsecured loans. Cultivators frequently borrowed more than they needed for purposes of cultivation, spending the surplus for marriage feasts and *shin pyu* ceremonies and sometimes on gambling and other nonproductive purposes. Once a cultivator forfeited his occupancy claim, he either moved on or lapsed into the status of renter-tenant.[6] Thus the expanding structure of debt itself kept agricultural expansion going.

Conditions on the Agricultural Frontier

A close-up view of the process of land reclamation in the Irrawaddy delta, as reported by a Burman settlement officer in the 1920's, will illustrate the anarchic conditions which prevailed on the agricultural frontier.[7] Violence was employed from the very outset as rival squatters extended their clearings. The combined efforts of the entire family were required for the arduous process of girdling or drowning out the multirooted mangrove trees, clearing underbrush, and the burning of stumps. Families meanwhile resided in temporary shelters where living

[5] Burma, *Report of the Land and Agricultural Committee* (hereafter cited as *RLAC*), pt. II, *Land Alienation* (Rangoon, 1939), pp. 39–42.

[6] Andrus, pp. 15–16; *RLAC*, pt. II, pp. 50–52.

[7] Burma, Settlement Dept., *Report on the Original Settlement Operations in Labutta Township, 1924–1925*, by Tin Gyi (Rangoon, 1926), pp. 6–10.

amenities were at a minimum. The initial objective was the acquisition of an occupancy tax ticket, which constituted a presumptive title claim usually worth substantially more as security for a loan than the cash indebtedness incurred in obtaining occupancy. The first debt of the squatter family was to the usurious Chinese trader, since the Indian Chettyar would, as a rule, not advance money on land security until a substantial equity had been developed. Seven to ten years of continuous cultivation beyond the initial clearance was usually required before a cultivator could obtain a reasonable income from crops in return for labor and capital expended. It was the rising level of land values rather than the immediate paddy output which sustained the development boom. Illness, bad management, natural misfortunes of rain and flood, plus the desire for ready money contributed to the spreading morass of squatter indebtedness. The cultivators usually sold their occupancy rights after a few years as a means of liquidating their debts and then moved on for a new try.

Such a scramble for land inevitably attracted criminal elements from all areas of Burma. Ex-*thugyi* leaders, who frequently employed semi-dacoit retainers to overawe opponents, were among the most ruthless of the land-grabbers in the area described in the Labutta Settlement Report. Pitched battles over desirable tracts involving scores of participants occurred periodically when rival bands clashed.[8] Men with capital not only financed the construction of dams and clearing operations, but also hired thugs to defend their claims. Individual squatters without funds and vulnerable to intimidation or expropriation had to struggle to develop the less promising areas or else accept aid from local capitalists on condition that they become in reality resident tenants.

In such new communities of Lower Burma, most government-appointed headmen and their "ten-house *gaungs*" commanded no respect or obedience as officials. There existed no governmental authority or social mores capable of regulating conduct in such localities. The only encouraging aspects of the Labutta situation were that the land was actually being developed and that the Christian Karen village of some 700 population located in the area, with its church and pastor, constituted an island of relative order and peace.[9]

[8] *Ibid.*, pp. 10–12. In 1921 a pitched battle occurred involving fifty to eighty on a side, each led by ex-thugyis. Crossbows and dahs were the weapons used.

[9] *Ibid.*, pp. 1–4, 6–12. Squatters were sometimes forced to execute a deed of sale of the land as security for a loan, accompanied by an oral promise from the lender permitting the redemption of the land on payment of yearly interest for a specified period.

159

During the course of this particular land survey, the settlement officer, acting under special authorization, decided some 900 disputed land claims, which were examined in the course of 530 separate hearings. He found among other things that the local Burman land records inspector was in collusion with two confederates and that the revenue surveyor added and erased designations of occupancy holdings at will, including the recording of his own son as occupant of an area which was really in dispute between two others. A mere gesture toward clearing and planting would often be recorded as occupancy. Adjudication of such disputes often had to be accomplished by the settlement officer quite arbitrarily on the basis of imperfect evidence; frequently all claims advanced to a given tract proved to be spurious. Of the 790 tenant families living in the area, 610 had occupancy rights covering only one year, while only 47 families had worked their holdings for as many as five years.[10]

The Indian Chettyars usually came into the rice development program of Lower Burma when cultivation and stable ownership had been established, but prior to the point of full development. As a rule the Chettyars avoided taking over ownership of land, preferring to keep their capital liquid. They frequently kept debtor-tenants on the land after foreclosures were possible, so long as substantial payments could be continued even at reduced rates of interest. Burman moneylenders usually accepted more risky security and extracted correspondingly higher interest rates than the Chettyars.[11] Over a long period of time, relatively few landowners in newly developed areas escaped bondage to the Chettyar. The exceptions included those cultivating land so poor that it did not provide adequate security or timid folk like the Karens who were less inclined to take chances.

A settlement report, prepared in 1908–1909, covering a longer-settled area of Lower Burma's Thaton District illustrated the circumstances usually encountered at later stages.[12] In the more productive parts of the district, according to the report: "Much of the land is in the hands of money-lenders and traders, who let it out on yearly tenancies. . . . Indebtedness is general; cultivating owners are often merely creatures of the Chetties." During the land boom of 1902 to 1905, resident

---

[10] *Ibid.*, pp. 12–16. The land tax in this area was set at approximately one-quarter of the rental price, which was usually less than half the total paddy output.

[11] Andrus, pp. 66–67.

[12] Burma, Settlement Dept., *Report on the . . . Settlement . . . of the Thaton District, Season 1908–1910,* by T. Couper (Rangoon, 1911).

Talaing (Mon) agriculturalists in Thaton District had mortgaged or sold older developed holdings in order to extend their acreage in new land. When the boom collapsed in 1905–1907, the speculators lost heavily. By 1908, almost half of the cultivated land was no longer owned even nominally by agriculturalists. Tenants working on yearly contracts, and lacking capital assets, tended to sow their rice rather than to transplant it. They also neglected their ditches and *kazin* balks (dikes) needed to irrigate the fields, and they made no improvements. Landlords in the district were therefore refusing to rent on shares, and the Chettyars were employing watchmen to guard their interest in the harvested crop. The group most completely dependent on the Chettyars in this area were the Indian cultivators, who often did not know where they stood with the lender. The latter usually took all except 100 baskets of the crop (the *wunsa* or food supply) at harvest time without even giving a receipt.[13]

Government became sufficiently interested in the deteriorating situation to authorize, in 1908, a general investigation of the land alienation problem. An able report, prepared by H. Clayton, indicated that virtually all sections of the country had been affected by the collapse of paddy prices during the 1907 world depression, that credit had contracted sharply, and that small proprietors in rice-growing areas were losing out to the lenders and traders.[14] A nearly contemporary report on Myingyan District, a populous area of Upper Burma, revealed that landlords and traders were collecting exorbitant rents and that the fixed land revenue demands were so high that they were driving many cultivator-owners into the predatory arms of the native moneylender. Extortionate interest rates had been substituted in Upper Burma for the exactions of the officials in the olden days, except that the lenders now had the law courts behind them and incurred no risks of reducing their social standing. The people of Upper Burma also preferred King Mindon's method of apportioning and collecting locally the *thathameda* tax because British-levied assessments allegedly did not take sufficient

[13] *Ibid.*, p. 7–11. A similar situation was described in Burma, Settlement Dept., *Report on the . . . Settlement of Kyaukpyu District of Arakan Division, Season 1914–1916,* by J. Claque (Rangoon, 1917), p. 38.

[14] *RLAC*, pt. II, pp. 50–52. Even after paddy prices had recovered substantially by 1914, nonagricultural ownership continued to increase. It amounted in 1914 to 43 per cent of all land in Hanthawaddy District, 33 per cent in Pyapon, 30 per cent in Insein, 29 per cent in Maubin, and 28 per cent in Pegu districts. See *RAB* for 1914–1915, p. 17.

account of losses incurred in poor years. The settlement officer (Mr. Furnivall) proposed, therefore, that taxes be greatly reduced in poor years, that money be made available on easy terms to cultivators through co-operatives, that the quantitative measures and various qualities of cotton be standardized, and that co-operative ginning and an open market for cotton be encouraged. These proposals were subsequently rejected by the Reviewing Committee allegedly because the evidence was not sufficiently weighty to warrant reopening a matter already considered negatively by the government.[15]

The general report on the administration of Burma for 1913–1914 affirmed, contrary to Mr. Furnivall's evidence, that very little land was being rented in Upper Burma and that the position of the resident agriculturalist had improved slightly during the course of the years.[16]

British Business Practices and Influence

A final difficulty faced by the rice cultivator and Chettyar alike was the policy of collusive buying at depressed prices adopted by the leading British milling firms, which alone could handle the increasing output. Whereas the Chettyars wanted to keep prices up in order to ensure interest collections and the solvency of their borrowers, the millers found it highly disadvantageous to bid against each other. The early tendency was to purchase the crop early through competitive bidding and thus escape paying demurrage charges on empty export grain ships which the millers needed to fill. Collusive buying began in 1882, when the price reached as high as 127 rupees for 100 baskets. The system was finally perfected in 1894, when, thanks to a depression, the price fell by some 40 per cent to 77 rupees only.[17] The relevant contemporary comment of a well-informed British official ran as follows: "A little more of the sterling probity, which used to be associated with the name of the English merchant, would do no harm in Rangoon rice dealings, and would win that respect from the farmer which heavy payments and cunning never will." [18]

Several other aspects of economic development directly affected the interests of the Burmese people. Burma's railway system, the construc-

[15] Burma, Settlement Dept., *Report on the First Regular Settlement Operations in the Myingyan District, Season 1909–1911*, by J. S. Furnivall (Rangoon, 1912), pp. 84–88, 91–93, 142.

[16] *RAB* for 1913–1914, p. 13.

[17] Albert D. Moscotti, "British Policy in Burma, 1917–1937" (Yale University dissertation, 1950), pp. 134–135; Shway Yoe, pp. 249–251.

[18] Shway Yoe, p. 251.

tion of which was started in 1870 and nearly completed in 1914–1915, was government-owned and built with Indian funds. The expenditure was justified largely on the basis of strategic and administrative considerations. Little if any of the capital was ever repaid, and the total railway debt, amounting to 344.5 million rupees was eventually charged to the separated Burma Government in 1937.[19] River transportation facilities were also provided initially by government funds, but they were later turned over to the Irrawaddy Flotilla Company, a Scotch firm, which operated at handsome profits a virtual monopoly of large-scale river freight service. The only other principal industrial development which occurred before World War I, besides expansion of rice and timber mills, was the Burmah Oil Company, organized in 1886. Skilled American drillers were employed by the company after 1904, and a pipe line from the upriver oil fields to the Syriam refinery was laid in 1908.[20] The oil company was unique among Burma's industries in that it made a sustained effort to employ Burmese personnel. Preliminary exploration of the large lead, zinc, and silver resources at Bawdwin in the Northern Shan States was undertaken before the war, but extensive development, along with the Mawchi tungsten mines in Karenni, the tin mines in Tenasserim, and the Lower Burma rubber plantations, took place after 1914. British industrial investment in Burma multiplied three times between 1914 and 1942.[21]

The British business community in Burma far outnumbered the civil servants, and in general the former set the tone of European sentiment. They favored a *laissez faire* policy by government, strong police control, easy money, and abundant Indian labor and were generally opposed to political or economic reforms. Few of them associated with the Burmese people or knew anything about Burma except as a place to do business.[22]

Attempts to Remedy Agricultural Conditions: Tenancy Measures

It remains to outline the successive proposals, largely abortive, made prior to World War I to improve the prospects of Burmese tenant farmers, to halt the alienation of land to nonagriculturalists, and to

[19] Andrus, p. 240.   [20] *Ibid.*, pp. 116–118, 122, 126.

[21] Helmut G. Callis, *Foreign Capital in Southeast Asia* (New York, 1942), pp. 88–89. British firms came to own 90 per cent of the foreign capital assets of Burma apart from land mortgages. Britain provided one-third of Burma's imports from 1903 to 1913, with only India's trade surpassing Britain's.

[22] Furnivall, *Political Economy of Burma*, pp. 165–170.

develop socially useful methods of agricultural financing, colonization, and land purchase.[23]

The first effort to encourage cultivator ownership was experimentation with the so-called patta system. This held out to select bona fide agriculturalists who were not entirely destitute of resources the option of accepting occupancy title on 15 to 50 acres to be exempt from taxes for a period of years during which they were forbidden to mortgage the land. The plan limited the credit available to the owner, but it also protected the land from alienation. The patta system never proved to be popular, partly because of delays entailed in completing land surveys and partly because of the competing attractions in the short run of the squatter-occupancy privilege of borrowing cash funds on land security. By 1900 it was apparent that only the well to do who needed no help acquired patta land. For this and other reasons, the system was abandoned in 1907.[24]

The government estates system was eventually set up in 1915–1916 as an alternative to the patta system. Estates were consolidated in various regions of the agricultural frontier where fuel areas had been reserved. Colonizers became tenants of the state and as such eligible for public loans secured by the land. Under the supervision of the States Colonies Department, rental levels kept pace with public improvements, and revenues from rentals were expended on further improvement of roads, building of bunds, and other land improvements. On a limited scale the system worked very well, but the total area involved never exceeded 320,000 acres in a total of 18 million acres under cultivation in Burma as 1939.[25]

The story of successive efforts to ameliorate by legislation the lot of the agricultural tenant was one of perennial failure. A land improvement act proposed in 1883 was only a perfunctory and ineffectual gesture.[26] In 1892 a bill was drafted which would have enabled cultivator-tenants to purchase their land at prices three times the year's rental if full title was available or at twice the rental if the occupant-landlord did not as yet enjoy full rights. The proposal was dropped because critics regarded it as too extreme. A third bill drafted in 1896 by Sir Frederic Fryer would have conferred on any tenant who had culti-

[23] These three subjects were reviewed successively in *RLAC*, pts. I, II, and III (Rangoon, 1939).
[24] *RAB* for 1921–1922, pp. 22–24.
[25] *ISCR*, XI, 178–180; Andrus, p. 82; *RLAC*, pt. II, pp. 40–43.
[26] Moscotti, pp. 11–12.

vated a given piece of land continuously for twelve years occupancy rights to such land at a rental fixed by the settlement officer and subject to change only on certification by a revenue officer according to prescribed rules. Such permanent tenancies would be heritable but not transferable. Tenants could be ejected only by a court decree based on failure to pay the prescribed rent or for diverting the land to non-agricultural purposes. The bill also would have made rental agreements entered into by ordinary tenants susceptible to review by the settlement officer. Permanent tenure, if achieved, would not only have controlled rents but would also have given the tenant an incentive to improve his land. This measure encountered determined opposition from certain government officers, who denounced it as gratuitous and unnecessary because a displaced tenant in Burma could always find other land.[27]

A subsequent bill of 1900, also sponsored by Fryer, abandoned the idea of promoting occupancy tenants in favor of a simple guarantee of security of tenure on payment of a fair rent as determined by a settlement report or revenue officer. This proposal was reviewed adversely by the Government of India in 1902. An alternative draft proposal, prepared in 1906 and presented for public consideration as the Burma Tenancy Bill of 1908, would have made possible the creation of a special class of "protected tenants" from those who held land habitually rented out by a landlord. The rents payable by "protected tenants" could be raised only by application to the revenue officer, who would be invested with power to fix fair rentals for terms up to five years. Protected tenancies were to be heritable but not transferable. Although the Burma Tenancy Bill was supported by Governor White, it enjoyed little Burmese support because the wishes of the tenants who would have profited from it were both unorganized and inarticulate. The interests represented in the legislative council and in other politically influencial circles, such as landlords, Chettyars, and the European mercantile community, all attacked the proposal with vigor. The measure was pondered by the council for several years, and a select committee finally proposed amendments. The project was finally shelved in 1914 by Governor White's successor.[28]

---

[27] *RLAC*, pt. I, pp. 3–5. These proposals clearly reflected the pattern of the British Parliament's experiments in dealing with land legislation for Ireland during the 1880's and 1890's.

[28] *Ibid.*, pp. 5–6.

Land Alienation Reform Proposals

Attempts to halt the trend of alienation of land ownership to non-agriculturalists were no more successful than efforts to improve the tenant's status. The basic proposal of the original Burma Agriculturalist Relief Bill of 1891 was to make the sale of land by a Burman agriculturalist conditional on his obtaining an instrument of transfer signed by a revenue officer. It prohibited sale or attachment of such land in execution of a decree issued by a civil court. Financial Commissioner Smeaton, the author of the bill, argued logically that Burman ownership could not be preserved unless the easy-spending agriculturalist was somehow prevented from borrowing too freely from moneylender and trader. This end could be achieved only by restricting the use of his land as security. The initial reaction of the Government of India to Smeaton's proposal was encouraging, but it was 1896 before a definite recommendation for legislation was drafted in Burma. Under the proposed terms, revenue officers would approve the sale of the land of an agriculturalist only to another agriculturalist and then subject to the pre-emptive right of purchase by the lineal descendants of the first occupant. (Here was a praiseworthy attempt to revive a principle of Burmese customary law.) Only usufruct mortgages would be allowed, extending up to fifteen years' time, during which the mortgagee could remain on the plot of land as tenant of the mortgagor. Leases would also be limited to fifteen years. Since Burma was due to attain legislative autonomy in 1897, the Government of India did not bother to reply to this 1896 proposal.[29]

It was ten years later, in May, 1906, that Governor White revived the attempt to curb the admitted evils of land alienation to nonagriculturalists. White undertook, among other things, to revive Burma's traditional rules giving to the vendor the right of repurchase after a period of years and placing coheirs in a favored position to redeem family land which had been sold. White would have permitted only usufruct mortgages and would normally have allowed particular contracts to imperil the produce of the land for only one year.[30]

Both the Government of India and the Secretary of State for India at London raised objections to the 1906 proposal. They argued that the definition of the term "agriculturalist" was too inclusive and vague; perhaps the Chettyars would refuse to grant loans on usufruct security; revenue officers, in any case, would have to shoulder too great discretionary authority. Within Burma a minority of officials and some

---

[29] *RLAC*, pt. II, pp. 43–45.   [30] *Ibid.*, pp. 45–48.

cultivators supported the measure, but the bulk of articulate opinion was negative. Numerous arguments were advanced. The property rights of the cultivator would be impaired; the proposal would retard the rate of bringing fresh land under cultivation; it might even force land out of cultivation thus impairing governmental revenues; it might ruin the Chettyars and the banks; it would affect adversely the rice millers. The physical and psychological effects of the panic of 1907 probably served to re-enforce such considerations.

The full report on White's Land Alienation Bill finally reached the governor in April, 1910. When he surrendered his post to his successor, Sir Harvey Adamson, later in the same year, White recommended that the bill be passed in a simplified form. In October, 1911, Adamson recommended instead that the bill be dropped for three reasons: (1) it was not practicable to define "agriculturalist"; (2) it would overburden the revenue officer by making an administrator out of him; (3) it would oust the Chettyar and thus disturb agricultural credit. The Government of India commented later that Adamson had probably overstressed the economic ill effects of impairing owner credit and that the objections as stated had not been made from the cultivator's point of view. Delhi admitted, nevertheless, that it was indeed difficult to find a definition for "agriculturalist." [31]

This topic can be concluded appropriately by citing Governor White's own thoughtful comment:

Gradually, but surely, the Burman is being squeezed off the land and . . . if, as seems likely, the proposed legislation is abandoned, the land will fall into the hands of non-agriculturalists and natives of India. Free trade in land . . . from an economic point of view . . . is probably sound. More rice will be grown for export; more land revenue and customs duty will be garnered. But . . . the standard of living will be lowered. The deterioration of the Burmese race, which will inevitably accompany their divorce from the land, will be a subject for regret when it is irremediable. Similarly, tenants in Burma . . . need protection. [32]

Attempts to Provide Better Credit Facilities

The only serious effort to provide an alternative source of credit to that of the Chettyars and traders was made through the Indian Co-operative Societies Act of 1904. [33] The co-operative credit movement developed from a recommendation contained in the Indian Famine

[31] *Ibid.*, pp. 48–50.　　[32] White, *A Civil Servant in Burma*, pp. 296–297.

[33] Moscotti, p. 12. An agricultural loan act had been proposed in 1884 in half-hearted fashion.

Commission report of 1901. In Burma there existed no popular under-standing or support for the co-operative idea when the Department of Agriculture undertook to foster the program. Because of the smallness of the share capital and member deposits in Upper Burma, the Upper Burma Central Union Co-operative Bank was established in 1910. It became in 1920 the Burma Provincial Co-operative Bank. The lending operations of this bank as an aid to co-operative societies were extended quite dangerously beyond its direct knowledge of circumstances to cover the needs of hundreds of local societies.[34] By 1915, some 1,250 credit societies were organized, which number increased to 3,319 by 1920 and to 4,057 by 1925.[35] But even at its maximum operation the co-operative movement provided only a fraction of credit needs for agriculture. By the 1920's the societies were running into serious diffi-culties, a problem which will be treated in a later connection. The credit societies could provide only a limited solution because the need for credit was heaviest in precisely those delta areas where the popula-tion was migratory and lacked the social cohesion and mutual trust needed for co-operatives to function. In this instance also, business elements represented in the legislative council supported the Chettyars and traders in resisting government efforts to protect cultivator-owners from usurious demands.[36]

Cultural and Religious Decline

The decline of indigenous Burmese culture under British rule be-came increasingly apparent in the decades prior to World War I. One factor was the disappearance of the royal court, which had functioned as the inspirational center for literature and learning, religion, music, and all forms of art expression. Exquisite craftsmanship and artistic performance lost much of their motivation when superiority was no longer appreciated and rewarded. The best work was often not as salable as the inferior, and the older tradition declined accordingly. Skilled craftsmen were reduced to the cultivator level when manu-factured imports displaced their products in the markets.

With the disappearance of trained secretarial posts at the king's court and at the headquarters of the many grades of *Wuns,* high liter-ary competence in the Burmese language also became an unremunera-tive luxury not widely esteemed. English became in time the language

---

[34] *RLAC,* pt. III, pp. 86–90.   [35] *Ibid.,* pp. 84–86.

[36] David G. Hinners, "British Policy and the Development of Self-Government in Burma, 1935–1938" (University of Chicago thesis, 1951), p. 21.

of the law courts, of the best secular schools, and of the legislative council, while use of Hindustani vied with Burmese in the hospitals and the urban bazaars. Burmese speech, reduced to its rudiments and shorn of its refinements, continued to be used mainly in rural areas and in domestic circles. Local communities in many areas ceased to be social units sponsoring entertainments, sports contests, and gala occasions. Restless spirits accordingly found their excitement in gambling, dacoity, or other antisocial activities.[37] The whole picture of cultural decline was a somber one.

The sad state of social and religious indiscipline was particularly apparent among the Burman Buddhists of Lower Burma. The participation of monks in the rebellion of 1886–1887, in violation of all the rules of the sacred order to eschew mundane affairs, was itself an overt demonstration of religious decay. For a time in Upper Burma, Sir Charles Bernard was able to enlist the aid of the Mandalay *thathanabaing* and other prominent *pongyis* in restraining belligerently inclined monks and in promoting the restoration of law and order. This was accomplished largely as a result of British promises not to interfere with religion and to continue the primate in office, even though the government refused support for his decisions. Sir Charles even persuaded the incumbent *thathanabaing* to visit Rangoon, where the government built a special resthouse for his accommodation on the slope of the Shwe Dagon eminence. Bernard discovered to his disappointment, however, that the Mandalay dignitary exercised little authority in faction-ridden Lower Burma, which remained reprobate religiously.[38] After Crosthwaite took over in 1887, he rebuffed the proffered assistance of the hierarchy by refusing its request for official recognition of its status and authority.[39]

Since the British authorities were not willing to take over the traditional responsibilities of the royal court in sponsoring the disciplining of the *Sangha* through its own agencies and since the monastic order without royal support was incapable of controlling disorderly members, an inevitable decision was reached. Government ruled that all wearers of the yellow robe must be treated as subject to the control of the secular courts and the police, just as were other citizens.[40] Thereafter

---

[37] Furnivall, *Political Economy of Burma*, pp. 227–234.

[38] Nisbet, II, 126–127.   [39] *The Cambridge History of India*, VI, 411.

[40] O. H. Mootham, *Burmese Buddhist Law* (Oxford, 1939), pp. 123–127. The *thathanabaing* was denied jurisdiction over civil cases in Upper Burma by Article 8 of the Civil Justice Regulations in 1886. The individual monk remained under the personal disciplinary authority of his *pongyi* superior only to a very limited and strictly religious sense.

even in cases where disputant or disorderly monks consented to the primate's or a *gaingyok*'s handling of their problems, the decision rendered carried no legal sanction. Ecclesiastical authority was virtually destroyed after 1891, when a secular judge overruled a disciplinary decision of the *Sangha*. This was a fateful step. When the last royally appointed *thathanabaing* died in 1895 and a division developed over the selection of a new one, the post was simply left vacant. The surviving regional *gaingyoks* and the *Sayadaws* at leading pagoda shrines continued to settle minor ecclesiastical squabbles in their respective districts, to hold examinations for probationers, and to try monks accused of misconduct. But the inevitable trend was in the direction of increasing laxity and decline, with Burman opinion becoming increasingly sensitive to any criticism leveled at religion or the monks.[41] At the turn of the century a sympathetic British observer reported that, although every rule of Buddhism was violated daily even by the *Sangha*, the religion still tended to make the Burman humane, tolerant, kindhearted, and charitable. Some saintly monks did good work preaching, but errant and wandering *rahans* tended toward sedition. When any monk started to practice magical incantations or to tattoo followers, it was time for the police to jail him.[42]

Apart from continuing to pay high popular deference to the monks, Burma's traditional structure of society disintegrated. The destructive process at the local level was much more rapid in the south than in Upper Burma, where traditional patterns of economy and landholding remained intact.[43] After 1900 the educational function of the monks declined rapidly, mainly because well-to-do Burmans began sending their children to the government and mission schools where English subjects were taught. The traditional *pongyi kyaung* education lost out primarily because it came to lead nowhere vocationally or professionally. On the other hand, students who were subjected to instruction in English and an alien curriculum struggled with a frustrating handicap, while at the same time they developed an attitude of contemptuous superiority toward their elders.[44] The academically

[41] Nisbet, II, 126–127; White, *A Civil Servant in Burma*, pp. 191–192. The government did give moral recognition to one of the candidates for *thathanabaing* in the form of a *sanad* setting forth the terms of recognition, but this recognition carried no substantive authority.

[42] White, *A Civil Servant in Burma*, pp. 192, 196–199, 264.

[43] White (*ibid.*, p. 183), writing in 1912, referred to the *pongyis* as "the most influential and respected class of the community . . . wielding indefinite but real power."

[44] The most undisciplined youth often came from Burman families in good cir-

competent could aspire to a post in the governmental bureaucracy, but few could hope to rise beyond the level of township *myook*, which was far inferior to the civil service stratosphere. Government service contributed envied social status to incumbents because of the authority and the high salaries attaching to it, but the prestige of the bureaucrat was destined to evaporate in the politically charged atmosphere of post-World War I.

In the economic field, few Burmans were a match in experience, resources, or general aptitude for competing British, Indian, and Chinese businessmen. In any case the effort to attain social prestige by amassing wealth violated all established Burmese traditions. The Burman landlord and moneylender were often more grasping than the Chettyar and enjoyed correspondingly little respect socially. The village *thugyis* enjoyed some prestige as perhaps the largest landowners of a given tract area and as the local representatives of governmental authority, but they were obliged to perform unpopular tasks, and their prestige was in no way comparable to that of the old hereditary *myothugyi*.[45]

One difficulty associated with the solitary pre-eminence enjoyed by the *pongyis* in the changing social order was that their personal prestige held up better than did their religious influence. In view of the increasing indiscipline and declining educational function of the *Sangha*, the overnumerous monks were making, in fact, a diminishing contribution to the national life.[46] The social loss incurred from the weakening religious influence was universally deplored, for Buddhism was potentially the humanizing, tempering, and integrating social factor, intangible but very important.[47] The situation was at its worst, of course, in Lower Burma's newly developed agricultural areas, where disorderly migrant communities were engaged in the demoralizing speculative scramble for economic advantage and usually included no *pongyi kyaungs* at all.

The displacement of monastic education by that of the government schools, especially after 1910, not only reduced the amount of religious and moral instruction imparted to the youth but also discredited in the eyes of the educated elite the prescientific lore of the *pongyis*. Even

---

cumstances. They ridiculed their elders, sometimes carried deadly weapons, got drunk, and fought each other at *pwés* (dramatic performances). See Nisbet, II, 233–243.

[45] *Ibid.*

[46] Fielding-Hall, *A People at School*, p. 244; Nisbet, II, 120–122.

[47] Fielding-Hall (*A People at School*, p. 247) called loss of religious vitality "the greatest possible calamity" for Burma.

where Buddhist families paid token deference to tradition by enrolling youth in monastic schools for short periods of time and by continuing the *shin pyu* ritual, religious instruction inevitably suffered in substantive content and in disciplinary effect. The artificial and often difficult requirements imposed by lay schools for obtaining passing marks,[48] as a condition for qualification for government jobs or clerkships, had no relevance to social ethics. Nor did the new schools help much in the clarification of Burma's emerging world orientation. Monastic morale itself suffered from the loss of educational responsibility and influence. In the course of time the yellow robe ceased to be a friendly, integrative social influence and became too often a cloak for antiforeign traditionalism and for ulterior political designs, which properly were not the concern of the *Sangha* at all. Buddhism's tradition of withdrawal from mundane affairs and its defensive posture intellectually disqualified it in large measure from making any positive contribution to the fashioning of the new social order. Nevertheless undisciplined, half-indoctrinated monks, as shall presently be apparent, did not refrain from exploiting their social influence in the political arena.[49]

An intimate picture of the transitional process through which Burmese society was passing is presented by Mi Mi Khaing,[50] the European-educated daughter of a Talaing government official. Her father was trained as a youth in a *pongyi kyaung* school and had fled from the school under threat of corporal punishment for disobedience. Journeying to Moulmein, he learned English and other knowledge which eventually qualified him to be a township *myook*. He sent his children to the English schools despite misgivings concerning the ex-

---

[48] *RAB* for 1913–1914, pp. 56–59, for 1914–1915, p. 99. The results of the Anglo-vernacular high school final examinations (tenth standard) for the two years 1913–1915 were 56.8 per cent and 46 per cent passed respectively. About 250 candidates per year qualified for matriculation in the University of Calcutta out of 360 to 440 taking the test. Almost half of the candidates for the B.A. degree failed to pass.

[49] Furnivall, *Colonial Policy*, pp. 199–200; Shway Yoe, p. 36. The lowered standards and discipline within the *Sangha* were reflected in the deflated value attributed to traditional modes of address. Thus the term *Sayadaw* (royal teacher, or *thathanabaing*) came to be applied to any monastery head; the venerable term *pongyi* ("great glory") came in time to be used for almost any wearer of the yellow robe. In post-World War II, even bus drivers were called *Sayas*. *Nga*, the traditional address used for *athi* commoners, was degraded after 1900 to apply only to criminals. Similarly the term *thugyi* was applied to the traditional *ywagaung*. See Mya Sein, p. 74.

[50] *The Burmese Family* (Bombay, 1946).

cessive length of the foreign educational program and the absence of religious-moral training. He gave food to the monks on their morning rounds. After he retired as an official, in 1935, he looked after the family plantations, contributed generously to pagodas and *zayat* (rest-house) construction in order to accumulate *kutho* (merit) and possibly to rationalize his acquisitiveness. While in retirement he gradually reimmersed himself in the nostalgic atmosphere of his Buddhist-oriented youth. He eventually gave up his Western shoes and socks, shifted from tables and chairs to mats and polished floors, and even dabbled in alchemy. But he still played tennis, drank lime juice, and used the knife and fork in preference to eating with his fingers.

Such a person's children could not possibly follow his pattern of life completely, for they lacked his early experience as a monastery *koyin*. Attendance at pagoda feasts gave place to the Rangoon cinema. There were also foreign-made goods to buy, a daily newspaper and English language books to read. Marriages were still arranged through the traditional go-between; the astrologers still did a profitable business; but there were few nostalgic religious memories for those born of *myook*-status parents after 1900.[51]

The Problem of Growing Lawlessness

The evaporation of community vitality and the accompanying inability of custom or government to control the antisocial forces unleashed by the expanding economy of Lower Burma spelled out in an alarming increase of crime, especially during the decade prior to World War I.[52] Much of the crime was apparently the work of youthful wanderers, lacking access to land and periodically unemployed. Village elders had the habit of putting such idlers to work on unpaid village services. Their departure from home might be good riddance locally, but it created difficulties elsewhere. They usually took to theft and then to dacoity, partly to find excitement and sometimes to obtain funds by which to hire persons to go their surety as "bad livelihood" suspects who otherwise could be jailed by the police for as long as six months' time. They also quickly learned that successful thievery could pay the cost of keeping on good terms with the local police.[53]

Some evidence of increasing criminality had appeared during the late 1870's among the carelessly selected immigrant laborers from India who virtually monopolized labor opportunities in the transportation,

[51] *Ibid.*, pp. 42–44, 66–73, 120.   [52] Donnison, pp. 35–36.
[53] G. E. R. G. Brown, *Burma as I Saw It*, pp. 85–86.

manufacturing, and public works fields. The coolie traffic at the outset was not far removed from slave trade.[54] From 1875 to 1877, the Indian jail population was proportionately nearly five times as numerous as that of the Burman Buddhists. By 1880 the virus of lawlessness had spread to the uprooted migrant Burman population which had been caught in the confused economic toils of commercialized rice production. Official observers in 1880 were concerned over what they called the reckless passionate character of the Burman, his fascination for riotous excitement, and the "indisposition of the people to . . . resist criminals." [55] Criminal statistics covering the five years 1880–1884, when compared with those of the preceding half decade, revealed that the number of murders had increased by 34 per cent and that of dacoities by 77 per cent. The gathering disorder eventually merged with the rebellion of 1886–1889.

Conditions in Upper Burma improved markedly in terms of order as soon as the fury of the rebellion had subsided. Social controls were re-established, and for the next decade and a half crime was held effectively under control. The exceptions were caused by Kachin depredations in the northern districts and by periodic lapses in localities suffering famine conditions.[56] Under normal conditions of stable government, neighborly relations, and resident land ownership on a permanent family basis and in the absence of commercialized agriculture and speculation in land, epidemic crime had never been a serious social problem in Burma.[57] The people of Upper Burma disliked many aspects of British rule, such as prevailing water and forestry regulations and the general leveling of society gradations, but such political resentment did not prior to World War I contribute to lawlessness. On the other hand, the large number of emigrants from the same area who sought to improve their fortunes by migrating southward contributed more than their full share to the growing disorder.[58]

In Lower Burma, the situation deteriorated steadily after 1890. Chronic debt and conditions of semianarchy on the agricultural frontier as well as transiency and seasonal unemployment contributed to

[54] J. T. Wheeler, *Journal of Voyageing up the Irrawaddy* (Rangoon, 1871), p. 26. Shipmasters active in the coolie traffic in 1870 sold the services of their passengers to Rangoon employers to recoup transportation costs and to realize a profit.

[55] *British Burma Gazetteer,* I, 509, 513–514. In 1884, cognizable crime was 50 per cent higher than in 1879.

[56] *RPA* for 1880–1884, 1889–1894, 1897. Violent crimes in Upper Burma numbered 3,409 in 1889 and only 296 in 1894.

[57] F. B. Leach, *The Future of Burma* (Rangoon, 1936), p. 121.

[58] *The Cambridge History of India,* VI, 440.

disorderly conditions. During the two long breaks in the agricultural season, one at the end of the rains after the rice was transplanted and the other during the latter half of the dry season following the harvest, foot-loose paddy farmers normally found excitement and some profit in lawless escapades. In the absence of agencies for mediation and settlement, petty disputes were magnified into passionate conflicts to be settled by antagonists with their dahs (long knives). Criminality, it should be noted furthermore, was confined almost entirely to the male population. Sometimes criminal elements got control of entire village tracts.[59] Concealment was usually easy. The police authorities encountered increasing difficulty collecting dependable evidence against offenders. During the pacification period and as late as 1896, youthful offenders had confessed offenses quite freely, and the voluntary surrender of criminals to the authorities was common. By 1902, as already noted, an increase in cases of perjury and false witness was widely reported.[60]

Police and courts faced a losing battle. Jailing, whipping, collective fines on villages, and the disciplining of errant headmen had little effect. Nor did the passage of the Habitual Offenders' Restriction Act and the Criminal Tribes Act do any good. The more vigilant the police were, the more criminal offenses were brought to light. Obviously much petty crime went undetected. From 1904 to 1912, cognizable offenses increased 17 per cent and noncognizable crime 40 per cent. In 1912, violent crime was twice the level of 1904. More than half of the serious crimes in Burma in 1913–1914 were committed in the Pegu and Irrawaddy divisions. From 1906 the annual police reports for Lower Burma repeated a dismal refrain concerning the inferior quality of the police recruits, the almost total failure of headmen to act against gambling and excise violations (liquor and drugs), and the alarming village apathy with respect to the defense of villages from armed attack. Convictions were made more difficult by perjury, concealment, and the faking of evidence, sometimes on the part of headmen themselves.[61] In 1913–1914, some 637 headmen were fined for being derelict in their duty, while 221 village tracts were fined collectively.[62]

[59] J. S. Furnivall, *Political Economy of Burma*, pp. 26–27, and "Reconstruction in Burma" (MS., 1943), pp. 16–24; *RPA* for 1905, p. 13.

[60] Fielding-Hall, *The Soul of a People*, p. 101.

[61] *RPA* for 1905, 1906, 1909, 1911, 1913; *RAB* for 1914–1915, pp. iv, 29.

[62] *RAB* for 1913–1914, pp. 13–15. Headmen convicted and fined were, of course, a small proportion of the total subjected to criticism. There were more than 17,000 headmen all told.

Sir Herbert Thirkell White, who was governor of Burma from 1905 to 1910, was more baffled by the growth of crime than by any other aspect of the country's problems. He explained that he could understand crimes of passion and impulse, but not the increasing prevalence of theft and embezzlement. His statement follows:

Children are treated with indulgence, not always according to discretion. . . . No orphan is left desolate. No stranger asks in vain for food and shelter. Yet these good people . . . produce dacoits who perpetrate unspeakable barbarities on old men and women. Sudden and quick in quarrel . . . with a strong if uncultured sense of humour, they can be cruel and revengeful. . . . The courts reveal a mass of criminality as shocking as it is surprising. Murders, dacoities, robberies, violent assaults are far too numerous.[63]

An Explanation of Burman Lawlessness

It has been noted (Chapter II) that whereas girls in old Burma early found an assured and useful status in the home the boys were usually pampered in childhood and were subjected to their first arbitrary discipline in the monastic school. As youth, they tended to drift away from family ties to find fellowship among persons of their own age. When confronted by disagreeable inhibitions, a Burman youth could either bully his way through or could by-pass the frustration by joining up with a dacoit band in order to experience the desired thrill of uninhibited power. Violence and cruelty, whether perpetrated in dacoity or in heated resentment of alleged personal indignity, were therefore not necessarily the expression of sadistic tendencies; often they were only an expression of fierce hostility toward frustration crossing one's path. Burmese youth could also attain the valued experience of individual autonomy in the free gaiety of association as equals (the "Ko" of formal address), none of whom enjoyed superior status or exerted power over their fellows.[64]

Under British rule the public service and the police afforded legitimate, and sometimes illegitimate, outlets for the exercise of power. The first was accessible to the student, the second to those lacking high educational qualifications. Even a petty official like a post-office clerk might like to show his authority by keeping the stamp purchaser wait-

[63] White, A Civil Servant in Burma, p. 66.
[64] For a full statement of this interpretation, see L. M. Hanks, Jr., "The Quest for Individual Autonomy in Burmese Personality," Psychiatry, XII (1949), 285–286.

ing. The police could employ threats, blackmail, and personal abuse on occasion. But all of these were poor substitutes for what had been destroyed. Within the system of jealously guarded social gradations of old Burma, each person had carried about in his own head a set of criteria which determined appropriate behavior toward royalty, government officials, military leaders and captains, *pongyis, myothugyis* (whether *ahmudan* or *athi*), local *gaungs* and village elders. The Buddhist *Sangha* itself provided a complete hierarchy of status permitting escape from outside competition. It afforded an avenue for eventual social recognition of one's superiority in wisdom, holiness, religious learning, and magical lore. At the same time, exit from the *Sangha* was always easy and carried no stigma. Under British rule, by contrast, the upper rungs of the social ladder including the high government offices, the wealthy merchant status, and positions as large landowners and business executives were pretty largely closed to Burmans. With the exception of the favored ("heaven-born") few who achieved posts in the civil service and a larger number who got minor government jobs, social mobility tended to be downward, descending from the small landowner or trader to the artisan, the landless cultivator, and finally to the unskilled laborer. It was the sense of suffering social degradation quite as much the economic hardship entailed in being classified as a coolie along with *Kalas* from India that made the Burman unhappy and resentful under the new order. The creation of the post of village headman compensated very meagerly for the social loss sustained in the general leveling of Burmese society.[65]

Although traditional deference for officials, *pongyis*, elders, and teachers carried over for a time, the degrees of respect to be accorded tended to blur as status disintegrated. In village situations, where bachelor youth had to provide labor gratis at the behest of the newly elevated headman, the boys became adept at circumventing what was distasteful. Since reverence for law in the abstract had never been part of the Burman tradition, the growing dissipation of respect for personal authority meant the elimination of customary restraint. Infliction of personal insult usually brought quick retaliation. Personal prestige was frequently sought in feats of strength or daring, perhaps in violence or personal intrigue, or in sheer Robin Hood adventure divorced from all established loyalties. Until later challenged by nationalist-motivated rebellion, police duty was attractive to many Burmans as affording

[65] *Ibid.*, p. 287.

opportunity for bravado in face-to-face encounter, for harsh handling of captured criminals, and, incidentally, for the collection of gratuities from bullied clients in order to supplement low salaries.

Those persons who lacked a spirit of daring could, of course, cultivate rice or possibly retire on a pension, but they were not admired for their peaceful moderation. Little premium, as a rule, was placed on deferred values or the calculated long look ahead; action usually took place not as sustained effort but in a narrow time span. Thus were both anxiety and sense of guilt minimized and delightful moments cherished as they occurred. Careless of system, evasive of responsibility, oblivious to consequences, the Burman male enjoyed those "exalted seconds" when through spoken utterance or physical violence he could gratify his yearning for freedom from threat and frustration.[66]

Such generalized considerations could not, of course, be regarded as applicable to every instance of lawless violence, but they probably go far to explain the eventual coalescence between crime and political disaffection. This situation was to become far more serious after the war when the rise of nationalist sentiment tended to dissolve all reverence for status, especially that of headman and police, as set up under the new categories of British rule.

Beginnings of a Renaissance of Burmese Cultural Traditions

Efforts to stimulate a renaissance of Burmese cultural and national traditions after 1895 owed more at the outset to Westernized factors than to traditional social forces. The lead was taken by an educated Burmese minority in touch with Western political institutions and ideologies, a group supported by a number of Westerners genuinely interested in Burma's welfare. In the late 1890's educated lay Burmese leaders in the Moulmein area and elsewhere began to sponsor nonclerical Buddhist schools, which adopted a Western-type curriculum modeled on that of the Christian mission schools. The Sasanadara Society of Moulmein, which was dedicated to educational and social uplift, started in 1897 the Sam Buddha Gosha Anglo-vernacular High School. The founders tried to finance the venture by encouraging the limiting of expenditures on such occasions as funerals, marriages, and *shin pyu* and ear-boring ceremonies. Similarly and shortly thereafter, the *Buddha Kalayama Meikta Athin* of Myingyan (later of Mandalay) founded the lay Buddha Thana Noggaha School, where religion was taught and where the Buddhist pre-Sabbath and Sabbath

[66] *Ibid.*, pp. 288–300.

178

holidays were observed. With the aid of a European monk, a similar type Asoka Society was formed at Bassein. In 1904 the Rangoon College Buddhist Association began to hold meetings and to publish lectures and sermons in pamphlet form.[67]

The attitude of the Buddhist *Sangha* toward education in secular subjects was such that the monks were able to contribute virtually nothing toward the needed mediation between the traditional order and the new educational demands. The monks were "above all advice" and as a rule accepted no responsibility for secular education; the stricter members banned the teaching of geography and arithmetic as sin. Most of the monasteries refused to accept lay teachers; they regarded the task of keeping attendance and other records as an indignity; they complained that school inspectors lacked proper deference. The decline of popularity of the *kyaung* schools was reflected in the fact that attendance fell off and that 80 per cent of their students attended only two years or less.[68] In 1891–1892, government-recognized monastic schools numbered 4,324 compared to 890 lay schools. The numbers were: 3,281 monastic to 1,215 lay in 1897–1898; 2,208 to 2,653 in 1910–1911; 2,977 to 4,650 in 1917–1918. Lay schools were obviously taking over.

The Young Men's Buddhist Association was organized in 1906 by educated Burmans concerned with refashioning valuable elements of the Buddhist tradition into an articulate movement in the new context of Western concepts and learning. The Y.M.B.A. (an obvious imitation of the Y.M.C.A.) constituted in itself tacit admission that little creative adjustment to the cultural impact of the outside world could be expected from the traditionalist and declining Buddhist *Sangha*. Nor was it interested in preserving, museum fashion, the quaint garbs and customs of Burma's indigenous tribal peoples.[69] The organizers of the Y.M.B.A. included U May Oung, a graduate of the University of Cambridge and late of London's Inns of Court, and U Kin, a man of unusual talents who was subsequently knighted by the British king.[70]

[67] Maung Maung Pye, *Burma in the Crucible* (Rangoon, 1951), pp. 2–5. U May Oung and his wife were active in the Sasanadara Society and its school at Moulmein.

[68] Burma, Education Dept., *Report of the Vernacular Education and Vocational Reorganization Committee, 1936* (Rangoon, 1936), pp. 134–138.

[69] Mary Caroline Minto, *India, Minto, and Morley, 1905–1910* (London, 1934), pp. 169–170. Viceroy Minto was greeted on the occasion of his visit to Burma in 1907 by a series of eleven picturesque exhibitions of distinctive native peoples, each assembled under a triumphal arch and dressed in tribal costume.

[70] Other founders included U Ba Pe, Sir Maung Gyee, U Ba Dun, U Ba Yin, U Sein Hla, U San Ba Ba. See Maung Pye, pp. 4–5. U May Oung's speech of

The Y.M.B.A. was at first essentially a student affair devoted to the discussion of religion and related subjects. It later expanded its interests to include a revival of Burmese art and literature, operating through a number of strong branches in urban centers of both Upper and Lower Burma. Annual meetings were arranged for a General Council of Buddhist Associations. The *Sasanadara* Society of Moulmein affiliated directly with the Y.M.B.A. in 1917.[71]

At the outset the Y.M.B.A. was suspected of political designs by the authorities, so that civil employees of government were forbidden to participate in it. During World War I there developed a tendency on the part of younger members of the Y.M.B.A., who lacked the moderation and, according to some, "the sterling character of the founders," to talk about such forbidden political topics. This trend was successfully resisted at first, but political-minded elements finally broke down the taboos.[72]

Another organization devoted to a revival of Burma's cultural renaissance was the Burma Research Society. It was conceived in 1909 by John S. Furnivall, then a settlement officer, and organized with the aid of U May Oung and M. Duroiselle, French lecturer in Pali at Rangoon University. According to Mr. Furnivall, the society was planned on a strictly nonpolitical basis and was also expressly enjoined from considering even economic questions. This was done so that government servants could be members. Even so, the financial commissioner for a time refused his approval of the organization for fear that the society might be a "deep-laid scheme to encourage nationalism and . . . subversive tendencies." Governor White was generally sympathetic with the project and accorded his assent to it after striking out the suggestion contained in the prospectus that increasing attention

---

1910 before the initial meeting of the Burma Research Society, of which he and J. S. Furnivall were cofounders, revealed a mind informed, intelligent, and yet becomingly modest. He became in the 1920's a justice of the High Court and a member of the governor's executive council. See *JBRS*, I (1911), 1–10, and XVI (1926), 158.

[71] Fielding-Hall (*A People at School*, pp. 255–256), writing of Burma in 1906, cited as the only encouraging development in the field of religion the appearance of lay societies for the propagation of Buddhism.

[72] Furnivall, *Colonial Policy*, pp. 142–143; Hinners, pp. 22–24; N. C. Sen, *A Peep into Burma Politics (1917–1942)* (Allahabad, 1945), pp. 6–8; K. M. Kannampilly, "Parties and Politics in Burma," *India Quarterly*, III (1947), 238–240. Early leaders of the political-minded faction of the Y.M.B.A. were U Ba Pe and U Chit Hlaing, both of whom figured actively in Burma's politics during the 1920's and 1930's.

should be given to Burma's archaeology; such a suggestion, he observed, might be construed as a criticism of the government for neglecting Burma's past. White was listed as a patron of the society and presided over some of its meetings.[73]

The Burma Research Society was dedicated to the study of all aspects of Burma's cultural past: literature, languages, remains, religion, foreign visitors, arts, industries, music, drama, folklore, relics, customs.[74] Part of the idea was to learn more about Burma in order to get away from the strait jacket of conformity to governmental and cultural patterns developed in India. Members were expected to participate actively and to contribute financial support. The appeal of the society was not widespread, for it concerned mainly only those Burmans who had contact with the modern world and a minority of Europeans who dared to admit a sympathetic interest in Burma. Such an interest, according to Furnivall, was itself considered bad form in some circles. It afforded a common meeting place where such persons could be encouraged to share a sympathetic interest in Burma's historic culture and life and to promote its present development. In Furnivall's phrase: "It was, on a very modest scale, an event of political significance; morally and potentially of great significance." [75]

Although prevented by the terms of its charter from considering current problems, whether political or economic, and although subsequently outflanked, as was the Y.M.B.A. itself, by more radical leadership in promoting national consciousness, the Burma Research Society made a very substantial and unique contribution to an understanding of Burma's history, customs, language, and literature. It aroused an interest and a demand for knowledge; it collected facts and organized knowledge to meet that demand; it afforded opportunity for discussion of the facts.[76]

It must be observed that the net results of all such efforts contributed inadequately to prepare Burma for meeting its manifold problems after World War I, but this is said not in disparagement but in recognition

[73] John S. Furnivall, "Twenty-five Years, a Retrospect and Prospect," *JBRS*, XXV (1935), 40–42. U May Oung became president of the society in 1923.
[74] See U May Oung's address at the opening session, *JBRS,* I (1911), 1–10.
[75] Furnivall, *JBRS*, XXV (1935), 42.
[76] *Ibid.*, pp. 42–45. Writing in 1935, Furnivall urged that the columns of the *Journal* be opened to all facts relative to life in Burma and to a discussion of such facts, as well as to the orientation of Burma to Southeast Asia and the outside world. He feared, and rightly so, that extremist partisan agencies less concerned with facts would fill the gap and that the Research Society would have difficulty surviving if it did not broaden its interests.

of the efforts made by liberal British advocates of constructive measures of governmental reform (Smeaton, Fryer, White, Furnivall, Clayton) and of the creators of such socially integrative agencies as the
Y.M.B.A. and the Burma Research Society. Far too little time was
available, and also too little scope, for the work of this constructive
mediator group before events of commanding political and economic
importance overtook their pioneering efforts. Several generations of
endeavor untroubled by world crisis might have sufficed to enlist an
impressive company of forward-looking Burmans in a program of national regeneration. It is, of course, almost equally probable that quieter
times might have generated only more exploitation, stagnation, and
lassitude, since economic distress and political influences from India
played major roles in arousing a new type of national feeling. In any
case events in Europe and in India connected with World War I vetoed
the prospect of a longer period of adjustment.

Part Three

THE RENAISSANCE OF
BURMESE NATIONALISM

VI

World War I and the Rebirth of Burmese Nationalism

THE direct impact of World War I on the development of political consciousness in Burma was relatively slight. Actual participation in the fighting was limited to some 4,650 of Burma's military police (mainly Indians), who volunteered for service in Europe, and to a contingent of some 8,000 indigenous Burmese, partly a labor corps, who saw service in Iraq. A war loan subscription of some £2 million was raised. The indirect effect of the war on Burma was nevertheless important, for it did much to break down the country's provincialism and to extend the political horizons of many of its people. It demonstrated, among other things, that the livelihood of the nation was vulnerable to world conditions subject in no wise to the control of the Burma Government, much less of the people themselves. The Burmese people also heard about Allied war aims; they took cognizance of President Wilson's statements about self-determination; they became aware of political developments in India; they read for the first time an account published in Burma of the Russo-Japanese war of 1905; they saw German prisoners-of-war used to help complete Burma's railway into the Southern Shan States. Widespread economic dislocation aggravated markedly the problems of government both in policing and in revenue collections.

At the end of the war, Burma found itself carried along in the wake of a major revolutionary upheaval and constitutional reform program centering in India. This provided Burma, ready-made, with both the

185

objectives and the methods of political agitation. World War I clearly constituted, therefore, a dividing point in Burma's political history. It gave new direction and power to emergent forces only potentially present before the war. The present chapter will trace the birth of political nationalism among the intelligentsia during and immediately following World War I.

Economic Effects of World War I

World War I precipitated a near paralysis of the rice industry of Lower Burma. The problem was a shortage of shipping to move the surplus crop. The shortage was caused partly by higher priority given to exports of timber, oil, wolfram, lead and zinc, and other minerals and, especially after 1917, to the drainage of shipping from the Indian Ocean to make good the ravages of German submarine warfare around the British Isles. The overseas outlet for rice contracted sharply, and leading rice mills shut down for lack of shipping to move the output. Considerable unemployment resulted in industry as well as in the paddy-growing areas. Moneylenders called in their loans and crop credits were unobtainable.[1] Against an average twenty-year rate of expansion of riceland acreage of more than 600,000 acres per half decade, the total increment from 1915 to 1920 was only 300,000 acres, and most of that occurred after the end of the war. During the same half decade the acreage devoted to rice in Upper Burma decreased by 368,000 acres.[2] The demand for agricultural products of Upper Burma, apart from rice, was lively, and prices kept pace with the generally rising cost of living, even though the area experienced exceptionally poor harvests during the season of 1915–1916.[3]

The wartime economic dislocation brought to the population of Lower Burma unrelieved and ever-deepening economic distress. The price of unhusked paddy payable to the cultivator declined from around 120 rupees per 100 baskets before the war to 97 rupees in 1915, 91 in 1916, and 80 to 85 in 1917 (below 80 in remote areas). This was less than it cost to raise and harvest the crop, since prices for everything except rice rose sharply.[4] Even when the paddy price bounded up

---

[1] RPA for 1915, p. 6.

[2] J. R. Andrus, Burmese Economic Life (Stanford, 1948), p. 43; RAB for 1917–1918, p. vii. From 1920 to 1925, by contrast, some 730,000 additional acres of riceland were brought under cultivation. At this rate, the acreage increment for 1919 alone would account for about one-half of the total for the half decade from 1915 to 1920.

[3] RAB for 1915–1916, pp. v, 22–24, for 1917–1918, p. vii.

[4] RAB for 1916–1917, p. ii, for 1917–1918, p. 12.

to 115 in 1918, the increase came too late to benefit many cultivators, especially those occupying the half-million acres where erratic rains ruined the crops.[5] Alienation of land to nonagriculturalists increased alarmingly, and tax delinquency became a serious problem. Collection of enhanced tax demands as a result of completed settlement surveys in 1915 and 1916 (amounting to a 24 per cent increase in Bassein District, 40 per cent in Toungoo, and 29.6 per cent in Henzada) had to be postponed. Collusion between headmen and villagers to avoid payment of the direct capitation tax of 5 rupees per household was reported for 1916–1917 in Tenasserim, Arakan, and Irrawaddy divisions. Headmen were everywhere reluctant to impose fines which they felt the people were too poor to pay.

Remissions of the tax payments were not enough to relieve distress, nor were they as much as the government could have afforded to do in view of emergency conditions. Only two-thirds of the gross revenue of 1,272 lakhs of rupees (127.2 million) for 1916–1917, for example, was actually spent. Government apparently did not want to encourage even destitute Burman cultivators to develop slovenly habits about paying taxes, whether the revenue was needed or not. In 1917–1918 land tax collections had to be postponed, and regulations for the sale of land for back taxes were liberalized.[6] Some relief was found in the multiplication by two and a half times of the number of agricultural co-operative societies from 1915 to 1920 (1,250 to 3,300) and in the dubious expansion of the operations of the Central Union Co-operative Bank beyond its actual knowledge of the circumstances of new borrowers.[7] The only encouraging aspect about government operations in Lower Burma during the war period was that the tide of lawlessness receded somewhat. This was probably due in part to the migration of many unemployed Burman cultivators upcountry where jobs could be had.[8]

Upper Burma during the war suffered far less of economic distress than Lower Burma, though it apparently experienced far more social

[5] *RAB* for 1918–1919, pp. iii–iv, 11–12. To the crop failure in 1917–1918 was added the influenza epidemic and the death of 26,000 cattle by rinderpest.

[6] *RAB* for 1915–1916, p. iv, for 1916–1917, pp. ii, 14–15, 45–46, for 1917–1918, pp. vii, 12. Settlement surveys completed in 1916–1917 increased the tax demand in Lower Burma districts only 8 per cent to 15 per cent as compared with 30 per cent to 40 per cent increases in the reports of the previous year.

[7] *RLAC*, pt. iii, p. 84.

[8] *RPA* for 1915–1917 and 1921. In 1917 as compared to 1916 the number of violent crimes increased by 87 instances in Upper Burma and declined by 53 in Lower Burma; as late as 1921 such crime in Upper Burma was still increasing by 69, while decreasing in Lower Burma by 64 instances.

187

disruption. Cultivators were able to shift from unprofitable rice cultivation to such crops as cotton, sesamum, onions and peppers, sugar, and tobacco, for which high prices were obtainable. British industrial investment in Upper Burma increased, principally in oil wells and mines. Population movement was into the cities of Upper Burma, because prosperity was adversely affected in many local areas by crop failures. This condition of relative prosperity also attracted numbers of destitute cultivators from Lower Burma. In urban centers such as Mandalay, Sagaing, Meiktila, and Pakkoku, money was plentiful and thievery widespread; gambling became a mania, and speculative purchase of urban real estate was the rule.[9]

A concomitant of this quasi-boom atmosphere in Upper Burma was the rapid increase of crime, an activity in which Lower Burma, theretofore, had maintained a notorious pre-eminence. Burma's steady increase in the total of cognizable crime during the course of the war (from 41,000 in 1914 to 45,000 in 1915 and to 48,000 in 1917) was due entirely to social disruption in Upper Burma, for lawlessness actually declined in Lower Burma. This trend persisted until 1921, when new political unrest complicated the problem generally.[10] Serious police trouble developed first in Yamethin and Myingyan districts in 1914–1915. The general aggravation of criminal violence during the following year was attributed to poor harvests and to the curtailment of agricultural loans.[11] Lack of popular co-operation with the police, rising costs of living, depressed trade conditions were cited in 1916–1917 as primary factors. In Katha District of northern Burma, the police reportedly lost all rapport with the people.[12] Some improvement in police recruitment because of unemployment was counterbalanced by a marked decline in police discipline.[13] Villages generally gave less information about the movement of criminals and even began suppressing evidence against offenders when the villages themselves were the victims.

[9] *RPA* for 1915, p. 6, for 1919, pp. 8–12. The Mandalay commissioner in 1919 (*RPA* for 1919, pp. 8–12) reported an influx of disorderly people for criminal purposes, coupled with increased laxity on the part of officials, especially the court magistrates.

[10] *RPA* for 1914–1921.

[11] *RAB* for 1914–1915, pp. v, 29, for 1915–1916, pp. v, 22–24. In 1915–1916, fifty villages were assessed collective fines in Yamethin and Myingyan districts alone.

[12] *RAB* for 1916–1917, pp. vii, 32–36. Crimes of revenge, extortion, robbery, and housebreaking in particular were on the increase.

[13] *RAB* for 1915–1916, p. vii. In 1915–1916, 17 police officers and 452 constables were discharged for indiscipline, and 218 other officers and 1,729 constables were punished departmentally.

The following explanation by Mr. Clayton, the commissioner of Akyab, in 1919, was equally applicable to Upper Burma as well:

The instincts which lead to social conduct are most imperfectly developed. . . . [This is] evidenced by the friction that exists in very many villages, the frequent murders . . . and the general lack of community feeling and a sense of mutual responsibility. . . . The . . . reënforcement of the social instincts which every society has devised . . . are . . . custom, religion, and criminal law. The Government of Burma has relied almost entirely on the last named, and it is to the decay of the first two that I would attribute the present tendencies to crime. . . . The real solution is to be found elsewhere than in the progressive improvements of the methods of police administration.[14]

To Mr. Clayton's statement should be appended another from the government's general administrative report of 1918–1919, which carried a novel political note:

For the cultivating classes . . . the year was not a prosperous one. . . . The crops were indifferent and there was a serious recrudescence of rinderpest. . . .

The prospects before Burma are bright, but it needs the co-operation of all classes of the community if full advantage is to be taken of them. It would be deplorable if co-operation were to be jeopardized by the introduction of imported political strife [from India] so foreign to the nature of the people of the country, and so inimical to their true interests.[15]

Emergence of Burmese Nationalism, 1916–1918

At one of the periodic sessions of the General Council of the Young Men's Buddhist Associations, held in 1916, several younger member delegates who had received their education in India and Europe made an abortive effort, mentioned previously, to get the council to expand its interests to include political questions as well as the usual fare of religious and cultural topics. U May Oung and other charter members resisted successfully this endeavor. Shortly thereafter, however, the goal of the political-minded group was indirectly achieved by agitation to prohibit the wearing of shoes on all pagoda premises. This issue had been raised ineffectively twice before, in 1901 and 1912, but in 1916–1917, under the leadership of U Thein Maung, a barrister from Prome, the idea caught the popular imagination and was magnified into a question around which nationalist sentiment quickly crystallized. Most of the Y.M.B. branch associations, about fifty of them all told and

---

[14] *RPA* for 1919, p. 11.   [15] *RAB* for 1918–1919, p. viii.

located in important urban centers, shifted strongly behind the agitation. The controversy became tense by 1918. Government finally ruled that each local *pongyi* head of a particular pagoda could decide the question for his premises as he chose, attempting by this ruling, without success, to bring the troublesome discussion to a close. As late as 1919, Buddhist Associations were still memorializing the government to enforce generally by law the prohibition decreed by leading pagoda heads.[16]

This "no footwear" controversy was as close as most Burmans had got by 1918 to developing a popularly comprehensible political issue.[17] The question, although intrinsically unimportant, could and did unite all branches of the Y.M.B.A. in a common cause, ostensibly a religious one, capable of capitalizing on the hypersensitivity of the Burma Buddhist population to any suggestion of disrespect to their religion or to the revered Buddhist *Sangha*. The actual agitation centered at Rangoon, where the issue became a symbol of anti-British political sentiment. It provided an occasion in which the Buddhist Burman could tell the British overlord that there was something that the latter could not do. Equally prideful British spokesmen bemoaned the "victory" of the agitators and declared disdainfully that "Europeans who respect themselves or their health do not visit the [Shwe Dagon] pagoda platform."[18] It was on such a religious issue that Burmese nationalism first expressed itself.

The primary role played by religious considerations in the emergence of naissant Burmese nationalism can be attributed to the fact that religion afforded the only universally acceptable symbol to represent an accumulation of grievances, economic, social, and psychological, which were as yet for the most part inarticulate and incapable of direct political exploitation. The immediate occasions of Burmese economic distress, for example, did not involve politics or the British directly. The anarchistic struggle on the agricultural frontier pitted Burman against Burman, while the other primary targets for dissatisfaction were the

[16] G. E. R. G. Brown, *Burma as I Saw It*, pp. 168–169; Albert D. Moscotti, "British Policy in Burma, 1917–1937: A Study in the Development of Colonial Self-Rule" (Yale University thesis, 1950), pp. 19–20. In 1919, four European women were molested while walking on the Shwe Dagon platform.

[17] Moscotti (p. 20) cites the statement of the American consul at Rangoon in September, 1918, that apart from the shoe question the Burmese people were politically apathetic.

[18] G. E. R. G. Brown, pp. 168–172. The fixed determination on the part of the English residents not to visit the Shwe Dagon platform shoeless in obedience to Burmese caveat was adhered to down to World War II.

Chinese traders, Burmese landlords, the Chettyar moneylenders, and the presence of immigrant Indian coolies. Nor could natural disasters such as the failure of the rains, damage from floods, or scourges of rinderpest among the cattle be attributed to British rule as a cause. Apart from the collusive buying practices of the large rice millers, already cited, Burmans had few instances of grievance against the expanding British business and industrial operations. The latter stimulated trade, contributed additional revenue, and contributed no ostensible adverse effect upon the indigenous population.[19] Economic distress, furthermore, was more closely associated with lawlessness than with political rebellion, although the two tended to coalesce at the point of their common hostility to the police. Only under the subsequent impetus of political considerations generated at the outset by noneconomic factors did popular distress take on political overtones.

Popular political opposition to British control, although incipient and potential, had not become sharply defined by the end of World War I. The people in all sections had a common grievance in the levying of the capitation tax in Lower Burma (5 rupees per household) and in Upper Burma's *thathemeda* tax (carried over from King Mindon's time), which was roughly equal to the capitation levy but based on nonagricultural income. These direct taxes were already becoming hard to collect by 1916–1918; they were destined in the decade of the twenties to become a major cause of political unrest. Popular hostility toward the distrusted police constabulary and lack of confidence in the regular courts of law tended to widen the chasm developing between people and administration. The government was disliked as alien and unsympathetic to Burman viewpoints and needs. But there were compensating circumstances. The top officials of the British civil services, despite their aloofness, commanded respect for their personal integrity and enjoyed "face" far in excess of that accorded to indigenous elements of the administration. Burman members of the higher levels of the bureaucracy were also envied because of their high salaries and their influential social status, even though their prestige was destined shortly to suffer impairment amid the passions of political agitation.

The absence of any organized Burmese political protest prior to 1918 made it both convenient and possible for government to ignore basic

[19] The labor on docks, railways, and river steamers was almost entirely Indian. In the Bawdwin mines of the Northern Shan States the labor was Chinese and Shan; some Karens were employed in the wolfram mines of Karenni, and a fair number of Burmans were employed in the oil fields and in timber extraction. Industrial labor generally was 80 per cent Indian.

problems of economic or constitutional reform. Burmese economic unrest and social demoralization were constant factors, but political nationalism developed as an articulate revolutionary movement within a matrix of religious and cultural sensitivity. The basic mistake involved in the postwar measures of constitutional reform was that they permitted political unrest to become vocal and active without affording aroused Burmese opinion any effective opportunity to grapple with the real sources of grievance, which were economic and administrative.

The alleged primary influence of Western ideologies in stimulating nationalist aspirations is subject to challenge.[20] The ablest of the Western-trained Burman political leaders, such as U May Oung, were government servants or barristers. As such, they were usually far removed from rapport with the populace as a whole and were conditioned by professional legal training against employing revolutionary methods. The leadership of the educated group associated with the Y.M.B.A. in the initial stages of the political negotiations was not destined to last. It was quickly outflanked by the less Westernized leadership of the so-called General Council of Burmese Associations, which took over in 1920 from the General Council of Buddhist Associations. The latter were closer to the people and were ready to collaborate with the political *pongyis*.

Students of the Anglo-vernacular high schools and of the University of Calcutta were not politically important prior to 1921, but they were a potential center of leadership. Student unrest was attributable not so much to their assimilation of Western ideologies, as some have supposed, but rather to a growing consciousness of national humiliation under alien rule, coupled with resentment over being subjected to an exacting Western educational regimen. What aroused the students was the common experience of frustration and resentment associated with their feeling of being slighted, or dubbed as inferiors. The unfortunate decision to locate the new university at Rangoon, Burma's political nerve center and near the famous Shwe Dagon pagoda, made the students peculiarly susceptible also to the designs of politicians. Apart from the unquestioned broadening of horizons through the schools, it is difficult to find any evidences of positive or substantial contribution by Western education to the development of Burmese nationalist aspirations. Neither the students nor the people generally entertained considered opinions concerning particular issues of con-

[20] See Rupert Emerson, *Government and Nationalism in Southeast Asia* (New York, 1942), pp. 25–34.

stitutional reform. Since the tradition of popular self-government on a democratic basis was totally lacking, particular reform objectives were usually borrowed directly from India or were dreamed up after an event as subsequent rationalizations of political behavior based at the outset on emotional or religious grounds.

The influence upon Burman political consciousness of contemporary developments in India needs also to be assayed. Generally speaking, the overt efforts of Indian political agitators within Burma to extend their revolutionary apparatus to that country were singularly unsuccessful, and almost entirely so up to 1920. The Indian nationalist movement was very important in setting the pattern of direct challenge to British rule; it also provided the basic objectives of constitutional reform and the developed techniques of strike and boycott which were eventually employed in Burma. But the nationalist movement in Burma was never a part of the Indian Congress Party conspiracy, and the occasional Burman attempts to accomplish a union of effort were invariably anemic and spiritless. The Burman imitation of Indian methods of resistance (*hartal,* boycott, walkout, *swaraj*) was always qualified by the dislike of the Indian connection and of resident Indians (moneylender, bureaucrat, or laborer) on the part of the masses of the Burmese. Agrarian discontent in Burma, for example, was never organized along patterns provided by the Indian Congress Party; it was not done at all, in fact, until the political *pongyis* came along to apply in their own way techniques borrowed from India.[21]

The tentative and partial political involvement of the Y.M.B.A. in the shoe-wearing agitation of 1916 and 1917 became the entering wedge for much heavier religious involvement in politics in later years. The replacement of the Y.M.B.A. in late 1920 by an outgrowth of its own General Council, the so-called General Council of Burmese Associations, happened precisely because political leadership by that time had shifted away from U May Oung and other moderate founders of the Y.M.B.A.

Governmental Policies during the War

One of the most stimulating personalities to appear in Burma during the course of the war was Lieutenant Governor Sir Spencer Harcourt Butler, who had had previous experience in India. He was fond of

---

[21] See Moscotti, pp. 16–18. The *pongyi* leader (more political agitator than monk) most closely identified with the Indian Congress Party movement was U Ottama.

speechmaking and was an extrovert promoter of numerous ideas, some of them very good. He was nevertheless quite content to view Burma through his India spectacles and was impatient of conservative officials in Burma who explained to him from time to time that the reforms he advocated for the country were not feasible. He contrasted Burma's backwardness with India's alleged progress in industry and in university education particularly and invited Burmans to visit India to see what had been accomplished there. He brought over from India a colonel of the police and immediately complimented the new appointee on his initial and superficial conclusion that police problems in India and Burma were essentially the same.[22] Upper and Lower Burma, according to Governor Butler, must be united under a single High Court and not treated as separate countries. Rangoon, in Sir Harcourt's view, must become the center of Burma's life.[23]

Governor Butler was optimistic with regard to Burma's economic future. Burma's very backwardness was, in fact, its opportunity. "The best of all, and nothing less," he insisted, "should be good enough for Burma." A greater Rangoon with imposing buildings must arise; a university site of ample proportions (400 acres) was purchased a few miles north of the city in 1916. Geological explorations should be pushed and mining operations expanded under a "policy of prudent boldness." He appointed an advisory committee on economic development including heavy nonofficial representation to explore investment opportunities for private enterprise on the basis of "security, encouragement, and a prospect of profit commensurate with risks involved." Butler believed in Burma's "inevitable and far-shining destiny" and urged co-operation in a spirit of mutual trust by officials and nonofficials, Europeans, Burmans, and Indians in attaining that goal.[24]

Sir Harcourt was less enthusiastic about constitutional progress. A committee appointed by him in 1916, including Burman members, to consider the scope and range of desirable reforms reported that little change was necessary.[25] In 1915, membership in the legislative council had been enlarged very slightly (17 to 19) to include a Karen and an elected representative of the British Rangoon Trades Association.

[22] Sir Spencer Harcourt Butler, *Speeches* (Allahabad, 1923), pp. 47, 62–63. The speech in question was delivered in 1916.

[23] *Ibid.*, pp. 71–72.

[24] *Ibid.*, pp. 44, 48–54, 73–75. The last phrase of Butler's departure speech of December 12, 1917, was: "I believe in the future of Burma."

[25] Sir Spencer Harcourt Butler, "Burma and Its Problems," *Foreign Affairs*, X (1932), 654–656.

Butler was quite opposed to importing into Burma on the basis of analogy such "Indian exotics" as representative district boards.[26] But the governor's oratorical enthusiasm on the occasion of a general durbar celebration in 1917 suggested by implication that important changes were to come:

I believe that you look upon the Government as your Government, which is out to do the best for you. . . . The world . . . after . . . the war . . . will be very different from what it was before the war. Everything is being torn up by its roots. . . . I suggest to you that you adopt an attitude of welcoming change. We must be more susceptible to new ideas in administration. . . . The only way to get things done is to get the people interested around a table, talk it out, and agree to some course of action.[27]

Indicative of the psychological impact of the war period upon Burma was the report of the Committee on the Imperial Idea,[28] appointed on the initiative of Governor Butler in July, 1916. The committee, consisting of eight ranking British civil servants, four missionary educators, and two Burmans (including U May Oung),[29] was charged with devising means of realizing through the schools and colleges a spirit of justice, co-operation, and sacrifice in the interest of national development coupled with a sense of personal loyalty to the king-emperor and an appreciation of the imperial idea. Passive acquiescence in the imperial connection must be stimulated into an active and conscious loyalty to it, manifesting itself in personal integrity and love of one's own country, its history, traditions, and potentialities within the empire. The committee worked from August, 1916, to January, 1917, and submitted its final report on March 30, 1917.[30]

The background assumptions of the committee report, as ably stated in its Appendix A, clearly reflected the political idealism of the war period:

The present European war is the result of the meeting of two opposing and mutually destructive ideals, the idea of Commonwealth and that of the

[26] Butler, *Speeches*, p. 49.

[27] *Ibid.*, pp. 73–74. The date of this speech was July 16, 1917, on the eve of Secretary Montagu's momentous announcement of Indian reforms.

[28] The full title was *Report of the Committee Appointed to Ascertain and Advise How the Imperial Idea May Be Inculcated and Fostered in Schools and Colleges in Burma* (Rangoon, 1917). This will be hereafter cited as *RCII*.

[29] To these were added later a subcommittee consisting of four Burmans to promote the use of patriotic songs, poems, and plays and an advisory board of seven prominent Burmans (*RCII*, pp. 5–6).

[30] *Ibid.*, pp. i–v.

autocratic centralized state. The ideal of Commonwealth, the development of a society of free responsible men and women bound together to create ever better and fuller conditions of life for all in obedience to law, is identical with the Imperial idea. The task before this Committee is . . . to give this ideal a Burmese setting.[31]

The report affirmed that India's sacrifices in the cause of freedom, justice, and right, shared by Burma as part of India, had earned for it a respected place in the empire. The problem was how to utilize the schools to acquaint Burman youth with the Commonwealth idea and to fit them for fruitful participation in its life.

The main body of the report, a labored effort, paid somewhat more attention to encouraging loyalty to the king-emperor than to the alternative objectives of character development and national patriotism. Parents, especially mothers, were exhorted to inculcate responsibility, self-control, and moral courage in their offspring. Burman elders were assigned to the task of censoring popular dramatic performances (*pwès*) which exerted a bad influence. The Boy Scout program, made appealing to the Burman taste in order to make its preachment effective, was strongly urged as a means of teaching endurance, chivalry, first aid, and patriotism. This recommendation was coupled with an urgent appeal for volunteer scoutmasters.[32]

The report acknowledged some difficulty in bringing the schools into the operation. It discovered, for example, complete lack of contact and understanding between students' parents and the teachers in the Anglo-vernacular schools. The potential as well as the actual contribution of the schools themselves to moral and civil training was heavily discounted. The committee pointed out that the Christian Anglo-vernacular schools, with their 75 per cent Buddhist enrollment, introduced religious sanctions alien to Burman traditions, while religious and moral instruction in the government-aided Buddhist schools consisted of perfunctory memorization which carried little relevance for training in civic responsibilities. Thus the average graduate of the Anglo-vernacular schools admittedly emerged with virtually no knowledge of the meaning of citizenship or its moral foundations. Furthermore, little could be expected in the promotion of the government's ends from the 19,500 *pongyi kyaung* schools, less than one-sixth of which were registered even under primary school standards.

Positive recommendations were few. One proposed the organization of hobby clubs, debating societies, and athletic activities for the stu-

[31] *Ibid.*, Appendix A, pp. 51–52, by Mr. Clayton.   [32] *RCII*, pp. 10–13, 26–32.

dents. The report also advocated the preparation of a *Manual of Civics* in Burmese based on Buddhist teachings regarding national defense and governmental administration,[33] a not very helpful suggestion in view of the nature of Burma's historical traditions. Formal recommendations concerning means to develop patriotic appreciation of Burmese ideals and traditions were limited to a proposal that three experienced British civil servants (including Clayton and Furnivall) be assigned the task of preparing a three-volume Burmese anthology composed of literary selections reflecting Burmese ideals, manners, and hero tales, calculated to stimulate a spirit of patriotic loyalty.[34]

Positive proposals intended to encourage loyalty to the imperial idea included the frequent display of various formal symbols of allegiance to king and country,[35] plus several promotional schemes calling for Burman participation. The latter included celebration by fetes, tournaments, and speeches on Empire Day and the king's birthday, both of which were to be made official holidays. The significance of the empire could also be stressed at speech days, at prize givings and other school events. Perhaps poems, songs, or dramatic performances could be written in Burmese based on an appreciation of the empire and the king-emperor. A series of fifty free lectures covering the history, government, geography, economics, and strategic interests of the empire was also proposed.[36]

The majority portion of the committee was particularly disturbed over the fact that almost half of the Anglo-vernacular schools (72 of 157), including some of the most enterprising, were managed by foreign agencies, mainly missionary. The report urged that all Anglo-vernacular high schools have as superintendent or headmaster a person of British nationality with status equal to the India Educational Service. No precipitate changes were contemplated, however, and appreciation was expressed for the co-operation of missionaries in the educational field. No missionaries of enemy nationality or origin should be permitted to operate in Burma, and all mission societies should be required to certify that their personnel would "foster loyalty to the British Government and promote the imperial idea in Burma." With

---

[33] *Ibid.*, pp. 22–26, 36–40.

[34] *Ibid.*, pp. 34–36. But in the Burmese tradition, government was ordinarily a scourge, and the heroes were usually the daring souls who defied the king.

[35] These included the national anthem, the Union Jack, portraits of king and queen, plus current pictures of royal processions, of state ceremonies, and of the armed forces. See *RCII*, pp. 26–32.

[36] *Ibid.*, pp. 8–10, 32–34.

respect to military training, selected cadets might be admitted to school corps for drill during the school sessions only, but the character and composition of the European Volunteer Corps must not be sacrificed by taking Orientals into it.[37]

The committee believed that the projected university and normal school at Rangoon, if placed in proper hands, could become a center for radiating sentiments of national patriotism and imperial loyalty. Key staff posts in such fields as history, government, geography, economics, and literature should be filled by men of British descent from British universities, and a proportion of the American College staff must also be British. Geography and history should be taught from the empire point of view, while all university students should acquire through their civics courses "knowledge of obligations and rights as citizens of the British empire." [38]

The most important and realistic observations concerning the problem of reconciling the somewhat antithetical objectives of empire loyalty and Burman patriotism were presented in the special Appendix A, prepared by Mr. Clayton. He affirmed that whereas good government and material well-being could produce passive acquiescence in the imperial connection, only ideals could generate active loyalty to a society of free and responsible men. Liberty was the lifeblood and ideal of the true Commonwealth because only in freedom could a man serve his neighbor as he should. Active loyalty, according to Mr. Clayton, must stem from a "sane and enthusiastic national spirit . . . [based on] love of country . . . its past history, its religion, its traditions, its civilization, and its potentialities for the future." The slogan of "Burma for the Burmans within the Empire" should express the conviction that the country's future would depend on maintaining the imperial connections. Mr. Clayton continued:

If . . . Burma . . . is still under tutelage and has not yet reached the full enjoyment of liberty and citizenship of the Imperial Commonwealth, [the student] should be taught not to regard his people as a conquered nation but to understand that England has assumed the task of the education and government of his country not as a tyrant but as a trustee for civilization in order to . . . build up those conditions of liberty and opportunity for the individual in which the people can learn to govern themselves. . . .

It is from his own patriotism, his own attachment to the ideals and tradi-

---

[37] *Ibid.*, pp. iv–vii. Entering missionaries were later obliged to sign a pledge that they would "do nothing contrary to or in diminution of the authority of the lawfully established government."

[38] *Ibid.*, pp. 16–23.

tions of his own people that [the Burman] will come to appreciate the national feelings and ideas of other races in the Empire and will learn to regard them not as foreign barbarians . . . but as brothers, who, in spite of differing customs, language, and national ideals, are yet one with him in spirit in their loyalty to the great Commonwealth of which we all are members. Nationalism must therefore come first. . . . Imperialism without a nationalistic basis is Prussianism. . . . The use of flags and ceremonies and outward symbols will be of little assistance unless the spirit which alone can give life to such formalities . . . has become an integral portion of the national tradition and consciousness.[39]

What the effect of a perusal of the report of the Committee on the Imperial Idea must have been on the mind of an intelligent Burman can only be surmised. He would certainly learn among other things that the Anglo-vernacular school system and university training, already unpopular,[40] were to be regarded as instruments of imperial politics. He was also likely to be more strongly impressed by the ideals of freedom contained in the report and by exhortation to patriotic love of country and its traditions than by the repeated affirmations that Burma's national aspirations could be realized only through continued tutelage under the imperial connection. British political opinion concerning India and Burma had obviously come a long way since 1909 under the impetus of the wartime challenge to Prussian autocracy. The new orientation of the war period provided, in turn, a springboard from which Burman opinion could take off in directions of its own choosing. Governor Butler's concluding recommendation that the proposed permanent Standing Committee on the Imperial Idea include one member chosen by the General Council of the Young Men's Buddhist Associations [41] was symbolic of political developments in store.

Burma's Exclusion from Proposals for Indian Constitutional Reform

The momentous announcement presented to Parliament by the Secretary of State for India, Mr. Montagu, on August 20, 1917, reflected

[39] *Ibid.*, pp. 51–55.

[40] Usually some 55 per cent of the candidates for high school graduation failed to pass, and around 50 per cent of the high school graduates taking the Calcutta University matriculation examinations failed. In 1915–1916, only 32 of the 56 candidates for the B.A. degree from Calcutta were successful, and this was an above-average performance. See *RAB* for 1914–1915, p. 99, for 1915–1916, p. 105, for 1916–1917, p. 112.

[41] *RCII*, pp. iii–v.

the same currents of wartime idealism found in Burma's Committee on the Imperial Idea report. Secretary Montagu's key statement was as follows:

The policy of His Majesty's Government . . . is that of increasing association of Indians in every branch of the administration, and the gradual development of self-governing institutions, with a view to the progressive realization of responsible government in India as an integral part of the British Empire.[42]

These new objectives were clarified in the formal White Paper Report of the Joint Committee on Indian Constitutional Reform, issued April 22, 1918, to the effect that policy would be directed "with a view to the progressive realization of full responsible Government by the elected representatives of the people of the country." [43] The specific changes recommended were to enlarge the legislative powers of the provincial councils of India, subject to the governor's veto and to the exclusion of certain types of questions, but including provision for direct election of the enlarged councils with communal representation.[44]

The initial reaction in Burma to Mr. Montagu's announcement was apparently very apathetic, and no one could have anticipated at the time the rapid development of political interest in it during the ensuing two years.

A few score persons at most, mainly those associated with the Y.M.B.A., appear to have been concerned, and these entertained ideas decidedly at variance with the expression of national feeling which later emerged. The delegation from the General Council of the Y.M.B.A. which was sent to Calcutta to talk with Secretary Montagu and Viceroy Chelmsford in December, 1917, asked primarily for Burma's separation from India governmentally and its recognition as a distinct nation within the empire. They stressed among other things the individuality of Burma, its differences from India as to race, languages, social customs, and religion.[45] The delegation cited the loyalty of Burma to the empire and the absence of political unrest

---

[42] Great Britain, *Parliamentary Debates* (H of C), 5th ser., vol. 97 (1917), pp. 1695–1696. These are hereafter cited as *PD,C.*

[43] *RAB* for 1918–1919, pp. i–ii; Great Britain, Parliament, H of C, *Sessional Papers* (hereafter cited as *PP,C*), vol. VIII for 1918 (Cmd. 9109), pp. 285–287.

[44] *PP,C,* vol. VIII for 1918 (Cmd. 9109), pp. 285–287.

[45] *ISCR,* XVII, 395. The delegation included U May Oung, U Ba Pe, U Su, and U Phay, the last being a retired government official.

and otherwise encouraged the belief that a separate settlement for
Burma could be worked out at a leisurely pace without risking trouble.[46] A Karen memorial, also presented at the time, pleaded specifically for continuance of British control. The Karen spokesman denied
that the benefits of free government were appreciated by Burma's
peoples and discounted the agitation for "questionable political privileges and the ushering in of dubious political eras." [47]

Burmese testimony favoring separation from India apparently re-
enforced previous representations by the Burma Government to influence Secretary Montagu to abandon his initial intention of placing
a financially autonomous Burma directly under the viceroy.[48] In any
case the Joint Committee report stated as follows:

Burma is not India. Its people belong to another race in another stage of
political development, and its problems are altogether different. . . . The
desire for elective institutions has not developed in Burma. . . . The problem of political evolution of Burma must be left for separate and future
consideration.[49]

The report of the Joint Select Committee on the Government of
India Bill stated subsequently that Burma would receive a constitution
analogous to that granted India, but that its political development
should be adapted to local circumstances. Instead of awaiting the
final outcome of the reform proposals for the rest of India, the Burma
Government under the leadership of the new governor, Sir Reginald
Craddock, was authorized to formulate in tentative fashion a separate
scheme for Burma. This plan was published in December, 1918, for
purposes of discussion, and it was submitted in an amended form for
review by the Government of India in June, 1919.[50]

The Craddock Scheme of 1918–1920

One unfortunate aspect of Governor Craddock's tentative reform
scheme was its unimaginative and patronizing tone. It was appar-

[46] Moscotti, pp. 60–61. The popular desire to remove Burma from India's control
was shared by many British civil servants, who alleged that Burma's contributions
to the central revenues were too high in proportion to population and to the return
services enjoyed and that Burma's needs and point of view received little attention
from the central Indian Legislative Council. Burmans wanted to stop coolie immigration and Indian access to government jobs in Burma. See White, *A Civil Servant
in Burma*, pp. 288–292.

[47] Sir San C. Po, *Burma and the Karens* (London, 1928), p. 66.

[48] *Ibid.*, pp. 61–62.

[49] *PP,C*, vol. VIII for 1918 (Cmd. 9109), p. 162, par. 198.

[50] *RAB* for 1918–1919, pp. i–ii.

ently prepared by men with little appreciation of Burmese sensitivity and no understanding of nationalist psychology.[51] The governor's remarks were obviously aimed to impress readers in New Delhi and London rather than to gain the support of Burman readers. Craddock's preliminary statement argued that Burma must not be deprived of the "measure of reform to which its circumstances entitle it" because of the loyal acceptance of British rule by the Burmans. Burman confidence and trust in the guidance of their British officers and their corresponding abstinence from discordant political agitation "far from disbarring from a . . . share in the advance toward responsible government, rather the more justified the bestowal on them of the highest degree of self-government which they are competent to exercise." Burma's advantages over India in religious toleration and in the absence of caste, as well as in the lack of extremes of wealth and poverty, in the high status of women, and in having a ready-made electoral role in the capitation and *thathameda* tax rolls, were, he insisted, nevertheless balanced by deficiencies which no reasonable Burman would deny. These were mainly lack of experience in self-government whether in rural boards, municipalities, or legislative council, plus the recentness of the annexation of Upper Burma and the general lack of higher educational training. Burma offered ultimately a more promising field for self-government than did India, according to Governor Craddock, but the country could not be permitted immediately full electoral control of the administration.

On the basis of the initial unfavorable Burman reception of the Craddock report, the unpublished revised statement issued by Rangoon in June, 1919, warned New Delhi that Burma's national pride vetoed any attitude of niggardliness or delay in granting Burma reforms comparable to India's. Such a policy would wound pride and throw the Burman "into the arms of the agitator and revolutionary." Crad-

---

[51] Lieutenant Governor Craddock had been born in India and had lived there for thirty-three years. His public speeches in Burma in 1918–1919 reflected his overriding concern that Burma be spared the "poison" and turmoil of India's political agitation. He asked for Burman co-operation in devising a constitutional scheme suitable to Burma's peculiar capacities and needs. He denounced Gandhi as a "misguided saint" and defended the Rowlatt Act. He declared rather patronizingly that, under the guidance of trusted British officials, Burma could, in time, gain the needed experience in elective institutions and could also live down its unsavory reputation for dacoity and crime, gambling and thriftlessness, and aversion to hard work. See Sir Reginald Craddock, *Speeches 1917–1922* (Rangoon, 1924), pp. 26–27, 72–73, 161–166.

dock's public addresses and his initial reform statement had in fact afforded the initial impetus to this undesired end.[52]

The principal features of Craddock's scheme centered around the introduction of a considerable degree of self-government at the district level on the pattern developed in India since 1882. The direct taxpayers of the villages would elect circle boards and they in turn would choose the district boards. The latter would take over from the deputy commissioners the administration of matters of purely local concern. The locally elected boards under the scheme would also enjoy financial powers to levy additional taxes for local purposes. Membership in these boards would be entirely unofficial, a ruling made deliberately to disqualify the village headmen as participants.[53] Craddock explained that the village-tract headmen had become so much the mainstay of governmental administration at the local level that he felt obliged to reject the fairly plausible and theoretically desirable suggestion to make the headmanship itself an elective office. Such a move, he felt, would be "to court disaster by putting too great a strain on . . . existing institutions." [54] The governor's claiming the headman as an ally of the government and excluding him from the locally elected boards had the unfortunate result of setting up the village *thugyi* as a vulnerable political target for emerging nationalist sentiment to attack.

The powers of the representative aspects of the central provincial government under Craddock's scheme were to remain severely limited until such time as experience and political education were gained and the novice electorate could be made more fully aware of the duties and privileges of citizenship. A two-thirds majority of the assembly

[52] *PP,C*, vol. XXXV for 1920 (Cmd. 746), pp. 9–12; Great Britain, Burma Reforms Committee, *Report* (1922; hereafter cited as *BRCR*), A. Frederick Whyte, Chairman, p. 7. Hugh Tinker (*Foundations of Local Self-Government . . . in Burma*, pp. 112–115) points out that Burman national consciousness flared in anger and wounded pride at the inference of inferiority and backwardness in the British spokesman's reference to Burma's "loyal, simple-minded folk, with their beautiful clothes."

[53] Elected village committees might include the headman, but it was thought too risky to permit headmen to become involved in politics.

[54] *PP,C*, vol. XXXV for 1920 (Cmd. 746), p. 13: "The headman . . . cannot be regarded simply as the spokesman of the people of his tract. He has been invested with . . . powers and responsibilities . . . as an executive officer. . . . The wishes of the people are usually consulted, but the ultimate . . . responsibility for his nomination rests with the Deputy Commissioner. . . . The present system . . . will therefore remain in force."

(elected members would make up only 61 per cent of the total) would be required to check legislation determined by the governor to be of central importance. Affirmative resolutions which the council might pass would have the legal effect of recommendations only, but the governor would agree not to disregard clearly expressed wishes of the council except in matters essential for maintaining order and security.[55]

For rural representation in the legislative council, one representative for each of the 31 council districts would be elected indirectly by members of their respective circle boards acting in conjunction with members of municipal committees of the smaller towns not included in direct urban representation.[56] Craddock explained rather untactfully that direct elections were not feasible because Burman voters would be inclined to be too much influenced by partisanship, friendship, or personal interest, which would allegedly tend to conflict with public interest.[57]

The proposed 16 urban constituency representatives (19 as later decided) were finally apportioned 5 to Rangoon, 2 to Mandalay, and one each to 12 single-unit areas composed of groupings of cities. Governor Craddock explained that the greater wealth, education, and progress of the towns justified their heavier representation, especially since conservative sentiment in rural areas was inarticulate. The governor's original scheme also provided for 20 communal constituencies for Indians, Europeans, Anglo-Indians, and Karens, plus one for the university. As revised by June, 1920, the elected communal representation benefited only the European and Anglo-Indian communities, 3 members all told. The Burma Chamber of Commerce, the Rangoon Trades Association, and the University constituencies also would each elect one representative. In addition to the 56 elected council members, 36 were to be appointed by the governor as follows: 20 officials, 14 nonofficials covering unrepresented minorities or interests, and 2 expert administrative advisers on finance and other technical matters.[58]

---

[55] *BRCR*, p. 3.

[56] The first proposal to let district councils choose one of their own number for the legislative council was modified in the June, 1919, revision. See *PP,C*, XXXV for 1920 (Cmd. 746), pp. 3–4.

[57] *Ibid.*, pp. 9–12; *BRCR*, pp. 2–3. It was also anticipated that such rural representatives would probably not know English and hence would be unable to participate in the legislative assembly proceedings.

[58] *BRCR*, pp. 2–3; *PP,C*, vol. XXXV for 1920 (Cmd. 786), pp. 13, 16–19, 35.

To take the place of the old executive council of the governor, Craddock devised a novel plan under which 4 high-salaried nonofficial "apprentice Ministers" would be appointed presidents of 4 executive boards, one each for home affairs, revenue and finance, development, and local self-government. The development board alone would be required to have a European president. The respective boards themselves would include the ranking government officials concerned with the particular subjects of its concern. Routine professional matters would continue to be handled by official members, but any board president could, with the concurrence of the governor, overrule a decision of the board itself. A vote of no confidence by the legislative council in any board president could be grounds for the governor's request for that person's resignation. The presidents served at the governor's pleasure, of course, in any case, but it was anticipated that fuller powers would, in time, be accorded to the board presidents. The salaries to be paid those Burmans able to qualify as prospective executive ministers (4,000 rupees per month) [59] were fabulous according to Burman standards, but the incumbents would probably not be political leaders and would in any case enjoy no responsibility or authority to interfere administratively. This proposal was easily the most vulnerable aspect of the Craddock scheme and the first one to be abandoned.

The principal changes introduced into the June 2, 1919, revision of Craddock's scheme, aside from several already noted, were to reduce even more the nominal powers of the executive board presidents. It was specified that they would be consulted only on matters falling outside the routine powers presently exercised by heads of departments holding membership on the respective boards. The June 2 revision again affirmed that Burmans generally were indifferent to public affairs, citing the outdated report by Governor Butler's committee of seven Burmans in 1916 to the effect that the country was not ripe for general extension of the elective principle. Burma's political interest had arisen in 1917–1918, according to Craddock, only when national pride became involved and Burmans foresaw the possibility of being ruled by an Indian Government controlled by Indian politicians.[60]

Viceroy Chelmsford and the Government of India spent a leisurely

---

The original plan envisaged a council of only 75 members instead of 92 as revised in June, 1919.

[59] *PP,C*, vol. XXXV for 1920 (Cmd. 746), pp. 20–23.

[60] *Ibid.*, pp. 3–4, 39–50.

seven months studying the Craddock proposals. They criticized mainly the board president idea as conferring no real authority, and they questioned the elimination of an executive council exercising a measure of control. The two-thirds veto powers of the council were also criticized. Craddock reluctantly surrendered his board president idea and countered with the proposal that Indian legislation be extended to Burma only after consultation with the governor of Burma and its legislative council. He also proposed in further extension of the idea of separation that Burma's representatives not sit in the India Assembly and that the viceroy thereafter be entitled governor-general of India and Burma.[61]

Craddock was invited to New Delhi for conferences in early 1920. By March 25, a final version of the proposed reform was agreed upon, declaring that Burma's political development was a generation behind India's and that a constitution on the India model could not, therefore, be imposed on Burma. The lack of a necessary foundation of political experience forbade forcing the pace in the erection of an elaborate superstructure looking toward responsible government. A constitution for Burma "analogous" to India's must, in any case, have regard for the relative stages of political development of the two countries. The report also proposed that the district councils should delegate powers to circle boards and then supervise their exercise, that legislative council elections be by indirect voting as originally planned, and that legislation should proceed under rules similar to those provided for India. Since it was assumed (quite gratuitously) that no Burmans for years to come could be found capable of performing the functions of a minister, several nonofficial Burmans in the interim period should be associated, by governor's appointment, with a new executive council composed of three two-member departmental committees to be set up.[62] The final version of the joint proposal was printed as a Parliamentary White Paper in June, 1920.

The reform proposals thus developed at Rangoon and New Delhi over so many months were actually stillborn. During the prolonged interim, the Secretary of State for India and the Joint Committee for India reforms, acting on the basis of representations by a Burman delegation sent to London in 1919, had already committed the British Government to a Burman constitution "analogous to India's." [63] During the interim, also, rapid political developments within Burma an-

[61] *Ibid.*, pp. 4–5.   [62] *Ibid.*, pp. 5–6; BRCR, pp. 4–5.
[63] Moscotti, pp. 62–65.

tagonistic to Craddock's personality and point of view had greatly prejudiced the outcome. The measure of Governor Craddock's embittered frustration over such interference was indicated in his subsequent acid comment as follows: "Never was a country and its people more untimely ripped from the womb of political progress than Burma, when Mr. Montagu with his magical midwifery across the Bay of Bengal, started to disturb them from their placid contentment." [64]

Burmese Rejection of the Craddock Proposal, 1918–1920

Although Burma's desire for separation from India as represented by the spokesman of the Y.M.B.A. at Calcutta in December, 1917, was quite genuine, the same leaders shortly thereafter became even more concerned lest Burma be denied the benefits promised to India. These fears seemed to be confirmed by the recommendations of the original Craddock scheme. Moderate elements of the Y.M.B.A.[65] advocated acceptance of the Craddock proposal, but they were quickly pushed aside by the more dynamic younger faction led by U Ba Pe and U Thein Maung. A series of mass meetings was sponsored by the Y.M.B.A., in February, May, and August, 1919, at which the decision was reached to send a delegation to London to protest the Craddock scheme, the revision of which was at the time in process of secret consideration by New Delhi and London. Some £2,000 were raised for the trip, and U Ba Pe, U Tun Shein, and U Pu were selected as the delegation. The last-named delegate, U Pu, represented the newly organized Burma Reform League. They left for England in July, 1919. Burman opinion by August had come around to the view as determined by a mass meeting held at Jubilee Hall, Rangoon, that the country should be included in the India reform program if the alternative was to be such as Craddock had proposed.[66]

[64] Sir Reginald Craddock, *Dilemma in India* (London, 1929), p. 109, and *Speeches*, pp. 245–250, 304–309, 333–340. Craddock denounced the political activity of the Y.M.B.A. and alleged that the Burmese delegation to London was Indian-subsidized. His statement at a Rangoon durbar, August 8, 1919, ran as follows: " 'Young Burma' seems to think it has the monopoly, first, of deciding what the scheme should be and secondly for appropriating all the privileges, authority, and responsibility which the scheme confers. . . . But the young have not the monopoly of brains, nor of shrewdness, nor of patriotism."

[65] The moderate Tu-Tha-Thin faction was led by U Ba Tu, U Po Tha, and U Thin. See Moscotti, pp. 21–28; N. C. Sen, *A Peep into Burma Politics (1917–1942)* (Allahabad, 1945), p. 8.

[66] U Chit Hlaing presided over the mass meeting on August 17, 1919, which filled Jubilee Hall and necessitated holding three overflow meetings. The London delegation represented the General Council of Young Men's Buddhist and Allied Asso-

The Burmese delegation was only partially successful in getting its viewpoint across to interested parties in the British Government, for London was busy with other matters. At first it could only stage press conferences and make contact with Labour Party members of Parliament. Finally the delegation got an interview with Secretary Montagu and a brief hearing before the Joint Select Committee in charge of formulating the India Reform Bill. They repeated all of the favorable things that Craddock had said about Burma's prospects, adding claims for widespread education plus pride of country and race. They obtained from Secretary Montagu a vague assurance that Burman opinion would be consulted before any bill affecting Burma would be brought before Parliament. The Joint Committee turned a deaf ear to the delegation's plea that Burma be included in the India Bill, claiming that it was too late. It did issue an important public statement on November 17, 1919, advising against including Burma but expressing no doubt that the Burmese deserved and would receive "a constitution analogous to India's."

It was this Joint Committee's obiter dicta concerning Burma's governmental future to which Craddock objected most strongly. The Burmese finally persuaded a Labour Party member to introduce, on December 3, a motion to include Burma in the India Bill, but the motion was withdrawn on the basis of assurances from Montagu that Burma could later either become a governor's province in India or await the passage of a different constitution during the 1920 sessions of Parliament.[67] The delegation started home at the end of the year. They faced the task of making Burma's wishes more definite and articulate for later and more effective presentation to the Parliament and to Burma's friends in Britain. They were welcomed as conquering heroes upon their return to Rangoon in early 1920. Cheering throngs pulled their carriage from the dock through the streets.

On learning that the revised Craddock–Government of India memorandum concerning the Burma reforms had been sent to London in March, 1920, and would be reproduced as a White Paper to be used as a basis for Parliament legislation, the Y.M.B.A. and kindred

---

ciations, including the Burma Reform League, the Upper Burma People's Association, and the Moulmein Burma Association. See *ISCR*, XVII, 395–397; Manchester *Guardian*, Aug. 25, 1919.

[67] *ISCR*, XVII, 395–398; *BRCR*, pp. 3–4; Craddock, *Dilemma in India*, pp. 115–118.

associations hurriedly dispatched a second delegation to London in late May, 1920. This was done before Burmese nationalist demands had time to become fully crystallized. The new delegation, composed of U Thein Maung and two members of the first delegation, U Ba Pe and U Pu, reached London in July, 1920. It was at this juncture that the Congress Party in session at Nagpur made a concession in recognition of Burma's autonomy by constituting it one of the twenty-one provinces of the Congress Party Organization.[68]

The three Burmans in London attacked the revised Craddock scheme as being in no way analogous to the Indian reforms and charged bad faith on the part of its sponsors. They demanded Burma's separation from India under a dyarchy constitution, including a bill of rights. They challenged the aspersions of Craddock to the effect that democracy was unsuited to Burma and that men of ability were not available to man a government. Participation in local government through district councils lacking any real responsibility to an electorate was not, they insisted, training in self-government.[69] Members of the delegation were gratified to learn from Secretary Montagu, at a private interview on August 12, that he also disliked important aspects of the Burma-India proposals, particularly the system of indirect elections and the complete absence of ministerial responsibility to the legislative council. Subsequently the delegation received from Burma and forwarded to Montagu an enormous Burmese petition asking for separation from India under a different but analogous constitution.

Annoying delays ensued. Montagu fell ill, and the Burman question had to compete for attention with Parliament's consideration of the troublesome Irish constitution, Russian relations, the Punjab riots (Amritsar), and such urgent domestic problems as coal and unemployment. The delegation prompted various opposition members of Parliament to question Secretary Montagu repeatedly on the reasons for the delay in reaching a conclusion with respect to Burma. One inquiry concerned London's recent decision to found a newspaper in Burma to explain the government's policies. Another asked whether Montagu could not postpone the Indian elections (about to be boycotted in Burma), so that new elections could be held under more

[68] Marshall Windmiller, "Linguistic Regionalism in India," *Pacific Affairs*, XXVII (1954), 296–297.

[69] *ISCR*, XVIII, 397–398. Similar Burman arguments transmitted by mail to a friend in Parliament (Mr. Lawson) were actually presented before the Commons on May 18, 1920. See *PD,C*, 5th ser., vol. 129 (Dec. 13, 1920), pp. 1432–1433.

acceptable rules. The Secretary gave the several questioners little satisfaction.[70]

London's eventual decision to include Burma within the dyarchy system of India seems to have been arrived at more or less by default for lack of an acceptable alternative. The Craddock scheme was almost as unacceptable to London as to the Burmans, and all interested parties recognized that formulation of a separate alternative bill would be time-consuming and would probably not result in granting political rights which extended in any way beyond those already accorded to India. London newspaper rumors that dyarchy rights were to be given to Burma were challenged as premature by Montagu in October. But on December 9, Labour Party friends of the delegation finally obtained from the Secretary a statement to the effect that a short bill would be introduced during the forthcoming session of Parliament to include Burma within the scope of the Indian reforms.

A more complete statement of London's intentions came on December 13.[71] It was issued in the face of expressions of doubt on the part of Conservatives that the visiting Burman delegation really represented Burmese opinion and other suggestions that the situation had better be examined afresh locally. Montagu declared that the revised alternative scheme prepared by the Governments of Burma and India was not satisfactory, but that the differences between India and Burma made it impossible without making further inquiry to extend the India Act to Burma by notification as provided under section 15. The moot questions concerned principally the franchise provisions and the selection of subjects to transfer to Burman ministers who, under dyarchy, would be responsible to the council. He did not anticipate that any great delay would be involved, however, and promised that a short bill bringing Burma under the India Act with appropriate amendments would be introduced in the next session of Parliament. At any rate, the end result seemed assured.[72]

[70] PD,C, 5th ser., vol. 134 (Nov. 17 and 24, 1920), p. 1899, vol. 135 (Dec. 8 and 9, 1920), pp. 404, 441, 2072.

[71] PD,C, 5th ser., vol. 136, pp. 133–141.

[72] BRCR, pp. 4–5. In general Labour members supported Burma's cause, while Conservative M.P.'s warned of rising resentment on the part of British residents of Burma. The Burma Reforms Committee headed by Sir A. Frederick Whyte was appointed in 1921 to work out moot details. Parliamentary friends of the Burmese delegation during the November–December, 1920, sessions also were prompted to question the government concerning Burman representation on the rice-control advisory board and the issue concerning the evacuation of pagoda hill in Rangoon.

The Burman deputation left London satisfied with its accomplishments and convinced that any effort at the time to tack on to the dyarchy reforms a new provision for separation of Burma from India would only entail indefinite delay without appreciable gains, whereas Burma's association with the India Act could be simply and expeditiously accomplished.[73] On its arrival at Rangoon in early 1921, the delegation was destined to encounter a political situation far different from the one they had left in the previous May.

By the time London's decision to include Burma under the dyarchy reforms had been reached—a solution which was liberal and generous from the British point of view—the political atmosphere within Burma had shifted amazingly in the direction of violent revolutionary protest. Several new ideas concerning reform had been set forth in a sweeping demand formulated during the summer of 1920 and asking for direct elections based on taxpayer suffrage for at least four-fifths of the legislative council. A model for a Burma Free State (*Myanma Shwe Pyigyi*) had been discovered in the Irish Free State Constitution. Burmans had also become interested in the Bill of Rights contained in the new Philippines constitution. The new Burman demands included: (1) legislative control of the budget under dyarchy, (2) at least two ministerial posts to be held by Burmans responsible to the council, (3) election of the president and vice-president of the council by that body itself. Majority opinion would forego separation from India rather than risk delay in passing a separate bill which might be similar to the Craddock scheme, but Burmans would otherwise by-pass control by India as far as possible. They asked that Burma's foreign policy and defense be put directly under the viceroy, that Burma's governor be chosen from England and be a man with parliamentary experience, and, finally, that a royal commission visit Burma to study its problems directly.[74] Some persons acquainted with liberal Western ideas had obviously been doing some study and thinking on their own. A member of the Y.M.B.A. within the legislative council meanwhile got that body to approve a resolution demanding reforms for Burma equal to those enjoyed by a major province of India.[75]

See *PD,C*, vol. 134 (Nov. 17 and 24, 1920), pp. 52, 341–343, 402, 1864, vol. 135, pp. 1265, vol. 136, pp. 133–141.

[73] *ISCR*, XVII, 397–399.   [74] *Ibid.*, pp. 398–407.

[75] Moscotti, p. 65. This action occurred during the negotiation of the so-called Meston Settlement for Burma's financial autonomy, allocating to Burma 6½ per cent of the total India debt.

By mid-1920, time was already running out on the chance of devising any plan in London that aroused Burman nationalism would now accept with more than grudging acquiescence. The continued delay which actually ensued in reaching any decision seriously aggravated the problem. In 1919–1920, surveillance of Burmese political activity had added an enormous additional burden to the already-overworked Burma police force and its secret Criminal Investigation Department.[76] From 1920 to 1922, political agitation ceased to be the exclusive concern of the Burmese Western-oriented intelligentsia. The popular revolution for political freedom had begun.

[76] *RPA* for 1919–1920, pp. 35, 311.

VII

Nationalism as a
Popular Movement

POLITICAL developments in Burma moved rapidly from 1920 to 1923. What had been in 1919 the concern of the membership of a few score urban branches of the Y.M.B.A. and kindred youth groups spread with amazing speed to encompass the school population, a considerable proportion of the Buddhist *Sangha,* and the residents of many of Burma's 17,000 village tracts. Nationalism thus became a grass-roots popular movement which the Westernized elite could no longer fully direct or control.

The University Act of 1920

One of the most unfortunate misunderstandings that developed between the British rulers and the hypersensitive Burmese nationalists during the period of growing ferment concerned the University Act. A university committee, of which J. G. Rutledge and Mark Hunter, the superintendent of public instruction, were leading members, undertook the task of establishing proper standards for the proposed University of Rangoon by stiffening the high school final and college entrance examination systems and by keeping the university as free as possible from political influence. The governing bodies, as planned, were to be the university council and senate, both of which were to be free from governmental interference except in the unlikely contingency that the legislative council would refuse to vote funds for the university.

The university committee felt that the deficiencies in the standards of preparatory schools could best be rectified by requiring most of the beginning university students to spend a year in probationary residence.[1] It was also proposed that a more exacting standard for grading the high school final examinations be introduced. The proposed act itself provided for a unitary residential university in preference to a federated one in which the teaching colleges might be scattered and the university center would function mainly as the examining body. Qualitative gains, it was felt, would overbalance the restriction on the number of students able to attend the university (875 Burmans were enrolled in Calcutta in 1919), since the pressure to relax standards would probably come from the large number of poorly qualified students seeking entrance. A preview of what was in store came with the action of the intermediate (second-year) university examining boards in the spring of 1920 in sharply reducing the percentage of passes issued from 68 per cent to 40 per cent for B.A. students and from 74 per cent to 45 per cent for B.S. students.[2]

On August 1, 1920, a mass meeting was convened in Rangoon under the sponsorship of the Y.M.B.A. with some 400 persons in attendance, including a number of *pongyis*. Burman objections to the proposed University Act, already approved in New Delhi and London, were set forth in a series of resolutions. Why, it was asked, was the act being pushed through the legislative council in such undue haste without bothering to consult Burmese opinion? U May Oung was explicitly challenged for having seconded the measure in the council. The meeting cited a deprecatory remark by Governor Craddock to the effect that Burma had too few university graduates to govern itself and asked whether Mark Hunter's ideas regarding higher standards and a residential university were not deliberately calculated to keep that number low. Another resolution complained that Burman representation on the controlling bodies (5 members only in a council of 46, one of them appointed by the head of the *Sangha*, and 2 of 24 in the senate) was far too meager to reflect the wishes of the people. The probationary-year idea was roundly denounced, as was the resolution which favored raising the high school (tenth standard) requirements, especially in English, and making all who graduated from high school eligible to enter the university. The meeting concluded that

[1] Great Britain, Burma Reforms Committee, *Record of Evidence* (hereafter cited as *BRCE*), III (London, 1922), 55–64.
[2] *RAB* for 1918–1919, pp. 124–127, for 1919–1920, pp. xiv–xv, 174–177.

Mark Hunter should be fired and that his alleged restrictions forbidding teachers and students to attend public meetings and to read newspapers in school should be abolished.[3]

The University Act was nevertheless duly passed by the council on August 28, 1920. Governor Craddock, the chancellor, was scheduled to preside over the formal opening of the university in early December. Thus began a controversy of portentous political significance, which produced the first open clash between national student disaffection and governmental authority.

Indian Political Influence

During the autumn of 1920, the boycott agitation sponsored by the Gandhi-led Indian National Congress made its first serious impact on Burma.[4] Trouble had started in India, following the tragic Amritsar massacre incident of April 13, 1919. Some 6,000 to 10,000 cornered and defenseless persons meeting at Amritsar in defiance of police orders were fired upon point-blank by 50 soldiers under orders of General Dyer until their 1,650 rounds of ammunition were exhausted. Hundreds of dead and at least 2,000 wounded resulted. It was in large measure this event, condoned by too many Englishmen in India, which apparently destroyed Indian confidence in British good faith and drove Gandhi into the political arena. It also led to the rejection of Secretary Montagu's not illiberal dyarchy reform scheme set forth in the India Act of 1919, which otherwise might have received an appreciative welcome from many Indians. After Amritsar no constitution which left in the hands of provincial governors the most important ministries controlling the police and military was acceptable to Indian opinion.

After consideration of the various alternatives available, the Indian Congress Party in 1920, discounting London's assurances that dyarchy was experimental and would be reviewed after ten years, adopted Gandhi's policy of full nonco-operation. It accordingly moved to boycott the fall elections for both the provincial legislative councils and the central Council of State under the new constitution.[5] It was the Indian effort to obtain Burma's co-operation in boycotting the first re-

[3] Rangoon *Gazette*, Aug. 2, 1920.

[4] *RAB* for 1918–1919, p. 40. Police surveillance of Indian agitators began in 1918–1919, but the rapidity of developments in 1920–1921 caught the Burma authorities entirely by surprise. See *RAB* for 1920–1921, pp. xix–xx.

[5] W. Norman Brown, *The United States and India and Pakistan* (Cambridge, Mass., 1953), pp. 74–76, 78, 92.

form election of October, 1920, that brought the two nationalist movements together.

One grievance raised by the Burman nationalist leaders of the Y.M.B.A., which sponsored the election boycott, was that, in the absence of a reform scheme applicable to Burma, the country would have to vote for its representatives in the New Delhi Council under the severely restricted franchise regulations of 1909. Since very few Burmans were eligible to vote in any case, the boycott was easily applied. In vain did the Burman delegation in London appeal to Secretary Montagu to revise the election rules for Burma and to authorize later Burman elections for the council in India.[6] The substantive question involved was not significant because Burma's participation in the New Delhi Council was unimportant. But the psychological impact made by the first application of the boycott technique was sharpened by the feeling that, suffrage-wise, Burma was being discriminated against.

During November, 1920, following the boycott agitation, strikes were in the air at Rangoon, with mob spirit and some intimidation in evidence. Local grievances concerned such matters as bus fares, the price of tea, and agitation sympathetic to the national (nongovernment) school program in India. Near the end of November, the American Baptist Mission's Cushing High School experienced a strike arising out of disagreement over the length of a holiday declared in connection with observance of the Buddhist light festival marking the end of the lenten season. Once having walked out, the strikers raised the grievance that Christian chapel programs at Cushing had included religious references not flattering to Buddhism.[7] This strike was nearing settlement when it was engulfed by the university boycott.

The idea of boycotting the university apparently originated with the same Young Burma group which had sponsored the August meeting of protest. Behind it also was the hostility engendered by the pro-

[6] *PD,C*, 5th ser., vol. 133 (Dec. 8, 1920), p. 2072.

[7] American Baptist Foreign Mission Society (hereafter cited as ABFMS), MS. *Correspondence from the Burma Mission*, L. W. Hattersley to J. C. Robbins, Dec. 5 and 11, 1920, sent from Cushing High School, Rangoon. In denying the boys a Buddhist holiday vacation, the principal was trying to stiffen the allegedly overlax disciplinary situation. Previous to this time, Buddhist parents sent boys to Cushing, where the Bible and Christianity were openly taught, caring little so long as the missionaries did not baptize them. By 1920, lay Buddhists generally were repudiating the monastic schools as being inadequate for educational needs. The Cushing strike was settled by a committee of parents and Burman elders meeting with the principal. See also Tinker, pp. 260–261.

posal of the Imperial Idea Committee in 1916 to make the schools serve as propaganda media for Burma's loyal continuance in the empire.[8]

The University Strike and the National School Movement

The university strike began on December 4, 1920, three days after the new university was originally scheduled for its official opening and two days before Chancellor Craddock, politically an unfortunate choice, was to have presided over its formal dedication. The instigation of the strike came primarily from outside the resident university student body, which personally was in the favored position of having already met the entrance requirements and the residential regulations. The students' only material grievance was the probationary year's requirement for all except the brighter students, but virtually no one had applied to take the preliminary college course. Student enthusiasm for the strike was therefore lacking at the outset. The plea of the boycott leaders was that the University Act had been forced on the country against the wishes of the people and that, since the Burman political leaders in the council had not prevented its passage, it was incumbent on the youth to "smash" it. Reluctant students were eventually forced into line by patriotic pleas and by insistence that all must stand together.[9] Within a few days the strike was almost 100 per cent effective, and the university authorities were at their wits' end to decide what to do about it.

Most of the striking students assembled in the vicinity of the Shwe Dagon pagoda, where they were housed in quarters vacated by monks. The strike, once started, attracted considerable support from Burmese parents and schoolmasters, as well as from political leaders. Indian agitators were also making a concerted effort to foment noncooperation and defiance of all authority. The university strikers were provided with food as well as shelter; eventually they developed their own organization and picketing system. A faltering effort was made to continue classes at the pagoda quarters, with older students instructing the younger. A date line set by the university senate for the

[8] *RAB* for 1920–1921, p. 181. The principal of University College testified that student activities continued, right up to the day of the boycott, without any overt evidence of unrest.

[9] *RAB* for 1920–1921, p. 81; *ABFMS, MS. Correspondence,* Hattersley to Robbins, Dec. 11, 1920; American Baptist Mission Field Secretary (hereafter cited as ABMFS), *Annual Report* for 1920–1921, p. 27. Pleas to try out the proposed university regulations before denouncing them fell on deaf ears.

return of strikers without penalty was without effect except to encourage overt student resignations. The government eventually issued
a reasoned explanation of its position, calmly and frankly stated, but
too late to have any effect. It was not long before the student unrest,
under stimulus from Indian agitators, shifted to a demand for complete home rule for Burma and to a denunciation of dyarchy reforms,
which the Burman delegation, homeward bound from London, had
just succeeded in obtaining for Burma.[10]

Starting from Rangoon, the strike movement spread during the
early months of 1921 to all government schools as well as to several
score aided schools including a number operated by the American
Baptist Mission. Editors and monks eventually entered the picture by
advocating not only a national university but a complete system of
national schools free from British support and control. Handbills and
other propaganda items were distributed urging students to quit all
government-aided schools, and a subscription of 1.5 million rupees
was collected to start the new system. The Central Council of the
Young Men's Buddhist Associations, which was in control of strike
policy, changed its name at the time to the General Council of Burmese
Associations (G.C.B.A.). The more inclusive title was calculated to
enlist Christian and non-Buddhist (Indian) nationalist support. The
decision of the G.C.B.A. to set up a system of "national schools" carried terrific finality behind it. It was obvious to informed observers in
early January that nothing short of financial collapse would end the
nationalist educational experiment.[11]

In the course of the strike, two distinct movements, one political
and the other educational and cultural, coalesced. Stimulation from
the outside included the powerful political contagion of the Gandhian
movement in India, coupled with contemporaneous revolutionary developments in China, Turkey, and the Philippines. From within Burma
increasing uncertainty and distrust regarding London's intentions as
to Burma's new constitution added psychological fuel to the flames.
Political unrest was also rooted in immediate disgust on the part
of educated Burmans over the inadequate and outdated electorate
which was authorized to vote in the initial boycotted Indian Council
elections. Against such a background, allegations raised by Indian
agitators to the effect that the whole British scheme of reform was

[10] ABMFS, *Annual Report* for 1921, p. 27; ABFMS, *MS. Correspondence*, Ray-
mond Currier to J. C. Robbins, from Rangoon, Feb. 27, 1921.
[11] ABFMS, *MS. Correspondence*, Currier to Robbins, Jan. 10, 1921.

a hypocritical farce gained credence in Burmese minds. Thus the Indian-instigated nonco-operation movement against the new constitution was already in a fair way to capture Burma when the furor over the University Act arose in the latter half of 1920.

The political grievance behind the university strike was the conviction that the British had decided to give Burma a second-class constitution on the basis of the country's small number (less than 400) of university degree holders and had then decided to perpetuate this disability by abruptly raising the standards of instruction and removing them from possible Burmese alteration. Hence the repudiation of the University Act and the launching of the movement for national schools. The more promising lads who cast their lot with the strikers did so at considerable personal sacrifice. They knew that such rebellious action would cut them off from consideration for lucrative civil service jobs, which were at the disposal of the British. In an act of personal abnegation many of them actually pledged never to enter the civil services. An understanding missionary observer commented confidentially as follows:

No one with democratic sympathies . . . in his heart can fail to be immensely stirred by the whole thing. Mistaken and extravagant as it is in some of its phases, it yet breathes the air of mountain tops and calls to the imagination brilliant pictures of an uncertain but . . . wonderful future. Some of its best motives and ideals are Christian and some of its . . . most ardent members have been Christian boys, who . . . have returned to college only because they feel the futility of the present methods. Their hearts are still devoted to the "New Burma." [12]

[12] *Ibid.* The principal of Cushing High School in Rangoon also wrote as follows (Hattersley to Robbins, Dec. 19, 1920, and March 13, 1921): "The new generation of children in Burma is better educated than their parents. Burman parents never did discipline their children any too well. Now we see them entirely losing hold of their children. . . . Even those parents who agree with us [in opposing the strike] are for the most part helpless. [Only] if the boys should take a notion to come back would they do so. . . ."

"It is terribly impressive to visit Bahan . . . at the base of the Shwe Dagon pagoda . . . . There the boys [whose homes are in the districts] are camped about 1300 strong. . . . They are wasting their time . . . many of them engaging in vice. . . . Each school of Rangoon has its own *zayat* or rest bungalow, fine brick buildings . . . [which] the priests have vacated. . . . They have no board to pay, as the public provides lavish gifts for these poor boys who are [allegedly] suffering so severely in a good cause."

"The miserable part of the situation is that in large part we feel deep sympathy with the strikers. Many of the things they desire we also desire. . . . We want to hold the love of our boys. . . . But on the other hand we cannot condone lawlessness."

Mission school officials in centers other than Rangoon whose work was upset by politically motivated strike agitation had little or no sympathy for the program of national schools and for the political factors behind it.[13] The Burma Baptist Convention (all indigenous Christian groups) in October, 1921, acclaimed the newly promised privileges of democratic self-government as being in agreement with Christ's teachings. The convention urged all leaders to spread information concerning the proposed reform scheme and to aid the government in making it a reality.[14]

Except in a few centers like Rangoon where considerable financial support could be mobilized, the national schools encountered insuperable difficulties. Many of them met in *pongyi kyaungs* where desks, maps, and other necessary equipment were lacking. Sponsors also made the impossible promise to put their pupils through the ten standards in about five years. Discipline was almost entirely lacking, and large numbers of so-called students roamed about rebellious of all authority.[15] In many localities, monks who were obscurantist in terms of modern learning acted as teachers while using their influence to persuade Buddhist families to desert rival government and mission schools. The strike held pretty well during 1921. But thereafter national spirit proved to be no substitute for trained teachers, school facilities, and operating expenses.

Most of the national schools were discredited before the end of 1922.[16] The better students, especially those prepared to sit for their government high school and middle school final examinations, tended to return first. A fairly high percentage (63 per cent) of the reduced number of tenth standard candidates passed their high school examinations in 1921, and most of them were admitted to the university without requiring the probationary year's work. The proposed National University never got started at all. The Baptist College (later Judson College) recovered quickly its prestrike enrollment and by 1922 moved

[13] See ABFMS, *MS. Correspondence* from Henzada and Pyinmana, and ABMFS, *Annual Report* for 1921. Karen Christians generally did not share Burman political aspirations, and the policy of the mission was to oppose Christian participation in strike agitation and to stress the contributions which Britain was making at the time to improve Burma's government.

[14] ABMFS, *Annual Report* for 1921, p. 23.

[15] ABFMS, *MS. Correspondence,* Hattersley to Robbins, March 13, 1921.

[16] *Ibid.,* Annual report by John E. Cummings from Henzada mission, Dec. 23, 1921, and one by George Josif of the American Baptist Mission school at Pyinmana, June 4, 1921.

well ahead (195 students vs. 138 in 1921).[17] University College recovered less rapidly, but the best students who wanted an education returned.[18]

The political effects of the university strike and the abortive national schools movement were, nevertheless, incalculable. They marked the birth of revolutionary nationalism in Burma. December 4, "National Day," was eventually designated a holiday. The educational agitation brought the teaching *pongyis* into the national movement as never before, and a fateful pattern was developed for using the university and the schools as instruments of political opposition. These developments reversed completely the plans and expectations of Governor Butler's Imperial Idea Committee of 1916–1917 to make the schools serve imperial ends. When the visiting Parliamentary Burma Reforms Committee took evidence on constitutional questions in November, 1921, even those moderate Burman spokesmen who cooperated with it in defiance of the G.C.B.A. boycott reflected the popular discontent regarding education. They insisted that theoretical standards within the schools must not be allowed to take precedence over the interests of the Burman youth and that the Education Department must therefore be placed under Burman control. One spokesman declared that it was folly at a time of rising political concern for the government to persist in its policy of saying: "We will give you what you require. We won't give you what you ask." [19]

New Political Issues: The Rice Control Board

Two relatively new political issues also arose during 1920–1921 to exacerbate nationalist feelings. One was the rather artificially petulant Burman demand that all military units be evacuated immediately from the area of the Shwe Dagon pagoda. The government's reasoned explanation that the transfer would be made as soon as new barracks at the Mingaladon cantonment were ready to receive the troops did not satisfy the complainants because it carried overtones of the British not wanting to be hurried. The troops were eventually moved. This issue was essentially psychological, not substantive.

The second issue was solidly economic, for it concerned criticism

[17] Judson College, *Annual Report, 1921–1922* (Rangoon, 1922).
[18] *RAB* for 1920–1921, pp. 179–182.
[19] *BRCE*, III (1922), 57–59, 61–63. The university representative, in reply, pleaded that the university must be allowed to develop for five to ten years free of political interference to enable it to adapt itself educationally to Burma's needs.

of the policy pursued following the end of the war by the government's Rice Control Board, which had assumed temporarily a monopoly of all rice exports. The controls had been established in 1918–1919 for the purposes of benefiting nonagricultural consumers by keeping the domestic price down and of preventing the realization of undue speculative profits on the part of millers and brokers engaged in the exporting business.[20] The purchase price of paddy intended for export was fixed at 180 rupees per 100 baskets in 1919–1920, whereas speculators managed to raise the uncontrolled domestic price to around 235 rupees. Most cultivators actually sold their crops for 150 rupees or less, which was barely sufficient to provide an incentive for the recovery of production.[21] By 1921, a very sizable profit of some 92 million rupees had accrued from the Control Board's sale of rice overseas, mainly in India, by taking advantage of the temporarily exorbitant world price.[22] Although the policy of denying the millers maximum profits was defensible, the operations of the Control Board policy had squeezed the cultivators and had served long-term British interests by preventing producers from expecting too high a price and by providing cheaper rice for the British-employed industrial labor, mainly Indian. Lower Burma cultivators and their moneylender creditors, both of whom had experienced very rough going during the wartime collapse of trade, took a dim view of government's policy of depressing prices and thus preventing agricultural interests from recouping wartime losses when the world market revived.

The practical question at issue in 1921 was who should determine how the windfall from rice exports should be spent. The Government of India, on the one hand, was insisting that the profits be spent outside of Burma, since the Indian consumer had paid most of the bill. On the other hand, Burman nationalists demanded Burmese representation on the Control Board to see that the disposition of the fund would benefit the allegedly exploited Burman cultivator. To nationalist political leaders the rice control policy appeared to be another example of how the British-dominated government consistently disregarded the viewpoint and interests of the Burmese population. They ignored the fact that rice-sale profits were actually spent on railways

[20] *RAB* for 1918–1919, p. iii.

[21] *RAB* for 1918–1919, p. 22, for 1919–1920, p. x, for 1920–1921, p. xiii. At the same time the level of rents increased by 50 per cent over that of 1918–1919.

[22] Ganga Singh, *Burma Parliamentary Companion* (Rangoon, 1940), p. 14. Paddy had sold for as low as 80 rupees in 1916.

222

and other useful development projects.[23] Complaint over the rice control policy, when joined to agitation against the capitation and *thathameda* tax exactions, provided a basis of common concern for local nationalist political organizations. Those sponsored by the G.C.B.A., called *Wunthanu Athins*, spread rapidly throughout rural Burma during 1921 and 1922.[24]

London had been but vaguely aware during 1921 of the rising political tension in Burma. Unfortunately, the official explanations of it received by His Majesty's India Office clearly did not agree with the version furnished by opposition members of Parliament who were in personal communication with Burman leaders. Parliamentary spokesmen friendly to the Burmans persistently, during 1921, questioned Secretary Montagu about what he proposed to do concerning various causes of political tension in Burma. The puzzled Secretary answered as best he could, but he admitted repeatedly that he had been unable to keep abreast of what was happening in Burma.[25] The formal channels of India Office communications via official agencies at Rangoon and New Delhi were obviously not keeping London adequately informed. The newly appointed Burma Reforms Committee was intended to give the Secretary and the Parliament a firsthand report on the situation.

The Burma Reforms Committee Investigation of 1921

The parliamentary committee sent to Burma in the fall of 1921 to investigate reform proposals was headed by Sir Frederick Whyte, the president of the Indian Legislative Assembly. The committee included two members of the Burma legislative council (Dr. San C. Po, who was a Karen, and U Myint), one Burman member of the governor's council of state (U Po Bye), an Indian member of the Legislative

[23] Moscotti, pp. 146–148. Some 22.5 million rupees from the rice fund were spent for railway construction; 27.5 millions were spent for roads, and the remainder for agricultural interests such as flood protection, waterway maintenance, water supply and irrigation projects, and veterinary services. A sizable sum (10 million rupees) went to bolster rural credit facilities. Railway branches from Moulmein to Ye (in Tenasserim) and from Pyinmana to Taungdwingyi were built.

[24] *RPA* for 1922, pp. 16–19. Note the revival of the term *athin*, which in old Burma had been applied to regimental royal-service units.

[25] Colonel Wedgwood and Mr. Swan were frequent questioners. See *PD,C*, 5th ser., vol. 139 (March 16, 1921), p. 1416, vol. 140 (April 6, 1921), p. 245, vol. 142 (May 1, 1921), p. 799, vol. 143 (June 27, 1921), p. 1809, vol. 147 (Nov. 3, 1921), p. 1953.

Assembly (P. P. Ginwala), the British editor of the Rangoon *Gazette* (Frank McCarthy), and a senior British government official (R. E. V. Arbuthnot).[26] The committee was selected with a view to enlisting public confidence, but its prospects of success were clouded by the decision of the G.C.B.A. made in August–September, 1921, and confirmed at a conference held at Mandalay in October, prior to Sir Frederick's arrival, to boycott the committee's sessions and to refuse all co-operation except where it might contribute to the speedy attainment of home rule. The words "within the Empire" were expressly deleted from the home rule resolution, which was the first overt action suggesting that Burma's independence was possible. This boycott policy was adopted in the face of Secretary Montagu's explicit assurances of 1920 that the basic demands presented by the Burman delegation to England would be met and also in spite of London's official announcement dated October 7, 1921, that Burma would be advanced to the status of a governor's province under the India Act of 1919.[27]

The Burma Reforms Committee discovered to its dismay upon arrival that, far from being appreciative of London's generous if belated concessions, most Burmans distrusted British intentions. Parliament's delay, combined with local grievances plus Indian nationalist agitation, had influenced a large proportion of the population to accept the allegations of political extremists.[28] Events had clearly outrun Britain's leisurely timetable. The assignment of several responsible ministries to Burmans under the dyarchy scheme did refute Burmese fears that they would get less than India, but this concession no longer satisfied nationalist aspirations. One factor was that Indians themselves had already rejected dyarchy. Actually the proposed reforms were bewildering and little understood. They fitted neither the needs nor the defined desires of the Burmese people, being in a sense "hasty, ill-planned paper schemes" adopted at London under political pressure.[29] The spokesmen for the G.C.B.A. now demanded complete home rule.[30]

Whyte's major objective was to secure for the Burmese as broad a franchise and as representative a legislative council as circumstances would permit. All elections would be direct. Lesser questions concerned minority representation in the council, the number of nomi-

[26] Sen, p. 13.
[27] Moscotti, pp. 23–26.
[28] *BRCE*, II, 132; *ISCR*, XI, 267–268.
[29] See Tinker, pp. 214–217, 244.
[30] *ISCR*, XI, 267–268. One section of the G.C.B.A. in 1921 favored contesting seats in the election and then abstaining from attending the council. Hence came a deviation from complete boycott of the dyarchy program.

nated official members, and the specific functions which should be transferred to responsible local ministers and from the Central Indian Government to Burman control.[31] The committee held hearings during November and December, 1921, in Rangoon, Mandalay, Moulmein, and Bassein. Societies and persons actively associated with the G.C.B.A. everywhere refused to testify. Considerable courage was required on the part of those who refused to be silenced by the boycott. The two most prominent Burman political figures to appear were U May Oung and U Ba Pe. Despite the conservative and partial character of the testimony obtained, the three volumes of evidence reveal much with respect to political trends.

On the moot question of whether or not to include forestry administration among the subjects to be transferred to a responsible Burman minister under the dyarchy plan, Burmese testimony was unanimously favorable. The people resented being excluded from working the forests; they regarded existing rules as unnecessarily strict; they believed that the situation would improve if a sympathetic Burman minister were in charge. European witnesses testified that damage to the forest reserves might occur, but most of them believed that the political risk of not acceding to popular wishes in this matter overweighed possible damage to the forests.[32] On the educational question, U May Oung urged that both Anglo-vernacular and European education, as well as vernacular, be included among the transferred subjects, since reserving control of education to the governor would only accentuate existing dissension. Political factors, he declared, again outweighed possible sacrifice of standards. Popular acceptance of the university would not be possible unless the people were left free to amend the Act of 1920.[33] A few British officials, among them J. S. Furnivall, went further to insist that political considerations dictated that everything that did not jeopardize Burma's order and security should be handed over.[34]

The subject that attracted least interest was the provision for elected circle boards and district councils in the area of local government, a

---

[31] BRCR, p. 1.

[32] The BRCE was published in three volumes. The Burman point of view is clearly revealed in I, 99, 265–268, II, 99–177, and III, 39–40. For British views, see III, 97–98, 189–194, 212, 218–219. The government spokesman, Mr. Ormsby-Gore, feared that relaxation of forestry controls would cause loss of revenue and that political pressure would imperil renewals of contracts and leases by large British firms, who alone could exploit the timber resources.

[33] BRCE, III, 50–52.　　　　　　[34] Ibid., pp. 218–219.

proposal which had appeared originally in Governor Craddock's scheme. A number of Burmans favored permitting village headmen to be candidates in political elections, even for the legislative council, but the sentiment on this score was not unanimous. Some complained that corruption at lower levels of the administration was widespread, and none expressed any enthusiasm for the proposed system of local self-government.[35] Mr. Furnivall leveled the most trenchant criticism when he declared that the proposed local bodies had no interest in administering such matters as sanitation and medical services and that it was folly to make them responsible for matters in which no public interest was manifested.[36]

A fairly wide difference of opinion developed over the question of the franchise. Most of the Burman witnesses favored restricting the voting to payers of land revenue up to a given amount, with no sex disqualification but with age limits fixed at twenty-one or twenty-five years.[37] Several asserted that the rural population was not interested in voting and that political interest centered almost exclusively in the cities of Lower Burma. One Burman judge thought that young Burmans were entirely too rash and wanted to move too fast. Some European witnesses agreed with the conservative Burmans that restriction of the suffrage was advisable. Others pointed out that the original Craddock proposal had itself mentioned the capitation and *thathameda* tax rolls as ready-made voting lists (but to be used for indirect elections) and that no other feasible intermediate standard existed on which to base a voting restriction.

Mr. Furnivall presented one of the strongest arguments against a broad franchise. He proposed that the right of suffrage be conditioned on the payment of a land tax of from 25 to 50 rupees and that the burden of proof be placed on those engaged in trades or business to make their own case for being included. Such a policy would restrict the voters to 1 million as compared to the 2.5 million expected to qualify under the capitation-*thathameda* requirement. He insisted that the additional 1.5 million would not know what they were voting for, that they might follow sane advice for a time, but that they would sooner or later respond to the bidding of some political or religious fanatic spouting absurd propaganda or magic. He foresaw that the resulting political movement could sweep the country like wildfire, and to no

---

[35] *BRCE*, I, 99–100, III, 16, 103, 105.   [36] *BRCE*, III, 222.

[37] U Ba Pe almost alone among the Burmans urged that tenants as well as landowners be allowed to vote (*BRCE*, II, 99–100).

good purpose. Furnivall insisted that manhood suffrage would therefore be inimical to the interests of the responsible politically conscious Burmans and would, if granted, make the maintenance of order and security by the government, however constituted, almost impossible.[38]

The same spokesman went even further to attack the reform proposals themselves. He declared that they were a "sham" precisely because they contained provisions for a suffrage far wider than the politically sophisticated Burmans themselves desired and were coupled with too severe restrictions on Burmese exercise of actual power. He proposed, instead, giving real power to moderate political leaders elected to the council on the basis of a restricted suffrage. He would then let those who clamored for home rule take the responsibility for broadening the franchise in response to developed popular agitation for the vote. The masses of Burma, he declared, lived in a different world from that of the political aspirants and would respond to other leadership than that of elected representatives in the council. If the Burman found that the vote he was being accorded got him nowhere, he was all the more likely to take up his dah and resort to direct action.[39] Events were to demonstrate the correctness of this analysis.

U May Oung commented on the vital necessity of lifting the reform movement immediately from the talking stage to something concrete, especially in view of the fact that any projected scheme would have to be experimental. Basic popular discontent, he insisted, was really rooted in poverty, and no amount of purely political reform would allay it. The important thing was to get a helpful program of economic and social reform under way. Europeans in Burma, he insisted, knew very little of what was going on in the Burman mind. Revolutionary sentiment stemmed from the growing feeling that an alien government, itself an oligarchy of color and opposed to the interests of the people, was responsible for worsening conditions. He agreed with Furnivall that the only means of bridging the gap between rulers and ruled and of promoting material betterment was for "Asians of substance and education" to be given a greater share in every branch of the adminis-

[38] *BRCE*, I, 40–41.

[39] *BRCE*, III, 219–222, 228–230. Mr. Furnivall summarized his position as follows: "Give real power to the Burman party and they will appreciate the need for security. . . . I advocate . . . in general the transfer of every subject that is not essential to security and . . . the grant of complete Home Rule as soon as the technical adjustments can be made. . . . We should be investing the Executive Council with the responsibility of introducing Home Rule on practical lines. Let us then cease to fight over the name Dyarchy and call the system Provisional Home Rule."

tration and for provincial subjects to be transferred immediately to Burman ministers. The masses, he insisted, did not need and were not asking for the legislative vote, but rather for a more understanding administration bent on improving their livelihood and living conditions.[40]

The other important issue examined by Whyte's Burma Reforms Committee concerned communal representation in the elected seats of the legislative council. With very few exceptions,[41] the Burman witnesses were most emphatic and unanimous in condemning special representation for minority groups. An important factor influencing the G.C.B.A. to boycott the committee hearings, it was revealed, was inclusion of one Karen, an Indian, and an Anglo-Indian member on the committee. If one group should claim special privileges, then all would demand them; unrepresented elements, Burmans insisted, could best be covered by nominated members. U May Oung in particular challenged the case for communal representation advanced by the Karen member of the committee by saying that Burmans were becoming aware of the need for a broadly national effort, and their willing co-operation with Karens would bridge the ethnic gap if given a little more time. Separate representation, on the other hand, would keep the two peoples forever apart.[42]

The two Burman members of the Whyte Committee itself, U Po Bye, at the time a member of the governor's council of state, and U Myint of the legislative council, found themselves unable to sign that part of the final report covering communal representation. U Po Bye contributed a meaningful explanation of their position. Whether within or outside the G.C.B.A., he declared, Burman opinion would make the decision respecting communal representation the touchstone of the *bona fides* of Britain's intentions. Minority representation in special constituencies meant "divide and rule" tactics and the negation at the very outset of the newly awakened national interest in political liberalism and co-operation under a common citizenship. Under British rule, he argued, Burma had become the happy hunting ground for the economically more experienced Indians, Chinese, and Europeans, with the Burmese everywhere and increasingly losing ground. The 500 branches of the G.C.B.A. represented the voice of the nation, which

[40] *Ibid.*, pp. 35–36.
[41] The most notable exception was J. A. Maung Gyi, an Anglicized Burman, who favored communal representation (*BRCE*, I, 265–268).
[42] *BRCE*, III, 52–53, 64, II, 99, 131, I, 276.

affirmed that reforms dedicated to the interests of the resident population in Burma must henceforth follow lines desired *by* them not those
determined *for* them on an entirely different basis. Peoples with permanent interests in Burma, he concluded, must therefore throw in their
lot with the Burmans in good spirit.[43]

The almost equally appealing case made for special Karen representation reflected their deep-seated distrust of Burman rule and their
complete divorcement from the newly developed spirit favoring Burman nationalist unity. Sidney Loo Nee declared that however much
the leaders of the two groups might cultivate mutual respect by co-
operative effort, Burman absorption of the Karens was outside the
range of possibility. Karen clannishness alone could, and would, preserve the race, for they knew what to expect from the return of Burman rule. Real toleration or equality was negated in practice by the
superior airs of the Burman people. He wanted British rule to continue
and a Briton to administer Karen educational affairs.[44] The Karen position found impressive support in the statement by the British deputy
commissioner of the border district of Thaton: "The man who says
Karen and Burman interests are identical is either blind, ignorant, or
untruthful. . . . If I were a Karen, I would fight for proper communal
representation; if I could not get it I would clear out for Siam." [45]

The final recommendations of the Whyte Committee can be briefly
summarized. Whyte conceded that Burma had gone through an aston-
ishingly rapid political evolution since 1919, to the point where politics
had become the preoccupation of Burmese and Europeans alike. Burma's omission from the constitutional progress of India had shocked
the pride of the nation even though parts of the Indian plan were felt
to have little relevance to Burman conditions. In the atmosphere of rising political concern and without achieving any real appreciation of
new proposals, dyarchy had already become in the popular mind the
actual enemy of home rule.[46] Because of the obvious difficulties in
applying the land tax standard for determining electoral rolls, the committee recommended the application of the household capitation and
thathameda taxes as the basis for the rural franchise. The existing
municipal tax rolls, based on payment of 4-rupee taxes, rental pay-

---

[43] *BRCR*, pp. 21–24.

[44] *BRCE*, I, 227–237, by Sidney Loo Nee.

[45] *BRCE*, II, 197–205, by D. F. Chalmers. The speaker cited, in support, specific
examples of abuse suffered by Karens at the hands of Burmese magistrates and
court officers in Thaton District.

[46] *BRCR*, pp. 5–6.

ments, or ownership of movable property, could be used for the urban areas. Candidates for office must be twenty-five years old but need not be residents of the district contested.[47] Since the inquiry had demonstrated that proportional representation was completely unfamiliar and unworkable in Burma, the majority of the committee agreed that communal representation would be required for Europeans and Anglo-Indians and that reserved seats should be set aside for Indians and Karens, seven for Indians and five for Karens. Representation in the council of the Burma (British) Chamber of Commerce and the Rangoon Trades Association would continue, such representatives to be joined by an elected Chinese business representative who would stand for the entire group, an elected Burmese Chamber of Commerce member, and an Indian member who would be nominated.[48]

The committee also advised that the ministries of forests and education (both European and Anglo-vernacular) should be added to those transferred subjects as defined in the India reform schemes. This concession was accompanied by a labored explanation for New Delhi's and London's benefit. Since the university already had autonomy, the authorities ought to be able to maintain proper standards without incurring the political liability of reserving the university to the governor's control. The only reason the committee refrained from recommending the transfer of a number of additional Central (New Delhi) items to provincial (Rangoon) control was to avoid the legislative delay which such an action would entail. They reported a strong and growing feeling that Burma's place within India was unsatisfactory and that the desire for separation was becoming daily more urgent.[49]

It was almost a year after the completion of the hearings of the Whyte Committee before Parliament passed the necessary enabling legislation to bring Burma within the scope of the India Act. It was not until January, 1923, that the dyarchy system was finally inaugurated. More than five years had elapsed since the Y.M.B.A. delegation first talked with Secretary Montagu at Calcutta in December, 1917. The reform was at best a makeshift, opportunist measure which had little relevance to Burma's wishes or needs. It was destined to prove futile in practice because it was incapable of tackling the country's urgent economic problems. The episode demonstrated among other things the difficulty of a distant and overburdened Parliament, however well intentioned, giving prompt and adequate attention to Burma's affairs, especially when the basic official information available to London was

[47] Ibid., pp. 8–11.   [48] Ibid., pp. 11–13.   [49] Ibid., pp. 16–19.

for so long transmitted through channels basically hostile to the reform effort.

U Ottama and the Pongyi Politicians

Nationalist agitation in Burma attained a new political and cultural dimension in 1921–1922 with the emergence of the *pongyi* politicians. A substantial beginning was made in developing this trend through the national schools effort already described, but this movement was destined to subside. A far more powerful impetus was contributed by the activities of the radical U Ottama, a political-minded Burman monk who had traveled widely in Eastern Asia during portions of the preceding decade. He arrived in Burma in 1921 from India, where he had become intimately acquainted with the activities and principles of the Indian National Congress.[50]

U Ottama was in reality a political agitator dressed in a monk's robe. His political potency derived from his remarkable effectiveness in haranguing his listeners on the idea that Buddhism was threatened with eclipse by an alien government. He insisted that the *pongyis* themselves must leave the monasteries to defend the faith. He combined this traditionalist appeal with the Gandhian nonco-operation techniques current in India.[51] Conservative elements within the *Sangha* rejected U Ottama even to the point of refusing him asylum, mainly because of his political fanaticism and his flagrant violation of canonical laws.[52] He was essentially an agitator rather than an organizer, but he enlisted a large and enthusiastic following among the younger monks. During 1921 he toured Burma attacking dyarchy, demanding home rule, inciting people to revolutionary violence, and predicting that France or America would come to Burma's aid.[53] The *pongyi* agitators appear to have attracted a very considerable personal following among the women of the villages. They captured control of many of the G.C.B.A.-sponsored village *athins*.[54]

U Ottama's arrest in 1921 on a charge of incitement to sedition and his conviction and sentence to ten months' imprisonment by a Burman

[50] Sen, pp. 14–15. U Ottama had traveled from Japan to India and had been for a period of time a student in Calcutta University. In India he had once been elected president of the Hindu Mabasabha organization.

[51] Moscotti, p. 16.

[52] Maung Maung Pye, *Burma in the Crucible* (Rangoon, 1951), pp. 13–14.

[53] Sen, pp. 15–17; Hinners, p. 29. From Henzada came word in 1922 that the Buddhist priests of the area had largely lined up with the nonco-operators. See ABMFS, *Annual Report* for 1922.

[54] *RPA* for 1922, pp. 18–19.

magistrate vastly increased his political influence. The furor served to ignite smoldering discontent, and he became the first martyr of the nationalist cause. When he was eventually released in 1922, he resumed where he had left off. He ran afoul of the police once more at a Mandalay meeting of the All-Burman Union in 1924 and was accordingly committed for a three-year prison term. Released again in 1927, he took up the antitax campaign until once more confined to jail, this time for good. He developed mental unbalance while in prison and eventually died in 1939.[55]

U Ottama did for nationalism in Burma part of what Gandhi did for it in India by transforming an essentially political problem into a religious one. But the approach was more crude. Buddhism was allegedly being attacked; the monks were being mistreated by police and courts; the dignity and pride of the Burman nation was, therefore, being outraged. His following included for a time a few of the truly venerable monks including the *Aletaya Sayadaw,* who later joined the so-called "21 Party." The political *pongyis* as a rule used prophesies and magic as well as direct agitation to turn the hatred of the people against the foreign government, the police and courts, the tax collector, and even the village headman. The weapon of boycott was also widely advocated. Pious monks faithful to their vows could do little to deter the extremists, who themselves achieved control over the General Council of *Sangha Sametggi* (Associations), organized in 1922. The G.C.S.S. was used to direct the *pongyi* political program.

Pongyi methods carried relatively little direct appeal to the less radical Westernized intelligentsia within the Y.M.B.A. and G.C.B.A. But such leaders sensed the massive power of the political ground swell generated by U Ottama. In contrast with the situation in India, where the Congress Party found its main support among the middle class and business and professional people, Burma had no such indigenous middle class.[56] If nationalist politicians in Burma wanted popular backing, they had little choice but to line up with the political *pongyis,* who alone swayed the village *Wunthanu Athins.* Since a monk's denunciation could ruin the standing of political aspirants, most of them sought religious support. Members of the newly elected legislative council often talked to *pongyi* leaders before voting on critical ques-

[55] Moscotti, pp. 42–43. A distinguished group of Burman barristers volunteered to defend U Ottama at his second trial.

[56] Guy Wint, "The Aftermath of Imperialism," *Pacific Affairs,* XXII (1949), 63–6.

tions.[57] The popular movement developed, on the whole, quite independently of the more progressive politicians. Men like U May Oung had no chance when competing against *pongyi* medievalism. Those who attempted to use the new governmental reforms to promote their country's liberation (and their self-aggrandizement as well), whether boycotters or co-operators, lined up *pongyi* support.[58] Eventually these political opportunists sacrificed popular confidence and in the 1940's left the political field to more radical youthful nationalists, bolder and more sincere, but not half so well educated. U Chit Hlaing, leader of the boycotting G.C.B.A., was an exception, for he sacrificed a personal fortune for the cause. He became for a time the "Uncrowned King of Burma." [59]

At the village level, where the headmen were forbidden, as officials and presumably allies of government, to participate in politics or to stand for election even to a circle board post, the political *pongyi* stepped in to fill the vacuum of leadership. In 1922 it was the *Sangha Sametggi* which co-operated with G.C.B.A. to boycott the Burma visit of the Prince of Wales.[60]

The Burma Government faced a bafflingly difficult task attempting to cope with the grass-roots disaffection which developed so rapidly in 1921–1922. Governor Craddock's caustic rejoinder that the yellow robe was losing its color and that the *pongyis* were sacrificing "the veneration of the ages for the nine days' applause of a gaping multitude" was an impolitic as it was ineffective. The government seemingly had no recourse except to resort to vigorous repressive measures against the radical political agitators whether in *pongyi* robes or not. The authorities used the temporary Rowlatt Act of 1919 (to run for three years), under which local government could require any individual suspected of revolutionary action or intent to post a bond and to restrict his movements, including arbitrary imprisonment for fifteen days. The Habitual Offenders Act of 1919 and the Criminal Tribes Act as amended in 1924 gave to the police further extraordinary powers of parole, control, and detention of suspects. Eventually, the special

[57] Maung Pye, pp. 13–16.

[58] Moscotti, pp. 27, 34–36, 152–153. U Ba Pe's *Sun* appealed for *pongyi* backing just as the other nonco-operators did.

[59] Maung Pye, p. 6; Wint, "The Aftermath of Imperialism," *Pacific Affairs*, XXII (1949), 66–67.

[60] Maung Pye, pp. 34–36. U Chit Hlaing of the G.C.B.A. and several other nationalist leaders were detained by the police during the course of the royal visit. At no time, however, did political disaffection in Burma reach the pitch of violence attained at the time in India. U Chit Hlaing was not a man of violence.

Burma Antiboycott Act of 1927, aimed more directly at political offenders, supplemented the standing rules against sedition and incitement to violence by levying severe penalties for promoting boycotts for purely political purposes. Press incitation to disloyalty and violence and the distribution of Indian political pamphlets were also listed as seditious offenses.[61]

Character and Activities of the Village Athins

The *Wunthanu Athins* ("own race" organizations) were set up as village political associations by the G.C.B.A. in 1921–1922 in an effort to bring public questions to the attention of the rural population. At the outset, they reflected also a measurably genuine popular concern to abolish official fraud and corruption, to suppress drinking, and to act collectively for the suppression of crime.[62] Even several high-placed British civil servants professed to see in the new organizations a potential means of mobilizing Burmese opinion in behalf of community welfare and the suppression of lawless activity and corruption. One divisional commissioner affirmed that unless popular initiative could be developed through some such agencies as the *athins* it was idle to dream of curbing vice, improving education, or developing a well-ordered *Sangha* monastic order. It was evident, he maintained, that religion had become so perverted by ignorance and fanaticism that it could now contribute but little to social integration. Unless positive encouragement could be given to the responsible village *athins*, therefore, the irresponsible *pongyis* and women politicians, who were the deadly enemies of constructive local initiative, would turn the *athins* into a political weapon of the fanatics.[63]

But the majority official opinion concerning the *athins* became increasingly negative. Political agitation was their sole sustenance, and this precluded co-operation with officials. Many of the *athins* degenerated into centers of political intrigue and agencies concerned mainly with protecting fellow members from punishment by police or courts.[64] Some fell under the control of third-grade court pleaders or mischief-making ex-*thugyis* who had been dismissed for cause. *Athin* leaders usually tried to influence the villagers to boycott the headmen and the

[61] *RAB* for 1921–1922, pp. xix, 14; Moscotti, pp. 120–121. Increasing criminal activity of the *pongyis* was cited as "both evidence of and incitement to a depression of public morality."

[62] *RPA* for 1922, pp. 11, 18–19, 44–45.   [63] *Ibid.*, pp. 16–18.

[64] *Ibid.*, p. 16. Some *athins* collected funds to defend political assassins in court.

regular courts and to have recourse instead to their own "kangaroo" courts, which inflicted penalties often resembling a game of forfeits.[65]

Many *athins* became hindrances to local governmental operations and poisoners of public opinion, mainly because of the bad elements included in them.[66] They did stimulate patriotism and national pride and also held out the prospect of reduced taxation, but they clearly failed to generate any responsible public opinion capable of promoting tangible social improvements.[67] One cause of their failure was the denial to the village headman of any political role, which left open to political adventurers the opportunity of attaining *athin* leadership. Similarly the headman's disqualification as a candidate for election to the circle boards tended to undermine his political influence and dignity.[68]

Political agitation aggravated the problem of suppressing crime because unrest and lawlessness tended to coalesce. Novel ideas of constitutionalism and popular rule, especially when seemingly divorced from legitimate means of political expression, unquestionably served to undermine the traditional concept of absolute governmental authority. This was particularly serious at a time when the authority of parents, religious sanctions, and social mores was at a low ebb. The police were in many instances corrupt and undisciplined and hence were not trusted by the people, who refused to aid them. As a result, approximately three-fourths of the murders during the 1920's were going unpunished. Buddhist monasteries in both Mandalay and Rangoon were reportedly serving as sanctuaries for known criminals, underscoring the dire need of an ecclesiastical body to enforce discipline among the monks.[69] In the villages where the authority of the headman was challenged and criticized, community resistance to dacoit operations became an exceptional occurrence.[70] The headman's new duties under the reforms, covering sanitation, local road maintenance, and agricultural functions, were at best only casually undertaken, because incentive and local support were lacking.[71]

[65] *Ibid.*, pp. 14, 44–45. One such court reportedly required a convicted rapist to run around the town ten times with a cowbell around his neck, as an alternative to his leaving the village.

[66] *Ibid.*, pp. 18–19, 44–45. The *RPA* for 1921 (p. 40) condemned the *Wunthanu Athins* for undermining the authority of the headman and cited as causes the influence of political *pongyis* and women politicians.

[67] *RPA* for 1922, p. 19.   [68] *RAB* for 1919–1920.   [69] *RPA* for 1922, p. 19.

[70] *RAB* for 1922–1923, pp. 32–33.   [71] Mya Sein, pp. 173–175.

Efforts to Salvage the Declining Authority of the Thugyi

Governmental efforts to bolster the position of the headman, starting around 1912, took the form of amalgamating adjacent village tracts
whenever a post fell vacant. A more deliberate effort to enlarge tracts
in order to create units capable of efficient administration began in
1917.[72] A basic objective was to increase the amount of the commission
on taxes received by the headmen in compensation for official services,
so that more dependable men could be attracted to the posts. During
the course of the decade prior to 1921, the number of village tracts
was reduced by more than 2,300 (from around 18,000 to 15,660), and
within the two years directly prior to 1921 amalgamations reduced the
number by 770 more. In 1921 the average compensation had been
raised to 166 rupees (up from around 100 rupees in 1902), whereas
270 rupees was regarded as minimal and 300 rupees as desirable.

But the policy worked imperfectly. Any reduction in the land tax
revenue for a given area as a result of crop failure automatically diminished the headman's commission proportionately, without reducing
his duties in any way. Occasionally, as a result, headmen would receive as little as 90 rupees' compensation for an entire year's service.
The assistant *ywagaungs* also began to demand monetary compensation. There was no dearth of applicants for vacant headmanships, but
for reasons other than salary or a desire to serve. Many of the candidates admittedly lacked the essential qualities of personality and integrity required. Another serious negative aspect of the amalgamation
policy was that villagers invariably resented being put under the jurisdiction of nonresident headmen. It was clear by 1921 that the wholesale
reshuffling of village-tract headmen would have to be discontinued,
although the practice of amalgamating tracts continued nonetheless.[73]

In an attempt to remedy the fading authority of the headmen the
government began to sponsor monthly sessions of Associations of Headmen consisting of ten to twelve neighboring *thugyis*. They met under
arrangements calling for a revolving chairmanship. This measure promoted some intervillage co-operation in minor matters, but it contrib-

[72] *ISCR*, XI, 423. The Burman Village Act of 1907 consolidated the village system throughout Burma and limited the headman's compensation to his commission;
excessive subdivision was halted in 1910, and the enlargements of tracts started
in 1912–1913. Mya Sein, pp. 172–173.

[73] *RAB* for 1919–1920, pp. 51–52, for 1921–1922, p. x; Mya Sein, pp. 172–178.
The number of governmental village tracts by 1926 was under 12,000, or one-third
less than in 1910.

uted little to solve the basic problem of lack of village co-operation in suppressing crime, as its sponsors had hoped it would do. Relatively few of those headmen who had been accorded special judicial powers (some 12 per cent of the total) made effective use of their authority as local magistrates, even though they welcomed the added prestige derived from such designation. The magistrate-headman did not handle civil and criminal cases promptly, in part because of unwillingness to accept responsibility and in part from sensitivity about the possible adverse review of such decisions by higher judicial authorities. Some 700 headmen were punished for dereliction of duty in 1918–1919 as compared with 491 in the previous year, the increase being attributed to the manifold temptations to which they were newly subjected.[74]

The following statement from the report of the deputy commissioner of Akyab District in 1919 explains some factors contributing to the growing tension within the villages:

Friction . . . exists in very many villages; . . . murders [are] committed on the very smallest provocation, and [there is a] general lack of . . . a sense of mutual responsibility. . . . Under modern conditions the [traditional] standard of social conduct has largely disappeared. . . . It is to the decay of [custom and religion] . . . that I would largely attribute the present tendencies to crime. . . . The real solution is to be found elsewhere than in the progressive improvement of the methods of police administration.[75]

The Question of Land Tax Revision

In one area of government where remedial action might have relieved economic and political tensions, namely reform of the taxation system, Governor Craddock's administration refused to move. An able settlement report for 1922 covering a riverine area near Mandalay,[76] for example, revealed that 85 per cent of the cultivators were in debt, that the people generally lived from hand to mouth, and that only the luckiest made more than a bare living. In this situation even the reduced *thathameda* tax (based on declining nonagricultural income) was becoming increasingly difficult to collect. The settlement officer, therefore, could find no grounds on which to recommend the customary increase in the tax demand. The head of the governor's Land Revenue Department nevertheless criticized this conclusion severely, and the

[74] *RAB* for 1918–1919, pp. 40–42, for 1920–1921, p. x, for 1922–1923, pp. 32–33.
[75] *RPA* for 1911, p. 11.
[76] Burma, Settlement Dept., *Initial Report on the Second Revision Settlement in the Mandalay District, Season 1922*, by H. F. Searle (Rangoon, 1924).

governor personally proposed a rule-of-thumb principle that a minimum increase of 5 per cent should be levied with every resettlement survey.[77] Another settlement report for 1920 covering newly developed land in Hanthawaddy and Pegu districts, made by a Burman officer and submitted with Mr. Furnivall's support as chief settlement officer, received similar treatment. The average per acre demand as recommended in the report was enhanced by some 40 per cent, on the authority of the governor's revenue secretary.[78]

An authorized general study of land revenue problems,[79] published in 1922, urged that officials take more fully into account as part of the cost of agricultural production the labor of the cultivator and his family in arriving at a "rental produce" basis for tax demand. The report also proposed simplifying procedures for remitting taxes in case of crop failures, as well as converting both the objectionable and relatively uniform capitation and *thathameda* direct taxes into local rates assessed as house taxes according to the quality of the structure. Mr. Furnivall, the author of the report, argued that, with the introduction and growth of popular control of the government, it was increasingly imperative that, without reference to any mysterious governmental formulas, an intelligent landowner could understand the grounds on which he was assessed taxes. All such actions must be based on verifiable facts. Taxes, he insisted furthermore, must be adjusted to the government's necessities, not with any design to achieve a surplus. The preparation of voluminous settlement reports should also be curtailed, and more effort be devoted to local investigation. These numerous proposals merited, from a political point of view, far more attention than they received.[80]

Introduction of the Burma Reforms

The more progressive elements of the G.C.B.A. nationalists, who were prepared to operate through legal channels to achieve their political ends, continued until 1922 in close contact with friendly opposition members of the British Parliament. Their principal spokesman was Colonel Wedgwood, who visited Burma for three or four days in

[77] *Ibid.,* pp. 1–2, 6–7.

[78] Burma, Settlement Dept., *Report on the Summary Settlement of . . . Areas in the Pegu and Hanthawaddy Districts,* by Maung Dwe (Rangoon, 1921), pp. 1–3.

[79] Burma, *Report of the Committee Appointed to Examine the Land Revenue System of Burma,* by J. S. Furnivall (Rangoon, 1922).

[80] *Ibid.,* pp. 67, 82, 165–167, 222, 279–286. This able report was never acted upon. Mr. Furnivall resigned from the civil service shortly after its publication.

early 1922 and who apparently received thereafter regular communications regarding Burman reactions to the reform proposals. As a result of a series of questions addressed to the Secretary of State for India, Wedgwood learned that New Delhi had completed its review of the Whyte Committee report on April 11, 1922, and that a draft resolution covering the Burma reforms was placed before the Standing Joint Committee of Parliament in early May. On June 12, 1922, when Lord Winterton moved the adoption of the resolution to include Burma in the India Reform Bill, with amendments, Wedgwood was ready with a number of proposals. The only substantial government amendments concerned provisions permitting qualified women to vote, the transfer of forestry and European education to ministers responsible to the council, and Burma's special provisions for communal representation.[81]

Parliament's debate on the bill was dispirited and desultory. Many opposing speakers did not even bother to stay to hear Lord Winterton's replies to their objections. Some alleged that the transfer of forestry administration to Burman hands jeopardized not only Burma's forests but also the prosperity of the country. Others objected to the suffrage and election provisions as being too liberal. A few advanced the general charge that since dyarchy had already failed in India, it was compounding folly to apply it to Burma also.[82] A number of the Conservative participants, however, lined up solidly behind Lord Winterton's bill and the Burma Reforms Committee proposals, affirming that Burma's constitution was already five years overdue, that further transfers of executive authority would have to follow, and that communal representation should be held to a minimum.[83] Colonel Wedgwood strongly deprecated the dogfight which had developed between the Burmese nation and Lieutenant Governor Craddock. He declared that the stupid feud had served only to intensify the sullen, distrustful, and unco-operative attitude of the people. If the liberty-loving Burmans were treated generously, made free and self-respecting, their country, he insisted, could develop into a bright demonstration of the practical feasibility of home rule in Asia.[84]

The series of amendments to the bill which Colonel Wedgwood advanced with uniform lack of success can be assumed to represent the

---

[81] *PD,C*, 5th ser., vol. 151 (March 7, 1922), p. 1046, vol. 152 (March 28, 1922), p. 1107, vol. 153 (April 11, 1922), p. 244, vol. 153 (May 2, 1922), pp. 1138–1139, vol. 154 (May 3, 1922), p. 978, vol. 155 (June 12, 1922), pp. 49–54.

[82] *Ibid.*, vol. 155, pp. 61–71, by Major Glyn and C. Yate.

[83] *Ibid.*, pp. 71–84, by Mr. Ormsby-Gore in particular.

[84] *Ibid.*, pp. 55–61.

wishes of his Burman friends and informants. Those which came to a vote were defeated by better than a three to one majority. They included the following proposals: (1) abandon direct communal representation as a means of protecting minorities along with the mischievous assumption that brutal mistreatment by the majority must be anticipated; (2) broaden the eligibility rules for candidates for elections to include men and women of twenty-one years; (3) repeal the election regulation barring as candidates persons convicted of criminal actions carrying more than a six months' sentence (this proposal was made on the interesting assumption that such a group might include some of the future political leaders of the country); (4) extend the female suffrage; (5) leave open the door for Burma's future separation from India.[85] Lord Winterton closed the debate with the optimistic assertion that in transferring the Forestry Department to Burman control Britain was meeting the acid test of her sincerity and that the important consideration was to encourage acceptance of the constitution by as large a section of the people as possible. The bill was approved without difficulty.[86]

Immediately following the passage of the Burma Reforms Bill on June 12, the executive committee of the G.C.B.A. assembled to consider what policy to adopt with respect to the impending elections for circle boards and the legislative council scheduled for November, 1922. Eight members of the G.C.B.A. council refused to accept the majority decision to boycott the circle board elections, and these were subsequently joined by some thirteen other G.C.B.A. leaders to form the so-called "21 Party." This group, which included U Ba Pe and others long active in the nationalist movement, was apparently attracted by the tactics advocated by new leaders of the Swaraj party in India who, in contradistinction to Gandhi's tactics, favored participation in the reform-scheme elections and the use of seats won in the provincial councils as forums from which to publicize home rule demands. When such demands met with refusal, the nationalist members of the council would oppose all government measures and seek to wreck dyarchy from within.[87] The "21 Party" decided at a formal meeting in September, 1922, to contest the legislative council elections and to participate in council operations "so long as the speedy attainment of Home Rule is

[85] Ibid., pp. 84–96.   [86] Ibid., p. 94.
[87] W. N. Brown, pp. 93–94; Tinker, pp. 130, 136–137. The Gandhist policy of complete nonco-operation lost favor in India following his arrest in 1922. The Swaraj Party led by Chitta Ranjan Das and Motilal Nehru held the Indian political stage for several years thereafter.

not prejudiced thereby." Democratic privileges were not to be utilized because they were valid and valuable per se, but because they seemed to offer a short-cut path to self-determination. The majority elements of the G.C.B.A., known as the Hlaing-Pu-Gyaw [88] group from the names of its three principal leaders, were particularly interested in promoting the activities of the village *Wunthanu Athins* and in co-operating with the political *pongyis* and women politicians to boycott the elections.[89]

The task of the boycotters was an easy one because the people generally were completely uninterested in both the circle board and the legislative council elections. It required little or no intimidation, therefore, to reduce participation in 1922 to below 7 per cent of the eligible electorate. The "21 Party" (or Nationalist Party) won twenty-eight seats of the seventy-nine elected members of the council. This was more than half of the general constituency seats, but less than 30 per cent of the total membership in the council.

On January 1, 1923, Burma became a full governor's province under the dyarchy constitution. Lieutenant Governor Craddock was replaced by Governor Sir Harcourt Butler, brought in for his second round as head of the provincial government. A single High Court replaced the previously divided top legal agencies for Upper and Lower Burma. Elective nonofficial district councils and circle boards, the former chosen by the latter, took over many of the responsibilities for local government.[90]

Unfortunately the very considerable advance in self-government which Parliament's decision held out to Burma aroused no popular enthusiasm whatever and only grudging willingness on the part of a minority political element to co-operate at all in the experiment, and that for ulterior ends. Ambitious politicians saw an opportunity to enhance their personal interests in the central legislative council, while conscienceless grafters crowded into the district councils. Most Burmans were even less pleased with dyarchy in operation than in prospect.

[88] H-P-G stood for U Chit Hlaing, U Pu, and U Tun Aung Gyaw. Subordinate factions within the G.C.B.A. were led by U Su and U So Thein, both of whom eventually broke with the H-P-G leadership. The G.C.S.S. (*Sanghas*) also divided three ways in 1922–1923. See Maung Pye, p. 6.

[89] Moscotti, pp. 32–33. [90] *RAB* for 1922–1923, p. ix.

VIII

Constitutional Experiment and Political Unrest, 1923-1929

THE experiment in governmental reform which was inaugurated in Burma in 1922–1923 had three distinct aspects. The most significant political development was the installation of a legislative council renewable every three years, to which the ministers of the transferred subjects of the administration were responsible. It included 130 members, of whom 80 were elected. A second aspect of the reform program concerned the selection by popularly elected circle boards of 28 district councils. The latter were charged with directing and supervising various aspects of local government. The third concerned administrative measures designed to strengthen the faltering hands of the village headmen in the face of dual defiance of their authority by the local political associations (*athins*) on the one hand and by the rising wave of crime on the other.

The decade of the 1920's was, on the whole, a period of meager positive achievement. The welter of political unrest which attended these governmental changes was aggravated by tangible economic grievances and by a rising tide of communal opposition to the presence and activities of Indian residents of Burma. The drift of events rather than any conscious direction of policy was largely responsible for developments.

Selection of the First Council

Under Burma's 1922 constitution, 58 of the 80 elected members of the legislative council were chosen in general constituencies. Fifteen

242

were elected communally (8 Indians, 5 Karens, one Anglo-Indian, and one British), while the remaining 7 represented various business groups and the university.[1] An additional 23, including 2 ex-officio members of the executive council and one member to represent labor, were nominated by the governor. Under the dyarchy arrangement only those members of the governor's council of ministers in charge of the transferred subjects (agriculture, excise, health, public works [except irrigation], forestry, and education) were responsible to the legislative council. The reserved subjects, which were controlled by ministers responsible directly to the governor, included general administrative direction, law and order, land revenue, labor, and finance. Defense and external relations together with currency and coinage, communications and transportation controls, income tax, and civil and criminal law were the concern of the Central Indian Government at New Delhi.[2] The governor alone could legislate for the peripheral Scheduled Areas of Burma (Karenni, the Shan States, Kachin and Chin tribal regions). He was also empowered to veto legislation, to forbid the legislative council from considering "reserved" subjects, and to certify any essential expenditure which the legislative council might decline to include in the budget.

The governor's control of financial policy severely limited any discretionary power which ministers in charge of transferred subjects could exercise.[3] In practice, the bureaucratic heads of the twenty-odd administrative departments—who made up the government's executive council—actually managed budgetary allocations. Ministers temporarily in charge of the six transferred departments (two to each minister) could not compete effectively with well-established civil service officials and routine operating procedures backed by the governor's financial control. The result was that the activities of the ministers of transferred subjects were largely political, not administrative, in character. Any new proposal for so-called "nation-building" objectives invariably involved expenditures, and it could therefore be countered by pleas of financial stringency or by politically impossible demands for increased taxation.[4] The simultaneous establishment, in December,

[1] Voters within the university constituency included members of the faculty staff and residents of Burma who were graduates of three years' standing.

[2] The Central Indian Government appropriated all revenues from customs, income tax, and salt excises.

[3] F. B. Leach, The Future of Burma (Rangoon, 1936), pp. 40–42; Moscotti, pp. 69–71.

[4] D. G. E. Hall, Burma (London, 1950), p. 152; Harvey, British Rule, p. 78.

1922, of a High Court of Judicature at Rangoon, based on royal letters patent, created a supreme court of appeal and revision for Burma independent of both administrative or legislative control.[5]

The suffrage for the forty-four general rural constituencies created in 1922 was based on the payment of the direct capitation or *thathameda* taxes, averaging round 5 rupees per household. Voters must be at least eighteen years of age. There was no sex disqualification, although 85 per cent of the female voters qualified by paying the Upper Burma *thathameda* tax. In the fourteen urban constituencies, the suffrage rolls were virtually identical with the municipal election voting lists, which included persons paying taxes on immovable property and others assessed an income tax of 4 rupees or more. In proportion to total population the urban centers were considerably overrepresented. The voters for the circle board elections were predominantly rural, but they included also taxpayer residents of adjacent small urban centers, which were not yet recognized as municipalities.

In the elections of 1922 fewer than one in fourteen of the eligible voters (6.9 per cent) participated, with urban voting much heavier than rural. There was some intimidation of would-be voters by *pongyi* and other boycott leaders at the polling places,[6] but few wanted to vote and little pressure was needed. The boycotters encouraged a predilection; they were not running counter to any popular desire. Popular participation in government through elections was for most Burmans an unfamiliar and unsought experience; it was regarded as particularly gratuitous to be concerned about choosing a legislative council which could exercise no real power. The fact that the right to vote was based on payment of the disliked capitation and *thathameda* taxes operated reciprocally to increase the unpopularity of these taxes and to cast odium on the suffrage which their payment accorded. Opposition to these taxes, in other words, touched precisely those persons eligible to vote.[7]

The basic popular issue in the 1922 elections was whether or not Burma should reject the whole dyarchy reform program. The 93 per cent boycott constituted an emphatic answer in the affirmative. The objectives advocated by the lay G.C.B.A. and the *pongyi*-led G.C.S.S., namely home rule, freedom from foreign domination, and remission

[5] *ISCR*, XI, 6–7.
[6] Moscotti, pp. 116–118; *ISCR*, XI, 256–258. Usually boycotters accompanied by a *pongyi* appeared at polling places and influenced would-be voters to go home.
[7] *ISCR*, XI, 256–257. The usual antidyarchy argument in Upper Burma was the erroneous assertion that voting meant increased taxation.

244

of taxes, seemed for many unlikely to be attained through any leger-
demain exercised by distrusted politician lawyers maneuvering in a
dyarchy council. The alternative tactic was to challenge the authority
of the new government, especially its policing, court, and tax collecting functions, which were after all not under council control at all.[8]
The principal targets of nationalist criticism of the new constitution,
both outside and within the council, included the limitations placed
on ministerial responsibility and the provisions for communal representation. Even Burmans who accepted ministerial posts under the dyarchy
system supported routine opposition resolutions favoring full ministerial responsibility.[9]

The only organized nationalist group which contested seats in the
election of the first council was the so-called "21 Party," headed by U
Pu (of Yamethin), U Ba Pe, U Maung Gyee, and U Ba Si.[10] Because
the party was not formally organized until September, 1922, its defection from the G.C.B.A. came too late for that action to influence many
of the local political *athins*. Personalities were everywhere more potent
politically than principles in any case. Even in areas where the boycotting parties were influential, candidates with local influence frequently attracted a considerable vote. More than half of the members
returned by the fifty-eight general constituencies ran as independent
candidates. Karen Christians participated actively in the balloting, and
in two general constituencies (Tavoy and Tharrawaddy districts) the
Karen candidates actually won election.[11] The "21 Party," or the Nationalists, as they preferred to be called, elected twenty-eight candidates, which was the largest single party group. They were pledged
to agitate within the council for nationalist objectives but not to prejudice the attainment of home rule. The vast boycotting majority of the
qualified voters were apparently completely unconcerned about who
the members of the legislative council were or what they did.[12] These
grass-roots political elements not represented in the council were destined to become even more important in the next decade.

The majority progovernment coalition within the council lacked
cohesion. It included a number of Independent members, a large portion of those returned by the several communal and business constituencies, and most of the sizable group nominated directly by the

[8] Moscotti, pp. 116–118   [9] *Ibid.*, pp. 69–71.
[10] *PP,C*, Cmd. 4004, p. 71. This Command paper was also published as Great
Britain, Burma Round Table Conference, London, 1931–1932, *Plenary Sessions,
Proceedings* (London, 1932); hereafter cited as *BRTCP*.
[11] *ABFMS, Annual Report* for 1923, pp. 97–98.   [12] *ISCR*, XI, 268–269.

governor. A so-called Moderate or Progressive bloc composed of a score of progovernment members coalesced briefly during 1923, but the bloc quickly fell apart, and nothing took its place. Fourteen of the elected Independents of the first council showed little preference for either side, and only six of the elected Burmans stayed with the government coalition throughout the council's sessions. Independent and nonparty members were too diverse in their political sympathies and in their racial composition to pursue any settled policy, much less to unite to form a homogeneous party.[13]

Functioning of the First Council

Governor Sir Harcourt Butler conducted his relations with the first legislative council with marked tact and skill. He selected as minister for education, local government, and public health an able member of the "21 Party," U Maung Gyee, who assumed office with the consent of his party. The other minister selected for the transferred subjects of agriculture, excise control, and forests was a moderate Anglophile Burman member of the ephemeral Progressive Party, Joseph Augustus (J. A.) Maung Gyi. In another conciliatory gesture, the governor selected as home member of his council the respected Sir Maung Kin, already mentioned as one of the original founders of the Y.M.B.A.[14] When U Maung Kin died in 1924, Butler called U May Oung from a high judicial post to be minister of home affairs. When, in 1924, J. A. Maung Gyi was elevated to a position as judge of the High Court, another moderate nationalist, U Pu of Yamethin, was made minister of agriculture, excise, and forests. The governor's conciliatory policy and the hearty support accorded him by these well-chosen Burman ministers, especially the imaginative leadership of U May Oung, produced for a time some semblance of cordiality and co-operation on the part of the Burman members of the council.[15] The untimely death of U May Oung in 1926 (at the age of forty-six), one of the ablest Burmans of his generation, a man of sound judgment, a scholar, and an excellent debater, was a serious loss which the country and the government could ill afford, administratively or politically.[16] Another backset in terms of Burman co-operation was encountered in the decision made by British authorities in India, over the protest of Gov-

[13] *Ibid.*, pp. 267–269.
[14] One of the two ministers for "reserved" subjects was required to be a Burman.
[15] *RAB* for 1923–1924, pp. vii–viii, for 1924–1925, pp. vii–x; Sen, pp. 17–25.
[16] Sen, pp. 27–28.

ernor Butler, to disband the 70th Burma Rifles and to restrict army recruitment to the Karen, Chin, and Kachin peoples.[17] The tentative honeymoon under dyarchy was quickly over.

Minister U Maung Gyee accomplished a considerable improvement in public relations with respect to education. He sponsored an amendment to the University Act which accorded more power to an enlarged university council (including additional nonofficial members) while it left academic control in the hands of the faculty senate. The founding of an intermediate college at Mandalay in 1925 [18] blunted popular resentment over the unitary residential character of the university. Attendance at the university steadily increased. U Maung Gyee also inaugurated the policy of according government support to the better-qualified national schools. Thirty-four of them were granted aid in 1923, and others qualified later. This new policy split the advocates of the national schools between the more conservative boycotting nationalists and the so-called Progressives. The latter took the sensible view that national fervor was no adequate substitute educationally for discipline and facilities for instruction.[19] The breakup of the national school experiment was hastened by the decision of the chief *Sayadaw* at Mandalay in 1924 disapproving the participation of monks in any form of secular education and opposing any semblance of governmental control over monastic schools through the official grant-in-aid system. Individual *pongyis* continued to participate in the aided school program, but parents generally preferred lay teachers to the ineffective and frequently obscurantist monks.[20]

By no means all of the actions of the first council were reasonable and constructive. At the very outset, the Nationalist members seized the occasion of the budget debates to attack the police system. They insisted that the entire policing operation was too costly. The pay of

[17] Sir Henry Crow, "Burma," *Asiatic Review*, XXXVIII (1942), 260–262. The army's objections to Burmese recruits centered on their unsatisfactory conduct in the barracks, their alleged tendency to desertion and A.W.O.L., their wandering out of bounds, and their improper disposal of kits.

[18] *RAB* for 1925–1926, p. vi.

[19] *RAB* for 1923–1924, pp. vii–viii; ABFMS, *MS. Correspondence*, L. W. Hattersley to J. C. Robbins, from Rangoon, June 21, 1923, and John M. Cummings to R. L. Howard, from Henzada, Sept. 3, 1925. Only two of the national school candidates in all of the Irrawaddy Division passed the seventh standard examinations in 1925. Many parents allegedly complained that the "do-as-you-please" national schools lacked discipline and regularity of attendance. Cummings reported that the teacher's position in the national schools was intolerable, being "poorly paid, irregularly paid, and subject to many masters."

[20] G. E. R. G. Brown, *Burma as I Saw It*, pp. 91–92.

the higher-bracket salaries was too high in comparison to that of the inadequately paid constables (17 to 24 rupees per month and, after 1923, 22 to 30 rupees), who allegedly made good their income deficiencies by corrupt practices. Critics proposed that the number of European inspector generals be reduced from four to two.[21] The Criminal Investigation Department in particular was criticized for devoting too much attention to the suppression of political agitation while neglecting the basic work of crime detection. One Nationalist Party spokesman referred to the exciting and exhilarating popular sport of police baiting. Nationalists also objected to paying India for the cost of maintaining the military police. In connection with the demand that money be diverted from police expenditures to so-called "nationbuilding" undertakings, the Nationalist leaders obtained in March, 1923, by a 40 to 37 vote, approval of a cut of 10 lakhs of rupees (1 million) from the proposed police budget. This action forced the governor subsequently to certify a supplementary allotment to cover essential police expenditures. In the session of 1924, the inspector general of police barely managed to oppose successfully a similarly proposed budgetary cut of 5 lakhs of rupees.[22]

The first council approved resolutions sponsored by Nationalist Party Burmans requesting the appointment of committees to investigate the growing problem of crime, the release of political prisoners, and the possible outright repeal of the capitation tax. The government accepted without qualification the proposed appointment of the Crime Enquiry Committee. The resolution to release political prisoners was amended in council by adding the important qualification that such action be taken only if compatible with law and order. Other resolutions to obtain release of violators under the Antiboycott Act and those convicted in the Mandalay Riot case of 1924 (including U Ottama) were defeated by the government coalition. With reference to the requested repeal of the capitation tax, made in March, 1925,[23] Nationalist Party sponsors suggested that the government levy a substitute tax to be borne by persons most able to bear it. Government replied that the innovators must propose a specific alternative source of revenue and also pointed out that the prospective loss to local funds could be made good if the district councils would exercise their

[21] *ISCR*, XI, 273, 298, 459–460, XV, 466. A constable's pay prior to the war was only 9 to 11 rupees per month.
[22] *ISCR*, XI, 213–215; Moscotti, pp. 32–33.
[23] *ISCR*, XI, 213; Moscotti, pp. 32–33.

newly granted revenue powers.[24] All elected Burmans in the legislative council supported a sweeping constitutional resolution dated August 28, 1924, advocating that all aspects of government except foreign affairs and defense be assigned to the province and that all provincialized subjects be transferred to responsible ministers, with authority to Burmanize the services.[25]

The council also took up the question of village administration. Burman members proposed unanimously that headmen be elected and be made removable by a two-thirds vote of the villagers, that jury trial be introduced, that elected village committees share the powers of the headmen, and that the liabilities of the village tracts under collective responsibility be reduced. Conservative Burmans differed only in preferring to move gradually and along conservative lines.[26] In a specific instance, Nationalist Party leaders tried to cancel a communal fine imposed for failure of a village to prevent the escape of a criminal. They also opposed the suppression of the outlawed *"Bu athins."* They almost succeeded (37 to 39) in passing a resolution to lift the emergency ban against allegedly subversive *athins,* imposed under the Criminal Law Amendment Act. The resolution provided only that legislative councilors acquainted with the problem certify that the assumed emergency no longer existed.[27]

Far less difference in point of view prevailed between so-called radical and conservative Burman members within the council, almost all of whom were members of the Westernized urban intelligentsia, than between the Burman councilors as a whole and the boycotting majority of the electorate outside. Party differentiations within the council had little or no relevance to the issues which governed political attitudes outside the council. The council sessions could be utilized to bring local needs and grievances to the notice of government, but the council was not the focal point or fountainhead of popular political leadership. It was almost paradoxical that many actions of nationalist councilors were inspired by popular forces which themselves took no interest whatever in the council sessions.[28]

One unfortunate result of the opportunity afforded in the legislative

---

[24] *ISCR,* XI, 288.

[25] *Ibid.,* pp. 310–311. Only one nominated Burman refused to support this proposal.

[26] *Ibid.,* pp. 273–274.

[27] *Ibid.,* pp. 284–286. The *"Bu athins"* will be described later.

[28] *Ibid.,* pp. 337–338. The Simon Commission affirmed quite correctly that the council was not the principal means used to give expression to popular grievances.

council for uninhibited and frequently irresponsible attacks by Burman nationalists on the administration was to incite a strong defensive reaction on the part of the British community, especially the business elements. Foreign capital had an enormous stake in the future of Burma, and its representatives possessed correspondingly little understanding of popular viewpoints and needs. This hardening of antinative opinion among resident Britons resulted in their condemning as mischievous and unwarranted all politically motivated activity. Thus, for the first time, an open chasm began to develop between politically conscious nationalists and the British business community, which could be counted on thereafter to oppose all constitutional concessions.[29] There developed also during the first and second councils increasing evidences of popular aversion on the part of the Burmans to Indian residents, based on both racial and economic grounds, an attitude which was apparently shared by all shades of Burmese political opinion.[30]

Grass-Roots Politics and the Antitax Campaign of 1924

The grass-roots political movement operating outside the council[31] was itself a confused amalgam of various contributing factors. The boycotting faction of the G.C.B.A., led by U Chit Hlaing (a Mon from Moulmein), U Pu (from Tharrawaddy), and U Tun Aung Gyaw, was essentially an urban Lower Burma organization. Its youthful Western-educated leaders were nevertheless endeavoring to develop and to control a political organization reaching down to the village *Wunthanu Athins*. This (H-P-G) G.C.B.A. operated in uneasy alliance for several years with the traditionalist General Council of *Sangha Sametggi* (G.C.S.S.), a monastic organization turned political under the leadership of rabidly anti-British *pongyi* agitators, of whom U Ottama was probably the most influential. The political *pongyis* were frequently men of energy and ambition, who had been frustrated in efforts to obtain an education and a decent livelihood. Although not true monks, they capitalized on popular reverence for the yellow robe and established themselves as natural leaders.[32] The potentially revolutionary

---

[29] J. S. Furnivall, *Introduction to the Political Economy of Burma*, pp. 49–50.

[30] *ISCR*, XI, 270–271. Whereas Indian members of the council supported the government, the lone Chinese representative usually backed the nationalists.

[31] *Ibid.*, pp. 270–271.

[32] From a recorded lecture by Professor U Kyaw Thet. Political *pongyis* charged with sedition included U Withakhda of Pyapon and U Theindaung of Magwe.

movement represented by the village *athins* would have been difficult for Westernized lay politicians to have controlled in any case. In the competition with magical techniques and irresponsible political propaganda of the *pongyi* agitators, the educated politicians faced an impossible task—hence the effort of all nationalist leaders to remain somehow on good terms with the *pongyis*. No colorful political personality emerged within the H-P-G group capable of capturing popular imagination to the degree achieved by U Ottama. U Chit Hlaing probably came closest to doing it, but he had too many scruples to attempt a revolution.

The contest for grass-roots political control was waged at the level of the village *athins,* where the personal qualities and influence of the local leaders always outweighed refinements of political principles or tactics. The basic issue everywhere in the villages was simply opposition to foreign rule, but no agreement prevailed regarding leadership or tactics. Usurpation of political leadership by the *pongyis* threatened seriously to undermine the social stratification which had developed under British rule, extending downward from the top government officials to Western-trained professional men, merchants, and landholders and finally to minor officials and the police. The collapse of this structure would have left the *pongyis,* including the obscurantists and astrologer-magicians among them, in a commanding social and cultural position,[33] but to no good purpose. Even leaders of the H-P-G faction of the G.C.B.A., as well as Burmans in the legislative council, had a stake in the survival of the British-fashioned hierarchy, no matter how avidly they might oppose the dyarchy constitution in particular and foreign rule in general. This factor explains the rivalry from 1922 to 1925 between the G.C.B.A. and the G.C.S.S. for control over Burma's political grass-roots *athins.*

Convincing evidence that revolutionary elements were working at the village level was the appearance in 1922 of the so-called *"Bu athins,"* conspiratorial secret organizations dedicated to achieving home rule by illegal methods of violence, intimidation, and defiance of authority. The awesome oath taken by members of a *Bu athin* was reminiscent of those imposed by the courts of old Burma. It ran in part as follows:

[33] See L. M. Hanks, Jr., "The Quest for Individual Autonomy in Burmese Personality," *Psychiatry,* XII, (1949), 287. *The Times* (London), April 1, 1922, reported that a royal pretender, one Prince Mintha Saw Yan Baing, twice tried to raise a rebellion in the Northern Shan States, once in 1919 and once in 1922.

I will work for Home Rule heart and soul without flinching from duties even if my bones are crushed and my skin torn. . . . If I fail . . . may I die . . . and . . . suffer in Hell permanently. I will not bid for fisheries [licenses] or [government licensed] shops; I will not drink intoxicating liquor or take to opium; I will not co-operate with Government . . . ; if a member of a *Bu athin* is in trouble and requires my assistance, I will help him; I will not use wearing apparel of foreign make; I will not marry foreigners; if a member of a *Bu athin* . . . infringes the law, and the Government asks about it, I shall say no.[34]

The *Bu athins* sought to end the government's licensing of fisheries and the legalized sale of opium and liquor; they also resisted payment of taxes. They were declared illegal in August, 1923, and were thereafter outlawed wherever discovered.[35] The leaders of the *Bu athins* were usually men of local importance only, but they invariably worked in close co-operation with the *pongyi* radicals of the G.C.S.S. They were particularly strong in Tharrawaddy District, where they operated in some sections a shadow administration in disregard of legal agencies. Another group of revolutionary *athins,* dubbed "*Sibwaye*" [development] *athins,* undertook to force Chettyars to scale down their debts. Irish fashion, they resorted to cattle maiming, arson, and even murder to force villagers to co-operate with their anti-Chettyar program.[36] In such actions one can perceive the re-emergence of certain aspects of the traditional pattern of revolution of old Burma. Promoters mingled crime with political agitation, defied the agencies of the government, and organized local gangs for the purposes of mutual protection and counterviolence. In anticipation of overt defiance of authority, an abnormal increase of crime occurred prior to the rains in 1924, especially in the riverine districts of the Irrawaddy Valley extending from Tharrawaddy northward to Thayetmyo.[37]

The pattern of revolutionary action advocated by U Ottama's followers and by the *Bu athins* [38] was presented for formal approval at

[34] India Office Archives, *Views of Local Government on the Working of the Reforms* (London, 1927), p. 327; Moscotti, p. 185. The phrase *Mathibu* meant in Burmese "I do not know."

[35] Moscotti, p. 36. By 1927, some 303 *Bu athins* had been outlawed.

[36] *RPA* for 1924, pp. 11–12; Moscotti, pp. 36–38.

[37] *RPA* for 1924, p. 11. From 1923 to 1925, the number of murders for all Burma increased 33 per cent, dacoities 85 per cent, and robberies 90 per cent. See *ISCR,* XI, 466–467.

[38] According to *RPA* for 1924 (p. 48), U Ottama was president of the violent Hindu Mahasabha for Burma. But Ottama's approach was distinctly Burmese.

a conference of the G.C.B.A. held at Paungde in May, 1924. An estimated 30,000 persons attended. It proved impossible for moderates on this occasion to defeat the proposal for nonpayment of taxes, although opinion on the subject was by no means unanimous. Popular support of the antitax resolution was probably based on economic considerations mainly. The H-P-G leaders at first tried to disassociate themselves from this decision, but they later went along rather than sacrifice popular support and precipitate an open rift within the nationalist movement for home rule. When the political *pongyis* subsequently exploited the Paungde decisions to foment overt violence, to bring the government into contempt, and to prophesy the downfall of British control, the bonds of the tenuous alliance between more moderate G.C.B.A. leaders and the radical faction of the G.C.S.S. became sharply strained.[39]

A break came finally at Mandalay in August, 1924, when a riot was precipitated by the provocative actions of U Ottama. In defiance of police efforts to deter him, he led a procession of followers directly past the headquarters of the rival G.C.B.A. group. Several persons were killed in the ensuing disorder, including two policemen. U Ottama, U Tun Aung Gyaw, and other leaders on both sides were arrested. The subsequent conviction and sentencing of U Ottama to three years' imprisonment for sedition aroused great popular excitement and set the stage for widespread revolutionary disaffection which developed during the dry season (November to May) of 1924–1925.[40]

The popular campaign against the payment of the capitation tax was most vigorously prosecuted in the five districts where the *Bu athins* were strongest, namely Tavoy (in the south) and Tharrawaddy, Henzada, Prome, and Thayetmyo districts along the Irrawaddy River. Governmental authority was openly defied; headmen were intimidated or murdered; military police had to be used to quiet the disaffected areas. For a time the tension was very severe. But the *Bu athin* leaders possessed no firearms, and their membership was relatively small. Or-

[39] *RPA* for 1924, pp. 12–13, 48; Moscotti, pp. 33, 42–44; F. B. Leach, *The Future of Burma*, p. 35. The *RPA* for 1924 stated that one faction of the G.C.S.S. led by U Naga and U Nageinda backed the nonviolent position taken by the H-P-G leaders. Governor Butler felt obliged to denounce publicly the superstitious rumor that Britain's rule would end in 1925 after a full century (*The Times*, Dec. 15, 1924).

[40] *RPA* for 1924, pp. 13, 48; R. G. Brown, pp. 176–184; *The Times*, Aug. 19, 1924, and Oct. 6, 9, 10, 1924. The police dispersed a pro-Ottama meeting in Rangoon on October 8, when several resisting monks were injured.

ganized political resistance had pretty well subsided by the end of 1924.[41] Violent defiance of authority thereafter was indistinguishable from criminality per se. In October, 1924, criminals, enjoying asylum in a *pongyi kyaung* in the very heart of Rangoon, made unprovoked attacks with dahs on passing soldiers and on an American missionary and his wife. The victims barely escaped being killed.[42] The failure of the antitax campaign of 1924 plus the quarreling which developed within boycotting nationalist circles split the G.C.B.A. in 1925 beyond possible re-establishment of any semblance of unity.

The more progressive urban faction of the G.C.B.A. opposed *pongyi* dictation and eventually approved the formation of the Home Rule Party in 1925. U Pu of Tharrawaddy was the leader.[43] Chit Hlaing stayed with the G.C.B.A. for a time, but the third member of the H-P-G triumverate, U Tun Aung Gyaw, withdrew from politics. The G.C.B.A. continued to function theoretically as a mass organization behind the Home Rule Party, but the majority group broke completely with the *pongyis'* G.C.S.S. after February, 1925. Thereafter only the conservative faction headed by U Chit Hlaing continued to maintain any G.C.S.S. connection and that a tenuous one. In March, 1925, one *pongyi*-influenced splinter branch of the G.C.B.A., known as the So Thein G.C.B.A., became sharply hostile to Pu's Home Rule Party.[44]

A smaller *Swaraj* Party patterned on the Indian model also appeared as a partial defection from the G.C.B.A. under the leadership of U Tôk Gyi and a Bengali leader named N. C. Banerjee. U Tôk Gyi had been one of Burma's nonofficial representatives in the Indian Legislative Assembly. He resigned his assembly post in 1925 and returned to Burma to enter politics. Among the leaders of the *Swaraj* Party were two Europeanized Burmans U Paw Tun and Dr. Ba Maw, of whom more will be heard later. U Tôk Gyi died shortly after the

[41] *RPA* for 1924, pp. 11–13. Governor Butler toured Tharrawaddy and other disaffected areas denouncing the rebellious *athins* and affirming his determination to protect law-abiding citizens (*The Times,* Oct. 17, 1924).

[42] ABFMS, *MS. Correspondence,* letter from G. S. Jury to J. C. Robbins, Oct. 11, 1924. The lives of the American victims, the Reverend Mr. and Mrs. Gleason, were saved only because the attack occurred adjacent to the General Hospital. Several criminal characters were found in a neighboring *kyaung* by the police.

[43] Other leaders included U Ni, U Ba Soe, U So Nyun, and U Aye. U Ni later sponsored a splinter faction known as the National Parliamentary Party. See Sen, pp. 29–30.

[44] *ISCR,* XI, 269; *RPA* for 1925, pp. 51–53; Moscotti, pp. 43–44.

election of 1925, and U Paw Tun thereafter took over leadership of the *Swaraj* Party.[45]

The *Swaraj* group was noticeably handicapped by its too close Indian connections. It followed the tactics advocated by C. R. Das and Motilal Nehru of India, to demand freedom from within the provincial legislatures and then to fight dyarchy by every legal means when such demands were refused. The Home Rulers belatedly espoused the *Swarajist* tactics in the fall of 1925, just prior to their participation in the elections for the second council. The Home Rulers attracted less support than the "21 Party" Nationalists but more than the *Swarajists*. In the second council these three antidyarchy factions collaborated as a loose confederation called the People's Party, all members of which were pledged at the outset to refuse posts in the government.[46]

The confused political events of 1924–1925 thus brought to an end the first attempt to fashion a nationalist political movement bridging across the gap separating urban and rural leadership. The two groups corresponded roughly to the Western-oriented faction and the traditionalist *pongyi*-led elements of the population. The failure was attributable in part to minor incidents connected with personal rivalries and to quarrels arising over the failure of certain G.C.B.A. leaders at both high and low levels to account for moneys subscribed for party purposes.[47] Revolutionary prognostications of the political monks lost much of their effectiveness during the three years of U Ottama's imprisonment.[48] *Pongyi* influence revived following his release in 1927, for he again enlisted the backing of an impressive mass following in the village *athins*.

The spectrum of Burmese political factions as of 1925 beginning with the groups least inclined to co-operate with the government can be summarized roughly as follows: the G.C.S.S., the U So Thein G.C.B.A., the U Chit Hlaing remnant of the older H-P-G G.C.B.A., U Pu's Home Rule Party, U Tôk Gyi's *Swaraj* Party, U Ba Pe's Nationalist (or 21) Party, and and Independent Burman members of the legislative council.[49]

---

[45] Sen, p. 26.
[46] *ISCR*, XI, 269.
[47] *RPA* for 1923, p. 38.
[48] *RPA* for 1925, p. 52.
[49] *Ibid.*, pp. 51–52. Indian influence in Burma's politics became virtually nil from the time after 1925 when Banerjee of the *Swaraj* Party and Mandajit, the leader of the Hindu Sabha group, quarreled over accounting for funds and other matters.

Political Developments of 1926–1929

In the elections for the second legislative council in 1925 some 16.26 per cent of the electorate participated, or one in 6 compared with one in 14 in 1922. The increased participation was attributable to the decision of Home Rule leaders to stand as candidates and to an increasing sense of popular disillusionment over the political effectiveness of the boycotting tactics. The overriding political issue within the constituencies remained as before the basic question of opposition to foreign rule, and the nonparticipation of five-sixths of the eligible voters still reflected popular hatred of the dyarchy reforms. The choices of those exercising the ballot were again conditioned more by the local influence of the respective candidates than by any preference for alternative political principles or tactics.[50]

The outcome of the elections was a distinct disappointment to the nationalist cause, since the candidates elected by the Nationalists (25), the Home Rulers (11), and the *Swarajists* (9) totaled only 45, which was less than a majority. Burman candidates who were elected as Independents tended, once the second council convened, to gravitate to the conservative government-supporting group. They eventually came to be known as the Golden Valley Party, a name adapted from the exclusive Rangoon area of residence of some of its leaders. The three nationalist groups, known collectively as the People's Party with its "Burma for the Burmans" slogan, were themselves handicapped by lack of party funds and were also rent by personal and factional rivalries.[51] The People's Party adhered to no coherent program, except the pledge not to accept office, and it was responsible to no articulate constituency. The nationalist politicians within the second council, as previously, exercised little or no influence over the village *athins*. Defections from the ranks of the People's Party during the course of the second council reduced the opposition vote from 45 to 35 members only.[52]

Two political trends became apparent between 1925 and 1928. The first was a sharpening of the cleavage between the Burman members and the communally selected non-Burman group. Even on the govern-

[50] *ISCR*, XI, 261, 268–269. The requirements that an unsuccessful candidate for the council forfeit his 100-rupee deposit and that recovery of it in any case be conditioned on taking the oath of allegiance rankled with the nationalists.

[51] *Ibid.*, pp. 271–273.

[52] *Ibid.*, pp. 268–269. Lee Ah Yain, the Chinese who became the new minister of forests and agriculture in 1926, defected from the People's Party.

ment side of the council, conservative Burmans among the Independents gravitated to the Golden Valley Party, an exclusively Burman group, although financed by a wealthy Rangoon Chinese. The Independent Party, so called, was made up after 1928 of the non-Burman councilors (English, Karens, Indians, Chinese, Anglo-Indian members) who countered the incipient threat of rising Burman nationalist feeling by voting regularly with the government. The Burma-domiciled Oscar de Glanville, elected by the English constituency, became president of the Independent Party. The rising tide of communal (mainly anti-Indian) sentiment throughout the Lower Burma constituencies was reflected in a sharp increase of agitation demanding Burma's separation from India.

The other trend was in the direction of the attrition in nationalist ranks already noted, stemming from the impoverishment of their several party treasuries and the desire of individual politicians to share some of the perquisites of office.[53] Since People's Party members were pledged not to serve in the cabinet, such posts always fell to a more conservative group. Dr. Ba Yin took over the education portfolio, Lee Ah Yain (Independent, Chinese Chamber of Commerce) the forestry ministership, and J. A. Maung Gyi took over the home member's post in 1926 following the untimely death of U May Oung. In 1927, Oscar de Glanville became the first elected member to be chosen as presiding officer of the council. U Ba Pe became the deputy president.[54]

With the nationalist People's Party bloc lined up solidly in the opposition and both the cabinet and the governmental majority made up of nondescript heterogeneous elements, no forward-looking legislative program could be attempted. The smooth functioning of government from 1925 to 1929 was achieved by studiously refraining from introducing difficult or contentious legislation, no matter how urgent the need for it might be. Official policy was to oppose extravagance and waste, to maintain law and order, and to uphold established administrative routines, educational standards, and economic production.[55] Some advance was realized in the field of higher education by Governor Butler's sponsoring a university endowment drive. The

---

[53] *Ibid.*, pp. 269–270. Whereas the non-Burmans tended to vote independently in the first council, they regularly voted with the government in the second and third. In March, 1925, the Burman majority of the council levied a 5-rupee tax on sea passengers entering Rangoon, a move strongly protested by the Indians. See *The Times*, March 24, 1925. Governor Innes vetoed the measure.

[54] *RAB* for 1924–1925, pp. vii–x, for 1925–1926, pp. i–vi.

[55] *ISCR*, XI, 578–581.

Chettyars Association made a substantial contribution, and the Burmah Oil Company established an engineering college for the training of technicians.[56] Both of these moves were in response to agitation within the council for improved educational opportunities for Burmans desiring to enter the civil service and to qualify for technical posts in government and business.[57] But the council itself marked time as far as progressive legislation was concerned. Two abortive agricultural reform proposals will be considered later.

Nationalist efforts within the second council to repeal the capitation and *thathameda* taxes continued. A formal motion to cancel Upper Burma's *thathameda* tax, advanced in March, 1926, was referred to a committee for examination and report. Nothing was done because the abuses brought to light were limited almost entirely to actions taken by nonofficial local assessors, and the complainants again proposed no alternative source of funds. The boycotting G.C.B.A., both the So Thein and Chit Hlaing factions, refused to give evidence to the Tax Enquiry Committee. The tax-repeal proposal was eventually defeated in June, 1927, after the government promised that within five years the entire income from *thathameda* taxes would be allocated for expenditure by local government agencies.[58] No such consensus was reached with respect to Lower Burma's less flexible capitation tax, which continued to be a matter of acrimonious dispute. The council also attacked the revised "Land and Revenue Rules" of 1926 calling for an enhancement of the revenue demand with each new settlement survey.[59]

The tax-repeal proposals were eventually associated with the demand to alter the terms of the Meston settlement of Burma's debt to India, dating from 1902 and revised in 1920. Abolition of Burma's debt payments to India, it was argued, would make good the revenue losses incurred by abolishing the hated direct taxes and would also satisfy Burman nationalist resentment over being required to pay the costs of Burma's conquest by India.[60] This anti-Meston agitation fed

[56] Sen, p. 29.
[57] *ISCR*, XI, 292–297. In 1927, U Nyo made the initial contribution for a Rangoon University Student Union building. The cornerstone was laid on December 5, 1927.
[58] *Ibid.*, pp. 288–292; *RPA* for 1926, p. 74.
[59] *ISCR*, XI, 287–288.
[60] *Ibid.*, pp. 288–292; F. B. Leach, *The Future of Burma*, pp. 65–68. The Burma Government itself attacked the Meston settlement, charging that excessive payments to India had retarded Burma's development of needed facilities for communication, transport, and public buildings. The revision of 1920 was supposed

the rising desire among the intelligentsia for Burma's separation from India.

Increasing anti-Indian feeling was also reflected in the strongly negative response given by a majority of the council to a proposal by an Indian member that a fixed proportion of the government posts in Burma be reserved for Indians. Burmans declared emphatically that they wanted no Indians in government services, "cheap or dear," and countered by a request for preferential treatment to Burmans in the assignment of jobs. Government spokesmen agreed to the latter proposal after adding the proviso, "other things being equal." A clear case of attempted class legislation was the Burman move to establish a monopoly position for themselves in the posts of government prosecutor by making appointments conditional on the completion of ten years' legal practice locally plus "high proficiency" in Burmese.[61] Another resolution to permit meagerly prepared students of law to qualify as third-grade pleaders was advanced within the council against the strong opposition of Burmans in the High Court, the Bar Association, and the Pleaders' Association.[62]

Other activities of the second council were routine. Scores of questions were raised attacking the police.[63] Attempts were made to review within the legislature rulings and decisions covering land claims cases already properly adjudicated by the courts. Burmans also advanced an abortive proposal for setting up a standing advisory committee on political prosecutions, with a nonofficial majority, to review the initiation of such prosecutions by government. Some members of the council wanted legislative review of the widespread disregistration of cooperative societies after 1928 on grounds of thriftlessness and dishonesty. Such moves appeared fully to confirm the fears of non-Burman members, especially the British, that the transfer of the Home Minis-

---

to facilitate greater financial autonomy to Burma, but it did little to strengthen the financial position of the Rangoon government.

[61] The government settled for five years' legal practice and an "adequate" knowledge of Burmese. By 1927, the considerable Indian propaganda in Burma, both Congress Party and Muslim League, affected only the Indian residents. Burma's delegation of forty-two members to the Madras meeting of the Indian National Congress in 1927 was nevertheless headed by U Ottama, U Sandawbatha, and J. A. Maung Gyi. See RPA for 1926, p. 79, for 1927, p. 67.

[62] ISCR, XI, 273–274, 297–298. The defeat of this measure was alleged to have dashed the hopes of some 5,000 aspirants to qualify under the proposed relaxed ruling.

[63] Ibid., pp. 213–215. A resolution censuring the Rangoon police for dispersing a meeting held to protest the conviction of U Ottama missed passing by one vote only.

try to a Burman minister responsible to the council rather than to the governor would destroy all judicial processes.[64]

The elections of 1928 changed the political situation but little. Some 18 per cent of the eligible voters participated, but the People's Party coalition emerged no stronger numerically than in 1925 and even more riven by personal rivalries. Efforts to collect contributions of 10, 50, and 100 rupees from members as a party chest failed, and the People's Party became completely insolvent by 1929. U Pu (Yamethin) displaced Oscar de Glanville as president of the new council, with U Ba Pe becoming again deputy president of the council. But these were the only nationalist gains. Lee Ah Yain continued as minister of agriculture and forests, and one U Ba Tin became minister of education. Nationalist opposition within the council continued to be highly ineffective.[65]

During the three years of U Ottama's second imprisonment, 1924 to 1927, the influence of the political *pongyis* declined. Two widely separated efforts to revive the antitax campaign in Tharrawaddy and Meiktila districts in 1926 were easily put down. A *pongyi* named U Wizaya (Wisara) headed an abortive effort to challenge the new land tax assessment plan and eventually went to jail for resisting the government. Another young *pongyi* at Tavoy posed as a prince-pretender (the *Setkya Min*) to the vacant throne at Mandalay, until he was arrested for making anti-British speeches.[66] A favorite *pongyi* tactic was to circulate prophetic rumors that the British were about to withdraw and that the revived Burma Kingdom would then abolish all taxes.[67]

The release of U Ottama in February, 1927, and the convening of the joint sessions of the So Thein G.C.B.A. and the G.C.S.S. at Pegu a month later revived political tensions. Disaffection again centered in the contiguous Insein, Tharrawaddy, Henzada, and Prome districts. The *pongyi* party started a vernacular paper, called the *Wunthanu*. An example of *pongyi* propaganda was a pamphlet outlawed by the

[64] *Ibid.*, pp. 213, 287–288, 292–297.

[65] *ISCR*, I, 197, XI, 271–273; Sen, pp. 31–32.

[66] *RPA* for 1926, p. 74; *RAB* for 1926–1927, pp. i–xiii. Revenue collections of direct taxes were difficult in both 1926 and 1927.

[67] *ISCR*, XV, 461. A scourge of rinderpest carried off some 40,000 cattle in 1926–1927, causing great distress in Lower Burma especially. Conservative missionaries resisted rising pressure to turn over Christian affairs to indigenous leaders and praised the determination of the British Government not to be stampeded into granting too much power to the Burmans. See ABFMS, *MS. Correspondence*, J. H. Cummings to J. C. Robbins, from Henzada, Jan. 30, 1927.

government in 1927 exhorting all Burman Buddhists and all monks affiliated with the G.C.S.S. to stage mass meetings in towns and villages in order to perform religious rites, to pledge themselves not to forget the lawlessness of the English, and to meditate throughout the day on the law of impermanence [presumably of British rule]. The author was U Wimalasarn of the extralegal *Wunthanu* district council of Tharrawaddy.[68] U Ottama attended the 1927 Indian Congress Party meeting at Madras and later toured Lower Burma urging nonpayment of the capitation tax. He was eventually arrested in 1928 for the last time.[69]

Radicalism in Burma during the late 1920's owed little to Indian agitators and apparently nothing whatever to world communism which was so active prior to 1928 in neighboring China, Indochina, and Indonesia.[70] Political protests generally followed traditionalist patterns. A village hermit at Shwebo, U Bandako, in 1927–1928 began tattooing villagers and instigated a feeble rising, which was followed by a series of large dacoity operations. Sections of Pegu Division got similarly out of hand in 1928 as a result of revolutionary speeches made by a rebellious monk. Military police were obliged to take strong measures in both areas for a number of months in order to re-establish control.[71] But with U Ottama in jail, the year 1928 was on the whole far less turbulent politically than 1927. Many observers were convinced by 1929 that the following of the *pongyis* was declining from lack of popular confidence in their political wisdom. It was nevertheless obvious that villagers who had listened to U Ottama were impervious to any counterpropaganda by the government.[72] The death of the monk U Wisera in 1929 as a result of a hunger strike allegedly extending over 166 days again fanned popular feeling to a fever pitch. Popular unrest was far from subsiding.[73]

Circle Boards and District Councils

Although the Burma Rural Self-Government Act of 1921 which provided for the election of circle boards and district councils was not

---

[68] *Burma Gazette*, pt. II (1927), p. 921; Moscotti, p. 183.

[69] *RPA* for 1927, p. 67.   [70] *ISCR*, XV, 461–462.

[71] *RAB* for 1927–1928, pp. xiii, 23; *The Times*, Aug. 23, 1927, and June 27, 1928. After a prolonged trial Bandaka was transported for life.

[72] *RAB* for 1927–1928; *RPA* for 1928, p. 70.

[73] U Wisara's hunger strike was undertaken in an effort to force his jailers to return his *pongyi* robe.

an integral part of the dyarchy constitution of 1922, it shared in full measure the popular hostility attaching to the reform program generally. The phrase "dyarchy councils" became a term of opprobrium. Like other aspects of the reform program, the local government councils were superimposed more or less arbitrarily on the regular administrative system. The scheme suffered a fatal handicap initially, since it had been first proposed as part of the much-criticized program of Lieutenant Governor Craddock. Educated nationalist leaders in the urban areas resented particularly the abrupt allocation of onerous administrative responsibilities, without official direction, to elected and unsalaried local bodies, whose members were completely lacking in experience with such matters, while dyarchy denied to the more competent Burmans in the legislative council control at the center over finances and larger questions of policy. Especially disliked were the repeated affirmations by British spokesmen that the character of Burman performance of responsibilities in local self-government would be the criterion for their fitness to enjoy a larger degree of self-government in the future. It thus appeared that the British were making the prospect of achieving home rule for Burma contingent on the proper performance by inexperienced villagers of duties which they were loath to assume. The effort would be made under handicaps of political opposition which denied Burmans any interested public capable of holding the individual council members responsible for their conduct.[74]

Advisory district councils had been introduced in India in the 1880's, modeled more or less on the county council system in England. The deputy commissioners frequently served at the outset as council chairmen. The responsibilities of the India councils had been broadened in 1907 and again in 1921 to include substantive administrative functions such as authorizing expenditures for projects to be executed under council supervision by subordinate agencies of government at lower levels.[75] Under the 1907 Village Act for Burma, the deputy commissioners were authorized to use village-tract headmen as executive officers for local expenditures on public works and health projects as well as for routine policing and tax-collection duties. What the

[74] Moscotti, pp. 122–126; Tinker, pp. 218–219. Burmese public opinion locally failed to grasp the fact that the electorate rather than the officials of government were expected to take responsibility for redress of grievances arising from district council action.

[75] F. B. Leach, The Future of Burma, pp. 16, 19, 36, 97.

India Act of 1921 did was to transfer a number of such executive functions covering health and public works to the newly established district councils.[76]

The district council system was introduced full blown into Burma in 1921 in response to no popular demand and without providing any preliminary experience in such matters. The action was also taken at a most inauspicious time of political furor, which made failure inevitable. The new arrangement provided that groupings of village tracts (4 or 5 of them combined to make a single electoral district area) should elect, on a suffrage age basis of twenty-five years, members of circle boards. The boards would average 10 to a dozen members per circle unit. Each circle board, in turn, would elect 2 of its own members to sit on the district council. Since the district was considered too large to serve as a unit for detailed administration of local affairs, the sponsors of the act assumed that the several circle boards would each be allocated a fraction of the funds available for local expenditure and would then act as the executive agents of the supervisory councils. It was also assumed that the circle boards, in turn, would depute some of their assigned tasks to locally selected village-tract committees.

Some 28 of Burma's 37 districts were included within the system, and only 17 councils were entrusted with full responsibility for local government.[77] Omitted were the less-developed areas of northern Burma containing Shan and Kachin populations plus several peripheral districts adjacent to hill tracts, two of them being in the Arakan Division.[78] The structure of the official administrative hierarchy of the several districts, from deputy commissioner down to village headmen and including the locally assigned employees of the functional departments of the central secretariat at Rangoon, remained as before, except that administrative direction in many matters was shifted to local hands. The 1921 Act specifically stipulated that activities of the district councils should not infringe upon the basic duties or prerogatives of the village headmen, who as government officials were not sup-

[76] Burma, *Review of the . . . Report on the Working of Districts Councils . . . in Burma* for 1925–1926 (Rangoon, 1927), pp. 2–5. This is hereafter cited as *RDC*. Village road maintenance remained with the headman until 1924.

[77] Tinker, pp. 217–219.

[78] *ISCR*, XI, 423–424. The most important districts omitted from rural government reforms were Putao, Myitkyina, Bhamo, and Katha in Upper Burma and Sandoway and Kyaukpyu in Arakan.

posed to be candidates for circle board membership and were expressly forbidden election to the district councils.[79]

The administrative responsibilities of the councils included the operation of public health, medical and veterinary services, the maintenance of secondary roads (especially bridges), waterways, and other public works (except irrigation). They also included vernacular education and the regulation of ferry services, rickshaws, bazaar rentals, and cattle pounds. The British sponsors of the act hoped that in time all activities related to local welfare could be turned over to the councils and that a growing public demand for better schools, water supplies, bunds, and roads would be reflected in a willingness to raise the needed additional funds from increased local taxation, which could be levied on the authority of the councils.[80] The essential governmental operations of tax collection, maintenance of law and order, and the administration of justice remained the unqualified responsibility of the official hierarchy as heretofore, but district officials must not run the councils. The chairmen and vice-chairmen of the councils were also protected against official interference by the regulation that their proceedings could be annulled only by action of the central Department of Local Government.

Difficulties quickly developed. Because responsible middle-class leadership inevitably gravitated to the cities, the rural areas lacked competent personnel. Most councilors were appalled at the volume of paper work involved, and the very bulk of the audit citations of defalcations and bookkeeping errors discouraged any attempt to correct them. Public opinion did not condemn moderate bribetaking, and it was wholly unprepared to check wholesale corruption. Basic problems stemmed from contract letting, sale of appointments, transfers, and promotions and from failure to discipline offenders.[81] Burman ministers in charge of administering local government studiously avoided using their power to interfere in district council affairs, preferring to shift supervisory chores to the divisional commissioners. The latter were specifically authorized to settle disputes between adjacent councils and to confirm all appointments and dismissals of employed officers of local councils within their several divisional jurisdictions. They could also force councils to discharge undesirable officers. But the commissioners, like the Department of Local Govern-

---

[79] *RAB* for 1927–1928, p. 2. [80] *RDC* for 1923–1924, pp. 2–3.

[81] Tinker, pp. 222–225. Formation of twelve new municipalities between 1918 and 1924 robbed rural areas of possible leadership.

ment, were too remote and too unconcerned to take over responsibility for detailed administration, which was needed. District officials, especially the deputy commissioners, were permitted to act independently of council authorization only in emergency situations involving public safety, threatened epidemics, or breaches of the peace. Under ordinary circumstances they could do no more than inspect operations, audit accounts, and report their findings to the Department of Local Government, which adopted a hands-off attitude.[82] The councils were free, therefore, to make all sorts of mistakes either carelessly or willfully in the knowledge that they would probably not be held accountable either by Local Government or by their circle constituencies.

Only 6 per cent of the eligible electorate bothered to vote in the 1922 elections for the circle boards.[83] Approximately 600 of the 2,700 circle board constituencies neglected to put forward any candidates at all, and in nearly 800 additional ones no election contests were involved in the choice of candidates.[84] In 1925 the number of uncontested elections was greater than in 1922, as was also the number of constituencies failing to choose circle boards at all. Only a few districts in 1925 registered voting gains.[85] Except for the authority belatedly vested in the commissioners to fill board and council vacancies by direct appointment, a number of the local bodies would probably never have been constituted at all.[86]

The regulation debarring village *thugyis* from participating in the councils unless they surrendered their headmanships was a source of difficulty. From the outset a substantial proportion of the elected members of the circle boards were headmen, and many of them refused to resign their village-tract posts when selected to sit in the district councils. When the commissioners, acting under the terms of the law, disqualified all *thugyis* as council members, many boards refused to elect any alternate choices, thus forcing the commissioners to exercise their nominating powers, usually to confirm the original selections.[87] The result was that no fewer than 132 of the original list of 574 council members were village headmen, of whom 80 were nominated outright to fill vacancies while 52 were confirmed in their irregular election by boards.[88] In 1925 some 30 per cent of the elected

---

[82] *ISCR*, XI, 435–436.

[83] *RDC* for 1927–1928, p. 1. Voter participation in 1922 varied from 63.6 per cent of the electorate in Kyaukse to 1.8 per cent in neighboring Meiktila. Tinker (p. 222) puts voting in 1922 at 11 per cent of the rural electorate.

[84] *RDC* for 1923–1924, pp. 1–2.   [85] *RDC* for 1926–1927, pp. 48–49.

[86] *Ibid.*, p. 21.   [87] *RDC* for 1923–1924, p. 1.   [88] *ISCR*, XI, 426.

circle board members were again headmen, but at this time a largely new group entered the councils.

Partly because of the increased effort on the part of self-seeking candidates to gain district council seats, only 23 *thugyis* were elected in 1925. The effect was to divorce councils even further from the control of village opinion.[89] By 1926 it was admitted officially that the prohibition of participation by headmen had been a mistake and that it would also have been better at the outset to have authorized district officials to serve as council chairmen.[90] The almost universal failure of the councils to assign funds or functions to the several circle boards [91] left the district bodies effectively insulated from all popular contacts.

The ominous trend, perceptible as early as 1925, for corruptionists to gain control of the councils aggravated the problem of obtaining the requisite degree of co-operation between the district officials and the specialized departments. Such co-operation was needed to carry out measures relating to health, medical and veterinary services, public works, and education. Able engineers and health officers could not be hired by the local bodies. Whereas some two-thirds of the original councils availed themselves of the opportunity to "co-opt" as members such district officials as the civil surgeon, the veterinary and school inspectors, and executive engineers,[92] the trend in subsequent councils was to forego the assistance of such technical officials, presumably to avoid their interference. Nine of the councils in 1926–1927 included no co-opted officials at all.[93] As an extreme case, the chairman of the Insein council was re-elected in 1925 even though he was under prosecution at the time for embezzling funds during his previous term of service.[94] By 1927, when some improvement could be noted in perfecting council organizations and in choosing competent secre-

---

[89] *RDC* for 1925–1926, pp. 6–9, for 1927–1928, p. 2; Tinker, p. 222. Commissioners in 1925 nominated 324 headmen to circle board vacancies, and 676 other headmen gained such posts by election. Only 34 council vacancies were filled by the commissioners in 1928. Only 14 *thugyis* found places on the district councils in 1928.

[90] *RDC* for 1925–1926, p. 38.

[91] *RDC* for 1924–1925, pp. 5–6; Tinker, pp. 217–219. Only two district councils assigned substantial functions to the circle boards.

[92] *ISCR*, XI, 426–427; Tinker, p. 225. Four of the twenty-eight district councils employed health officers.

[93] *RDC* for 1926–1927, p. 3, for 1927–1928, p. 2.

[94] *RDC* for 1925–1926, pp. 10–15. In 1927 the Insein council voted no confidence in its own elected chairman (*RDC* for 1927–1928, p. 28).

taries, the *Wunthanu Athin* extremists unfortunately began to revive their active obstruction to the work of the local bodies.[95]

It is not surprising under the circumstances that the hated "dyarchy councils" became synonymous in the public mind with inefficient and corrupt administration.[96] The published reviews of the annual reports are replete with details bearing out the popular indictment. The most persistent deficiency related to the steady decline in the standards in keeping financial records concerning both district and school funds.[97] The auditors themselves were resisted by the councils precisely because they revealed the administrative abuses. It was partly a case of inexperience and ineptitude. Some of the councils required five years to prepare bylaws delegating powers and duties to their officers. The secretaries and clerks generally ignored instructions, while officials who had defaulted in one council office had no difficulty getting employed by another. The commissioners finally issued the not overly drastic regulation that secretaries whose reports for three successive years were classified as "very unsatisfactory" must be removed. Fraudulent contracts were let often to expensive and inexperienced Burman contractors; school funds were misappropriated and overcommitted, so that many teachers were left without pay. Outright embezzlement was uncovered along with double payment of bills and irresponsible use of borrowed funds.[98] The record was a dismal one.

The basic causes for the failure of the district council experiment included political factors which went deeper than the undoubted dishonesty or naïveté of many members. From the very outset in 1923, council members encountered social persecution, attacks on their business interests, damage to property, and even physical violence at the hands of boycotting elements.[99] Even where this kind of active resistance was lacking, the popular attitude was usually one of complete indifference. Candidates for council posts under these

---

[95] *RDC* for 1927–1928, pp. 7–8, 10–21, 28. In Magwe, Sagaing, and Monywa districts particularly, the councils in 1928 attracted public-spirited men who realized much improvement.

[96] F. B. Leach, *The Future of Burma*, pp. 98–99.

[97] *RDC* for 1925–1926, pp. 10–15. Of the 48 district fund audits reported for 1923–1926, 4 were classified satisfactory and 36 as unsatisfactory or very unsatisfactory. Only 12 such audits were run at all in the third year of this period. Of the 42 school fund audits for the same years, 3 were rated satisfactory and 26 unsatisfactory or very unsatisfactory.

[98] *RDC* for 1925–1926, pp. 10–15, for 1926–1927, pp. 3–21, for 1927–1928, pp. 15–21.

[99] *RDC* for 1924–1925, p. 4. Four council members were killed, and two others were assaulted with dahs in 1924–1925.

circumstances became, too often, men motivated by reasons other than the social interest, for they were not answerable to any public opinion or interested electorate. Irresponsibility in the handling of finances became the rule rather than the exception.[100] Since council members served without salary compensation, many of them assumed that they ought not be held responsible for maladministration. Neglect of duty on the part of council employees as a rule also went unpunished. The situation was made to order for dishonest staff members and favor seekers.[101] Efforts of government to cultivate closer relations between the public and the legislative council membership, through the periodic meetings of the newly created Local Government Advisory Board, accomplished little.[102]

The money available for local government purposes was never adequate. Around 37 per cent of the district council funds were contributed by the provincial (all-Burma) departments directly charged with promoting basic functions of the councils, namely education, public works, health, and medicine. These moneys were supplemented by revenue from locally collected tolls and fees derived from regulation of markets, ferries, slaughterhouses, and cattle pounds. In Lower Burma, a 10 per cent assessment on land revenue was added to the local funds. Direct government grants to Upper Burma districts made good their loss of income because of failure to share in the land revenues. No district council ever undertook to exercise its authority to levy additional local taxation or to enhance locally collected fees.[103] A tentative proposal by government in 1928 to allocate income from direct capitation and *thathemeda* taxes to local purposes, if it had been carried out, would probably have encouraged in time a larger measure of responsibility.

Appropriations for vernacular education accounted for approximately half of the expenditures of the councils and were administered by the school board committees of the councils.[104] An initial difficulty

---

[100] *RAB* for 1927–1928, p. xi.

[101] *RDC* for 1925–1926, p. 11, for 1927–1928, p. 7; *ISCR*, XI, 437.

[102] *ISCR*, XI, 281–282. The minister in charge of local government was president of the advisory board, and six of the ten additional members were elected by nonofficial members of the legislative council. The board advised the minister on all aspects of local government. The advisory boards met three times a year.

[103] *RDC* for 1927–1928, p. 7; Tinker, p. 238. Councils were authorized under the Act of 1921 to levy taxes on income from houses, buildings, and lands or on local areas benefiting by such public works improvements as railways, embankments, or irrigation works.

[104] *ISCR*, XI, 439; *RDC* for 1926–1927, pp. 3–21. School expenditures increased

encountered by the board schools was the opposition of national school supporters, who boycotted all government schools. Even after the national schools movement collapsed, the board schools were plagued by irregular attendance, indiscipline, inadequate buildings, and underpaid, therefore incompetent, staffs. There was a genuine public demand for vernacular education including some English training, but the funds available needed to be multiplied ten times to provide compulsory, free, primary instruction. School funds in most districts were perennially overcommitted even in areas where they were honestly administered. As a result teachers' pay was chronically in arrears.[105]

In some districts the teachers began to follow the questionable expedient of seeking entrance to the councils in order to serve on the school boards. Some of the early school board reports, prepared by teacher members in English and apparently not read by Burmese-speaking members of the council, were highly critical of the councilors themselves.[106] One of the effective uses of school funds was in the allocations made, under a grant-in-aid system, to privately run (often missionary) schools. Because school registry for government aid was dependent on passing official inspection, the school boards and the school inspectors generally co-operated, although board members sometimes resented official interference.[107] Political considerations affected school operations at times, and the careful auditing of school accounts invariably aroused local resentment.[108]

The funds available for local public works projects frequently remained unspent because of the council's failure to co-operate with the Public Works Department. Councils refused, for example, to meet the allegedly excessive demands of the Public Works Department that some 24 per cent of the cost of works completed must be chargeable against the expense of maintaining the department's establishment, plant, and tools. Few councils hired competent engineers of their own, which left the execution of works projects to departmental agencies, if the work was to be done at all. Burmese contractors for public works bid high and were usually inefficient. The result was that roads, bridges, and bunds fell into disrepair, and many needed

---

from 44 per cent of the total annual expenditures of the councils in 1923 to 50 per cent in 1928.

[105] *RDC* for 1925–1926, p. 35.   [106] *RDC* for 1924–1925, pp. 16–21.

[107] *RDC* for 1924–1925, pp. 16–23, for 1926–1927, p. 17, for 1927–1928, p. 21. Twelve of the districts in 1925 had no schools which were exclusively under school board sponsorship.

[108] *ISCR*, XI, 440–445; F. B. Leach, *The Future of Burma*, p. 100.

projects were not undertaken.[109] Another unfortunate result was that intervillage roads, which, prior to 1924, were maintained by gratis labor recruited by the tract headmen, were thereafter entirely neglected because villagers refused to serve.[110]

Public health services (sanitation and disease prevention) were not in public demand and were correspondingly poorly developed. Popular hostility to the activities of official sanitary inspectors of the Health Department was reflected in the councils themselves. When government offered to meet half the cost of hiring full-time district health officers, very few local bodies were interested.[111] Hospitals and medical dispensaries were more generously treated, although the hospital committees were usually inefficient, and building facilities were everywhere grossly inadequate. The basic problem in the field of health services was clearly that of educating public demand.[112] Few observers would contest the conclusion that no aspect of the reform program was as disappointing as that of local government and that the unused circle boards were themselves the weakest aspect of the scheme.[113]

Problems of Municipal and Village Government, 1923–1929

The political ferment present in Burma in the 1920's also affected adversely municipal affairs. Burma's approximately three-score municipalities, many of which dated from before World War I,[114] had been indebted for many of their positive accomplishments to the participation of non-Burman (European) members on their governing committees. This leadership disappeared in many localities under self-government. Here as with the district councils most of the people were little concerned about the conduct of local affairs except to

[109] RDC for 1923–1924, pp. 6–8, for 1925–1926, pp. 18–19, 41, for 1927–1928, pp. 8–10. Expenditures for public works increased sharply (by 46 per cent) in 1927–1928.

[110] RDC for 1927–1928, pp. 18–21.

[111] RDC for 1923–1924, pp. 2–8, for 1925–1926, p. 31, for 1927–1928, p. 15.

[112] RDC for 1924–1925, pp. 16, 36, for 1926–1927, pp. 3–21; ISCR, XI, 432–434, 440–445. Veterinary assistants assigned to the districts remained under the direct control of the Veterinary Department, even though rentals, purchase of medicines, and other contingent costs were charged to district funds.

[113] RDC for 1924–1925, pp. 5–6, for 1925–1926, p. 17.

[114] ISCR, XI, 454. In 1926–1927 Burma had fifty-eight full municipalities plus fifteen "notified area" towns, to which latter group some sections only of the Municipal Act applied.

270

avoid as far as possible any additional taxation, regardless of urgency of the need for improved services.[115]

Standards of efficiency in municipal government, which had never been high, deteriorated rapidly after 1924. The 35 per cent unsatisfactory performance by town committees from 1919 to 1923 increased abruptly under political pressure to 44.7 per cent in 1923–1924, 74 per cent in 1924–1925, 85 per cent in 1925–1926, and 95 per cent in 1926–1927. In the final year the performance of only one municipality was adjudged fully satisfactory, and only two others fairly so. Local committees were particularly careless about supervising the municipal staff. Dishonest and incapable men were hired, and the corrective checks on misconduct provided by law through agencies of the Department of Local Government and the divisional commissioners were inadequate to cope with the growing problems. Lacking was a vigilant citizenry capable of generating indignation over the misconduct of officials. Outside of Rangoon, few municipal officials knew any English; few had experience in business and in the handling of money or any understanding at all of administrative routines and reports. Expansion of local amenities, such as water, lighting, and cleaning services, ceased, and in few places were the earlier standards maintained.[116] But such results might easily have been anticipated. In this connection the following informed comment on the problem is relevant:

Municipal self-government did not fail [as alleged by the government] because "self-government was an exotic plant to which the character and the people were unfavourable," but because there was no homogeneous organic community to govern itself, and because the committees were required to govern the people as the Government saw fit instead of as the people wanted. . . . To try to make people do of their own accord what they do not want to do is neither self-government, nor common sense.[117]

It was stressed in Chapter VII that one of the most deleterious effects of the political agitation of the early 1920's was to weaken the already-vulnerable authority of the village headman. The essential requirement for the effective operation of the *thugyi* system was the voluntary

[115] Tinker, p. 219. Of the municipal electorate, 28 per cent voted in 1921 and 44 per cent in 1924. But in Rangoon only eleven of twenty-five seats were contested in 1928.

[116] *ISCR*, XI, 462–466; Tinker, pp. 221, 225, 230, 236. The reports for 1926–1927 revealed "extensive embezzlements and defalcations," especially at Mandalay.

[117] J. S. Furnivall, "Reconstruction in Burma" (MS., 1943), pp. 11–12.

acceptance of joint responsibility by the whole body of the villagers especially in matters relating to law and order and to the general improvement of local amenities.[118] Government's policy of forbidding headmen to participate politically in the *Wunthanu Athins* in effect isolated them from the sympathy and co-operation of a majority of the villagers, who were expected to accept joint responsibility under headman leadership. Police reports as early as 1923 urged that the ban against political participation be removed. By 1927 such reports declared that the police could do nothing without the aid of the headmen and that under existing conditions politics was striking at the very backbone of law enforcement by turning public opinion against the headmen.[119] *Thugyis* also lost prestige because elected members of the new local bodies, from which headmen were legally barred, tended to regard themselves as superior. In the public mind, the headman became simply the "maid of all work" for the government, and as such he incurred the disdain of the grass-roots political leadership.[120]

Matters became particularly critical during the course of the antitax campaign of 1924, when village headmen usually found themselves opposed by the influential *Wunthanu Athins*. The headman's personal income was materially reduced by difficulty encountered in collecting taxes, and his authority was also directly impaired when fines were assessed on villages for suppressing evidence in relation to the illegal antitax agitation.[121] Thus political activity and criminal defiance of governmental authority leveled a joint attack on the headman.[122]

The report of the Crime Enquiry Committee presented to the legislative council in late 1923 recommended as an aid in the curbing of crime that elected village committees, numbering up to four members for each tract and operating under chairmen of their own selection, be authorized to share the policing and judicial authority of the *thugyis*. The committees would also share the authority to requisition assistance and to impose collective fines. Service on such committees would carry exemption from taxes. The report recommended also that the selection of headmen be by election and that those already on life tenure be obliged to offer themselves for election approval.[123] Some of

---

[118] *ISCR*, XI, 447.   [119] *RPA* for 1923, p. 39, for 1927, pp. 57–58.

[120] Mya Sein, pp. 177–178.

[121] *RPA* for 1924, p. 51; *RAB* for 1924–1925, pp. 17, 21.

[122] *ISCR*, XI, 207. The government offered liberal rewards for headman co-operation in rounding up dacoits.

[123] *Ibid.*, pp. 331–332; *RDC* for 1925–1926, p. 5. Committee authority as recom-

the nationalist spokesmen in the legislative council went further to propose limiting the headman's term to five years and making his appointment and removal subject to vote of the villagers. They also insisted on a sharp reduction in the legal requirement of communal responsibility for assisting the police.[124]

Government spokesmen felt that it was necessary to meet council demands part way in order to forestall more radical politically motivated efforts to eliminate entirely the office of headman as an obstacle to the activities of the village *athins*.[125] The Burma Village (Amendment) Act of 1924 authorized the election of village committees empowered to advise and assist the headman and to share his judicial powers. Magistrates were permitted by the act to transfer to village committees for trial any case of which the committee took cognizance in the first instance. The headman was ex-officio chairman of the tract committee, and his official responsibility and tenure remained related as before to the authority of the deputy commissioner of the district.[126] The village judicial committees established under the Amending Act of 1924 were made identical with the administrative committees mentioned in the Local Government Act of 1921, if and when the latter should ever become operative.[127]

Aside from relieving political pressure temporarily within the legislative council, the amending bill accomplished little. The village committees were never active; they heard occasional cases but generally exercised their judicial powers very sparingly. In many villages, committees belittled the headmen and undermined their control. Headmen continued to forfeit authority under the debilitating burden of performance of irksome petty tasks and the constant barrage of political attack as the alleged creatures of the official bureaucracy.[128] The government-sponsored voluntary district police advisory committees set

---

mended would include power to investigate, search, and arrest, to deliver arrested persons to the police, to furnish police intelligence, to disarm persons, and to approve local requisitions and fines.

[124] *ISCR*, XI, 274.

[125] *Ibid.*, pp. 314. Some of the minority groups in the council did not favor election of headmen for the suggested five-year terms.

[126] *RAB* for 1923–1924, pp. vii–viii, for 1924–1925, p. 14; *ISCR*, XI, 332. The headman's authority to requisition services and supplies were reduced, but he still could fine villagers refusing to do public duties.

[127] *ISCR*, XI, pp. 424–427, 447–448.

[128] *RAB* for 1924–1925, p. 14; *RPA* for 1923, p. 39, for 1929, pp. 76–79, for 1930, p. 44; F. B. Leach, *The Future of Burma*, pp. 121–122. Youthful police inspectors accorded scant respect to the headmen.

up in 1925 to enlist popular co-operation were so ineffective that by 1927 no police superintendent was able to get members to attend meetings.[129] The correlation between the waning authority of the headman and the growing problem of crime was summarized as follows by the Pegu District police superintendent in 1926:

Headmen are a very mixed lot, and while some assist the Police to the best of their ability, and a few assist occasionally, there are a large number who are definitely against the Police. . . . Practically every headman has a number of very doubtful followers—not a few of whom are actual relations— and whilst he may be willing to assist the Police in ordinary cases, he does his very utmost to assist his followers when suspicion falls on them. . . . Not a few of the more wealthy headmen in the district have doubtful pasts, and the majority of them are still ready to take a hand in crime if this can be done with any degree of safety.[130]

In 1927, the governmental majority in the legislative council reversed its policy of 1924 by curbing the judicial and other powers enjoyed by many of the village committees.[131] The council reinstated the responsibility of deputy commissioners for village defense as well as that of the community to co-operate in the punishment of those harboring criminals. On the occasion of this action, the nationalist opposition group within the council walked out of the chamber in protest.[132]

Political Factors Contributing to the Increase of Crime

It is more easy to demonstrate that criminal activity increased with the rising tide of political agitation following World War I than it is to establish a causal connection either way. The increase of violent crime in Burma is represented in the following figures: [133]

Year	Number of Offenses
1918	1,456
1919	1,721
1920	1,950
1923	2,048
1924	2,625
1925	3,257

[129] ISCR, XI, 216–217.   [130] RPA for 1926, pp. 65–66.

[131] RAB for 1928–1929, p. 26. Headmen and committees exercising judicial powers in 1929 numbered around 3,700 for criminal cases and 3,900 for civil cases, in a total of some 12,000 tracts.

[132] RAB for 1926–1927, pp. i–xiii; ISCR, XI, 316, 447. The village committees tried petty civil and criminal cases and acted as an "advisory body to the village headman in the performance of his administrative duties concerning the general welfare of the tract" (ISCR, XI, 447).

[133] RPA for 1919, p. 15, for 1921, p. 20, for 1923, p. 17, for 1925, p. 17.

Lesser crimes increased in roughly the same proportion. The number of offenses leveled off after the peak year of 1925, but rose in 1928 and again in 1931–1932. Possibly half of such crimes resulted from sudden explosions of temper, and many of the premeditated ones were in part the result of boredom and yearning for excitement.[134] By the mid-twenties Burma's jails were filled to overflowing, so that tickets of leave had to be granted before old sentences expired in order to make room for the newly convicted.[135] Nearly all of those consigned to prison were men (almost never women), of whom some 56 per cent were under thirty years of age. Around three-fourths of the convicted were literate, and 84 per cent were Buddhist Burmans.[136] Cities as well as rural areas were affected. In the city of Rangoon, minor (noncognizable) crime increased from 10,093 offenses in 1918 to 29,415 in 1927.[137]

In rural areas, criminal activity rose during the two long breaks in the agricultural season, one after the rice was planted and the other during the dry season following the harvest. Many peasant workers were unemployed, and idle hands got into mischief. Dacoit leaders, often disguised as traveling hawker-peddlers, attracted spirited young men to them by tales of plunder and excitement. Disparity between low wages and rising living costs was also an important contributor to criminal activity.[138] Matters became worse after 1922, because of the difficulty encountered by police in obtaining evidence against offenders even from the victims themselves. The *Wunthanu Athins* systematically protected members from punishment, and the *"Bu athins"* as well as the criminals were capable of inflicting physical intimidation not only on police and headmen but also on any villagers who cooperated with agencies of the law. Wealthy landlords often acted as patrons of the *athins,* partly for self-protection, and criminals readily accepted the aura of antiforeign nationalistic and religious concern to cloak their activities. Criminal elements were thus able to circulate in good patriotic company.[139]

The almost universal popular complaint raised against the police and the only slightly less virulent criticism of the magistrates were in some measure justified. It was no secret that many ill-educated, ill-housed, ill-paid policemen accepted petty bribes whenever opportunity afforded, which was often.[140] As for the magistrates, the historian, Har-

---

[134] *ISCR*, XI, 211–212, XV, 458–463.   [135] *RAB* for 1926–1927, p. xiii.
[136] *RPA* for 1932, p. 11.   [137] *ISCR*, XI, 210.
[138] *ISCR*, XI, 304, XV, 458–461; Moscotti, p. 33.
[139] F. Bigg-Wither, "Cleaning up Burma's Murder Zone," *Contemporary Review,* vol. 156 (1929), pp. 715–722; *RPA* for 1924, pp. 13–15.
[140] *RPA* for 1923, p. 11, for 1925, pp. 13–14.

vey, estimated on the basis of his own wide experience as a magistrate in Burma that perhaps 50 Class I judges in all of Burma were incorruptible and that the other 600 judges frequently accepted gratuities from litigants aggregating as high as eight to ten times their annual salaries. The judges could conceal their favoritism by being overstrict in applying rules of evidence or by their shift of emphasis while translating oral Burmese evidence into English for the formal court record. Some verdicts were sold outright.[141]

An attempt was made in 1924 to improve the quality of the police by offering higher pay, even though the staff was reduced. But an immediate increase of robbery and dacoity quickly forced the reinstatement of the staff, and standards remained much the same. Equally ineffective was the makeshift effort to differentiate between police assigned to administrative (law and order) responsibilities and those assigned to anticriminal operations.[142] Since simple imprisonment seemed to have little or no effect as a deterrent to crime, and mild sentences none whatever, an act was eventually passed, following the recommendation of the Crime Enquiry Committee, permitting punishment by whipping for those guilty of violent crimes.[143]

The explanation of what the baffled police reporters described as "the general apathy of the people and the almost entire lack of a healthy public opinion condemnatory of the criminal" was in part political. Popular irresponsibility stemmed from the traditional Burman concept that alien government, regarded as the enemy of the people, was losing its authority; increasing lawlessness was traditionally connected with impending political change. Why should persons who were not aligned by self-interest on the government's side (as were the bureaucracy, the police, the magistrates, and the headmen) assist the legal authorities and thereby invite discomfort and abuse to themselves from criminal elements? Dacoity and other forms of police baiting did not seem in many minds to differ qualitatively from the tactics employed by the predatory police themselves, except that the risks and the stakes were usually higher for the criminal-rebel than for the police. Little could be done to halt crime as long as this chasm between government and people persisted.[144]

[141] Harvey, *British Rule,* pp. 36–38; *RPA* for 1924, pp. 13–15.

[142] *ISCR,* XI, 211–212, XV, 461. The Village Patrol Beat for surveillance of known criminals was abolished in 1924.

[143] *RAB* for 1927–1928, p. xiii.

[144] *ISCR,* XI, 216. One nationalist spokesman in the legislative council remarked: "If Government wants to reduce crime, [it] should trust the people more. . . . The

Many of the Westernized Burman nationalist leaders could find release for their frustration by political activity, either within Burma or in co-operation with friends in England, designed to attain home rule by constitutional means. But most Burmans lacked the perspective, the faith, and the patience needed to follow legal methods. Many of them would retrieve the alleged damage sustained to their racial dignity and to their cultural and religious heritage under British rule by resorting to direct-action methods. Their minimum objectives were to recover control over their own land and to throw out the Indian immigrant (*kalá*) invaders. For a number of reasons, including the fact that London was making various constitutional concessions and that police control was faltering, many Burmans became convinced that government was losing its grip. Soothsayers were available to convince the doubting ones. In a situation where social controls were already impaired and where substantial and valid complaints against police and courts existed, psychological and emotional factors provided the variables in the equation. The impact of the preachments of U Ottama and his followers and the wave of popular resentment which followed his initial arrest, plus the *pongyi* propaganda generally, were far more potent in promoting confusion and unrest than were tangible economic grievances or Burman dislike of particular constitutional provisions. In this context of incipient revolution, the spread of crime and the refusal of the people to help curb it were largely the natural Burman by-product of political developments.

Economic Developments, 1923–1929

Although the years from 1923 to 1929 were relatively prosperous ones, so that acute economic distress did not contribute materially to mounting political unrest, almost nothing was acomplished by government to improve the peasant's impoverished condition. No concession was made in response to the perennial attacks made both within and outside the legislative council on the capitation and *thathameda* taxes (amounting only to some 55 to 60 lakhs in a total revenue of 1,100 lakhs).[145] A similarly negative attitude was taken by government, as previously explained, toward the demand for modifications of the rising level of tax rates in the permanent land settlement re-

---

people are not willing to co-operate if they are not trusted. . . . What I should like to [try as an experiment] is for Government to hand over the police work to the village committees." See also Moscotti, p. 33.

[145] *ISCR*, XI, 327, XV, 455.

ports.[146] The Burmese request that the Rice Control Board profits be used for agricultural loans to help peasants recover land alienated to moneylenders was also refused.[147] The only two ameliorative proposals advanced by government concerned a proposal of 1924 to establish a land mortgage bank and a subsequent measure of 1927 to halt land alienation. Neither was pushed to enactment.

The proposed land mortgage bank was supposed to be operated by a central board, which would sell interest-bearing bonds to obtain operating funds for two or three pilot regional banks. The banks would make loans on mortgage security to local co-operative societies, which would in turn guarantee payment of the borrowers' dues. Profits arising from the banking operations would be refunded to each participating co-operative society in proportion to the amount borrowed. The project was abandoned partly because it was adjudged unrealistic to "hope" that Chettyars and commercial banks would buy the bonds of a competing lending agency and partly because few of the debt-ridden peasant owners retained the 50 per cent equity in their land needed to furnish the required security.[148]

The Burma Agrarian Bill of 1927 was prepared by an able civil service official, Thomas Couper, who was assigned in 1924 the task of studying the problem of land alienation. The bill proposed three things: (1) to make payments for wages, cattle hire, and current rent the first charges against the produce of the land; (2) to see that ejected tenants were compensated for improvements made on the land; (3) to give small-scale tenants cultivating 30 acres or less with a record of fair treatment of their landlords the right to contract for leases covering up to seven years' duration. Publication of the draft of this bill aroused a storm of protest from landlords generally, while the potentially benefiting tenants were voiceless and inarticulate. The proposal was promptly abandoned.[149]

The latter half of the decade of the twenties witnessed a steady de-

[146] In 1927, a year of falling paddy prices, four newly published land settlement reports raised the revenue demand 29 per cent, 11 per cent, 28 per cent, and 36 per cent respectively in the districts affected.

[147] See p. 222 above.

[148] RLAC, pt. III, pp. 127–134, 157–162. Government also promoted in a small way through the Estates Department several tenancy copartnership co-operative credit societies, which had moderate success until overtaken by the depression.

[149] RLAC, pt. I, p. 6, pt. II, pp. 50–52. The similarity between the proposed Burma land reform and Gladstone's earlier three "F" reforms for Ireland is striking. The three "F's" called for fair rent, fixed tenure, and free sale of improvements for Irish tenant farmers.

cline in the price of paddy at Rangoon, from 202 rupees per 100 baskets in 1926 to 169 rupees in 1928 and 133 rupees in 1930.[150] Although much of this decline was attributable to world-wide trends toward depressed agricultural prices, Burman nationalists interpreted it as resulting in large measure from the operations of the much-criticized "Bullinger Pool." The pool was a private agreement between four principal European rice-exporting firms, entered into in 1921, to "observe a common policy in rice purchases and sales." By 1928, the Bullinger Pool had become a major target of Burmese nationalist criticism, which condemned it as the latest in a long series of examples of exploitation by British firms of agricultural interests, including the peasants, landlords, and moneylenders. Participating firms defended the pool as a legitimate business move taken in behalf of self-preservation and made possible not by enjoyment of any illegal advantage or monopoly but simply by the members' superior business skill, financial backing, and commercial reputation.[151] Regardless of the merits of the case economically, the revived practice of collusive British buying of rice in a falling market provided psychological tinder for a political explosion.

A final development contributing to agricultural unrest was the virtual collapse in 1928–1929 of the extensive network of co-operative agricultural credit societies. As previously explained, the activities and commitments of the agricultural co-operative societies had been badly overextended during the war. They reached the peak membership of 4,057 societies in 1924, at a time of maximum political ferment. Difficulties developed from the fact that popular education in co-operative procedures lagged far behind expansion of activities, leaving a backlog of ignorance and confusion as to proper methods of operation. Too early government divested itself of responsibility for control, and official supervision became perfunctory. Abuses multiplied. The rather elaborate audit forms provided for the co-ops were usually more confusing than helpful; loans in many instances exceeded available funds; collections were irregular and practices of renewing loans overlenient; officers of the societies themselves accepted oversized loans; fictitious figures were inserted into many reports. All of this and more were discovered as a result of a thoroughgoing investigation authorized in 1928. The official report, submitted in 1929, revealed that the Provin-

[150] See Ganga Singh, *Burma Parliamentary Companion* (Rangoon, 1940), p. 14.
[151] Peter Ady, "Economic Bases of Unrest in Burma," *Foreign Affairs*, XXIX (1951), 477–478.

cial Co-operative Central Bank was insolvent and that the whole co-operative operation was in a state of collapse. The world depression completed the debacle. The process of liquidation of the co-operatives began in 1932, with government bearing most of the loss. Only about one-third of the societies were salvaged in any form.[152]

The Visit of the Simon Commission, 1929

Such was the disturbed economic and political situation in Burma at the time of the arrival of the members of the India Statutory Commission in February, 1929. The commission had been appointed by London in 1928 in pursuance of the provision of the India Act for review of the operation of the dyarchy constitution after ten years. The group was provided in advance by the Burma authorities with a thoroughgoing analysis of the workings of Burma's government (volume XI of the *ISCR*), and it also took additional oral evidence during the course of its sojourn within the country. The substance of the commission's findings and recommendations will be analyzed in the following chapter. It is relevant at this point to consider only its reception within the country and the political situation which it found.[153]

Prior to Sir John Simon's arrival in 1929, Burman nationalists made a concerted, if futile, effort to achieve agreement so as to present a united front to the commission. The "Unity League" effort came to grief over lay opposition to the attempts of the political *pongyis* to dictate terms. There were also genuine differences of viewpoint with respect to the desirability of immediate separation from India. The lay-controlled "Burma for the Burmans League" advocated separation from India, the curtailment of Indian immigration and moneylender operations, freedom from *pongyi* domination, and enactment of legislation designed to enable the reputable *Sangha* to discipline and control more effectively the offending wearers of the yellow robe. This group also became known as the Separation League.

The *pongyi*-led party, reacting angrily through its executive "Hundred Committee," opposed lay interference with religious matters, de-

---

[152] *RLAC*, pt. III, pp. 84–95.

[153] Sir Reginald Craddock, *Dilemma in India*, (London, 1929), p. 118. The ex-governor of Burma here blasted the whole Montagu reform scheme and criticized the Government of Burma's account (*ISCR*, vol. XI) of its working as being far too generous and optimistic. He cited a plethora of damaging allegations formulated by an *ad hoc* nonofficial Association of Professional and Business Men in Burma, who opposed any extension of self-government to Burma whenever constitutional revision should be undertaken.

manding implicit obedience to the monks on the part of the village *athins*. They advocated nonseparation from India and co-operation with the National Congress movement in India. It was the Hundred Committee which instigated the complete boycott of the Simon Commission.[154] Although mass support clearly lay with the *pongyis,* the efforts of the boycotting group, abetted by Indian politicians, to organize processions and hostile demonstrations in Rangoon and Mandalay against the commission were unimpressive. The close Indian connection of the Burma boycott leaders was strengthened in March, 1929, by Mohandas Gandhi's visit to Burma.[155]

The report submitted to the Simon Commission by the official and fairly representative Burma Committee agreed in some particulars with views of the Separation League. It was more cautious than the nationalists of the league in its urging the necessity of providing checks on the popular assembly. A majority of the official committee also favored continued representation in the council of communal groups and the official bloc. U Ba U of Mandalay presented a minority statement opposing communal representation, advocating full self-government and greater representation for the rural voter. Another dissident member was M. M. Rafi, a Muslim Indian lawyer, who opposed Burma's separation unless full self-government was also accorded.[156]

But from the popular point of view the prospects of coming to agreement on any reform proposals were discouraging. U Wisara's death in prison in 1929 fanned popular excitement at a most unfortunate time. He became Burma's *pongyi* martyr second only to U Ottama.[157] While the commission was hearing evidence in early 1929, military police were being used in Tharrawaddy and other districts to suppress political agitation against payment of the capitation tax.[158] The political situation was obviously unstable.

---

[154] *RAB* for 1928–1929, pp. iv–ix, xi; Moscotti, pp. 44–46.
[155] *RAB* for 1928–1929, p. xi.   [156] *ISCR,* III, 510–519.
[157] *Burma, Report of the Rangoon Town Police* for 1929, p. 5.
[158] *RAB* for 1928–1929, pp. i–iii.

IX

Reform Proposals and Rebellion, 1929-1931

THE three years from 1929 to the close of 1931 witnessed three arresting developments. The first was London's official reappraisal of Burma's dyarchy government in operation. The second was an outbreak of riotous violence directed against alien Asian elements of the population. The third was the first serious overt effort at anti-British revolution since the pacification of the late 1880's. These events demonstrated a growing divergence in point of view between Burmans and the locally resident British and also among the several Burmese political factions as well. The sense of crisis was greatly intensified, but hardly caused, by the demoralizing impact of world depression on all aspects of the commercialized rice industry of Lower Burma. The period affords a revealing opportunity to observe developing political currents within the country.

The India Statutory Commission

The India Reform Act of 1919 provided that after the new constitution had been in effect for a decade its operation would be examined with a view to introducing needed changes. Because of the unexpectedly fast pace of political developments in India, the British Parliament acted as early as 1927 to appoint from its own membership a commission of seven members headed by Sir John Simon to conduct the promised appraisal. The commission visited India in the cold season of 1927–1928. It encountered a determined boycott instigated by Congress Party leaders, based ostensibly on London's failure to appoint representative Indians to the commission. Repercussions of this Indian quarrel with the Simon Commission were observable in Burma during 1928. The subsequent Burman boycott of the commission was inspired in part by the agitation of Congress Party partisans in Burma and partly by growing popular distrust of British intentions regarding Burma's political future. The commission reached Burma in January, 1929, shortly after the election of the third legislative council on November 28, 1928.[1]

Prior to the arrival of the commission the newly elected council selected from its own membership a Burma committee of seven men to sit with the British commission. This committee included three Burmans, none of whom were associated with the largest nationalist People's Party, plus four representatives of minority groups: a Karen, an Indian Hindu, an India Muslim, and an Anglo-Indian.[2] Unrest on the part of the majority Burman group in the council at being denied an opportunity to be represented on the commission was intensified by their failure to obtain either of the two ministerial posts for transferred subjects in the new government.[3] U Ba Pe's People's Party had won 40 of the 59 general constituency seats and also picked up following the election 5 more from the ephemeral National Parliamentary Organization. Their voting strength was sufficient to elect Tharrawaddy U Pu speaker of the council over the candidacy of the Burma-domiciled Briton, Oscar de Glanville. But the People's Party could not outvote the majority coalition made up of a dozen Independent Burmans plus the minority representatives and appointed members.[4] The political atmosphere in early 1929 even among the moderate nationalists of the council was not encouraging for the accomplishment of the task of the Simon Commission.

The principal differences between the attitudes of the educated Burmans both within and outside the legislative council and the *pongyi*-influenced boycotting factions of the G.C.B.A. stemmed from the total

[1] N. C. Sen, *A Peep into Burma Politics, 1917–1942*, pp. 34–37.

[2] *ISCR*, XV, iv–vi. U Aung Thwin was chairman of the Burma committee. The other members were U Ba U, U Ba Shin, M. M. Rafi, Sra Shwe Ba, M. Campagnac, and E. Eusoof.

[3] U Ba Tin became health and education minister and Lee Ah Yain continued as minister of agriculture and forests (Sen, pp. 29–33).

[4] Sen, pp. 29–36, 46–49. U So Nyun and U Aye were elected at this time by the National Parliamentary Organization, but they joined the People's Party.

opposition of the latter groups to dyarchy per se and presumably also to any alternative British-sponsored reform proposal. The G.C.B.A. was particularly susceptible to influence from India on the assumption that Burma's political advance was conditioned on achievements in India (in the U Ottama tradition). The obvious preference in British circles for Burma's separation from India was represented by some as a prima-facie attempt to disrupt co-operation between nationalist movements on the opposite shores of the Bay of Bengal. Three factions of the G.C.B.A. (those led by U Chit Hlaing, U Maung Su, and U Ba Shwe respectively) meeting in general session at Mandalay in mid-1928 amalgamated their forces to back the Indian-advocated boycott. A fourth more radical faction led by U Soe Thein refused amalgamation and sent its views to a meeting of nonboycotters in Rangoon. This split came even though the Soe Thein group agreed with other G.C.B.A. factions in opposing separation from India. Six other parties including the India-influenced *Swaraj* and Home Rule groups plus the youthful ultrapatriotic *Dobama* ("We Burmans") Party joined the boycott of the commission. U Chit Hlaing aggravated unrest by advising his followers to cash all their India currency notes on the ground that separation would render them immediately valueless.[5] Thus the vast majority of the politically conscious Burman electorate was influenced to distrust Britain's intentions and to refuse to co-operate with the Simon Commission.

Except for several Burmans of standing who volunteered to testify as individuals before the commission and the spokesmen for minority peoples, the only organized Burman groups which refused to honor the boycott were the "Burma for the Burmans League" and the somewhat larger Separation League. Both were *ad hoc* organizations, without mass backing, sponsored by the intelligentsia at Rangoon. The first was organized on August 28, 1928, and the second appeared somewhat later. The sponsors included minor officials of the government, vernacular newspaper editors, a Burman manager of the Burmah Oil Company, and several of the opposition leaders in the legislative council. The two leagues were distinct but their viewpoints and aims, which will be examined in a later connection, were very similar.[6] Both of them agreed with the majority of Burma's official committee in favoring separation from India and in resisting the obscurantist fear-mongering agitation of the G.C.B.A.

[5] *RPA* for 1929–1930, p. xii.   [6] *ISCR*, XVII, 385, 407.

British Testimony before the Commission

By far the most substantial contribution to the findings of the commission regarding the working of dyarchy was made by a selected group of British Indian civil servants experienced in the Burma administration. The commissioner of Tenasserim Division, J. J. Anderson, prepared a thoroughgoing and objective description (volume XI of the *ISCR*) of the operations of the government. Virtually all of the evidence contained in volume XV and a portion of that in volume XVII were contributed by seven high-level British members of the government.[7] This group was not only informed factually but was also sympathetic to the objective of achieving self-government for Burma as quickly as was feasible. They argued that if change should be regarded as necessary because dyarchy did not work, London's policy ought to take the direction of according a greater degree of responsible government. Their position was summarized as follows:

It is neither possible nor desirable to go back upon the announcement of August, 1917, that it is the object of His Majesty's Government ultimately to establish completely responsible government in British India, nor is it possible or desirable . . . to move back toward autocracy. And if the Commission holds that further advance in Indian provinces is a matter of political necessity, the same advance should be made in Burma. . . . If Burma is separated from India, the goal . . . would be full responsible government . . . as an integral part of the British empire.[8]

It was mainly in the matter of timing that British spokesmen for the Burma Government differed from nationalist leaders. The former were convinced that the transfer of such matters as law and order and finances could not as yet be safely made to ministers responsible to an elected council. They argued that both the electorate and the council lacked the requisite experience. They rejected the idea that the council should be indefinitely excluded from such matters, and they did not subscribe to the mischievous theory that Burmans were on trial as to their fitness for self-government. The circumstances demanded a forward policy under which a workable government should be devised

[7] *ISCR*, XV, iv–vi, XVII, 383 ff. H. W. A. Watson and A. R. Morris represented the forestry services. Other government spokesmen were the finance secretary, A. E. Gilliat; the finance minister, S. A. Smyth; the chief secretary, J. Claque; the inspector general of police, R. W. Macdonald; and the collector of Rangoon, R. K. Harper.

[8] *ISCR*, XI, 583.

largely on a unitary basis according full provincial autonomy for Burma as related to India with as much responsibility entrusted to the council as it was capable of carrying. As safeguards against the danger of actual breakdown in government, some powers must be reserved to the discretionary authority of the governor. These should include authority to ensure tranquility, financial stability, the integrity of the public services, and the prevention of unfair discrimination against minority racial, religious, and economic interests.[9]

The second British group from which testimony was taken was the Burma Chamber of Commerce. It was a venerable organization dating from 1877, and its members possessed a very substantial and continuing stake in the future economic development of Burma. Spokesmen for the Chamber of Commerce also professed sympathy for Burma's political aspirations and conceded under questioning that if India was given a constitutional advance Burma also must receive similar concessions. They nevertheless argued strongly on both commercial and financial grounds that Burma must be separated from India. Burma's financial obligations to India were deemed excessive; India's tariffs on both exports and imports served no Burman ends. Burma's parliamentary representation, consisting of a meager 5 members among 144 in the India Assembly and 2 seats among 59 in the Council of State, was denounced as useless. Burma's opposition to separation, according to the Chamber's spokesman, Mr. Wroughton, rested solely on the fear that, apart from India, Burma would get no constitutional advance whatever. He declared that the Burmese were a proud race and in many ways a capable one and that Burma had done as well as any province of India under dyarchy.

But from this point on, the Chamber spokesmen diverged from Burman nationalist expectations. The new government, they insisted, must be capable of maintaining order, must encourage friendly co-operation between component racial groups, and must also promote an atmosphere for commercial activity free of undue discrimination or state interference with trade. They insisted that finances and law and order clearly could not as yet be entrusted to Burman hands with safety; the structure of government must be kept simple because experienced political leadership was lacking; the official element should continue active in the legislative council; British personnel in the civil service should be protected from unwarranted attack and not be further reduced in size; minority interests must continue to enjoy special suffrage

[9] *Ibid.*, pp. 583–586.

privileges and representation. Essential safeguards covering police, finances, minority protection, and foreign capital should therefore be vested in the governor's authority. Finally, the new government should place no limitation on Indian immigration and permit no impairment of free trade between India and Burma.[10] Such adverse testimony from the Burma Chamber of Commerce representatives afforded grounds on which Burmans could discount the Chamber's alleged sympathy for constitutional progress.

A third nonofficial British group, newly organized as the Association of Professional and Business Men in Burma, proved to be uncompromisingly hostile to every suggestion of constitutional advance for Burma. Dyarchy, in their view, had been a mistake which unfortunately could not be canceled, but London must not be influenced by the political clamor for an extension of self-government. Such a goal was impossible to realize in the complete absence of public spirit, popular co-operation with government, and official responsibility. Rural self-government agencies were denounced as grossly incompetent both administratively and in financial matters; municipal elections allegedly involved private political arrangements, control of blocs of voters by employers and Indian procurers of labor, plus wholesale practices of false personation and intimidation. The elected members of the legislative council were described as self-seeking lawyers of limited professional status, while the local political bosses (the labor maistries and the *pongyis*) were declared completely incapable of comprehending political issues. The association presented a dark picture of universal lawlessness, ineffective courts of law, and lack of popular assistance to the police. It concluded that in the absence of educated political opinion and popular comprehension of the privileges and obligations of citizenship, advance in the immediate future toward full responsible self-government was folly which would result disastrously for both country and people.[11] This intemperate blast disclosed the scope of the real rift between the opinion of the resident British business community and that of indigenous nationalist elements.

[10] *ISCR*, XVIII, 359–361, 378–382. The principal spokesman for the Chamber of Commerce was Mr. Wroughton of the Bombay Burma Company. He pointed out quite correctly that the disciplining of police officers guilty of irregularities was already difficult and that "bad hat" activities were apparently proving fascinating to many Burmese people and were eliciting a measure of sympathy if not a kind of popular hero worship.

[11] *ISCR*, XVII, 362–367, 383–384.

The Burman Rejoinder to British Testimony

The provocative testimony of the Association of Professional and Business Men and to a lesser degree that of the Chamber of Commerce dissipated any prospect of achieving that measure of agreement with moderate nationalist elements which government spokesmen had tried so carefully to establish. The first rejoinder came from Burman members of the Simon Commission itself. Chairman U Aung Thwin of the legislative council committee undertook to explain the prevalence of criminality in terms of the lack of subsidiary off-season industries for the cultivators and the consequent widespread idleness and unemployment following the rice harvest, coupled with the Burman's craving for excitement and adventure. U Ba U pointed out that the legislative council's criticism of the police had not been without justification and that it had resulted in reorganization and higher pay for the police. He pointed out that Burma's kings prior to final British conquest had also attempted to inaugurate their own constitutional reforms. Political apathy did not extend to all elections, he insisted. Where the issues were understood and were relevant to the interests of the voters, as in the selection of village headmen, U Ba U affirmed that elections were keenly contested. He resented particularly the British slur to the effect that members of the council consisted mainly of junior pleaders with no professional legal experience.

It fell to the Muslim Indian representative, M. M. Rafi, to answer the British attacks on the shortcomings of local self-government under dyarchy. Popular acceptance of the district councils, he declared, had been hindered by the unpopularity of concomitant dyarchy reform at the center. The local government law had assigned no specific functions to the circle boards; it had provided no funds or facilities for supervising the work of inexperienced councilmen; the "hands off" policy of local government had actually denied to the councils the effective co-operation of general administrative officials. Rafi raised the countercharge that government apparently wanted the local bodies to flounder about. He also challenged the allegations of wholesale personation in municipal elections, and in this he was supported by Mr. Harper, the government's representative on the commission as collector of Rangoon.[12]

The regular Burma Provincial Congress Committee as a whole was committed to the eventual attainment of full responsible government

[12] *ISCR*, XV, 435–443, XVII, 373–376.

and was strongly in favor of separation from India. Burma's external relations, it argued, should be directly with the British. A majority of the committee favored a unicameral legislature, communal representation, and the continuance for five years only of the official and nominated blocs in the council. All six of the governor's ministers must be made responsible as a group to the council, with the governor empowered to veto legislation and to exercise emergency powers as heretofore. Constitutional amendments, under the proposed arrangement, could be advanced by the legislature subject to the approval of the Secretary of State for India and Burma in London.[13]

More representative of educated Burman nationalist opinion was the statement presented by the "Burma for the Burmans League" already referred to. The memorandum which it submitted to the Simon Commission demanded immediate separation from India and dominion-status home rule. It argued that Burma had become a happy hunting ground for Indian immigrants whose presence denied work opportunities for Burmans. British Indian rule had brought poverty and idleness to the Burman people, hence evil deeds, destruction of religion, and their threatened extinction as a nation. The people were unable to live on their earnings, much less sow the seeds of merit by charitable gifts as in the olden days. Heavy expenditures on police activities contributed to heavy taxation, while tribute to India and remittances sent to India by alien residents cost the country as estimated 2 crores of rupees (20 million) annually, enough coin allegedly to fill 5,000 bullock carts.[14]

The memorandum submitted by the league also called for lowering entrance requirements to the university and for the admission of private (nonresident) candidates to the intermediate (second year) and bachelor examinations. A league resolution calling for the introduction of legislation for controlling the Sanghas was considered at the August meeting. It was withdrawn for later consideration on the grounds that needed reform of the Sangha had better come from within the order rather than be imposed by laymen from the outside.[15] Most of the spokesmen for the "Burma for the Burmans League" were openly critical of the misguided and politically suicidal boycotting agitation

---

[13] ISCR, III, 510; Moscotti, pp. 72–75.

[14] U Mya U argued that Indian remittances and moneylender profits amounted to 68 million rupees per year. Indian Chettyars, it was alleged, had recently started moneylending operations in Saigon with 400 lakhs of rupees (4 million) earned in Burma.

[15] ISCR, XVII, 385–387, 394.

being conducted against the Simon Commission. They were much more concerned to develop a positive case for separation and for reform. Most of them were willing to guarantee protection of non-Burman economic interests, but insisted that unrestricted entry of foreigners must end.

U Mya U, the principal league spokesman, declared that a Burman army led by British officers and backed by resources of the empire would be competent to safeguard the country's security. He did not discount the seriousness of popular concern that a separated Burma might decline to the level of a crown colony, but he affirmed in rejoinder that Burma's existing constitution was already far in advance of colony status and that current trends in India, the Philippines, and Ceylon were all toward self-government. A separated Burma would be able to work for dominion status later and could, he predicted, obtain it. The counterproposal to play safe by staying with India would leave Burma's defenses, its finances, and its government under Indian control and serve to perpetuate the policy of "Burma for the Indian." He insisted, therefore, that now was the time to break away and save the Burman race by becoming, as a free people, a "unit among the other races within the great British Empire." He denounced the *Swaraj* Party (led by U Paw Tun and Tharrawaddy U Pu) as traitorous to Burma home rule.[16]

Hostility to Indians was apparently the primary concern of the "Burma for the Burmans" group. It was willing to defer dominion status to some future time, to protect foreign economic interests, and to remain indefinitely an integral part of the empire in order to achieve immediate separation. U Mya U was challenged by M. M. Rafi during the course of the commission's cross-examination on the difficulty of defending a separated Burma, its diminished prospects for constitutional reform, its need for Indian labor and for the financial services performed by the Chettyars.[17]

A somewhat more representative and politically sophisticated group was found in the "Separation League." It shared the objective for immediate separation from India, but was more directly concerned to develop an agreed draft of a constitution for separated Burma. The Separation League was a coalition group including some representatives of the "Burma for the Burmans League," the Karen National Association, the People's Party, the British Burman Association, and the

---

[16] *Ibid.*, pp. 387–393, by Mya U of Mandalay. [17] *Ibid.*, pp. 413–416.

Burma Provincial Congress Committee. Even U So Thein's G.C.B.A. co-operated to the extent of submitting its views.

The formal memorandum submitted by the Separation League denounced the efforts of Indian politicians to foment distrust of the good faith of the British Government in order to perpetuate Burma's costly India connection. This had meant for Burmans loss of land to Indian owners, loss of status on the part of Burman women married to Indian Muslims, loss of opportunity for military service, loss of employment opportunities, and financial losses in terms of tariffs and overseas payments. To dispel this India-inspired distrust of British intentions, London would have to declare explicitly that Burma would be admitted to such political advancement as would be conceded to India. Parliament must not repeat the mistake of 1918–1922, when reforms were so long delayed that Burman nationalism was caught up in the meshes of the nonco-operation movement of India before the changes could even be appraised, must less implemented.

The dyarchy scheme for division of powers, according to the Separation League, had been tactfully handled by Governor Butler at the outset. It had degenerated under the second and third councils to the point that the cabinet contained no ministers who were in fact responsible to the elected portion of the council, but were only well-paid servants of government itself. In order to remedy this situation the Separation League proposed the enactment of an abbreviated version of its proposed new constitution, based on that of the Irish Free State. This document displaced the shorter analogous proposal drafted by the "Burma for the Burmans League." [18]

The constitution of the "Burma Free State," or *Myanma Shwepyigyi*, was patterned on the British model, but it contained a number of features superficially reminiscent of old Burma. It proposed in the first place that Burma's boundaries include the Naga Hills, Manipur, and Cachar states on the borders of British India. The proposed Parliament, or *Wunthanu*, would include a chamber of deputies, or *Hlutdaw*, and an upper chamber, or *Byedaik*. The Burma Free State would take its place as a coequal member of the British Commonwealth of Nations, with both English and Burmese as official languages. A bill of rights was set forth in clauses 6 to 10. Members of the proposed *Hlutdaw* would be chosen by a limited adult (21 years or older) electorate for a four-year term by proportional representation; members of the

[18] *Ibid.*, pp. 407–413.

291

Byedaik would be selected for nine-year terms (one-third renewable every three years) from a prepared panel of names of honored citizens, by the combined votes of the *Hlutdaw* and the *Byedaik* itself voting secretly and also according to proportional representation. The *Wunthanu* as a whole would control the use and access to all lands, waters, mines, and minerals and all potential power resources. Leases or licenses in the public interest could be accorded for periods not to exceed ninety-nine years. The oath prescribed for members of the *Wunthanu* would include loyalty to His Majesty George V and to the British Commonwealth, but members would not be liable for prosecution for statements made during formal sessions of Parliament.

The *Hlutdaw*, under the proposed constitution, could be dissolved on the advice of the executive council, and a new election held within thirty days following dissolution. The *Hlutdaw* would exercise exclusive jurisdiction over money bills, but the purposes of all appropriations must have been previously recommended by the representative of the crown on the advice of the executive council. The king's representative could withhold assent to all legislation. Only the *Wunthanu* could raise armed forces and consent to Burma's involvement in war save in the case of actual invasion. Amendment of the constitution could be accomplished by ordinary legislation, subject to royal assent, or after an eight-year period by popular referendum. All members of the executive council, consisting of a president, vice-president, and finance minister, must be members of the *Hlutdaw* and be responsible collectively to it, but the larger ministry, up to a total of twelve members, might include departmental heads responsible individually to the *Hlutdaw*. The governor-general as crown representative would be appointed and paid as in Ireland, and the High Court and judges should continue to be appointed by the crown on the advice of the executive council.[19]

Oral testimony submitted during the course of the hearings revealed the strong opposition of the Separation League to any kind of communal representation and to the continued presence of a foreign bureaucracy. All loyal citizens of Burma would be treated alike under the law, but Indian immigration would be curbed.[20] The constitutional proposals of the Separation League had the merit of being based on homework, but they were probably unintelligible to Burmans unfamiliar with British governmental practices. It nevertheless was the clearest indication of Burman constitutional aspirations that the com-

[19] *Ibid.*, pp. 400–406.   [20] *Ibid.*, pp. 406–416, by U Hla Tun Pru.

mission was able to obtain. It indicated that students of government in Burma were looking beyond the political leadership of India and were trying to fashion an independent and workable pattern of home rule on their own. The example of the Irish constitution was destined to emerge again prominently during the course of the Burma Round Table Conference of 1931–1932. What the distrustful and largely inarticulate anti-Separationist boycotters had in mind, aside from keeping hold of Mother India's hand out of distrust of London, was not made apparent to the commission at this time.

Views of Minority Ethnic Groups

The Separation League's inclusion of a vaguely worded provision for proportional representation no doubt explained the association of the Karen National Association with the league's program. The Karen Association represented some ten branch groups located in the Irrawaddy delta and Sittang Valley extending from below Prome on the west to Toungoo on the east. Its own memorandum was drafted by informed and educated Karens who were also obviously doing their own thinking. It differed from the position of the Separation League in a number of details but mainly in their insistence on communal representation for Karens both at the center and in local governing bodies in proportion to population. They proposed that the Karen seats allotted to the council be included in a single Karen voting constituency covering all of Burma and that similar proportional allotment be made for local body representation on a district-wide basis. The Karens asked specifically for an equitable share of the district school funds and for their own school inspectors. The Karen Association opposed special representation on the council for commercial groups and the university. It also requested that more polling places be set up and that guarantees be provided against false personation of voters and against improper counting of votes.

The Karen National Association attacked the dyarchy system in operation. It alleged that the cheap profiteers elected to the legislative council lacked public spirit and represented nobody, since the population as a whole was unconcerned about the council. Political parties were denounced as blighting, mushroom growths "nourished by the manure of self-interest," while the governor's appointees to the council were "pure puppets." The pay of cabinet ministers should not exceed 1,000 rupees per month. The association favored full responsible home rule even at the risk of bloody revolution for a time, as a means of

293

ridding the country of political hypocrites and their blind followers. It favored freedom of the press and of speech even though both press and platform admittedly lacked solid virtues. It castigated the chairmen and secretaries of district councils as thieves, denounced the office of commissioner as an expensive luxury, and insisted that supervision of local bodies must be undertaken by the central authorities. The memorandum declared, finally, that efforts to maintain law and order were farcical, that justice was a mockery, and that the swearing and drinking of the dreaded *Nyaungye* oath of olden times should be revived for use in the courts.[21]

The parallel statement presented by representatives of the Karen elders, Sydney Loo Nee (Sgaw) and Sra Shwe Ba (Pwo), was more typical of the provincialism of the Karen population as a whole. It stressed Karen loyalty to British raj and the legitimacy of their concern to preserve separate Karen nationality. The authors asked that eleven new Karen electorates be added to their five under the existing dyarchy council and that a reservation of some 16 per cent of the public service appointments be made for Karens. They were particularly concerned to preserve Christian Karen schools. Under questioning by the commission the Karen elders admitted that a number of their more extreme demands were of questionable merit, such as the abolition of the High Court and all established governmental services, as well as the party system. They preferred home rule for a separated Burma under direct British control.[22]

The memorandum submitted by Indian interests supported Burma's political aspirations. It pointed out, however, that the majority G.C.B.A. groups, who were not represented in the Burman deputations, were opposed to separation from India. Indian spokesmen also rebutted Burman allegations that the Indian connection had milked Burma of taxes, profits, and remittances and that free immigration threatened to swamp the country. They insisted that the Chettyars had contributed greatly to Burma's economic development. The Indians asked specifically for sixteen reserved seats in the new council, for the elimination of high-proficiency Burmese language examinations for the civil service, and for legal safeguards to protect Indian economic interests.[23]

The statement of the Burma Muslim community differed only

[21] *Ibid.*, pp. 422–431.   [22] *Ibid.*, pp. 418–422, 431–434.
[23] *Ibid.*, pp. 443–448.

slightly from that of the Indians. The group generally was concerned to end alleged legal discrimination favoring Burman Buddhists and to preserve Muslim communal interests. Muslims demanded a fair share of government jobs and 10 per cent representation in all levels of public bodies including municipal government, village committees, and district education boards. The Muslim League spokesmen went further to insist that one-eighth of all governmental grants for educational, charitable, and religious purposes be allocated to Muslim interests. The league also made a special case for protection of coastal shipping interests (important in the Arakan) and for equal treatment for Muslims seeking agriculture and business loans. They did not strongly oppose separation from India, however. Muslim interests centered in the Arakan region where around a third of the population was Mohammedan.[24]

The Anglo-Indians, Anglo-Burmans, and Europeans domiciled in Burma were in close agreement. They were concerned about special representation on the council, on the Rangoon Corporation, the semi-official capital Development Trust, and the port commissioners' bodies. They also wanted a fair share of government appointments and access to a separate military unit. They favored separation from India and the exclusion of all undesirable aliens, especially among the Chinese. The only constitutional advance they proposed concerned placing transferred subjects under four ministers instead of two, all to be supervised by a minister in chief chosen by elected members of the legislative council.[25]

The Shan chiefs and Burman landowners also presented special memorandums. The Shan *Sawbwas* wanted confirmation of their arbitrary hereditary authority under customary law, with a minimum of direct British supervision and all quite independent of the reformed government. The Federation of the Shan States dating from 1922, under which education, public health, and police were centrally controlled, should be abolished.[26] The Burma Landowners' Organization included an alleged 700 to 800 members, all of whom possessed a minimum of 300 acres of land. Although its spokesmen admitted that landowners were already liberally represented in the existing council, they asked for the reservation of two special council seats which would not have to be contested in general constituencies. The landowners favored separation from India, more adequate flood protection, and

[24] *Ibid.,* pp. 434–438.   [25] *Ibid.,* pp. 462–465.   [26] *Ibid.,* pp. 459–461.

295

lowering of the export duty on rice. They also attacked proposed legislation covering landlord-tenant relations.[27]

The extensive hearing accorded by the commission to non-Burman minority groups added very little to the understanding of the political situation within the country. It tended on the contrary to solidify the conviction of many Burman nationalists that majority wishes would be neglected because so much heed was being paid to divergent minority points of view. The testimony revealed that the distrustful views of the anti-Separationist mass organizations were known. But the commission gained no inkling of the vehement opposition being generated within the boycotting groups or of the wide popular acceptance being accorded the views of the extreme anti-Separationists.

Conclusions of the Simon Commission

The conclusions of the commission reflected its findings. It argued the unwisdom and futility of Burma's continued costly representation in the Central Government of India.[28] It reported that Burma would never acquiesce in being ruled by a self-governing India and that all thinking Burmans favored immediate independence. The only grounds advanced for postponing separation was the belief entertained by those elements which allegedly derived their political inspiration from Indian sources that Burma's future progress might be hastened by its close association with India. The commission hoped that an early decision for separation, accompanied by guarantees concerning the status which the new government would enjoy, would improve the atmosphere for consideration of practical problems. Financial and political considerations all favored separation, but legislative council members clearly preferred separation even if it produced no financial gains. The only valid negative considerations appeared to be Burma's defense requirements, its need of Indian labor and trade, and the possible reluctance of India to accord immediate separation.[29] Burman opposition to the presence of Indian labor was heavily discounted in the following terms:

The steady excess of Indian immigrants over Indian emigrants may be the measure rather of economic development than of any Indian penetration of Burma. . . . Whether [the Indian] stays or returns, he often plays a part

[27] *Ibid.*, pp. 457–458.
[28] Of Burma's four members in the India legislature, one was a European and one an Indian.
[29] *ISCR*, II, 181–184.

in the economy of Burma which the Burman is not willing to undertake for himself.[30]

Disturbing to many Burmans was the failure of the commission to reaffirm explicitly the proposal by the Rangoon government that Burma's new constitution would probably resemble in "material particulars" the proposals for India. It declared instead that since the essential demands for administrative efficiency and problems connected with the control of backward tracts would make disastrous any premature efforts to dispense with British aid Burma's special case would be subjected to further examination and then decided on its own merits.[31]

The Simon Commission's review of the Burma political situation was certainly informed, but few would deny that the disparate evidence gleaned on a hurried visit and subject to varying interpretations by interested parties was somewhat distorted and out of focus. What it did not gauge was the undercurrent of unrest beneath the surface calm. Continued student disaffection was evidenced in 1930 by the strike of Buddhist students at three mission schools in Rangoon against attendance at Bible classes and by the appearance also in 1930 of the radical youthful patriotic *Dobama* ("We Burmans") Party, destined to achieve future political leadership. Considerable commotion attended the publicized ceremonial cremation of the body of the political *pongyi* martyr, U Wisara, in February, 1930. The government also encountered increasing difficulty in 1929–1930 in collecting capitation and *thathameda* taxes especially along the reaches of the Irrawaddy Valley from Insein and Tharawaddy districts on the south and northward as far as Mandalay.

Nevertheless, the official administrative report of the Burma Government for 1929–1930 reflected no sense of apprehension or alarm. It cited evidence that various Burman political factions, both within and outside the legislative council, were riven by differences of policy and by personal rivalry. The boycott of the cremation ceremony of U Wisara by the So Thein G.C.B.A. as well as the signal failure of funeral orators to raise funds for political purposes seemed to be reassuring.[32] There was nothing in the Simon Commission report or in the government appraisal of the immediate situation to suggest an impending political storm.

---

[30] *ISCR*, I, 78.

[31] *ISCR*, II, 90; Moscotti, pp. 75–77.

[32] *RAB* for 1929–1930, p. xii; Sen, pp. 29–33. Resistance to tax payments was also strong in Thaton District.

Reactions to the Commission's Report: Separationists and Anti-Separationists

Although the report of the India Statutory Commission, published in June, 1930, was officially declared to have been well received in Burma,[33] the grounds for such optimism were meager. Spokesmen for the special minority groups were doubtless happy to see their views fully recorded. But majority Burman opinion, largely unrepresented in the report, had all the more reason to resent the coverage given to the views of minorities. Disliked particularly were the opinions of non-official British groups so hostile to nationalist goals and so deprecatory of Burma's capacity for self-rule. Burmans became increasingly aware that the British business community, against whom the mass of the population hitherto had harbored no serious economic grievance, was their most formidable political enemy.[34] The basic conclusion that Burma should be separated from India was destined to be sharply challenged by subsequent events. The several factions of the G.C.B.A. which had boycotted the commission's hearings treated the report with complete contempt, accepting neither its premises nor its findings. Only on the dangerous assumption that the wishes of the inarticulate rural population did not matter politically could anyone have felt confident that progress was being made in self-government.

At the official level, preparations to implement the findings of the commission proceeded in due course. The Burma governor, Sir Charles Innes, explained formally before the legislative council on August 2, 1930, the likely prospect that Burma would achieve separation under a constitution not inferior in status to that granted to India. Immediately thereafter Governor Innes departed for London on sick leave and designated a Burman, Sir J. A. Maung Gyi, as acting governor.[35] On August 11, the council approved resolutions favoring the separation of Burma from India coupled with a wistful bid for full dominion status. The contrary action of three amalgamated branches of the G.C.B.A. in October and November denouncing the separation pro-

[33] *RAB* for 1929–1930, p. xii.

[34] Maurice Collis, *Trials in Burma* (London, 1945), pp. 68–73, 212. Collis points out that the Rangoon business community, to which the governor and his reserved councilors were actually responsible, consisted mainly of the three exclusive British clubs which no Burman could enter: the Boat Club, the Pegu Club, and the Gymkhana Club. Even the British in government service, who realized that some knowledge of the Burmese point of view was necessary to their jobs, achieved relatively little toward such understanding.

[35] *Ibid.*, pp. 235–238.

posal was unofficial and seemingly without great political significance. Accordingly, the Burma delegation selected to represent the country at the first India Round Table Conference, which convened in London in November, 1930, was solidly in favor of separation.[36] The deliberations of the conference as they affected political developments in Burma will be considered in a subsequent chapter. What is needed at this juncture is an assessment of political dynamics operating within Burma below the official level of the legislative council.

Except for the ultracautious Burmans and those who had a clear personal stake in the continuance of British rule (the civil servants), the basic views and aims of all Burman nationalists were much the same. All wanted genuine home rule, free of interference from both Britain and India. All disliked the dyarchy system, the payment of direct household capitation and *thathameda* taxes, the police system, and the operation of the courts of law. All resented the presence of the Chettyar moneylender and the Indian laborer, and most of them believed that deterioration of the position of the Burman as landowner and wage laborer was due to the presence of the Indian. Many Burmans also resented British aloofness and "face," particularly the lack of any attempt on the part of Europeans to achieve an understanding of the Burman point of view coupled with perennial moral preachment regarding the evils of lawlessness.[37] For many thoughtful Burmans the very salvaging of the Buddhist faith, so sadly deteriorated under alien rule, and the recovery of the moral fiber and social integration of the nation were dependent on the early achievement of self-rule. Nationalist groups differed, therefore, not so much in objectives as in the methods to be used for attaining their ends and also in the immediate concerns stressed by particular individuals and factions.

The Separationist faction was small but informed and highly vocal. It included many of the better-educated nationalists, especially those with experience outside of Burma, who saw the political problem in fairly broad perspective. They regarded Burma's separation from India

[36] The delegation consisted of U Aung Thwin, U Ba Pe, M. M. Ohn Ghine, and Oscar de Glanville.

[37] A classic instance of the clash of "face" is presented by Collis (*Trials in Burma*, pp. 73–105). As judge of the Rangoon court Collis incurred the wrath of British members of the Pegu Club for "letting a white man down" by criticizing severely the conduct of a British employee of Steel Brothers accused of mistreating a servant. Collis also tried for manslaughter two British military personnel who ran down in a car a Burmese woman pedestrian. Collis insisted that any other course than strict impartiality headed straight for trouble with the Burmese and complained that his British friends preferred "face" to evenhanded justice.

as an urgently necessary step both for national reasons and for considerations closely associated with the interests of their own class. Financial and trade considerations, the need for immigration control, and the advantages of cutting loose from India's political leading strings once for all were to them compellingly strong. These considerations were buttressed by the class interests of the educated Burman calling for exclusion of Indian competitors from government service and from the professions, especially law. The better-informed Separationists also envisaged with some confidence their ability to obtain for Burma an increasing measure of self-government whether inside or outside the empire. They proposed to realize their objectives by utilizing the legal channels available to them, such as the legislative council and freedom of speech, the press, and assembly. They intended also to exploit fully the opportunity for direct access to friendly Labour Party circles in England and especially in the Parliament. In spite of their meager following in Burma, the Separationists provided effective leadership in the negotiations at London.

By far the largest segment of Burma nationalist opinion subscribed to the contrary anti-Separationist point of view. It stemmed mainly from distrust of British intentions regarding Burma's political future. Fear of being isolated from India in the common struggle for self-rule dated back to the bitter fight over the "Craddock Scheme" in the early 1920's. Elements of the G.C.B.A. which had boycotted the dyarchy elections and the Simon Commission owed much to the leadership and example of the Indian Congress Party transmitted through U Ottama and others.[38] The anti-Separationists also lacked the confidence entertained by their better-informed Separationist opponents that historic tides were moving progressively toward colonial emancipation throughout the Commonwealth, nor did they believe in the efficacy of employing direct political channels to London apart from India. Indian influence was responsible for the circulation of rumors at Rangoon during Simon's visit in early 1929 that the Burma Government's official support for separation was in fact a ruse to give to Burma constitutional reforms inferior to India's. Many Burman nationalists were therefore inclined to co-operate with India a little longer rather than venture out in the cold world all alone.[39]

[38] Burma, Home Dept., *Interim Report of the Riot Inquiry Committee* (Rangoon, 1938), pp. 23–24. This is cited hereafter as *IRRIC.*

[39] Collis, *Trials in Burma*, pp. 56–60. Indian friends of Collis in Rangoon were reportedly gleeful in February, 1929, over the credulous Burman response to such allegations of British perfidy toward Burma.

Another effort on the part of Indian nationalist spokesmen to muddy the political waters in Burma came in early 1930, when the Congress Party mayor of Calcutta, J. M. J. Sen Gupta, visited Rangoon. He delivered a fiery anti-Separationist speech, incurring thereby his arrest and trial on a technical charge of incitement to sedition. Sen Gupta's arrest was accompanied by a minor riot, involving only Rangoon Indians, allegedly instigated by local Congress Party politicians. The provocative action was robbed of much of its appeal because Sen Gupta was given a fair trial and a token ten-day sentence, but it did achieve a temporary improvement of Burma-Indian relations and strengthened anti-Separationist sentiment. Fearful minds could conclude that, since government had prosecuted Sen Gupta simply for making a speech against separation, then the British must have some sinister reason for stopping such talk and for advocating Burma's separation from India.[40]

The failure of the Simon Commission report, which appeared in June, 1930, to spell out in precise terms its recommendations for Burma's future constitution played into the hands of the anti-Separationists. Some Burman politicians at Rangoon, probably at Indian suggestion, interpreted the departure of Governor Sir Charles Innes for London on sick leave in August, 1930, as part of a deliberate endeavor to promote a constitution for separated Burma inferior to that of India and one designed to protect the vested interests of the Burma British community. This distrust communicated itself in less articulate fashion to the villagers and produced a highly charged atmosphere. Hatred of the allegedly perfidious government at Rangoon tended to heighten discontent.[41]

The membership of the anti-Separationist movement lay in three groups. The first was composed of the amalgamated elements of the G.C.B.A., consisting of the U Chit Hlaing, U Maung Su, and U Ba Shwe factions. These groups convened at Mandalay in October to November, 1930, and denounced both the legislative council and the Simon Commission for recommending Burma's separation from India. Their basic position was that separation from India must be rejected unless Burma were offered full dominion status. The dissident U So Thein faction of the G.C.B.A. went even further to demand complete

---

[40] Burma, *Report of the Rangoon Town Police* for 1930, p. 10; Collis, *Trials in Burma*, pp. 106–109, 166. Gandhi's famous march to the sea began on April 6, 1930, a month after Sen Gupta's trial at Rangoon.

[41] Collis, *Trials in Burma*, pp. 236–238, 288.

independence, but it was pursuing at the time secret political plans of its own and therefore refused to associate itself with the other anti-Separationist factions.[42] The anti-Separationist cause was also supported by the important elements of the *pongyi*-led *Sangha Sametggi* and by Tharrawaddy U Pu's Home Rule Party. The latter was represented by eight to ten members in the legislative council.[43]

The characteristic aspect of the anti-Separationist movement continued to be political collaboration with the Indian National Congress program. The movement in Burma received substantial encouragement from across the bay in March and April, 1931, when the Karachi meeting of the Indian Congress Party negated the official British view by explicitly recognizing Burma's right to "remain an autonomous partner in a free India with a right to separation at any time." A year later, in March, 1932, the India Legislative Council itself supported the Congress Party view to the effect that a decision by Burma to remain a part of India would not be irrevocable, as London was insisting.[44]

The weakness of the anti-Separationist movement derived in part from the lack of any unifying ideological commitment which was widely shared by the unwieldly mass of its adherents. Many elements of the group, although sympathetic to Indian nationalism, were at the same time hostile to Indian political as well as economic influence in Burma proper. The anti-Separationists also lacked an effective positive program of action geared to Burma's needs and traditions. Petitions sent by U Chit Hlaing to India to abolish all direct taxes were as ineffective as the earlier boycott of elections had been. Nonpayment of taxes, strikes, and hartals merely victimized participants and did not relieve Burman frustrations. It is not surprising, therefore, that other more violent forms of Burman protest tended to overshadow the negative anti-Separationist program of action.

[42] *PD,C*, vol. 247 (Jan. 26, 1931), p. 578. U So Thein's telegram flatly refusing to accept any British reform scheme short of complete independence was read in Parliament.

[43] *BRTCP*, pp. 68–80. Tharrawaddy U Pu at the Round Table Conference in London (Dec. 3, 1931) explained the influence of the *pongyi* politicians as follows: "The All-Burma *Sangha*'s Council . . . is a very important factor which no statesman can forget. They are the real leaders of Burma. . . . This *Sangha*'s . . . Council has about 100,000 . . . members or adherents . . . [who] boycott elections . . . and the Council. . . . The villagers worship and . . . obey the village *Sanghas* from childhood. . . . We, the anti-Separationists . . . have *pongyis* . . . in every village . . . [who] influence their particular villagers" (*ibid.*, p. 80).

[44] *PP,C*, vol. VIII for 1933–1934, "Records . . . of the Joint Committee on Indian Constitutional Reform," pt. II, pp. 121–129.

Economic Distress and Racial Friction

The most ominous Burman political development which occurred during 1930 was not the anti-Separationist agitation, but the widespread resort to overt violence. Such actions were usually antiforeign in character, directed especially against alien Indians and Chinese, and the grievances prompting them were mainly economic. Particularly affected were unemployed Burman laborers forced under depression conditions to compete with Indian coolies, harried agricultural tenants who were being outbid by Indian cultivators, Burman landowners recently dispossessed by Chettyar moneylender creditors, and the victims of usurious Chinese shopkeepers. The series of interracial explosions of 1930 and early 1931, involving murder, arson, and other forms of physical intimidation, were confined almost entirely to Lower Burma, where the Burman clash with the alien usurer and the Indian laborer was most direct. Politically, these riots tended sharply to undercut the efforts of Indian Congress Party agents to foster co-operation with Burman nationalists under the banner of anti-Separationism. An increasing number of Burmans who were caught in the economic pinch of gathering depression tended to subordinate concern over remote constitutional issues, ill-understood at best, to more direct methods of obtaining short-term relief.

The serious break in Burma's agricultural prosperity came in 1930, although the point of diminishing returns for the cultivator had been reached earlier.[45] Within Burma's expanding economy, down to 1928, Indian labor tended to take over commercial and industrial employment, while Burmans gravitated to the newly developed areas of rice cultivation. By 1928, the high costs entailed in reducing waste areas to cultivation began to force an increasing number of Burmans to compete with Indians for a share of the urban employ, at first in the skilled-labor fields [46] but finally also in the areas of common labor. The closing down of European plantation and mining operations at the outset of the depression in 1929 reduced non-Burman employment and threw more Indians on the labor market.

[45] In 1929, prior to the depression, some 230,000 acres in Lower Burma passed into the hands of nonagriculturalists through mortgage foreclosures (*RAB* for 1929–1930, p. 17).

[46] By 1929, indigenous races had taken over some 36 per cent of the skilled labor of Rangoon but only 23 per cent of the unskilled. See J. J. Bennison, *Report of an Enquiry into the Standard of Living of the Working Classes in Rangoon* (Rangoon, 1928), pp. 91–93.

In 1930 came sharp cuts in the price for boat paddy at Rangoon. From a high of 194 rupees per 100 baskets of paddy in 1924, the price fell to 169 in 1928, to 159 in 1929, and to the hardship level of 138 in 1930. The cost of producing the 1930 crop was high because the old agreed rates for labor still applied plus the fact that the per acre rental obligations were payable in kind at the depressed price level. The share left for most cultivators, after costs were paid, was scarcely enough in many cases to cover interest on loans much less the family food supply for the ensuing year. Tenant farmers in early 1931 over-sold their food stocks and ran out of rice before the end of the year. The subsequent collapse of Rangoon paddy prices in 1931 by almost half, to a mere 77 rupees, which was far below production costs, was catastrophic. Moneylender credits were withdrawn, mortgages were foreclosed, and large areas went out of cultivation. Thus during the half decade from 1929 to 1934, almost 2 million acres of Lower Burma paddy land passed into the possession of nonresident, nonagricultural-ist Chettyar owners.[47]

The Chettyar community normally tried to avoid acquiring title to land, preferring to keep its assets liquid. Its organization was efficient and internally honest, with agencies located in all of the larger towns of Lower Burma. It profited from well-established banking connections. Subagents capable of dealing with individual landowners in terms of personal acquaintance and knowledge of their security assets functioned throughout Lower Burma. Chettyars lent on good security, at from 15 to 30 per cent per annum. Burmans could not match the resources and administrative efficiency of the Chettyars, while European bankers as a rule refused to go to the trouble of becoming acquainted with villager borrowers. If the necessitous borrower lacked both securities and credit, he was obliged to have recourse to the local Chinese shopkeeper to piece out the year's food supply and to obtain other supplies. Paddy so borrowed was usually repayable by two baskets for one at harvest time.[48] Both types of usurers in normal times fattened off the debt-ridden Burman cultivators.[49]

[47] India, Census Commissioner, *Census of India, 1931*, vol. XI, *Burma*, pt. I (Rangoon, 1933), report by J. J. Bennison, pp. 16–17; *RLAC*, pt. II, pp. 35–38. In 1930 the government remitted up to one-third of the land revenue in the newly settled areas, but this afforded no relief to the destitute tenants.

[48] Furnivall, *Political Economy of Burma*, pp. 128, 130–147. Aside from the Chettyars, few Indian businessmen in Burma made any effort to learn Burmese.

[49] The Chettyars were Madrasis. The Chinese in Lower Burma were almost entirely Cantonese and Fukienese. Few of the Chinese were common laborers or engaged in domestic service, where many Indians were so employed.

Although Burman cultivator resentment against Indian moneylender and Chinese shopkeeper creditors was reaching the breaking point in 1930, it was at the level of the competition among semidestitute laborers, Burman and Indian, that racial trouble first developed. The first clash occurred at Rangoon in May of 1930. A group of Indian Coringhi shipping coolies, acting allegedly at the instigation of Congress Party agitators, struck for better wages on May 8. Burmese laborers were brought in on a temporary basis as strikebreakers. When the starving Coringhis eventually agreed to return to work on May 26, the Burmans were summarily dismissed. According to the official version, the outbreak began when a large number of Coringhis set upon a group of protesting Burmans.[50] The discharged Burmans also became infuriated when the Indian dock workers ridiculed them before their own womenfolk, who had come distances to bring the noonday lunches. Fighting spread quickly throughout Rangoon and raged unchecked for two days. The tattoo *sayas* did a flourishing business. Rough Burmese mobs decorated with magical charms hunted down panic-stricken Indians in a savage, fanatical frenzy. The official report indicated around 100 killed and about 1,000 injured, almost all Indians; contemporary observers reported from 300 to 500 killed.[51]

The riots were not politically motivated, for mobs avoided the police and were not hostile to the British residents. Most of the Indian victims were of unknown identity, and none of the injured received any compensation. Only two Burmans who got into a fight with the police were prosecuted. The authorities afforded temporary asylum for some 7,000 Indian laborers and later managed with local Indian help to return them unharmed to their homes.[52] A perceptive British judge at Rangoon described the mood of the victorious rioters as follows:

The Burmese proletariat walked with a lighter step. They had shown the Indians their place. This was Burma, a land which had been independent for hundreds of years before it fell to the English. Too many Indians had crowded into it from their starving villages across the bay. They could . . . undersell the Burmese, and there was a swarm of them too in the public services, particularly in the railways and the prison Department. Well, they had been taught a lesson.[53]

[50] *PP,C*, vol. XIX for 1931–1932 (Cmd. 3997), "Statement on the Moral and Material Progress and Condition of India for 1930–1931," pp. 552–553.

[51] *Ibid.*, p. 553; Collis, *Trials in Burma*, pp. 183–203.

[52] Collis, *Trials in Burma*, pp. 204–208.   [53] *Ibid.*, p. 209.

Within less than a month following the riot, a mutiny occurred in the Rangoon Central Jail on June 24, the exact date of the release of the Simon Commission report. It originated as a plot of Burmese inmates to murder the newly appointed Indian prison superintendent, who had tightened discipline. The mutineers turned down a chance to escape from jail in order to attack the superintendent. Military police called in to quell the outbreak were all Indians, and their killing of three Burmese convicts and the wounding of sixty others added tinder to the racial feud.[54]

Such riotous outbreaks continued into 1931. Burmese attacks against the Chinese occurred at Rangoon in early January. During succeeding weeks, they spread in concentric circles from Rangoon into nearby districts, gradually merging with the political rebellion which will be described below. By March, 1931, swarms of homeless and destitute Chinese traders and shopkeepers from outlying areas had been driven into the capital city, where they had to live by their wits or by theft.[55] In March and April of 1931, savage Burman attacks against resident Indian cultivators developed along the Pegu-Toungoo district border, whence the disorders spread southward into Hanthawaddy District. As a direct-action effort to expel Indian cultivators through physical violence and arson, this move was not, in any real sense, part of the contemporary antigovernment Saya San rebellion.[56]

Racial violence plus the depression itself had the effect of halting the tide of Indian labor immigration to Burma. This had exceeded 400,000 entries by sea for each of the four years from 1926 to 1929. In 1930 and 1931, the number of Indian departures exceeded entries by 30,000 and 57,000 respectively, and from 1933 the annual immigration figure stabilized at around 250,000 entries annually, with about as many returning to India.[57]

Another less violent form of antiforeign feeling was the instigation by *pongyi* politicians during 1930 of organized opposition to the teaching of Christianity to Buddhist children in the mission high schools of Rangoon. *Pongyi* leaders actively hindered efforts to settle the Buddhist student strike at Cushing High School which was occasioned in part by the school's refusal to permit students to attend pagoda holidays. A *pongyi* in nearby Letpadan published a tract reviling the Christian

[54] *Ibid.*, pp. 211–234.

[55] Burma, *Report of the Rangoon Town Police* for 1931, pp. 6–8.

[56] *RAB* for 1930–1931, p. ix; *RLAC*, pt. ii, pp. 52–55; F. B. Leach, *The Future of Burma*, pp. 47–48.

[57] Furnivall, *Political Economy*, pp. 87–88.

God. Mission schools at Moulmein and elsewhere were accused of using inquisitorial methods. The protests apparently enjoyed little support from Buddhist parents of students, but they carried fanatical nationalist overtones and boded ill for the future of missionary education. During the ensuing year, 1931, the so-called "conscious clause" was interpreted by the government as forbidding compulsory religious instruction of students in Christian schools without the express consent of parents.[58]

Development of Anti-British Sentiment

It was doubtless inevitable that the government itself and the British community resident in Burma should in time also run afoul of the increasingly aggressive mood of the Burmese nationalists. The British, of course, were not defenseless and exposed as were the hapless Indians and Chinese; most of them had no occasion to come into direct contact with the Burmese people. As employers and businessmen their dealings were largely with more docile Indians. Burmans were denied membership and even physical entry to the European clubs at Rangoon and to the Rangoon Golf Club at nearby Mingaladon. Part of the technique of sustaining British "face" was to maintain one's social distance. British refusal to visit the Shwe Dagon pagoda platform at Rangoon following the Burmese-sponsored ban on footwear was a case in point. Except for a number of able and perceptive members of the Indian civil service, few British residents achieved any understanding of the Burman point of view concerning political matters or of the factors responsible for growing social disintegration and lawlessness. All politically motivated activity was from the British businessman's point of view both mischievous and disreputable.[59]

British "face" plus the very lack of direct European contact with the Burmese public prevented the latter from developing sentiments of violent personal hostility to the British comparable to that entertained for the Indians. And yet the changing Burman mood was generating its own consciousness of "face" and offended racial dignity. This was true at the lower as well as the higher social levels. At one of the Rangoon trials in 1929 over which Judge Maurice Collis presided, involving a British employee of Steel Brothers who had mal-

---

[58] *RAB* for 1929–1930, pp. vi–ix; ABMFS, *Annual Report* for 1930 and 1931, by W. E. Wiatt (Rangoon, 1932).

[59] Collis (*Trials in Burma,* pp. 34, 58, 68–73, 89–93) gives an excellent characterization of the attitude of the British community in Rangoon.

treated and humiliated a thieving Burmese servant to the point where the victim jumped from a second-story window to his death, the charge of murder was brought before the court by an able lawyer, U Paw Tun, hired by nationalist funds. The court proceedings were attended ominously by rude, half-educated political *pongyis* and by their uncouth women followers wearing coarse homespun jackets.[60]

A more tangible Burman grievance against the British community was dramatized by the sustained attack inside and outside the legislative council on the highly unsatisfactory report presented by the official Enquiry Committee appointed to examine complaints relative to the "Bullinger Pool." The committee's report declared that the firms involved had violated no law and also characterized their collusive rice-buying arrangement as merely good business practice. While the millers continued to profit handsomely, the Burman landowner-cultivator was caught in the maddening squeeze between the usurer and the millers. To the extent that government defended the "Bullinger Pool" arrangement and undertook no measures of relief, it came to share the growing popular hostility toward the European firms.[61]

Other grievances against British rule were of longer standing. Most immediately important was resistance to the continued collection of the hated direct capitation tax. This was coupled with the policy, already noted, of raising the rate of land tax with each successive settlement survey.[62] Burmans also disliked the Indian Penal Code and courts, which supported the moneylender and the rack-renting landlord but offered no effective relief to the debt-ridden cultivator. Officials who were in a position to bring charges under it used certain sections of the code as a means of extorting bribes for reducing the seriousness of charges levied or for dismissing them. Finally came the

---

[60] *Ibid.*, pp. 73–105.   [61] Hinners, p. 35; Harvey, *British Rule*, pp. 67–70.

[62] A case in point was brought out by R. S. Wilkie (Burma, Settlement Dept., *Report on the Third Settlement of the Pyinmana Subdivision of Yamethin District . . . Season 1931–1933* [Rangoon, 1933]). The report as amended by the Department of Local Government raised the land revenue demand by 18 per cent on the basis of enhanced rental values. This was done in the face of the fact that approximately three-fourths of the households were reported to be indebted to an average level of some 300 rupees. The report also explained that high rents were due to population pressure and consequent rack-renting as well as to competitive bidding for access to the limited area of arable land. The Chettyars were active in the area and flourishing, while cultivators admittedly realized little surplus over costs in good years and retained no *wunsa* (food reserve) at all if crops were bad. In Thaton District in 1931, some 80 per cent of the cultivators were in debt to an average of 431 rupees. See *Report*, pp. 1–15, 35, 40–42.

alarming process, which began in 1929, of the wholesale transfer of land titles to Chettyar nonresident nonagriculturalists.

Behind these more obvious grievances was the growing awareness among the better informed that European firms, who continued to pay handsome dividends even during the depression years, were for the most part opposed to constitutional concessions, ameliorative economic regulations, and limitation of Indian labor immigration. Governor Innes' action in vetoing the proposed "Sea Passengers' Tax," which was passed by the legislative council for the purpose of collecting 5 rupees from all adults entering Rangoon by sea, suggested that the government was unsympathetic.[63] During the latter half of the 1930's some of the youthful members of the ultranationalist *Dobama* Party began to talk in Marxist terms of imperialist exploitation and the assumed interconnection between colonialism and capitalism.[64] Many thoughtful, educated Burmese were aware that religion and social morality were disintegrating and that the *pongyi*-led nationalism defied all rational control. What they resented most was British preachment decrying Burmese lawlessness and disorder without assessing the causes and British use of disorder as reason for postponing self-government. British-Burman relations grew increasingly tense as the decade progressed.[65]

The Saya San Rebellion

The rebellion led by Saya San which broke out in Tharrawaddy District of Lower Burma on December 22, 1930, differed qualitatively from other contemporary forms of nationalist political protest. Its leaders had virtually nothing in common with the Separationists and very little with the anti-Separationists in their rather timid dependence on Indian nationalist leadership and Gandhian techniques. The rebellion also differed in spirit from the frenzied racial xenophobia which characterized the preceding and subsequent outbreaks of rioting, even though Indians were sometimes molested by the rebels.

The Saya San rebellion differed from the spontaneous antialien riots mainly because it was a deliberately planned affair based on tra-

[63] E. J. L. Andrew, *Indian Labour in Rangoon* (London, 1933), pp. 33–34.

[64] Moscotti, pp. 131–133, 141–142. In 1930 the Chinese Communist center at Shanghai sent agents to Burma. They made little headway, and four were deported. A red flag was found in a captured rebel camp in 1931. See *The Times*, Aug. 20, 1930, and Jan. 2, 1931.

[65] Collis, *Trials in Burma*, pp. 34–35.

ditional Burmese political and religious patterns. When the average Burman considered displacing British rule he thought automatically in terms of a revival of kingship. Pretenders had appeared repeatedly in Upper Burma since 1910, but had usually been suppressed without difficulty.[66] In 1928 one U Rathe Bandaha had led an abortive rebellion from Shwebo and Sagaing, complete with tattooing, magical medicines, and royal throne.[67] Had the G.C.B.A. leader, U Chit Hlaing, been a revolutionary, which he was not, he could doubtless have headed another such effort. Maurice Collis tells of one occasion in May, 1928, when the local *Wunthanu Athins* at Sagaing provided their visitor, U Chit Hlaing, with a caparisoned elephant to ride accompanied by a military retinue. But the crowd drifted away when the "uncrowned king" rebuffed the gesture and began to talk instead about constitutional and economic reforms.[68] Saya San was himself a native of Shwebo, even though he staged his uprising in disturbed Lower Burma. His effort was associated with a revival of the entire panoply of royal regalia and religious sanctions, Brahman, Buddhist, and animist. As an exhibition of traditional political bravado, the rebellion captured the imagination of the Burmese people to a degree quite impossible for the Separationist or anti-Separationist factions to attain.[69]

The Saya San movement stemmed particularly from the dissident U So Thein branch of the G.C.B.A., which advocated complete independence and declined to co-operate with the advocates of mere home rule.[70] It was political rather than racial in motivation, for the rebels were quite as ready to attack nonco-operative Burmese headmen and landlords as they were the occasional Indian who got into their path. As an ex-*pongyi* and a member of the executive committee of the So Thein G.C.B.A., Saya San was commissioned in the late twenties by that body to investigate the complaints of the people concerning such matters as the capitation tax, agrarian debt, and denial of popular access to forest reserves where needed bamboo and firewood

[66] One pretender was put down at Sagaing in 1910 and subsequently another at nearby Myinmu (one Maung Thant). See Maurice Collis, *Into Hidden Burma* (London, 1953), pp. 162–164.

[67] Burma, Legislative Council, *Proceedings* (hereafter cited as *BLCP*), XXIV (Feb. 16, 1933), 244–246; Collis, *Trials in Burma*, pp. 34–35.

[68] Collis, *Into Hidden Burma*, pp. 162–164.

[69] *PP,C*, vol. XII for 1931–1932 (Cmd. 3900), "Report on the Rebellion in Burma Up to 3rd May, 1931," pp. 1–2.

[70] For U So Thein's telegram to London containing this demand, see *PD,C*, vol. 247 (Jan. 26, 1931), p. 578.

could be obtained. Following the presentation of his report of findings in 1928, he allegedly withdrew from all official connection with the So Thein G.C.B.A. and began the task of organizing in great secrecy his separate political societies in preparation for armed rebellion.[71] The preparations were apparently entirely unknown to the government.

The rebellion centered in Tharrawaddy District, which had been throughout the twenties a center of disaffection. Saya San's preparations extended also into other districts. A special communication sent to the Shan *Sawbwas* solicited their co-operation on the basis of the new leader's "ardent desire to advance religion and the nation." [72] A cadre army, sans modern weapons, was drilled and indoctrinated, while a jungle capital was prepared in a remote foothill area of the Pegu Yoma some twelve miles east of Tharrawaddy town. On October 28, 1930, at the auspicious moment of 11:33 P.M., which had been selected by learned astrologers, Saya San was proclaimed quite secretly to be the *Thupannaka Galon Raja*. The *galon* was a fabulous bird capable of destroying the *naga* (snake) foreigner. The White Umbrella, ancient Brahman symbol of divine kingship, was raised over the new rajah's head. To this was added the Crown and Sword of Victory, as well as sacred slipper and whisk symbols.

Enlisted in support of the new jungle king were the magicians with their protective medicines and the practitioners of cabalistic tattooing (in *galon* figures) supposed to impart invulnerability, together with a variety of amulets and charms.[73] The aid of guardian *nat* spirits was also solicited. The rebels allegedly hoped to enlist in their cause the potent ghost of the British commissioner of Pegu Division, whom they scheduled for assassination. They had to be satisfied with a mere British forestry officer as victim, and his ghost apparently did not measure up to the task. Most of the organizers under Saya San were political *pongyis* who worked through the local *Wunthanu Athins*.[74] The political-religious character of the movement was clearly reflected in the following oath required of all members of the "*Galon*" societies:

We are banded together to drive out all unbelievers . . . till we are free of the rule of the English. . . . I will obey all superiors of the Galon society

---

[71] *BRTCP*, pp. 70–80.   [72] *BLCP*, XXIV (Feb. 16, 1933), 244–246.

[73] *PP,C*, vol. IX for 1931–1932 (Cmd. 3997), pp. 129–137; Tun Pe, *Sun over Burma* (Rangoon, 1949). Saya San was himself a quack doctor and the author of a widely circulated book describing traditional medical nostrums.

[74] Collis, *Trials in Burma*, pp. 273–278; *PP,C*, vol. XII for 1931–1932, pp. 1–12.

. . . so that our religion may be saved from the unbeliever. . . . Grant that I may help destroy all . . . unbelievers. Protect and help our religion, O ye greater and lesser Nats. . . . Grant to us liberty and to the Galon King dominion over this land.[75]

Hostilities began in Tharrawaddy District on December 22, 1930. On the previous day at a durbar held in Tharrawaddy town, the acting governor, Sir J. A. Maung Gyi, had flatly rejected a popular petition asking him to reduce taxes. Within less than a week's time, some 1,500 rebels assembled in the area, and the group eventually reached approximately double that size. But the entire *Galon* army possessed at the outset only 30 guns, and its supply of firearms was meagerly augmented by scattered attacks on permit holders, especially village-tract headmen and outpost police.[76] The unpopular forestry service was a prime target. Six forestry officers including one European were killed, and some 100 forestry houses were burned. As in olden times, the appearance of a pretender to the long-vacated Burmese throne, buttressed by traditional trappings of authority, attracted a motley crew of dacoits and other adventurers hungry for excitement; most of them had apparently not been parties to the organized conspiracy.

The movement did not at first seem very formidable, for the military police encountered no serious resistance in achieving the initial objective of capturing and destroying the rebel "palace" in the jungle. But this seemingly convincing demonstration of the ineffectiveness of charms, amulets, and "invulnerable" tattooing as protection against modern firearms did not, as expected, produce the dispersal of the rebel army. It broke up into several large gangs capable of conducting continued resistance from hide-outs in the jungle. Numerous smaller groups numbering ten persons or less, including criminal characters, terrorized nonco-operating villagers and some defenseless Indians and Chinese by perpetrating dacoities, arson, and outright murder.[77] Heroic endeavors were made to manufacture crude firearms from pipe lengths and bicycle tubing. The locale of the most formidable resistance continued to be in Tharrawaddy District and in neighbor-

[75] Moscotti, p. 186. See also C. V. Warren, *Burmese Interlude* (London, 1937), pp. 92–94.

[76] *PP,C*, vol. XII for 1931–1932 (Cmd. 3900), pp. 1–12; see also *PD,C*, vol. 253 (June 15, 1931), pp. 1408–1409. By May, 1931, there were 12 headmen and 27 police killed and 3 headmen and 18 police wounded.

[77] *PP,C*, vol. XII for 1931–1932 (Cmd. 3900), pp. 10, 13, 18–20; *PP,C*, vol. XIX for 1931–1932 (Cmd. 3997), pp. 129–133; *PD,C*, vol. 253 (June 15, 1931), p. 1409.

ing Insein District, where the embers of rebellion were not finally extinguished until April, 1932.

Immediately following the outbreak of violence in Tharrawaddy, sympathetic rebellions occurred elsewhere. At Yamethin, in central Burma, a rising was instigated on January 4, 1931, by a *pongyi* agitator recently arrived from Saya San's headquarters in Tharrawaddy. It was a feeble affair numbering only 40 to 50 men, who were rounded up by the police within a few days' time. A more formidable rising, the preparations for which had been made by Saya San himself, began in Pyapon District, south of Rangoon, on January 7. The effort was short-lived because the police were ready for it, having been forewarned. The authorities were nevertheless confronted boldly by a mob of approximately 700 men armed only with dahs and spears, who advanced on the police contingent in solid phalanx. An hour and a half of sustained firing was required to disperse the group. Several score were killed, and the remaining 600 men, unable to find jungle cover, were quickly rounded up. The disaffection in Pyapon, it was discovered, centered in Dedaye township where the Chettyars had recently taken over much of the land.[78]

Trouble started in Bassein and Henzada districts in late February. The rising was not very substantial in Bassein, although the police arrested a considerable number of men bearing the telltale tattooed markings. Some 300 rebels attacked the police in Henzada District on February 21. The group was dispersed, but most of them succeeded in escaping to the jungle where they maintained desultory resistance. From Henzada the movement spread up the Irrawaddy Valley into Prome and Thayetmyo districts. In all of these areas itinerant *pongyi* agitators attracted attention by their denunciations of popular grievances, but they enlisted relatively few active participants. The discovery of tattooing procedures in Toungoo, Myingyan, and Mandalay districts led to police arrests, which nipped in the bud incipient overt risings. The only Upper Burma district seriously involved in the rebellion was Thayetmyo, and there the disaffection was confined for the most part to a remote corner township. The early posting of government troops at strategic points in Upper Burma, at Meiktila, Yenangyaung, and Shwebo in particular, helped forestall further trouble. By August of 1931, the Mandalay District was reported to be entirely quiet.[79]

[78] *RLAC*, pt. II, pp. 52–55; Collis, *Trials in Burma*, pp. 277–278.
[79] *PD,C*, vol. 251 (May 11, 1930), pp. 798–799, statement by Wedgwood Benn; ABFMS, *MS. Correspondence*, from Herbert Hinton, Aug. 16, 1931.

Upper Burma was spared the acute economic distress which the collapse of the price of paddy had produced in Lower Burma. The rebellion reached its peak by the time of the onset of the rainy season in May and June of 1931, and it gradually declined thereafter.

Suppression of the Rebellion

Efforts of the government to counter political unrest by other than military means were not particularly effective. Governor Innes returned to Burma in January, 1931, fresh from attending the Indian Round Table Conference. But he was able to convey to Burmans no specific assurances concerning the nature of their new constitution.[80] He conferred repeatedly with responsible Burman leaders and twice addressed the legislative council on the subject of the rebellion. Burmans complained that they were powerless to intervene in the interest of quieting unrest as long as popular uncertainty prevailed concerning London's intentions.[81] Governor Innes did afford economic relief by reducing by one-tenth to one-third the land revenue demands in the fifteen districts hardest hit by the depression. He also held in abeyance for a time the forcible collection of loans as well as taxes and provided 20 lakhs of rupees (2 million) for agricultural loans.[82] The government offered amnesty to all rebels who would surrender their arms, give information valuable to the authorities, and then return home. The *Aletawya Sayadaw* and other reputable *pongyi* leaders from Rangoon were used to transmit these offers to the rebel bands, and with some success.[83]

Foremost among the government's administrative moves to counter political unrest was the appointment of a special commissioner, Mr. Booth-Gravely, to be in charge of the five districts most seriously affected by the rebellion. Within these districts, sixteen administrative units were set up, manned by police and including special trial tribunals.[84] To broaden the scope of the jurisdiction of these special tribunals the government sponsored the enactment of the Criminal

[80] *RAB* for 1930–1931, pp. v–vii, 10; *PD,C*, vol. 254 (July 9, 1931), p. 2310. Secretary Wedgwood Benn here explained to Parliament, in reply to a question, that Burma's future constitution had simply not been decided upon.

[81] *RLAC*, pt. ii, pp. 52–55.

[82] *RAB* for 1930–1931, p. 10; *PD,C*, vol. 254 (July 9, 1931), p. 2310.

[83] *PP,C*, vol. XIX for 1931–1932 (Cmd. 3997), pp. 135–137; *The Times*, July 25, 1931.

[84] *PP,C*, vol. XIX for 1931–1932 (Cmd. 3997), pp. 135–137. The tribunals functioned without juries, but their decisions were subject to appeal.

Law Amendment Act of 1931. The act was scheduled to run for five years. It specified that special judicial commissioners could arrest without legal warrants and try by summary procedure under rules of their own choosing persons thought to have violated or to be about to violate certain sections of the Indian Criminal Code. The legal prohibition of the possession of arms and penalties for assisting the administration of justice were specifically cited. The government's justification for the act was based on the farfetched assumption that the Bengal Revolutionary Association, which had circulated certain inflammatory pamphlets in Burma, was somehow responsible for the rebellion. One of the sweeping applications of the act was to outlaw the So Thein G.C.B.A. and its affiliated *athins* as promoters of the rebellion.

The proposed act touched off a bitter debate within the legislative council, thereby nullifying the previous attempts of the governor to obtain the political co-operation of Burmese leaders against the rebellion.[85] The debate afforded opportunity for the opposition in the council to voice its grievances. It denounced the act as an insult to Burma, as a "lawless law," intended to paralyze all political activity in Burma and related in no way to the minor and scattered Bengali agitation cited as justification for it. U Ni declared that the interminable delays attending London's decisions regarding constitutional reform were in large measure responsible for the revolutionary violence in Burma as well as in Bengal. The relatively moderate Indian representative, E. P. Pillay, asserted that:

It is this . . . insensible type of legislation which, more than anything else, has been the cause of constant friction between the Government and the country. . . . Instead of preventing terror, [such legislation] inspires it.

U Ba Pe summed up the indictment by declaring that only by establishing the fact that the government promoted the welfare of the people could order be restored. He continued:

What is the use of having a government that has not the wisdom to promote . . . the welfare of the people? . . . If Government is so bankrupt

[85] Great Britain, *The Burma Criminal Law Amendment Act* (London, 1931), pp. 5–7, 14–17; Moscotti, pp. 50–53; Burma, Labour Statistics Bureau, *Report of an Enquiry into the Standard of Living . . . of the Working Classes in Rangoon*, by J. J. Bennison (Rangoon, 1928), pp. 18–20. Although U So Thein apparently at first tried to halt the rebellion, his G.C.B.A. later enrolled volunteers for it (*The Times*, Feb. 11, 1931).

315

of ideas, why not call for a conference of the leaders of the various communities in Burma and get their views on the question? [86]

The contrary arguments advanced by government spokesmen served only to exacerbate nationalist sensibilities. Sir Frederick Leach, for example, denounced as a stain on Burma's good name those who, by implication, were willing to allow Burman territory to be used for purposes of revolutionary agitation and anarchy. Oscar de Glanville, ex-president of the council and subsequently one of Burma's representatives to the Burma Round Table Conference, warned:

The extent of Parliament's grant of governmental responsibility depends upon the people of Burma and to a very large extent upon the opposition in this House.[87]

The vigorous military measures taken to counter the rebellion were calculated to demonstrate that invulnerable tattooing and magical charms, however venerable, were no match for modern firearms.[88] But realization of this fact did not quiet the uprising. By June, 1931, some 8,100 government troops were deployed in the campaign. These were augmented following the cessation of the rains in the fall by the arrival of seven additional battalions from India, six Indian and one British, comprising some 3,640 troops.[89] Early in the rains Saya San was forced to flee northward, and he hid for a time in a *pongyi kyaung* some fifteen miles north of Mandalay. Flushed from this asylum in early August, he escaped into the nearby Shan hills only to be captured a short distance northeast of the summer capital of Maymyo. Saya San's right-hand lieutenant, U Myat Aung, was also captured in Pegu District in November, 1931.[90] Following the loss of its leaders, the rebellion degenerated more than ever into unco-ordinated gang

[86] Great Britain, *Burma Criminal Law . . . Act,* pp. 19–26, 52, 55. Subsequently a speaker in Parliament echoed U Ba Pe's appeal as follows: "Would it not be possible to . . . get into closer touch with the mind and thought of the Burmese people? There seems a strong case for more people on the spot studying . . . their thoughts and political ideas" (by Rennie Smith in *PD,C,* vol. 254 [July 9, 1931], pp. 3410–3411).

[87] Great Britain, *Burma Criminal Law . . . Act,* pp. 26, 30. Opposition motions to amend the act were defeated 48 to 37 and 46 to 39.

[88] *PD,C,* vol. 254 (June 12, 1937), p. 12. On June 12 the military police decapitated fourteen rebels and displayed the heads publicly in an effort to convince the doubting.

[89] *Ibid.;* also vol. 260 (Nov. 23, 1931), pp. 3–4.

[90] ABFMS, *MS. Correspondence,* from Herbert Hinton, Aug. 16, 1931; *PD,C,* vol. 260 (Nov. 23, 1931), pp. 3–4.

operations of varying sizes. It was in April, 1932, that the larger resistance groups were finally broken up.

From the limited number of persons involved, it is clear that the rebellion was in no sense a mass rising of the Burmese people in any way comparable to the troubles in 1886–1887.[91] The secrecy with which Saya San's preparations had to be enshrouded, the alert counteractivity of the police, the rebels' lack of firearms with which to oppose trained government forces, and the fact that the acute economic distress on which the movement fed was confined to Lower Burma— all militated against widespread popular participation. To the majority of the educated Burmans, Saya San's quixotic effect was sheer madness, worse than futile.[92] In the key center of Tharrawaddy town, Karen volunteers were recruited to aid in the pacification. Thus the pattern of Karen military co-operation with the government against Burman rebels, set in 1886, was revived in 1931. Armed Karen irregulars assisted in repelling rebel attacks on isolated villages and also participated in offensive operations against rebel bands.[93]

Saya San was convicted of seditious treason and executed on November 28, 1937. An Anglophobe European-trained lawyer of Mon antecedents, Dr. Ba Maw, volunteered his services as counsel for Saya San's defense. The decision was appealed to the High Court and then to the privy council. It was a daring political move, which Dr. Ba Maw exploited skillfully for personal political ends. It afforded him a springboard to a colorful political career, first as education minister, then as first head of the cabinet after 1937, and finally as chief of state during the Japanese occupation. Dr. Ba Maw identified himself politically with the anti-Separationists, although he had little or nothing in common with them culturally.[94] A meagerly educated but

[91] *PP,C*, vol. XIX for 1931–1932 (Cmd. 3991), pp. 135–137; *PD,C*, vol. 262 (May 9, 1932), pp. 1817–1818. Government forces inflicted some 3,000 casualties, killed and wounded, and themselves suffered 50 killed, including police and officials, plus 88 wounded. Of the 8,300 persons arrested, only a small fraction were tried and some 350 were convicted. Seventy-eight were sentenced to death, and 270 were transported to the Andaman Islands. A score of headmen and several score Indians also lost their lives.

[92] *PP,C*, vol. XIX for 1931–1932 (Cmd. 3991), pp. 135–137; *PD,C*, vol. 262 (March 9, 1932), pp. 1817–1818.

[93] ABMFS, *Annual Report* for 1931, p. 73; *PD,C*, vol. 255 (July 13, 1931), pp. 3–4, vol. 260 (Nov. 30, 1931), p. 774.

[94] *The Times*, Aug. 25 and 29, Nov. 4 and 30, 1931; Kyaw Min, *The Burma We Love* (Calcutta, 1945), pp. 9–15. Dr. Ba Maw's father, U Kye, had engineered a rebellion in Thaton District following 1886 and had been obliged to flee to Siam.

317

politically cunning third-grade pleader from Tharrawaddy, named U Saw, also volunteered his legal talents to defend Saya San. U Saw eventually appropriated the *galon* symbol of the rebels for his own political movement. Both Dr. Ba Maw and U Saw vaulted into political prominence during the ensuing decade, outdistancing other politicians who were not in accord politically with the mass movement.

Political Significance of the Rebellion

The psychological and political significance of the rebellion was more far-reaching than the limited extent of active popular participation would indicate. Daw Mi Mi Khaing has recorded [95] how she, as a schoolgirl from a civil service official family far removed from nationalist agitators and attending a Catholic mission institution in 1931, sensed strongly the wave of patriotic fervor which attended the mad rebellion. The sheer audacity of Saya San's personal conviction that he was born to be the ruler of a resurrected Burmese Kingdom fired the girl's imagination and stimulated her latent pride of race and of culture. She reports how her fellow Anglo-Indian students complained bitterly that the proud Burmans now wanted all others to bow to them. Even though Saya San was admittedly a charlatan and his followers frequently dacoits, he became for her as for other Burmans the intrepid spirit, the embodiment of physical courage and hardihood.[96] Thus the perpetrators of the uprising breathed new vitality into Burmese nationalism simply by demonstrating the courage of their political commitment against impossible odds. The heat of their frenzied resistance welded a connecting bond, between the culturally disparate *pongyi*-led masses and the Westernized elite. Although the uprising did not reconcile political differences, it undoubtedly constituted an important landmark in the development of Burmese nationalism.

The rebellion failed to resolve political differences simply because

---

Maung Ba Maw and his older brother Maung Ba Han were educated at St. Paul's Catholic school in Rangoon. Both became Christians, Ba Maw a nominal Catholic and Ba Han a follower of the Plymouth Brethren sect. Both graduated from Calcutta University and completed their legal education including doctorate degrees at European continental universities, Ba Maw at Bordeaux and Ba Han at Heidelberg. They had previously encountered irritating experiences in England. Dr. Ba Maw's Anglophobia apparently stemmed primarily from personal resentment. He was a vain person who, prior to 1931, had been something of a laughingstock because of his affectation of European ways.

[95] Mi Mi Khaing, *The Burmese Family* (Bombay, 1946), p. 94.
[96] *Ibid.*

it took no cognizance whatever of the basic alternatives as presented by either London or India. It paid little attention to the Indian National Congress program; it ignored the successive Round Table Conferences which were being held at London; it shut its eyes to the existence of regular and legal procedures for accomplishing political ends. The several G.C.B.A. groups therefore continued to be divided over what tactics to follow. U Chit Hlaing's followers eventually denounced both the rebellion and the no-tax campaign, and the U Ba Shwe faction joined them in a decision to participate in the legislative council election contest of 1932 and to settle constitutionally for dominion status. The more radical U Maung Su group, on the other hand, continued flatly to oppose both election participation and council entry. The latter group, in imitation of Saya San, demanded nothing less than complete national independence, and it continued to co-operate with the Congress Party program of civil disobedience and nonpayment of taxes.[97] In 1932, a loose political federation was formed between the U Chit Hlaing G.C.B.A. and the *Swarajists,* led by U Paw Tun.[98]

The government could take little advantage of these differences because its own policies were at the time mostly negative, offering few if any issues capable of attracting popular support. The police suppressed several inflammatory pamphlets and arrested distributors of a subversive sheet entitled "Freedom First." The editors and publishers of two vernacular papers in Rangoon were arrested and convicted of sedition. Special police precautions had to be taken during the course of the trial of the editors.[99] Positive proposals that might have alleviated the causes of the rebellion quickly ran aground. The constitutional issue could not be decided in Rangoon in any case, and Governor Innes was apparently not in sympathy with policy trends prevailing in London. He flatly rejected the unpublished recommendations of a special McCallum-Nichols Enquiry Committee that the peasant disaffection be countered by enacting into law the land alienation reform proposals dating back to 1906. The governor demurred on the traditional grounds that there was still no feasible way to define the "agriculturalist" group to whom land alienation would be restricted

[97] *RAB* for 1930–1931, p. viii.

[98] *RAB* for 1931–1932, pp. ix–x. The anti-Separationists of 1932, led by Dr. Ba Maw, U Kyaw Myint, and Yanbye U Maung Maung, continued to receive some financial aid from the Indian Association of Burma, although the latter was concerned mainly with protecting Indian interests.

[99] Burma, *Report of the Rangoon Town Police* for 1931, p. 5, for 1932, pp. 4–5.

and that the proposed restrictive measures would create uncertainty and impair agricultural credit and freedom of contract.[100]

British authorities could and did continue to take effective advantage of the divergencies and rivalries within the nationalist movement, both in the Burma legislative council and in successive conferences held at London. But this was costly in terms of failure to develop any integrated and responsible party group within Burma capable of cooperating with government and to command at the same time a measure of popular support. Such an objective was, of course, not easy to realize. Burmans often distrusted each other more than they did the British, and the opportunism, obstruction, sometimes violence of their reactions reflected the prevailing distrust. Too many Burman leaders habitually clamored for extreme constitutional concessions not as privileges capable of realization, but as means of attracting a following or as preliminaries to essentially revolutionary ends. The vogue was for nationalist spokesmen, whether in Burma or at London, to challenge flatly the British monopoly of constitutional control. Elected Burman representatives at the village, district, or legislative council level, on the other hand, usually acted in terms of personal self-interest without acknowledging any meaningful responsibility to the Burmese population. Popular distrust of leadership thus provided a meager foundation for representative government. It was awareness of this incipient anarchic threat behind the Burmese revolution, which would probably defy control by any revised instruments of self-government, that made indigenous minority groups such as the Karens fear Burman control and cling so persistently to British protection.

The British reform proposals failed not because London's eventual concessions to Burman self-rule were ungenerous and inadequate, but because they were so tardily realized and did not enlist the confidence and co-operation of any responsible conservative Burman elements.[101]

Perhaps the most serious impairment of governmental prestige which the rebellion produced was at the village level, where the special victim was the authority of the headman. He became the target of attack by armed rebel gangs and the butt of criticism by political agitators. The local *Wunthanu Athins* denounced him as tax collector and defied his authority as a police officer and local magistrate.[102] At best the villagers were apathetic to the headman's authority; at worst they

---

[100] *RLAC*, pt. II, pp. 52–55.
[101] For an elaboration of this theme, see Moscotti, pp. 155–165.
[102] *RAB* for 1930–1931, pp. 11–15.

were openly hostile. Because of the dire financial stringency of the times and the relaxation of discipline generally, many headmen defaulted in their obligations to the government in 1931–1932. Even criminal looting operations began to carry a political flavor because they could avoid public censure if directed against the government's side.[103] Noteworthy also was the remarkable increase of crime during 1931–1932 in Upper Burma districts, especially Yamethin, Meiktila, Pakokku, Myingyan, Thayetmyo, and Minbu. Here as in Lower Burma, police work was increasingly ineffective. The evidence was cumulative that governmental authority at the village level was disintegrating.

[103] *RAB* for 1931–1932, pp. ix–x, 76–77.

X

Formulation of a New Constitution for Burma,

1931-1935

THE most important political issue which Burma faced from 1931 to 1936 was whether or not the country should be separated from India and, if so, on what terms. The question was considered in preliminary fashion at the India Round Table Conference of 1930–1931 and more fully by the Burma Round Table Conference held a year later. It became the major issue in the bitterly contested election of 1932, when adherents of the erstwhile boycotting elements of the G.C.B.A. won a resounding but futile victory for the anti-Separationist cause. The failure of the Government of Burma and London authorities to dispel popular distrust of British intentions regarding the nature of the new constitution aggravated popular unrest.

With the formulation and general acceptance of the new constitution of 1935, the older nationalist tactics of election boycott, traditionalist rebellion à la Saya San, and anti-Separationist agitation faded from the political horizon while the various factions of the G.C.B.A. disintegrated. The same period witnessed the emergence of the youthful student-led Thakin or *Dobama* Party, which was destined in time to fill the political vacuum.

Burma at the India Round Table Conference

The future political status of Burma was treated as a question of minor concern by the first India Round Table Conference, which met at London from November 12, 1930, to January 19, 1931. Burma was represented by four members of the legislative council, U Ba Pe, U Aung Thin, M. M. Ohn Ghine, and Oscar de Glanville, a Briton domiciled in Burma. U Ba Pe championed the radical nationalist point of view, and De Glanville a more moderate one. The other two spokesmen agreed with U Ba Pe but were relatively inarticulate.

At an early session of the whole committee of the conference it was decided without apparent dissent and after only some fifteen minutes' casual consideration that Burma under the new reform scheme would be separated from India. A special subcommittee was accordingly selected to consider constitutional matters relating to Burma. Separation had been recommended by the Simon Commission and had also been approved in early August, 1930, by vote of the Burma legislative council. All four Burman representatives favored separation, and there appeared to be little or no Indian opposition to it.[1]

The decision of the conference leaders to ignore unofficial protest representations sent to it by the anti-Separationist faction in Burma, including a cable in October followed by a vehement documentary denunciation of separation in November, was understandable, but highly unfortunate.[2] The Burma representatives at London stressed the importance of taking cognizance of anti-Separationist sentiment, but their views also went unheeded. The Burma subcommittee included, besides the four Burma delegates, several British and two Indian members, plus Burma's governor, Sir Charles Innes, then in England on sick leave. Earl Russell acted as chairman.[3]

The viewpoint of the British Government as presented by Chairman Russell at the first session of the subcommittee on December 5 was simply stated. The separation of Burma from India was regarded as settled and was therefore no longer open to discussion. Only items relating to the terms of separation such as finances, trade, defense, and protection of minority interests need be considered. The question of the new constitution of separated Burma could be approached later

[1] Great Britain, India Round Table Conference, Nov. 12, 1930–Jan. 19, 1931, *Proceedings of Sub-Committees*, pt. II (London, 1931), pp. 154–157. This is hereafter cited as *IRTC*.

[2] *The Times*, Dec. 3 and 17, 1930. Secretary Benn later explained that the anti-Separationist diatribe was only one of many documents received through irregular channels and was not deemed worthy of special attention. See *PD,C*, vol. 247 (Jan. 26, 1931), p. 578.

[3] *The Times*, Aug. 6, 1930. In August, 1930, prior to leaving Burma, Governor Innes had assured the legislative council that, with separation, Burma would not be accorded a lower role than India.

either through a special Burma Round Table Conference, as suggested previously in full committee, or by sending another special commission to Burma. With regard to the nature of the new constitution, the chairman declared that His Majesty's Government at the time was prepared to say that "the prospects of constitutional advance held out to Burma as a part of India would not be prejudiced by separation." Discussion of these various topics, which extended over December 5, 8, and 9, developed into an effort on the part of British spokesmen to keep the issues distinct and separate, while spokesmen for Burma undertook to telescope them.[4]

With respect to the separation issue there was little disagreement. The Indian spokesmen and one Briton suggested that the whole committee had acted too hastily and that the considerable body of opinion in Burma opposing separation needed to be reassured that the decision was reached only after due consideration. British spokesmen in reply doubted that any considerable body of anti-Separationist opinion really existed in Burma. De Glanville stigmatized such sentiment as did exist as essentially subversive, since it hoped to exploit Indian aid in overthrowing British control. The three Burman delegates themselves opposed bringing the issue again before the whole conference, although they insisted that opposition within Burma would be strong unless specific assurances were given that separated Burma's new constitution would be equal to that of India. They argued that the dissident group, no matter how subversive, should be permitted to state its case openly and freely in order to counter false rumors. Chairman Russell ruled finally that it was already too late for opponents of separation to express their opinions.

Conditions of separation caused a minimum of difficulty. De Glanville and U Ba Pe agreed that the sending of a new commission to Burma would only inflame public opinion and foment boycott and rebellion. A special Burma Round Table Conference was therefore required on which all political elements would be represented. Questions raised concerning the means of implementing separation encountered no difficulty, with the exception that Burmans objected to the proposal that no future discrimination should be levied against the entry of Indian labor.[5]

---

[4] *IRTC*, pt. II, pp. 154–157, 160.

[5] *Ibid.*, pp. 155–157, 160–168. The subcommittee agreed that the interests of Indians and other minorities should be protected, that financial questions not amenable to negotiation be arbitrated, that defense arrangements be made prior to separation, and that a trade convention be negotiated.

The attacks of non-British members of the subcommittee focused mainly on Chairman Russell's carefully noncommittal statement concerning the new constitution. U Ba Pe wanted more explicit assurance that Burma's future constitutional status would be the same as India's, including a reaffirmation of the British pledges made in 1917 and 1919. The three legislative council rulings of August, 1930, favoring (a) separation, (b) appointment of a constitutional commission, and (c) the grant of dominion status, must, he said, be taken together. Misgivings about (c) were responsible for opposition to (a). Other critics preferred the word "unaffected" to the phrase "not be prejudiced," used by Chairman Russell. De Glanville backed U Ba Pe in saying that a declaration by the Prime Minister was needed to the effect that British pledges previously made to India as a whole applied also to Burma.[6] He proposed specifically that the phrase "toward responsible government" be added following "Constitutional advance." Shiva Rao of India also supported U Ba Pe, and his Indian compatriot, Mody, almost pushed to a vote a motion to amend the phrase to read: "Burma's claim or right to responsible government would not be prejudiced." [7]

Chairman Russell's insistence that the phrase as originally given was unambiguous and in any case the only one that could be made at the time was supported so vehemently by Governor Charles Innes that pride of authorship seemed to be involved. Innes affirmed flatly, in contradiction to views of the legislative council representations, that his own familiarity with Burmese opinion made him confident that the statement proposed by Russell would not cause great unrest in Burma. In rejoinder to U Ba Pe's sharp dissent, the governor declared with obvious irritation that he knew the situation in Burma. He added that His Majesty's Government was, in fact, not yet seized of the problem of Burma's constitution, since it had not yet heard the views of Local Government (Innes himself), of the Simon Commission, or of the Government of India. At the moment, London's mind was therefore perfectly blank on the subject. The constitution, he promised, would receive free discussion later. Chairman Russell did give as his personal opinion, in reply to U Ohn Ghine's query as to the implications of the proposed statement, that separated Burma would be at least as well off as India, but he refused to make any official commitment on the matter.[8]

---

[6] *Ibid.*, pp. 159–160, 168–170.   [7] *Ibid.*, pp. 169–170.
[8] *Ibid.*, pp. 170–174. U Ohn Ghine replied: "If that is clear, it is all right." U Aung Thin conceded that separation would come first. Only U Ba Pe held out for clarification of Britain's aims.

The most abrupt British negative was reserved for U Ba Pe's insistent demand for dominion status. Russell said that Burma's new constitution must be settled before any "status" could be awarded and declared that U Ba Pe could be sure that the statement he desired concerning equality with India would not be made. British members commented that until the position of Burma was examined there was no assurance that "Burma can carry the same status as India" and that any pledge of equality could lead only to unfortunate comparisons later. In the end, Chairman Russell even refused De Glanville's request to include in the subcommittee's formal report the recommendation to call a Burma Round Table Conference. He explained that the Governments of Burma and India must be consulted before making decisions, but he did promise that the views of Burman members would be reported to the Secretary of State for India by special minute.[9] The reason for refusing De Glanville's request could be inferred from Governor Innes' flat declaration before the group that he would express his own views on the Round Table Conference issue only to His Majesty's Government.[10]

The official statement regarding Burma made by the Labourite Secretary of State for India, Wedgwood Benn, before Parliament on January 20, 1931, was longer and slightly more explicit than that of Chairman Russell. It ran in essentials as follows:

The Government has decided to proceed with the separation of Burma. . . . The prospects of constitutional advance held out to Burma as part of British India will not be prejudiced by this decision, and . . . the constitutional objective after separation will remain the progressive realisation of responsible government in Burma as an integral part of the Empire. . . . They intend to take such steps in the framing, in consultation with public opinion in Burma, of a new Constitution as may be found most convenient and expeditious.[11]

One of the most disturbing results of the conference from the Burman nationalist point of view was the clear impression gained that Burma's own governor, Sir Charles Innes, was actively intervening to oppose Burman wishes and to prevent London from giving the as-

[9] *Ibid.*, pp. 175.
[10] *Ibid.*, p. 168. The report of the subcommittee, presented to the whole conference on January 16, recommended vaguely that separated Burma be accorded suitable constitutional advances with safeguards for minority and business groups.
[11] *PD,C*, vol. 247 (Jan. 20, 1931), pp. 29–30. Premier MacDonald made a briefer statement on January 19.

surances needed to dispel distrust of British intentions. It was widely rumored that Innes was himself sponsoring the drafting of a constitution which would put Burma on the approximate level of a crown colony.[12] The governor's attitude toward Burma's nationalist aspirations were, of course, not improved by the outbreak of the Saya San rebellion during the course of the Round Table Conference. He had to hasten back to Rangoon in late January to face the troubled situation, as already explained. For some months after his return, the harried governor had neither time nor inclination to give thought to plans for convening the mooted Burma Round Table Conference.[13] It is not surprising that one of the basic nationalist demands, when the conference convened in the fall of 1931, was that Sir Charles be replaced as governor.

London's decision to call a special Round Table Conference for Burma was not made without considerable prodding. Maurice Collis and other British friends of Burma were active in late May and June. More important were the efforts of the daughter of U May Oung, Ma Mya Sein, who at the request of nationalist friends proceeded to England in June, 1931, prior to her attendance at an international conference in Geneva as representative of women of the British Empire. Although she lacked official status, Ma Mya Sein made the most of British concern over the fanatical Burma rebellion then in progress to publicize the urgent need for British and Burmans to come to a meeting of minds and for prompt action at London to dispel uncertainty over Burma's future constitution. She talked to interested groups and individuals in the press, in business, in academic and professional circles, in society and politics. Her contacts included Lady Astor, Malcolm MacDonald, son of the Prime Minister, Geoffrey Dawson of *The Times*, and, finally, the outgoing Secretary of State for India himself, Mr. Wedgwood Benn.[14]

By late July, 1931, members of Parliament in correspondence with Burmans were asking Secretary Benn whether assurances could be given that pledges of constitutional advance accorded to India also

[12] Collis, *Trials in Burma*, p. 157. A Mr. Lister was allegedly the draftsman. When Burman delegates to the Round Table Conference asked later to see the Burma Government's constitutional memorandum, the request was refused.

[13] *Ibid.*, pp. 281–282, 289. Collis tells how leading Burmans requested Governor Innes, as Collis was proceeding to England on April 30, 1931, to do something to clear up the uncertainty about the proposed Burma Conference.

[14] *Ibid.*, pp. 289–290; also from personal testimony made by Daw Mya Sein. The Manchester *Guardian* (June 25, 26, 1931) gave full publicity to the activities and point of view of Daw Mya Sein.

included Burma and that Burma's new constitution would not be inferior to India's. Benn replied (July 20) that "all the pledges made to Burma as part of India stand," but he was not able a week later to tell whether the mooted Burma Round Table Conference would again consider the advisability of Burma's federation with the rest of India.[15]

Probably because of delay in clearing the decision with Rangoon, Benn's formal announcement of the decision to call the conference was not made until August 21, 1931, on the very eve of his retirement as Secretary. Ma Mya Sein returned to England from Geneva to become the youngest of the twelve Burman delegates.[16] Sir Samuel Hoare took over the Secretaryship for India in September under the so-called National Government still headed by J. R. MacDonald. But invitations sent earlier by Benn held, and on September 28, Secretary Hoare announced the names of the delegates selected.[17]

The Burma Round Table Conference

The Burma Round Table Conference was made up of 33 persons in all, 9 members of Parliament, 12 Burmans, and 2 representatives each from 6 minority groups—Indians, Karens, Chinese, Shans, Anglo-Indians, and British. Six of the Burman representatives were selected from Separationists in the legislative council, and 5 were anti-Separationists, partly from outside the council. The twelfth Burman member, Ma Mya Sein, whom the British preferred to call Miss May Oung, was a Separationist but remained neutral on this issue during the conference. Before the Burman delegates left Rangoon, they made a concerted effort to agree on a common program of action. At a conference with the *Bagaya Sayadaw*, a respected *pongyi* of the anti-Separationist side, a resolution was adopted unanimously which required the delegates to reject out of hand any proffered constitution short of full and immediate responsible government. In the face of such rejection they were to return to Burma for further consultations.[18] The anti-Separationists were unhappy over being in the minority, and all Burmans were worried because Governor Innes again preceded the delegation to England (in September, again on sick leave), reportedly in order

[15] *PD,C,* vol. 255 (July 20 and 27, 1931), pp. 1046, 1963. The most inquisitive M.P. was Mr. Freeman.

[16] *PD,C,* vol. 257 (Sept. 28, 1931), p. 2; Collis, *Trials in Burma,* p. 291.

[17] *PD,C,* vol. 257 (Sept. 28, 1931), p. 2.

[18] Great Britain, Burma Round Table Conference, Nov. 27, 1931–Jan. 12, 1932, *Proceedings of the Committee of the Whole Conference* (London, 1932), pp. 76–77. See also *BLCP,* XXI (Feb. 19, 1932), p. 238.

to prejudice the views of the new National Government prior to the arrival of the conference delegation.[19]

Burman and British views concerning the purpose of the conference differed widely. To the Burmans, it was to approve or reject a specific constitutional document for Burma. The British intended only that the conference should afford a hearing, previously denied, to the anti-Separationist faction and should canvass the views of all interested parties with respect to the nature of the future constitution. Such information would assist Parliament in its responsibility as the sovereign authority to formulate and to enact legislation with reference to the Burma reforms. The problem, therefore, from the British point of view was not one capable of negotiation. Lord Peel, as chairman, took the position that Parliament's hands were free, that it was neither bound by previous promises nor committed currently with respect to the specific nature of the new constitution.[20]

The Burman factions agreed on their basic demands. Their prepared statement declared that the restoration of peace and the establishment of relations of understanding and confidence between government and people required nothing less than a Burmese cabinet fully responsible to an elected legislature. Such a government must be installed not later than April 1, 1932. Because it was fruitless to negotiate with the existing Government of Burma, London should send out a new governor who could be expected to give expression to real feelings of amity on the part of the British people toward Burma. Finally, to prepare a suitable atmosphere for holding elections under the new constitution, the Government of Burma was urged to grant amnesty to all rebels, remit all capitation and *thathameda* taxes, and set up a joint British-Burman commission to examine the causes of the rebellion and to recommend economic and other remedial measures calculated to promote pacification.

U Ba Pe, the Separationist spokesman, argued that the present government was powerless to halt economic and social disorganization and that only a fully responsible government could get at the roots of social disease and enlist popular co-operation.[21] He proposed that all seats in the new lower house be filled by election from general (noncommunal) constituencies; minority groups could find special representation in the one-fourth of the upper house to be appointed by the governor with the advice of his cabinet. Full financial powers should

---

[19] Collis, *Trials in Burma*, p. 181.   [20] *BRTCP*, p. 39.
[21] *Ibid.*, pp. 31–34, 39.

be vested in the lower house, with no powers whatever reserved to the governor.[22]

The anti-Separationists set forth their views at great length. They declared that Burma was "bound to India by holy ties of suffering under foreign yoke, and nothing less than Dominion status shall cut those ties." [23] It was unsafe for Burma to separate from India unless assured of fully responsible self-government with dominion status. The existing government was antagonistic to free speech and association, completely out of touch with the people, indifferent to the poverty of the peasants, and apparently concerned only for the profits of exploiting capitalists.[24] Unless a satisfactory constitution were devised, the anti-Separationists refused to be bound by any majority decision regarding separation. When told by the chairman in response to a query that the constitution evolved as a result of conference discussion would be put into effect whether the anti-Separationist party liked it or not, Tharrawaddy U Pu said defiantly: "We demand responsible government, and we are determined to achieve it. We consider it our birthright to rule ourselves fully." If the British were not going to grant Burma's demands, let them say so at the outset and thus save time.[25]

Lord Winterton's reply for the British delegation to such quasi-treasonable talk was to speak irrelevantly on what a charming, romantic, and beautiful country Burma was. He explained: "I have always admired the Burmans' intense devotion to the soil of their country and their love of colour, laughter, of beauty and their artistic perception." Chairman Peel flatly refused to answer several of U Pu's queries.[26] He also resisted sharply the presumption advanced by the twelve Burman delegates that they alone had a right to speak for Burma and that their opinions must therefore carry peculiar authority.[27]

The announcement made by the Prime Minister on December 1, 1931, at the close of the concurrent Indian Conference, to the effect that India would be accorded responsible self-government with safeguards and reservations covering external relations, defense, and financial stability cleared the air somewhat. It had the effect of undercutting the extreme demands of the Burman delegation for a constitution en-

---

[22] *Ibid.*, pp. 7–17.

[23] *Ibid.*, p. 65, by Tharrawaddy Maung Maung of the Home Rule Party.

[24] *Ibid.*, pp. 37–39, by U Ni and U Su.

[25] *Ibid.*, pp. 14–31, 67–68, 81. The basic objective of the Burmans at London was to obtain a constitution like that of the dominions which could develop of its own momentum without referring every change to London for approval.

[26] *Ibid.*, pp. 20–21.   [27] *Ibid.*, pp. 233–236.

tirely lacking safeguards and reservations and dashed any hope of the anti-Separationists that retention of the Indian connection would realize their political desires. The announcement also strengthened the insistence of Oscar de Glanville and other minority representatives that communal representation and other safeguards must be included. British delegates worked hard to obtain unanimous acceptance of the need for safeguards, and almost succeeded. At the end, U Pu alone held out against them.[28]

But the Burman delegation failed to realize any compensatory advantage from their acceptance of reserved powers for the governor. When De Glanville predicated his appeal for safeguards on his confident affirmation that all promises previously given to India applied with equal and full force to Burma, he was brought up sharply by Wardlaw Milne, the British spokesman. Said Milne:

I cannot agree that . . . every word of [the statement of December 1] applies to Burma. To my mind the statement is very definitely made regarding India; and . . . I do not think we have any right to suggest that the statement . . . gives a promise in regard to Burma at all.

Milne added that the British Government had come to no decision as yet concerning the future character of Burma's government and was in no way committed on the matter. The constitution must be suited to Burma, whether superior or inferior to India's.[29]

This statement destroyed at one stroke earlier assurances, such as that of Secretary Benn in July, which were sorely needed to keep distrustful Burman anti-Separationist sentiment in check. U Ba Pe at a later stage tried in vain to influence the chairman to concede that the latest statement regarding India's constitution applied equally to Burma. Lord Peel simply affirmed that they were conferring to consider what safeguards and reservations should apply to Burma.[30] Speaking with reference to obvious British determination to exercise untrammeled sovereignty over constitutional matters, Dr. Thein Maung made the following considered comment:

I would like to remind the members of the British delegation that they should bear in mind the decisive fact of the logic of events, that it is safer to go forward than to stand still, and to confer institutions perhaps somewhat prematurely rather than to arouse discontent by withholding them. The success of the working of representative institutions depends, not so

[28] *Ibid.*, pp. 48–54, 166–167, 260–262.   [29] *Ibid.*, pp. 48–54.
[30] *Ibid.*, p. 109.

much upon their logical excellence, as on their being able to attract and make use of the forces of public opinion.[31]

Statements made during the course of the conference by all the Burman delegates, and especially those of the Separationist group, reflected the strong feeling of resentment against the prominent place which Indians and other foreign residents had acquired in Burma as laborers, capitalists, traders, and, in particular, government servants. U Ba Pe proposed that requirements for citizenship and adult suffrage be the same and that enjoyment of such status be restricted to members of indigenous races and to persons permanently domiciled in Burma by some twelve years' residence. All active citizens, he declared, must agree to "sink or swim with the rest of the population." When British delegates denounced the proposal as a denial of equality of treatment for British subjects throughout the empire, U Ba Pe and others denied both the fact and the need for such equality.[32]

A strong suggestion of class as well as national interest also emerged in the Burman insistence that indigenous candidates be given a more favored position with respect to civil service appointments. Burmans would have had the ministers share with the governor control over the Civil Service Commission. They even advocated that service complaints be routed through political channels to the ministers in charge of the particular administrative area involved, rather than through the commission itself as heretofore. All members of the civil service, even Englishmen, they argued, should be recruited in Burma by the commission, but the latter body should be denied the power to dismiss or punish incumbents. This deliberate effort to inject politics into the hitherto sacrosanct status of the "twice-born" civil service persisted down to World War II. Spokesmen also criticized the exorbitant salaries paid to ministers as well as to regular members of the civil service. Others urged, as a means of diverting idle youth from dacoity, the recruitment of Burmans into the armed services plus the right of the legislature to discuss matters of defense.[33]

Spokesmen for the minority groups played a relatively minor role in the sessions of the conference. The Burman emphasis on the prior claims of the indigenous races attracted support from the two Karen

[31] *Ibid.*, p. 84.

[32] *Ibid.*, pp. 31–34, 54–55, 82, 194–197, 248–249. U Ni supported U Ba Pe. Ma Mya Sein objected that Burmese women married to foreigners lost their status of equality enjoyed under Burmese law.

[33] *Ibid.*, pp. 110–111, 116–117, 138–141, 150, 163–164. Mr. Harper of the India civil service supported the antidacoity argument.

delegates, who also strongly advocated separation from India under a system of full self-government not inferior to India's constitution.[34] The Indian representatives, especially Mr. Haji of the Scindia Navigation Company, sided with the anti-Separationists. The semblance of rapport between the Karens and the Separationists on the basis of indigenous versus alien interests was more or less dissipated by the revival of the Karen demand made before the Simon Commission for an electoral constituency in each of the sixteen districts of Lower Burma, as compared with five seats previously enjoyed. No other minority group made so extreme a demand for increased representation. U Ba Pe argued in reply that the Karens were not a distinct racial group and that the viewpoint of a majority of the Karens was the same as that of the Burmans. Also objectionable to the Burmans was the prophetic Karen advocacy of a five-sided Federation of Burma including states for Burmans, Karens, Shans, Kachins, and Chins to be somehow welded together into a "solid nation." The Karens and other minorities insisted that the governor be entrusted with power to redress inequities and injustices in case of discrimination on racial or religious grounds and to obtain proper representation on public bodies and in the public services.[35]

The conference reached no formal decisions, but instead confined its report to recording the views expressed. General agreement was arrived at that Burma should have a bicameral legislature with a partly nominated Senate and that the cabinet should be responsible to the legislature and subject to unspecified safeguards and reservations vested in the governor. The governor would also enjoy a veto power over legislation. It was understood, furthermore, that minority peoples would be accorded special communal electorates and special protection of their rights along with those of existing commercial interests.

Sequel to the Round Table Conference

Prime Minister MacDonald contributed something to quieting Burmese fears by the following forthright statement made on January 19, 1932, at the close of the conference:

His Majesty's Government are prepared, if and when they are satisfied that the desire of the people of Burma is that the Government of their country

[34] *Ibid.*, p. 60.
[35] *Ibid.*, pp. 60, 74. The Karen delegates asked for the creation of a separate Karen army regiment. Ma Mya Sein resisted pressure from minority group leaders that she demand "minority rights" for Burmese women.

should be separated from that of India, to take steps, subject to the approval of Parliament, to entrust responsibility for the Government of Burma to a legislature representative of the people of Burma and a ministry responsible to it, with the conditions and qualifications which I am about to specify. The responsibility will extend not only to provincial subjects, reserved as well as transferred, but also to subjects which have hitherto been the responsibility of the Government of India. The people of Burma will be in a position to decide whether or not they are in favour of separation from India. His Majesty's Government consider that the decision might best be taken [by London] after a general election at which the broad issue had been placed before the electorate.

Matters reserved for ultimate authority of the governor according to MacDonald, included the Scheduled (hills) Areas, financial policy, currency and coinage, external and internal security, (Anglican) ecclesiastical affairs, and the civil services. Since members of the Indian Federation could not be accorded the privilege of withdrawal when and as they pleased, Mr. MacDonald specified that the choice before Burma would be separation from India on the basis of the constitution as proposed or permanent and unconditional federation with India.[36] The constitution, he added in an aside, would be not merely a static instrument but also "a potentiality and that potentiality would belong to you." [37]

In order that the Prime Minister's statement might exert maximum reassuring effect, it was translated into Burmese and thousands of copies were distributed in Burma. Among informed Burmans who were willing to consider the British proposal open-mindedly, it carried an impressive impact. This was demonstrated by the fact that all of the anti-Separationist delegates to the conference except U Chit Hlaing decided, while en route home by boat, that the wisest course was to go along with the Prime Minister's proposal.

When the Prime Minister's statement was debated by the Burma legislative council in late February, 1932, the sentiment expressed was overwhelmingly favorable to an amended motion put forward by U Ba Pe. This was to the effect that while the proposal did not completely satisfy the political aspirations of the people of Burma it did afford a "workable basis for determining the future constitution of separated

---

[36] *Ibid.*, p. 182. Prime Minister MacDonald specified that the governor normally should seek the advice of the largest party in the lower house in appointing his ministers.

[37] *BLCP*, XXI (Feb. 18, 1932), 221, 251.

Burma." Both Tharrawaddy U Pu and U Ni supported U Ba Pe's position to the great discomfiture of the anti-Separationist faction, which they had been selected to represent at London.[38] De Glanville was happy to note that "opinion has now veered round in favor of Separation." Even M. M. Rafi, Indian council member from Moulmein, declared: "If the constitution gives real power, as indeed I believe it does in certain directions, I for one would not hesitate to welcome it, to work it, and to expand it." [39] Opponents of U Ba Pe's motion had no answers to the Separationist arguments that the Prime Minister's proposal would be immediately beneficial to Burma commercially, financially, and in terms of expanded exercise of governmental powers. In comparison with these gains, the expectation that at some future day Britain and India would be willing to accord Burma more generous terms was highly speculative.[40]

Anti-Separationists, with the Rangoon Indian representative, E. P. Pillay in the vanguard, denounced the proposed constitution as worthless and unworkable and ridiculed childish home rule champions who had been so easily satisfied with the few political crumbs thrown to them.[41] Others simply vented their wrath on political turncoats who had deserted their cause, or they challenged the ecclesiastical reservation (for Anglican chaplaincy) as if it threatened the Buddhist religion.[42] Even the argument against the probable allocation of some 60 or more crores of rupees (1 crore equals 10 million) of India's funded debt to a separated Burma was turned to account by the resourceful U Ba Pe. He associated India with Burma's conquest and condemned her for wanting money for such a disservice to Burma. He added that Burma might pay the 102 crores if India would return Assam and Manipur to Burma. Even so, some two-thirds of the regular debt of 60 crores, he pointed out, was productive capital in the form of railways, telegraph, and telephone services.[43]

[38] *Ibid.*, pp. 218–230, 238, 242.

[39] *Ibid.*, pp. 234, 251–256, 260. De Glanville also congratulated U Pu for having the political courage to change his mind. The Anglo-Indian and Karen spokesmen also favored separation on the British plan.

[40] *Ibid.*, pp. 224–230. Burma's ability to retain funds from customs revenue and the income tax, which previously went to the India Government, constituted the greatest financial gain. All of the powers of the center except the reserved group would devolve on Burma, more than doubling the particular items under local control (40 to 90), according to U Ba Pe.

[41] *Ibid.*, pp. 248–251.

[42] *Ibid.*, pp. 215, by U Chit Pe. U Ba Pe (p. 224) answered this argument about the ecclesiastical reservation.

[43] *Ibid.*, pp. 229–230.

The Prime Minister's proposal to submit the Separationist issue to a general vote was unfortunate on several counts. For one thing, the election interlude and its sequel postponed any affirmative action on the Burma reforms for a year and a half.[44] Then British insistence that rejection of the proffered separation meant Burma's permanent and irrevocable political association with India, an alternative which no Burman wanted, seemed to confirm the suspicion that the British must have ulterior motives to press so vigorously for separation. This view became more plausible when, at the Karachi meeting of the Indian National Congress in April, 1932, a resolution was approved that Burma should be permitted to join the Indian Federation with the privilege of subsequent secession.[45] The combination of Indian political intrigue and popular suspicion that anything the British, especially business interests, wanted so badly could not possibly serve Burma's national aims revived the anti-Separationist movement during 1932, rescuing it from imminent oblivion in February and raising it to political dominance in November. The election thus elicited from the anti-Separationists a maximum of partisan furor and a minimum of judicious appraisal.

The Anti-Separationist League

A prime mover in the transformation of the futile and fragmented boycotting G.C.B.A. groups into the Anti-Separationist League appears to have been an Indian representative at the London Conference, Mr. S. N. Haji, whose Scindia Navigation Company had a large financial stake in both passenger and freight service between Burma and India.[46] The anti-Separationists also had the backing of the pro-Congress Indian Association of Burma organized in 1931 and headed by Mr. Tyabji. As the story eventually emerged, Mr. Haji persuaded U Su, the anti-Separationist conference delegate closest to the *pongyis* and to the G.C.B.A.,[47] to forget his postconference conversion to the Prime Minister's proposal and to undertake to rally the boycotting G.C.B.A. and the *pongyi* politicians against the British-sponsored sepa-

[44] *PD,C*, vol. 261 (Feb. 8, 1932), p. 458. Secretary Hoare explained that action on the Burma reforms had to await the outcome of the election.

[45] *PD,C*, vol. 267 (June 27, 1932), pp. 1600–1601.

[46] John L. Christian, *Modern Burma* (London, 1943), pp. 237–238. Haji tried to obtain approval by the India Legislative Council of a resolution reserving India coastal shipping, including the India-Burma run, to ships of India registry.

[47] *BRTCP*, pp. 84–85. U Su had boasted at the conference that only those politicians unable to influence the *pongyis* opposed their political activities.

rationist constitution. U Su later declared that Haji paid him 1,000 rupees per month for seven and one-half months for his services to the cause and also financed anti-Separationist political meetings and the printing of election pamphlets.[48]

U Chit Hlaing, who was too honest to have been a willing partner to Haji's machinations, eventually lent his influence to break the traditional boycott policy. The other principal promoter of anti-Separationism was Dr. Ba Maw, an intelligent but ambitious European-educated lawyer-politician, who was at the moment vaulting into the limelight as the defender in court of the captured rebel, Saya San.[49]

The launching of the Anti-Separationist League came in early July, 1932. It followed immediately on the heels of a statement by Secretary of State Hoare in London negating the April Karachi resolution of the Indian National Congress that Burma might join the proposed Indian Federation with the option of subsequent withdrawal.[50] At the organization meeting in Rangoon, the league leaders challenged London's insistence that federation with India would have to be permanent and unconditional and advocated continued union with India until Burma possessed a satisfactory constitution. Dr. Ba Maw drafted resolutions to this effect, which were promptly voted.[51] A concerted and generally successful effort was then organized to enlist the active participation of all elements of the G.C.B.A. plus the local *Wunthanu Athins* and the General Council of the *Sangha Sametggi* or *pongyi* association.

Two principal anti-Separationist factions emerged. One of them was aligned with the venerable U Chit Hlaing, who simply stressed the unsatisfactory nature of the proposed constitution and favored federation with India. The other, affiliated with Dr. Ba Maw, advocated Burma's federation with India as merely a temporary measure calculated to advance the cause of independence.[52] The Congress Party's

[48] *BLCP*, XXV (May 3, 1933), 330–332. This story broke in the *New Light of Burma* in 1933. U Su persuaded U Ni to explain the details to the council.

[49] The president of the India Association of Burma, S. A. S. Tyabji, a Congress Party Indian, later denied allegations that his Association had helped finance the anti-Separationist campaign. He nevertheless favored federation and probably served as a channel for communication with Congress leaders in India. See *PP,C*, vol. VIII for 1933–1934, pp. 146–148.

[50] *PD,C*, vol. 267 (June 27, 1932), pp. 1600–1601. Hoare insisted that granting Burma the right to secede would negate the very basis of the proposed Indian Federation and would also prejudice the constitutional powers of Parliament.

[51] *PP,C*, vol. VIII for 1933–1934, "Records of the Joint Select Committee," p. 129.

[52] *Ibid.*, p. 57.

Karachi resolution by itself apparently played a minor part in the actual campaign.[53]

The Election of 1932

Because the refinements of the constitutional and separationist issues were beyond the comprehension of most of the electorate, rival political leaders were obliged to fashion their arguments to appeal to popular prejudices. The trump card of the anti-Separationists was that Britain was trying to force separated Burma to accept another worthless dyarchy-type constitution, no doubt for some nefarious political purpose, and that their Separationist opponents were therefore playing the British game. Separationists countered by arousing popular hostility to the presence of Indian laborers and moneylenders,[54] while charging that Indian money was financing Dr. Ba Maw in particular. The anti-Separationists capitalized on the fact that anti-Indian feeling was strong only in Lower Burma and that it was easier to appeal to popular economic and political frustration by a sweeping condemnation of Britain and all her works than to argue apologetically that the proposed constitution, although not entirely satisfactory, was nevertheless worth trying. Toward the end of the campaign *pongyi* politicians injected the spurious but devastating charge that the proposed (Anglican) ecclesiastical reservation, never popular with Burmans, actually threatened the destruction of Buddhism itself. Separationist proponents cried "foul," but their explanations never caught up with this irresponsible accusation.[55]

From the standpoint of the more sophisticated minority of the Burman nationalists, the arguments were heavily weighted in favor of separation. They advocated the allocation and use within Burma itself of internal tax revenues, import tariffs, and private monetary remittances to India, plus the curbing of Indian participation in the public services. The local British community was strongly Separationist for reasons of its own, which did not include opposition to Indian interests in Burma. They believed that separation would improve Burma's finances and economic development and thereby stimulate business and commercial activity. Freeing Burma from the disturbing influence

[53] *Ibid.*, pp. 130–140. Dr. Ba Maw later stated that the political issues were Burmese, not Indian, and that no anti-Separationist leaflet or poster had mentioned the Karachi resolution.

[54] *BLCP*, XXII (Aug. 10, 1932), 114–118. Debates of this session included attacks on the Chettyars.

[55] Sen, pp. 44–49.

of Indian nationalist politics was also desirable from the British point of view. Some proponents of separation undoubtedly believed, furthermore, that Burma under the Colonial Office might be more amenable to sensible direction, economically and politically.

Burman distrust was based not so much on doubt of the good faith of Prime Minister MacDonald as on their firm conviction that the British community within Burma was no friend of Burmese nationalism. Local British support of the Separationist cause amounted, therefore, to the kiss of death in many constituencies. London's refusal at the conference to concede explicitly Burma's parity with India in constitutional progress and Round Table Conference assertions that Burma's possibly inferior constitution would conform to Burma's needs (by whom defined?) underscored anti-Separationist anxiety over the possible results of premature severance of ties with the Indian nationalist movement.[56]

The election of November, 1932, produced a resounding victory for the Anti-Separationist League. They elected 42 candidates (most of them affiliated with Dr. Ba Maw's faction rather than U Chit Hlaing's) to 29 Separationists and 9 neutrals. The popular vote was 415,000 to 250,000 in favor of the anti-Separationists, who scored heavily in Upper Burma.[57] The election saw the virtual disappearance of the Independent conservatives or Golden Valley Party, even though Sir J. A. Maung Gyi managed to retain for a time his post as home minister. Another result was the emergence of Dr. Ba Maw as a rising star in the political firmament, to be reckoned with in the future.[58] *Pongyi* political influence was for the moment stronger than ever. But the boycotting technique was now discredited along with Saya San's revolutionary tactics, and the actual exercise of popular political influence would henceforth center in that portion of the elected council leadership which was willing to stay on good terms with the *pongyis*. Dr. Ba Maw exploited the new situation with consummate skill.

[56] Collis, *Trials in Burma*, pp. 281–282. Furnivall has alleged (*Colonial Policy*, p. 167) that London used unconditional and permanent federation as a threat to force acceptance of separation, without considering seriously the possibility of conditional federation.

[57] *PP,C*, vol. VIII for 1933–1934, p. 7; ABMFS, *Annual Report* for 1933 (New York), p. 19.

[58] Sen, pp. 47–48; *BLCP*, XXII (Aug. 11, 1932), 155; *RAB* for 1932–1933, p. i. In spite of his predominantly antidyarchy backing, Dr. Ba Maw permitted his second in command, U Kyaw Din, to take over in December from J. A. Maung Gyi the transferred forestry ministership previously vacated in August, 1932, by the sudden death of the Chinese incumbent, Sir Lee Ah Yain.

In retrospect, the political events of 1931–1932 contributed much to bridge the gap between the elite nationalist leadership of the legislative council on the one hand and the grass-roots *athins* and the boycotting G.C.B.A. on the other. The bridging operation came from both sides. The Saya San rebellion of 1931, which owed nothing to council leadership and very little to most of the organized G.C.B.A., had aroused a sympathetic response even among Burmans who deprecated its futile madness. It strengthened the voices clamoring in London for a Burma Round Table Conference. Popular fears and aspirations were carried to the London Conference by nationalist spokesmen of various parties, who had reached prior agreement on Burma's basic political demands. The rise of the Anti-Separationist League indicated, of course, that a yawning chasm still persisted between the elite and the masses, but the bridging process nevertheless continued. The election referendum was sufficiently relevant to popular concern to end the futile G.C.B.A. policy of mass boycott and to bring all political elements within the same general context. Political integration thus moved measurably forward despite prejudiced interpretations and false allegations.

Separation or Federation

The British Government, obviously dumfounded by the 1932 election results in Burma, refused to accept them as final until after Burmans were made to understand that, as part of the proposed Indian Federation, Burma would be treated exactly as any other province and would therefore have no means at her disposal to withdraw.[59] The first session of the newly elected council was called for early December, at which time the constitutional alternatives were debated. Feeling was so tense that the council chambers and precincts were heavily guarded by the police.[60]

At the start of the postelection legislative council session, U Chit Hlaing, venerable G.C.B.A. leader making his initial appearance in the council, was elected president unanimously. He immediately ran into difficulty because his official parliamentary counselors advised him that any motion outside the two alternatives offered by London would

[59] *PD,C*, vol. 270 (Nov. 16, 1932), pp. 1136–1137, statement by Hoare; Manchester *Guardian*, Nov. 9, 1932. On July 4 Hoare had resisted the urging of Sir Reginald Craddock to call off the Burma election entirely. See *PD,C*, vol. 268 (July 4, 1932), pp. 6–7.

[60] Burma, *Report of the Rangoon Town Police* for 1932 (Rangoon, 1933), pp. 4–5.

be out of order. The first motion advanced by U Ba Shwe of Mandalay, a follower of U Chit Hlaing, to federate unconditionally with India lost by a vote of 51 to 27, with Chit Hlaing's group the principal supporters. Dr. Ba Maw opposed the motion and denounced as fraudulent the argument that anti-separation meant permanent federation. The countermotion by U Ba Pe favoring separation on the basis of the Prime Minister's proposal also lost, but by a closer margin of 44 to 33 votes. The crisis came when President U Chit Hlaing ruled that any alternative to these two motions was out of order and therefore inadmissible. He was thereupon attacked savagely by Dr. Ba Maw for trying to override the verdict of the election and was accordingly ousted from the council presidency. Dr. Ba Maw also denounced as unfair, highhanded, dishonest, and unconstitutional the attempt of the Prime Minister to limit Burma's choice to two alternatives only.[61]

The final double-barreled resolution, moved by Dr. Ba Maw's follower, Ramri U Maung Maung, was accorded unanimous approval on December 22. It proposed that in the absence of a satisfactory constitution, Burma would federate with India on condition that it be permitted the right to secede by act of its own legislature.[62] The action amounted in effect to a rejection of London's two alternatives and a move to dicker with both India and Britain for the best possible terms.

As a sequel to the December action, Dr. Ba Maw and U Chit Hlaing made a furtive and unpublicized visit to India in January to confer with members of the central Legislative Assembly and with available Congress Party leaders.[63] The Indian reaction to the approaches of the Burmans was mildly encouraging but not entirely satisfactory. The Burman visitors persuaded some thirty-seven assemblymen to sign a manifesto dated February 7, 1933, declaring that Indian opinion recognized Burma's special position and would not object to Burma's exercising the right of secession "on terms acceptable to the Federation." The acting president of the Indian Congress Party and several of his associates indicated their agreement. But liberal Indian opinion was

[61] *BLCP*, XXV (1933), 62, 78–79, 245, 250. Oscar de Glanville took over as head of the council on Dec. 16, 1932. U Chit Hlaing was ousted on a motion by Sir J. A. Maung Gyi (*The Times*, Dec. 14 and 17, 1932).

[62] *BLCP*, XXV (1933), 252. Minor reservations included a financial adjustment based on economic conditions within Burma, plus provision to provincialize important governmental functions of the central authority so that Burmans could acquire experience in handling all phases of government.

[63] *The Times*, Feb. 6, 1933. The most important Congress Party leaders were in jail at the time.

by no means unanimous on the subject. Srinivasa Sastri of Madras feared that granting such a privilege to Burma would release centrifugal forces that could weaken and paralyze the federation.[64] Subsequently several responsible Indian leaders preparing to go to London to attend the Joint Select Committee hearings issued a press statement stating that if Burma eventually wanted to secede "she would consult the other federal units . . . [who] will also have a say in the matter." [65] These statements obviously fell considerably short of the December 22 conditions.

Meanwhile a full transcript of the December debates was forwarded to London by Burma's new governor, Sir Hugh Lansdown Stephenson, who succeeded the ailing and unpopular Sir Charles Innes in January, 1933.[66] During the regular February session of the legislative council the anti-Separationists were still riding high. Over British protests they approved a resolution calling for a public examination of the causes of the Saya San rebellion. The judgment of the courts must be reviewed, they insisted, by the higher tribunal of the people. The issue was made to order for Dr. Ba Maw, Saya San's defender in court, who won "loud and continuous applause" when he asserted that the essential consideration was the political atmosphere within the villages which enabled Saya San to gain a popular following. British spokesmen argued that the preparations for the rebellion, dating from 1928, antedated the depression and the whole Separationist issue and that Saya San simply wanted to be king. The resolution was approved, 59 votes to 25. During the course of the debate, Burma's finance minister declared that even if Burma were permitted to secede from India, "her Constitution would still remain a matter for consideration by the British Government." [67]

On March 20, 1933, came the important announcement from Secretary Hoare in London that His Majesty's Government was awaiting a clear indication of the views of Burma's legislative council with respect to the two alternatives open to them. He added that the longer Burma delayed her choice, the longer would be the postponement of the pros-

[64] *PP,C*, vol. XVII for 1934–1935, "Moral and Material Progress and Condition of India during the Year 1932–1933" (London, 1934), pp. 55–57; *The Times*, Feb. 7, 1933.

[65] *BLCP*, XXV (1933), 256–257. The Indian spokesmen were Abdur Rahim, Sapru, and Jayakar.

[66] *BLCP*, XXIV (Feb. 9, 1933), 1–3.

[67] *Ibid.*, XXIV (Feb. 16, 1933), 233–234, 239–247; *The Times*, Feb. 17, March 1, 1933.

pects of her constitutional development. He hoped that in the event that Burma should elect for separation Parliament's Joint Select Committee would find it possible "to examine their proposals for a constitution . . . in consultation with representatives of Burma in the same way as it is proposed that representatives of India should be taken into consultation." Hoare added that except for its being on a unitary instead of a federal basis, Burma's proposed constitution would be almost identical with India's.[68] A reassuring British White Paper was issued at the time and reproduced in Burma summarizing the constitutional pledges made to Burma back to 1919 and setting forth a detailed description of the proposed new constitution, with all variations from the India draft italicized.[69]

Dr. Ba Maw and U Chit Hlaing joined hands with the conservative Sir J. A. Maung Gyi on March 22 in asking the governor to call a special session of the legislative council to enable Burma to reply to Secretary Hoare's request.[70] The sponsors apparently intended to formulate a basis for reopening negotiations with London. U Ba Pe refused to be associated with the request, since he could not possibly command the votes needed to approve his objective of separation on London's terms. The governor set April 25 as the date for convening the special session.

The Burman sponsors of the session drafted a compromise resolution designed to attract the unanimous approval of the council. Ramri U Maung Maung was designated to move the adoption of the compromise proposal, just as he had done in December. The resolution reaffirmed Burma's opposition to separation on the basis proposed by the Prime Minister but requested that a new representative conference be convened to undertake to formulate "a constitution affording a basis for the automatic growth of Burma towards full responsible government as a separate political entity, within a reasonable period." [71] Dr. Ba Maw himself helped draft the resolution.

For reasons which are not altogether clear Dr. Ba Maw decided on

[68] *PD,C*, vol. 276 (March 20, 1933), pp. 2–4.

[69] Great Britain, India Office, *Scheme of Constitutional Reform in Burma if Separated from India* (Rangoon, 1933), pp. 2–3, 9–28. Noteworthy was the explicit exemption of Burma from all laws of Parliament applying to "Colonies" under an act of 1889.

[70] *BLCP*, XXV (1933), 3, 82–83; *The Times*, March 23, 1933.

[71] *BLCP*, XXV (1933), 15–17, 79–80. This motion by Ramri U Maung Maung was the only one presented to the special session. J. A. Maung Gyi pointed out that the word "separated" was deliberately avoided in favor of "a separate political entity."

the very eve of the opening of the special session to withdraw his support from the compromise proposal and to plump for unconditional federation with India. This was done despite the fact that a number of his own followers, including Ramri U Maung Maung, refused to go along and that the majority G.C.B.A. groups and the *Sangha* political organizations also opposed the move. U Chit Hlaing's group in choosing between the given alternatives had consistently favored federation, but this position had been the cause of the rift within the two anti-Separationist factions in December, 1932. The most plausible explanation was that Ba Maw had decided to line up with the all-India revolutionary movement in the expectation that Burma would obtain generous treatment at the hands of the proposed India Federation once the Congress Party nationalists had captured political leadership in it. In other words, Dr. Ba Maw demonstrated more hope that the Indians would permit Burma to secede later than that Britain would ever give Burmans the kind of constitution they wanted.

Congress Party leaders in Burma, who had in 1932 maintained at least a pretense of neutrality in what was then described as a matter for Burmans alone to settle, went all out for federation in April, 1933. All eight Indian members of the council fell in line, including M. M. Rafi, who in February, 1932, had actually favored accepting the Prime Minister's proposed constitution for a separated Burma. That 1932 statement of intention had been far less explicit than the currently circulated White Paper. When chided during the debates for shifting his stand, Rafi explained that he must heed the wishes of his constituency. He defended the Congress Party high command from the charge of making irresponsible promises to Burma on the ground that they were honorable men who would not repudiate their own principles of self-determination.[72]

The difficulties which Dr. Ba Maw encountered when he tried to propagate his new-found enthusiasm for federation among the G.C.B.A. groups and participating *pongyi* politicians ruled out the possibility that their influence was the explanation for his decision. The details of these negotiations were revealed during the debates. When he had attempted to persuade the G.C.B.A. at a meeting held in Sagaing to oppose flatly Burma's separation from India, he ran into objections from representatives of the Thetpan *Sayadaw's Sangha Sametggi*. The latter refused to go along unless the same resolution condemned also the White Paper covering India's new constitution. In

[72] *Ibid.*, pp. 256–257, 327–329.

the course of the quarrel U So Thein was ousted from G.C.B.A. leadership in favor of a new *Thamada* (president), U Po Sin, who agreed with the Thetpan *Sayadaw*. The *pongyi* position as set forth in a pamphlet prepared and distributed by the tens of thousands by U Nyannoktara was antifederationist and solidly behind the December 22 resolution.[73] Another fragment of the G.C.B.A. headed by U Su, the collaborator with Mr. Haji in 1932, had by 1933 gone over entirely to the Separationist side. By the time of the convening of the special session on April 25, the popular anti-Separationist camp was completely at sixes and sevens. Dr. Ba Maw was not even sure how many of his own followers within the council would respond to his directions.

The debate of April 25 to May 6, 1933, presented the peculiar spectacle of the spokesmen for the majority anti-Separationist faction—the very leaders who had sponsored calling the session—refusing to participate in the deliberations. Dr. Ba Maw made no effort to speak and absented himself much of the time. U Chit Hlaing not only failed to enter the debate, but even refused to support Ba Maw's belated request for an extension of time. U Chit Hlaing actually stalked out of the chamber in the midst of the only serious effort of the anti-Separationist proponents to state their case.[74] Supporters of Ramri U Maung Maung's compromise motion to seek a representative conference with London, together with the outright advocates of separation, had no difficulty in holding the floor almost continuously in their apparent determination to talk the session to death. Limitation of the discussion to two weeks' time had been agreed at the outset, and no one complained seriously when the governor refused Dr. Ba Maw's meagerly supported request to extend the session so that all sides might present their case.[75] U Ba Pe held the floor for two and a half days and concluded this marathon performance by refusing either to support or to reject the motion under discussion. He also declined to offer an amendment of his own. Several able speeches were made in favor of separation,[76] but much of the discussion was made up of political infighting between rival politicians.

Since the Separationists clearly did not have the votes to carry their

[73] *Ibid.*, pp. 81–83, 474, 480–482. Some 50,000 of these pamphlets were allegedly printed and distributed.

[74] *Ibid.*, p. 405.   [75] *Ibid.*, pp. 224–225, 447.

[76] *Ibid.*, p. 372, notably by Sir J. A. Maung Gyi, U So Nyun, and U Ba Pe. A convincing statement was also submitted by the Burma Chamber of Commerce representative concerning the substantial financial benefits which a separated Burma would enjoy (*ibid.*, pp. 10–12).

cause and Dr. Ba Maw had rejected the compromise resolution asking that a representative conference be convened to formulate a more acceptable constitution, the Separationists had no recourse except to forestall any possible straight endorsement of federation. The divided state of the Ba Maw–Chit Hlaing majority in the council enabled the Scparationists to carry the fight to their political opponents.

The opposition attacks on Dr. Ba Maw were particularly vigorous. How, they asked, could one account for his sudden conversion to out-right federation, a policy which he had opposed so emphatically in the December debates and which the G.C.B.A. and the *Sanghas* also op-posed? How indeed, except in terms of considerations ulterior to Burma's desire to get a more satisfactory constitution. He was invited to tell what he had learned on his recent hurried trip to India.[77] Since responsible political leaders in India as well as London discounted any hope that Burma could be given preferred rights of secession in the proposed Indian Federation, how, asked U So Nyun, could anyone assume that withdrawal could be easily arranged some fifteen or twenty years hence after Indian interests had become even more firmly entrenched in Lower Burma? [78] Burma's proposed constitution, he argued, would be fully equal to India's and in many respects would contain additional advantages.

A frontal attack was made by U Ba Pe on the allegedly nefarious machinations of Mr. Haji and other Indian interests in Burma. U Ni told in full U Su's story about Haji's role in financing the original organization of the Anti-Separationist League in 1932. Copies of threat-ening letters were produced in the council which had been sent to members of the council allegedly by Mr. Haji through a G.C.B.A. in-termediary. They were intended to intimidate members who might be expected to vote in favor of separation. U Ba Pe was not seriously challenged when he declared that Messrs. Tyabji, Rafi, and other In-dian members of the council were acting on explicit instructions from Indian sources to advocate full federation.[79]

The rejoinder of the anti-Separationists was feeble. This was partly because Dr. Ba Maw and other informed and articulate leaders refused to take up the challenge of the Separationists. U Ba Shwe of Mandalay spoke derisively and vaguely about turncoats who had repudiated the

---

[77] *Ibid.*, pp. 15–17, 79–80, 238–247, by Ramri U Maung Maung, J. A. Maung Gyi, and U So Nyun respectively. There is a suggestion here that Dr. Ba Maw had made a second trip to India.

[78] *Ibid.*, pp. 17, 248.   [79] *Ibid.*, pp. 256–257, 330–332, 373–378, 452.

guidance of the G.C.B.A. He advocated the defense of Buddhism and the Burmese race. His only effort at a constructive proposal was to suggest quite naïvely that Dr. Ba Maw, U Ba Pe, and U Chit Hlaing confer on matters of policy.[80] The secretary of the Chit Hlaing G.C.B.A., U Khin Maung, in winding up the debate, repeated Ba Shwe's diatribes about dishonest and cheating anti-Separationist turncoats. In response to badgering, he refused to answer questions concerning the acceptance of Mr. Haji's money by the G.C.B.A. and then subsequently virtually admitted its acceptance by arguing that they were not federationists because given money by Mr. Haji. He attacked the Separationists for fomenting racial ill will and accused them also of threatening their opponents. It was in the midst of U Khin Maung's effusive speech that U Chit Hlaing ostentatiously stalked out of the chamber.[81]

The session ended on May 6, as scheduled, with almost a score of persons still asking to be heard, but apparently with no one really sorry that the affair had ended. The original motion of Ramri U Maung Maung was never put to a vote, and no substitute for it was proposed. Dr. Ba Maw immediately attempted to make political capital out of the proroguing of the council session by telegraphing members of Parliament and the India Office that, except for the governor's arbitrary action, some 46 (otherwise reported as 44) council members, including the 8 Indians, would have voted for outright federation. When questioned about the matter in Parliament, on May 8, Secretary Hoare discounted the report and indicated that his news was that the leaders of all the principal parties favored terminating the debate.[82]

British Initiative on Constitutional Reform

The British Government concluded, quite understandably, that the anti-Separationists during the second debate had "evaded all opportunities which were openly offered them to bring the matter to a clear decision." It was not possible, therefore, to accept any ex-parte statement as to what might have happened as if it were a clear decision of the council.[83] In July, 1933, the question of what to do about the Burma reforms was accordingly referred by Secretary Hoare to the Joint Select Committee of Parliament, together with a tentative sketch of the main lines of a possible constitution if Burma should be sepa-

[80] *Ibid.*, pp. 62–63. The anti-Separationists included many unable to speak English.

[81] *Ibid.*, pp. 474–480, 482, 488.

[82] *PD,C*, vol. 277 (May 8, 1933), pp. 1203–1204.

[83] *PD,C*, vol. 278 (June 1, 1933), p. 2074.

rated from India.[84] The decision of the committee, announced on August 7, 1933, was that the policy concerning separation was one for Parliament to decide. The Prime Minister's proposal of January, 1932, to defer the decision until after Burmese opinion was consulted had officially lapsed because no clear expression of opinion was available from Burma.[85] The committee nevertheless decided that Burma's political leaders should appear before the Joint Committee. The new Burmese delegation reached London in December, 1933.

The Burma hearings before the Joint Committee, held from December 6 to 22, 1933, were predicated on the initial affirmation by Secretary Hoare that the United Kingdom had "never abdicated its right to come to any decision it thought proper in regard to separation." Parliament was prepared to exercise that right in the absence of a clear expression of opinion from Burma.[86] Since this position amounted to a direct challenge to the anti-Separationists, their testimony occupied most of the time of the first two sessions, December 6 and 7. The question of Parliament's constitutional powers emerged as the basic issue.

The arguments of the three leading anti-Separationist spokesmen were in agreement on the point that the mandate of the 1932 election rejecting the Prime Minister's proposal must be honored. U Kyaw Din, Ba Maw's second in command, who had recently accepted the forestry ministership, admitted that some of the doubts concerning Britain's intentions had been removed since 1932, but that Burmans were still unsure about what would happen twenty years hence. He nevertheless favored separated Burma's status as an equal partner in the empire. The legislative council had therefore decided that Burmans had better express their own desires rather than rule on any arbitrary alternatives set by London.[87] U Chit Hlaing argued simply that the results of the election of 1932 committed the British Government. Governmental pressure on the new legislative council and London's subsequent limitation of alternatives, in his view, had been arbitrarily imposed.[88]

Dr. Ba Maw spoke at much greater length and introduced several novel considerations. He argued that His Majesty's Government had itself decided to refer the matter of separation to full electorate be-

[84] *Great Britain,* India Office, *Scheme of Constitutional Reform in Burma,* pp. i–ii.

[85] *PP,C,* vol. XVII for 1934–1935, p. 57. [86] *Ibid.*

[87] *PP,C,* vol. VIII for 1933–1934, pt. ii, "Records of the Joint Committee on Indian Constitutional Reform" (London, 1934), pp. 116–117; *The Times,* Dec. 9 and 15, 1933.

[88] *PP,C,* vol. VIII for 1933–1934, pt. ii, pp. 8, 119–121, 180.

cause the 1930 council was not representative. It was precisely on the basis of the urgings by him and by U Chit Hlaing, namely that Burmans must take advantage of London's wish to refer an important matter to their vote, that a rebellious people had been persuaded to abandon nonco-operative policies and participate in the election of 1932. He denied that considerations relative to the Karachi resolution of the Indian Congress exercised any significant influence on the minds of the voters. Lower Burma voted for separation because of economic distress and local friction with Indians, while Upper Burma voted simply to reject London's offered reform. Dr. Ba Maw argued, further, that Burma had already been accorded special status by being allowed to vote on the separation matter and that its right of secession from the Indian Federation could be inferred by analogy from special provisions covering the Indian princes. He declared nevertheless that he preferred federation without secession rights to the "non-Burman idea of separation" proposed by London.[89] Dr. Ba Maw's views were not at all convincing when, in reply to searching questions by Major C. R. Attlee, he alleged that federation would benefit Burma financially and would not endanger the desired Burmanization of the public services. He felt that Burma could not stand alone unless all powers of government were accorded it under full dominion status.[90]

The Separationist delegates had relatively little to say. U Ba Pe declared that Burmans differed only in the method and timing, not in their objective, of separation from India. As against permanent federation with India all Burmans were separationists. The committee, therefore, had better proceed with its discussion of the proposed constitution. The Karen spokesman supported U Ba Pe. All parties agreed that the Joint Committee should come to a decision as quickly as possible. No record was preserved of the final nine days' discussion by the committee on the constitution itself, although newspaper reports indicated that the hearings were friendly and constructive.[91]

The report of the Joint Committee, submitted to Parliament in 1934, was ex parte to the extent that it ignored the factor of distrust of Brit-

---

[89] *Ibid.*, pp. 129–140. S. S. Tyabji, speaking as president of the profederationist Indian Association for Burma, denied allegations that the association had participated actively in the campaign by financing the anti-Separationists (*ibid.*, pp. 146–147).

[90] *Ibid.*, pp. 173–175.

[91] *Ibid.*, pp. 118, 151–157, 164; *The Times*, Dec. 15 and 23, 1933. Sra Shwe Ba declared that "as long as Burma is kept dangling on India's dhoti, so long will there be no cohesion among the indigenous races in Burma."

ish intentions as being a basic consideration responsible for the anti-Separationist movement. It declared that the anti-Separationists had rejected every offer made and had asked for impossible concessions in the hope of extracting a more liberal constitutional scheme. The demand for the right of secession at will from federated India was particularly objectionable since it challenged by implication the power of Parliament to regulate Burma's constitutional status and her relations with other possessions of the commonwealth.[92] Dr. Ba Maw's intransigent position, in co-operation with the Indian Congress Party, can probably best be explained in terms of this constitutional issue.

In addition to recommending Burma's separation and to submitting a detailed commentary on the Burma White Paper, the committee made another proposal of ominous future import, which reflected British and Indian, rather than Burmese, desires. Ostensibly to ease the adjustment of trade and labor relations during the early years of separation, the committee proposed that existing governments be authorized to reach temporary agreements on tariffs and immigration policy covering a period of years until a firm negotiated agreement could be reached between the new governments.[93] Thus was autonomous Burma denied immediate control over immigration and tariff policies, two important considerations arguing for separation. In 1934, opinion in Britain swung sharply over to the separationist point of view, but the anti-nationalist interests of the British business community in Burma were also prominently represented in the discussions.[94] It was on December 11, 1934, that the Undersecretary of State for India finally moved the approval of the Joint Select Committee report for the separation of Burma joined with the compromise proposals covering trade and immigration control for an interim period.[95]

During the subsequent debate on the Burma Reform Bill in April and May, 1935, the Undersecretary was on the defensive almost throughout because of his alleged too little concern for the safeguarding of vested British interests.[96] Someone asked how a Burmese min-

[92] *PP,C*, vol. VI for 1933–1934, "Report of the Joint Committee on Indian Constitutional Reform" (London, 1934), pt. i, sec. 6, "Burma," pp. 245–281.

[93] *Ibid.*, p. 281.

[94] Sir Charles Innes delivered an address entitled "The Separation of Burma" (printed in the *Asiatic Review*, n.s., XXX [1934], 193–215) in which he presented ably the reasons for separation. In the discussion following the speech great emphasis was placed on Burma's need for Indian labor, capital, and markets.

[95] *PD,C*, vol. 296 (Dec. 11, 1934), pp. 235–246, by Undersecretary Butler. The motion was supported by a detailed argument for separation.

[96] *PD,C*, vol. 299 (March 18, 1935), p. 801. Ex-Governor Craddock asked the

ister could be safely entrusted with control of the police, and especially the military police. A Socialist M.P.'s protest against the provision for 8 British seats among the 132 members of the new House of Representatives brought a counterclaim concerning "what Burma owes to Britain, all that Britain has done and the millions of pounds we have poured into the country, and the fact that we have not subtracted such great profits." [97] Another Labour Party protest against the Scheduled Areas provision, which allegedly conferred exclusive privileges on British firms exploiting valuable mineral resources, was answered by ex-Governor Craddock himself.[98]

The debate was concluded and Burma's new constitution approved on May 30, 1935, almost six and one-half years after John Simon's visit to Burma in January, 1929. Again as in 1918 and 1922, the inordinate delay involved in coming to a decision had aggravated the political problem.

The Constitution of 1935

The Government of Burma Act of 1935 made two major contributions to broadening democratic self-government. In the first place it discarded the dyarchy system in favor of a cabinet of nine members fully responsible to an elected House of Representatives. In order to implement the new system the governor was specifically directed in his draft instructions to select his cabinet in consultation with the person who in his judgment was most likely to command majority support in the legislature. Except in matters which appeared in the governor's judgment to jeopardize his specific responsibilities, he was instructed to abide by the advice of his ministers.[99] The constitution itself provided that the ministry must resign office as a group whenever it ceased to command a majority in the House of Representatives.[100]

Undersecretary to restore the rule permitting the governor of Burma to appoint the president of the legislative council, because of recent disorderly scenes within the council at Rangoon.

[97] *PD,C,* vol. 300 (April 10, 1935), pp. 1257–1258, 1260–1261. Morgan Jones protested and Sir H. Croft replied. Liberalizing Labour Party amendments to the constitution were usually voted down by overwhelming majorities (here, 196 to 37).

[98] *Ibid.,* pp. 1262, 1280–1284.

[99] *PP,C,* vol. XX for 1936–1937, "Draft Instrument of Instructions to the Governor of Burma," pp. 2–17. The governor was also directed not to relieve his cabinet ministers of responsibilities properly their own. He was to foster a sense of joint responsibility among them for making and executing substantive policy decisions.

[100] Great Britain, *Government of Burma Act, 1935,* 26 George V, ch. 3.

A second major change related to the addition of 33 new general constituencies to the House of Representatives plus an increase in the number of Karen constituencies from 5 to 12. Both of these changes reflected the concern of the special Delimitations Committee sent out to Burma by London in 1935 that rural areas be more adequately represented than before. Practically all of these new seats were non-urban.[101] The 12 Karen constituencies and also the 8 Indian ones were now made single-member units. Members of these minority groups living outside the designated unit areas could vote only in the general constituencies. Other minority representation was on an all-Burma basis. Six of the 11 business-group representatives were British. Two labor constituencies were also included, one at Rangoon and vicinity and the other at the oil-field center at Yenangyaung.[102] The general taxpayer requirement for suffrage remained the same as before.

The new constitution balanced these popular features by providing for a conservative Senate of thirty-six members to act as a check on the lower house. Eligibility for the Senate was virtually limited, by means of high-income qualifications, to well-to-do businessmen, professional people, landlords, and officials.[103] The Senate enjoyed the power of veto over legislative enactments, but was subordinate politically and in financial matters to the lower house. Half of the senators were elected by the House and half were appointed by the government. The pattern of ethnic composition of the two houses was to be kept similar. Whereas the rural-oriented and stronger House of Representatives would ensure that basic problems relating to agrarian distress would be tackled, the propertied Senate would presumably curb radical gestures in the direction of expropriation of existing property rights.

An even more effective curb on the plenary power of the cabinet and the House of Representatives was found in the extensive executive powers vested in the governor. Reserved to the governor's control was the administration of the so-called Scheduled Areas (the Shan

---

[101] Sir Laurie Hammond, *On the Delimitation of Constituencies in Burma* (London, 1936), pp. 4–13, 20–26.

[102] *Ibid.* Only permanent employees working in registered factories or members of labor unions of two years' standing and with at least 250 members could vote in the labor constituencies. Around 25,000 Indians and 10,000 Burmans were thus enfranchised. The new House of Representatives numbered 132.

[103] *Ibid.* Senatorial candidates must have been assessed during the previous year on income of at least 12,000 rupees ($4,500), or have paid land revenue of 1,000 rupees (500 rupees in Upper Burma), or have served previously in the government as a high official.

352

States and other peripheral hill tracts) as well as jurisdiction over defense, foreign relations, monetary policy, and Anglican ecclesiastical affairs. It was mandatory on the governor to maintain order, to protect Burma's financial stability and credit, to protect racial and religious minorities from discrimination, to safeguard the legal rights and interests of the public services, and to see that Burma's tariff laws did not discriminate unfairly against the commerce of India and the United Kingdom. To assist the governor in the performance of these duties were provided several high officers subject to his exclusive control, an advocate general, a financial adviser and staff, and three counselors who could represent him in Parliament. The most sweeping safeguard was found in Article 139 of the constitution, which expressly authorized the governor to assume "any or all of the powers vested in or exercised by any body or authority in Burma" when, in his opinion, circumstances imperiled governmental authority. The governor was himself the judge of the extent of his legal jurisdiction, and he was not obliged to justify, by reference to any specific provision of the constitution itself, his disregarding of any advice coming from his ministers which appeared likely to jeopardize his executive responsibilities.[104]

The governor's legislative powers were equally impressive. He could (a) prohibit Parliament's discussion of reserved subjects, (b) restrict its consideration of matters adversely affecting his mandatory responsibilities, and (c) withhold consent to the introduction of any bill touching constitutional matters, criminal trial procedure, or tax liability of persons domiciled in the United Kingdom. He could also veto any legislative enactment or withhold his consent pending consultation with London. Even after the governor's approval, the home government could veto an act within a year after its passage. The governor could issue ordinances for the Scheduled Areas and authenticate over his signature any schedule of expenditures impinging on his special responsibilities. If needed for the proper discharge of his duties, the governor could also enact laws on the constitutional level not subject to repeal by subsequent legislative action.[105] The constitution of 1935 was thus in no sense a radical instrument; it was definitely not intended to satisfy nationalists bent on promoting revolutionary objec-

[104] Great Britain, *Government of Burma Act, 1935*, pp. 234–235; *PP,C.* vol. XX for 1936–1937, pp. 3, 5, 7.

[105] Great Britain, *Government of Burma Act, 1935*, pp. 234–238; Christian, pp. 81, 84–86, 91; Hinners, pp. 62–66. Only the governor's council could initiate financial measures.

tives whether in the political or the economic field. It could and did afford valuable experience in parliamentary practice and an opportunity, hitherto denied, to come to grips with agrarian problems.

The constitution tended inevitably to encourage political feuding over the plums and perquisites of public office. Since the primary concern of every cabinet group was to maintain a working majority in the House, a particular minister's value to the government was measured, not in terms of administrative capacity, but by the number of parliamentary votes that he could control. Ministers usually left the administration of their several assortments of departments and bureaus to the permanent staff, while they concentrated on cultivating friends and keeping political fences in repair. Nevertheless the very fact that cabinets were required to defend themselves against political attack within the House and in the press for lack of accomplishment in the public good exercised a salutary influence, even if such attacks were not always made on the highest of motives.

The cabinet system, under the 1935 act, was superimposed upon an established administrative civil service whose personnel and procedure were susceptible to interference but hardly subject to political control. The governor appointed the Civil Service Commission and shared in the commission's responsibilities for recruiting and administering the services. Appointments to the Class I civil service and police officers and to the top civil medical and engineering services were made by the Secretary of State in London.[106]

Three supplementary actions taken by London in 1935 with reference to Burma's new constitution were destined to arouse considerable friction. The first concerned the settlement of the debt of separated Burma to India at 50.75 crores of rupees (507.5 million). This sum represented 7.5 per cent of India's total central governmental liabilities. The debt was to carry interest at 3.5 per cent and was to be repaid in forty-five annual installments. The largest single item was 33.5 crores to cover the value of the India-owned Burma Railways. Another substantial portion of the sum, particularly objectionable to Burmans, was allocated to cover the cost of the India Government's conquest of Burma. The arrangement was attacked in the legislative council.[107]

[106] Great Britain, *Government of Burma Act, 1935*, pp. 262–281; Hinners, pp. 69–71.

[107] W. S. Desai, *India and Burma* (Bombay and Calcutta, 1954), p. 65. In view of Burma's favorable trade balance, informed persons did not view the debt to India as burdensome. Burmans voted to assume 5 per cent only of India's debt, but nothing on the cost of the conquest (*The Times*, Aug. 15, 1935).

The matter of Burma's debt was destined to be the subject of further negotiation in the postwar period.

The second matter had to do with London's issuance of an order in council, to be effective for a minimum of three years after separation from India, freezing the existing tariff schedules and import quotas of India and Burma. Regulations covering outside imports as of 1937 could be lowered only by mutual consent of Burma and India, while free trade would continue in goods of either Indian or Burmese origin. The governor could authorize emergency exceptions.[108]

Associated with the same order was a regulation covering the identical time period forbidding Burma and India from levying any new restrictions on the migration of Indians to Burma. This order voided for the time being the constitutional provision that separated Burma could regulate the entry of Indians.[109] The so-called "compromises" intended to soften the economic shock of separation operated mainly to the benefit of India and the British employer and trader in Burma and negated for the time being two important advantages of separation from the Burman point of view. The new constitution became fully operative in the spring of 1937.

[108] Great Britain, India Office, *Trade and Immigration Relations between India and Burma after the Separation of Burma,* Cmd. 4985 (London, 1935), pp. 4–8. Tariffs on goods not produced in either country could be lowered on two months' notice. This freezing agreement could be continued for a fourth year by mutual consent of the governor and the viceroy.

[109] *Ibid.,* pp. 11–12. The agreement also specified that the Reserve Bank of India was to serve as the central bank of Burma for the three (or four) year period and stand guarantor of Burma's currency notes. The constitution permitted no restriction on the entry of British subjects domiciled in the United Kingdom.

XI

Political Doldrums,

1933-1936

THE performance of the fourth and last council under the dyarchy system of government, which was in force from 1932 to 1936, was both uninspired and uninspiring. Almost nothing creative was accomplished. Major local political decisions lay with the governor, and formulating the new constitution was the task of the London Parliament. Burmans generally contemplated apathetically the passing of the hated dyarchy regime, for they were in no mood to appreciate the potentialities and importance of the new reform constitution. The entire system of representative government seemed to many observers to be a sham from the standpoint of reflecting the people's views and redressing popular grievances. The spectacle of politicians of the council scrambling unashamedly for political preferment tended to confirm the low popular estimate of the council system. Few persons except aspirants for office approached the elections of 1936 under the new constitution with any great interest. Except for the appearance of a potentially important youthful Thakin Party (the *Dobama Asiayone*) and the fateful university strike of 1936, the period was one of political doldrums.

Political Situation in the Villages

The political discouragement experienced by village-level nationalist followers after 1932 was understandably profound. They had resorted successively to election boycott, to resistance to taxes, to defiance of authority of headmen and police, and finally to the traditional methods

356

of political rebellion on a limited scale, all to no avail. With *pongyi* leaders U Wisara and U Ottama gone, the one dead and the other insane and imprisoned, the *athins* had rallied in 1932 to the appeal of the Anti-Separatist League to abandon their futile boycott tactics and to register their rejection of Britain's proposal to separate Burma from India short of dominion status. But London had seemingly ignored the election mandate, and many of the councilors elected on the anti-Separationist ticket had themselves seemingly betrayed the people's cause. Popular spokesmen in the council continued to agitate for abolition of direct taxes and for the right to elect village headmen for limited terms, but formal council resolutions covering such topics were regularly ignored by the government.[1] As public interest in the council declined, the politically ambitious shifted their attention exclusively to personal aggrandizement. The eventual acceptance of high office under the seductive dyarchy regime by popularly elected leaders seemed to confirm distrust of the entire system of British-fashioned representative government.

The fourth council's failure to do anything effective to ameliorate the dire economic distress of the country was not due to lack of reform proposals. The council's leadership was simply unable, within the bounds of its conservative and minority party backing, to undertake any thoroughgoing agricultural reform effort. The moderately well-to-do Burman landlord group, widely represented in the council, had previously resisted an officially drafted tenancy relief reform measure in 1927.[2] The same landlord group was even less ready in 1934, after having suffered severe losses during the depression, to countenance a similar relief measure.[3] A predepression Land Improvement Act of 1929

[1] *RAB* for 1932–1933, p. 31; *BLCP*, XXIX (Feb. 21, 1935), 137–138. An antitax resolution and one asking for three-year election of village *thugyis* were rebuffed by the government as impracticable in August, 1934, and again in February, 1935.

[2] *RLAC*, pt. I, *Tenancy*, pp. 6–7. Thomas Couper had drafted the "Burma Agrarian Bill" of 1927. It was published in the *Burma Gazette* and aroused such a storm of protest from landlords that the government decided not to proceed with it. Couper's proposal was threefold: (1) the first charge on produce of land should be for wages of laborers, unpaid cattle hire, and current rent; (2) ejected tenants would be compensated for improvements made; (3) good-conduct tenants cultivating 30 acres or less (the majority group) could obtain leases up to seven years' duration based on a fair rental assessment.

[3] The 1934 proposal was contained in an able *Pegu District Settlement Report* (Rangoon, 1934) prepared by Mr. Binns. It proposed that wages due laborers be made the first charge on the new paddy crop, that the landlord's claims should not differ from that of other creditors, that tenants be free to order their own farming procedures, and that remission of rents be obligatory in years of extensive crop failure.

designed to help finance improvements in water facilities and drainage proved so cumbersome to administer that it was used scarcely at
all.

A number of abortive relief proposals were made during the course
of the depression. One recommendation to revive the Land Alienation
Act drafted in 1906, previously mentioned, was negatived by Governor
Innes and left unpublished. The governor was concerned about the
danger of impairing credit, violating freedom of contract, and creating
uncertainty in land transactions.[4] Another committee, appointed in
1932 in response to a council resolution to propose measures to protect
land and produce from forced sale, came up with no recommendation
at all. An official proposal of 1934 to establish a land mortgage corporation to finance cultivator repurchase of lands, the same to be thereafter
restricted to agriculturalists, died for lack of affirmative support. The
Burma Agriculturalist Debt Conciliation Act, finally approved in 1936
as a voluntary scaling-down scheme to be applied by mediatory boards
including nonofficials, was never put into operation.[5]

Two relief measures, in addition to the *ad hoc* remission of taxes,
were effective in a limited way. The first was the Agriculturalists' Loans
Act of 1931. It made money available at 6.25 per cent to the extent of
4.6 million rupees in 1931–1932 and a less amount thereafter. The second measure was the heroic effort made by the registrar of lands, U
Tin Gyi, to salvage something from the wreckage of the co-operative
society system. As previously explained, the credit of the mismanaged
co-operative program collapsed in the late 1920's. Forced liquidation
by the government of the assets of some 2,600 dissolved societies was
such an impossible task that U Tin Gyi undertook to scale down outstanding debts by some 70 per cent (from 52 lakhs to 14.5) and to arrange for repayment over a period of years. For the barely surviving
1,400 societies, U Tin Gyi devised a rent-purchase scheme under which
debts were amortized over fifteen years and those societies repaying
obligations promptly were advanced funds on a generous basis.[6]

The recovery of the surviving co-ops proceeded apace from 1934 to
1937. By 1938, when U Tin Gyi died, more than 600 societies had been
fully reconstructed. Nine hundred others were well along toward that

[4] *RLAC*, pt. ii, pp. 52–55.

[5] *Ibid.* The Conciliation Act was proposed by Commissioners B. W. Swithinbank
and H. F. Searle. Searle was in charge of settlement and land records.

[6] *RLAC*, pt. ii, pp. 73–84, pt. iii, pp. 101–110. Surviving co-operatives were
granted funds at 1.25 per cent interest to lend at 6.25 per cent. The co-operatives'
indebtedness was amortized at 3.75 per cent.

goal, and 19 new societies had been formed.[7] The episode was not important in terms of its total impact on the problem of agricultural debt, but it demonstrated the kind of administrative talent and dedication to public service which was needed to disprove the popular view that government was alien and hostile to the interests of the people. Burma could well have afforded to trade several dozen legislative council politicians for each additional U Tin Gyi.

Sweating out the depression did not improve the popular mood. From 1930 to 1936 one-quarter of the paddy land of Lower Burma changed hands through mortgage foreclosure, with the Chettyar community acquiring four-fifths of the newly transferred land to add to its 6 per cent holdings of 1930. Much more could have been legally acquired by them.[8] Wherever debtors could continue to make substantial payments, the Chettyars scaled down payments due and let indebted cultivators keep their lands. Many of the cultivator "owners" who avoided foreclosure had very little equity left in their holdings.[9] Chettyar loans ceased, and many landlords refused advances to tenants except in kind and for direct consumption purposes, all at enormous interest rates.

Personal losses were heavy. The peasants' jewelry was all sold or pawned by 1934. Landlords lost very heavily because they were caught between mortgage requirements and taxes and the frequent cheating by tenants through default or secret sales outside. Land taken over by the government for nonpayment of taxes was usually unsalable and, if unused, quickly returned to the jungle. Cultivators generally ceased buying all luxury products and reduced consumption of fish from once every five days to once a month. Still there was no abject destitution in the countryside and relatively little hunger. Resident Indian "owners" actually increased in numbers in Hanthawaddy District from 9 per cent control of paddy land in 1930 to 11 per cent in 1934. To Burman hatred of the Chettyars was being added jealousy of Indian competition in agriculture itself.[10] By 1934 the price of rice had increased some-

[7] *RLAC*, pt. III, pp. 106–110.

[8] Andrus, *Burmese Economic Life*, pp. 68–70. Chettyars in 1934 owned 36 per cent in one section of Pegu District and 31 per cent of the land in Insein District in 1935.

[9] In a typical section of Hanthawaddy District surveyed in 1933, 93 per cent of the cultivators were in debt to an average of three and a half times the net yearly earnings per household. This was true even after foreclosures had liquidated many of the larger debts and after uncollectible portions had been scaled down.

[10] Burma, Settlement Dept., *Report of the Third Revision of the Hanthawaddy District*, by U Tin Gyi (Rangoon, 1934), and *Pegu District Settlement Report*,

what from the all-time low of 60 rupees per 100 baskets, considerably below production costs, to around 90 rupees. The alienation of land to noncultivators finally leveled off in 1936 and then receded slightly.

The status of the village-tract headman continued to deteriorate during the early thirties. There was less defiance of his collector activities than before, but he became increasingly involved in politics. A number of deputy commissioners in 1935 recommended abandoning outright the prevailing policy of amalgamating village tracts (which then numbered 11,000 as against some 18,000 in 1900) in favor of letting every local village elect a headman of its own. But the holding of village-tract headman elections made the *thugyis* increasingly party men beholden to their friends at the expense of opponents. The general administrative report for 1934–1935 commented in understatement: "Where, as in some few cases he [the headman] numbers criminals among his friends, the results are highly unsatisfactory." A New Village Amendment Act of 1935 gave the deputy commissioner authority to reject forthwith improperly chosen headmen, but only on grounds that the principles governing elections were violated.[11] The portent of weakening official status of the headman and his increasing responsibility to local opinion was destined to be spelled out in ominous terms in the stormy events of 1938.

Legislative Council Politics

The initial mood of the Burman element of the legislative council elected in 1932 was one of assertive defiance of government. This expressed itself in the council's attempted obstruction of virtually all official proposals. Appropriations for obviously necessary services such as police were voted down, along with grants for rural improvement including maintenance of drainage and irrigation facilities. A major objective of nationalist policy, and a novel one, was to obtain control for the popular parties of the three prized plums of power, the two transferred ministerships and the presidency of the council. This development signalized a weakening in the determination of nationalist leader-

---

by B. O. Binns, pp. 31–38. Resident Burmans owned only 39 per cent of Hanthawaddy land in 1933. Household debt in Pegu District averaged twice the annual income.

[11] *RAB* for 1934–1935, pp. 36–38, for 1935–1936, pp. 23, 26. The report commented: "The general run of public opinion favours illicit distillation and trade." For this reason, headmen ignored excise law violations.

ship not to accept office under dyarchy, and it precipitated an unseemly scramble for political power in the election of 1936.[12]

The first anti-Separationist to accept a place in the government was Dr. Ba Maw's second in command, U Kyaw Din, who took over as minister of education in early 1933. After an initial period of hesitation, Dr. Ba Maw consented to U Kyaw Din's elevation on the ground that it did not compromise his basic objective of anti-separation.[13] But difficulties developed when U Kyaw Din's associations with the governmental stratosphere influenced him to do some thinking on his own. As a participant in the Joint Select Committee hearings at London in late 1933, he advocated forthright acceptance of London's proposal for a separated Burma, to the annoyance and chagrin of all anti-Separationists, especially Dr. Ba Maw.

The return of the committee to Rangoon precipitated a bitter public debate. Outside the council the controversy developed into a permanent split between the *pongyi*-led General Council of *Sanghas Sametggi* and the already fragmented, lay-directed G.C.B.A. Inside the council an open attack on U Kyaw Din was made by three major parties, those of Dr. Ba Maw, U Chit Hlaing, and U Ba Pe.[14]

The debate on the motion of no confidence in the ministry covering both U Kyaw Din and Sir J. A. Maung Gyi came off in late February, 1934. U Kyaw Din was attacked by rabid anti-Separationists as a traitor and turncoat who had allegedly boasted that he could use some of his handsome 60,000-rupee annual salary to buy off the opposition. His role at London was a special target of the attack. Some critics (U Ni and U Tha Gyaw) insisted that acceptance of a ministerial post inevitably forced any incumbent to sacrifice his political principles as an offering to the evil dyarchical spirit; they therefore distrusted all aspirants to high office. Others advanced lurid charges of disorderly and undignified conduct on the part of U Kyaw Din and alleged that he had done nothing constructive as the education minister.[15] U Ba Pe and Dr. Ba Maw, acting in collusion, presented identical arguments to the effect that U Kyaw Din must resign because he entirely lacked party support within

[12] Hinners, p. 48.

[13] *RAB* for 1932–1933, p. i. Sir J. A. Maung Gyi was acting governor for a time in 1930–1931 and took over as forest minister following the death of the incumbent, Sir Lee Ah Yain, in August, 1932.

[14] *RAB* for 1933–1934, p. xxi. Oratorical vehemence brought repeated speaker's warnings and one prosecution of a legislative council member in February, 1934.

[15] *BLCP*, XXVII (Feb. 20, 1933), 174–191.

the council and also possessed no following in the country. As a constitutional matter, they argued that the ministers of transferred subjects must enjoy popular backing both within and outside the council.[16]

Few Burman speakers rose to defend either minister.[17] U Kyaw Din's own defense was halting. If he had changed his views regarding separation, he argued, Ba Maw had also done so by becoming a federationist.[18] Sir J. A. Maung Gyi entered no defense at all but left the outcome to his *karma*. The approval of the no-confidence motion by the close vote of 49 to 47 found almost all Burmans voting in the majority. This move was followed by an abortive Burman effort to oust Oscar de Glanville as president of the council. It failed by the narrowest of margins, 41 to 42, amid scathing comments from official benches regarding the allegedly petty and puerile criticism advanced in support of the ouster. A motion to unseat the Karen deputy president, Saw Pe Tha, was withdrawn.[19]

On April 9, 1934, U Ba Pe took over the ministry of forests and Dr. Ba Maw that of education following a successful no-confidence motion. U Chit Hlaing had to wait until early 1935 before succeeding De Glanville as president. With this abandonment of the nonco-operation policy the leaders of the three nationalist parties aggravated still further the drift toward internal rifts and defections. So bitter were the enemies of Dr. Ba Maw that they endeavored, in June, 1934, to embarrass him as education minister by provoking a strike at a leading government high school coupled with an unsuccessful effort to extend it to the university. The net result was to impair school discipline [20] and to set the stage for a more formidable series of school strikes some two years later. The rift within the anti-Separationist forces of the council was never healed, although Dr. Ba Maw usually managed to fend off periodic no-confidence motions more readily than U Ba Pe. The self-seeking objectives of both men were fully exposed.

The feuding within the Burman majority of the council was bridged over temporarily when the attack on Sir Oscar de Glanville as presi-

[16] *Ibid.*, pp. 192–193, 201–203. Dr. Ba Maw also denounced U Kyaw Din's attitude in England before the Joint Committee as "destructive of Burma's legitimate rights and claims." Dr. Ba Maw, in this connection, was called to task for divulging secret information.

[17] *Ibid.*, pp. 173–175. Mr. Pillay (Indian) denounced the attacks as personal and acclaimed the honesty and integrity of both ministers. British spokesmen hesitated to intervene.

[18] *Ibid.*, pp. 198–201.   [19] *Ibid.*, pp. 207–243.

[20] *RAB* for 1934–1935, pp. xii–xiv.

dent of the council was renewed at the session of August, 1934. The controversy developed amid scenes of wild disorder. U Saw, acting as a leader of the People's Party and as council lieutenant of U Ba Pe, precipitated the furor by defying repeated rulings by President de Glanville on points of order. Acting in accordance with his constitutional powers, De Glanville, on August 11, ordered U Saw's forcible expulsion from the council and its precincts for the duration of the session.[21] When the president learned later that dissident elements of the council planned to stage a "Parallel Council" meeting in the corridor adjacent to the chamber and to steal the mace from the speaker's dais, De Glanville asked for extra police protection. This action was immediately denounced as an attempt to intimidate the council.[22] When the angered council then voted to remove the president, Governor Stephenson withheld his necessary concurrence. Thereupon members of the three main Burman parties boycotted the chamber sessions and recorded in the adjacent lobby an adverse vote on every item of official business. The council was eventually prorogued but not until after its essential business was accomplished.[23]

The inevitable renewal of the nationalist attack on the council president, in February, 1935, accomplished De Glanville's downfall. His opponents charged that he had issued rulings arbitrarily, that he did not know the Burmese language, and that he lacked the confidence of the majority of the council. U Saw again provocatively challenged the president's authority by refusing seven times in one speech to honor the chairman's requests that he use English instead of Burmese so that his accusations could be answered.[24] The defense of the president's conduct in office, undertaken by official spokesmen and by Indian representatives, was presented ably and in a dignified manner, but the political demand to Burmanize the presidency was not to be denied.[25] The motion to remove De Glanville as president and to invite the necessary concurrence on the part of the governor was passed, 56 to 38, with virtually every Burman voting with the majority. This time Governor

[21] A moot point developed as to the precise boundaries of the chamber "precincts."

[22] BLCP, XXIX (Feb. 21, 1935), 157–159, 174–176. The August scene is here fully described. Councilors objected especially to actions of two European police officers who took seats in the rear of the council chamber briefly, until asked by De Glanville to go elsewhere.

[23] RAB for 1934–1935, pp. xii–xiv.

[24] BLCP, XXIX (Feb. 21, 1935), 149–152, 164.

[25] Ibid., pp. 178–182. Tyabji's substitute motion to set up a committee to define the term "precincts of the Council" lost by vote of 58 to 38.

Stephenson did not withhold his concurrence. U Chit Hlaing was selected as the new president on February 27, 1935, with little opposition.[26]

During the course of the same session which witnessed the ousting of De Glanville as council president London afforded a final opportunity for Burma's representatives to debate the proposed new constitution. The bill had already passed its second reading in the Commons and was awaiting final approval. In the emotion-charged atmosphere it proved impossible to elicit any calm, informed Burman discussion that might have been useful for London guidance. A British member made suggestions favoring the entry of Indian labor. The Chettyar spokesman praised the constitution but challenged criticisms of his community appearing in Parliament's report.[27] U Saw, speaking for the People's Party, declined to participate in the debate because the bill was past changing now, and he refused to recognize De Glanville as speaker in any case. One Burman spokesman was called to account by De Glanville for denouncing the Joint Committee's report as hypocritical and dishonest and an affront to Burma. Another alleged that Britain was forcing separation down Burman throats in order to make the country a sheltered field for capitalist exploitation.[28] The debate degenerated into a contest of epithets and a tedious repetition (mainly in Burmese) of the federationist point of view. At the end of the debate the council voted 47 to 37 against outright federation, 49 to 23 against asking for a fuller measure of self-government, and overwhelmingly without a division in support of a demand for dominion status forthwith.[29]

Political Leadership, 1933–1936

Although popular political leadership at the *Wunthanu Athin* level clearly lacked interest in constitutional problems and in the activities of the legislative council, the political *pongyis* had by no means abdicated their local influence. The political importance of the unruly *pongyis* was concretely demonstrated on February 21, 1935, when they took over the gallery of the council en masse. Their purpose was to witness the rejection of Sir J. A. Maung Gyi's request for permission to introduce a proposal designed to enlist the aid of the civil courts

[26] *Ibid.*, pp. 184–185, 196–197.

[27] *Ibid.*, XXIX (Feb. 18–20, 1935), 64, 76–78, 90–92.

[28] *Ibid.*, pp. 93, 115–120, 125, by U Ba Thein. U Ohn Myaing declared that the report lied in saying that Burma wanted separation.

[29] *Ibid.*, XXIX, 132–134.

to enforce decisions of the monks' own board of learned *Vinayatheras* covering civil disputes arising within the order. The proposal had previously received the approval of leading *Sayadaws* of Rangoon. The negative vote was 51 to 12. Only five Burman councilors dared to defy the body of *pongyis* sitting in the visitors' gallery.[30] The group departed immediately as soon as the vote was recorded. Politicians in search of votes thus still found it expedient to appease the political *pongyis*. Even the more sophisticated younger men, who discounted the superstitious lore of religious leaders, dared not leave to their rivals the exclusive exploitation of magic and omens.[31]

Two political developments within the council overshadowed all others in the period directly prior to the election of 1936. The first was the widening rift between Dr. Ba Maw and U Ba Pe, occasioned mainly by the latter's campaign attacks made against the former outside the council. In retaliation against these attacks, Dr. Ba Maw's following in 1936 joined that of U Chit Hlaing and some Europeans to endeavor to drive U Ba Pe from power. The attack was politically motivated although several specific charges were levied. U Ba Pe's insincere advocacy of an antiopium measure sponsored by the League of Nations and his unwise subsidy grant to a pottery-works venture were the charges most frequently mentioned. The no-confidence motion lost 34 to 42.[32]

This unseemly center-stage feud between ministers linked together in the same cabinet was surpassed in importance by the emergence of U Saw as a new political figure, destined, as was Dr. Ba Maw, to achieve the Premiership under the new constitution. U Saw and Dr. Ba Maw differed in many respects. Whereas the doctor's degree in law of Dr. Ba Maw was earned in a French university, U Saw had passed the sixth standard only and had failed in his subsequent efforts to matriculate at Calcutta and London universities. Both were ambitious opportunists hungry for power, but Dr. Ba Maw depended on his unusual native intelligence and political agility to further his interests, while U Saw utilized the uninhibited ruthlessness and political cunning of a man possessing, at the same time, administrative capacity of a

[30] *Ibid.*, XXIX (Feb. 21, 1935), 146–147. Contemporary observers reported that this *pongyi* invasion of the council galleries was instigated by U Paw Tun, a home ruler.

[31] George Appleton, "The Burmese Point of View," *Asiatic Review* (1948), XLIV, 236.

[32] *BLCP*, XXIX (Aug. 18, 1936), 331–346.

superior order. Dr. Ba Maw was inordinately vain, a sophisticated Europeanized person; U Saw was thoroughly Burman, earthy, shrewd, and possessed of a keen, if coarse, sense of humor. Dr. Ba Maw was leftist by inclination and was influenced by a resentful Anglophobia born of unhappy experiences in England. U Saw, the son of a well-to-do but not too reputable landlord father, was more conservative economically and not above collaborating with the imperialists themselves if it would further his political ambition.

U Saw's rise to political prominence was only slightly less meteoric than Dr. Ba Maw's. He showed no promise of leadership for several years after he entered the legislative council in 1928 as a young man of twenty-eight. When Saya San's rebellion broke out in his native Tharrawaddy District, U Saw adopted for himself the rebel's *"galon"* (mythical bird) symbol. He also sent a seditious brochure [33] to the Secretary of State for India in July, 1931, which included observations on the causes of the rebellion and denounced the allegedly lawless methods used to suppress unrest. London took no notice at this time of U Saw's efforts to attract attention.[34] As already indicated, U Saw volunteered to defend Saya San in court, but as a third-grade pleader he could not compete in the trial with the brilliant performance of his European-trained rival. Elected as a Separationist in 1932, U Saw attached himself shortly thereafter to the *Sun* (*Thuriya*) newspaper press, of which U Ba Pe was senior editor. For several years thereafter he acted as U Ba Pe's major lieutenant in the People's Party. He gained further prominence in August, 1934, by his provocatively unruly conduct in the legislative council and even more by his eventually successful effort to exclude Oscar de Glanville from the presidency of the council in early 1935.

In 1935, U Saw visited Japan, ostensibly on newspaper business. He returned an ardent admirer of Japan and the Japanese. Shortly thereafter he managed to raise enough money to buy out the *Sun* press and to transform that paper into his personal political organ. On numerous occasions he used his paper in irresponsible fashion to foment trouble. The *Sun* was openly pro-Japanese at a time when Chinese opinion in Rangoon was strongly otherwise.[35] U Saw was returned to the legislature as a candidate on U Ba Pe's coalition ticket in the election of 1936, but shortly thereafter organized his own *Myochit* (Love of Country)

[33] Kyaw Min, *The Burma We Love* (Calcutta, 1945), pp. 28–36.
[34] *PD,C*, vol. 261 (Feb. 8, 1932), p. 458.
[35] F. Tennyson Jesse, *The Story of Burma* (London, 1946), pp. 169–171.

Party. U Saw's penchant for ruthless self-centered intrigue harked back to the darker traditions of the court politics of old Burma.[36]

The wide cultural gap which separated Burma's elite English-speaking political leadership from the traditionalist Burmese-speaking masses made it virtually impossible to define political issues in terms that could be communicated meaningfully to the popular electorate. Even when communicated, such problems as the University Act, election boycott, resistance to taxes, anti-separation, or "Buddhism in danger" were potent as symbols of inarticulate political restiveness rather than as clear-cut issues. The finer questions of constitutional reform were incomprehensible to the people. The English-speaking politicians who participated in the legislative council, in the governmental administration, and in the successive conferences at London were drawn almost entirely from well-to-do families possessing sufficient means to educate their sons along Western lines. Of this group, only U Chit Hlaing, a Mon from Moulmein, enjoyed a genuine popular following, mainly because of his selfless dedication to the nationalist cause. Had he been a man of violent temperament and sufficiently lacking in political scruples to have posed as Burma's new king, he could have gathered a formidable following. But even he was unable to retain popular allegiance after accepting membership in the legislative council and election to its presidency.[37]

Virtually all of the Europeanized nationalist leaders during the dyarchy period eventually compromised their resistance to British rule by coveting, or by accepting, posts within the governmental system. Of the original founders of the Y.M.B.A., U Kin was knighted by the British king and U May Oung became High Court judge and governor's minister. Sir J. A. Maung Gyi and others of his Golden Valley Party went over entirely to the British side. U Ba Pe's long-sustained anti-British point of view began to weaken when he accepted London's separationist constitution in 1932, and it was compromised when he entered the ministry in 1934. Dr. Ba Maw, despite his grass-roots G.C.B.A. backing in the election of 1932, cut himself off from popular confidence when he sought and gained high office in early 1934. U Paw Tun, although long associated with the *pongyi*-led boycotting

---

[36] Kyaw Min, pp. 28–36; Jesse, pp. 171–172. The *Sun* newspaper almost certainly accepted subsidies from the pro-war Japanese consulate. Pro-Japanese items in the *Sun* would cease at times when the consul ran out of money, according to persistent rumor.

[37] U Chit Hlaing dissipated a substantial personal fortune in his support of the G.C.B.A. political program.

factions and an ardent home rule advocate, took office after 1937 under Premier Ba Maw and his successors. As Sir Paw Tun, he eventually was Governor Dorman-Smith's right-hand man from 1942 to 1946. U Pu headed a ministry briefly in 1939–1940, until pushed aside by the aggressive U Saw. Political coalitions within the politician group were formed and dissolved at will, usually on a purely personal basis, all without reference, except briefly at election time, to the wishes of the majority Burmese-speaking urban or village electorate.

It was this wide rift which developed between the nationalist political leadership at Rangoon and the people generally that afforded opportunity for the eventual rise to prominence of the youthful revolutionary Thakin Party or *Dobama Asiayone*. This will be the theme of later chapters.

The Karen Nationalist Movement

Brief consideration needs to be given to the growing political importance of the Karens. Attention has already been called (Chapter IV) to the emergence in 1881 of the National Karen Association, which was designed to bridge the gaps between Christian and non-Christian Karens and between Karen linguistic divisions as well. The N.K.A. was also intended to relieve American and other missionaries of the onerous burden of representing the Karens in political matters. Karen security under British police protection, their growing measure of economic well-being as paddy farmers in the plains, and their rapid educational progress under Christian missionary auspices—all combined to generate even prior to World War I a considerable measure of political self-consciousness. The movement, although essentially political, owed most to the educated Christian Karen minority, mainly Sgaw, which provided the leadership in virtually all areas of progressive Karen activity.[38]

The atmosphere of awakened nationalist consciousness prevailing in

[38] The Pwo Karens of Amherst and Thaton districts and the delta were becoming Burmanized, whereas the Bwe Karen hill tribes were animist and backward. The following statement is taken from W. C. B. Purser's *Christian Missions in Burma* (Westminster, 1911), p. 165:

"Christianity has transformed the Karens beyond all recognition. It has not only given them a literature and education; it has changed a multitude of mutually hostile tribes into a united and compact people. The Karens are now a nation with national hopes and aspirations, and with . . . the nucleus of an organization that will in time bind together the widely scattered members of the race."

all of Asia following World War I had a double effect in stimulating Karen political awareness. In the first place the contagion of nationalism infected Karens as well as Burmans. Then Karen anxiety over the ominous prospect of again being subjected to majority Burman rule added a sense of urgency theretofore lacking in the postwar political activities of the N.K.A. leadership. The possibility of an eventual clash in Lower Burma between conflicting Karen and Burman nationalist movements, which before the war had appeared remote, suddenly took on a serious aspect. Missionaries long identified with the promotion of Karen religious and educational interests faced a particularly difficult problem in determining what attitude to take.

The alternatives were stated in median terms by two American missionaries to the Karens writing in the early 1920's. One of them argued that a virile and virtuous people, such as the Karens, possessing traditions of past political greatness and concerned to maintain their national identity probably deserved a chance to survive as a nation. He defended as easily understandable the missionary policy of taking advantage of those Karen traditions which had prepared the way for their acceptance of Christianity. He also pointed to the missionary invention of a Karen writing system based on the Burman alphabet as proof that no deliberate attempt had been made to alienate the two peoples as far as education and communication were concerned. He insisted, furthermore, that only as educational, medical, and other social services came to the naturally suspicious Karens through trusted Christian channels could positive and permanent gains have been achieved at all.[39] It was this policy of following the line of least resistance and of greatest immediate profit to the mission, while the ultimate political problems involved were ignored, that constituted a possible basis for criticism of the Christianizing program from the Burman point of view.

An alternative point of view, set forth by the Reverend Harry Marshall, a second-generation Burma missionary of scholarly attainments, was more consonant with traditional American Baptist principles of complete separation of church and state. He declared that the future of the Karen race lay

not as a separate people, living apart and seeking advantages for themselves . . . but [in] forgetting racial feeling as far as possible and throwing themselves into the life of the land. . . . [By] adding their quota to

[39] E. N. Harris, "The Conservation of a Race as a Missionary By-product," *Biblioteca Sacra,* LXXVII (1920), 151–164.

the general good, they will not only be raising themselves but also the common life which they must share with their neighbors.[40]

It was easier to recognize the theoretical correctness of Dr. Marshall's point of view than to apply it rigorously in the face of growing Karen national ambition buttressed by fear of the prospect of resubjugation to Burman control. In any case, the situation was heavily conditioned by history, and political decisions of the Karens were, by the 1920's, almost entirely outside of missionary control.

Burman-Karen relations were not improved during the period of gestation of the Montagu-Chelmsford reforms because of the strenuous activities of Karen leaders of the N.K.A. from 1917 to 1921. In Burma, Calcutta, and London, they attacked as premature the granting of "questionable political privileges" to Burma, whether at the center or at local government levels. When it became apparent that the reform measures would be enacted, N.K.A. spokesmen based their demands for six communal seats in the council and special minority safeguards squarely on their often-demonstrated loyalty to the British crown.[41] They were eventually awarded five communal seats in the council, and two Karens were appointed to the Senate. They developed additional grievances during the twenties over alleged neglect of Karen schools by the elected district councils and because of intimidation suffered at the hands of Burman *Wunthanu Athins,* who attempted to enforce non-payment of taxes.[42]

The first authoritative statement of Karen nationalist aspirations was made by a respected Christian Sgaw Karen, Dr. San C. Po, in a book published in 1928, on the eve of the Simon Commission investigation. Dr. Po insisted that because his people could not expect fair treatment at Burman hands, London should set aside the Tenasserim Division as a separate state federated to Burma but administered by the Karens apart from Burma proper. The proposed Karen state would welcome the assistance of British civil service officials trained in the Karen languages, but would enlist the help of Burman officials only where qualified Karens were not available. The author based his plea on the demonstrated loyalty of the Karens to the British crown and warned

---

[40] Harry I. Marshall, *The Karen Peoples of Burma* (Columbus, Ohio, 1922), p. 34.

[41] *PP,C*, vol. IV for 1919, p. 303, vol. XXXV for 1920, pp. 5–6, vol. III for 1919: Great Britain, Parliament, *Joint Select Committee Report on the Government of India Bill*, Appendix X, pp. 81–82.

[42] San C. Po, *Burma and the Karens* (London, 1928), pp. 70–76.

that, if Karens were denied the boon of self-government, a new generation of extremists would appear capable of destructive folly. Karen
nationality, he affirmed, was rooted in patriotic sentiment and in historic
sharing of trials and triumphs and was no less valid than Burman nationalism. The Karens, he concluded, wanted to be free to sing as successive verses: "My Country 'Tis of Thee" and "God Save Our Gracious
King!" [43]

Coming as a public statement from a man of Dr. Po's respected standing, his plea to partition Burma had to be taken with some degree of
seriousness as representing Karen nationalist views, despite the admitted fact that Karens constituted a minority element in most districts
of the Tenasserim Division.[44] Probably because it became apparent that
Britain would never be party to any plan so inflammatory to majority
Burman sentiment, the demand for a separate Karen state was not raised
by the Karen delegations selected to confer with the Simon Commission in 1929 or in subsequent discussions in England. Burman ire was
nevertheless aroused because of Karen insistence that, since they could
not expect equitable treatment from Burman officials, they must therefore be granted special safeguards including a communal representative in the council from each of the sixteen districts of Lower Burma.
The enhancement of communal representation (Karens finally got
twelve seats) was one of the most objectionable features of the 1935
constitution from the Burman point of view.

During the suppression of the Saya San rebellion in 1931, Karen
volunteers in Tharrawaddy District, as previously pointed out, actively
supported the military police in a spirit reminiscent of 1886. The Karen
school compound at Tharrawaddy became a veritable arsenal. The
prospective clash between Karen communalism and Burman nationalism was explained by the field secretary of the American Baptist Mission, writing in December, 1931, as follows:

I wish the whole communal question could be shelved so far as Burma is
concerned. The Christian Burmans are favorable to such a policy, but I
fear the Karens are not, and possibly they are justified under present circumstances. I fear the help they have given government during this rebellion

---

[43] *Ibid.*, pp. 76–84.

[44] Karens made up almost all of the population of the sparsely populated Salween
District and a bare majority (52 per cent) in Thaton District. Elsewhere they
ranged in 1931, in Tenesserim Division, from 6.9 per cent in Tavoy District
and 11.8 per cent in Mergui to 20.5 per cent in Toungoo District and 20.7 per
cent in Amherst. See India, Census Commissioner, *Census of India, 1931*, vol.
IX, pt. I, pp. 192–193, 212–213.

is going to make it harder for them if separation comes, and some of them know it. The rebellion has made the feeling much stronger than ever. . . . Burman [Christian] leaders are beginning openly to advocate a closer identification of Christians with the Nationalists. They are beginning to feel as do the Chinese that . . . a stigma is [involved] in being too closely attached to the missionary.[45]

But the circumstances were not all discouraging. The National Karen Association leadership, acting as an indigenous element of Burma's population, associated itself with separation from India, which action provided a basis of rapport with majority nationalist sentiment in Lower Burma. After the election of 1932, a Christian Karen, Saw Pe Tha, was elected deputy president of the legislative council. The existence of a block of twelve Karen seats in the House of Representatives after 1937, even though co-operation among the incumbents was far from perfect, gave the Karens enhanced political importance. Premier Ba Maw, in 1937, selected Saw Pe Tha as a member of his cabinet. On December 21, 1938, occurred the first official celebration of Karen National Day. The declaration issued at the time was not entirely clear in its implications, but it suggested a role of co-operation in the task of achieving a united Burma.[46]

Most observers during the later thirties believed that Karen-Burman relations were improving. This was certainly true in government circles and among the educated elite. The minority Karen group and the larger Burman group attending Judson College came to know and to respect each other as personal friends. This was in part a result of the efforts of the administration to bridge racial barriers both in classes and in extracurricular activity. How far this preliminary *rapprochement* at the urban elite level penetrated to the villages it is impossible to say, but

[45] ABFMS, *MS. Correspondence,* letter from W. E. Wiatt to R. L. Howard, Dec. 30, 1931, from Rangoon. Pwo and Sgaw Christian Karens were unable to submerge their mutual jealousies in order to co-operate even in a proposed federated seminary in 1938 (W. E. Wiatt to J. C. Robbins, July 21, 1938). Both Karen groups wanted missionaries attached to them alone.

[46] ABFMS, *Annual Report* for 1938, pp. 23–24. The declaration ran in part as follows:

"We are emerging from isolation into the stream of national affairs. . . . Our two million Karens have a significant part to play in Burma's destiny. . . . We owe our existence as a people not to political arrangements, but to certain distinctive qualities . . . simplicity, love of music, honesty, steadiness, a sense of God. We believe that we can best keep and develop these characteristics in free association with other peoples. . . . We can share the responsibility with other peoples for making Burma a united people."

serious friction was not in evidence. Burman ire during the thirties was directed for the most part against other targets than the Karens. It was at least possible in 1938 to envisage a gradual ending of national and religious animosities during the course of a decade or two of continued cultural integration as Burma developed experience in self-government. This dream was rudely shattered by events of World War II and after.

The Burma Student Movement and the Schools

A final political element which developed into a factor of potential power during the 1930's was the All Burma Student Movement, centering at Rangoon University and extending into the leading Anglo-vernacular and vernacular preparatory schools. Reference has been made earlier to the tendency of youthful Burmans to spell out their resentment and frustration in terms of indiscipline and violence, including dacoity.[47] The politically motivated university and schools strike of 1920–1921 and the subsequent abortive effort to establish a national system of schools[48] had left as a residue the skeleton of a student organization and also the tradition that education, particularly that portion of it conducted in English, was a matter of nationalist political concern. The University Student Union building on the Rangoon campus, financed by privately contributed funds and permitted the privilege of wide freedom of discussion within its precincts, provided a center after 1928 for student activities for the entire country. The organized Student Movement and the Thakin Party both dated from 1930.

The Student Movement was never a matter of broadly popular concern because the number of families directly involved in its affairs were too few. In the thirties many of Burma's youth continued to attend monastery schools, although government-sponsored vernacular schools were in growing demand. The Anglo-vernacular high schools, which prepared for the tenth standard diploma and for university entrance, were patronized by a minority of middle-class Burmese families. The University Student Union became important politically because it was located at Rangoon within easy reach of party politicians and also because it brought together into intimate acquaintance potential leaders from all parts of the country. From Rangoon, student leaders could maintain direct connections with all of the important preparatory

[47] Chapter V, pp. 173–178.   [48] Chapter VII, pp. 218–221.

schools where student frustration and unrest were fully as rife as at the university itself.

School diplomas were important, not because the learning transmitted was valued per se, but because they qualified the holders for jobs above the level of peasant or common laborer. The few highly competent honors graduates of the university could aspire to the India or Burma civil service. Because of such possibilities, they usually kept to themselves any personal political sentiments which might later prove to be embarrassing. The ordinary B.A. graduate could study law or, if personally circumspect, could expect to obtain a subordinate post in government or business. But some 40 per cent of the university students who qualified for the B.A. examinations regularly failed to pass. Casualties among candidates for the intermediate (sophomore) examination regularly exceeded 50 per cent, while failures in the all Burma high school tenth standard tests usually approximated two-thirds. The fourth standard and seventh standard tests were less rigidly applied, but as increasing numbers began to qualify under them, the educational requirements for job eligibility were progressively raised. As Mr. Furnivall has aptly said: "The diplomas were subject to the law of diminishing returns, which, translated into human values, is the law of increasing discontent." [49]

Anglo-vernacular school training with its lessons to learn, its bells to obey, its rules to observe, and its dire examinations to pass, failure of which meant return to the rice fields, was not designed to stimulate appreciation and loyalty. At the same time it was sufficiently Westernized to increase student estrangement from parents who had not experienced it and to render many students incapable of family control.

Young men who were blocked in their efforts at upward social mobility by their failure to pass the requisite school examinations could have recourse to several alternatives. They could recover their lost sense of uninhibited power (1) by turning to dissipation, (2) by banding together as dacoits, or (3) by engaging in nationalist political intrigue.[50] The last, no doubt the best of the three, was still a poor instrument for developing social responsibility or for reforming an educational system. Lacking was a proper stimulus for youth achievement in extracurricular school activities and sports. The Boy Scout movement, even where pro-

[49] J. S. Furnivall, *Problems of Education in Southeast Asia* (Institute of Pacific Relations, Secretariat Paper no. 9, Dec., 1942), pp. 8–9.

[50] L. M. Hanks, Jr., "The Quest for Individual Autonomy in Burmese Personality," *Psychiatry*, XII (1949), 285–289.

moted, was alien, artificial, and, from the Burman point of view, denationalizing in its tendencies.[51]

Burma's youth problem as associated with educational unrest came to a definite crisis in the troubled half decade from 1932 to 1937.[52] This fact was recognized by successive annual reports of the Educational Department itself, which emphasized the need to revitalize the curriculum by substituting practical, useful knowledge and activity for "dull routine, meaningless disciplines, and dead knowledge." But apparently little was done officially except to set aside one period each day for religious instruction varying in content with the nature of the school.[53]

The Thakin Party or Dobama Asiayone

Among the seemingly unimportant but potentially significant political developments of the early 1930's was the organization of the Student Movement and the *Dobama Asiayone* (We Burmans Society). The latter organization was formed in 1935 by the amalgamation of the All Burma Youth League (1931) and the *Dobama* Society (1930). The league had undertaken after 1931, under the leadership of Maung Ba Thaung, to revive the remnants of the national school organization of the early twenties and to extend its contacts into the nonnational high schools as well, both vernacular and Anglo-vernacular. In connection with this effort, a university student touring in Upper Burma observed a village where the head *pongyi* had become resentful over the decline of Buddhism, which he attributed to English domination. He had accordingly advised all householders to affix the term *"Thakin"* to their names.[54] *Thakin* was the word for "lord" or "master" customarily used

[51] Frank Haskings, *Burma Yesterday and Tomorrow* (Bombay, 1944), pp. 54–84. Haskings founded the New Life League for Burma in 1940 modeled in part on China's New Life Movement.

[52] Burma, Education Dept., *Ninth Quinquennial Report on Public Instruction in Burma for the Years 1932–1933 to 1936–1937* (Rangoon, 1938), p. 45. To quote: "In recent years freedom and preparation for free citizenship have received fuller recognition in the theory and practice of education in the schools, but the boys in the upper standards have reacted to this freedom by showing less temperance and less tolerance of the ordinary rules of school life. . . . Respect for parents has declined and the boys are resentful of authority and the experience of age . . . [as] a reflection of the intense national spirit and social unrest . . . [of] the last ten years."

[53] Burma, Education Dept., *Annual Report on Public Instruction in Burma,* for 1935–1936 (Rangoon, 1936), pp. 17–18, 35.

[54] Recorded lecture by Professor U Kyaw Thet (1954), Rangoon-Hopkins Center.

in Upper Burma for addressing Englishmen. Transferred to Rangoon University, the idea developed into the student practice of addressing each other as "Thakin." The term became a symbol of youthful defiance of British rule and an affirmation of the national credo that the Burmans themselves must be masters of their own country.

The *Dobama* Society, previously organized in 1930 at Rangoon by a few student friends, developed in time into an elite student nationalist group. The leaders of the Youth League were Maung Ba Thaung and Maung Nu, while Maung Ohn Khin was the prime organizer of the *Dobama* group. The Youth League and the society joined ranks in 1935 as fellow Thakins to harness the energies and enthusiasm of Burman youth to the nationalist cause.

The Thakins as a rule were not recruited from the university honors students, who were the most likely candidates for the civil service appointments. As ardent nationalists they professed to disdain Burmans who sold their nationalist birthright for social position and a good salary. They were even more contemptuous of the middle-class politicians who solicited popular support as a means of their personal advancement. Their principle was to "live dangerously," to take risks, and to seek no personal advantage at the sacrifice of nationalist ends.[55] Many of the student leaders came from families of humble circumstances. They were therefore more familiar than were the lawyer politicians with the distress of the people. Times were hard and jobs difficult to come by, especially so for students. Nevertheless, their initial youthful efforts to reach the peasants were unrewarding because the villagers were distrustful. The Thakins realized their best results in organizing fellow students; they developed a cadre of followers in most of the important high schools. The *Dobama* song, composed by Thakin Tin and destined later to become the national anthem, captured student imagination in proclaiming the prior rights of Burmans to the riches of their own land. Many of them found the reading of Marxist anticapitalist literature far more interesting than their school subjects.

After their early Marxist indoctrination began to take effect, the Thakins turned their efforts to organizing Burman labor groups, stevedores, mill workers, oil-company employees. But here also they were handicapped because industrial employment in rice and timber mills was seasonal in character and more than 80 per cent Indian. Only the Burmah Oil Company made a particular practice of employing Bur-

[55] *IRRIC*, pp. 43–48. U Kyaw Nyein, minister of industries, took an honors degree in English.

mans, albeit at the prevailing low rates of pay. Thakins Ba Swe and Ba Hein, in 1935, organized Burmah Oil Company employees at Yenangyaung to demand reinstatement of several discharged employees plus a two-thirds increase in wages paid to all laborers.[56] Thakin Ba Swe's efforts attracted the attention of some members of the legislative council, but his subsequent attempt to dramatize the movement by staging an oil-workers' march on Rangoon was a fiasco. Thakin labor agitators subsequently raised a demand, which was never pressed, for 100 per cent Burmese labor on the Rangoon docks.[57] Student efforts to organize labor were revived in 1937.

Thakin ideology, always strongly nationalist, was otherwise a hodgepodge, extremely fluid. They studied whatever came to hand, Dr. Sun's *San Min Chu I,* the Sinn Fein movement literature of Ireland, Nietzsche, and Karl Marx. While official British circles were publicly attributing Communist infiltration in the early thirties to immigrant Chinese and Bengali revolutionaries,[58] the Burman contact with Marxism was actually via England itself. Maung Thein Maung of the Burma Youth Movement met Communist friends in London in 1931 and joined Palme Dutt's "League against Imperialism." [59] Dr. Thein Maung, a Ba Maw supporter, brought back a set of Marxist writings upon his return from the Burma Round Table Conference in 1932. The editor U Tun Pe, acting as custodian of the estate of the executed rebel, Saya San, used the funds derived mainly from sale of San's medical book to purchase a full set of the writings of Marx, which circulated among members of the *Dobama Asiayone.* A Burma book club, sponsored by J. S. Furnivall, also featured English publications, some of them leftist in character. A more radical Red Flag Leftist Book Club had over 200 members in 1937. It purchased works on the history of socialism, in particular Strachey's *Theory and Practice of Socialism* and Palme Dutt's *World Politics.*

By no means all of the Thakins became convinced Marxists, but the outstanding Burman Communist leaders, Thakins Soe, Than Tun, and Thein Pe, joined the Thakins in the thirties, and the able Thakin Mya,

[56] *BLCP,* XXIX (Feb. 21, 1935), 146–147. Demands also included abolition of company stores, allegedly profit sharing.

[57] *RAB* for 1934–1935, p. xiv.

[58] *RAB* for 1933–1934, pp. iv, 29.

[59] Dutt was the Anglo-Indian Communist leader, long resident in England, who was for almost two decades the agent for transmitting Comintern directives to India. He gained election to Parliament on one occasion. The Burma Government was apparently aware that the Thakins were receiving Communist literature and had Communist connections in England and India. See *IRRIC,* pp. 45–48.

founder of the Socialist Party, was one of three Thakins elected to the House of Representatives in 1936.[60]

The *Dobama Asiayone* as a whole was essentially a nationalist rather than a Communist organization, although it was revolutionary in spirit. Marxism tended to buttress its all-out opposition to capitalist imperialism. The idea of opposing economic exploitation was not exclusively theirs. Burma's politician spokesmen at successive London conferences repeatedly attacked the Burma Government for operating to the benefit of foreign capitalists.[61] They and others demanded that foreign corporations Burmanize their stockholders, boards of directors, labor forces, and business trainees.[62] But criticism of British business operations was not an important element of popular discontent and not even the basic concern of many Thakins. Thakin Nu's prewar novel, entitled "Man the Wolf of Man," blamed the country's ills quite as much on the apostasy of Burmans who aped the British and on absentee landlords with their dishonest measuring baskets as he did on the imperialist exploiters. The Thakins in Nu's narrative were true friends of the people, exalting revolution but crying "Down with the begging bowl" as well as "Down with capitalism." [63]

The broader student movement which Thakin leadership exploited so skillfully was not basically a Marxian affair. Many Thakin nationalists even at the end of the thirties were willing to accept outside help from any quarter, Congress Party India, Nationalist China, Communist China, or even Fascist Japan, in order to realize their primary objective of political independence. Outlawed Communists did use the *Dobama Asiayone* as a cover for their sectarian activities until the Thakin organization was itself proscribed in 1940.

The University and Schools Strikes of 1936

Students at Rangoon University during the dry winter season of 1935–1936 did not seem to be noticeably unhappy or embittered. Like many campuses elsewhere, it was for many a delightful place to spend a few years, making new friends of both sexes, attending dra-

[60] Thakin Thein Pe was the best educated of the Communist leaders. Thakin Than Tun's education was limited to the Teacher Training College, and Thakin Soe was only a clerk and laboratory assistant of the Burmah Oil Company refinery at Syriam in 1935 when he got into politics (U Kyaw Thet lecture, referred to in note 54 above).

[61] *BRTCP*, pp. 39–40.

[62] *PP,C*, vol. VIII for 1933–1934, pt. II, p. 198, a statement by U Ba Pe before the Joint Select Committee.

[63] Thakin Nu, "Man the Wolf of Man," unpublished manuscript.

matic performances and variety musical concerts, and earning a "Pass" B.A. degree by working hard only around examination time. Students listened to debates on the relative merits of democracy and fascism and occasionally to impassioned harangues at the Student Union on agrarian unrest, striking laborers, and nationalist expectations. Such serious interests were punctuated by tennis tournaments, the cold-season regatta on the lake, and other more frivolous amusements. Some fanatical male students, backed by the monks, decried in futile fashion the threatened degradation of Burma's womanhood as a result of the vogue of wearing transparent muslin blouses.[64] Students were studying for tests in their usual desultory way by preparing answers to expected questions based on examinations from previous years and hoping for the best. There was little to suggest that a student upheaval was either premeditated or imminent.

A short time before examinations were scheduled to begin several provocative speeches were delivered by Thakin Nu, a law student of University College and president of the Student Union, denouncing a particular University College lecturer for alleged immorality and demanding his dismissal. When this demand was transmitted to Principal Sloss by Thakin Nu's emissary, Thakin Kyaw Nyein, the principal replied that he would not be intimidated by any student or organization. This statement was distorted to make it appear that the principal was actually defying all political organizations in Burma, and the garbled version of the interview was used with great effect by student orators to foment a rebellious spirit.[65] Serious tension developed when Principal Sloss, with the concurrence of the college governing board, summarily expelled Thakin Nu, but still there seemed to be no evidence of planned student retaliation.[66]

The matter was revived when the *Journal* of the Student Union printed an inflammatory follow-up article entitled "Hell Hound at Large." When Thakin Aung San, the *Journal's* editor and also secretary of the Union, refused to reveal the name of the author, he also was disciplined. Union leaders thereupon, on February 25, called a strike and blockaded all halls where examinations were scheduled by lying

[64] Mi Mi Khaing, *The Burmese Family*, pp. 94–98. Mi Mi Khaing's observations as a faculty member in Teacher Training College, where Than Tun was then a student, checks with the author's impressions from the main university campus.

[65] The *Nation*, on Dec. 29, 1955, published a statement of confession and apology to Mr. Sloss by Premier Nu covering his unfortunate handling of the situation of 1936.

[66] *BLCP*, XXIX (March 1, 1936), 823–824, by Tyabji.

down across entrances and across roadways leading to examination buildings. No person familiar with the customs of Burma would dare inflict indignity by stepping over such prostrate forms. The result was that the examinations could not be held.

Whether the university strike was premeditated or not, Thakin leadership in the Rangoon University Student Union had been gratuitously provocative. The All Burma Student Movement, of which Thakin Aung San was president, was ready to get into the act as soon as the trouble started, ostensibly in order to "break the shackles" of the alien educational system. The imminence of the dreaded final examinations helped ensure student co-operation both in the university and in the high schools. The strike was also timed to coincide with the final week of the legislative council session. All of these circumstances appear to have been more than coincidental, but the conflagration still required the igniting influence of arbitrary actions on the part of University College authorities to set it off.

To the Burman nationalist students generally, and especially to those not well prepared for the examinations, the strike brought the excitement and exhilaration attending a gesture of freedom and defiance. Nearly 80 per cent of the men resident in the University College dormitories and somewhat more than 20 per cent of the Judson College students vacated their quarters and moved to the slopes of the Shwe Dagon pagoda hill, where sympathizers provided their food and lodging.[67] From this headquarters, selected students were assigned picketing duty within Rangoon and at the university. Selected cadres were dispatched to provincial high schools, both vernacular and Anglo-vernacular, located at all important urban centers, where they succeeded in persuading students of some thirty-two schools to join the strike.[68] Thus not only the university examinations but also high school final tests everywhere had to be postponed until June. Some observers were alarmed that so large a number of students were abroad in Rangoon and elsewhere without parental or any other kind of supervision. But Burman sentiment generally made heroes of the strikers and accorded them full moral and material support. The transformation of a student protest against disciplinary authority into a political event of province-wide impact was the achievement of the Thakins and the Student Movement leadership.

[67] Mi Mi Khaing, pp. 97–98; BLCP, XXIX (March 1, 1936), 832–833.
[68] Burma, Education Dept., Annual Report on Public Instruction in Burma, for 1935–1936, p. 35.

The strike looked otherwise to the school authorities and to the teaching staffs. To the University College authorities, it was a contest of "face," involving the impossible admission that the exercise of disciplinary authority was contingent on student approval. The Education Department was particularly angry with the sympathizing public while at the same time admitting the need for some educational changes. Its comment on the situation ran as follows:

The importation of ideas associated with industrial strife into the educational world falsifies a relationship which is essentially one of co-operative learning and doing. . . . It is self-evident that those who foment indiscipline among children and adolescents have sold their sense of responsibility for an expedient. . . . Steps must be taken to sublimate in constructive study and work the sense of frustration that is the cause of indiscipline in present-day . . . youth. . . . One . . . reflection emerges clearly; it is that the system and methods of examination must be changed as soon as possible. Modern methods of measuring and recording intellectual and other abilities and aptitudes must . . . replace to a considerable extent existing written examination.[69]

For the staffs of the colleges of the university and of the high schools, which had no part in causing the trouble and whose best-prepared students were victimized by it, the strike was an abominable nuisance. Indian, Karen, and Chinese students in particular had no reason to share the Burmese nationalist enthusiasm, although only scattering attempts were made to evade the examination boycott. When the issue in early March shifted ostensibly to reform of the University Act, virtually all of the university students fell in line.[70]

The official governing body of the university, the university council, got into the act when it became apparent that the examinations would have to be postponed. After several meetings, the council voted to request the chancellor, who happened to be the governor, to appoint an investigating committee to examine into the causes of the strike. The council rejected an alternative motion sponsored by Burman legislative council members, U So Nyun, U Kun, and apparently also Dr. Ba Maw, to appoint to the committee designated persons thought

[69] *Ibid.*, pp. 1, 13.

[70] *Ibid.*, pp. 8, 13. The disturbing effects of the strike on University College students in particular was shown in the poor results of the examinations held in June, 1936. Only 41 per cent of the intermediate and 54 per cent of the bachelor candidates of University College passed. Judson College by comparison scored normal 56 per cent and 76 per cent pass averages. The results of the postponed high school examinations were even more tragic.

to be capable of winning the confidence of the students themselves.[71]

Meanwhile Thakin Aung San, as strike leader, appealed to sympathetic members of the legislative council to support the student cause. The council debated the question on March 4, the final evening of the legislative session. The legislative council leaders most eager to make political capital of the educational crisis were members of the People's Party, who wanted to embarrass the education minister, Dr. Ba Maw. U Saw and U Kun moved that the legislative council itself approve a designated list of names, including those of the movers, to examine into the basic root causes of discontent at the university. Several emotionally charged speeches insisted that the legislature had never intended, by approving the University Act of 1920, to abdicate to an autonomous university council its responsibility to act in such an emergency situation. The debate revealed that the merits of the quarrel between Principal Sloss and the Student Union leaders were of little concern to the politicians. When Mr. Tyabji, himself a member of the university council, started to discuss the circumstances of the strike by saying that the provocative speeches of Thakin Nu and the printed article appearing in the *Journal* presented a prima-facie case for disciplinary action of some sort, he was abruptly cut off on the ground that he was speaking irrelevantly to the motion in hand.[72] Supporters of the motion attacked the British Education Department secretary in particular for saying that government took no stand on the question of the strike or on university council policy. They also accused Dr. Ba Maw of acting one way as a member of the university council and another as education minister in the legislative council.[73]

Dr. Ba Maw's official view was that, by reason of the terms of the University Act, the university council had full authority over all internal affairs including discipline and examinations. Hence the only area of possible activity by the legislative council was to re-examine the University Act itself. In supporting such a review of the act, Dr. Ba Maw cited the statement submitted by the Mandalay boycotters' council charging that the university was "completely dominated by

[71] *BLCP*, XXIX (March 1, 1936), 814–815, 834. The motion actually approved was proposed by U Kyaw Zan, ex-mayor of Rangoon.

[72] *Ibid.*, pp. 823–824, 834. Indian speakers in particular deprecated striking methods as a means of redressing educational grievances. Mr. Campagnac argued that it was the parents who should take up the matter of any real grievances. Immature students, he insisted, could not be permitted to run the university and demand the dismissal of disliked professors; they would abolish all examinations if permitted authority.

[73] *Ibid.*, pp. 813–846.

Government officials with ultra-imperial outlook" and that the government was opposing the efforts of Burman students to acquire an education which would afford them the ability to criticize the existing constitution. Dr. Ba Maw refused to support the motion under debate because it trespassed on the internal affairs of the university, but he offered to convey to the university chancellor the views of the council as a guide in selecting three of its members to serve on the proposed legally authorized university investigating committee. It was a clever defense, but the minister obviously lost nationalist backing as a result of the incident. U Saw's motion was passed by a chorus of "ayes" against but a single "no." Government supporters abstained.[74]

The committee selected by the chancellor to investigate the causes of the strike recommended that a number of student demands be acceded to, and the strike was accordingly called off before the reassembly in June.[75] The sequel to the demand to revise the University Act can be quickly told. A university commission recommended in May, 1937, that poor students be assisted by scholarships, but it rejected the student demand for nonofficial control of the university council. Thakin Aung San and others then carried the matter directly to the new House of Representatives. He urged that the chancellor be elected by the council itself, which must, by amended law, henceforth include a majority of nonmembers of the university staff and the civil services, along with representatives of the students themselves and the legislature. The University Act as amended in 1939 went far to meet these student and political demands. It even included legislative review of examination results. U Tin Tut took over as the first elected university chancellor in December, 1939.[76] Rangoon University was destined to pay a heavy penalty in the postwar period as a result of infiltration within its own controlling authority of the influence of both student and party politicians.

The Election of 1936

The election campaign of 1936 was feverishly waged by the rival candidates, but it aroused little popular enthusiasm. The acceptance of ministerial posts in 1934 by the two leading political figures, U Ba Pe and Dr. Ba Maw, and U Chit Hlaing's accession as president of the council in 1935 had destroyed the foundation of the popular alignments of 1932. A faction of U Ba Pe's People's Party turned against

[74] *Ibid.*, pp. 837–845.   [75] *RAB* for 1935–1936, p. xvi.
[76] Hinners, pp. 83–86; *New Burma*, Dec. 27, 1939.

him, and Dr. Ba Maw was virtually abandoned by his erstwhile
G.C.B.A. anti-Separationist following. U Chit Hlaing maintained his
hold on one of the G.C.B.A. factions, although his political star was
clearly descending.

U Ba Pe undertook to recoup his political fortunes by sponsoring
the amalgamation in early May, 1936, of his fragmented People's Party
with four groups from Upper Burma to form the so-called *Ngabwinsaing* (Five Groups Alliance) Party. Its titular head was one Prince
Hteik Tin Wa, a distant relative of the royal family, who was serving
at the time as chairman of one of the Upper Burma branches of the
G.C.B.A.[77] The alliance was made up of office-hungry politicians;
otherwise it completely lacked homogeneity. It enjoyed good financial
backing and was, on the whole, a moderate group ready to function
under the new constitution. They developed virtually no contact with
the village peasantry,[78] yet managed because of widely dispersed local
support to win forty-six seats.

Dr. Ba Maw was less successful. After his initial negotiations for
co-operation with the Hlaing-Myat-Paw faction of the G.C.B.A. broke
down over differences concerning the distribution of seats, he undertook to create a new "*Sinyetha*," or "Poor Man's," Party. The party
itself was composed mainly of the education minister's personal followers; the name, one commonly used, was selected to catch the peasant imagination; the program as gradually formulated was a salad
mixture, which offered to the villagers everything they were supposed
to be demanding, topped with a touch of reddish Marxist dressing.[79]
Sinyetha meant, among other things, village reconstruction and tax
reductions, regular periodic election of village headmen, freer agricultural credit through land mortgage banks, lower land rents, repurchase of alienated land with government aid to the extent of 4
acres per household, and compulsory free education.[80] As an effort to
outline what Burmese peasants ought to favor if issues could be substituted for personalities, the effort was commendably clever. It fell
short of its mark precisely because too many Burmans distrusted the

[77] *RAB* for 1935–1936, pp. xiv–xvi; Christian, *Modern Burma*, p. 234.
[78] K. M. Kannampilly, "Parties and Politics in Burma," *India Quarterly*, III
(1947), 240–241.
[79] When invited to explain before the University Student Union, on September
26, 1936, what the *Sinyetha* policy meant, Minister Ba Maw spent the afternoon
prior to the meeting in conference with an invited and informed economist asking
about the practical applications of Marxist principles to Burma.
[80] Hinners, pp. 75–76; Christian, p. 242; Rangoon *Gazette*, Oct. 5, 1936.

author and discounted his promises.[81] Dr. Ba Maw bid for backing in Mandalay by urging that the Parliament's Constituencies Delimitation Committee shift one of Rangoon's 4 seats to Mandalay.[82] Even his attempts to utilize the help of friendly *pongyi* politicians brought meager returns in popular support. In spite of a colorful campaign effort, the *Sinyetha* Party won only 16 seats, to the great satisfaction of his numerous political opponents including those in official circles.

Minor parties cut no important figure in the contest. U Chit Hlaing's party developed no political program except hostility to the constitution. They captured a modest 12 seats. Sir J. A. Maung Gyi made a futile effort to broaden the affiliation of his conservative Golden Valley Party.[83] The Thakins decided belatedly to enter the election contest under the name of the *Komin-Kochin* ("One's Own King–One's Own Kind") Party. U Ba U of Mandalay was the president and Thakin Aung San was the secretary-general of the new party. Youthful Thakin campaigners toured extensively, but they attracted little popular attention by their attacks on the new constitution, an approach similar to that of U Chit Hlaing's G.C.B.A. The *Komin-Kochin* candidates proposed also to enter the legislature in order to disrupt its proceedings. They came off with 3 seats only, one of which was appointed. The leader was Thakin Mya, the able and respected founder of the Socialist Party, a man several years older than Thakin Aung San. U Ba U later defected to Dr. Ba Maw's party.[84] Independent candidates garnered some 13 to 17 seats depending on the definition of the term "independent." The Karens' 12 communal members (badly integrated as a group) and the 9 Europeans raised the total to 115 seats. The rest of the 132 members represented minority racial groups, business, and labor.

If the 46 members elected on the *Ngabwinsaing* ticket had constituted a homogeneous group instead of a mere collection of office seekers, U Ba Pe, U Saw, and their associates would have made up the nucleus of the new cabinet. But leaders of all five groups wanted cabinet posts, and there were not enough to go around. U Ba Pe's efforts to form a cabinet ran aground when the followers of several leaders who

---

[81] At Mandalay and elsewhere, Ba Maw's opponents attacked him in 1936 by circulating a cartoon picture showing him split down the middle, one-half Burmese, one-half European.

[82] *PP,C*, vol. IX for 1935–1936, Appendix IV, p. 35. The committee was headed by Sir Laurie Hammond.

[83] *RAB* for 1935–1936, p. xiv.

[84] *Ibid.*, p. xiv; Sen, pp. 52–54; Moscotti, pp. 57–58. The other elected *Komin-Kochin* candidate was Thakin Lay Maung.

were omitted from his lists, particularly U Pu and U Maung Gyee, defected from the party.[85]

In the end Dr. Ba Maw managed to form a coalition cabinet, including representatives of three disparate groups, U Pu of *Ngabwinsaing*, U Paw Tun of U Chit Hlaing's party, and Sir Htoon Aung Gyaw, leader of a dissident Arakan splinter group. The Karen leader, Saw Pe Tha, was also included. Thus Burma's first government under the new 1935 constitution included Dr. Ba Maw as the Premier, two *Sinyetha* followers, Dr. Thein Maung (commerce and industry) and U Tharrawaddy Maung Maung (education), U Pu of *Ngabwinsaing* (lands and revenue), U Paw Tun of Hlaing-Myat-Paw (home), Saw Pe Tha (agriculture and forests), and U Htoon Aung Gyaw (finance).[86]

[85] Prince Hteik Tin Wa of the *Ngabwinsaing* Party attempted, in November, 1936, to prevent the formation of any ministry at all.

[86] Sen, pp. 55–56.

XII

Burma under the New
Constitution, 1937-1941

BURMA'S brief experience with responsible parliamentary government from March, 1937, to the outbreak of the Far Eastern war in December, 1941, was not without its promising aspects even though it brought to light numerous deficiencies and problems. The encouraging developments related to the fact that the government at long last came to grips in a determined and vigorous way with basic issues such as agricultural and credit reform, improvement of village administration, and regulation of Indian immigration so often by-passed previously. Leaders of government were usually genuinely concerned to accomplish something in the general good. No quick and easy solutions were found for many difficult problems, but their very consideration introduced a wholesome sense of reality into public affairs.

As might have been anticipated now that the stakes of power were high, one problem concerned the unremitting struggle for control between rival politicians. The lack of any genuine responsibility of party groups to the electorate plus the absence of any generally accepted standards of permissible public conduct or tactics gave to the political arena something of the atmosphere of a jungle. No holds were barred in the efforts made to embarrass political opponents whether within or outside the legislature. Members of the government were subjected in the legislature to a constant barrage of questions and personal attacks, punctuated with periodic no-confidence motions. Outside the legislature, the vernacular press employed even more sinister tactics in misrepresentating facts and in fomenting popular passions and overt violence.

A second major problem concerned the enormous difficulty of developing any popular awareness that government was intended to serve the needs of the people rather than to exploit them. This situation was fully exposed by an official inquiry made in 1940 which revealed the appalling amount of bribery and corruption within the bureaucratic governmental system. Administratively as well as politically, the public good was being lost sight of. Generally speaking, the successive governments from 1937 to 1942 acted more responsibly than might have been expected, while the opposition groups acted more irresponsibly. Unfortunately, the time afforded was too brief to work out any real improvement in any of the major problem areas, to develop any definition of political ethics, or to bring popular judgment to focus on the conduct of rival groups vying for political power. The process of salutary, if somewhat painful, experience in self-government under the 1935 constitution was aborted by the conquest of Burma by Japan in early 1942.

That intelligent Burmans were not unaware of the deficiencies arising out of their own political immaturity and were not afraid to judge themselves realistically was a wholesome sign. The following statement, relevant if not entirely justified, appeared in the public press of Rangoon in September, 1939:

We are a nation of adult infants. . . . It often prompts such statements as "Our Burmese Kings . . . conquered Siam, Assam, and Manipur." . . . Our personal achievements . . . evoke a similar childish emotional response. . . .

Proportionately, we have more places of worship than any other country . . . and yet we are the least religious. . . . We have a religion which forbids its priests to meddle in worldly affairs, yet some . . . are more worldly and more debauched than any other religious brotherhood. . . . We do not experience pleasure or fulfilment in the thought that we are grown up individuals prepared to meet struggle and hardship. We think that the longer we remain impervious to life's warning the luckier we are; that if life would only spare us its blows, we should be happy.

Children do not . . . like to think connectedly; they do not like to think at all. . . . Grown up Burmans have similar . . . dislikes. They leave it to their priests, students, and newspapers to think for them. . . . We refuse to grow up and think for ourselves; we are unable to purge ourselves of the fear of ridicule. . . . Burmese politics have no meaning save to keep Burmese newspapers busy. . . . All our politicians are out to wreck the constitution but at the first available opportunity, the loudest-lunged . . . will not hesitate to swallow his spit. . . . This is a picture of the Burmans as one of them sees them, but we need not despair. Recognition and detection of the causes of a malady are half the cure.[1]

Dr. Ba Maw's Government and Its Program

U Ba Pe's loosely knit *Ngabwinsaing* Party, despite the election of forty-two of its members to the House of Representatives, quickly fell apart because of differences over the distribution of the political spoils of office. U Ba Pe's inability to form a government gave Dr. Ba Maw his golden opportunity. By a judicious division of the cabinet posts, giving one to U Pu of the old People's Party, another to U Paw Tun from U Chit Hlaing's group, a third to a dissident Arakanese leader, U Htoon Aung Gyaw, and a fourth to Saw Pe Tha (Karen), Dr. Ba Maw garnered enough support outside his own party's fourteen votes to form a government. The cabinet included two of Dr. Ba Maw's abler followers, U Tharrawaddy Maung Maung and Dr. Thein Maung. U Chit Hlaing was confirmed as speaker of the House. In order to enlist the support of the Chamber of Commerce groups and of the British bloc, which was also required to make up his majority, the new Premier had to hold in abeyance most of the radical socialistic proposals included in his election-time *Sinyetha* platform. His success in assembling a majority-supported cabinet, which took over as the government in March, 1937, was a tribute to his political skill although hardly to his dedication to espoused principles of governmental policy. With some plausibility he could and did continue to attack his office-hungry *Ngabwinsaing* opponents for being landlords and industrial promoters ambitious to displace British and Indian business.[2] But Dr. Ba Maw's radicalism was again, as in 1934, secondary to his attainment of political power.

The new government had to concern itself with a number of problems which carried over from the dyarchy period. Among these was what to do in the field of education, a subject with which the new Premier had himself been intimately concerned as the previous minister of education. The University Act was up for amendment, and the lengthy (1936) report of the Campbell Committee on the promotion of vernacular and vocational training was under consideration.[3] Pro-

[1] *New Burma*, Sept. 8, 1939, by U Thant of Pantanow.
[2] Sen, *A Peep into Burma's Politics*, pp. 55–56; Christian, *Modern Burma*, p. 239.
[3] Burma, Education Dept., *Report of the Vernacular Education and Vocational Reorganization Committee, 1936* (Rangoon, 1936), pp. 432–436. By A. Campbell.

ponents of what remained of the national schools were worried about the continued decline of these institutions in popularity. The press in general echoed student complaints concerning curriculum content, examinations, the use of English instead of Burmese, and the allegedly undue deference to Western expectations and standards. The demand for prison reform and for agricultural relief also carried over, as did the perennial objection to English as the official language of the legislature.[4]

On a few relatively minor questions the new government was able to make immediate concessions to popular sentiment. Abolishment of the capitation and *thathameda* taxes was initiated by stages, and they disappeared by January, 1942. In their place was substituted a system of state lotteries, from which the government would take a speculative two-fifths of the gross proceeds. Dr. Ba Maw also legalized more than 100 *Wunthanu Athins* in Tharrawaddy District which had been outlawed following the Saya San rebellion. Some political prisoners were released at the time of the coronation of George VI, and a gesture was made toward returning security deposits previously required of the vernacular press. Other minor concessions were the reduction of postal rates and the decision not to transfer the seat of government to Maymyo for the hot season.[5]

The Ba Maw government also initiated several substantial steps in the direction of basic agricultural reform. The Premier appointed a Land and Agricultural Committee, consisting of ranking political leaders plus leading civil servants, both Burman and British, to undertake a series of inquiries. Four able reports were eventually forthcoming, dealing with tenancy (I), land alienation (II), agricultural finance, colonization, and land purchase (III), and the regulation of moneylending (IV). Part III of the report was made the subject of further examination in 1939 by a separate Agricultural Finance Committee. A Village Administration Emergency Committee was also set up in 1937. Only the first two of these six reports were completed in time for action on them by the Ba Maw government.

The Tenancy Act, as drafted in accordance with committee recommendations[6] and presented to the legislature in August, 1938, was de-

---

[4] *New Burma*, Aug. and Sept., 1937; Christian, p. 235.

[5] Christian, pp. 236, 239; Sen, p. 56; Hinners, pp. 79–82; Burma, Legislature, House of Representatives, *Proceedings* (hereafter cited as BL,HRP), IV (Aug., 1938), pp. 295–300.

[6] RLAC, pt. i, *Tenancy*.

signed to make tenancies secure and end the evil practice of granting leases for one year only and at highly competitive rates. Under the act, any tenant who was refused a renewal of his lease could obtain, on formal application, such renewal on the basis of a "fair rent" scale as determined by a local revenue official, provided only that the tenant had treated his landlord fairly in the past. Such rental obligations could be made chargeable against the crop only after payment of wages for laborers and repayment of crop loans had been given priority. Landlords were also required by law to compensate the departing tenant for any improvements made by him during the course of his occupancy. This bill was referred in August, 1938, to a Select Committee with instructions to report at the February, 1939, session of the House. It was finally enacted into law in May, 1939.[7]

The Burma Alienation of Land Purchase Bill, also introduced in August, 1938, was similarly referred to a committee for later action, beyond the lifetime of the Ba Maw government. It was designed to prevent the transfer of land by an agriculturalist to a nonagriculturalist, following the pattern of the Punjab law of India. Thakin Mya was one of the few members of the House who urged immediate consideration of the bill.[8] Efforts to act on the other basic committee reports occurred after the fall of the Ba Maw cabinet, but his government deserved the credit for preparing a solid basis for remedial action covering difficult but urgent economic problems. The question of implementing these reform recommendations will be considered in a subsequent connection.

Opposition Tactics, 1937–1938

Dr. Ba Maw's government encountered its most inveterate political opposition from the factions headed by U Ba Pe and U Saw. The first was a past master of political intrigue within the legislature, and the second included in his political repertoire irresponsible press agitation and the use of *agents provocateurs* designed to foment popular unrest and to provoke overt violence. In 1938, U Saw broke away from the *Ngabwinsaing* group and set up his own *Myochit* (Love of Country) Party.

[7] *BL,HRP,* IV (Aug. 29–30, 1938), 359–366, 393. In February, 1938, U Saw attempted without success to obtain passage for a simple Paddy Rents Control Bill, which would have limited rents arbitrarily to a maximum of one-fourth of the gross paddy output.

[8] *Ibid.* (Aug. 30, 1938), pp. 396–401.

At the very outset of the legislative session of 1937 this opposition group challenged the action of the governor in certifying, without consent of the legislative council and prior to the coming into effect of the new constitution, the "Burma Frontier Force Act." This action covered a problem falling within the governor's assigned responsibilities and constitutional authority. Whereas the proposed frontier force was to consist of a nucleus from the regular (non-Burman) military police supplemented by Burman recruits, the nationalist opposition members demanded the immediate Burmanization of the entire body. Although the issue was of minor intrinsic importance and the opposition proposal was quite impracticable, the matter had to be referred to London for final settlement.[9] This was the first instance of the exercise of arbitrary legislative power on the part of the governor under the new constitution.

Leftist critics outside the legislature denounced Dr. Ba Maw's abandonment of his *Sinyetha* program. In reply, he retorted that political power must not be turned over to the enemies of the people. Dr. Ba Maw described his program for the first six months as rudimentary socialism, adapted to Burma's needs, attacking national wrongs, and preserving as many of his principles as was possible under the circumstances. Under a coalition ministry his full policy could not be attempted—he needed more time. On the anniversary of U Wisara's death, he declared that *Sinyetha* would use the "beggar's bowl" to attain its victories over the capitalists represented in the *Ngabwinsaing* and the united G.C.B.A.[10]

Much time was consumed during regular sessions of the House of Representatives by the opposition's posing of hundreds of questions designed to draw from the cabinet damaging admissions of ignorance or negligence which might be used to belabor the government.[11] These chronic attacks were punctuated, whenever a likely occasion developed, by no-confidence motions. At times the press agitation of the opposition included, as one of its targets, U Chit Hlaing, the speaker.[12] Although the European and business groups refused to participate in this type of political infighting and on several occasions prevented the downfall of the ministry, they never accorded full support to Dr. Ba Maw. They disliked his personal vanity and leftist tendencies, his ex-

[9] *PP,C,* vol. XX for 1936–1937, p. 19; Hinners, pp. 83–86.

[10] *New Burma,* Sept. 22, Oct. 3 and 29, 1937.

[11] In 1937, the British group in the House stood and gave a rousing cheer on the occasion of the thousandth question.

[12] *New Burma,* Sept. 3, 1937; Sen, pp. 55–56.

travagant schemes for social and economic reform, and the implied threat to economic stability in his taxation policy.[13]

The Anti-Indian Riots of 1938

A serious anti-Indian riot began on July 26, 1938. The occasion was the fomenting of a popular furor in Rangoon over the republication of a book by a Muslim author, one Shwe Hpi, critical of the Buddhist religion. The book had appeared originally in 1931, when it had aroused little attention. The appearance of a new edition in 1937 was actively exploited by elements of the vernacular press hostile to Dr. Ba Maw, U Saw's *Sun* leading the chorus, in a deliberate effort to instigate public hysteria and violence. Alleged insult to the Burmese race and religion were charged. Quotations from the book hostile to Buddhism were cited and misleading accusations were made to the effect that Muslim men took Burmese women as wives and then outraged their religion. Such statements were accompanied by cartoons putting police authority in contempt. Government's attention was drawn to the situation in mid-July, 1938, and the matter was referred as a routine item to the home minister, U Paw Tun, who on July 25 ordered a translation made of the book preparatory to proscribing its circulation. Official efforts to calm the growing excitement were accorded no co-operation whatever by the press.[14]

On July 26, 1938, a mass meeting was called in the Shwe Dagon pagoda area by the All Burma Council of Young *Pongyis* Association. The meeting was attended by agents of U Saw. The Young *Pongyis* group included monks who were not amenable to ecclesiastical discipline and who customarily used the yellow robe as a cloak for their political activities so as to escape police interference.[15] A protest procession was organized, which proceeded from the pagoda area toward the Soortee (Indian) Bazaar in downtown Rangoon. When the police attempted to halt the procession, it degenerated into a mob bent on taking vengeance on Muslim Indians. Rioting spread throughout the city. The sight of Indian police assaulting yellow-robed *provocateurs* inflamed opinion. Resentment was fanned on the following day by unsubstantiated press rumors that *pongyis* making their morning rounds had been assaulted by Muslims. On July 27, the situation within the

[13] Hinners, pp. 79–82.

[14] *BL,HRP*, IV (Aug. 26, 1938), 294–333. U Paw Tun's explanation has been followed in the text.

[15] Burma, Home Dept., *Final Report of the Riot Inquiry Committee* (Rangoon, 1939), pp. 12–13, 276–277. This is hereafter cited as *FRRIC*.

city got entirely out of hand and the anti-Indian rioting began to spread outward from Rangoon. A semblance of quiet was restored within the capital by August 1,[16] but it was some time before disturbances elsewhere could be brought under control.

The furor varied in intensity from place to place and not always in proportion to the local anti-Indian sentiment. Many areas where few Indians lived were the scenes of much trouble, such as the Thakin-infested oil-fields area at Yenangyaung, the Mandalay-Sagaing region, and the original home of the Alaungpaya dynasty in far-northern Shwebo.[17] Political opportunists fomented the riots everywhere. Both the rapid spread of the disorders and their aftermath of persistent unrest demonstrated, in the words of the committee, "that the real origin of the disturbances and the real cause of their protraction was . . . political." [18]

The police were entirely unprepared both in morale and in numbers to cope with the virulence of the outbreak.[19] The spirit of the rioters was boldly antigovernment, but they used the defenseless Indians as scapegoat targets. The verifiable casualties inflicted by rioters included 192 Indians killed and 878 injured, in a total casualty tabulation of 1,084. Some 155 of the 171 casualties from police action were Burmans. The 4,306 persons cited for offenses committed during the rioting admittedly included only a small fraction of the number of persons involved.[20] When a second outbreak occurred at Rangoon from September 2 to 8, the governor promulgated the Rangoon Emergency Security Act, which permitted the arrest of suspects and imprisonment up to fifteen days without trial. This act continued in force until late October, 1938.[21] A prodigious amount of looting of Indian homes and

[16] *New Burma*, report of July 29, 1939; Burma, *Report of the Rangoon Town Police* for 1938, pp. 6–8.

[17] The Riot Inquiry Committee spent one month in Rangoon, 6 days at Yenangyaung, 5 at Sagaing, 10 at Mandalay, and 3 at Shwebo, plus a total of 15 days in 12 other centers. See *IRRIC*, pp. 3–5.

[18] *FRRIC*, pp. 287–288.

[19] *Ibid.*, pp. 227–236, 247–249. Lack of vigorous police action in the initial stages of the rioting was attributable in part to standing regulations that only an officer in charge of a station could command dispersal of an unlawful assembly and that a magistrate's consent was required before an order to fire could be given. Hostile popular sentiment and uncertainty of official support in case of violation of regulations made the police hesitant to act.

[20] *Ibid.*, pp. 270–271, 281.

[21] Burma, *Report of the Rangoon Town Police* for 1938, pp. 7–8; Hinners, pp. 95–99.

shops occurred in the Rangoon area. Not until the second week of September were peace and security fully restored in the capital.[22]

Countermeasures of the government included the outlawing of two inflammatory newspapers, the Burmese *Sun* and the Indian *Saithan*. On September 22, the governor appointed the Riot Inquiry Committee consisting of a British justice as chairman, a British secretary, two responsible Muslim Indians, and two Burman representatives. The committee was authorized to report on the causes of the riots and reasons for the ineffectiveness of police measures taken to oppose it. It was also directed to recommend measures to prevent their recurrence.[23] The situation which the committee uncovered during the course of its labors was so disturbing that it paused at Mandalay to prepare an interim report covering items demanding prompt and vigorous attention.[24]

The Reports of the Riot Inquiry Committee

The committee's two reports declared that the immediate causes of the outbreak were the provocative and irresponsible role of the Burmese press and the activities of troublemaking agitators, both lay and *pongyi*. Such provocative activities not only long preceded the rioting but continued after the initial outbreak to foment defiance of the civil and police authorities and to fan hysteria by rumormongering. The committee also criticized the role of *pongyis* and the monasteries generally in promoting the rioting, although it was careful to distinguish between the undisciplined political-minded wearers of the robe and the elderly and truly pious monks. It cited more than 132 specifically authenticated cases of misuse of the yellow robe in acts of incitation to violence, actual assaults, looting, arson, and murder. Many *pongyi kyaungs* (monastic living quarters) were being used as refuges for hooligans and as depositories for loot, the natural hesitance of the police to violate such premises being counted upon.[25] The Thakin

[22] ABFMS, *MS. Correspondence*, W. E. Wiatt to R. L. Howard, at New York, Sept. 10, 1938.

[23] Mr. Justice H. B. L. Braund headed the committee; F. S. V. Donnison was secretary; U Po Han and U Khin Maung Dwe represented the Burmans, and Senator A. Rahim and M. A. Rauf the Indians. See *IRRIC*, p. 1.

[24] *Ibid.*, pp. 1–5, 8–11.

[25] *FRRIC*, pp. 276–280, 294. U Khin Maung Dwe registered an unimpressive dissent to the effect that no proof existed that the *pongyis* had looted for their own personal gain. The committee's evidence seems conclusive. It attributed the lack of civic responsibility in part to popular surrender to the superstitious influence of some of the *Sangha*.

Party was freed from any responsibility for causing the outbreak aside from its persistent effort to foment indiscipline within the schools and to discredit the government's authority. Once the riots started, however, the Thakins provided anti-imperialist slogans and otherwise improved the opportunity afforded by the disorders for extending their membership affiliations and their prestige as nationalist champions.[26]

The committee attributed the obviously virulent anti-Indian feeling behind the violent upheaval in Lower Burma to persistent efforts of the press to poison Burman-Indian relations and also to economic unrest, rooted in unsolved problems of land tenure. Opposition to Indian landlord and moneylender operations and the burning popular resentment over the competition of immigrant Indian labor with Burmese in both the agricultural and industrial fields were additional factors. The final report cited the recently released partial report of the Land and Agricultural Committee to emphasize that land reform was long overdue and that some immediate move must be made to quiet deeply ingrained Burmese sensitivity especially in Lower Burma to the continued unrestricted entry of Indian immigrants.[27] By comparison with this basic economic issue, the question of the disadvantage suffered by Burmese women married to Muslim men in the loss of the full legal equality of the sexes under Burmese Buddhist law was obviously a minor consideration.[28] The offspring of such a union had to be reared as Zerbadi Muslims, and some genuine apprehension was uncovered that this requirement would fragment further Burma's social structure and create an additional minority problem; [29] but the numbers involved were not sufficiently great to be alarming.

The final report of the committee emphasized among other things the impenetrable barrier of suspicion and distrust with which the police were regarded by all classes of the population. The summary statement may be cited:

If there is anything more than another which is responsible for the stubborn resistance of crime to all attempts to decrease its volume in Burma, it is, we think, the universal distrust of the police. . . . Of all things which, in our opinion would make for tranquility in Burma and . . . lay the foun-

[26] *IRRIC*, pp. 43–48.

[27] *Ibid.*, pp. 11–14, 21–26, 34–36; *FRRIC*, pp. 273–276.

[28] ABFMS, *MS. Correspondence,* Wiatt to Howard, Sept. 10, 1938. Wiatt believed that economic factors, including desire for loot, were far more important than religious sentiment.

[29] *IRRIC*, pp. 28–33.

dation for . . . nation building movements . . . a complete and thorough overhaul of the police system by . . . impartial . . . experts is . . . the most to be desired. . . . We have met throughout with . . . abhorrence of the police and an almost universal prejudice even among respectable people against them. If confidence in the police could be established . . . the people would be more ready to accept the rule of law . . . and . . . insist upon tranquility.[30]

Equally ominous with the popular dislike of the police, and not unconnected with it, was the depressing revelation that the public generally had sympathized with the rioters and endeavored to shield them from punishment. Convincing evidence was assembled that the village headmen almost invariably refused protection to Indians or else asked money for giving it. In many instances *thugyis* actually led the rioters in their attacks.[31] In several localities, as at Prome, where the local elders acted commendably to assist the officers of government in restoring order, they did it in spite of being dubbed "cowards" by many of the citizens. The public attitude toward the rioters was reflected in the leniency of the courts in dealing with offenders. Only 1,800 of the 4,300-odd arrested persons were tried, and only half of those tried were convicted. The ministry itself advised the courts to try only the more flagrant cases. One instance was cited where the secretary of a cabinet member brought influence to bear on the deputy commissioner of his home district to release some prisoners. The committee reported as follows:

The virtual immunity of rioters in general from arrest and punishment have left behind it a legacy of contempt for law which subsequent events are proving will be hard to eradicate. . . . Indian victims . . . ask themselves whether they can be safe henceforth in a country where they may be killed . . . with impunity.[32]

Alongside the committee's concluding homily about the importance of developing among the Burmans a spirit of "orderly conduct, tolerance, and honest dealing" as an essential condition for the realization of nationalist ambitions was the obvious fact that the people of Burma were moving steadily in the direction of revolution. Because the govern-

[30] *FRRIC*, pp. 225–227.

[31] *Ibid.*, pp. 269–270. The report declared that "the sympathies of . . . the vast majority of respectable [Burmese] men and women lay, and still lie, with the rioters and not with their victims or the police."

[32] Appendix XIV (p. lxvi) of the *FRRIC* gave twenty-nine specific instances in which dereliction of duty by headmen had been fully authenticated. See also *FRRIC*, pp. 272–273.

ment had delayed too long in ameliorating economic and administrative grievances, the public dislike of police authority had turned to defiance.[33] The cautiously hedged-about advances in self-government accorded by the 1935 constitution were proving not sufficient to contain the rising political tide within constructive channels, especially with *agents provocateurs* abroad.

Four constructive measures came out of the Riot Inquiry Committee's reports. One was James Baxter's valuable statistical study of Indian immigration to Burma,[34] unfortunately two decades overdue. The second was the initiation of preliminary talks with Indian authorities looking toward the limitation of Indian entry. A third was the eventual appointment of high-level official committees to examine the subject of bribery and corruption in Burma's government.[35] Another committee was appointed to examine problems of village administration.[36] These four items will be considered later.

Aftermath of the Riots of July, 1938

During the August, 1938, session of the House of Representatives, U Saw's *Myochit* Party led the fight to oust Dr. Ba Maw's government on the grounds that it was negligent and that continuing popular unrest demonstrated the government's loss of popular confidence. Far from admitting his own responsibility in fomenting the disorder, U Saw claimed credit for drawing popular attention to Shwe Hpi's objectionable book and blamed the government for acting tardily in suppressing it. Other partisan opponents attacked Dr. Ba Maw for being contemptuous of the masses and for abandoning his *Sinyetha* policy of pretended concern for the poor. Home Minister U Paw Tun was somewhat apologetic in explaining his role in the crisis, but he accused U Saw's paper, the *Sun*, of causing the trouble. Dr. Ba Maw's defense was that political prejudice and personal ambition motivated his attackers. When the no-confidence motion came to a vote on August 26, the European bloc, despite its dislike of Dr. Ba Maw, stood firmly behind the government, and the motion was defeated 66 to 61.[37] U Saw had failed in the

---

[33] *Ibid.*, pp. 269–270, 287–291.

[34] James Baxter, *The Report on Indian Immigration* (Rangoon, 1941); *IRRIC*, pp. 26–27.

[35] Burma, Home Dept., *Report of the Bribery and Corruption Enquiry Committee, 1940* (Rangoon, 1941). This is hereafter cited as *RBCEC*.

[36] Burma, Home Dept., *Report of the Village Administration Committee, 1941* (Rangoon, 1941).

[37] *BL,HRP*, IV (Aug. 26, 1938), 294–333; Hinners, pp. 95–99.

immediate realization of his political objective, but his paper and his *Myochit* followers continued to foment unrest in the succeeding months. In this endeavor they gained an ally in the Thakins and their Student Movement allies.

In many respects the methods employed by the Thakins both within the legislature [38] and outside contrasted sharply with the political tactics of Dr. Ba Maw's principal opponents. Eschewing U Saw's objective to foment disorder for its own sake and to the detriment of many innocent victims, the Thakins undertook throughout 1938 to organize students, workers, and peasants for the realization of specific objectives. They refused to accept the bribes of office to which the older politicians were amenable or otherwise to compromise their undeviating advocacy of nationalism and economic change. Their willingness to sacrifice themselves for such ends was itself condemnatory of the office-seeking politicians, who were usually unsparing in their disdain for both the idealism and the radicalism of the youthful Thakins.[39] By the same token the youthful group began to command an increasing measure of popular respect.

But Thakin efforts to dramatize their political and economic principles were often misguided and sometimes costly. One of their less successful ventures was the attempt to organize labor groups in various occupational areas. In February, 1938, the Thakins had attempted unsuccessfully to co-operate with Indian Congress Party agents to influence Indian dock coolies at the port of Rangoon to strike against their labor-gang recruiters. There followed similar attempts to organize the city's rickshaw pullers and the renters of bazaar stalls, all of them Indians. More effective was a Thakin-planned strike of Burmese bus drivers on the route to suburban Insein. The strikers stopped traffic by blockading a road junction and assaulted the police with bricks and

[38] The two Thakin members of the House of Representatives, Thakin Lun Baw and especially Thakin Mya, supported their nationalist and socialist principles without indulging in irresponsible antics. Thakin Mya urged immediate agricultural reform, and Thakin Ba Sein (an appointed member) denounced a committee proposal to aid large landholders in setting up special land mortgage banks on a joint-stock basis. Social progress, he said, counseled the liquidation of large holdings. See Burma, *Report of the Agricultural Finance Committee* (Rangoon, 1939), pp. 21–22.

[39] U Kyaw Min's attitude toward the Thakins (*The Burma We Love*, pp. 50–55) is typical of the older politicians. To him the Thakins were recruited from the frustrated half-educated unemployed, who regarded labor as beneath their status and blamed their difficulties on British-fashioned education. Before popular audiences who "wallowed" in their fervid oratory, they posed as martyrs; "to others who were more realistic they were little fools."

stones. They finally resumed work only when the government intervened to grant their demands.[40]

In 1938 also, several of the Thakin leaders, notably Thakins Lay Maung, Ba Swe, and Ba Hein, undertook to organize the Burman employees of the Burmah Oil Company not only in the oil-fields area (Chauk and Yenangyaung) but also at the Syriam refinery near Rangoon.[41] Oil was one of the few British industries in which Burman labor was extensively employed, and prevailing working conditions up to sixty working hours per week for sometimes as little as 13 rupees per month (£1) seemed to call for remedial measures. The organizers distributed pamphlets condemning capitalists, foreigners, and the existing government. The effort failed because the Thakin-sponsored Burman labor movement was wholly artificial and because labor's leverage for collective bargaining was in any case virtually nil in the presence of a surplus of cheap Indian labor. Nothing daunted, Thakins Ba Swe and Ba Hein attempted in 1938 to dramatize the labor cause by leading an oil-field strikers' march to Rangoon. They were arrested at Magwe shortly after the march had begun and were temporarily imprisoned.[42]

The close alignment between the activities of the youthful Thakins and the All Burma Student Movement was demonstrated when on December 12, 1938, shortly after the imprisonment of Thakins Ba Swe and Ba Hein, an epidemic of school strikes began. Many schools were obliged to close as a result of the hysteria, and they remained closed intermittently, with only partial attendance when in operation, down to the end of the school year on March 6, 1939. Some parents, many school authorities, and even the teachers themselves connived at student indiscipline to the great distress of the government.[43] In Thakin-sponsored demonstrations at Thonze and at the Shwe Dagon pagoda, the Communist hammer and sickle flag was for the first time prominently displayed,[44] while resolutions passed at meetings in Rangoon called for the "dictatorship of the proletariat" and the establishment of a "foreign bureau" to maintain labor contacts across national lines.[45]

---

[40] Burma, *Report of the Rangoon Town Police* for 1938, pp. 7–9.

[41] *IRRIC*, pp. 43–48.

[42] *Ibid.*; Hinners, pp. 86–88; U Kyaw Thet, recorded lecture.

[43] Burma, Education Dept., *Annual Report on Public Instruction in Burma*, for 1938–1939 (Rangoon, 1940), pp. 1–3, 15. A few of the examinations were held in March, but they were repeated in June, as had been done in 1936.

[44] The Rangoon *Gazette* of December 16, 1938, contained pictures of the Communist banners; see Christian, p. 238.

[45] ABFMS, *MS. Correspondence*, W. E. Wiatt to P. D. G. Lerrigo, from Insein, Jan. 21, 1939.

An unfortunate student incident occurred on December 20, 1938, when a group of university students tried to picket the entrances to the secretariat at Rangoon, in support of the demand to release Thakins Ba Swe and Ba Hein from prison. The Indian police guarding the grounds were at first watchful and patient, even though onlookers as well as students were hostile.[46] The picketers were about to disperse when violence flared which lead to the death of Maung Aung Gyaw, a Judson College student. Some fifty girl marchers in the vanguard were halted by police after entering a forbidden street area. Trouble began when the police then undertook to prevent the men students from following the girls. Apparently concerned in part about the safety of the girls, the men began to attack the police with stones and such other missiles as were at hand. During the ensuing melee, one policeman broke his club over the head of Maung Aung Gyaw who later died from the blow. He became eventually one of the Thakin martyrs of the nationalist struggle.

The secretariat incident caused quite a political furor and was subsequently fully investigated by a committee of the legislature. All members of the committee but one agreed that the police had acted within the law, although too savagely and overmuch in a spirit of panic. The police were criticized for raiding a nearby newspaper office, presumably to destroy photographic evidence of the affair.[47] Thus at some cost to themselves and to their immediate following, the Thakins and the students for a second time had dramatized their economic objectives and their political opposition to British rule.

As a result of the secretariat incident, the government, on December 22, again invoked the Rangoon Emergency Security Act. On the very first day of the emergency, U Saw got himself arrested and imprisoned briefly for leading a public procession in violation of police regulations. Subsequent Thakin and *pongyi* efforts to foment strikes at the Port Commission's workshops, in river transportation, and in the oil industry had to be suppressed by force. Not only at Rangoon but in such distant places as the lower Chindwin Valley and Thayetmyo the police used batons to disperse unruly crowds. The arrest of Thakin leaders at their strike headquarters at the Shwe Dagon pagoda area on January 23, 1939, and police seizure of allegedly incriminating papers [48] did noth-

[46] Burma, *Report of the Rangoon Town Police* for 1938, pp. 7-9.

[47] Burma, Home Dept., *Report of the Secretariat Incident Enquiry Committee* (Rangoon, 1939), pp. 1-17; *BL,HRP*, VI (Sept. 8, 1939), 752-762.

[48] *PD,C*, vol. 343 (Feb. 6, 1939), pp. 644-646; *The Times*, Jan. 13, 14, and 20, Feb. 14, 15, and 17, March 9 and 14, April 28, 1939. See also Hinners, pp. 95-99.

ing to quiet popular recrimination against the government. The situation reached the point in early February, 1939, that British-officered troops at Mandalay had to fire to disperse a student-*pongyi* mob numbering in the thousands, with the result that fourteen rioters were killed.

It was under such circumstances of spreading disorder that the European bloc in the House of Representatives apparently concluded that Dr. Ba Maw's government was proving itself unable to attract requisite popular support and must therefore go. Shortly after the February session of the Parliament opened, they voted with the Opposition factions to unseat the government. Another reason for the Europeans shift away from Ba Maw was that he had become involved in a quarrel with the European chairman of the Public Services Commission over alleged political interference in appointments and promotions and had actually moved to abolish the commission entirely.[49]

Out of office, Dr. Ba Maw reverted to his 1936 *Sinyetha* reform program and to his traditional Anglophobia, aggravated now by the fact that the shifting of British votes had produced his downfall in 1939. His subsequent alignment with the radical Thakin nationalists will be treated in a later connection.

U Pu's Ministry, 1939–1940

The ministry headed by U Pu, which took over following Dr. Ba Maw's downfall in February, 1939, did so under allegedly unfavorable astrological auspices.[50] It was at best a heterogeneous coalition affair. Three of the eight members carried over from Ba Maw's government (U Pu, Paw Tun, and Htoon Aung Gyaw). The other members were U Saw and U Aye of the *Myochit* Party, U Ba Pe and U Tun from the *Ngabwinsaing* remnant, and Saw Po Chit, Karen independent. Barring one shake-up in January, 1940, when U Ba Pe was dropped, this cabinet lasted for some nineteen months. Its policies for the most part were conservative. It penalized press indiscretions, repressed revolutionary activities of the Thakins, and banned the circulation of some thirty leftist books. It also co-operated with Allied efforts to furnish war

[49] Hinners, pp. 97–99. The European Public Services commissioner had resigned in protest. Conservative elements, such as the landlords, industry, and the Chettyars, had been worried for some time over Dr. Ba Maw's radical reform proposals.

[50] *New Burma* (July 7, 1939) reported an astrologers' controversy over whether the exalted position of Mars would counteract Saturn's unfavorable position to prevent the predicted early resignation of the ministry.

supplies to China via the Burma Road by reducing the Burma duty on goods re-exported to China from the 3.5 per cent set by Dr. Ba Maw's regime to a mere 1 per cent.[51] The government weathered repeated no-confidence motions during which its conservative alignment and its sterility in the area of reform were under attack both within and outside the House.[52]

The strong man in the U Pu ministry was U Saw, the minister of agriculture and forests. As a man of ambition and of great political cunning, U Saw was more feared than respected. His power stemmed from a number of factors. He was owner-editor of the *Sun* and undisputed head of his own *Myochit* Party. He had at his beck and call a partisan *"Galon"* army, which dated from the Saya San rebellion and which had been used for partisan political purposes during the riot episode of 1938. He also enjoyed important backing from wealthy conservative Burman landlords and businessmen and from Indian riceland interests. Finally U Saw maintained close co-operation with the All Burma *Pongyis* Council, a branch of the old united G.C.B.A. whose influence afforded him a mass following unavailable to any of his rivals.[53] Europeans liked him because he was less radical than others and would not hesitate to utilize repressive laws to put down subversive activities, especially those of his political rivals.

In comparison with U Saw's rising star, the deposed Dr. Ba Maw became a voice in the political wilderness. He tried to revive his shopworn *Sinyetha* program, but his pretensions were heavily discounted, and he possessed no effective means of appealing to the peasant masses. His European habits and training, his inordinate personal vanity, and his repeatedly demonstrated willingness to sacrifice principles for office were formidable handicaps. The press-dubbed "proletarian Pharaoh" uttered his Marxist clichés and his feigned sympathy for the underdog to a most unresponsive audience. Dr. Ba Maw eventually

---

[51] *New Burma* in August, 1939, had been obliged to post a 500-rupee deposit for criticizing the police as indecent; another paper had been fined 1,000 rupees for reprinting Indian Communist propaganda. The China traffic gave Burma's railways their first surplus in nine years (*The Times*, Oct. 16, 1940).

[52] *BL,HRP*, VI (Sept. 12, 1939), 865–867. The no-confidence motion lost by 68 to 51 votes. Editorial comment on the occasion of the death of U Ottama (*New Burma*, Sept. 10, 1939) declared that the pure patriotism of the *pongyi* nationalist leader had been exploited in his day by designing politicians who were still living in ease and comfort as betrayers of the nationalist cause.

[53] Hinners, pp. 99–101; *New Burma*, July 15, 1939. U Paw Tun also cultivated *pongyi* support politically.

took advantage of the outbreak of the European war to embark upon a program of subversive agitation which led him into alliance with some of the revolutionary Thakins and finally to jail.

Failure of the Land Reform Program

The frustrations encountered in the Burma Government's efforts to introduce a thoroughgoing program of land reform were attributable in part to administrative deficiencies and to lack of time prior to the onset of World War II. The government also faced the inherent difficulty of dealing with so baffling a problem within the political and legal framework of the Burma constitution of 1935. Of the four aspects of the problem examined by the Land and Agricultural Committee, namely (1) tenancy, (2) land alienation, (3) agricultural finance, colonization, and land purchase, and (4) the regulation of moneylending, only the first was enacted into law in time to get a real testing administratively. Reform measures to correct land alienation trends and to provide financing were debated for two to three years before enactment, only to be overtaken by the war. A proposed bill to regulate moneylender operations was never enacted. The committee's analysis and recommendations were themselves realistic and sound and served subsequently as a basis for policy decisions in the postwar period.[54]

The Tenancy Act, passed in May, 1939, was intended to ensure more security of tenure at lower rentals by enabling leaseholders to appeal to revenue or settlement officers of the government to set a "fair rent" standard. The measure proved unworkable because it was physically impossible for the officials designated as rent determiners to make the thousands of examinations requested by as many tenants. Even when a judgment was rendered, the local influence of landlords, often supported by a bribe, made the actual rental reductions very small. When the government attempted to authorize blanket reductions in lieu of the examination of individual cases, the courts set the regulation aside as extending beyond the scope of the law. When the Tenancy Act was itself amended in March, 1941, to correct several obvious deficiencies, the propertied Senate refused to accept the amendments.[55]

The Land Alienation Act, proposed by Dr. Ba Maw in 1938–1939,

[54] All four parts of the Land and Agricultural Committee report were republished by the Burma Government in 1949.

[55] Hinners, pp. 101–104; Andrus, pp. 81–82.

forbade the transfer of land held by an agriculturalist to a nonagriculturalist. It thus tended to limit the credit available for the cultivator-
owner to crop loans or to loans based on mere personal security.
Although mortgage loans from one "agriculturalist" (a person earning
half of his income from cultivation) to another were still permissible,
in actual fact few of them were in the lending business. Existing
mortgage obligations were unaffected by the proposed law, except
that alienation of land by mortgage foreclosure should thereafter run
for fifteen years only and the land would then revert to the original
mortgagor unencumbered. Probably because no more than 15 per cent
of the land of Lower Burma was agriculturalist-owned and not heavily
mortgaged and because the fifteen-year limitation afforded no immediate relief, no one was particularly enthusiastic about so futile a
measure. The act permitted nonagriculturalist owners to continue borrowing on mortgage security as before. The act as finally passed in
1941 was never put into effect and never tested in the courts.[56]

The committee's third report, on agricultural finance, colonization,
and land purchase, which was designed to encourage cultivator-
ownership or tenancy under state proprietorship, received very considerable attention. The report proposed that the state should purchase
from nonagriculturalist proprietors at market prices compact areas of
land to be divided into family-sized units and settled under the Government Estates Department. Permanent hereditary tenancies and
eventual individual ownership were alternative goals. Defaulting members and irresponsible co-operative societies also, according to the
report, would have to be eliminated rigorously. The several estates
units would have to be organized to meet credit, milling, marketing,
and consumer needs. The scheme required the setting up of an extensive governmental administrative machinery plus a system of land
mortgage banks and intermediate co-operative societies capable of
accepting responsibility for the repayment of loans to the government. Another important limiting factor was the providing of necessary
funds to purchase lands and finance production.

To provide credit needs for agriculture outside the government
estates, the report proposed establishing system of land mortgage banks
on a co-operative basis, prepared to lend up to 50 per cent of the
value of the land put up as security.[57] A reviewing committee of the

[56] RLAC, pt. II, Land Alienation, pp. 56–61; Andrus, pp. 77–81.

[57] RLAC, pt. III, Agricultural Finance, Colonization, and Land Purchase (Rangoon, 1939), pp. 147–154.

legislature cautioned that the land mortgage bank proposal must be approached very cautiously especially in view of the absence of the needed co-operative societies and the scarcity of land unencumbered by 50 per cent mortgages. It also proposed trying out several proposed pilot banks as a preliminary measure.[58]

A land purchase bill, as first proposed by Agriculture Minister U Saw in late August, 1939, was designed for political effect to demonstrate some tangible accomplishment on the part of the government in behalf of the landless cultivators. It followed a simplified pattern which made no provision for establishing the agricultural co-operatives or the governmental machinery needed. It proposed to lend money to the nonexistent co-ops at 3.75 per cent interest and to finance the whole affair from existing but obviously temporary revenue surpluses plus the unfunded debt represented by outstanding post-office savings certificates. It took no account of the imminence of war in Europe. It also plumped directly for tenant ownership through annuity payments to the government and made no mention of providing the necessary facilities for milling and marketing and for disbursing land mortgage credit. This poorly conceived proposal received rough handling at the hand of critics, British, Indian, and Burman, and was finally ordered printed and circulated for study until the next legislative session.[59]

In the perspective of postwar developments, the most interesting comments on U Saw's measure were made by Dr. Ba Maw and Thakin Mya. The ex-Premier declared that nothing short of a new agricultural order and a new Burmese economy based on an extension of the system of state tenancy was required. Wastelands must be improved at government expense; the debt load must be lifted from the peasants, and subsidiary occupations must be provided. To pay the rich for lands which they later could recover from private owners would profit only the well to do.[60] Thakin Mya spoke as the president of the All Burma Cultivators' League along frankly socialistic lines. He proposed that immediate relief to the debt-ridden cultivators be achieved not by some grandiose purchase scheme but by taxation reform, by scaling down debts including arrears of rents, and by the postponement for the time being of the execution of civil court decrees against agriculturalists. He proposed, furthermore, that any land purchase scheme be delayed until the tenancy

[58] Burma, *Report of the Agricultural Finance Committee,* pp. 6–22. This committee preferred not to encourage the idea of individual ownership.

[59] *BL,HRP,* VI (Aug. 29, Sept. 1, 1939), 182–187, 370–372. B. N. Das argued pointedly that co-operative mindedness was wholly lacking in Burma.

[60] *Ibid.* (Aug. 29, 1939), pp. 187–195.

and land alienation acts had been operative for two to three years. In the interim administrative agencies must see to it that revenue and rent settlement officers really reduced rents on the application of tenants. All cultivable wasteland should be reclaimed, deforested, irrigated or drained at government expense, and such land should be socialized in preference to the promotion of private ownership.[61] Thakin Mya's formula was the clearest prewar statement of Thakin views on the agricultural reform question.

The Land Purchase Act, finally passed in late 1941 just prior to the Japanese invasion, was, of course, never implemented. Chettyar evacuation during the war and postwar decisions amounting to partial expropriation of the Chettyar community's vast land and mortgage holdings at government-fixed rates finally cut the Gordian knot in a revolutionary solution of the land alienation problem.[62] A final prewar reform bill designed to register moneylenders, to inspect their accounts, to limit rates of interest to 12 per cent for secured and 18 per cent for unsecured loans, to disallow compound interest on loans, and to limit accrued interest to the amount of the original loan was never enacted into law.[63] It too was irrelevant to postwar revolutionary conditions, because the Chettyars never attempted to return.[64]

Village Reform Proposals

The Village Administration Enquiry Committee was originally constituted in 1937 and did much of its work in 1939–1940. After a period of inactivity, its work was revived in January, 1941, and its report was submitted on March 25 following. The directive under which the committee completed its task specified that the village-tract *thugyi* should become the elected representative of the villagers to co-operate with judicially competent elected village committees.[65] The recommendations reflected popularly desired changes which the bureaucratic administration, heretofore convinced that the village headman constituted the very foundation of local government, had never dared contemplate.

The Village Administration Enquiry Committee report proposed that village headmen should be elected by three-year-resident adult suffrage

[61] *Ibid.* (Sept. 1, 1939), pp. 400–406. [62] Andrus, pp. 82–83.

[63] *RLAC*, pt. IV, *Regulation of Moneylending*, pp. 177–188.

[64] The only other important economic reform measure enacted was the Payment of Wages Act, adapted from the India act of 1935. This act attempted through inspectors to forestall employers from withholding wages as a means of controlling their workers. See Hinners, p. 104.

[65] The committee included B. W. Swithinbank and seven Burmans.

under stringent rules designed to prevent fraud. The deputy commissioners would be empowered to disqualify candidates only for specifically defined reasons, not on mere standing, character, or hereditary grounds as before. The headman should normally retire at age sixty, but he would be subject to dismissal at the discretion of the deputy commissioner on the basis of open-air hearings held in response to an inquiry petition signed by three-fourths of the village-tract electorate. In view of the discontinuance of direct capitation and *thathameda* taxes after January 1, 1942, headmen should henceforth be compensated at fixed rates ranging from 180 to 400 rupees, supplemented where necessary by the allotment of *thugyisa* plots exempt from taxation. Headmen should also be paid expenses for nonroutine trips to township or district headquarters, should be accommodated at *zayat* resthouses away from home, and should also be allowed to keep a firearm without license fee. Rewards and titles should add to the dignity of his office.[66]

The committee also recommended that village committees elected to assist the *thugyi* in judicial matters should serve hereafter for five years instead of three and should exercise exclusive jurisdiction over small civil suits (50 to 100 rupees) in the tract of the defendant.[67] Village committees should retain locally elected fees for the time being. In criminal cases, the offended villager would still be free to seek remedy before a regular magistrate if he wished to do so, and township officers should review, on the basis of written reports, all findings and orders of village committees in criminal cases. A final recommendation was that *ywagaungs* (one for 20 houses and 3 per 100) be appointed as unsalaried rural policemen to act until a rural constabulary could be financed and established. Two guns for defense should be allotted to each important village. The *ywagaung's* post would carry exemption from ordinary village duties, and the incumbent should be eligible for traveling expenses and rewards and be allowed to wear *dalwes* (arms) without a license. The village police authorities should be required to report the arrival and departure of visitors as a means of keeping track of suspected criminals.[68] The report was important as a feasible Burman-designed plan to breathe vitality back into the moribund

[66] Burma, *Report of the Village Administration Committee* (Rangoon, 1941), pp. 1–10.

[67] Only 44 per cent of the village committees enjoyed judicial powers at the time.

[68] Burma, *Report of the Village Administration Committee*, pp. 10–20. Proposed miscellaneous regulations covered police jurisdiction over *pwès*, festivals, *pongyi-bayans*, cattle sales, and leper colonies.

village administrative unit. The Japanese invaded Burma before the report could be acted upon.

Bribery and Corruption

The 1941 report of the Bribery and Corruption Enquiry Committee, of which B. W. Swithinbank was chairman, was a revealing and realistic document which stripped away much of the reputation of British colonial rule for superior standards of honesty and efficiency.[69] The investigation was planned not as a punishment of the guilty but as an effort to diagnose a disease and prescribe a remedy for it. All the evidence obtained from some 338 voluntary witnesses, including many public-spirited persons, was kept confidential as far as names of informers and accused were concerned, and it was explicitly established in the authorization that no disciplinary action would be taken in consequence of the information obtained. With few exceptions members of the legislature gave no assistance to the committee. It owed most to public-spirited and knowledgeable members of the legal profession and to the Thakin Party generally, which was particularly cited for affording hearty co-operation.[70]

The committee attributed the dismal situation which it uncovered partly to traditional administrative abuses carried over from the time of the Burmese kings, but mainly to the destruction of institutions of local self-government and the proliferation of bureaucratic agencies lacking responsible oversight and inspection. In Burmese times, persons who were obliged to seek the services of government officials and clerks paid customary gratuities as a matter of course, objecting only when demands were excessive or when injustice resulted. Petty bribes made legitimate business move more smoothly or tipped the scales when discretionary authority was involved. Larger bribes which could buy favors at the expense of justice were frowned upon. The prudent person stayed away from the clutches of the royal officials and handled his affairs through action of the village elders, through mediatory courts, or through the hereditary *myothugyi*. Under British rule, most top-level officials in both the general administrative services and the specialized branches of government, including all of Class I of the Burman services, were customarily honest and just; but they were too

---

[69] The corruption inquiry was authorized on a motion by a Karen member of the House. Other committee members were W. A. Wright, J. A. Maung Gyi, U Thwin, U Kun, and U Po Yin.

[70] *RBCEC*, pp. 1–5, 7.

remote to be accessible to the average person. Below the top level there developed a miasma of administrative corruption and chicanery.

The report explained the situation as follows:

Where in Burmese times [a villager] may have passed his life without seeing more than [a] half-dozen officials, he was now exposed to an ever-increasing variety of functionaries, [such as] Township officers administering three separate legal systems (Civil, Criminal, and Revenue) all of which were equally strange to him; Police, Vaccinators, Veterinary Assistants, Cadastral Surveyors, Revenue Surveyors, Road overseers, Irrigation overseers, Epidemic Sub-Assistant Surgeons, Sub-Inspectors of Excise, Fisheries officers, and Forest Rangers, and superior officers who controlled these; persons of whose duties and power he had only a vague idea, who had to administer regulations with which [the villager] was almost unacquainted, and many of whom administered them with a view to extortion. . . . Government had no conception of the price which the taxpayer has paid for [these services] in addition to what he paid in taxes.[71]

Whatever gradual gains had been realized in improving administrative standards since 1900 had been more than offset by the increase of opportunities for officials to prey on the people. The specific evidence made available in the report went far to explain popular distrust of "Government" as something strange and hostile and the people's fear and hatred of the police in particular.

Much of the official graft was in the nature of petty exactions imposed by clerks (often working prolonged apprenticeships gratis), by miserably paid constables working for a pittance salary of 15 to 20 rupees per month, or by subordinate township and revenue officers, who handled large sums of money and exercised considerable discretionary authority. The bribes ranged from nominal sums up to substantial payments intended to obtain excuse from income tax liability or remission of land revenue because of alleged crop failure. Chettyars, it was found, regularly paid gratuities to judges who were handling their numerous cases in court. Bribes included in addition to money such items as free house rent, motorcars, ponies, whisky, women, food, jewelry, and on down to mere personal flattery. The report estimated that from 50 to 70 per cent of the subordinate magistrates made a business of selling justice and that police offenses varied from refusal to record evidence of crime without a fee to denial of bail and to exacting

[71] *Ibid.*, pp. 7–8.

protection money from keepers of illegal brothels and gambling and opium dens. Excise officers in particular amassed quick fortunes and were allegedly 100 per cent corrupt.

Corruption poisoned the very efforts made by the government to relieve the distress of the needy. Revenue officers withheld percentages of government loans granted to needy cultivators and defrauded the treasury of enormous sums of tax revenue by certifying falsely concerning crop failure. Efforts of tenants to obtain "fair rent" assessments under the Tenancy Act usually failed allegedly because landlords paid a bribe to the revenue officer. The mountain of evidence included land records dishonestly recorded and fishery lease violations ignored; also indicated were false certification of rubber quotas, of mining licenses, and of reports of extraction of timber for royalty payments. Jail privileges, approval of headman elections, service in public hospitals, incorrect records of vaccination of people and cattle, favorable medical examination reports, school inspections for grant-in-aid allocations, public works contracts, and even altered reports of the outcome of the Buddhist scripture examinations—all of these were obtainable corruptly by payment of illegal gratuities.[72]

The remedial proposals made by the committee included the application of both Western and indigenous remedies. Payment of adequate wages to clerks, constables, and deputy *myooks,* plus the revival of extensive touring and inspection by high-level officials as well as action by civic groups, were obviously British suggestions. The Burmese members proposed in addition that magistrates and clerks, as in the traditional *myoyon,* perform their services not in private but in open court and in full view of the public and of each other. They also recommended that judges be required to take publicly the oath to do justice, in the presence of the town elders and a *Mahathera* (*pongyi* of twenty years' record) at every new posting. They also suggested that any abrupt adjournments of court in the middle of a case should constitute prima-facie grounds for suspicion of ulterior purposes. Officials who were held in general public disrepute should automatically be suspected of graft and be subjected to scrutiny of private conduct as well as their bank accounts.[73] The formidable administrative deficiencies revealed by the report obviously added a new dimension to the problem of implementing any reform legislation however wisely conceived. It was clear that the basic problems of official peculation were

[72] *Ibid.,* pp. 10–39.　　　　　　　　[73] *Ibid.,* pp. 43–47, 50.

411

of long standing, and also that increasing political interference with the civil services had operated to aggravate the decline of service standards.[74]

The Changing Political Climate in Asia

The political temperament throughout Eastern Asia was changing rapidly during the late thirties. The new climate was sharply reflected in Burma, where it tended increasingly to outrun nationalist sentiment as reflected in the elected legislature. The contagion of the anti-European aspects of the Kuomintang revolution in China contributed to heightening nationalist sentiment in Burma throughout the 1930's. After Japan began in 1937 its all-out effort to conquer China, the tension sharpened noticeably, and Burmese opinion was largely in favor of the Chinese cause. Because of continuing popular antipathy to Indian residents, as demonstrated in the riots of 1938, Burmese sympathy for the Indian Congress Party was less widespread; it was confined largely to leftist revolutionary elements such as the Thakins. But Britain was the common imperialist overlord of India and Burma, and important political developments within India had an inevitable reaction across the bay. Burma's successive good-will mission exchanges with China in the late thirties were unofficial affairs including moderate political leaders, whereas contacts with Indian revolutionaries were mainly covert and radical. Both sources contributed materially to the changing political climate.

The pervasive influences from outside Burma were reflected even in such nonpolitical operations as the Christian missionary program. Burman members of Baptist churches, for example, opposed communal privileges and demanded not only closer identification of Christians with nationalist Burman objectives, but also complete freedom from missionary leading strings. They went so far as to threaten to refuse to accept any more missionaries unless mission funds for use in Burma were turned over to the control of the indigenous churches.[75] The democratic basis of Baptist church polity made the American Baptist Mission church groups peculiarly vulnerable to the changing political

[74] FRRIC, pp. 263–264.

[75] ABFMS, MS. Correspondence, W. E. Wiatt to R. L. Howard, Dec. 30, 1931, same to J. C. Robbins, July 21, 1938. As field secretary of the ABM, the Reverend W. E. Wiatt doubted the ability of local churches to handle mission funds for promotional purposes or to select incumbents for such key posts as Judson College principal or the head of the Insein Seminary.

412

climate. The difficulty was that Christians from minority groups reacted somewhat differently from the Burmans.

The rising tide of Asian nationalism inevitably produced repercussions from among all ethnic groups jealous of their own positions. Karen Christians, both Sgaw and Pwo, usually demanded that missionaries assigned to them be identified unreservedly with their own peculiar interests and points of view.[76] Karen spokesmen opposed nationalist pressure to Burmanize the civil service by the elimination of British personnel.[77] Arakanese nationalists, using the public press, underscored periodically the reality of their own local patriotism, which arose from the long history of political independence of the area. The Arakanese spokesmen wanted no brown Burman bureaucracy to replace the white one.[78] Even more objectionable from the Burman point of view was the desultory agitation to revive old Mon literature and culture. The Burmese press in 1939 blamed on European meddling a contemporary instance of divisive resurgence of Mon culture. The critics declared that Mons were now Burmans and that minority guarantees were totally unacceptable especially at a time when all ethnic groups must be knit together in a national unity.[79] The political temperature of minority sentiment was rising along with that of the Burmans.

The influence from India in the late thirties was for the most part radically leftist in character, either Communist, Socialist, or ultra-nationalist after the pattern set by Bengal's Subhas Chandra Bose. As early as 1937, Dr. Thein Maung's English-language paper, *New Burma*, reproduced lengthy portions of the address of the Communist M. N. Roy, delivered before the Radical Youth's Conference at Madras. Roy's theme was that capitalism was helping destroy the old feudal order, but that it contained the seeds of its own destruction. He argued that the freedom struggle must be waged on the basis of an anti-imperialist ideology with the goal of economic liberation.[80] The *Dobama Asiayone* after 1938 regularly sent delegates to the annual meetings of the Indian

[76] *Ibid.* Judson College in 1939–1940 resisted political pressure, backed by Burman Christians, that a representative of the government be included in its board of trustees.

[77] Burma, *Report of the Committee on Expenditure on the Public Services, 1939–1940* (Rangoon, 1940), pt. I, pp. 87–98.

[78] *New Burma*, Aug. 1, 1937.   [79] *Ibid.*, Aug. 25, 1939.

[80] *Ibid.*, Aug. 4, 1937. Successive issues of the *New Burma* (Aug. 6, 8, and 11, 1937) published in three installments an article entitled "Twenty Years of Bolshevism"; the fourth and final number was entitled "Soviet Foreign Policy—A Changed Face to the World" (Aug. 14, 1937).

Congress Party, where they developed contacts with Pandit Nehru and the Socialist Jayprakash Narain and with Indian Communist elements operating within the Congress-Socialist ranks. Marxist and Communist literature was regularly brought back to Burma.

Communist slogans were in evidence, as already indicated, during Thakin-led phases of the 1938 riots and again in the Thakin-inspired strikes and student furor of December, 1938, to April, 1939.[81] The fourth annual *Dobama Asiayone* meeting in 1939 copied the Indian Socialist Party program in its entirety. The left-wing Indian Congress Party leader, Ranga, visited Burma on the invitation of the Thakins in July, 1939, to address labor and peasant meetings. At the Thonze meeting, Ranga praised the people of Tharrawaddy District for their heroic revolutionary effort of 1931 and congratulated the peasants in particular for having come at long last to grips with British imperialism. He argued for reduction of rents, for peasant ownership of land, and for Burman operation of all mills, fisheries, and forestry work and predicted that the next rebellion would bring liberation because every Burman worker and peasant would take up the fight.[82]

During 1939, overt Communist propaganda from India began to produce a rift within *Dobama* ranks. The first official Communist cell, organized at Rangoon, included within its membership Thakins Ba Hein, Soe, Aung Than, Goshal, and Thein Pe.[83] Evidence of the rift among the Thakins was contained in a "Moscow party-line" appeal appearing in the *New Burma* of August 2, 1939, to form an "Anti-Imperialist United Front" in order to resist participation in the impending "imperialist war," which was prophesied to start later in August. Political opportunists such as the *Wunthanu* groups, the *Myochit* Party, and even Thakin leaders were declared not capable of organizing the needed antiwar rally, and much less so were the older party leaders in the government. The *Dobama Asiayone*, despite its enjoyment of some mass backing, was allegedly only a medley of socialists, nationalists, and fascists, who followed the mistaken Congress Party tactics and whose lack of organizational ability had been demonstrated by the fiasco of the oil workers' strike. It was time, continued the arti-

[81] Christian, p. 238, citing the Rangoon *Gazette*, Dec. 16, 1938.

[82] *New Burma*, July 21, 23, 26, and 28, 1939. Ranga's speech before a Rangoon labor group, largely Indian, was very poorly attended. Editorially, Dr. Thein Maung's paper expressed disagreement with Ranga's views on the Indians' role in Burma, but the paper published his speeches almost in full.

[83] It is doubtful that the group at this time developed any direct contact with Communists in Moscow or even in England.

cle, for radicals, socialists, democrats, progressives, and revolutionaries to sink their minor differences and to lead the masses in an antiwar rally.[84] It will shortly be clear that the Communist-directed minority of Thakins was able to influence but not to control nationalist Thakin policy toward the war.

The "Freedom Bloc"

The outbreak of war in Europe on September 1, 1939, had an immediately sobering effect throughout Burma's political spectrum. The government's presentation of the threat inherent in a victory for fascist aggression gained a respectful hearing. The Central Working Committeé of the *Dobama Asiayone* declared on September 9 as follows:

We condemn Fascism not only when it suits our convenience, but always, because it is in contradiction to . . . principles and ideals we stand for. . . . Both our rulers and ourselves have their respective duties, the one to the other.

The statement then forbade any member of the *Asiayone* to identify himself with riots, strikes, or other direct action without the express consent of the Working Committee. Members were ordered to avoid inflicting injustice or otherwise adding fuel to the flames of passion; they were also to respect humanity and those moral sanctions shared by all thinking persons.[85] One effect of this decision was the abrupt cessation of educational unrest and school strikes, which had plagued Burma's educational institutions during nine months prior to the outbreak of war.[86] It was obviously a time for deliberation and considered action—but in what direction?

The sequel to the initial action of the *Dobama* group was the promulgation in late September, 1939, of a nine-point program on the basis of which it offered to co-operate with any party for nationalist ends. The principal demand was that the governor should agree to consult his ministers even in those areas related to his special authority, pending the election of a Constituent Assembly to frame a constitution for an independent Burma. Other points called for negotiating a revision of the debt settlement with India, for the vesting of monetary and

[84] *New Burma*, Aug. 2, 1939. That *New Burma*'s editors were themselves not antiwar did not prevent their giving the "Anti-War Anti-Imperialist Front" a generous hearing on September 3, 1939.

[85] *Ibid.*, Sept. 10, 1939.

[86] Burma, Education Dept., *Annual Report on Public Instruction in Burma,* for 1939–1940 (Rangoon, 1940), p. 1.

financial control in the House of Representatives, and for assignment of Burma's defense preparations to the council of ministers. Recruitment of defense units should be entirely from the indigenous population, and funds needed for defense purposes must come from income and large-scale business taxes.[87]

Under Dr. Ba Maw's experienced editorship, the cumbersome nine-point program of the Thakins was reduced to three only and was made the basis for the so-called "Freedom Bloc." The three points were: (1) Britain's recognition of Burma's right to independence, (2) preparations for calling a Constituent Assembly, and (3) bringing all the special authorities of the governor immediately within the purview of the cabinet.[88]

The "Freedom Bloc" was an ultranationalist organization, deriving its name from the "Forward Bloc" fathered by the Bengali revolutionary, Subhas Chandra Bose, with whom Ba Maw had apparently been in communication. It was an amalgam of the *Sinyetha* Party, affiliated political *pongyi* groups, minor elements of the defunct *Ngabwinsaing* Party, and the *Dobama Asiayone*, except for those extremists who insisted on following the orthodox Communist line of policy. Dr. Ba Maw was designated the president-dictator (*Anashin*), and Thakin Aung San was named the general secretary. Other leaders were Thakins Nu, Ba Swe, Mya, and Hla Baw, who was president of the *Dobama Asiayone* at the time.[89]

One of the clearest early statements of "Freedom Bloc" policy came from Thakin Aung San, even though it was presented in halting English. Thakin Aung San declared that politics must rise above ideological bickering, emotional demagoguery, and even economic ends in order to advance stage by stage toward the realization of human values and activity at life's best level. He acknowledged that scientific socialism was a worthy goal, but, he insisted, attempted socialist action in Burma prior to the achievement of nationalist ends was sheer adventurism. Mass activity, he declared, must replace dependence on parliamentary methods, but it must be cleansed of demagoguery and be based on the broadest possible political front. He said: "Let the ways of the hooligan and blusterer, and the magician and mystic be thrown overboard. Then only can politics be real." He concluded by urging all progressive youth to advertise and to activate the "Freedom Bloc."[90] Thakin Aung San's repudiation of doctrinaire Marxism was unacceptable to such pro-

[87] *New Burma*, Sept. 27, 1939.
[89] *Ibid.*

[88] *Ibid.*, Oct. 6, 1939.
[90] *Ibid.*, Oct. 13, 1939.

Communists as Thakins Ba Hein, Soe, and Thein Pe, who would not offer to co-operate with the "imperialist war" on any terms. Personal rivalry (Ba Sein versus Aung San, for example) also emerged to disrupt the unity of the *Dobama Asiayone*. The responsible Democratic-Socialist organizer of the All Burma Cultivators' League, Thakin Mya, became president of the *Asiayone* in 1940, and pro-Communist Thakin Ba Hein in 1941, but the allegiance of the Thakins was becoming divided.[91]

The immediate tactic of Freedom Bloc leaders was to demand that U Pu's government accept their program or resign office. The Premier was thus put sharply on the defensive, and his embarrassment was aggravated when his own agricultural minister, U Saw, as *Myochit* Party president, issued a policy statement almost identical with that of the Freedom Bloc in content and timing.[92] When U Ba Pe in particular objected to U Saw's tactics, the latter used the issue to drive his rival from the cabinet in January, 1940.

During the last two months of 1939, Dr. Ba Maw carried his appeal to the people of the central valley of Burma, addressing large gatherings, often with a *pongyi* presiding. He demanded the resignation of U Pu's government and skirted subversive incitement in almost every address. An especially inflammatory statement made at Amarapura in early December caused the government to consider whether to arrest him. Dr. Ba Maw's principal argument was the same as Thakin Aung San's, namely that socialistic principles must be put to one side in favor of union of all nationalists behind independence, which was itself the prerequisite of all economic improvement. Thakin Nu was present on the occasion of the *"Anashin's"* address at the Shwe Dagon pagoda in November, and the *Sayadaw* U Thawma presided at Ba Maw's Kamayut meeting on December 21. Dr. Thein Maung, confidant of Dr. Ba Maw, gave full press coverage to all Freedom Bloc propaganda activities, called on U Pu editorially to resign, and exhorted all progressive elements to support the Bloc.[93]

In view of the fact that Freedom Bloc agitators were in no position to attain their extreme demands by direct methods, it was quickly apparent that they intended to fish in troubled international waters to find sustenance for their cause. The visit of Dr. Ba Maw's lieutenant, Dr. Thein Maung, to Japan immediately after the launching of the Freedom Bloc movement suggests the possibility that Japanese aid was from the outset part of Ba Maw's calculations. The objects of the

---

[91] Hinners, pp. 105–108. [92] *New Burma*, Oct. 20, 1939.
[93] *Ibid.*, Oct. 11 and 25, Nov. 1, Dec. 15 and 22, 1939.

visit were ostensibly to sell Burma rice, to inspect schools, and to see the sights, but the elaborate attention given the visitor by the Japanese belied such pretensions. Dr. Thein Maung reached Tokyo on November 7 via Dairen and Kobe and remained in Japan for more than a month. At a dinner accorded the visitor at the Peer's Club, with Baron Sonada presiding, Dr. Thein Maung urged closer cultural relations between Japan and Burma and added, "As the West has failed us, we must now answer the call of the East." His newspaper in Rangoon, *New Burma*, featured his Japan reports under the titles "Eastward Ho!" "The West Has Failed Us," and "On to Japan." The paper also began to include overt Japanese propaganda in such articles as those by Yone Noguti entitled "Asia Is One" and "New Order in Asia," stressing among other things the theme that the Japanese were also Buddhists.[94]

The Thakin faction within the Freedom Bloc was clearly divided, but it was on the whole much less favorable to a possible Japanese *rapprochement* than was Dr. Ba Maw's group. Thakin Ba Sein, a conservative rival of Thakin Aung San, was almost alone in advocating use of the Japanese to end British rule, while the pro-Communist Thakin Ba Hein at the other extreme opposed all fascists including the Japanese. Thakins Nu and Aung San in 1939 were publicly strongly pro-Chinese as opposed to Japanese imperialist aggression. Thakin Nu joined with political moderates, such as U Ba Lwin and U Ba, both educationists, the highly respected Fabian Socialist U Ba Choe, and Daw Mya Sein in participating in late 1939 and 1940 in a good-will mission to China. The mission carried friendly greetings to Generalissimo and Madame Chiang Kai-shek.[95] U Ba Choe translated Dr. Sun Yat-sen's *San Min Chu I* (Three Principles of the People) into Burmese. The Chinese nationalists sent a return mission in 1941.[96] Subsequently some of the Thakins conceived the idea that Communist China might even be of possible assistance.

Four Thakins again attended the Indian Congress Party meeting at Ramgarh in 1940 to maintain contacts with Indian friends, both Congress and Communist.[97] The 1940 meeting of the *Dobama Asiayone* at Tharrawaddy adopted the "no war effort" slogan of the Congress Party. At the same time, pro-Communist Thakins within the Freedom Bloc sponsored classes in Marxist doctrine utilizing Dr. Ba Maw's li-

[94] *Ibid.*, Oct. 18, Nov. 19, Dec. 1, 8, 10, 13, and 17, 1939.
[95] *Ibid.*, Dec. 13 and 19, 1939.
[96] Christian, p. 323; *The Times*, Dec. 8 and 13, 1939.
[97] K. M. Kannampilly, "Parties and Politics in Burma," *India Quarterly*, III (1947), 240–241.

brary. The Freedom Bloc as a whole was leftist and revolutionary in character, but it subordinated ideology to nationalism and was obviously prepared to accept outside assistance from any quarter in support of its basic objective of the independence of Burma from British rule.

Overt antiwar propaganda on the part of Freedom Bloc leaders was resumed in May and June, 1940, following the end of the *Sitzkrieg* or phony war in Europe. The arrest of three Thakin agitators in May, 1940,[98] under the governor's newly promulgated Defense of Burma Act aroused protests even from the government ministry. The act extended the arbitrary police power of the governor to cover actions that prejudiced British relations abroad, fomented enmity and strife within Burma, or were in opposition to Burma's safety and defense. The act was to run for the duration of the war plus six months, and offenders under it were to be tried by special tribunals. A bold speech by Dr. Ba Maw on June 9 in which he advocated neutrality in the European war and denounced his political enemies within Burma's Parliament as gangsters begging for crumbs from London [99] was the prelude to the Freedom Bloc's open break with the law in July and August.

The occasion for defiance of governmental authority was Premier U Pu's virtually unqualified pledge to support the war effort. This was made on the basis of the governor's agreement in July, 1940, to recruit local defense forces under the direction of U Maung Gyee, newly appointed Burmese defense counselor. Such a move would have gone far to quiet Burman opinion if it had been made six months earlier, but it was singularly ineffective in the context of the collapse of France and the tragedy of Dunkirk.[100] The Burma Government's temporary closing of the Burma Road on July 16, 1940, an act intended to mollify Burmese opposition groups and one long advocated by the Thakins, tended now only to encourage the antiwar agitation. Leading members of the Working Committee of the *Dobama Asiayone*, Thakins Lay Maung, Than Tun, and Soe, as well as many Thakin district leaders were arrested in early July for urging villagers not to aid the war effort.[101] Thakin Nu was arrested following his address at Jubilee Hall, Rangoon, on July 16. He was sentenced on July 24 to one year's imprison-

---

[98] Christian, p. 238.   [99] Hinners, pp. 118–119, 121–123.

[100] *Ibid.*, pp. 111–114, 120–123. U Pu's prowar policy was conditioned solely by his unilateral assertion that Burma's help in the war would be fully effective when rights were granted equal to those of the other self-governing members of the empire.

[101] *New Burma*, July 7, 10, and 17, 1940.

ment. Dr. Thein Maung was similarly arrested for subversive utterances on July 27.[102]

Dr. Ba Maw, in a final dramatic move, resigned from the House of Representatives in late July, declared his decision to risk all in behalf of his country's freedom, and courted arrest by delivering a speech at Mandalay attacking U Pu's policy of supporting the war. IIis arrest on August 6 caused something of a political sensation. In a martyr-toned farewell to the Buddhist monks, the laity, and the people of Burma, he turned over to others the burden of bearing the torch of freedom. Thakin Mya, president of the All Burma Cultivators' League, was designated as the future leader of the Freedom Bloc. The simultaneous arrest of several Japanese agents in both London and Burma suggested that the British police were acting on broader evidence of subversion than was stated in the warrant issued for Dr. Ba Maw's arrest.[103] The ex-Premier's trial started on August 20, and he was sentenced on August 29 to one year's imprisonment, a decision confirmed on appeal two months later. Dr. Thein Maung escaped conviction largely through the skillful efforts of his defense counselor, Dr. Ba Han, older brother of Ba Maw.[104] During the early stages of the trials an all-parties opposition meeting convened in Rangoon to attack U Pu's policies of repressing political agitation and of co-operating with the war effort on the basis of a mere hope that Burma would eventually attain independence. The second week of September saw U Pu replaced as Premier by the more vigorous U Saw.

The Ministry of U Saw, 1940–1941

U Pu's government was defeated on September 7, 1940, on a no-confidence motion sponsored principally by U Ba Pe. Despite growing popular unrest instigated by the Freedom Bloc, which had managed to hold the political spotlight since late 1939, responsible Burmans within the legislature were not ready to sabotage the war and to risk British defeat in the then dubious state of world affairs. U Pu's ministry might therefore have weathered the storm had it not been for the action of U Saw during the final stages of the debate in abruptly with-

[102] Ibid., July 24 and 28, 1940.
[103] Ibid., Aug. 7 and 9, 1940; Daily Telegraph, July 30, Aug. 7, 1940.
[104] New Burma, Aug. 21, Sept. 25, 27, and 29, 1940. Following the acquittal of Dr. Thein Maung, his paper, New Burma, began a series of pro-Japanese articles which discussed cultural trends in Japan (by Oshikawa), presented a "Portrait of Prince Konoye," and interpreted the recently concluded Japanese treaty with Thailand as intended merely to exclude European influence from the Far East.

drawing from the cabinet and shifting his *Myochit* following to the Opposition side. Because alternative groups were either at loggerheads among themselves or were semiseditious, the governor, on September 9, asked U Saw himself to try to form a cabinet. U Saw succeeded in the task by following Dr. Ba Maw's 1937 tactics of attracting the support of minority groups, the Indians, the Karens, and the Europeans. He kept three members from U Pu's old cabinet, U Paw Tun, U Ba Than, and U Tharrawaddy Maung Maung, and brought back Saw Pe Tha to represent the Karens.[105]

The policies which the new Premier announced on September 26 were by no means devoid of nationalist sentiment, but they were a far cry from the advanced position he had taken in 1939. He abandoned the demand for Burma's independence, in favor of dominion-status home rule to be achieved by legal evolutionary means. He would reduce governmental expenses and Burmanize the civil services in all areas. As an earnest of his sincerity he accepted voluntarily pay reductions from 5,000 rupees per month to 3,000 rupees for the Premier and from 5,000 rupees to 2,500 rupees for the other ministers. He proposed also to introduce free compulsory primary education, to make Burmese the medium of instruction at the university, to promote a national youth movement, and to assist in the founding of a Buddhist university (*Sasana Takkathe*) designed to promote a religious revival. As the price for the needed backing in the legislature, U Saw also agreed to support minority rights, to curb radical agitation, and to give positive support to Burma's defense measures.[106]

No part of U Saw's policy was implemented with more enthusiasm than the suppression of internal agitation and unrest. He carried Dr. Ba Maw's trial through to final conviction and, when the initial year's sentence expired, did not hesitate to continue the prison terms for both him and the convicted Thakins. He hounded into prison or hiding all of the Communist Thakins and all except the most discreet members of the Freedom Bloc. Overt antiwar agitation ceased in the press. Thakin Aung San escaped the warrant issued for his arrest only by fleeing the country. Now that U Saw was fortified by the enjoyment of governmental authority, he agreed to ban all private armies, his own *"Galon"* forces as well as the so-called "Dhama Tat" of Dr. Ba Maw, the "Bama Tat" of the Thakins, and Defense Counselor U Maung Gyee's so-called "Green Army." By October, 1941, he had used the Defense of Burma Act to silence all hostile newspapers and to imprison

---

[105] Hinners, pp. 122–123.   [106] Christian, pp. 244–245.

such political enemies as U Ba Pe, U Ba U (Mandalay), the ex-mayor of Rangoon U Ba Win, and Rangoon labor representative in Parliament, U Ba Hlaing.

After U Saw became Premier, pro-Japanese articles disappeared from his newspaper, the *Sun*. He agreed in October, 1940, not only to reopen the Burma Road to China traffic but also to abolish all customs duties on goods in transit over the road.[107] In April, 1941, he went along with British plans to extend the Lashio branch of the Burma Railways to the China border. Britain compensated the Burma Government for the cost of new port installations at Rangoon and for the customs losses and police staff needed for Burma Road traffic. London also accepted responsibility for the cost of extending the Lashio Railway branch into China after U Saw had protested the bilateral agreement made between Britain and China. Burma was given an option to buy the railway, was accorded the right to impose customs and immigration controls along the railway, and was guaranteed against monetary loss from its operation.[108]

Premier U Saw was, at the same time, not oblivious of the need to develop a program of positive accomplishment which could provide a broad basis for popular support. In this effort he made the most of his colorful personality. For one thing he revived traditional Burmese practices respecting deference shown to royalty in the popular relations toward his own authority.[109] He pushed to conclusion most of the reform measures already initiated by his predecessors. He enlisted the aid of Dr. Thein Maung's committee for a Buddhist university to devise a system of advanced instruction in the Pali scriptures. The plan called for fourteen junior colleges and nineteen senior colleges scattered widely throughout Burma and heading up in an examining authority at Mandalay.[110] He pushed the passage of a long-needed Rural Self-Government Act of February, 1941, which shifted responsibility for supervising the operations of local elected bodies both rural and urban from the remote divisional commissioners to specially designated in-

---

[107] Hinners, pp. 121–130; F. Tennyson Jesse, *The Story of Burma* (London, 1946), p. 169; Sen, p. 65; *PD,C,* vol. 370 (April 1, 1941), p. 868, vol. 377 (Feb. 22, 1942), p. 1570.

[108] Hinners, pp. 130–136.   [109] U Kyaw Thet's recorded lecture (1954).

[110] Burma, *Report of the Pali University Enquiry Committee* (Rangoon, 1941), pp. 1–34. The Pali University was designed to revive religious scholarship and to diminish the growing discord and jealousy prevailing between rival sects. The curriculum and the study program as well as examinations were to be under the control of the *Sayadaws*. Six college units were to be located at Mandalay, three in Rangoon, and three in Pakokku.

spectors who were to range widely.[111] U Saw also negotiated with the Government of India the Saw-Bajpai Agreement of July, 1941, under which Burma's right to limit Indian immigration was conceded in return for preferential treatment for goods of Indian manufacture imported by Burma.[112] This agreement was inoperative because it was never fully ratified, but it set a pattern for postwar Burma policy.

One of the most characteristic expressions of U Saw's nonsubversive brand of nationalism was found in his pressure for the complete Burmanization of the civil services. The full demand was presented in the 1940 *Report of the Committee on Expenditure on the Public Services.* Sir J. A. Maung Gyi was chairman, and U Tin Tut, senior Burma civil service officer, was the committee adviser. This report was prepared as a kind of Burman rejoinder to a discouraging British-sponsored Fiscal Committee's recommendation, which urged a thoroughgoing effort to raise funds by local taxation in order to replace the disappearing capitation and *thathameda* levies.[113]

Sir J. A. Maung Gyi's report recommended as an essential economy measure that except for certain technical services which Burmans were not yet trained to fill, such as medicine and engineering, all new recruitment to the civil service should be made exclusively from persons domiciled in Burma. The report complained that the new European recruits in contrast to those of former days made no effort to learn the language or to understand the people. They were also too expensive to maintain, with the extra overseas service allowances, the additional Burma pay, and the educational aids supplementing already large regular salaries. The authors insisted that rioting danger was now nil in view of the passage of the agricultural reforms and the availability of Burmans of responsibility, honesty, and initiative to take over the police as well as other services. The prestige which British officers had once enjoyed as members of the conquering race had allegedly been destroyed in recent years, and Burmans must therefore prepare to take over governmental administration at all levels. The report concluded:

---

[111] Hinners, pp. 129–130.

[112] The agreement ignored most of the findings of James Baxter's *Report on Indian Immigration,* which stressed the positive contributions of Indian labor to Burma's economy and minimized Indian-Burman competition in the labor field.

[113] Burma, Fiscal Committee, *Interim Report on Local Taxation* (Rangoon, 1940). This report argued that wheel taxes could be increased to keep up the roads, that water, lights, and sanitation facilities should be maintained by house taxes assessed at four levels, and that municipalities should also levy local rates for education. Some twenty of the twenty-eight districts, it pointed out, levied no local taxes at all for roads and lighting.

Some [European civil servants] are able to adapt themselves to the changed Constitution and to work with Ministers with commendable tact and efficiency, while others find it difficult to attune themselves to what in the ministerial sphere is in effect a Burmese Government intended to be run with Burmese ideas and in sympathy with Burmese public opinion. These difficulties are likely to increase with the progressive grant of responsible government to Burma.[114]

It mattered little that the lone British member of the committee, backed by the Karen member, dissented sharply from both the factual assumptions and the tone of the report. The important fact was that the most conservative Burman opinion available (Sir J. A. Maung Gyi) had asked in the name of economy that the British let Burmans run their own country.[115] The sands of colonial control were running out in 1941.

[114] Burma, *Report of the Committee on Expenditure on the Public Services, 1939–1940*, pt. i, pp. 1–8.
[115] *Ibid.*, pp. 87–98.

424

§ *Part Four* ℬ

RE-EMERGENCE OF
INDEPENDENT BURMA

XIII

Japanese Occupation

THE Japanese conquest and occupation of Burma from 1942 to 1945 constituted a milestone in the political history of the country no less important than the British annexation of 1886. World War II transferred the problem of Burma's political future from the more or less parochial context of direct relations with London and local party feuding to that of events of world import connected with a major shifting of the balance of power. Events of the war both in Europe and in the Orient disrupted completely the normal process of political evolution throughout the colonial countries of Southeast Asia. The war also precipitated everywhere nationalist revolutions to throw off the political and economic domination of European colonial powers. Although the Japanese were the immediate agents of change by virtue of military conquest and their political concessions were designed to enlist co-operation of the Burmese peoples in the achievement of Tokyo's war aims, the emergent revolutionary nationalism was a deep-currented, popular movement with abundant vitality of its own. Because the anti-imperialist spirit generated by the war experience was also revolutionary economically as well as politically, it tended to contribute to the vogue of Communist techniques of political organization, agrarian reform, and forced-draft economic development.

In Burma, the political groups best able, by virtue of their superior daring, nationalist principles, and adaptability, to take advantage of the new situation were the components of the Dr. Ba Maw–Thakin

Party "Freedom Bloc." Under circumstances of continued peace, such a group could have risen to political dominance only after decades of political struggle, if indeed it could have done so at all. During the course of the war, the Freedom Bloc group managed to achieve a virtual political and military monopoly within the limits permitted by the Japanese occupation. Thakin elements of the *Dobama-Sinyetha* coalition turned against the Japanese during the final months of the British reconquest. Thus the wartime monopoly, somewhat qualified, persisted into the postwar period under the banner of the Antifascist People's Freedom League. The Freedom League alone acquired the essential internal cohesion, the mass following, and the capabilities of physical resistance needed to champion the nationalist cause.

Another important consequence of the war was the elimination of the prewar economic predominance in Burma of the British and Indian capitalist communities. British efforts to recover control of industrial, mining, and transportation operations, most of them heavily damaged by the war, were certain to be resisted strongly by the Burmese nationalists. The Chettyar moneylender community was eliminated once and for all, and their vast holdings of land titles and mortgages were taken over by Burman authorities, thus cutting the Gordian knot of the baffling problems of tenancy and land alienation. Finally, the successive periods of interregnum from 1942 to 1948 released internal forces of criminal violence and political disorder which would continue for a decade and more beyond the termination of the war to retard economic reconstruction, to plague the successive governments of Burma and the population generally. Chapter XIII will be devoted to the early aspects of the conquest and occupation.

Prelude to World War II in Burma

Two brief episodes from the prewar period need to be considered as having a bearing on the war itself. One concerned the secret departure of Thakin Aung San [1] for China in late 1940 disguised as a Chinese crewman aboard a Norwegian boat. The ostensible purpose of his journey was to make contact with the Chinese Communists to see if they could be of any assistance in Burma's struggle for independence. He apparently had no clear idea how he was to accomplish this end.

[1] Ian Morrison, *Grandfather Longlegs* (London, 1947), pp. 62–69. Thakin Aung San was born the son of landowner parents in Yenangyaung in 1915. He became president of the Burma Student Movement in 1936 and secretary of the *Dobama Asiayona* in 1938.

He carried a letter of introduction from the Indian Communist Party to the party in China, together with a small amount of cash. It was a madcap adventure, but arrest awaited him if he remained in Burma. Other aid from abroad seemed remote at the time. Many Thakins were unalterably opposed to the fascist Japanese, while both Indian and Chinese nationalists offered a forlorn hope. Thakin Aung San was arrested in Amoy by the Japanese. He obtained release only on the basis of urgent representations made to Japanese agents at Rangoon by the pro-Japanese Thakin Ba Sein to the effect that Thakin Aung San had really been seeking aid from Japan. Thus began the overt collaboration with the Japanese on the part of the leader of Burma's "Thirty Heroes."

The Thakins themselves differed sharply over the Japanese collaboration proposal. The pro-Communist group, led by Thakins Thein Pe and Ba Hein (*Dobama* president in 1941), refused to go along. On the occasion of Thakin Aung San's brief and furtive ten-day return visit to Burma in 1941, he nevertheless enlisted the co-operation of Thakins Mya, Ba Swe, and Kyaw Nyein in forming the pro-Japanese People's Revolutionary Party. Thakins Ba Sein and Tun Oke were also prominently pro-Japanese. The conspiracy spread widely among Student Movement leaders. In 1941, Thakin Ne Win proceeded to Japan, where he received instructions on the role to be played by the proposed Burma Independence Army. Most of the training of the thirty comrade-collaborators took place on Hainan Island. The cadre of a Burma Independence Army assembled at Bangkok in late 1941, and vigorous recruitment efforts followed the outbreak of war. This army re-entered Burma in the wake of the Japanese invaders of 1942.[2]

The second episode was Premier U Saw's visit to England in October to November, 1941, to ask the British Government for a definite promise of postwar dominion status for Burma. The immediate objective of Rangoon was to bolster Burma's co-operation in the war effort by giving the people a stake in the outcome. The Burman desire to contact London was in part a reaction to the objectionable statement made by Burma's new governor, Sir Reginald Dorman-Smith, upon his arrival in June, 1941, that Burma's chances for constitutional advance would depend on the effort which it expended in prosecuting the war. Nationalist hopes were subsequently raised by the promulgation in August of the "Four Freedoms" of the Atlantic Charter, Article 3 of which affirmed that peoples would have the right to choose their own form of government. When opposition spokesmen in the Burma Con-

[2] *Ibid.*

gress asked U Saw on August 17, 1941, whether Article 3 applied to Burma, he replied that he assumed that it did. The question was obviously one of such overriding political importance that some measure of assurance would have to be obtained if cabinet and governor were to continue to co-operate administratively as well as in defense preparations.[3]

Premier U Saw and his Burman associates were pleased by the fact that Governor Dorman-Smith was personally friendly toward them, less reserved in his social relations than some of his predecessors had been, and apparently not hostile to Burma's political aspirations. The governor recognized in U Saw a political realist whose ambition to exercise power took precedence over other considerations and whose valued co-operation in defense preparations and in suppressing anti-British subversive elements must be retained if possible. The governor from the outset shared with the cabinet ministers his personal responsibility for defense preparations by including them in his defense council. He also sought to gain time by postponing for one year the general elections scheduled for November, 1941, in full awareness of the fact that U Saw had no intention of allowing any political opponent to outbid him in demanding political freedom for Burma. It was with a view to strengthening, if possible, U Saw's political position domestically that the governor arranged with London in late August that Burma's Premier and his secretary, U Tin Tut, be invited to Britain to talk with the Secretary of State for India, Mr. Amery, and with Prime Minister Churchill, ostensibly to convey a "message of good will" from Burma. London refused Rangoon's suggestion that the invitation indicate explicitly that the discussions would also concern Burma's postwar constitutional prospects.[4]

It was after the invitation had been extended that the British Prime Minister, on September 8, publicly exempted from the application of the Atlantic Charter all elements of the British Empire, without any reaffirmation of Britain's previous empire policy statements.[5] Even though the prospects of Burma's obtaining any explicit guarantee were admittedly dim, the governor tendered U Saw a farewell dinner, wished him well in his endeavor, and received in return U Saw's profession of

[3] Hinners, pp. 134–136; Maurice Collis, *Last and First in Burma (1941–1948)* (London, 1956), pp. 27–34.

[4] Collis, *Last and First in Burma,* pp. 24–30; *The Times,* Sept. 1, 1941. The governor was not unaware that U Saw was also a corrupt politician.

[5] New York *Times,* Sept. 15, 1941.

firm friendship whatever the outcome. Burma's two emissaries arrived in London by air on October 11.[6]

U Saw lost no time telling the London press that, although he was not the bearer of an ultimatum, he wanted a clarification of Britain's policy respecting complete self-government for Burma as a condition of full co-operation in the war effort. If the Atlantic Charter did not apply to Burma, were they fighting for their eventual freedom or not? A number of private "letters to the editor" suggesting that Burma was on trial and implying its unfitness for early self-rule were answered by the mission immediately and with spirit.[7] U Saw's official conversations with the defense and home ministers and with Secretary Amery were conducted in a friendly atmosphere, for London had no desire to offend one who had served well from the British point of view as Burma's Premier. At the eventual meeting with Mr. Churchill at Chequers, U Saw was finally told that it was not feasible to discuss Burma's future constitution in wartime. Mr. Churchill nevertheless promised orally that if Britain won the war the issue of Burma's constitution would be dealt with in a liberal manner.[8]

The following official statement by Secretary Amery issued on November 4 was so qualified and cautiously worded as to be completely unsatisfactory from the Burman point of view:

It is to that high position of Dominion status—a position to which we would not lightly admit outside people without full consideration of the character of their Government or the responsibility which it might involve—that we wish to help Burma to attain as fully and completely as may be possible under certain contingencies immediately after the victorious conclusion of the war.

Our purpose is clear, and I can give U Saw the assurance that we sincerely mean what we say. . . . With a situation at the end of the war which no one can yet foresee, it is out of the way to give a categorical assurance of such a nature as might result in gross misunderstanding and disappointment.[9]

[6] Collis, *Last and First in Burma*, pp. 32–34; *The Times*, Oct. 11 and 14, 1941. Collis explains (p. 34) that Premier U Saw was invited to London as one "set up by a British agency to manage in the British interest the internal affairs of Burma."

[7] *The Times*, Oct. 14, 17, and 30, Nov. 4, 1941; *News Chronicle*, Oct. 27, 1941. U Tin Tut no doubt composed these newspaper rejoinders.

[8] Collis, *Last and First in Burma*, pp. 35–36.

[9] *The Times*, No. 5, 1941; Hinners, pp. 137–139; *PD,C*, vol. 376 (Nov. 27, 1941), p. 884. Collis' assertion (p. 36) based on Governor Dorman-Smith's records

British official policy toward Burma remained unchanged after the Far Eastern war broke in early December, 1941, even though Secretary Amery was subjected to sharp criticism in Parliament for turning U Saw away with a "troubled mind." U Saw's assertion that he left England without bitterness was belied by subsequent statements attributed to him in the United States. After spending several weeks in the United States, he was halted at Hawaii on his return trip to Burma by the outbreak of war in the Pacific. He had to retrace his journey via the United States and Europe. At Lisbon he was detected communicating with Japanese legation officials, and it was learned through cable intercepts to Tokyo that he had promised that Burmans would assist an invading Japanese army and that he personally, if still in power, would do what he could to help. He was accordingly arrested by British police upon his arrival in Egypt on January 19, 1942. He spent the ensuing four years as a prisoner in British Uganda. He returned to Burma in early 1946. U Tin Tut was also detained for several months, but since there was no evidence of treasonable action against him, he was released in May, 1942.[10]

The Anglophile Sir Paw Tun took over the Burma Premiership following U Saw's detention. He brought U Htoon Aung Gyaw into his cabinet as finance minister. These two along with U Tin Tut became the ranking Burman members of Governor Dorman-Smith's wartime staff at Simla, India. During the Japanese invasion the ministry as a whole remained loyal to the governor.[11]

Japanese Plans for Burma

Burma was apparently of minor importance in Japan's early plans for the projected New Order in Eastern Asia. Tokyo's primary concern was to exclude Western influence from Eastern Asia and to work out a satisfactory settlement with China which would establish the hegemony of Japan in the region. Economic pressure plus offers of territorial bribes to China (Tonkin and north Burma) were combined with military sanctions to obtain Chungking's acquiescence.[12] Japan's first es-

---

that Secretary Amery tried to help the governor by obtaining from Mr. Churchill a more explicit statement lacks corroboration elsewhere.

[10] Collis, *First and Last in Burma*, pp. 37–39, 68–69, 209. U Saw was visited in Uganda in June, 1942, by his friend Dorman-Smith, who was en route to England at the time.

[11] *Ibid.*, pp. 47–48.

[12] F. C. Jones, *Japan's New Order in East Asia: Its Rise and Fall, 1937–1945* (London, 1954), pp. 87, 140–141, 148–149, 234. The map found in Chiang

pousal of the New Order following the capture of Canton in November, 1938, made no reference whatever to Southeast Asia. The coveted prize in the southern areas was control over strategic Singapore and preferred access to the valuable resources of Malaya and the East Indies islands, especially oil, rubber, tin, and the great variety of agricultural products of the Indies. The Philippines and French Indochina, flanking the entrance to the South China Sea, were of secondary strategic and economic importance (coal, hemp, sugar, rice). Siam by comparison was not regarded as essential to Japan's ends, while more remote Burma was distinctly less so.[13]

A primary condition for any Japanese commitment to an imperialistic adventure in the areas bordering the China Sea, with its attendant risk of naval war with both the United States and the United Kingdom, was the neutralization of the highly respected Soviet military power in Eastern Siberia. The Japanese Navy was equally respectful of American and British sea power.[14] This meant that Tokyo must await the appropriate opportunity to act and must take no unnecessary risks, especially so for nonessential objectives like Burma. Hitler's surprise agreement with the Moscow authorities in August, 1939, discouraged Tojo's plans as far as Soviet immobilization was concerned, but it did make Britain and France more ready to acquiesce in Japan's domination of China.

The complete destruction by Germany of French and Dutch power in Europe in the summer of 1940 and the dire threat imposed on Britain after the Dunkirk tragedy opened up a new field of adventure for Japan in Southeast Asia. It also brought the pro-Axis army clique finally into full control at Tokyo. Germany's victory appeared to be so overwhelming that it seemed essential that Japan at once stake out its claims in Southeast Asia. While the crucial air battle raged over England and a force of 5,000 Japanese massed opposite Kowloon, the British in July, 1940, canceled traffic temporarily over the Burma Road.[15] French weakness in Indochina combined with obliging German pressure on the Vichy Government enabled the Japanese to occupy Tonkin and to get French officials elsewhere in Indochina to do Tokyo's bidding. When the Dutch Government in exile proved to be stubbornly

Kai-shek's wartime version of *China's Destiny* (in Chinese) indicated large portions of north Burma within the bounds of China.

[13] *Ibid.*, p. 79; Willard Elsbree, *Japan's Role in Southeast Asia, 1940–1945* (Cambridge, Mass., 1953), pp. 15–17.

[14] Jones, pp. 128, 242, 250–251. [15] *Ibid.*, pp. 114, 124, 155, 163–166.

433

intractable, the Japanese were content to spin out the negotiations awaiting eventual Soviet military involvement in Europe, which came with Hitler's invasion of Russia in June, 1941.

Only when the German invasion of England failed to come off in late 1940 did Tokyo realize that Siam would have to be occupied as a prelude to the essential conquest of Singapore from the land side and as preliminary to the relatively incidental elimination of British control from Burma also. This called for eight months' additional preparation. Tokyo's final decision to take over Southeast Asia even at the risk of war with the United States and Great Britain, and in spite of naval misgivings, came in July, 1941, following Japan's failure in efforts to negotiate with the Dutch for favored economic control over the Indies. Included in the context of this additional and final program of preparation in 1940–1941 were the arrangements made for the collaboration of Thakin Aung San and his youthful associates in the expulsion of British rule from Burma. Prior to 1941, Tokyo evinced little serious interest in Burma,[16] although the possible contingency of invasion certainly was contemplated and planned much earlier.

Japanese gathering of military and political intelligence in Burma dated at least from the middle thirties. Tokyo's efforts to promote cultural contacts got under way with the establishment at Tokyo in 1935 of the nonofficial International Students Institute. U Saw's visit to Japan in 1935, his purchase of the *Sun* newspaper upon his return, presumably in part with Japanese funds, and that newspaper's subsequent publication of Japanese-sponsored propaganda was clearly a part of the program of preparation. Dr. Thein Maung's visit to Japan in the autumn of 1939 and the subsequent vigorously pro-Japanese tone of his newspaper, *New Burma*, thereafter reflected the intensification of Japanese efforts which followed the outbreak of the European war. But prior to late 1940, Japan assumed that resistance by the British from Burma would have only to be neutralized and that Burma need not be militarily occupied. It was anticipated that Russian or German influence would also assist Japan by effectively neutralizing India, which was therefore not included at all in Tokyo's early plans. Japan lacked the forces needed to overrun India if Tokyo was concerned to avoid the risk of overextending its resources outside the Pacific area.[17]

[16] *Ibid.*, pp. 218, 238, 242–246, 351.

[17] Jones, pp. 330, 402. It is noteworthy that Subhas Chandra Bose, the Bengali revolutionary who eventually headed the Japanese-sponsored Indian National Army, fled to Berlin in 1939 and remained there until May, 1943.

The rationalization of Japan's imperialist urge, presented in terms acceptable to both the militarist and the democrat, can be succinctly stated. Alone of all the Asian countries, Japan considered itself capable industrially, governmentally, and militarily of eliminating the centuries-old Western dominance of Eastern Asia. Other peoples of the area, especially those of Southeast Asia, lacked the essential industrial and military elements of national power, which could enable them to survive as truly independent states. It was therefore considered desirable and necessary that East Asian peoples attain deliverance from Western control within the framework of a Co-Prosperity Sphere operating under Japanese protection and direction. Component nations would be "independent" only as parts of the framework established and maintained by imperial Japan. Even this qualified form of independence would have to be deferred for some time, and perhaps indefinitely, in the case of front-line areas such as Burma. The Japanese language would become the *lingua franca* of the Sphere, and the Japanese monetary system would provide the common denominator of credit and exchange. Japanese business and technology would develop the natural resources and promote trade throughout the area.[18]

Tokyo's lack of concern for the territorial integrity of the various states of Southeast Asia was demonstrated in the bribe offer made to Thailand to "restore" to its control Burma's easternmost Shan States and parts of Cambodia. These two proposals were actually carried through by the Japanese. It was to Japan's interest that the aid of Burma nationals be enlisted to destroy British rule, but not that they be stimulated to the point of insisting on maintaining Burma's territorial integrity or of establishing its complete sovereignty as an independent state. Except for Malaya, which would have to be ruled directly, the Japanese planned to govern in most areas through local agencies, even to the extent of utilizing resident French and Dutch assistance in Indochina and the East Indies respectively. The methods to be used and the timing would depend on the circumstances.[19]

The Japanese objective as of late 1941 was to ensure freedom of movement and access to all military resources of the various countries of Southeast Asia, but not to become involved more than necessary in governmental problems. The changeover from military to civilian rule would await the emergence of favorable circumstances locally. Concerted efforts were to be made everywhere to force the economically important overseas Chinese communities in Southeast Asia to shift their

[18] Elsbree, pp. 8–11.   [19] *Ibid.*, pp. 15–17.

435

allegiance from the Kuomintang to the pro-Japanese puppet regime of Nanking. The position of Burma as a front-line area came under special scrutiny by Tokyo in 1942. The Total War Research Institute, a group headed by Premier Tojo himself, recommended that the army retain indefinitely full control over economic activities and transportation facilities in Burma and that the qualified Co-Prosperity Sphere type of "independence" would there be deferred longer than elsewhere. It was also agreed that no liberal or Communist agitation in favor of self-determination would be tolerated and that intellectuals or agitators refusing to be converted from such concepts would have to be wiped out.[20]

Burma was included in the general indoctrination plan sponsored in 1942 by the army-controlled Greater East Asia Ministry, which took over from the Foreign Office the affairs of Southeast Asia. It absorbed the older International Students Institute and, with government funds, began to invite influential political and social figures and able youth to visit Japan. A succession of Burman good-will missions was sent to Japan, and some fifty state scholars were enrolled in Japanese schools. The objective was to spread the vogue of the Japanese language, to afford opportunity for others to catch the Japanese war spirit, to enlist active efforts to realize the Greater East Asia Co-Prosperity Sphere objective, and to educate a select group of youth in needed technical skills. Japan was to become the "light of Asia" and its unquestioned leader in all fields.[21]

This Japanese blueprint for exploiting nationalism for imperialistic ends was both too contradictory and too subtle to be workable. It was based upon the dubious premises that it was Japan's manifest destiny to emancipate and to lead Eastern Asia and that, since the colonial areas lacked the requisite social cohesion and economic foundations for generating really strong popular movements, local nationalist agitation need not be taken very seriously.[22]

The Japanese Conquest

At the outset of their invasion of Burma, the Japanese enjoyed the advantage of the strong tendency of Burmese nationalists to discount heavily the evil things told them by the Chinese about the Japanese. Burmans were attracted particularly by Japan's self-appointed role as

[20] *Ibid.*, pp. 18–24, 26–34.
[21] Jones, pp. 333–337. Some of the Burmese youth were selected from leading families and were virtually hostages in Japan.
[22] Elsbree, pp. 38–41.

liberator of Asia, by her alleged status as a kindred Buddhist country, and by the fascinating combination of military victory and economic achievement. As between the English and the Japanese, most Burman nationalists favored the latter.[23]

It cannot be assumed that the Japanese Government told the non-descript handful of youthful Burman collaborators associated with Thakin Aung San very much concerning their detailed plans for Burma's future role in the Co-Prosperity Sphere. Tokyo did not regard their potential assistance as particularly important. Only two dissident Thakins, Ba Sein and Tun Oke, appear to have enjoyed intimate contact with the Japanese in Burma. Thakin Tun Oke fled to Japan in 1940, and Thakin Ba Sein was apprehended while attempting to flee the country. Thakin Aung San, as has already been indicated, joined up with the Japanese only after his original plan to contact the Communist Chinese ran afoul of the Japanese police at Amoy.

The Japanese adviser-supervisor of the "thirty heroes" who assembled on Hainan Island for training was one Colonel Suzuki (alias Minami), who later became known as *Bo Mogyo* (thunderbolt). The latter name was adapted from a Burmese saying concerning lightning striking the spire of the palace, symbolic of the destruction of British rule.[24] *Bo Mogyo* was also advertised as a son of the late Prince of Myingun returned to liberate the Burmans.[25] The cadre assigned to the task of organizing governmental agencies in the wake of the Japanese army was headed by Thakin Tun Oke, and the group to be associated with recruitment of the Burma Independence Army and direct military aid was headed by Thakin Aung San. Since nearly all of the leaders of the Thakins in Burma were jailed during 1941, preparations on the Burma side for active collaboration were limited prior to the invasion itself.[26] Dr. Ba Maw and Thakin Nu had been jailed prior to Thakin Aung San's initial departure for China.

Exactly what the Japanese promised the "thirty heroes" it is impos-

[23] Thakin Nu, *Burma under the Japanese* (London, 1954), pp. 1–2.

[24] Burma, Intelligence Bureau, *Burma during the Japanese Occupation* (Simla, 1943, 1944), I, 1–3. This is hereafter cited as *BIB*. Another version of the legend was that the spire of the Shwe Dagon was struck by lightning during the British war of 1824, symbolic of the fall of royal power.

[25] Tun Pe, *Sun over Burma* (Rangoon, 1949), pp. 43–44. A Bangkok *pongyi* had allegedly authenticated *Bo Mogyo*'s connections with Burmese royalty. The allegation that the Japanese seriously intended to set up a Burmese prince as puppet monarch in 1942 (*Burma Tribune*, Oct. 4, 1950) apparently lacks substantial confirmation apart from this propaganda rumor.

[26] Nu, *Burma under the Japanese*, p. xxiv; Thein Pe, *What Happened in Burma* (Allahabad, 1943), pp. 24–36.

sible to say. Certainly it included the expulsion of British control and some sort of independence for Burma, for Burman collaboration could have been obtained on no less terms. But there could have been no genuine alliance between groups so unequal in status and in bargaining strength. "Free Burma" must, of course, co-operate in the Japanese military campaign, close the Burma Road into China, and grant to the Japanese broad commercial concessions. It could only hope that it would be able to improve its position after the British were gone.[27]

The principal Japanese attacking force entered Burma in late December, 1941, via the difficult Myawaddy Pass directly east of Moulmein. They overran Tenasserim quickly and encountered their first serious resistance from a holding party at Moulmein. British preparations for Burma's defense were far from adequate. It was believed at Rangoon as late as October that border difficulties of mountainous and jungle terrain would discourage a Japanese invasion, especially in view of Singapore's more vital importance strategically. Re-enforcements promised for Burma after the war began were either diverted to Malaya or simply failed to arrive. British staff organization and intelligence facilities were particularly deficient, and without substantial re-enforcements no counteroffensive was possible. Britain's military resources in 1942 were not unlimited.[28]

Japanese tactics in Burma tended to avoid direct frontal assault along the main routes of travel. They resorted instead to a series of flanking operations which enabled them repeatedly to set up road blocks behind the main British-Indian defense positions and thereby force successive withdrawals. In such operations they were assisted by Burmese guides familiar with the adjacent jungle terrain, while British intelligence concerning such movements were generally lacking. The most important single disaster suffered by the defending British forces occurred at the crossing of the lower Sittang River east of Pegu on February 23, 1942. Here the field commander's recommendation to withdraw promptly to stronger defense positions to the west of the river was overruled at headquarters. Threatening Japanese infiltration forced the early demolition of the only bridge crossing and left ten of twelve British battalions on the left bank. This meant the loss of nearly all the heavy equipment of the units concerned.[29] Once the Japanese cut the main railway and highway routes north of Pegu in

---

[27] Thein Pe, pp. 24–36.   [28] Collis, *Last and First in Burma*, pp. 42–49.
[29] *Ibid.*, pp. 93–96. It is difficult to credit Collis' generous conclusion that no one made a mistake at the Sittang crossing.

438

early March, Rangoon and the entire delta had to be evacuated. A small advance Japanese unit actually cut the road to Prome temporarily prior to General Alexander's withdrawal from Rangoon.[30] Bolstered by the late arrival of an armored division, the British-Indian army together with a few Burmese contingents retreated northward up the main Irrawaddy Valley. The Chinese army, which entered the fighting belatedly in mid-March, undertook to defend the Sittang Valley east of the Pegu Yoma and also the Southern Shan States.[31]

The natural hesitation of the government to give up Rangoon and the awkward problem of moving military supplies ahead of the retreating army along transportation routes already clogged with tens of thousands of refugees, mainly Indians, proved incapable of solution. One of the major tragedies of the evacuation of Lower Burma was the exodus of some 400,000 panic-stricken Indians, many of whom died on the overland route to India.[32] A primary deficiency of the civilian administration was its overlong delay in providing a disciplined and dependable service unit to man the Rangoon docks, which were repeatedly abandoned by Indian coolies following the early Japanese bombings. After the destruction of the Allied air force, including the famous American-led Flying Tiger Corps, the British retreat became a rout. For a time the Chinese army staged a determined stand in the Toungoo area. They also gave effective assistance to the hard-pressed Indian troops in the oil-fields region north of the Pegu Yoma—so belatedly, however, that the British forces barely escaped entrapment.[33] But a Japanese penetration into Burma's Shan plateau from northern Siam brushed aside the Chinese defenders and eventually cut the escape route via Lashio. The entire Chinese army was obliged to break off the fight in the central valley. In retreat, the panic-stricken Chinese forces became an undisciplined rabble.

By the time the rainy season broke in late May, 1942, the Japanese victory was devastatingly complete. British-Indian military prestige

[30] Ibid., pp. 107–113.

[31] Ibid., pp. 84–87, 119. In December, 1941, General Wavell invited a single Chinese army to enter Burma, but the invitation was only halfhearted, since the British would have to supply its needs in large measure. Chiang Kai-shek's failure to co-operate until March, 1941, when the cause was lost, was maddening to both General Stilwell and to the British commanders.

[32] BIB, I, 23–24. A considerable number of Indians took refuge in the heavily Indian-populated Zeyawaddy area in the upper Sittang Valley.

[33] Collis, Last and First in Burma, pp. 139–144. Although General Stilwell was titular commander of the Chinese forces in Burma, he had no effective control since every major order had to be confirmed in Chungking.

had been shattered by an Oriental army both in Malaya and in Burma. The debacle also discredited in British minds their own time-honored conception of their protecting, civilizing, and supervising role in Asia.[34] For the most part the stunned Burmese population took no part in the fighting and were not hostile to the retiring British-Indian forces. The British authorities in Burma had entirely underestimated the ability of the Japanese forces to invade Burma in force.[35] After the border was pierced, the British-Indian forces devised no measures of defense capable of withstanding the Japanese tactics of rear infiltration; once Rangoon was abandoned there was no feasible stopping place or source of supply short of the difficult overland routes to India. Finally Burman nationalist assistance to the invaders, in particular that of the political *pongyis* and the Thakins, was more effective than could have been anticipated, especially since almost all the leaders of the "Freedom Bloc" had been jailed as early as 1940.

The nucleus of the Burma Independence Army was introduced into Burma at Victoria Point and Tavoy in late December, 1941. It was given several hundred rifles, which were to be distributed to Thakin followers as recruitment proceeded. The B.I.A. gathered the rest of its arms along the way. It became inevitably a motley, undisciplined array, officered only by untrained Thakins and including a considerable proportion of criminal riffraff bent on looting and other forms of self-aggrandizement. The basic task of the group was to appoint local governing committees, operating under Thakin leadership and supported by B.I.A. contingents, in communities abandoned by government forces and now in the wake of the Japanese advance.[36] The authorization from the Japanese military under which the B.I.A. units operated was at best very general and not always recognized as authentic locally. All B.I.A. officers appropriated the ancient title *"Bo"* or Colonel. Few of the youth leaders had had previous experience in government or understood their basic tasks. Even the best of them, working under the adverse circumstances, had little chance to succeed. There was much of

---

[34] Collis relates (p. 105) a ghoulish story of the last British evacuées of Government House in Rangoon as they gave vent to their frustration by breaking up the wall portraits of previous British governors of Burma.

[35] Sir Archibald Cochrane, "Burma in Wartime," *Asiatic Review*, XXXVII (1941), 681–694. The ex-governor here reported that Burmese volunteering was good, that government ministers were co-operating, and that the jungle mountains of the Siam frontier were formidable.

[36] *BIB*, I, 4, 23, II, 154–155.

requisitioning, of ordering about, and also of summary punishment.[37]

Following the Japanese capture of Moulmein, a body of several hundred of the B.I.A. proceeded by boat directly across the Gulf of Martaban to the undefended lower reaches of the Irrawaddy delta. There they proceeded to assume control of abandoned major centers of administration in areas unvisited by the Japanese.

The military contingent of the B.I.A. actually joined battle with British forces at several points to the north of Pegu and subsequently in the Irrawaddy Valley across the river and north of Henzada.[38] The Japanese generally discouraged Burman participation in direct hostilities. Their principal role was to act as interpreters and guides, as avenues of intelligence, and as *saboteurs* and arsonists behind the British-Chinese lines. B.I.A. elements also included many political *pongyis*, who were among the most fanatical opponents of the British and Chinese armies not only behind the lines but also in the actual fighting.

The revolutionary Burman nationalists displayed genuine enthusiasm for the triumph of the invaders.[39] Such slogans as "Burma for the Burmans" and "Asia for the Asiatics" carried a powerful appeal which increased in effectiveness as the campaign progressed. At its peak strength the B.I.A. numbered in the neighborhood of 30,000 young men, the majority of them recruited by Thakin leaders through the Student Movement cadres.[40] Thakin Nu describes the initial exultant emotions of the Mandalay Burmese, in 1942, rejoicing over the prospect of freedom, reviving songs of olden times, and mouthing the rumor that *Bo Mogyo* was the son of the Myingun Prince. The mood was quickly dissipated by the abrupt and insulting tactics of the Japanese soldiery.[41]

The Japanese advance into Upper Burma was so rapid that the governmental operations of the B.I.A. failed to keep pace. Many of the regular administrative officials carried on after a fashion for some weeks before they were eventually pushed aside by the officious B.I.A.

[37] Tun Pe, *Sun over Burma*, pp. 23–27. An eyewitness here describes the B.I.A. *"Bos"* at Zawgyi town in 1942, their heads turned by new-found glory and their newly taken wives decked out in looted clothes and expensive jewelry. They punished looters with a rough type of formal justice, but suffered no check in their own thefts. They took too much for granted and were unprepared for inevitable popular rejection.

[38] Notably at Pyinbongyi and Shwegyin in the Pegu area and at Paungde and Shwedaung above Henzada. See *BIB*, I, 3–4.

[39] *Ibid.*, p. 1; Nu, *Burma under the Japanese*, pp. 1–16.

[40] *BIB*, I, 59.   [41] Nu, *Burma under the Japanese*, pp. 20–21.

It was noteworthy that the Japanese prevented the Burmese forces from entering the Shan States at all. The Shan *Sawbwas* took an oath of allegiance directly to the Japanese. As soon as the campaign was over, the Japanese army set up peace commissions of its own to calm the people, to explain Japanese aims, to keep order, and to watch for Burmese disaffection.[42]

The Baho *Administration of 1942*

Within a little more than two weeks after the British evacuation of Rangoon on March 7, 1942, the Japanese commander of the B.I.A., Colonel Suzuki, installed Thakin Tun Oke in the capital as chief administrator of the so-called Burma *Baho* Government. Associated with Thakin Tun Oke in the task of supervising and reducing to a semblance of order the B.I.A. administrative units scattered throughout Lower Burma was Thakin Ba Sein. Thakin Tun Oke's Miscellaneous Order no. 1, dated April 7, affirmed the sole administrative authority of the *Baho* officials and defined administrative procedures along patterns of British rule.[43] Actually the chief administrator's authority extended little beyond the bounds of the capital of Rangoon, itself policed by the Japanese, and his revenue sources were likewise limited to the city.

For several months after the *Baho* regime was installed and until the Japanese military forces were free to intervene, each local B.I.A. governing committee was virtually on its own. By early June the always officious and sometimes thieving and predatory B.I.A. had made itself thoroughly unpopular everywhere.[44] The best of them could do little to stop the orgy of looting and banditry, coupled with the violent settling of old grudges, to which the entire country was subjected during the interregnum.[45] On the occasion of the formation of a Central Administrative Committee at Maymyo on June 4, 1942, General Iida, the Japanese commander in chief, issued an order transmitted through Thakin Aung San forbidding the Burma Independence Army thereafter

---

[42] *BIB*, I, 4, 27.   [43] *Ibid.*, p. 1–3.

[44] Tun Pe, *Sun over Burma*, pp. 26–27, 40. By the early summer of 1942, Burmans were outspokenly anti-B.I.A. and anti-Japanese, saying that the British sucked Burman blood but the Japanese went to the marrow of the bone.

[45] Tun Pe (*ibid.*, pp. 8–9, 24) describes a "night caravan" of looters moving into a town to "harvest" items of value from abandoned homes. From such universal "scrounging," the next step was outright banditry—the lifting of money, watches, jewelry, and pens from travelers held up at gun point.

442

to take any part in politics or to assume any further authority in governmental administration. The circumstances of the selection of this committee will be considered later.

One of the most unfortunate episodes of the misapplication of assumed governmental authority on the part of youthful B.I.A. representatives occurred in the heavily Karen-populated section of Myaungmya District in the western delta. Trouble began during the interregnum when B.I.A. representatives in March, 1942, undertook to collect the guns of members of disbanded Karen regiments, who had begun to return to their homes. To the nationalist B.I.A., the Karens were suspect because of their traditional pro-British alignment and their general unwillingness to accept the legal status of the governing committees sponsored by the B.I.A. Some friction also developed from the failure of the B.I.A. to restrain criminal elements. As the tension increased, Burmans eventually questioned the loyalty of even the Burmese-speaking Buddhist Karens. The impressive presence of Senator Sir San C. Po narrowly averted trouble at Bassein. A *modus vivendi* was also achieved for a time at Myaungmya through B.I.A. co-operation with ex-Minister of Justice Saw Pe Tha. Distrust was nevertheless rampant on both sides. The presence of a dah-wielding *pongyi* among the B.I.A. alarmed the Christian group particularly and revived memories of the communal feud of 1886.

Open strife developed in late May, 1942, within Myaungmya, where areas adjacent to the town were Karen-controlled. Within the town the B.I.A. forces, with the help of Saw Pe Tha, maintained strict police regulations restricting the movement of Karens but not otherwise threatening them. Serious trouble began following the accidental discovery by the B.I.A. of a secret plan initiated unilaterally by a Christian Karen leader, Saw San Po Thin—possessed of more valor than discretion—to precipitate a three-pronged attack on the city intended to "rescue" Saw Pe Tha and other Myaungmya Karens from Burman "oppression." The alarmed Thakin leaders, assuming erroneously that Saw Pe Tha was playing a double game as party to the conspiracy and not waiting to investigate, promptly proceeded to shoot Saw Pe Tha together with his English wife and family and to take other Karens into custody as hostages. Outside influence, including that of Dr. San C. Po, succeeded in persuading two of the proposed attacking columns to abandon the planned "rescue," so that Saw San Po Thin's isolated attack on May 26 was easily repulsed. Thereupon the exasperated Burman

443

leaders initiated a routine program of daily executions. The Catholic Mission headquarters at Myaungmya was burned, and the unarmed inmates of an orphanage were killed.

For several weeks after May 26, batches of Karen hostages, selected by lot, were shot daily. The feud spread to the immediate countryside, where infuriated Karen partisans, assuming that Burman policy was one of deliberate extermination, inflicted atrocities on the Burman population in retaliation. From the Myaungmya center, the trouble spread in varying degrees of intensity throughout the delta area. Such communal strife was equally violent in Karen-inhabited Salween District. The civil war persisted until mid-June, when the vigorous intervention of the Japanese military authorities put an abrupt end to it.[46] A very tense situation persisted even after peace was formally restored.

The tragedy of Myaungmya was that the ill-considered action of a relatively few persons on both sides had opened old wounds and revived mutual distrust, which subsequent efforts of both the Japanese and Dr. Ba Maw's government were unable to dissipate. The explosion at Myaungmya was but the most serious of many evidences of the general inadequacy of the B.I.A. administration and the feeble authority wielded by Tun Oke's *Baho* administration. The Japanese action in suppressing the overassertive B.I.A. control was one of the few popular moves which it initiated during the course of the occupation. It was mainly to counteract conditions of increasing anarchy within the country that the Japanese began preparations in late May, 1942, to reorganize the Burma Government under Dr. Ba Maw's leadership.[47]

In late July, all contingents of the Burma Independence Army were assembled in Rangoon, ostensibly to re-equip and reclothe it. On July 24, the entire force was demobilized, save for a cadre of officers headed by Thakins Aung San and Boh Let Ya, who accepted responsibility for co-operating with the Japanese in the selection of the new Burma Defense Army (B.D.A.). Applicants for re-enlistment were carefully screened, and the 4,000-man B.D.A. was formally installed on August 26. Major General Aung San (so commissioned by the Japanese) was

[46] Morrison, pp. 183–201. Morrison's account has been supplemented by Karen and Burman sources.

[47] *BIB*, II, 39. Only ruthless military suppression by the Japanese halted the orgy of looting and robbery which developed during the interregnum. Government reports covering the first ten months of the completed occupation reported some 8,000 recorded dacoities and around 2,100 murder offenses. In all abandoned premises looters systematically stripped all valuable objects, including not only furniture, but also lighting fixtures and wiring, hinges, locks, and other hardware.

formally in command, but the whole army program operated under strict Japanese military control.

Establishment of Dr. Ba Maw's Provisional Government, 1942

It was demonstrated before the end of the military campaign that ex-Premier Ba Maw was regarded by both sides as a key person. As a refugee following his escape from the Mogok jail, he was the object of search by both the British and the Japanese. Not one of the members of U Saw's ministry remaining behind in Burma [48] could match Dr. Ba Maw's administrative experience, nor did they have any standing with the ultranationalist Thakin and *Wunthanu-pongyi* collaborators who had assisted the Japanese army. Dr. Ba Maw was himself an ardent nationalist, notoriously anti-British, and, if his close association with Dr. Thein Maung of *New Burma* was any criterion, sympathetic with the Japanese liberation program.[49] Dr. Ba Maw's personal vanity and his consuming ambition and covetousness for power made him vulnerable to Japanese blandishments at the outset, even though these same qualities later magnified their difficulties in dealing with him.

The Japanese commander in chief, General Iida, took Dr. Ba Maw into custody as a willing captive at Maymyo in late May, 1942. General Iida asked Dr. Ba Maw to head a new civil administration to restore order and to take the place of the vengeful and sadly mismanaged *Baho* regime.[50] At a conference of political leaders held at Mandalay on May 21, Dr. Ba Maw, in the company of Dr. Thein Maung, took the position that Burma's friend from the East had indeed come to her rescue.[51] In an effort to associate the *Dobama* group with Dr. Ba Maw's proposed leadership, two of the most influential of them, Thakin Nu and Boh Let Ya, were transported from Rangoon to Mandalay in the company of Colonel Suzuki to confer with the former *Anashin* of their prewar Freedom Bloc. On this occasion Dr. Ba Maw feigned disinterest and was annoyingly uncommunicative to Colonel Suzuki, apparently

[48] U Saw was jailed in Africa. U Paw Tun and U Htoon Aung Gyaw fled to India with the governor.

[49] Dr. Ba Maw's limited prewar professional connections as a lawyer with the Japanese dentist and chief spy in Rangoon, Dr. Suzuki, were assumed by some during the war to have established the presumption of his overt collusion with the Japanese. There appears to be no substantial evidence to buttress this charge. It is highly probable, however, that his chief confidant, Dr. Thein Maung, continued in touch with Japanese agents.

[50] Jones, pp. 352–353.   [51] Tun Pe, *Sun over Burma*, pp. 14–15, 31.

in a calculated maneuver to maintain face before the Japanese officer.[52]

An arrangement was finally concluded with General Iida at Maymyo on June 4 to form a coalition Preparatory Committee, partly *dhama* (Ba Maw's following) and partly Thakin, to set up a central governmental administration for Burma that would displace the demoralized *Baho* regime, floundering as it was in a morass of recrimination.[53] For reasons which will be reviewed later, both the *Baho* leadership and other leading Thakins such as Nu, Than Tun, and Mya, not previously associated with the Japanese, participated in the deliberations of the committee. U Ba Pe was brought from Shwebo to Maymyo as another potential participant,[54] but he consistently refused throughout the occupation to work with the Japanese. Most of the committee members saw little choice but to accede for the time being to the Japanese proposals, since refusal to co-operate would make them personally suspect. The Japanese spokesmen made it clear from the outset that the primary function of the provisional government would be to mobilize the resources of Burma in support of military victory and to ensure perpetual friendship between the two countries. Since independence could not be granted during wartime, the proposed Burmese Government would be subordinate to Japanese military authorities. Eventually full independence would be accorded within the framework of the Japan-sponsored Greater East Asia Co-Prosperity Sphere.[55]

For Burman nationalist participants, the arrangement provided at best a humiliating and unwelcome role. The initial session of the committee broke up in disagreement, mainly because Japanese specifications accorded them so little leeway.[56] Dr. Ba Maw's personal following fell in line quickly, along with a reputable element of the *Sangha*. Unsophisticated *Sayadaws,* such as the one at Maymyo, reportedly accepted without question the current propaganda representation that the Japanese had entered Burma at Thakin Aung San's request to drive out the British and to give freedom to Burma.[57] Dr. Ba Maw's followers as well as the *Baho* leaders developed in time a positive stake in a Japanese victory. It was Bandoola U Sein and Dr. Thein Maung whom Dr. Ba Maw first selected to publicize the "Trust Japan" program throughout Upper Burma.

[52] Nu, *Burma under the Japanese*, p. 27.   [53] *Ibid.,* pp. 23–24.
[54] *Ibid.,* p. 31. U Nu describes U Ba Pe's bewilderment upon his arrival at Maymyo and his despairing remark: "Burma is dead."
[55] *BIB,* I, 5–6.   [56] Nu, *Burma under the Japanese*, p. 25.
[57] Tun Pe, *Sun over Burma*, pp. 10–11.

The executive administration as finally installed on August 1, 1942, included five followers of Dr. Ba Maw (Dr. Thein Maung, finance; Bandoola U Sein, reconstruction and public works; U Tun Aung, justice; U Ba Win, education and health; Saw Hla Pe, information, commerce, and industry). The other posts were held by two carry-overs from the *Baho* regime (Thakins Tun Oke, forests, and Ba Sein, labor), plus two of the regular-line Thakins (Mya, minister without portfolio, and Than Tun, agriculture).

The Thakin group was miffed because they shared very meagerly in the 120 major governmental appointments subsequently made by Dr. Ba Maw, and the leaders talked for a time about resigning in protest. Thakin Nu was omitted from the list of ministers at his own request. He became during the ensuing year the general secretary of the combined *Dobama-Sinyetha* Party, which Thakin Mya was mainly instrumental in organizing. The party was definitely not a Japanese idea. It included the nucleus of the mass organizations of labor and peasant groups which the leftist Thakins had previously sponsored.[58] Some of the Marxists, such as Thakins Kyaw Nyein and Ba Hein, eventually abandoned their original antifascist scruples and participated in the Ba Maw regime. Only the all-out pro-Russian Communists, Thakins Thein Pe and Soe, followed strictly the Moscow-inspired policy of no co-operation whatever with the fascist Japanese. Thakin Thein Pe fled to India, and Soe went underground in the delta area and maintained guerrilla resistance against the Japanese throughout the course of the occupation.

As a closely knit group with common objectives, sharing each other's confidence although differing in opinion as to tactics, the high-level Thakin leaders emerged as an effective political group. Thakins Mya and Nu in particular enjoyed the confidence of Dr. Ba Maw and were influential in promoting the *Dobama-Sinyetha* Party; Thakin Than Tun demonstrated intelligence combined with an unusual degree of dedication and administrative capacity; Thakin Aung San, as head of the Burma Defense Army, was a young man of unquestioned integrity, an intimate friend of Thakin Nu since the university strike of 1936 and brother-in-law of Thakin Than Tun. Thakins Mya and Than Tun had been associated from prewar times in the promoting of associations of cultivators, and they resumed such activity during the war. Because of personal defections and the fact that many Thakins resented what

[58] Nu, *Burma under the Japanese*, pp. 1–16, 38.

447

they regarded as the too-close identification of their leaders with Dr. Ba Maw's regime, the *Dobama Asiayone* as such practically disintegrated during the course of the occupation.[59]

The concerted attempt made by Dr. Ba Maw after August, 1942, as head of the executive administration to recall to their former posts all the regular administrative officials aroused considerable resentment among the ousted *Baho* civilian agencies. Also disgruntled were the disbanded Burma Independence Army personnel. The disaffected elements were eventually mollified by the putting of old officials on three months' probation and by the assignment of party representatives to act as political watchers at every administrative center. Usually a Ba Maw follower and a Thakin-B.I.A. member were jointly assigned.[60] This kind of political interference contributed to the eventual demoralization of virtually all routine administrative services.

Burman-Japanese Relations, 1942–1943

Before the conquest of Burma by the Japanese forces had been concluded, most Burmans who had made contact with the invaders, including the more responsible leaders of the B.I.A., had become very much disillusioned about Japan's promises of independence for Burma. Thakin Nu and other nationalists toyed with the idea of joining up with the Chinese.[61] When the retreating Chinese forces became hopelessly demoralized, some Thakins had actually attempted to contact the retiring British forces in the Arakan area. Thakin Thein Pe from India publicized what appeared at the time to be a most improbable story of concerted Burman nationalist opposition to the Japanese. The political situation was very confused.[62]

The Burmese population generally had abundant reasons for disliking the Japanese. Instead of welcoming Burmese efforts to establish friendly relations, Japanese commanders committed the uncalled-for insult of slapping the faces of village elders and officials even up to the level of the *Kayaingwun* or district commissioner. It mattered little that Japanese underlings were treated by their officers in the same disre-

[59] *Ibid.*, pp. 81–87.

[60] *Ibid.*, pp. 43–44; *BIB*, I, 32–33. The *dhama* member was usually the local political chief, and a Thakin nominee served as his secretary.

[61] Nu tells (pp. 1–16) of the release of Thakins from the Mandalay jail by Chinese friends and their tentative agreement to proceed to China until the plan was thwarted by the Japanese cutting of the Lashio road.

[62] Thein Pe, *What Happened in Burma*. In January, 1942, the British proscribed the entire Thakin Party as treasonous. See *PD,C,* vol. 378 (March 19, 1942), p. 1641.

spectful manner. The military authorities also conscripted Burmans and Karens for menial labor service; they requisitioned rice and killed the peasants' cattle for food. Booted Japanese soldiers occupied *pongyi kyaungs* and used the sacred precincts for latrines and for slaughtering purposes. They employed monks' robes to bind the feet of their horses, used monastery altars for drying clothes, and sometimes destroyed images and scriptural scrolls. Burmese *pongyis* themselves were disdained by the Japanese as overnumerous and generally useless idlers. Japanese practices of forced inoculation at railway stations and road blocks contributed to public resentment.

But the acme of Burmese revulsion was reserved for the actions of the ruthless *kempetai* (military police) and their renegade informers. The military police operated as a law to themselves. They enlisted spies to serve them and were completely devoid of humanitarian sensibilities in their treatment of arrested victims.[63] One of the reasons for the willingness of leading Thakins to participate in Ba Maw's government was that it provided a partial cover from the *kempetai* for themselves and for their friends.[64] The ordinary Burman enjoyed no such privileged status. Many learned to speak the Japanese language in order to facilitate their communication with the dreaded Japanese military authorities. Japanese officers themselves acted as *agents provocateurs,* while political enemies of Dr. Ba Maw and the Thakins frequently turned Japanese informers in order to gratify personal antagonisms and resentments. Notorious among those ready to serve the Japanese were the hireling police, who allegedly hobnobbed as with new-found military friends.[65]

Efforts of the Japanese authorities to re-establish themselves in the regard of the people were notoriously ineffective. Shortly after the occupation of Rangoon, *Bo Mogyo* received visitors on the Shwe Dagon platform. A Japanese attempt, made in October, 1942, to sponsor a United *Pongyi* Association for the purpose of promoting co-operation with Japan's program and purging its enemies, died a-borning. The derogatory implication of the Japanese proposal that the new association would "carry out a positive religious program of benefit to the Burmese people" was not lost upon the *Sangha.*[66] In July, 1943, the

[63] *BIB,* I, 14–15, 28–29, II, 31; Tun Pe, p. 42.

[64] Nu, *Burma under the Japanese,* pp. 51–53. Thakin San We was assigned to the *kempetai* headquarters, while Thakins Chit and Hla Maung kept actively busy getting their friends out of difficulty.

[65] *Ibid.,* pp. 56–57; Tun Pe, pp. 10, 12, 41–42.

[66] *BIB,* I, 14–16, 28–29. General Aung San at this juncture agreed, in general,

Japanese tried again to revitalize their prewar reputation as a Buddhist country by convening a Greater East Asia Buddhist Conference at Tokyo, dedicated to the promotion of cultural, philanthropic, and social ends. To tie Burma into the project the local Japanese authorities collected what were alleged to be treasured *dattaw* Buddhist relics, miraculously multiplied, to enshrine in a Japanese replica of the Botataung pagoda of Rangoon, which had been destroyed by Allied bombing.[67] Burman Buddhists exhibited no enthusiasm for promoting a pilgrimage shrine in Japan.

Two other projects sponsored by the Japanese were somewhat more successful than their misguided efforts to ingratiate themselves religiously. One which had limited relevance only was the protection and encouragement afforded to the delta Karens by the Japanese military following the Myaungmya incident. The Japanese-sponsored Karen associations were essentially anti-Burman and pro-Japanese. The Karens were particularly attracted by the results shown in a kind of rough census taken by the Japanese, which more than doubled the previously calculated size of the Karen population. The pro-Japanese *rapprochement* on the part of the Karens tended in many instances to take the place of the prewar British-Karen alliance. Substantial Karen leaders such as Bassein's Dr. San C. Po co-operated with the Japanese efforts at pacification and also in curbing pro-British activities among the Karens. Many Karen girls volunteered to serve as nurses in the army hospitals.

Partly to counteract growing Japanese influence among the Karens, Dr. Ba Maw in 1943 sponsored a rival Karen Center Organization or Board headed by Saw Ba Maung. Dr. Ba Maw utilized Saw Hla Pe, the then minister of forests, as cabinet liaison. Beginning in 1944, the budding Antifascist League sponsored a third organization of Karen youth utilizing as leader Saw San Po Thin, who had previously harbored parachutists and whose misguided planning had precipitated the tragic Myaungmya affair. The Communist Than Tun was apparently one of the most influential Burman proponents of Karen reconciliation.[68] But neither the overt efforts of Dr. Ba Maw nor the covert approaches of the anti-Japanese conspiracy accomplished much to

---

with the Japanese indictment that the *pongyis* were overnumerous and frequently useless.

[67] *BIB,* II, 110–113. The *dattaw* were reported to have been carried to Japan by Dr. Ba Han on his visit of May, 1944.

[68] J. S. Furnivall, "Twilight in Burma: Independence and After," *Pacific Affairs,* XXII (1949), 161.

dispel the deep-seated Karen distrust of the Burmans. Many Karens were obviously predisposed to accept any affiliation which seemed to contribute a measure of security.

By far the most popular Japanese-sponsored organization was the apolitical East Asia Youth League. Its popularity was due in part to the fact that it developed under the leadership of U Ba Gyan and other Judson College graduates [69] who were familiar with the rural reconstruction program of social service as developed by Professor J. R. Andrus and elsewhere by U Ba Lwin, principal of the Myoma High School of Rangoon. The league was actually an essentially indigenous rather than Japanese undertaking. It was started on June 28, 1942, and was financed from the outset by Burmese philanthropy. It concerned itself with such matters as safety shelters, sanitation measures, and library and educational activities and with the general mobilization of the youth of Burma for constructive nonpolitical objectives. Dr. Ba Maw was at first more or less indifferent to the program, but later became somewhat jealous of the popularity of the league. Eventually he tried unsuccessfully to absorb it into his own official National Service Association (*Myanma Wunthanu Aphwe*), or Circle Army, launched in December, 1942.[70]

The East Asia Youth League included Indians, Karens, Mons, and Shans, as well as Burmans. The attitude of the Thakin leaders toward it was indicated by Thakin Nu's frank deprecation of its avoidance of political activity and its expenditure of time and effort in social service activities. The league was not antagonistic to the Burmese Government, but it refused to be swallowed up by it. It was one of the few popular movements from which the Japanese sponsors realized public appreciation. The league eventually affiliated in late 1944 with the Thakin-sponsored resistance effort and thereby contributed an important element of popular support to the budding Antifascist People's Freedom League (A.F.P.F.L.).[71]

The clear trend of Burmese opinion throughout 1942 was strongly anti-Japanese. The personal indignities suffered, outraged religious

[69] Ko Ba Gyan, Hla Maung, and Ba Shin were three Judson College leaders. Others were U Kyaw Myint, U Zaw Weik, and U Tun Hla.

[70] Dr. Ba Maw's "Circle Army" or *Wa Tat* was based on a Burmese legend according to which a magician astrologer demonstrated his superiority over the king by drawing a circle which multiplied itself in spite of royal efforts to erase it. The circles of service units should likewise magically multiply. The idea was cleverly conceived, but the needed spirit was lacking.

[71] Nu, *Burma under the Japanese*, pp. 86–87; also personal testimony from East Asia Youth League leaders.

451

sensibilities, and arbitrary exactions in the form of goods and labor services were all added to dire economic distress and to the virtually unanimous skepticism concerning Japanese promises of independence for Burma. Despite the government's ameliorative efforts and the success of Thakins Mya and Nu in amalgamating the *Dobama-Sinyetha* political factions, the executive administration came to share the growing popular hostility to the Japanese.[72] The official denunciation of all political opposition to the executive agencies as treason and Dr. Ba Maw's affirmation of "One Party, One Blood, One Voice, One Command!" were completely uninspiring especially when the voice and command seemed always to carry a Japanese accent. Efforts of the *Dobama-Sinyetha* leaders to capture popular imagination by transferring to Rangoon some of the "Soil of Victory" from Shwebo, home of the Alaungpaya dynasty, and by devising and raising a Burmese national flag encountered either sharp Japanese discouragement or flat veto.[73]

One of the most convincing of Dr. Ba Maw's efforts to conciliate responsible Burman opinion was his appointment to the Supreme Court in February, 1943, of such reputable men as U Mya Bu, U Ba U, U Maung Gyee, and U Myint.[74] But this worthy move was of no political consequence in comparison with the contemporary Japanese requirement that a 30,000-man labor force be recruited from Lower Burman districts to help construct the new Siam-Burma Railway.[75] All the sincere efforts of Thakin Mya and Labor Minister Ba Sein, who were sent by Dr. Ba Maw to examine working conditions and to provide amenities and inspectors at the Burman end of the railway line, did little to lessen popular resentment against this meagerly disguised form of slavery. Thousands of Burmans as well as European prisoners died working on this project.[76]

Thus despite the endeavors of the Burmese administration to alleviate popular dislike of the Japanese and to enlist confidence, it was clearly apparent by the first month of 1943 that Burmans could never

---

[72] *BIB,* I, 7–8, 47. Burma's rice surplus was not salable after 1942. Cattle disease began in 1943 to take a dreadful toll.

[73] *BIB,* II, 150. On December 2, 1942, some "Victory Soil" was deposited by Ba Maw near Rangoon's Royal Lakes, and in it was to be planted the tree symbolizing the Burman kings' rule over the Zambudipa ("Southern Island") of Hindu cosmology. The Japanese preferred erecting a "Heroes' Shrine" commemorating those who died in the three Anglo-Burmese wars.

[74] *BIB,* I, 40.   [75] *Ibid.,* pp. 49–50; Jones, p. 355.

[76] *BIB,* I, 49. Thakins Ba Sein and Mya made an on-the-spot investigation of conditions at Thanbyuzayat, headquarters for the Burma labor force.

be persuaded to support Japan's military effort unless they were given a more tangible stake in a Japanese victory. A liaison conference held at Tokyo in early January decided on independence for Burma and the Philippines. On January 22, 1943, Premier Tojo announced to his House of Representatives that Japan's aim was independence for Burma (as well as for the Philippines), and on January 28, he promised Burma independence within a year.[77] Japan here played its trump cards early in the game. On March 11, Dr. Ba Maw and his pro-Japanese confidant, Dr. Thein Maung, accompanied by Thakins Mya and Aung San departed for Tokyo to confer regarding the circumstances which would attend Burma's advance to independent status. All four of the visitors were decorated by the Japanese Government.[78] U Kyaw Nyein accompanied Dr. Ba Maw as personal secretary. While the group was at Tokyo, Premier Tojo told them that, as a condition of the grant of independence, Burma would have to declare war on Britain and the United States.[79]

"Independent" Burma Allied with Japan, 1943–1944

Although Japan's offer of independence to Burma was never entirely convincing, it certainly had the effect of stimulating collaboration and of bringing to the support of the government an impressive array of responsible Burmese leadership. Upon Dr. Ba Maw's return from Japan in April, 1943, he sponsored his famous "Four Armies" combination. These were the Blood Army (the fighting forces), the National Service Association (Circle) Army, the Leadership (Political *Dobama-Sinyetha*) Army, and the Sweat Army (Labor Corps or *Let Yon Tat*).[80] None of the proposed collaborationist services was new, but the aura of patriotic endeavor was now thrown around them; the clear implication was that only as Burmans contributed to the Japanese victory would the promised freedom become a reality. The failure of the British-Indian attack on the Akyab front in the spring of 1943 and the refusal of London to offer any comparable

[77] Jones, p. 353. [78] *BIB*, I, 9; New York *Times*, March 31, 1943.
[79] Jones, pp. 353–354.
[80] *BIB*, II, 133–137. The *Wa Tat* or Circle Army, originally conceived in December, 1942, as an agency of voluntary civilian service, was now made into a bureau of the government, with Bandoola U Sein serving as head of a central advisory council. The East Asia Youth League refused at first to be absorbed into the *Wa Tat*. The Labor Corps, or *Let Yon Tat*, was recruited by assigning quotas to headmen in the traditional Burmese fashion and with the customary favoritism. Recruits constructed buildings, roads, and revetments, as well as railways. They were paid meagerly in accordance with their skills.

promise of postwar independence for Burma buttressed the feeling that Burmans had nothing to lose by trying to make the best of the ostensible opportunity afforded by Tokyo. There was no dearth of political candidates for membership on the Preparatory Committee, although by no means all of those actually selected were enthusiastic.[81]

On May 8, 1943, the names of the Burma Independence Preparatory Committee were announced. To the dozen or so members of the executive administration were now added six respected political leaders of widely varying views: U Chit Hlaing, U Set, Thakin Kodaw Hmaing, Thakin Nu, U Aye, and Dr. San C Po. The list also included the former solicitor general, U Thein Maung, two Burmans representing commerce and industry (U Mya of Yamethin and U Aye Maung of the Burmese Chamber of Commerce), plus the editor U Tun Pe. The committee was an impressive array of talent, even though it operated under strict Japanese supervision in its appointed task. Dr. Ba Maw acted as chairman. The sessions of the Preparatory Committee were secret, and the records of its proceedings were destroyed.[82] According to Dr. Ba Maw's postwar testimony, the Japanese adviser of the committee, Colonel Ishamira, actually drafted Burma's declaration of independence and the alliance treaty with Japan, plus a secret military agreement requiring of Burma full co-operation in promotion of military aims and permitting Japanese nullification of any governmental action of which they disapproved.[83]

In July, 1943, Dr. Ba Maw and Thakin Nu journeyed to Singapore, where they met Premier Tojo and the Bengali revolutionary Subhas Chandra Bose, who had just been delivered to Penang Island in June by a German submarine. He was designated to become the leader of the Indian National Army to assist Japan in conquering India. At Singapore it was made clear that "independent" Burma would be used as a base for the prospective Japanese–Indian National Army invasion of India. Dr. Ba Maw took advantage of the meeting to protest to Premier Tojo the overbearing attitude of the Japanese army authorities in Burma. Tojo promised that civilian advisers would be sent and that the army would thereafter respect Burmese opinion.[84] Prior to the meeting at Singapore, Premier Tojo had announced at Bangkok on July 4, 1943, that the easternmost Shan States of Keng-

---

[81] Nu, *Burma under the Japanese*, p. 62; Hinners, p. 161.

[82] Tun Pe, *Sun over Burma*, p. 70.   [83] Jones, p. 354.

[84] Elsbree, pp. 58–60. The need to do something to enlist Burmese co-operation was so obvious that the local armed forces raised little objection to Tokyo's decision. See also Jones, pp. 354–355.

tung and Mongpan had been given by Japan to Thailand; the Burmans were not consulted at all.[85] On July 26, Tokyo's special envoy and ambassador to Burma, Renzo Zawada, arrived in Rangoon.

On August 1, 1943, the Japanese military administration for Burma was formally dissolved and Burma's independence was solemnly proclaimed. The eventful ceremony was followed by Burma's declaration of war against the United Kingdom and the United States and by the reading of the terms of the Burma's Treaty of Alliance with Japan pledging co-operation in the war and in building the Greater East Asia Co-Prosperity Sphere. Tokyo's radio labored the point that the latter action was taken entirely on the initiative of the independent Burmese authorities.[86]

The sessions of the Independence Preparatory Committee were characterized by persistent but largely futile efforts of several democratic-minded members, led by U Thein Maung, to preserve as much as possible of the traditions of liberal government. About all U Thein Maung accomplished was the provision for a popularly elected legislature at some future date, and the statement in Article 3 of the constitution that the powers and authority of government were derived from the people. This article constituted a repudiation of the monarchial authority, whether British or Burmese, even though the alleged popular sovereignty was to be exercised in accordance with subsequent provisions of the instrument. The committee also witnessed the irrevocable break between the *Baho* faction, led by Thakins Ba Sein and Tun Oke, and Dr. Ba Maw's leadership. In an effort to block Dr. Ba Maw's elevation to dictatorial control, Thakins Ba Sein and Tun Oke had advocated a return to monarchy and were accordingly dropped, at Dr. Ba Maw's insistence, from the new list of ministers. Because of their persistent opposition to Dr. Ba Maw they were subsequently taken into custody by the Japanese and transported to Malaya and then Indonesia for the duration of the war. The rift was effectively camouflaged by the announcement that the two were being sent as ambassadors to China and Manchukuo respectively.

Opposition tendencies within the Preparatory Committee were curbed by careful Japanese surveillance of the sessions of the committee and by occasional overt interference.[87] The committee did ob-

[85] *BIB*, I, 27, II, 78–79.

[86] *BIB*, I, 9–11. S. C. Bose attended the ceremonies of August 1, 1943, as Dr. Ba Maw's guest.

[87] Hinners, p. 161; Nu, *Burma under the Japanese*, p. 62. On one occasion General Kawabe intervened actively.

tain modification of the original Japanese assertion, as of March, 1942, of their priority claims for ten years or more on all British properties in oil, timber, minerals, and other natural resources. The committee insisted that all abandoned lands revert to Burman ownership unconditionally along with all other natural resources, transport facilities, and buildings and grounds as well, subject only to Japanese lease, rent free, during the war of items needed by the military. The Japanese finally agreed, except only with respect to the matter of oil.[88]

The constitution as drafted by the committee was essentially fascist and Japanese in character. Dr. Ba Maw as head of the state (*Naing-gandaw Adipadi*) was accorded "full sovereign status and powers" (Article 4). As such he appointed both the cabinet and genro-type privy council of elder statesmen. The requirement that the *Adipadi* consult the Prime Minister in making these appointments was meaningless because Ba Maw himself occupied both offices. The cabinet was responsible to the *Adipadi,* and the privy council functioning as an advisory body had to be consulted only on such matters as constitutional changes, budget, taxation, national loans, and treaties. Legislation was to be passed by the sovereign *Adipadi,* after his discretionary consultation with his ministers and the privy council. The constitution made tentative reference to the eventual calling of a representative Constituent Assembly and provided that the cabinet and privy council should elect a successor to the *Adipadi* whenever a vacancy occurred. The oath taken by all government officials was that of loyalty to the people of Burma and to the *Anashin Adipadi,* or dictator head of state. In practice, whether by design or not, the governmental system gravitated in the direction of royalty. Before the end of 1943, the *Adipadi* was referred to by the additional title of *Anashin Mingyi Kodaw,* or king.[89]

The cabinet which took over on August 1, 1943, included the following: Dr. Ba Maw as Prime Minister; Thakin Mya as Deputy Prime Minister; U Ba Win (home affairs); Thakin Nu (foreign affairs); Dr. Thein Maung (finance), to be replaced later by U Set after Dr. Thein Maung was selected for the key post of Burmese ambassador to Tokyo; General Aung San (defense); U Thein Maung (justice); U Hla Min (education and health); Thakin Than Tun (agriculture, later trans-

[88] *BIB,* I, 3. The original declaration was made by *Bo Mogyo* on March 23, 1942 (II, 6–7). The chorus of the *Dobama* song was made the national anthem of Burma.

[89] *BIB,* II, 10–14, 247.

port); U Mya of Yamethin (commerce and industry); Thakin Lay Maung (communications and irrigation); Bandoola U Sein (welfare and publicity); U Tun Aung (co-operation with the Japanese); Thakin Lun Baw (ex-member of the House of Representatives, as public works recovery minister). Although the cabinet, with a few exceptions only (U Set, U Thein Maung, and U Mya), was composed exclusively of *Dobama-Sinyetha* partisans (minus Thakins Tun Oke and Ba Sein), virtually all other political groups were represented in the twenty privy council posts. The council included five ex-senators, five ex-members of the House of Representatives, the former Speaker U Chit Hlaing, and the elderly *Dobama* patron, Thakin Kodaw Hmaing, plus one ex-minister, two editors, and five ex-officials and businessmen.[90]

The powers of Dr. Maw's regime were so narrowly circumscribed in all matters relating to the conduct of the war that some nationalists like Thakin Kodaw Hmaing doubted the wisdom of the decision of the younger Thakins to accept office.[91] Dr. Ba Maw himself postponed the formal celebration of the recognition of Burma's independence until September 25, 1943, when the Japanese made good their commitment to cede to Burma all of the Shan States except Kengtung and Mongpan, which had previously been accorded to Thailand.[92] Some of the cabinet ministers under the new scheme took responsibility for routine administrative duties and procedures, which gave to the younger members considerable experience in governing. One of the perennial problems was the resentment demonstrated by civil service officials over the interference locally by political representatives of the so-called Leadership Army. A four-day conference including the deputy commissioners (*Kayaingwuns*) of eighteen Upper Burma districts was staged in October, 1943, to iron out disciplinary procedures and difficulties of official-politician relations.[93]

The burden of propagandizing for support of the war effort fell mainly on Premier Ba Maw and his immediate followers, especially Bandoola U Sein. Dr. Thein Maung took over the important liaison connection with Tokyo as Burma's ambassador to Japan. The Thakins

[90] Nu, *Burma under the Japanese*, pp. 10–12.

[91] *Ibid.*, p. 127. Thakin Kodaw Hmaing, a venerable author who was sixty-six years old in 1943, accused the younger Thakins of sacrificing their principles for office. He had been a lecturer in the National College of 1920.

[92] United States, Office of Strategic Services, *Japanese Administration of Burma* (Washington, 1944), p. 30.

[93] *Ibid.*, p. 27.

endeavored for the most part to build up their political organization without compromising themselves overmuch with Japanese propaganda. Particularly successful in this respect were General Aung San as head of the Burma Defense Army and Thakins Than Tun and Mya in promoting peasant and worker organizations. Thakin Nu did participate in the propaganda program, however. From both the administrative and the political points of view, the government of "independent Burma" was something more than a puppet affair, how much so will be examined later.

The Burmese People and the Occupation

Although the Japanese authorities undertook with a measure of success to correct some of the early mistakes of 1942 which had alienated the Burmese people, such efforts were more than offset by an accumulation of economic grievances affecting all areas of the country and Lower Burma especially. The basic cause was the disruption of trade channels both internally and overseas. The Japanese army took over all large river-transport and railway equipment, leaving only a few freight cars for civilian use. It also stripped the rails from many double-track lines in order to find materials for the new Thanbyuzayat road into Siam. The basic food needs of the people—rice, fish, salt, cooking oil—were therefore badly distributed. The Japanese decision to divert Upper Burma sesamum cooking oil to lubrication purposes left Lower Burma painfully short of this essential item of food. The price of oil at Rangoon multiplied thirteen times. Even in normal times, Burma had been short of cooking oils. The breakdown of overseas trade left Lower Burma with a surplus of some 3 million tons of unsalable rice, an unremediable situation which plunged Lower Burma into economic stagnation.[94]

Equally tragic for the cultivators was the loss of one-third to one-half of the draught cattle population due in part to epidemic diseases (principally rinderpest) and in part to Japanese cattle requisitions for transport purposes as well as for beef and leather. Even after the close of the war in 1945, the Burma rice crop was only some 42 per cent of normal largely because of the cattle shortage. The failure of the Japanese to import into Burma adequate amounts of consumer goods, especially cloth, to match the enormous issue of military cur-

[94] The Japanese took out 200,000 tons of rice in 1942. The government in early 1943 undertook to purchase some 52 million baskets, a year's supply, but it lacked the means (BIB, II, 59–62, 68–71, 176).

rency stimulated price inflation at a time when paddy farmers were living by subsistence agriculture. Many Lower Burma cultivators had no alternative other than to seek employment either in Dr. Ba Maw's Sweat Army (*Let Yon Tat*) or in the Japanese army labor battalions, the *Heiho Tat*.

Another series of grievances developed in the field of business opportunity. War contractors preyed on the people, and a swarm of Japanese business and manufacturing interests invaded the country.[95] Most of them were concerned with army procurement and therefore paid no taxes to the government. This situation made fairly clear what Burma's proposed independence within the Co-Prosperity Sphere would mean for the future business opportunities of the Burmans. The supreme Japanese economic adviser, Ogawa, who arrived in early 1944, was considered hopelessly impractical.

Only two of the economic aspects of the occupation were in any way favorable to Burman interests. One was the fact that Japanese efforts to promote economic self-sufficiency and to train Burmese state scholars in Japan in such fields as banking, engineering, and industrial management suggested ways in which Burman economy could be strengthened by diversification and educational preparation could be broadened.[96] The other favorable factor was that Upper Burma cultivators, who were relatively prosperous because of their diversified output, were able to pay off accumulated debts in cheap Japanese currency. The promise of eventual relief to Lower Burma debtor peasants as a result of the evacuation of their Chettyar creditors and absentee landlords was of no help immediately. An enormous amount of paddy land (estimated at 2 million acres) went out of production and reverted to semijungle.

The efforts of the Burmese Government to alleviate economic suffering, although ineffective on the whole, were sufficiently vigorous in the field of agriculture to leave behind the impression that the minister

[95] *BIB*, II, 218–222. The names of fifty-five Japanese firms doing business in Burma in wartime are listed. They covered all aspects of economic activity. Some of them, such as the Mitsui Bussan Kaisha, engaged in a dozen or more lines. Even so, the Japanese firms were somewhat less active in Burma than elsewhere in Southeast Asia probably because the eventual severance of overseas contact made economic operations unprofitable.

[96] United States, Office of Strategic Services, *Japanese Use of Burma's Industry* (Washington, 1945), pp. 1–8, 13, 65. The Japanese set up a central bank in January, 1944, in an effort to mobilize local savings. Japanese firms in Burma manufactured many items previously imported and in 1944–1945 sponsored a bold effort to expand cotton cultivation and cloth manufacture.

of agriculture, Thakin Than Tun, was sincerely concerned.[97] All land revenues for 1942 were remitted, and paddy-land rents were reduced by half. An effort was also made to train managers of co-operatives, to introduce co-operative farm credits and cultivation, to redistribute land, to diversify crops, and otherwise to implement the prewar agrarian reform program.[98] Near the end of the war, Thakin Than Tun shifted his efforts to the even more difficult transportation problem, again with fairly impressive results. By 1945, no wartime cabinet minister, except possibly Deputy Prime Minister Thakin Mya, matched U Than Tun's reputation for administrative ability and integrity. Dr. Ba Maw interposed his influence on numerous occasions to shield his countrymen from excessive Japanese exactions, but such actions, if known at all to the people generally, were more than overbalanced by his persistent trumpeting of Japanese propaganda and his active involvement in the Japanese war procurement program.[99]

[97] Nu, *Burma under the Japanese,* p. 85. Nu pays tribute to Thakin Than Tun for demonstrating brains, drive, and all-round administrative ability.

[98] *BIB,* I, 47–49, 114–119.

[99] For a succinct summary of Burma's economic grievances during the Japanese occupation, see Maung Ba Han, *The Planned State* (Rangoon, 1947), Appendix A, entitled "Interim Report of the Burma Special Research Commission," pp. iv–xvi.

XIV

"Independent Burma"
in Wartime

THE final twenty months of the Japanese occupation of Burma featured the role of *Adipadi* Dr. Ba Maw and his Thakin associates in the government. It also witnessed the all-out attempt of the Japanese to invade India using Burma as a base. Finally came the emergence of the Thakin-sponsored Antifascist League, to resist, in cooperation with the returning Allied forces under General Mountbatten, continued Japanese control.

The Role of Adipadi Ba Maw, 1943–1945

The structural organization of the "independent" Burmese administration of 1943 was basically the same as in British times, although with several differences. The most noteworthy change was the presence of Japanese advisers for every important civilian office and the requirement that they be consulted regarding all important decisions. Behind the façade of governmental forms, Japanese control of both political and economic spheres was real, except in minor routine matters. Japanese officials censored both the press and the radio. Even the Supreme Court was subordinate to Japanese military courts in all matters affecting Japanese personnel and general security. A second change from British times was the revival of traditional Burmese terminology. All Burman military leaders of any consequence and many of no consequence at all assumed the title *"Bo"* (Colonel); the head commander became *"Bogyoke."* The district commissioners were called *Kayaingwuns;* the district superintendent of police became the *Ye Boh Hmee;* a Class II revenue official became the *Akunwun.* The seven divisional commissionships of British times were at first abolished and later revived in the form of four regional viceroys. Village headmen, now called *Okkitas,* were assisted by *thamadi* assessors. A final major change was the presence of political party "observers" called *gaung saungs,* at all levels of district administration. The Public Service Commission was headed during the first year by Dr. Ba Maw's brother, Dr. Ba Han, and thereafter by the ex-mayor of Mandalay, U Ba Hlaing. Both men were Christian Burmans.[1]

To deal with special aspects of governmental problems, *Adipadi* Ba Maw set up a dozen or more boards. Four of them were designated to give attention to various aspects of the state services; two concerned economic problems and finance; the others, severally, covered publicity and national welfare, literature and translation, commerce and commodity distribution, enemy properties, labor, and the mobilization of national resources. In May, 1944, the *Adipadi* named Dr. Ba Han chairman of a research commission, along with two other Burmans of training and ability, U Soe Nyun and U Ba Nyein, and sent the group on an important mission to Japan. They also visited other parts of the Greater East Asia Co-Prosperity Sphere, especially Manchukuo, the Philippines, and Thailand.[2] Dr. Ba Han prepared an interim report of his mission immediately upon his return to Rangoon in August, 1944,[3] which suggested that the major concern of the commission had been to obtain amelioration of Burma's economic grievances by the Japanese and to establish direct contacts with other subordinate members of the Co-Prosperity Sphere.

There is no evidence that the plethora of special boards ever accomplished substantial results. Throughout the duration of the occupation the Burmese Government lacked real authority and had great difficulty making its rulings effective in the districts. Shortage of transportation and poor communication facilities were basic problems, but administrative corruption and widespread lawlessness were equally serious difficulties.[4]

Adipadi Ba Maw's plan for national mobilization of Burma's manpower resources was based upon a revolutionary concentration of

[1] *BIB*, I, 15–19, 21.   [2] *Ibid.*, pp. 22–25.

[3] Maung Ba Han, *The Planned State* (Rangoon, 1947), Appendix A.

[4] Dr. Ba Maw's own review of governmental problems (*Burma's New Order Plan* [rev. ed.; Rangoon, 1944], pp. 1–8), as of October, 1943, complains of administrative inefficiency, bickering, nonco-operation, and corruption.

power along fascist lines. He professed at the time to be completely contemptuous of democratic methods and principles. He declared that action and results must take precedence over "talk about democratic votes . . . democratic rights, democratic bunk." He added:

We have . . . accepted a revolutionary task. . . . [When] the work is done and the peril averted . . . people may go back to their old political play acting if they should still want to be amused in that way. . . . Man's will and work and sacrifice [must be] the basis of an all-time national plan.

He undertook to implement his program by mobilizing the entire population under ten functional categories working in the closest possible co-operation with the Japanese army. All ten groups were to be cemented together by the unifying force of "One Blood! One Voice! One Command!" As incentives for all-out effort, he proposed that enemy-owned properties including land be distributed in recognition of meritorious service and that nonagriculturalists be given preferential consideration for state employment. Community zeal could be rewarded by providing public works facilities, such as roads and wells.[5]

Except within a limited circle of partisan personal followers and others who were sufficiently in his confidence to appreciate his abilities and his services, Dr. Ba Maw's leadership as *Adipadi* carried a hollow ring. As a Westernized Burman and an amazingly adaptable one, he lacked popular roots politically. Associates declared that his egotism and vanity tended to conceal his essentially humanitarian impulses. Dr. Ba Maw was not ruthless enough to play the dictator's role. On the other hand, his desire for political power made him willing to accept the support of nondescript personal flatterers, political *pongyis*, and especially superstitious persons like Bandoola U Sein, his minister of religious development and propaganda.[6] Dr. Ba Maw's labored efforts to accommodate himself to popular Buddhist and animist sensibilities alien to his own training were unconvincing and, in the minds of some, robbed him of certain essential qualities of personal integrity.

[5] *Ibid.*, pp. 1–9, 22–28.

[6] Tun Pe, *Sun over Burma*, pp. 54–58, 75, 99. U Tun Pe describes Bandoola U Sein's astrological warning not to use the word *hti* (lottery) because it was the symbol of Saturn and therefore involved danger to the country. He also alleged that England, Holland, etc., would be defeated because "lan" in Burmese could mean "pushed back." Thakin Nu (*Burma under the Japanese*, p. 81) cites Dr. Ba Maw's consulting a palmist prior to August 1, 1943, to see whether he was destined to be assassinated.

In no aspect of his public relations program did the *Adipadi* make a more persistent and yet ineffectual effort to ingratiate himself than in the field of religion. His original move, in 1942, to fuse the *Sangha Asi Ayon,* of which he personally was head, with the *Dobama-Sinyetha* Party affected only the political *pongyis.* In May, 1943, he undertook the more ambitious task of uniting the four main Buddhist sects in a *Maha Sangha* Association. It was to be controlled through a representative National Council of Chief Sayadaws (of thirty years' standing) plus district *Sayadaws* (of twenty years' standing), all to be selected by the monks themselves. Leaders of several rival *pongyi* factions assembled at Rangoon at his invitation for what was a stormy twelve-day session. The progovernment Lower Burma faction won a tentative victory. They elected the *Aletawya Sayadaw* as chief monk and set up a working committee responsible to the association and to the *Adipadi.* The result was to intensify rather than to resolve the religious rift, partly because of the government's thinly disguised objective of exploiting the monks for propagandist purposes. The *Maha Sangha* Association was intended among other things to consolidate Burma's independence, to promote the Greater East Asia Co-Prosperity Sphere, and to strengthen Burman-Japanese friendship. Even the political-*pongyi* followers of the *Adipadi* were interested in their own ends and took no interest in the social service work of the Circle Army or the East Asia Youth League.[7]

As *Adipadi,* Dr. Ba Maw identified himself completely with the Buddhist faith. He took the oath of refuge in the Three Jewels (Buddha, *Dhamma, Sangha*) and pledged himself to "defend the Buddhist faith like the royal defenders of old." He fed the monks at his residence and informed both the people and the *nats* at a Shwe Dagon meeting that he would promote religion in Free Burma. Such sentiments, if sincerely entertained, would have been acceptable to Burmese Buddhists, but some members of his own cabinet could not accept his toadying to political *pongyis* who forgot their religious commitments not to interfere in governmental administration. Thakin Nu's comment was that the *Adipadi* was apparently more concerned that his government avoid giving offense to *pongyi* followers than to avoid offending Japanese sensibilities.[8] Thakin Nu's criticism of Dr.

[7] *BIB,* II, 110–111, 141–142; United States, Office of Strategic Services, *Japanese Administration of Burma* (Washington, 1944), p. 16.

[8] Nu, *Burma under the Japanese,* pp. 90–91. U Nu cites in this connection an instance in which he was rebuked by Dr. Ba Maw for telling Japanese editors

Ba Maw on this count is almost the only caustic note in his entire story. He said:

I firmly believe that men who lean on *pongyis* in politics are mere opportunists. The men who drag *pongyis* into politics should be pitied because they do not know how sinfully they are acting. . . . Although the *pongyi* can escape penalty by doing penance, this does not relieve the guilt incurred by the man who made use of him.[9]

Thus, despite all the frantic efforts of Bandoola U Sein as minister of religious development and propaganda (itself a telltale combination), the *Adipadi* apparently added little to his public respect or support by his labored concern to identify himself with the Buddhist faith and the welfare of the *Sangha*.

The nonofficial East Asia Youth League was in some respects an embarrassment to the government's public relations program. The social service activities of the 600 branches of the league in areas of health, emergency service, and education won the thankful confidence of many people. Thus, except in a few areas, the political propagandizing of the government and the activities of the much-publicized Circle Army suffered by comparison with the nonpolitical league, which resolutely refused to be swallowed up by the government. The league did aid recruitment for the Burma Defense Army (renamed in 1943 the Burma National Army), but the army eventually developed a truly national character of its own. In 1944 the name of the East Asia Youth League was changed to the All Burma Youth League. Its first political act was to join the secret Antifascist People's Freedom League (A.F.P.F.L.) as a constituent member unit. The A.B.Y.L. continued as an active element of the A.F.P.F.L. to the end of 1948.[10]

A final aspect of Dr. Ba Maw's efforts to accommodate himself to Burma's political traditions was his revival of customs of the Burmese

---

that 95 per cent of Burmans distrusted the Japanese for being too greedy and domineering.

[9] *Ibid.,* pp. 91–92.

[10] Ba Gyan, "The All Burma Youth League," *Burma,* III (1953), 56–60. The league co-operated actively with the A.F.P.F.L. until December, 1948, when its units were temporarily broken up by the insurrections. U Ba Gyan, its head, was included in the cabinet until then. It was reorganized in December, 1950, under the leadership of Justice U Thein Maung as chairman of the board of directors. It continued as a nonpolitical social service and youth-training organization. Twelve of the forty-five members of the Union Youth Affairs Council, which was sponsored by Premier Nu in 1950, were associated with the program of the A.B.Y.L.

Court. The trappings of royalty (the court music, the dwarf announcer addressing the *Adipadi* as if king) were used by him as early as the initial independence ceremony of August 1, 1943. Court customs came to be increasingly in evidence at the end of the occupation period. Dr. Ba Maw eventually included the term *Mingyi* (great prince or king) as part of his title, and his championship of the Buddhist faith was also in the royal fashion. Manipuri Brahman priests were brought to Rangoon from Mandalay in late 1944 to help solemnize the marriage of the *Adipadi's* daughter Tinsa Maw and Bo Yan Naing, presumably the dynasty's heir apparent.[11] The consort of the *Adipadi* began receiving visitors while seated on raised dais in the pattern of the chief queen's court. Other aspects of royal protocol were revived along with classical patterns of court entertainment. Songs composed in honor of the *Mingyi Adipadi* connected his father with the resistance to the British in 1886 and with other aspects of the nationalist tradition.

On the occasion of the launching of the *Mahabama* (Great Burma) Party in August, 1944, to displace the *Dobama-Sinyetha* amalgamation of 1942, the *Adipadi* planted a sacred tree in the "Soil of Victory," brought from Alaungpaya's home at Shwebo and deposited near Rangoon's Royal Lakes in 1942. This tree symbolized the ancient tradition that Burma's kings would rule not only Burma proper but over the entire "Southern Island" (*Zambudipa*) described in Hindu cosmology.[12] The effect which Dr. Ba Maw's pretense at royalty (in preference to adherence to democracy) may have had on the Burmese people generally is very difficult to gauge. Informed Burmans were not favorably impressed, and his political enemies did not hesitate to attack him because of his royalist pretensions.[13]

Apart from a limited circle of Burmans connected with the government and others who were aware of the *Adipadi's* numerous efforts to shield his countrymen from Japanese exploitation and punishment,[14] the Burmese population apparently viewed Dr. Ba Maw with attitudes ranging from distrust to hatred. They discounted his Buddhist pretensions; they disbelieved his propaganda pronouncements; they resented his dictatorial authority which repudiated democratic liberties and attempted popular regimentation; they associated him, no doubt

[11] Colonel Bo Yan Naing was serving at the time as chief of operations of the Burma National Army.

[12] Nu, *Burma under the Japanese*, pp. 83–84; also from eyewitness oral testimony.

[13] Tun Pe, *Sun over Burma*, pp. 71, 73.

[14] Nu, *Burma under the Japanese*, pp. 32–34, 49–51.

Shwe Dagon Pagoda, Rangoon

Dr. Ba Maw

more than he deserved, with onerous military exactions and economic privations. Finally, it was probably asking too much of Upper Burmans in particular to accept as prospective king a Westernized person of Mon extraction.

Dr. Ba Maw's Relations with the Japanese

Dr. Ba Maw's relations with Tokyo were far more friendly than those with the local Japanese military command within Burma itself. It was Premier Tojo (not the local military leaders) who backed Dr. Ba Maw's elevation at the outset and who decided also that Burma must be accorded a larger measure of independence if it was to serve Japan as a military base for invading India. Premier Tojo met Dr. Ba Maw personally both in Japan and at Singapore prior to August 1, 1943. From that date to the end of the war Burma was represented in Tokyo by the Japanophile Dr. Thein Maung, a close personal follower of the *Adipadi*.

During 1943 and 1944, a procession of Burmese missions, including politicians, educationists, newspapermen, business people, and students, made their way to Japan.[15] The fifty Burmese state scholars studying at the International Students Institute at Tokyo were granted living allowances, language instruction, and counseling service. The Burman recipients were apparently reasonably happy with their lot in Japan despite thought control, a limited course of study, and close supervision.[16] The Japanese propaganda program overreached itself in subjecting such students to a mythological version of history intended to buttress Japan's leadership claims. Tokyo also denied Burmese students free contact with the Japanese people.[17] Burmese visitors were apparently most impressed by the remarkable technological development of the Japanese as an Asiatic people and by their disciplined concentration on the war effort. Burmans visiting Manila en route to Japan were even more impressed by the Filipino leaders, who flatly refused to scuttle their democratic institutions and ideals or to declare war on the United States.[18]

[15] *BIB*, II, 49. The first large mission was led by the seasoned missioner, U Ba Lwin, the prewar friend of China.

[16] *BIB*, II, 49; Willard Elsbree, *Japan's Role in Southeast Asia, 1940–1945* (Cambridge, Mass., 1953), pp. 106–108. The topics studied included agriculture, railways, rubber production, engineering, business administration, finance and banking, and military training.

[17] *BIB*, II, 49; Tun Pe, *Sun over Burma*, pp. 77, 90–91. The Burmese students sent to Tokyo were apparently less unhappy than the Filipinos.

[18] Tun Pe, *Sun over Burma*, pp. 91–93.

When one turns attention from the fairly understanding relationship between the Burma Government and that of Japan to the situation within Burma, the reality underneath the façade of full co-operation becomes one of rivalry and recrimination. The friction centered in the personal feud between the unbending Major General Isamura, third-ranking Japanese leader in charge of Burma-Japanese relations, and the equally assertive and proud *Adipadi* Dr. Ba Maw. In the contest for face, the Japanese had the advantage in possession of superior authority and coercive power. But the general faced a resourceful and determined opponent in Dr. Ba Maw, who tried the patience of his Japanese associates on numerous occasions. For example, the *Anashin Adipadi* blocked Isamura's proposal to make the study of Japanese compulsory in Burma's schools. Serious friction flared in late 1942, when General Isamura canceled abruptly the plans of the *Dobama-Sinyetha* Party leaders for designing and raising ceremonially the new Burma flag. The banner finally selected (broad yellow and green horizontal stripes with a red rising sun in the corner) was brought to Rangoon from Mandalay in the company of the previously mentioned "Soil of Victory" from Shwebo. The *Anashin* and his council planned to sign the banner, each using his own blood, prior to its elevation at Rangoon. Similar flags for the districts were to have been first raised on the same sacred site in Rangoon, while local flags would be consecrated in similar fashion by preliminary association with the district flags. When the Japanese military authorities abruptly vetoed the whole procedure, the feud began in real earnest.[19]

The Japanese leadership in Burma was most unsympathetic toward Premier Tojo's move, made in early 1943, to grant a larger measure of Burman independence under Dr. Ba Maw's leadership. In June, 1943, the local Japanese tried in vain to interest the personable Thakin Nu in taking over the leadership from the disliked *Anashin,* possibly as a ruse to sow dissension within the *Dobama-Sinyetha* alliance.[20] On the occasion of Dr. Ba Maw's visit to Singapore in company with Thakin Nu in July, 1943, General Isamura went out of his way, protocol-wise, to put the Burma leaders in their subordinate place.[21]

After Tokyo's grant of "independence" to Burma, the *Adipadi* demanded and obtained the formal cession to Burma, in September,

---

[19] Nu, *Burma under the Japanese,* pp. 44–46. According to Thakin Nu, Dr. Ba Maw's angry rejoinder on the day following the veto was that Burmans themselves must take personal risks in order to make themselves strong like the Japanese.
[20] *Ibid.,* pp. 57–60.   [21] *Ibid.,* pp. 64–65.

1943, of most of the Shan States. Shortly thereafter, he began to casti-
gate the Japanese army for interfering in Burma's political affairs and
for establishing Japanese business firms in an economic monopoly.
On February 17, 1944, occurred the first of several alleged attempts
on the part of agents of General Isamura to assassinate the *Adipadi*.
The government at the time found itself able to bring to justice
neither the guilty Japanese military agents nor even their arrogant
Burman "bad-hat" accomplice. One of Dr. Ba Maw's few triumphs
over Isamura was in a matter of protocol on the occasion of the
marriage of Tinsa Maw to Bo Yan Naing, which took place at the
time of the siege of Imphal in 1944. The arrangers accorded the place
of honor to Subhas Chandra Bose as titular head of Free India, over
the claims of Isamura, and managed to justify the move as an alleged
contribution to Indian morale.[22]

In June, 1944, Dr. Ba Maw published a revision of his 1943 booklet
entitled *Burma's New Order Plan*. In the new edition he declared
flatly that Burmans would not fight unless they were given a tangible
stake in the outcome of the war. Burmans, he said, were suspicious
of independence which denied them the concrete right and the power
to administer their own affairs in their own way. Daily proof must
be afforded that the country was already free and that the people
must fight to keep it so. He pointed out four minimum essentials for
Burmese-Japanese co-operation: (1) the Japanese must not mix in
Burma's political affairs; (2) they must abstain from taking opinion
polls calculated to sow distrust of the government; (3) they must
accord to Burmese government servants, for purposes of negotiation,
some equivalency of rank with that of officers within the Japanese
army; (4) both the Japanese army and business firms must utilize
Burmese liaison officers as a means of reducing friction with the people. The *Adipadi* also complained that the army must permit the publication of more complete and accurate war news.[23]

The exasperation of the Japanese over the publication of such representations, which were capable of seriously embarrassing their position
if disclosed abroad, can be easily understood. Dr. Ba Maw's central
objective in the booklet was, however, to bolster the morale of the

[22] *Ibid.*, pp. 80–84. In July, 1943, Mongpan and Kengtung had been given to
Thailand. Burmese officials were required previously to apologize on the occasion
of the bayoneting of a Japanese national who failed to heed the order of a Burman
police officer.
[23] Dr. Ba Maw, *Burma's New Order Plan*, pp. 32–56. This item apparently did
not reach British or American wartime intelligence agencies.

Burmese people in the face of rapidly deteriorating living and working conditions.[24]

Almost contemporaneous with the publication of *Burma's New Order Plan* was the sending to Japan in May, 1944, of the high-level Special Research Commission, composed of Dr. Ba Han, U Soe Nyun, and U Ba Nyein, already referred to. In addition to asking Japan for trained technical assistance, the commission's major concern was apparently to convey to Tokyo the reality of Burma's impending collapse economically and to outline to the Japanese authorities the basic economic grievances suffered by Burma's population at the hands of the army.[25] Dr. Ba Han's commission also visited Manchukuo and made a concerted effort to enter into direct contact with other peoples of Southeast Asia. Particularly significant was its contact with Filipino leaders who were even more restive than the Burmese under Japanese domination.[26] Dr. Ba Han did not improve his personal relations with the Tokyo Japanese by refusing, as a Christian, to participate in the Shinto religious ceremonies.

It was too late to salvage the situation when, in September, 1944, the Tokyo authorities, responding to continued Burmese pressure, attempted to ameliorate some of the popular grievances deriving from Japanese army exploitation. The new commander in chief, General Kimura, gave assurances in response to the request of the cabinet that the offensive behavior of low-ranking officers would be curbed. He assured the Burmese of his concern, but little improvement resulted. In October, 1944, Dr. Ba Maw, becoming more bold because of the rapidly deteriorating Japanese military situation, advanced Burma's claim to enemy property initially confiscated by the Japanese, as an allegedly essential factor in giving Burma a larger stake in victory. He also demanded more newsprint, more freedom of the press and of assembly, and limitation of the profits of Japanese firms to a mere 6 per cent of investment plus a relaxation of their economic monopoly.[27]

In November, 1944, Dr. Ba Maw visited Tokyo again and allegedly urged without avail that the Japanese armies, clearly beaten, evacuate Burma in order to spare the country further destruction and suffering.

---

[24] *Ibid.*, p. 30.   [25] Elsbree, pp. 60–64.

[26] Maung Ba Han, *The Planned State*. Appendix A, entitled "Interim Report of the Burma Special Research Commission" was prepared within ten days of the group's return to Rangoon on August 2, 1944. Appendix B related to their visit in Thailand.

[27] Elsbree, pp. 64–70.

He found the Tokyo authorities adamant in demanding continued Burman military co-operation and concerted efforts to stimulate confidence in an ultimate Japanese victory.[28] In the early spring of 1945, on the very eve of the complete Japanese military collapse, the *Adipadi* finally undertook to legislate concerning important economic matters without obtaining prior Japanese approval.[29]

Save at the outset of the occupation, in 1942–1943, when Burmans were given no choice but to act in conformity with the desires of the Japanese army, it appears that the indigenous Burmese Government normally undertook to achieve national ends in preference to those of the Japanese. This was somewhat less true of those who owed their elevation to power entirely to the Japanese and who developed a personal stake in a Japanese victory because they could envisage no prospect of personal advantage from British reconquest. This was not the case for most of the Thakins in the government and army, and it was not true in any sense for men like Justice U Thein Maung, who struggled from the outset to maintain liberal democratic principles as well as Burman nationalist ends. The Japanese were able to use Dr. Ba Maw for a time and after a fashion because of his opportunism, his lust for power, and his pronounced fascist and anti-British inclinations. But in the final analysis, the *Adipadi's* ambition and personal pride plus his genuine concern for nationalist objectives prevented his playing the puppet's role.[30] Proof lay in his perennial insistence that the national spirit be taken into account, in his persistent endeavors to escape the limitations imposed by the Japanese military authorities so that Burmans could make their own decisions, and, finally, in his concerted opposition in 1944 against Japanese economic exploitation. Such policies were appreciated and respected by persons in a position to know, but the people generally were not aware of them. Finally, and to his credit, Dr. Ba Maw refused to betray to the Japanese the developing resistance movement of the Antifascist People's Freedom League.[31]

The Role of the Thakins in the Government

Some of the reasons for Thakin participation in the pseudoindependent Government of Burma were the same as Dr. Ba Maw's. They

---

[28] Jones, *Japan's New Order in East Asia,* pp. 356–357.
[29] Nu, *Burma under the Japanese,* pp. 107–108.
[30] Elsbree, pp. 72–75; Nu, *Burma under the Japanese,* p. 54.
[31] Nu, *Burma under the Japanese,* pp. 93–97.

were concerned, as was he, to avoid a rift within nationalist ranks, which could only have played into Japanese hands. They also enjoyed personally, as did he, the exercise of even the limited measure of power accorded to them, especially the deference accorded to them as persons in authority by government underlings and by the public.[32] The Thakin leaders also shared, although perhaps to a somewhat less degree than Dr. Ba Maw, Burman resentment over Japanese slights and humiliations. As the front man, the *Adipadi* alone had the thankless and always onerous task of the final implementation of Japanese requisitions, while trying to maintain a measure of personal dignity and face. The Thakin members of the government obviously smarted under popular accusations that they too were indulging selfish motives in accepting office under such humiliating circumstances.[33]

Recriminations and jealousies arose even within the Thakin group. Their views tended to range through the entire political spectrum from the conservative Thakin Tun Oke to the Communist rebel Thakin Soe. These differences actually shattered the original *Dobama Asiayone* organization beyond remedying. The party name survived the war only in the Tun Oke–Ba Sein fragment.[34]

But in several important respects, the Thakin ministers differed from their *Adipadi* chief. Thakins Mya, Nu, Than Tun, Aung San, Lay Maung, and Lun Baw, despite major *Dobama* defections, still commanded the allegiance of a youthful nationalist following which the *Adipadi* could not match. Ministers Mya and Than Tun, together with Thakin Tin, were the leaders of the All Burma Cultivator's League dating from 1938. Thakin Lun Baw was associated with Thakins Mya and Ba Swe in leading the incipient Socialist-sponsored labor organizations.[35] Defense Minister Aung San was the acknowledged leader of the Burma Defense Army (renamed the Burma National Army in September, 1943) along with Bo Let Ya and Bo Ne Win. The army group in co-operation with Thakin Than Tun also enlisted in 1943–1944 substantial support from an anti-Japanese Karen youth organization in the delta. Thakin Nu was able to place Thakin

---

[32] *Ibid.*, pp. 54–59, 74–75.

[33] *Ibid.*, pp. 61–62, 77–78, 87. Thakin Nu's book labors overmuch his defense of the Thakin decision to team up with Dr. Ba Maw, indicating clearly that public criticism of this action was a sensitive point. Thakin Kodaw Hmaing's criticism of the participation policy drove Thakin Mya to tears on one occasion. See also Tun Pe, *Sun over Burma*, p. 48.

[34] Some of the disgruntled Thakins actually turned informers for the *kempetai*.

[35] Nu, *Burma under the Japanese*, pp. 128–130.

San Swe in the actual headquarters of the Japanese *kempetai*, where he could intervene when any of the group got into trouble; Thakin Nu also assigned Thakins Chit and Hla Maung as trouble shooters to smooth out local instances of friction.[36] The Thakin leaders in the Ministry enjoyed, finally, the inestimable advantage that they trusted each other, not only as personal friends but also in sharing a selfless dedication to achieve freedom for Burma which was at the time devoid of desire on the part of any of the group to dominate over the others.

Because they were indispensable politically to Dr. Ba Maw,[37] Thakins Mya, Nu, and Than Tun were able to serve notice on him prior to his election by the Preparatory Committee as *Adipadi* that they intended to maintain their own "inner circle" and not to accept his personal control over their political activities.[38] Thakins Than Tun and Aung San, the boldest of the group, used their ministerial posts as covers for their activities in plotting the actual overthrow of Japanese control.[39] Once the resistance movement got under way apart from Dr. Ba Maw, starting in late 1943,[40] the Thakin leaders could also count on the active support of the popular and widespread East Asia Youth League.

The Burma Defense Army, under the leadership of Defense Minister Aung San and General Ne Win, developed distinctive Burmese traits and characteristics, despite very close Japanese associations and control.[41] The change of name on September 16, 1943, to the Burma National Army (B.N.A.) carried the psychological implication that they would attack all national enemies. But the development of morale within the force was not easy. Overbearing Japanese officers slapped Burmans who failed to salute. The food was often bad, the discipline rugged, the officer leadership generally poor, the garrison and air raid duty irksome and unexciting. The force was issued only a limited number of light arms. Recruiting was slow even when aided by the hard-working East Asia Youth League. The B.N.A. personnel, for

[36] *Ibid.*, p. 35.   [37] *Ibid.*, pp. 61–62.   [38] *Ibid.*, pp. 66–67.

[39] *Ibid.*, pp. 61–62. Thakin Than Tun was the working leader of the resistance program.

[40] *PD,C*, vol. 433 (Feb. 17, 1947), Supplement, pp. 19–20. Arthur Henderson here confirmed the fact that General Aung San was in contact with the Allies at the end of 1943.

[41] Tun Pe, *Sun over Burma*, p. 68. The vice-minister for defense was Thakin Aung Than; Colonel Thakin Hla Maung became chief of staff; Boh Yan Naing, the eventual son-in-law of the *Adipadi*, was chief of operations. See *BIB*, II, 154–156; Nu, *Burma under the Japanese*, pp. 128, 130.

obvious reasons, came to hate the Japanese thoroughly, so that it was not difficulty to enlist them in the budding resistance movement.

As early as the spring of 1944, secret lectures were in progress within the B.N.A. to the effect that it would soon have opportunity to fight the Japanese. Only then did morale begin to improve.[42] The depressing military outlook for Japan and Germany by June, 1944, contributed to the improvement of Burma morale. The Japanese invasion of Manipur was overtaken disastrously by the rains; Normandy was successfully invaded; an attempt was made on Hitler's life; Premier Tojo resigned in July, 1944, following the failure of his gamble in Manipur; the Japanese home islands were brought within bombing range.[43] In June, 1944, occurred also the first expression of overt Burmese resistance to the Japanese, which was promptly crushed by the *kempetai*. Dr. Ba Maw protested the ruthless methods employed, but he was only threatened for his pains.[44]

The organization of the Antifascist People's Freedom League in 1944, a matter to be described shortly, can best be understood as the effort of the anti-Japanese Thakin leaders both within and outside the government to reintegrate the shattered nationalist front in order to rid Burma of Japanese control and then to carry on the independence struggle after the British returned. Its nucleus was an amalgam of Socialist and Communist Thakin leadership, the B.N.A., the East Asia Youth League, and the mass peasant and worker organization affiliated with the older Socialist and the emerging Communist parties.

The Indian National Army and the Japanese Invasion of India

The intensive Japanese program of political and economic mobilization for Burma carried out in 1943 was specifically in preparation for the attempted invasion and conquest of India in the following year. The Japanese had missed a golden opportunity in 1942 to invade south India from Singapore by sea, for reasons that will be indicated below. The British then had virtually abandoned militarily the coast of the Bay of Bengal following the debacles of Malaya and Burma. The eventual Japanese overland penetration into Manipur and Assam, at-

---

[42] *BIB*, II, 162–165. British intelligence by early fall of 1944 learned that the B.N.A. would probably turn against the Japanese once the latter were on the run.

[43] Jones, pp. 424–442; Tun Pe, *Sun over Burma*, pp. 102–103. Such military events, which filled Dr. Ba Maw with grim forebodings, had an encouraging aspect for the B.N.A.

[44] Jones, p. 356.

tempted in 1944, was undertaken in the face of terrific difficulties of terrain which necessitated stripping Burma of all available river boats and much animal transport. The animals, as a rule, were driven to the limit of their endurance, then killed to provide meat for the invading troops. The campaign was a desperate gamble especially in view of the fact that the onset of the monsoon rains in late May would render the principal military supply roads across the Chin Hills from Burma quite impassable. The success of the Japanese effort was dependent in any case on their ability to stimulate a co-operative anti-British rebellion within the adjacent Indian province of Bengal. For this purpose the Japanese associated with their invasion effort the presence and influence of the outstanding Bengali revolutionary, and an ex-president of the Indian Congress Party, Subhas Chandra Bose. The details of the military campaign are of little concern to the political history of Burma, but some attention needs to be given to the role of the Indian Independence League and the Indian National Army.

That the Japanese planned to utilize anti-British nationalist sentiment in India to help cancel out British influence was demonstrated by the organization in 1942, among captured Indian troops and the sizable Indian civilian population in Malaya and Burma, of the Indian Independence League (I.I.L.) and the Indian National Army (I.N.A.). The league was widely dispersed throughout Southeast Asia, and for the most part its main branches in Burma as elsewhere functioned primarily to protect Indian rights and interests. The I.N.A. in 1942 was located mainly at Singapore, where large numbers of captured Indian army personnel from Hongkong and Malaya were assembled. Most of the defeated Indian troops in Burma had evacuated into India.[45] Rash Behari Bose (no relative of Subhas Chandra Bose), an Indian long resident in Japan, was the key person in the initial efforts to rally the co-operation of the I.I.L. and the I.N.A. The project was essentially Premier Tojo's idea and was not favored by the generals (Terauchi and Sugiyama). For various reasons the Japanese temporized when in June, 1942, an actual opportunity came to invade India by sea and the fairly sizable Indian National Army force at Singapore could have been used to advantage.[46]

It was at the first general meeting of the executive committee of

[45] *BIB*, II, 144–145.
[46] Elsbree, pp. 32–34. The Japanese in the summer of 1942 had full naval control of the Bay of Bengal. They could have captured Ceylon and Mauritius and cut off Allied contact with India and Persia by sea.

the I.I.L., held at Bangkok in June, 1942, that the matter of the invasion of India was considered. The key person was one of the organizers of the league and the commander of the I.N.A., one Mohan Singh, who had held the rank of captain in the British-Indian army. One of the basic demands of the conference was that, prior to any Japanese attempt to invade India in co-operation with the I.N.A., Tokyo should recognize the absolute independence of India and summon Subhas Chandra Bose from Berlin to be the Indian leader. Partly as a result of Tokyo's hesitation and partly because of difficulties in meeting the I.I.L. demands, the opportunity to invade India by sea slipped away never to be regained.[47] After June, 1942, the Indian camp at Singapore began to disintegrate.

In December, 1942, when the Japanese proposed to shift some 900 I.N.A. officers from Malaya to Burma preparatory to invading India by land, the full break came. General Mohan Singh, with the backing of the I.I.L. council, flatly refused to move to Burma unless Tokyo clarified once for all the future independent status of India. Other demands included the equality of Indian troops with the Japanese, I.I.L. custody of Indian property in the conquered areas, and avoidance of Japanese interference in the political affairs of India. Singh and others resigned from the I.I.L. council following the arrest as a spy by the Japanese of one of his military aides. When Rash Behari Bose sided with Tokyo's rejection of the league's demands, Singh undertook to dissolve the I.N.A. and was accordingly arrested along with other Indian officer sympathizers.[48] The arrested group was sent to a Japanese prison camp in New Guinea, which was eventually overrun by General MacArthur's American forces.[49] The I.N.A. fell almost completely apart after the Mohan Singh incident of December, 1942.

It was following the fiasco of 1942 that the Japanese pushed Rash Behari Bose aside and persuaded the German Government to send Subhas Chandra Bose to Malaya by submarine. He arrived at Penang in June, 1943. He immediately undertook with considerable difficulty to revive the enthusiasm of the I.I.L. Subhas Bose met Dr. Ba Maw at

---

[47] The Japanese fleet returned to Pacific waters in 1943, apparently little interested in helping Germany to the extent of intercepting Allied aid to the U.S.S.R. via the Persian Gulf. Germany had conceded to Japan priority as far as 70 degrees east longitude, which ran to the west of India. See Jones, p. 402; Maurice Collis, *Last and First in Burma*, pp. 184–185.

[48] W. S. Desai, *India and Burma* (Bombay, 1954), pp. 79–80.

[49] The full account of this episode must await the availability to scholars of the classified files at Washington.

Singapore in July, 1943, as previously mentioned, and came to Rangoon as the latter's guest on August 1, 1943. On October 21, 1943, at Singapore, the provisional government of Free India (*Azad Hind*) was established with Bose as head. Both Dr. Ba Maw and Bose attended the subsequent Greater East Asia Co-Prosperity Sphere meeting at Tokyo on November 5 and 6. It was with the *Adipadi's* consent that the headquarters of *Azad Hind* was eventually shifted to Rangoon on January 7, 1944. Bose raised funds for liberating India to a total of 215 million rupees (some 150 millions of the sum came from Burmese Indians alone), but his attempts to revive the I.N.A. as a fighting force ran completely aground. The supposed two I.N.A. divisions located in Burma were militarily a joke. Although relations between Subhas Bose and Dr. Ba Maw were cordial,[50] the Indian-sponsored program was never popular among the Burmese, who wanted nothing more than that Bose and the Japanese should move on into India, as indeed they tried to do in early 1944.

In the attempted invasion of India, the I.N.A. troops were used near the fighting front mainly as decoys to suborn such Indian forces as the Japanese army might be able to isolate. The first noteworthy failure came on the Akyab front early in the campaign of 1944, when an Indian force which was temporarily cut off from the main body refused to heed the I.N.A. appeal. A second failure was registered in Manipur, which was invaded by the Japanese in March, 1944. Here the Japanese had planned to stage a triumphal I.N.A. entrance into captured Imphal.[51]

It was a close call for the Allied armies in Manipur, for the invading Japanese force established control of all land routes to Imphal and as far as Kohima in Assam. Only the determined British-Indian defense, rebuffing all I.N.A. appeals, and the timely air-borne troop transport and the supply services to Imphal, provided mainly by United States Air Force planes diverted from the China run, kept the Japanese from triumphing at Imphal. When finally cut off from their own supplies by the monsoon rains, the Japanese army in Manipur disintegrated as a fighting force. The dry season of 1944–1945 saw a British-Indian-African army reconquer Burma.[52] In April, 1945, the I.N.A. itself flatly refused to obey Japanese orders to attack the revolting Burma National Army,

[50] Desai, *India and Burma*, pp. 81–87; Elsbree, pp. 156–159.

[51] Elsbree, pp. 34–36, 157–159; Tun Pe, *Sun over Burma*, p. 98. Advance press copy was furnished Burmese newspapers in anticipation of Imphal's fall.

[52] Vice-Admiral Earl Mountbatten of Burma, *Report to the Combined Chiefs of Staff . . . 1943–1945* (London, 1951).

and in the final two months of the campaign I.N.A. personnel deserted to the British side in large numbers. The I.N.A. surrendered on May 18. Subhas Bose accompanied the retreating Japanese to Bangkok on April 24 and subsequently died in an air crash on Formosa on August 18, 1945.

It was Burma's misfortune to have been exploited as a base for the Japanese attack on India and to have suffered from 1943 concentrated Allied bombing attacks on all railway and other transportation facilities and strategic centers. The city of Akyab was obliterated by bombing, and Mandalay by artillery fire. All cities along the main north-south routes of transportation suffered partial to total demolition, and the countryside was strewn with arms of all descriptions. Some were dropped by the defeated British forces in 1942; others were flown in to aid local opposition to the Japanese; still others were left behind by the departing Japanese. Wartime Burma paid a heavy price both in material losses and in social demoralization as a consequence of its fateful role as a battleground. When the smoke had cleared away it was the Thakin-led A.F.P.F.L. nationalist front which survived politically to continue the struggle for the independence of an economically wrecked country. It remains to outline briefly the steps in the emergence of the resistance movement.

The Antifascist People's Freedom League

The prime architects and leaders of the A.F.P.F.L. were the youthful Thakins Aung San and Than Tun, the first by virtue of his forthright personality and leadership of the Burma National Army and the second by reasons of his imagination and intelligence coupled with an unusual capacity for sustained endeavor. The two were related by marriage (their wives were sisters). They were bolder and more reckless than their close friends, Thakins Nu and Mya, who were almost ten years their seniors. Thakin Than Tun occupied the key position of liaison between the essentially nationalist Thakins (Aung San and Nu), the Socialist organizers of the peasant and worker associations (led by Thakins Mya and Ba Swe), and the more doctrinaire Communist underground (Thakins Thein Pe in India and Soe in Burma). Thakin Than Tun's own Communist convictions apparently matured during the course of the war; he emerged in 1945, at the war's end, as head of the Communist Party of Burma and as secretary of the A.F.P.F.L. Both of the younger leaders were self-effacing men of unquestioned dedication to nationalist ends, who enjoyed enviable reputations for personal integrity.

The story of the formation of the A.F.P.F.L. can be put together only in a fragmentary way. One of the first overt steps, apparently taken in late 1943, was the reconciliation achieved by Thakins Aung San and Than Tun with the minority anti-Japanese group among the delta Karens. This group was led by Saw San Po Thin, who also harbored Allied agents parachuted in by plane. The official government-sponsored Karen Central Organization, headed by Saw Ba Maung, tended also in a less overt way to gravitate toward the nationalist anti-Japanese position, although other important Karen elements continued to be pro-Japanese and to harbor their distrust of Burmans generally.[53]

Apparently the second major step toward the A.F.P.F.L. was the linking up with an associate sent by Thakin Thein Pe from India, one Thakin Tin Shwe, who was dropped by a British plane in the early spring of 1944. The reply to New Delhi was sent back by Thakin Nyo Tun, who was picked up by prearrangement off the Arakan coast by a British gunboat. Thakin Nyo Tun's arrival at New Delhi was eventually confirmed in a British radio message containing the agreed phrase "Grandfather Hare has reached the House of Orion." [54] Thakin Than Tun also tried, but without success, to link up with the Chinese nationalists. Shortly after this understanding with British authorities in India had been entered upon, Thakins Than Tun and Aung San arranged for Thakin Soe to come out of hiding temporarily (wearing a B.N.A. captain's uniform) in order to work out an agreement for the collaboration of his anti-Japanese guerrilla group operating in the delta jungles. Eventually the Communist Thakin Ba Hein, who had been an active participant in Nyo Tun's mission, joined Soe in the underground resistance.[55]

It was only after the preliminary steps had been completed that the Burma National Army, under the direction of Thakin Aung San as

---

[53] Nu, *Burma under the Japanese*, pp. 98–101; J. S. Furnivall, "Twilight in Burma: Independence and After," *Pacific Affairs*, XXII (1949), 161. Saw Hla Pe as minister of forests was the cabinet link with the Karen Central Organization.

[54] Nu, *Burma under the Japanese*, pp. 102–104. Thakin Tin Shwe brought letters not only from Thakin Thein Pe but also from the leader of the anti-Japanese Communist Party secretary in India, P. C. Joshi. Thakin Tin Shwe was, according to Nu, betrayed to the Japanese police after the contact was made.

[55] *Ibid.*, pp. 104–105; Tun Pe, *Sun over Burma*, p. 101; Hinners, p. 197. General Aung San later denied Soe's exaggerated claim that he had actually started the A.F.P.F.L.

minister of defense, was linked up to the resistance movement in a definite way. A nationalist orientation had been started within the army fairly early in 1944. The signal of the break with the Japanese propaganda line was General Aung San's forthright declaration at the Jubilee Hall meeting in August 1, 1944, the first anniversary of Burma's "independence," to the effect that Burma's freedom was on paper only and a long way from reality. The audience cheered, but Dr. Ba Maw was displeased over such indiscretion.[56] This was followed by the clandestine publication and distribution within the Burma National Army of a secret manifesto approved by the A.F.P.F.L. inner circle (Thakins Mya, Nu, Than Tun, Aung San, and Chit) to prepare to sabotage the war effort and to attack the fascist Japanese dacoits and their renegade agents among the Burmese. The Antifascist League pledged itself to co-operate with the "democratic" allies (a tell-tale Communist cliché?) and to achieve for Burma by peaceful means a free constitution and essential social services.[57]

The 1944 manifesto entitled "Drive Away the Fascist Japanese Marauders" was an impressive document. It listed as the objectives of the antifascist organization a constitution drawn up by the people of Burma including freedom of thought, speech, the press, assembly, and religion, plus protection against illegal detention and the outlawing of discrimination on grounds of race, religion, sex, or minority status. The constitution should also guarantee security of employment and free popular access to forest supplies and fisheries. The state would pension its employees, aid the uplift of backward communities, promote education, and provide a progressive and equitable agricultural reform scheme. As a prospective program of action, the members were urged to prepare to destroy Japanese transport and supplies, persuade laborers to desert, hide carts and boats, inform concerning Japanese movements, and conduct guerilla operations. The leftist authorship of the manifesto was reflected in the victory flag displaying a white star on

---

[56] Tun Pe, *Sun over Burma*, p. 103.

[57] Nu, *Burma under the Japanese*, p. 106; A.F.P.F.L., *The New Burma in the New World* (Rangoon, 1946), pp. 16–18. A commitment of similar character was made by Thakin Thein Pe in India calculated to remove the doubts of the British authorities concerning the wisdom of accepting the aid of the Thakins. He allegedly advocated British-Burman co-operation for generations to come based on the equality and justice of dominion status. Even radical A.F.P.F L. plans to abolish landlordism and to nationalize economic facilities would be held in abeyance during the reconstruction period. See A.F.P.F.L., *From Fascist Bondage to New Democracy* (Rangoon, 1945), pp. 19–29.

a red background, the latter to denote the bravery and blood of the masses and the unification of the world's peoples. Readers were exhorted to set up a "People's Government." The statement was signed "Comrades." [58]

The East Asia Youth League and the cadres of peasant and worker organizations (sponsored by the Socialist and Communist parties) were drawn into the A.F.P.F.L. conspiracy during the late months of 1944. Its eventual transformation into a broad nationalist front had to await the overt military break which came in late March, 1945. The self-appointed supreme council of the A.F.P.F.L., consisting originally of nine persons (later increased to fifteen), undertook to extend the A.F.P.F.L. outside the capital by appointing district chairmen, who were eventually to form the nucleus for a national council.[59] The vitality of the resistance movement stemmed from the new patriotic Burman determination to be free of foreign control, a spirit generated from their common experience of dire suffering under Japanese occupation. The Burma National Army became the hope of the country, and the people gave it enthusiastic support.[60]

Adipadi Ba Maw was by no means unaware that the "inner circle" Thakins were engaged in political activities quite independent of his own more cautious efforts to wring from faltering Japanese control additional concessions for Burma. He learned of Thakin Soe's temporary emergence from the jungle and of the fact that contact had been attempted with India. But it may be doubted that he realized the full extent of the A.F.P.F.L. program. He was himself strongly opposed to the return of the British and repeatedly warned "traitors" and the occupiers of Chettyar lands that they would lose all if the British returned. In November, 1944, Bandoola U Sein took over the active leadership of the *Mahabama* (Great Burma) Party. Thakin Nu himself had helped organize the new party after August, 1944, when he gave up his empty role as foreign minister. Bandoola U Sein continued

[58] A.F.P.F.L., *From Fascist Bondage*, pp. 13–18; Maung Pye, *Burma in the Crucible*, pp. 177–183.

[59] Hinners, pp. 197–199; A.F.P.F.L., *The New Burma*, pp. 16–18.

[60] The following statement by Maung Maung (*Burma's Teething Time* [Rangoon, 1949], pp. 17–19) will illustrate the postwar mood: "Suffering . . . evoked the national spirit of the people and set their patriotism afire. . . . The Burmese people found for once that they could not be happy-go-lucky, relying on their star to light the way. They drifted no more. . . . They would not have Burma down. . . . Never [before] in history has Burma been so united, so fixed in the determination to get her independence or die."

481

to the end to trumpet the pro-Japanese propaganda line and to stress counterespionage activity.[61]

Dr. Ba Maw apparently regarded the Thakin leaders as unsophisticated youth who were entirely too rash in their undertakings. But however unhappy he may have been about their resistance plot when finally informed of it, he refused to betray it to the Japanese. The *Adipadi* preferred to stress the need to achieve Burma's own freedom, both political and economic, without compromising that objective by such reckless dealings with the returning British-Indian forces. Thakin Nu himself co-operated with Deedok U Ba Choe and the conservative Henzada U Mya in carrying out certain aspects of the government's propaganda program as late as the latter half of 1944.[62] Even after it became obvious in the spring of 1945 that the Japanese cause in Burma was lost beyond recovery, the Anglophobe Dr. Ba Maw refused to make any gesture in the direction of welcoming British re-entry. It is also significant that two of the most responsible leaders who had been a party to the entire A.F.P.F.L. nationalist conspiracy, Thakins Nu and Mya, elected to evacuate to Moulmein with the *Adipadi*. Many persons in a position to know the nationalist viewpoint and objectives of *Adipadi* Ba Maw tended to acclaim, as does Thakin Nu, his "grit and determination" to fight for Burma's political and economic independence, however much they may have disliked his egotism, vanity, opportunism, and chameleon tactics.[63]

It was the confidence of the A.F.P.F.L. leaders in Dr. Ba Maw's integrity as a nationalist that led them later to invite him to join their popular front party after his eventual return from Japan in 1946. It was apparently at that point too much of a comedown for one who had enjoyed for a time the semiroyal status of *Adipadi* to condescend to participate on a basis of something less than equality with the "boys" who had meanwhile seized the political leadership in postwar Burma.

The military role which the revolting Burmese army played in the total effort of the defeat of the Japanese forces was minor, but it was nonetheless strategically important and timely. On March 28, 1945,

[61] Hinners, pp. 200–201, 205.

[62] Nu, *Burma under the Japanese*, pp. 93–97.

[63] *Ibid.*, pp. 95–97. Wrote Thakin Nu: "Dr. Ba Maw had not the slightest contact with the English and Americans. . . . 'Well,' he told Nu, 'it looks as if Thakin Than Tun and his lot are playing with fire. So be careful. I don't want to stop anyone from doing what he thinks right. But you had better not tell me more about it. . . . The only thing I care about myself is independence.'"

when the Burmans turned on the Japanese, the main theater of fighting was still in the Upper Burma plain around Meiktila. British forces were dangerously behind schedule in their efforts to reach Rangoon before the monsoon rains made a morass of their own overland supply routes. So doubtful was the British command of reaching the port city in time that General Leese recommended, as of March 26, that the plans, previously discarded in February, for an amphibious assault on Rangoon from the Akyab-Kyaukpyu area be revived. Failure to acquire Rangoon as a supply channel before the rains disrupted air and surface supply services from India could have forced a general British withdrawal overland from ground hardly won. Burman co-operation was also welcome because Kuomintang Chinese forces in the Northern Shan States area were refusing at this juncture to cut off the Japanese retreat route at Loilem, as requested by the British command.[64] The forced Japanese evacuation of the Irrawaddy delta area before the end of April also changed their defeat into a rout as far as the considerable forces to the west of the Pegu Yoma were concerned.

It was on March 17 that the main contingents of the 10,000-man Burma National Army, led the General Aung San, left Rangoon for the "front." They departed under the inspiration of the salute of Japanese planes and the oratory of *Adipadi* Ba Maw. The people cheered for a different reason, for it was rumored that the B.N.A. commanders acted on orders drafted by the A.F.P.F.L. rather than by the Japanese.[65] Thakin Than Tun's departure from Rangoon on the following day for the purpose of a rendezvous with a British Major Carew at Toungoo was actually expedited by a timely suggestion from the *Adipadi* himself (promoted by Boh Let Ya) that the Thakin leader proceed to Toungoo for propaganda work. It was not until March 28, when the families of Thakins Than Tun and Aung San disappeared from Rangoon, that the Japanese became aware that they had both gone underground. On March 29 Rangoon received the news that 5,000 men of the Burma forces in the Toungoo-Pyinmana area and around Prome, as well as throughout the delta, had struck the Japanese in the rear. The action tied down a large number of Japanese troops

[64] Mountbatten, pp. 139–145. The amphibious force reached Rangoon on May 5 as scheduled, some eleven days after the Burmese action had forced the Japanese to evacuate the port.

[65] Maung Pye, pp. 81–87. The B.N.A. in June, 1945, changed its name to the "Patriotic Burmese Forces." As a veterans' group it came later to be known as the P.V.O., or "People's Volunteer Organization."

who might otherwise have been used to block the advance of the British 14th Army.[66] Thereupon the Burmese troops remaining in Rangoon were completely disarmed. The details of the latter phases of the campaign will be considered in the subsequent chapter.

Dr. Ba Maw's final cabinet meeting was held on April 22, and on the following day the *Adipadi,* accompanied by his personal followers and by Thakins Mya, Nu, and Lun Baw, evacuated the capital via Pegu en route to Moulmein. The British forces occupied Rangoon on May 5.[67] Although the Thakin inner circle which had planned the A.F.P.F.L. remained unbroken, it was the bolder General Aung San and Thakin Than Tun who emerged as its leaders with respect to both the Burman nationalist following and Lord Mountbatten and his British field commanders. Units of the Burma army subsequently saw active duty in the hill country to the east of the Sittang River into which the remnants of the defeated Japanese army withdrew. Some of the Japanese soldiers who were cut off from news concerning Tokyo's capitulation in August held out until October, 1945, before they surrendered.

Once having thrown off the cloak of secrecy, the A.F.P.F.L. undertook to broaden its base to include virtually all nationalist political elements. In May, 1945, the supreme council was enlarged to include three representatives from each of the five major component parts, namely the People's Revolutionary Party, with its Socialist-Communist core, the Burma National Army, the All Burma Youth League, the Karen Central Organization, and the *Maha Sangha.* To these were added ten representative political leaders of older established nationalist parties including U Saw's *Myochit,* Dr. Ba Maw's *Mahabama,* Thakin Ba Sein's *Dobama Asiayone* fragment, and the Fabian group led by U Ba Choe. The council also promised self-determination to all national minorities in an effort to enlist their allegiance as well.[68] It was on the basis of this broadened affiliation, backed by several mass organizations and by actual military participation throughout the final months of the Burma campaign, that the A.F.P.F.L. put forward its claim to speak for the Burmese nation as a whole.[69] The difficulties encountered in that attempt will be examined later.

[66] Mountbatten, pp. 144–145. The B.N.A., according to British reports, fought the Japanese throughout Lower Burma, killing a division commander and 700 men.

[67] Nu, *Burma under the Japanese,* pp. 106–111; Maung Pye, pp. 70–71.

[68] Hinners, pp. 210–212.

[69] The A.F.P.F.L. council was enlarged from the original 9 to 15 and then to 36 members.

XV

The Problem of Postwar British Policy

THE determination of British postwar policy for Burma was tardy and halting because the London authorities comprehended with great difficulty the profound changes which wartime experiences were producing in Burma. London's attention tended to focus on military aspects and on the disastrous impairment of Burma's productive capacity which presumably must be made good with British help before any kind of normal postwar governmental functioning could be resumed. The economic problem was very real. Several million acres of riceland had reverted to jungle; the cattle population had declined by one-third; and industries and transportation facilities and even the cities were in large measure destroyed. What London failed to appreciate fully was that a new sense of Burman national solidarity had been born from the common experience of wartime suffering. British prestige had been heavily compromised by defeat at the hands of Japan, and Burmans were determined to cancel their status of political subservience. The wartime elimination of British and Indian business interests afforded the Burmese an opportunity to strike out for economic independence as well and thus to end, once for all, alien economic domination. Thoughtful Burmese recognized that the deficits in Burmese capital, technical skill, and administrative and business experience were stubborn obstacles to be overcome, but few if any felt that these were serious enough to postpone independence.

The divergence between the official British and the Burman national-

ist points of view was aggravated by London's apparent willingness
to let the Burmans stew for a while in the aftermath of the harsh Japanese occupation so as to enhance their appreciation of British rule.
London was far more susceptible, of course, to the influence of representatives of British firms intent on returning to their vast economic
stakes in Burma than to any pressure emanating even remotely from
the Burmese people. Mr. Churchill in particular found the question of
Burma's postwar status so distasteful and hypothetical that he blocked
until May, 1945, repeated efforts of the exiled Burma Government and
the Secretary of State for India and Burma to obtain an earlier statement. At the outset, the British army command in India was almost
as conservative as London, for it tended to regard as traitors all Burmese collaborators with the Japanese, on whatever basis. The army
gave no credence to Governor Dorman-Smith's optimistic view that,
if properly encouraged, the Burmese people could be expected in time
to welcome the restoration of British control.

Much clearer in their appreciation of what was happening in occupied Burma was the membership of the exiled Burma Government at
Simla, India. It included a number of moderate Burmese nationalists
and a larger group of experienced British civil servants, some of whom
were genuinely sympathetic to the nationalist point of view. Governor
Dorman-Smith at the outset also accepted the moderate nationalist
point of view, for he regarded himself as a true friend of Burma and
was concerned to make good Britain's failure to protect the country
from invasion. He was also sensitive to British criticism of his administrative record of 1941–1942 and to the unconcealed aspersions cast by
members of the army command and the government in India on the
worth-whileness of the "holiday" activities of the Burma Government
at Simla.[1] His situation was particularly frustrating because London
withheld approval of all proposals for postwar policy with respect to
Burma. Any decision regarding Burma would be heavily conditioned
by what would happen in India, despite separation of the two countries.

Two new liberalizing factors entered the picture in 1944–1945. The
first was the personality of Lord Mountbatten, who took over in late
1943 the post of Supreme Allied Commander for Southeast Asia. His
influence was felt decisively during the course of the reconquest of
Burma in the dry season of 1944–1945, when the returning British
forces first became aware of the markedly altered political climate

[1] Maurice Collis, *Last and First in Burma*, pp. 187–191.

486

within the country. Lord Mountbatten was inclined to encourage the co-operation of patriotic nationalist elements not only as a step to facilitate the British reconquest but also in his role as Allied leader obliged to contemplate using Burma as a base for the eventual explusion of the Japanese from all Southeast Asia. The second factor was the accession to power in London, in July, 1945, of Mr. Clement Attlee's Labour Government. The Labour Party was far more understanding of Burma's and India's political aspirations than was its predecessor Conservative Government. The outcome would certainly have been different and might easily have been tragic lacking the inclination of Lord Mountbatten to accept political and military realities and Mr. Attlee's sincerity of purpose to redeem Britain's promises respecting freedom for Burma.

London's Negative Attitude

It is not difficult to account for the general unwillingness of the British Government throughout the war period to undertake the distasteful task of formulating a new policy regarding Burma's political future. The United Kingdom was engaged in a war of survival, and Burma was well down on the list of urgent priorities. Because Burma's postwar status would inevitably influence, and be influenced by, what happened in India, London had an additional reason for caution. This was especially true after the failure of the Cripps mission in the spring of 1942 to bring India actively into the war effort on the basis of postwar reform promises.[2] The physical impossibility, in 1943 and early 1944, of Britain's making any serious military or naval effort to oust the Japanese from control of Burma, despite American proddings, made it appear to some a matter of doubtful wisdom to compete with Japan's propaganda moves by promises which could not be backed up immediately by a substantial display of military strength. London authorities after 1942 were even inclined to believe that the inevitable American defeat of Japan in the Pacific war might enable the British to return to Burma without serious fighting. Under such a possibility, there existed no urgent military reasons to make postwar promises to Burma.[3] Strongly buttressing British inactivity was the disinclination of Prime Minister Churchill and his Secretary of State for India and

---

[2] *PD,C*, vol. 378 (March 12, 1942), p. 1188. On this occasion Secretary Amery refused to include a reference to Burma in any statement he made concerning the Cripps mission to India.

[3] Collis, *Last and First in Burma*, pp. 187–191.

Burma, Leopold S. Amery, to sponsor the liquidation of the British Empire.

Immediately following the military debacle in Burma in the spring of 1942, Governor Dorman-Smith was invited to London for consultation. During the course of his two months' visit in the United Kingdom from June to August, 1942, the governor expressed the conviction that since the mass of the Burmese people had evinced no hostility toward the defeated British forces (only 4,000 Burmese had allegedly assisted the Japanese) it was incumbent on Britain to acknowledge its obligation to make good the failure to protect Burma from invasion.[4] The governor returned to India in September, 1942, with a commission from Mr. Amery to select a group from the personnel of the exiled Burma Government at Simla to formulate concrete plans for material and governmental reconstruction following the war, including proposals for future policy reforms.[5]

While the work of the Simla planners was getting under way, Secretary Amery rebuffed repeated efforts by Opposition members of Parliament, some of them prompted by Burman friends, to elicit assurances concerning postwar self-government for Burma and British willingness to negotiate with representative Burmans on the matter. The government's official policy, according to Mr. Amery, was to concede self-government to Burma "as soon as circumstances permit." But he insisted that order would first have to be restored and that the circumstances attending liberation could not be anticipated.[6] Even after Premier Tojo's promise of independence of January, 1943, and Dr. Ba Maw's subsequent visit to Tokyo in March, the Secretary not only refused to set any time limit for granting Burman self-rule but also refused even to say that constitutional alterations were being considered.

Following the Japanese grant of "independence" to Burma on August 1, 1943, and Dr. Ba Maw's declaration of war on the United Kingdom, Labour Party spokesmen tried in vain to obtain a reaffirmation of the 1931 pledge that Burma's separation from India would not prejudice Burma's constitutional prospects. They argued that Burmese opposition to the Japanese would be far more resolute "if the Burmese people knew what they were fighting for as well as what they were fighting against." Secretary Amery replied that the government's policy was clear, that Allied victory was the best reply to the Japanese, and that

[4] *PD,C,* vol. 381 (July 9, 1942), pp. 933–934, vol. 382 (July 22, 1942), p. 154.
[5] *PD,C,* vol. 386 (Feb. 2, 1943), pp. 760–761.
[6] *PD,C,* vol. 385 (Nov. 19, 1942), p. 489.

the wisdom of making any statement at all was a matter of timing for the government to decide.[7]

Simla's Planning Program

The legal Government of Burma, in exile at Simla, India, performed three major tasks. The first was administrative. It concerned the affairs of several thousand evacuated government servants (many of them kept on half pay), relief measures for other *évacués,* and settlement of contractor claims. Simla also administered throughout the war in token fashion the Fort Hertz area in the extreme northern part of Burma and a portion of the Chin Hills. Simla's second function was to staff the Burma Intelligence Bureau, which evaluated information coming out of the occupied country and prepared the two-volume report entitled *Burma during the Japanese Occupation.* The Intelligence Bureau also sponsored broadcasts beamed to Burma. The bureau gave special attention to developments within the particular governmental departments of its several members. The objective was to ascertain the point at which the routine functions of government would have to be resumed once Burma was reoccupied.

More closely relevant to the political prospects of postwar Burma was Simla's third activity, a planning operation directed by the special Reconstruction Department under the chairmanship of F. B. Arnold. The department included a number of able younger members of the Burma civil service [8] who were sympathetic to the Burmese point of view, as well as several representative and informed Burmese assigned at Simla.[9] Premier Sir Paw Tun (appointed on January 20, 1942) and Finance Minister U Htoon Aung Gyaw, the two members of the 1941 cabinet who elected to accompany the governor to India, also took an active part in the work of the planning department.[10] The mandate under which the Reconstruction Department operated was liberal in character and broad in its scope, and much effort was put into its task.[11]

The activities of the Simla Reconstruction Department were never

[7] *PD,C,* vol. 392 (Nov. 11, 1943), p. 1287, vol. 395 (Dec. 2, 1943), pp. 516–517. The questions were raised by Members of Parliament Sorenson and Dugdale.

[8] Notably R. E. McGuire, B. O. Binns, and H. F. Oxbury.

[9] U Tin Tut, U Kyaw Min, U Hpu, U Ba Tin, and Daw Mya Sein were members of the Simla staff.

[10] The two Burman ministers became advisers to the governor after December 10, 1942, when Dorman-Smith, by proclamation, assumed full emergency powers under Article 139 of the constitution. The governor's emergency powers were subsequently extended repeatedly by action of Parliament at London.

[11] Maung Pye, *Burma in the Crucible,* pp. 72–77.

publicized, but enough was disclosed to indicate the general tenor of its recommendations. Its basic concern, underscored by the governor himself, was to find a basis on which essential Burmese co-operation could be assured during the critical postwar period. The department assumed that representative Burmans must share in the formulation of any future constitution and that it must in any case stay abreast of whatever was granted to India. Burma spokesmen also asked to be accorded an active role in carrying out postwar economic policy, which must include governmental regulation of the business operations of non-Burmese firms and the control of transmittal of earnings abroad and of labor immigration. Burman members also maintained that foreign firms which had suffered damage or destruction as a result of the war should not be accorded compensation from Burma revenues except in cases where such damage was caused by the Burmese themselves.

The Reconstruction Department agreed, furthermore, that for political reasons the Chettyars must not be allowed to return either as landowners or as moneylenders. It was also assumed that the public services, including the university, should be completely Burmanized at an early date and that all communal representation and special minority privileges be abolished. Burmans also insisted that they share in the control of the hill areas.[12] The department authorized a number of special studies to be made. One on public power policy recommended an 80 per cent nationalization of Burma's facilities for electric power.[13] The same trend toward nationalization was discernible in other recommendations as well. Detailed attention was paid to the postwar economic problems of transportation, agriculture, minerals and oil extraction, timber, milling services, and foreign trade.

During the first half of 1943, Governor Dorman-Smith and Secretary Amery agreed that an indefinite extension of the governor's emergency authority (for perhaps five to seven years) would be needed to put the country back on its feet economically. It was also decided that the reconstruction program would be broken down into a number of projects to be carried out by the experienced personnel of prewar British firms but financed by grants from the British Treasury and supervised by the Burma Government. The arrangement was conceived at Simla as a means of allaying Burmese fears, allegedly unfounded according

---

[12] Ibid.; Burma, Towards a Greater Burma: Speeches on Reconstruction (Simla, 1944).

[13] Merz and McLellan, Report on Post-war Organization of Electricity Supply (London, 1945).

to Amery, that recovery measures would witness the economic entrenchment of foreign firms and would enable them to exercise undue political influence. The proposal also appealed favorably to the Secretary and to the British business community, who saw in the prolonged period of executive control a guarantee that disruptive political influences would not block the recovery program. Dorman-Smith also liked the scheme because it would afford him a coveted opportunity to co-ordinate Burma's economic and governmental development along presumably constructive lines. The projects scheme was not approved at London in early 1943, however, partly because the Treasury refused to commit itself to the sizable monetary grants involved and because Mr. Churchill disliked the idea of making any statement of postwar intention at all, however cautious.[14]

Despite Secretary Amery's recognition that some reassuring definition of British policy would be required to make Britain's return to Burma palatable, he and the governor appear to have differed rather sharply in point of view. Mr. Amery was concerned mainly with placating British business interests while biding his time until the Prime Minister and the War Cabinet were ready to move. The governor, on the other hand, faced the impact of Burmese nationalist opinion at Simla. He must somehow meet the problem of enlisting genuine co-operation from the Burmese people upon his return. This problem became increasingly urgent during 1943 because London offered no rejoinder to Japan's grant of "independence" to Burma. *Adipadi* Dr. Ba Maw was seen enlisting almost every shade of Burmese political opinion in his new regime. The governor accordingly determined to make a second visit to England. He reportedly made the following public statement at New Delhi in July, directly prior to his departure:

We must recognize this as an unexampled opportunity to correct abuses and defects which were apparent under our [prewar] administration. . . . Burma belongs to the Burmese and when the time [shall come] for full self-government, we must try to hand over [a] country for which we have done a good job of work.[15]

The governor apparently accomplished little at London in his second wartime visit from August to November, 1943. Not only was Mr. Churchill adamant in his refusal to issue any statement concerning postwar Burma, but he took sharp exception to Dorman-Smith's refer-

---

[14] Collis, *Last and First in Burma*, pp. 189–191.
[15] *Daily Express*, July 21, 1943.

ence to "handing over the country to the Burmese." Mr. Amery also ruled that it was inopportune to speak of self-government for Burma. He countered the governor's argument that military necessity counseled the clarification of postwar plans by pointing out that no early invasion was contemplated. The governor thereupon took his case for enlisting Burmese co-operation to the Labourite Ernest Bevin, to the East India Association, to members of the Commons, and even to the royal family, but to little avail.[16]

One of the apparent results of the second London visit was the selection of a special parliamentary subcommittee on Burma policy under the standing Imperial Affairs Committee of the Commons. Under the chairmanship of Mr. Somerset de Chair, the group was directed to examine the means of postwar reconstruction in Burma and especially the problem of encouraging capitalist enterprise "to resume operations in spite of losses." [17] The governor's visit also encouraged Burman residents in England to enter their urgent pleas in the press for some declaration of postwar policy comparable to the Cripps offer to India in order to enlist Burman co-operation with the eventual United Nations liberation effort.[18]

Probably the most distraught person at Simla during the latter half of 1943 was the titular Burmese Premier Sir Paw Tun. It was his often-expressed and prophetic opinion that if nothing were done by London to attract the support of Burma's moderate nationalists the double-dealing and traitorous Thakins, even though heavily discredited by their role in the B.I.A., could eventually make good their claim to be the spokesmen for the nation. He believed that an immediate pledge of full dominion status for Burma after five years' effort devoted to re-establishing the country's economy would enlist the co-operation of the moderate majority of nationalists. Sir Paw Tun regarded the Thakins as presumptuous blackguards and had no sympathy for the efforts of Britain's secret Force 136 to enlist the military co-operation of malcontents within Burma who presumed to represent Burman opinion. Whether or not London's silence was responsible for sabotaging any possibility of realizing Simla's reconstruction plans, it is, of course, impossible to say. By August, 1944, the Burman group at Simla were themselves declaring that the country would not willingly revert to its

[16] *Asiatic Review*, XL (1944), 15–23; Collis, *Last and First in Burma*, pp. 192–204, 209–212.

[17] *Financial News*, Nov. 9, 1943.

[18] *The Times*, Dec. 20, 1943, letter by Ma Hla Ye.

prewar status and would definitely forego material reconstruction in favor of political freedom if a choice between the two had to be made.[19]

The planning work of the Simla government suffered from the fact that the mandate under which the Reconstruction Department operated was so elastic, and its actual responsibility so limited, that its deliberations eventually became divorced from reality. The governor went along with the department's recommendations up to a point, but he apparently tended in 1944 and 1945 to favor contrary influences. The divergences came on such questions as Indian immigration, Chettyar land claims, and the need for separate administration for Kachin, Chin, and Shan-inhabited areas.[20] In the absence of any specific indication from London regarding the postwar Burma policy, the department's activities degenerated in time into a theoretical (almost academic) exercise, devoid of practical political significance. The older Indian civil servants were properly doubtful of being able to enlist the co-operation of Burmese nationalists on any basis of concessions which would be acceptable to London, while the representatives of British business firms, particularly those influencial in London, favored the re-establishment of economic activities in reconquered Burma even at the cost of turning back the political clock.

The basic question, which only London could decide, was whether the primary postwar objective should be to prepare Burma for self-government or whether political progress should be subordinated to the re-establishment of economic processes in general and British business interests in particular. The alternatives were described by Mr. John S. Furnivall in a forthright statement prepared in England at the request of Mr. Arnold's department, as follows:

We have a choice of two policies. One alternative is to keep the people weak by depriving them of arms and multiplying divisions so that foreign rule is necessary and they are least able to resist it. The other alternative is to build up a society . . . so that it can be as strong as possible and capable of self-government. Both will involve bloodshed. By burning enough villages, killing enough men (and, of course, women and children), dropping enough bombs, and bribing enough "yes-men," we can "pacify" the country; how long it will take and how much it will cost is uncertain. . . . [Such a course] will save us the trouble of thinking; the multiplication of police, magistrates, and jails will provide us with more jobs and allow Government

[19] Collis, *Last and First in Burma*, pp. 207–208, 223; *Christian Science Monitor*, June 29, 1944; *Manchester Guardian*, Aug. 5, 1944.
[20] Collis, *Last and First in Burma*, pp. 198–199.

officers to draw their pay and European firms their profits. The latter alternative requires faith and courage; to make the people strong is to make them dangerous. . . . The project . . . does not . . . imply excessive belief in the immediate capacity of the people to govern themselves without assistance . . . but it does imply a belief—rather perhaps a hope—in our powers to give them the necessary assistance.[21]

Conservative Pressure and the Blue-Print for Burma

In sharp contrast with the theoretical discussions of the Burma reconstructors at Simla was the articulate statement prepared in England by business spokesmen for the Burma Chamber of Commerce in 1943 and 1944. It argued that priority in postwar Burma must be given to tangible economic recovery in preference to political experimentation. Burmans would simply have to adjust their thinking to the essential conditions for meeting the country's needs for capital, technical aid, and the restoration of transportation. It would be unwise, therefore, for London to embarrass future decisions by making definite promises concerning Burma's political future. The primary need was to set up a strong government capable of opposing disruptive political influence, so that economic rehabilitation could be accomplished. The emergency rule of the governor under Article 139 (as proclaimed on December 10, 1942) should be extended indefinitely, and all civil servants associated with Dr. Ba Maw's regime should be required to clear themselves of taint of disloyalty. British firms previously active in Burma must be compensated from future Burma revenues for damages suffered from "denial" (scorched-earth) measures and should also enjoy preferred status in the role of reviving economic production. Nor should there be discriminatory treatment of Indian firms and labor. Chettyar land titles and mortgages would have to be honored and no restrictions placed on Indian labor immigration. In fact, large numbers of imported Indian coolies would be essential from the outset.[22]

The most important development in 1944 with respect to postwar Burma was the preparation and publication of the report of the Commons Committee on Burma Policy. The findings were based mainly on interviews with retired Burma officials and directors of Rangoon business firms.[23] The committee's so-called Blue-Print for Burma was published in November, 1944, its appearance having been delayed for a

[21] John S. Furnivall, "Reconstruction in Burma" (MS., 1943), pp. 110–111.
[22] Chatham House Paper no. IV, Aug., 1943; Great Britain and the East, Oct. 23, 1943, pp. 11–12, and July 1, 1944, p. 39.
[23] Collis, Last and First in Burma, pp. 229–231.

number of months at the request of the government, which was much concerned over the outcome of the attempted Japanese invasion of India. Publication had the immediate effect of provoking a spate of negative press comment and eventually led to a parliamentary debate on December 12, 1944.[24]

The authors of the *Blue-Print* [25] argued that a primary requirement for obtaining Burmese co-operation would be to fix a time limit, not to exceed six years from the resumption of British control, for completing necessary economic reconstruction prior to granting full self-government to Burma. During this maximum six-year period of personal rule by the governor, Burmans should be trained to participate in business operations and the governor should be authorized to seek Burman aid in laying the groundwork for a new constitution. The proposed constitution would also have to be examined by a representative Burman assembly. A second major prerequisite for Burmese co-operation would be to eliminate as far as possible noncultivator ownership of land and Chettyar moneylender operations. Chettyar evacuation, according to the *Blue-Print,* had already effected a partial solution of Burma's agrarian problem. A loan secured by Burma's revenues might be used to liquidate Chettyar claims at perhaps 30 per cent of face value. Final treaty arrangements with self-governing Burma should permit enlistment of British-ruled non-Burmese hill people in the imperial armies and should include indemnification for losses suffered by British commercial firms operating in Burma at the time of the Japanese conquest. As a slap at Mr. Amery's unco-operative India Office, the *Blue-Print* proposed that Burma's affairs be transferred forthwith to the Office of the Secretary for Dominion Affairs.[26]

The debate on the *Blue-Print* began in the press before it reached Parliament. A number of Burman-authored letters to *The Times* condemned the plan as "a travesty of His Majesty's Government's pledges" and denounced as impossible a return to the rule by governor's ordinance for any period approaching a six-year term. From both political and psychological points of view, the façade of "independence" under the Japanese would be more attractive to Burmans than the *Blue-Print* proposal. An *ad hoc* Burma Association in London wanted no period of direct rule by the governor, but rather the declaration of a general

---

[24] *PD,C*, vol. 406 (Dec. 12, 1944), pp. 1078–1128.

[25] Messrs. Somerset de Chair, Reed, Shephard, MacDonald, and others.

[26] *PD,C*, vol. 406 (Dec. 12, 1944), pp. 1078–1128. The *Blue-Print* was attacked strongly by Indian interests for its suggested sacrifice of Chettyar claims. See Hinners, pp. 179, 185.

amnesty and the early convening of a popularly elected Constituent Assembly.[27] The eventual debate in Parliament on December 12 indicated how far apart official British opinion and that of the Burman nationalists had drifted.

As the principal spokesman for the government, Secretary Amery made no concession whatever to the growing demand for a policy declaration even along the conservative lines of the *Blue-Print* proposals. He indicated blandly, instead, that Burmans had not forfeited by their collaboration with the Japanese their claim to British assistance in moving toward the ultimate goal of self-government within the commonwealth. But the manner and the date would be determined in due course by London. Mr. Amery also declined to promise that Burma's constitutional progress would keep pace with India's. Basing his opinion in part, no doubt, on the secret intelligence that Burman nationalists were actively preparing to turn against the Japanese, Mr. Amery expressed confidence that the Burmans would welcome liberation from Japanese control and would also appreciate the spirit of friendship and good will behind preparations to make good the damages suffered from Britain's failure to defend Burma. He declared flatly that former Indian residents of Burma would be allowed to return and that Chettyars would have their lands restored.[28]

The Final Policy of Simla, 1945

The outcome of the parliamentary debate on the *Blue-Print* proposal was entirely negative. The more liberal aspects of the Reconstruction Department's plans at Simla were jettisoned. Governor Dorman-Smith's subsequent efforts to agitate through the Indian press for a liberal postwar policy in Burma involved his acceptance of Mr. Amery's principle of restoring Indian interests in Burma on a nondiscriminatory basis plus his advocacy of importing 200,000 coolies for reconstruction purposes. The conservative Indian civil service officers who took over the planning at Simla in 1945 were skeptical of Burmese capacity for self-

[27] *The Times*, Nov. 21 and 24, 1944, Dec. 8, 1944, Feb. 8, 1945; *Daily Herald*, Feb. 8, 1945; *News Chronicle*, Feb. 8, 1945. The rift is observable in a Burma Chamber of Commerce warning that Indians must not be discriminated against and in Thakin Than Tun's first wireless exchange with Force 136 denouncing the *Blue-Print* as unacceptable.

[28] *PD,C*, vol. 406 (Dec. 12, 1944), pp. 1078–1128. Speaking for Labour, Mr. Creech Jones urged that plans for responsible government for Burma be initiated as soon as possible and that Burmans be accorded a considerable role not only in shaping the new constitution but also in determining the kind of economic rehabilitation given them.

rule; they also doubted with good reason that the six-year limitation proposed in the *Blue-Print* would suffice to guarantee Burmese co-operation. The final tentative decision of the Simla government, subject to London's confirmation, was to give priority to "law and order" con-siderations and to the restoration of essential economic operations. The political objective of complete self-rule would be deferred for a number of years until orderly conditions and a sufficient degree of economic recovery would permit the resumption of constitutional progress.

As a substitute for the thorny proposal to compensate from Burma revenues those British firms who had suffered losses through "denial" measures, Simla revived in altered form the rejected projects proposal of 1943. The six main fields of economic rehabilitation previously con-sidered were broken down into twenty-odd administrative "project" units (one each for agriculture, timber, oil, and other major facets of the economy). Each of the "projects" would employ competent persons with prewar experience in Burma to direct that particular phase of the recovery operations. British firms previously active in Burma were to be accorded priority privileges. Funds to prime the economic pump would be provided by a British Government loan of £80 million to £100 million on a noninterest-bearing basis. The Burma Government would then pay wages and salaries of personnel and purchase the capital goods needed by the various "projects" agencies, while any profits realized would revert to the fund. Eventually, the control of specific economic operations would be turned over to private firms, whose future status would be governed by agreements to be negotiated by Britain with the future Burma Government. The economic rights of Indian laborers and businessmen previously resident in Burma would also be fully recognized. This policy proposal was finally approved by London in May, 1945.[29]

Within the framework of this general policy not only the Simla government but also the Civil Affairs Section (CAS) of the imperial army, which was re-entering Burma in early 1945, began to fill up their ranks in large measure with ex-civil servants and business people for-merly resident in Burma. Such persons, with occasional exceptions, usually lacked sympathy for the Burmese point of view. It was Simla's expectation in May, 1945, that military occupation of Burma would probably persist until near the end of 1945, during which time primary attention would be focused on the restoration of communica-tions and public utilities and on the promotion of health measures. It

[29] One of the prime fashioners of the final "projects" proposals was Mr. O'Dell.

was also expected that for some eighteen months following the ending of military control the civil government would exercise rigid supervision of all economic activities within Burma.

It was remarkable that, after so many months of considering what measures were needed for enlisting essential Burmese co-operation with the returning British administration, a plan was finally adopted at Simla so completely divorced from that objective. No less a person than ex-Premier Sir Paw Tun in May, 1945, denounced the final Simla plans as "rubbish," the absurd and highhanded work of men who were both ignorant and incompetent. He insisted that the program was irrelevant not only to the realities of the political situation in Burma, but also to the declared British policy of promoting Burma's self-government. Most of the Burmans at Simla agreed fully with U Paw Tun's estimate.[30] The program appeared to be tantamount to vesting both administrative and economic control in the hands of the very British Burma Chamber of Commerce group who traditionally had been contemptuous of Burman political aspirations and most directly interested in reviving the provocative Chettyar moneylender operations and Indian labor immigration. The situation was doubly ominous because the same group promised to continue to be influencial in government circles in London after the war.

One of the most thoughtful statements of the conservative point of view was made by Mr. F. Burton Leach, a senior Indian civil service official with long experience in Burma.[31] The author conceded that "independence" was a magic word and that the dominion status offer made to India would probably have to be matched in Burma. Also on the side of freedom was the discredit which British prestige had sustained and the suggestive standard set by the United States in freeing the Philippines. Mr. Leach nevertheless believed that Burma's military vulnerability, situated as it was between India and China, and the overpowering need for assistance in economic rehabilitation over a period of possibly six years argued convincingly for the ultimate goal of self-government within the Commonwealth. Commercial firms, he affirmed, were entitled to compensation for property destroyed by military order, and Chettyar claims would have to be settled (possibly to the extent of £30 million). Burmans meanwhile would need to qualify themselves for high posts in industry, and some guarantees

---

[30] Statement reported by observer in Simla, May, 1945.
[31] F. B. Leach, *The Problem of Burma* (London, 1945).

General Aung San

Premier Nu

would have to be devised for the 5 million minority peoples.[32] Events were to prove that political realities in Burma permitted no such leisurely approach.

The Influence of Lord Mountbatten

The ultimate decision with respect to Britain's postwar policy in Burma had also to take into account the personality and viewpoint of Lord Mountbatten, the Supreme Allied Commander for Southeast Asia (SACSEA). As a colorful and outstandingly able member of the British royal family, Admiral Mountbatten was not an individual whose views could easily be brushed aside. As an Allied theater commander, responsible to the Combined Chiefs of Staff and with large contingents of the United States Air Force and some ground forces serving under his orders, he was obliged also to give primary consideration to military ends and to do so in a broader context than Burma alone. He was personally sensitive, as London was not, to American opinion, which, with respect to postwar colonial questions, was in most respects out of sympathy with the views of Messrs. Churchill and Amery. The ground forces which reconquered Burma were almost entirely imperial troops (Indian, British, African, and Gurkha), but the large United States Air Force contingent based in India played an important role, especially in the area of supply services. This was true both in the defense of Manipur and after the fighting shifted in 1944–1945 into the plains of central Burma. The extreme northern areas of Burma, along the Ledo Road to Mogaung and Myitkyina and thence to Bhamo and Lashio, were reconquered by an American-directed Chinese army, aided by local Kachin guerrillas.[33] The Supreme Allied Commander (SEA) and his Allied army, furthermore, were assigned military responsibilities within Southeast Asia extending far beyond the boundaries of Burma. In fact, it appeared that Burma itself would probably have to serve as a base of operations. Political decisions made in Burma prejudicial to continuing military operations would, therefore, inevitably be matters of broad Allied concern.

The agency within the Southeast Asia Command responsible for conducting clandestine operations of both a guerrilla and intelligence

[32] Ibid., pp. 8–12.

[33] The 670,000 British combat troops (European, Indian, African) serving in the Southeast Asia Command constituted 91 per cent of the total ground forces. British forces made up 80 per cent of the total Allied strength including air power. See PD,C, vol. 414 (Oct. 9, 1945), p. 82.

nature within Burma proper was known as Force 136 of the Special Operations Executive, an agency of the London War Cabinet.[34] Force 136 armed and directed Karen guerrilla groups and established the contact from December, 1943, with the budding Antifascist People's Freedom League (A.F.P.F.L.). Lord Mountbatten exercised responsibility for the conduct of civil affairs in reoccupied Burma from January 1, 1944. The Civil Affairs Section (B) was placed under Major General C. F. B. Pearce, a former Burma civil servant. Partly because the limited number of competent Burma-trained persons had to be shared between the CAS(B) and the Simla government, General Pearce recruited many of his staff from former employees of British firms operating in Burma (Steel Brothers and the Burmah Oil Company, for example), who were unfamiliar not only with political realities in Burma but also with governmental administrative procedures. General Pearce and his CAS(B) were therefore ultraconservative. The gulf between the viewpoints of Force 136 and CAS(B) with respect to effectiveness and the advisability of utilizing the assistance of indigenous anti-Japanese groups within Burma was unbridgeable.[35]

Force 136 and CAS(B) clashed seriously in early 1945. On the basis of protests from General Pearce made in early February, 1945, the field commander in central Burma, Lieutenant General Leese, forbade the further distribution of arms for the use of the Burma National Army. Pearce alleged that such distribution imperiled the present and the future security of Burma, an attitude shared by Governor Dorman-Smith and Sir Paw Tun. Communist authorship of some of the anti-Japanese A.F.P.F.L. leaflets distributed in the vicinity of Mandalay plus the ultranationalist views of the Thakin leaders of the A.F.P.F.L. contributed to CAS(B)'s concern. When the decision was appealed to Admiral Mountbatten by Force 136 on the ground that Burmese guerrilla operations would be useful both militarily and in influencing the population as a whole toward the British side, the Supreme Allied Commander (SEA) on February 24 overruled the order of General Leese. He directed that arms in limited numbers could still be distributed, not to the A.F.P.F.L. as an organization, but to approved individuals who would accept responsibility for sur-

[34] Collis, *Last and First in Burma*, p. 197. The United States OSS Detachment 101 was confined in its operations to General Stilwell's campaign in northern Burma. A similar United States Detachment 221 operated from Akyab to Rangoon, but only in the later stages of the war.

[35] Vice-Admiral Earl Mountbatten of Burma, *Report to the Combined Chiefs of Staff . . . 1943–1945* (London, 1951), pp. 142–144, 189.

rendering them at the end of military operations. On March 5, Admiral Mountbatten left to local commanders the decision as to when and how the B.N.A. guerrillas would be brought into active co-operation with British military operations. Actually some 3,000 arms, a small fraction of those already in Burman hands, were distributed to anti-Japanese groups after February, 1945.[36]

Lord Mountbatten's important decision was apparently at the outset based exclusively on military considerations. He reasoned that, since the already armed B.N.A. was determined to act against the Japanese regardless of British permission, it seemed to him far more sensible to try to utilize them as allies than to divert several divisions of British troops to the militarily profitless undertaking of putting them down. This consideration became doubly urgent after March 22, when General Leese indicated doubt that the British 14th Army, fighting against desperate Japanese resistance in Upper Burma, could reach the port of Rangoon before the onset of the rains in May, which would render virtually inoperable the supply services for his army overland from India. The utilization of some 5,000 B.N.A. troops strategically placed in the rear of the retreating Japanese troops on both sides of the Pegu Yoma was regarded by Mountbatten as a kind of windfall needed to facilitate the early capture of Rangoon. The Supreme Allied Commander (SEA) also indicated that, under existing circumstances, the reaction in the United States as well as in Britain would be highly critical 'if proffered Burman aid were rebuffed.[37]

The final decision to co-ordinate the impending Burman attack on the Japanese rear with the advancing operations of the British 14th Army came on March 25. General Leese then reported that the psychological and tactical moment had arrived, a conclusion strongly supported by General Slim but protested by CAS(B) officers. On March 27, Lord Mountbatten reported to the British Chiefs of Staff his decision to encourage the assistance of the B.N.A. forces on military grounds. He agreed to withhold any promise of amnesty for past

[36] *Ibid.*, pp. 142–145. The A.F.P.F.L. leaflets emphasized the objective of enlisting mass support from all classes, nationalities, and creeds and insisted that the A.F.P.F.L. flag must have a red background to reflect the boldness of the group and the unity of the blood of the poor masses of all nations. See also Collis, *Last and First in Burma*, p. 197.

[37] *Mountbatten*, pp. 142–145. This decision and later ones by Lord Mountbatten contributed to the recognition given him in the Union of Burma's Honour's List for 1956, when he was awarded the highest Agga Maha Thiri Thudhamma designation. In fact, Lord Mountbatten had long advocated a policy statement from London, according to Collis (*Last and First in Burma*, pp. 222–224).

treasonable actions, but proposed to tell A.F.P.F.L. leaders that their aid to the Allies both militarily and in civilian reconstruction would later be taken into account. Members of the B.N.A. were to expect eventually to be disarmed, although suitable volunteers from the group would be enrolled in the future regular Burma armed forces.

The situation was essentially a *fait accompli,* for the British War Cabinet gave its reluctant consent on March 30, two days after the Burman revolt broke. London's provisos included the assertion that the British attached little importance to the A.F.P.F.L. military contribution and that former collaborators with the Japanese had to atone for numerous mistakes before establishing themselves in the favor of Britain. Britain, furthermore, was not prepared to discuss with General Aung San or any other nationalist spokesmen issues touching the future political institutions of Burma, but would insist that the political progress of Burma within the Commonwealth could only be achieved by unity and discipline under British leadership.[38]

Subsequent developments in the campaign demonstrated conclusively that Lord Mountbatten's decision was militarily justified. The British army's thrust down the Sittang Valley toward Rangoon was greatly accelerated as a consequence of Burmese help, and Rangoon itself was rendered untenable by April 22. In the Toungoo area, the B.N.A. attack on the Japanese rear was co-ordinated with the action of a Karen guerrilla unit under Force 136 to defeat Japanese efforts to strengthen their sagging front by re-enforcements sent from Thailand via Mawchi. Burmese attacks in the delta area, mainly a Karen battalion led by Saw San Po Thin, tied down other Japanese troops which could have been used to block British progress toward Rangoon.[39] The British 14th Army advanced from Yamethin to Pegu, a distance of some 220 miles, in eighteen days (April 11 to 29), and they covered in five days only the crucial 150-mile stretch where the B.N.A. attack occurred (Pyinmana to Nyaunglebin). A United States glider-borne engineering unit, using bulldozers, developed in co-operation with Indian army engineers nine air strips in the course of eleven days during the most rapid period of the advance. The most effective contribution of the Burmese army to the Allied victory was in causing

[38] *Ibid.,* pp. 144–145.
[39] *Ibid.,* p. 153; Burma, *Report of the Frontier Areas Committee of Enquiry, 1947* (Rangoon, 1947), pt. II, p. 169, hereafter cited as *RFACE.* The initial B.N.A. attack killed some 700 Japanese, including a general and a division commander.

the complete breakdown of the Japanese army's lines of communication and transport to the delta area.[40] Japanese forces, re-enforced by contingents from the delta and from Moulmein, made a final determined stand at Pegu (April 29 to May 1). When defeated, they retreated to the east of the Sittang River. Rangoon was occupied by British sea-borne forces from May 2 to 5, just as the first monsoon rains struck the city.[41] Rangoon port became thereafter the vital channel for supplying the British 14th Army.

The capture of Rangoon afforded opportunity for reconsideration of the question of the status of the B.N.A. collaborators. The general standard set for testing the loyalty of Burma public servants who had participated in the Japanese-sponsored Burma Government, as revised by CAS(B) on April 21, were such that the A.F.P.F.L. leaders, and especially Thakin Aung San, could not possibly qualify. Aung San had not only given overt aid to the Japanese military forces in 1942, but had actually taken an oath of allegiance to the enemy Japanese when appointed general of the B.D.A. He and Dr. Ba Maw were at the top of the black list (drawn up along with "gray" and "white" classifications) of persons to be arrested on sight.[42] The April 21 directive indicated that the burden of proof of acting under duress was to fall on those making such claim. Since the original justification for using B.N.A. assistance to expedite the capture of Rangoon no longer applied, General Pearce of the CAS(B) urged the immediate arrest of Thakin Aung San as a war criminal. When CAS(B) was again overruled by Lord Mountbatten on the ground that such action would provoke a minor civil war in an area in which much fighting was still to be done and which had to serve as a basis for continuing operations, General Pearce and a number of his associates resigned from the army and resumed their civil service posts at Simla. That this crisis had not been anticipated is indicated by the fact that General Hubert

[40] General Ne Win's statement of May 7, 1945, in A.F.P.F.L., *From Fascist Bondage to New Democracy* (Rangoon, 1945), p. 34.

[41] Mountbatten, pp. 153–154. A small United States American air-borne group from OSS Detachment 221 landed at Mingaladon airfield on May 2 and was at the port of Rangoon to greet the first British arrivals by sea.

[42] Disloyalty classifications included those who had given military aid to the Japanese, had published or spoken to further Japan's war effort or to put the legal (British) authorities in contempt, had taken an oath of allegiance to the enemy (except to Dr. Ba Maw, under circumstances amounting to duress), or had committed acts of sabotage against loyal subjects, the legal government, or the British army.

503

Rance, Pearce's successor as chief of the CAS(B), was not able to reach Burma until June 17 and that some of the CAS(B) agencies from Calcutta did not reach Burma until August, 1945.

On May 16, Lieutenant General Slim and Thakin Aung San agreed that the B.N.A., as a recognized ally, would be placed under the control of the British field commander, who would be provided data as to the strength and disposition of the Burmese forces. The question of allegiance was not resolved. General Slim refused to recognize General Aung San's claim to be the military representative of the alleged A.F.P.F.L.-sponsored provisional government of Burma. The Burman leader in turn refused to accord allegiance to anybody except the A.F.P.F.L. and specified that any decision about the future status of the B.N.A. would call for consultations with the A.F.P.F.L. executive council. Lord Mountbatten's view was that it was realistic at the time to deal on a *de facto* basis with the A.F.P.F.L. as a "coalition of political parties commanding the largest following in the territory." Governor Dorman-Smith's veto prevented General Slim from assuring General Aung San at the time that the returning governor would consider the inclusion of representatives of the A.F.P.F.L. in his executive council.

On May 22, the Chiefs of Staff at London again bowed to Mountbatten's common-sense political improvisation and accepted the B.N.A. as a temporary ally eligible for regular pay and rations. The Burman force was subsequently to be reassembled and reorganized as an auxiliary military body for service outside Burma. When civil government should return, B.N.A. volunteers would be permitted to enroll in the regular Burma army after the police had winnowed out criminal elements. On May 30, Governor Dorman-Smith himself agreed not to censor the political activities of the B.N.A., which was to be renamed the Patriotic Burmese Forces. He also sent a Simla liaison to army headquarters at Rangoon. The B.N.A. participated in the Allied victory parade at Rangoon on June 15.[43]

Before continuing the story of events in Burma, it is necessary at this point to pause to consider the long-awaited British Government White Paper on Burma, published on May 17, 1945.

The Burma White Paper of May 17, 1945

The impatience of all elements of Burma's government in exile at Simla over London's neglect of Burma policy approached exaspera-

[43] Mountbatten, pp. 200–201; Collis, *Last and First in Burma*, p. 239.

tion in the spring of 1945. The psychological opportunity to make a real appeal for moderate Burman support afforded by the A.F.P.F.L. decision to turn on the Japanese was lost beyond recovery. Subsequent far-reaching *de facto* decisions made by the military command were in complete disregard of Simla's wishes. Some at Simla alleged that Churchill was exclusively responsible for London's maddening inactivity, but the larger problem of postwar British policy for India was certainly a contributing factor.

In early April, 1945, Governor Dorman-Smith, accompanied by U Tin Tut and U Htoon Aung Gyaw,[44] proceeded to England for the third time, determined to be in London at the same time as Viceroy Lord Wavell, so that Burma and India could obtain comparable concessions. It was alleged that the governor threatened to resign if no suitable arrangement could be arrived at to relieve Simla's extreme embarrassment. Weeks passed and nothing happened. Burmese apprehensions in particular were aggravated on May 10, when Secretary Amery replied to a parliamentary inquiry concerning the probable political repercussions which might attend the return of Burma's oil fields to foreign companies by saying that His Majesty's Government had no intention of preventing the "nonforeign" British oil companies from resuming operations under unexpired leases previously granted by the Government of Burma.[45] In addition to the pressure being exerted by the Simla government, London faced also United States advocacy of the highly objectionable (to London) United Nations trusteeship principle, which was designed to bring the government of dependent peoples under the purview of world opinion.[46]

The basic misconception which seemed to underlie the logic of the White Paper on Burma, finally published on May 17, was that the returning British authorities would be welcomed by a chastened Burmese population grateful for deliverance from the Japanese. The small minority which had favored the Japanese in 1942 and were now aiding the British were presumed to be sadder and wiser as a result of their tragic blunder. Against the background of this erroneous assumption were posited two ex-parte British affirmations, namely (1) that Burma's progress toward self-government had been interrupted and set back by events of the war and (2) that the restoration of

[44] U Htoon Aung Gyaw visited America as well.
[45] *PD,C*, vol. 410 (May 10, 1945), p. 1995.
[46] See "The Colonial Issue," *Economist*, vol. 148 (1945), pp. 401–402. The French were also much perturbed over the trusteeship idea.

Burma's economic and social life, which constituted the foundation of any democratic political structure, must precede the revival of the political institutions of the prewar period. Thus the establishment of orderly conditions, the replacement of buildings, utilities, agriculture, communications, and industry, must first be realized. Since these tasks were beyond the financial resources of the ravaged country to perform, they would have to devolve on the civil government functioning under the direction of the governor.

On the basis of such premises, the White Paper decided that the plenary powers of the governor under Article 139 of the 1935 constitution would be extended for three years, in the hope that by then order would have been established and full economic rehabilitation realized. After a new electoral law was enacted and electoral rolls prepared, constitutional government could be re-established on the prewar model.[47] The White Paper also explained that the timing of the resumption of political progress would depend in large measure on the degree of co-operation accorded by all sections of the Burmese people in restoring normal conditions. The rigors of the governor's arbitrary rule under Article 139 would be lessened at the outset by the issuance of orders in council authorizing the governor to avail himself of the advice and assistance of a small executive council, mainly official, but to include nonofficial Burmese as opportunity should offer. Subject to the governor's supervision and control, such councilors could share in the administrative task. Perhaps an interim legislative council might even be authorized. Such temporary arrangements would lapse with the termination of Article 139, to occur as soon as conditions made possible holding elections under the regular constitutional provisions.

Burma's prospects for further constitutional advance as set forth in the White Paper were hedged about by ample qualifications. Contingent on continuing improvement of the economic and financial position of the country following the restoration of the 1935 constitution, a preparatory study could be undertaken and completed covering advisable constitutional changes. After these proposals had been considered and after various parties and sections of the Burmese people

[47] Great Britain, *Burma: Statement of Policy by His Majesty's Government, May, 1945* (London, 1945); Maung Pye, pp. 202–203. Governor Dorman-Smith and his friends had agitated for a flat three-year maximum period of governor's rule, with an earlier re-establishment of executive and legislative councils and preparations for framing a new constitution soon after civil government returned. See *PD,C,* vol. 411 (June 1, 1945), pp. 495–550.

had reached "a sufficient measure of agreement" on them, the actual formulation of a suitable constitution could be undertaken. This constitutional process would be accompanied by discussion of agreements with London authorities covering matters on which Britain would have continuing obligations in Burma. Parliamentary approval of the newly formulated constitution would come only after it had been accorded "a sufficient measure of support in Burma" to justify such action. Thereupon His Majesty's Government and the representatives of Burma would enter into final agreements respecting Britain's continuing political obligations and financial advances previously made by London. The Shan States and the tribal areas would continue under the governor's rule until the inhabitants signified a desire for some suitable form of amalgamation with Burma proper. Full self-government within the British Commonwealth would follow the tangible establishment of the necessary administrative organization and the completion of treaty arrangements. The final goal for Burma would be the status of full equality with the dominions and with Britain herself.[48]

Mr. Amery's oral discussion of the White Paper on June 1, when the House of Commons debated Burma policy, was far more conciliatory than the "cold officialism" of the document itself.[49] Undoubtedly one factor in causing the change of tone was that events in Burma had already outrun the tardy planning of London. The Secretary gave assurances that, from the outset, reconstruction would accord with Burmese ideas of what they would wish to do once accorded full power. The basic concern of British economic plans, he explained, was to put Burma back on its feet from a revenue point of view. An interest-free loan carrying no maturity date would provide consumer goods and needed capital equipment. This equipment would eventually be paid for by the companies using it. Furthermore, no reprisals would be taken against anyone "who, in the interest of his own people, had to conform to Japanese orders." Segments of the B.N.A. currently espousing the British cause were being allowed to "work their passage home" and thus make restitution for previous errors. Mr. Amery understood that it was the intention of the governor to seek advice from Burmans of all points of view, not from the vocal minority alone.

[48] Great Britain, *Burma: Statement of Policy*.

[49] The Manchester *Guardian* for June 2, 1945, admitted that the rigidity of the India Office had done much harm, which could not be canceled out by Mr. Amery's speech.

Mr. Amery's final reference in the debate was in deprecation of two articles which had appeared in *The Times* on May 29 and June 1, sponsored by Burmese residents of London calling themselves the Burma Association. The association demanded dominion status for Burma on a fixed date, with constitutional government to be re-established as early as possible and new elections held within twelve months. The association's statement also demanded a general amnesty covering all alleged collaborationists with the Japanese coupled with a shouldering of the cost of rehabilitation by Britain.[50]

The debate on the White Paper was a fairly tame affair. This was due in part to Mr. Amery's conciliatory verbal assurances and in part to the tendency of potential critics to rely considerably on the leeway to be accorded to Governor Dorman-Smith by the promised orders in council. Such leeway, it was assumed, would liberalize the approach and telescope the procedures set forth in the White Paper itself. The authors of the *Blue-Print* of 1944 proposed only minor changes, since the Secretary's verbal assurances had exceeded their expectations.[51] The criticism of several Labour Party spokesmen was undercut by the fact that both Sir Stafford Cripps, who had participated in drafting the White Paper, and Creech Jones tended to give full weight to Governor Dorman-Smith's liberal sentiments and credence to Secretary Amery's alleged good intentions. Sir Stafford believed that the proposed three-year period could be shortened and thought that the permissory orders in council provided the best means available for bringing representative Burmese into early association with political and economic planning for the country. He hoped that the Burmese would be patient, believing that the authors of the White Paper had Burma's good at heart. Creech Jones sharply criticized the delay in restoration of constitutional government as well as the prospective continued domination of Burma's economy by outside interests. But he also believed that the White Paper was a constructive and practical approach and that little more could be done at the time in view of the continued state of war in the Burma area.[52]

Other Labour Party spokesmen (Cove, Hynd, Sorenson) attacked the alleged "die-hard, stodgy, wooden-headed imperialism" of which

---

[50] *The Times*, June 1, 1945.

[51] Mr. Somerset de Chair even surpassed Mr. Amery's concern for business interests by demanding full compensation for "denial" losses. Sir Stanley Reed wanted a definite date for dominion status and return of the land to the cultivators. Mr. Shepard wanted Japanese military currency to be partially redeemed.

[52] *PD,C*, vol. 411 (June 1, 1956), pp. 495–550.

Amery was the alleged embodiment and Churchill the romanticist prophet. The White Paper, they alleged, denied to the Burmese any political initiative until British commercial interests were re-established and safeguarded. Such methods of administering overseas territories by making the defense of capitalist investments the paramount consideration, it was argued, were not shared by Britain's American ally and would inevitably attract criticism from abroad. *The Times* articles were cited to demonstrate conservative Burmese dissatisfaction with the plan. The Secretary, it was alleged, had consulted not the Burmese but big business. They declared that the younger nationalist leadership of Burma, whose wishes the governor would be obliged to take into account, would demand the right to participate fully in economic and political planning. With such participation lacking, the White Paper proposal would inevitably stimulate rebellion, rioting, and implacable hostility to British rule.[53] Approval of the White Paper by Parliament was easily attained.[54]

British press on the Burma debate was mildly critical. The Manchester *Guardian* (June 2) deprecated the officialism of the White Paper. *The Times* editorial emphasized the problem of not allowing nationalist enthusiasm to blind people to the value of British assistance in rebuilding Burma to the economic stature required for sustaining independence. Britain's allies and India were watching the policy in Burma as a test of the sincerity of London's professed aim to promote colonial self-government. Achievement of a genuine accommodation with Burma would also convince other Asiatic peoples that the West recognized the existence of the renaissance of nationalism in the Orient.[55]

So sharply critical was the reaction of Burmese opinion to both the content and tone of the White Paper of May 17, and so far had events

---

[53] *Ibid.*, pp. 549–550. In his closing remarks, Mr. Amery promised to give wide publicity to his oral comments and acclaimed Governor Dorman-Smith's industry and sympathy for the Burman point of view.

[54] The debate in the House of Lords on June 7 was brief and entirely apologetic in character. Speakers affirmed that irresponsible criticism would only encourage the Burmese to oppose the plan, which had already been badly received abroad. Cripps's assurances and Dorman-Smith's sympathy for Burma's political aspirations plus Simla's plans for economic restorations with Burmese co-operation would, it was hoped, go far to dispel distrust. Lord Listowel and the Earl of Scarborough participated.

[55] *The Times*, June 2, 1945. *The Times* editors on May 15, 1945, had suggested the somewhat contrary idea that Indian-Burman friction was so great that only continued broad political control over both of them by Britain could suffice to keep the tension within bounds.

in Burma outdated it by the time of its approval at London, that it came to have in actuality little more than academic importance. Burmese objections centered on the fact that London's proposal would turn back the political clock temporarily to the pre-1920 period. It would also give priority to economic recovery operations designed to reinstate British prewar firms and would leave to non-Burmese decision the question of when and how constitutional progress would be resumed. The White Paper's stipulation that Indian Chettyars and laborers would be restored to prewar status would have been enough by itself to have guaranteed Burmese rejection. The reference to "continuing British obligations" including control of the peripheral hill areas, coupled with emphasis on a prior achievement of a "sufficient measure" of Burmese agreement on future constitutional changes, conjured up the familiar bogey of "divide and rule" tactics.

The White Paper's point of view was in particularly sharp disagreement with the A.F.P.F.L. policy statement issued May 25, shortly after London's policy publication. The statement affirmed that the tremendous rise of nationalist sentiment in Burma made impossible any return to the spiritual or political level of 1941. Nothing short of complete independence would satisfy Burma's people, and Burma expected every honorable nation to uphold her political aspirations. The drafting of a new constitution must be entrusted to a popularly elected assembly as soon as war conditions would permit. The A.F.P.F.L. agreed nevertheless to co-operate for the time being in expelling the Japanese, in restoring order, and in rehabilitating economic processes.[56]

When first published in the Indian Communist paper *People's War* on June 17, 1945, presumably through the co-operation of Thakin Thein Pe, the A.F.P.F.L. statement took on some Communist Party twists apparently not found in the original version. It declared in melodramatic fashion that if in the hour of victory over fascist slavery, in which Burma had supported the Allied cause, the country were denied freedom then this would mean that fascism was not dead and that the war must be continued. General Aung San was quoted, quite out of character, as follows: "Down with forces of reaction and aggression in the world! Long live freedom and democracy!" Thakin Thein Pe himself, in the article, wanted Britain to make clear the extent to which the further exploitation of Burma's resources would be devoted to the rehabilitation and prosperity of the Burmese people. He refused

[56] A.F.P.F.L. *From Fascist Bondage to New Democracy*, pp. 36–38, 46, 52–53.

to believe that the White Paper was the last word from London.[57] The rigidity of London's formal policy pronouncement undoubtedly strengthened Communist influence within the A.F.P.F.L. and encouraged the easy change-over from antifascism to anticolonialism.

The governor made an early and valiant attempt to bridge the widening gap between British and Burmese points of view. As a dinner guest of Burmese leaders at Simla on June 19, he declared that it was nonsense that Burma's elections had to wait until 1948 and that a popularly elected legislature and a council of ministers were needed to share and to shoulder the responsibility for government.[58]

The precise character of British policy was clouded by the fact that Mr. Churchill's government was defeated in the general parliamentary election of July, 1945, so that the final implementation of the program fell to the successor Labour Government of Prime Minister Clement Attlee. Until October, 1945, the actual initiative in Burma lay with the military commanders Admiral Louis Mountbatten and General Hubert Rance, chief of CAS(B).

The Cas(B) Period

The B.N.A., regrouped on June 11, 1945, and rechristened on June 30 as the Patriotic Burmese Forces, participated actively in the final phases of the Burma campaign, especially in the fighting in mountains to the east of the Sittang Valley. The defeated Japanese forces were obliged to hold positions in the lower Sittang area and to make periodic counterattacks across the river in order to allow time for the considerable Japanese forces trapped to the west of the Pegu Yoma to effect a juncture with the main Japanese army. The defeat of the maneuver was made doubly sure when Allied commanders, on July 4, captured a detailed copy of Japanese withdrawal orders. When the attempted breakthrough took place according to schedule from July 20 to August 4, a slaughter ensued. Of the 6,271 known casualties inflicted by Allied forces during the two-week period, some 3,200, or more than half, were accounted for by Burmese guerrilla forces. Burmese troops continued through September, in the Southern Shan States and along the Sittang-Salween watershed, to fight isolated Japanese forces who were unaware of Tokyo's August surrender.[59]

General Rance's CAS(B) functioned throughout this period under severe handicaps. Deficiences of staff were matched by difficulties in

[57] People's War (Bombay), June 17, 1945.
[58] Times of India, June 20, 1945.   [59] Mountbatten, pp. 170–173.

obtaining desperately needed civilian supplies, especially clothing and transportation facilities. The needs of the fighting forces enjoyed priority, and what civilian supplies were obtained had a way of disappearing from the docks or being otherwise dissipated because of lack of dependable facilities for distributing them to the destitute peasants. Rural distress was also aggravated by the cancellation of all Japanese military currency. The issuance of British military currency unmatched by imported consumer supplies precipitated price inflation up to four times prewar levels. Arms were widely dispersed throughout the Burmese population, and CAS(B) officials dared not even venture into many areas, particularly sections of the Myaungmya area of the lower delta, where the Burman-Karen feud had revived following the departure of the Japanese. During the period of the attempted Japanese breakout, Rangoon was invaded by some 50,000 refugees, who brought with them the threat of famine and epidemic disease to the capital.

The CAS(B) suffered in morale and efficiency because it was makeshift and temporary. Once Japan had surrendered, not only the Simla authorities but the Burmese and London as well pressed hard for an early transition to civilian control. When the formal transfer to Simla's officials began on October 16, the army's tasks of restoring basic transportation and communication facilities were far from completed, and very little had been done to collect illicit arms and to establish orderly conditions. It was to the credit of General Rance that despite the many deficiencies of CAS(B) he won for himself personally in the course of the troubled four months of his service as chief of the agency the generous respect of all Burmese groups who dealt with him.[60]

During the period of military occupation a policy controversy between Lord Mountbatten and Governor Dorman-Smith concerning the proper attitude to take toward the A.F.P.F.L. and its Burma National Army and the date of the change-over became increasingly acute. To the governor and to the mature Burmese spokesmen of his entourage the turncoat Thakins were still the "silly little fools" of the prewar days, who might because of recent actions be excused from their treasonable deeds of 1942, but who possessed neither the right nor the capacity to pose so presumptuously as spokesmen for the Burmese nation. From Simla's point of view, the B.N.A. was little more than a bandit outfit.

[60] *Ibid.*, pp. 191–194; *PD,C*, vol. 413 (Aug. 23, 1945), pp. 778–779. Undersecretary Henderson on August 23 told of efforts to expedite the restoration of civilian control of Burma.

From many parts of Burma came alarming news that the Burmese forces were acting in complete contempt of the Burmese police, whom the nationalists despised for having toadied to their Japanese masters during the war.[61] General Aung San's insistence in May that his personal allegiance and that of his army was to the executive council of the A.F.P.F.L., itself Communist-influenced, was viewed by Simla as a flagrant repudiation of British authority.

When the governor flew to Rangoon harbor on June 20 for interviews with Burmese leaders aboard a cruiser, it was primarily due to Lord Mountbatten's insistence that he gave a special private interview to Thakins Aung San and Than Tun, as the acknowledged leaders of the A.F.P.F.L. Other Burmese representatives who were invited to confer with the governor included ex-Premier U Pu; ex-Ministers U Ba Pe, U Aye, U Ba Than, Dr. Ba Yin, and U Soe Nyun; two former High Court justices (U Mya Bu and U Ba U); an ex-president of the Senate; a landowner; an editor and banker; representatives of the Indian, Chinese, and Karen communities and U Set, a former mayor of Rangoon and an ex-vice-chancellor of the university. The implication was obvious that the governor believed that other Burmans besides the Thakins had a right to be consulted.[62] The governor apparently made a favorable impression by assuring the group that the proposed three-year interval of governor's rule might be considerably shortened and by agreeing with the Burmese that military rule was a necessary evil which ought to be abrogated as soon as possible. A leading British paper quoted him as follows: "Great Britain has no intention of sending a Governor back to Burma in order to reëstablish the old regime. On the contrary, he is being sent back to set up a new regime under which Burma will be completely self-governing. . . . Burma's fight for freedom is over." [63]

Following Governor Dorman-Smith's return to Ceylon, he insisted to Admiral Mountbatten that the B.N.A. be accorded no general amnesty and even revived General Pearce's proposal of May that General Aung San be arrested and tried for treason. Lord Mountbatten

[61] A summary CAS(B) report (no. 85) of June 9, 1945, covering Thayetmyo, Kyaukse, Yamethin, Magwe, Toungoo, Myaungmya, and Pyapon reported police stations attacked and officers slain, villagers terrified, and the authority of CAS(B) generally ignored by the B.N.A.

[62] Accompanying the governor were his personal advisers, Sir Paw Tun, U Tin Tut, and Mr. Hughes (who remained in Rangoon as the governor's personal representative). General Rance was also present, as were four officers from Lord Mountbatten's staff. Reported from Kandy, July 11, 1945.

[63] Manchester *Guardian*, June 21, 1945.

demurred on the ground that such action would so crystallize anti-British sentiment in Burma that no influential group of Burmese could be found to assist in civil administration. It was finally agreed that the B.N.A. would be reduced from 25,000 to 10,000 men, that records of all personnel would be carefully examined by CAS(B), and that those cleared would be demobilized with two months' pay or else be allowed to rejoin the new Patriotic Burmese Forces, which would serve henceforth under direct British commanders. General Aung San himself would serve as deputy inspector general of the P.B.F. with the rank of brigadier.[64] No move could be made to implement this demobilization policy while the fighting continued.

Lord Mountbatten's attitude toward Burma's nationalist leaders stemmed from the assumption that, since His Majesty's Government's declared policy was to move toward self-government soon after the conclusion of the war, the reputation which British administration would enjoy in world opinion would depend on how the A.F.P.F.L. was treated.[65] He did not regard nationalist aspirations sincerely entertained as criminal, and he tended also to excuse treasonable Burmese aid to the Japanese in the confused situation of 1942, barring only those who had treacherously intrigued with the enemy. The recent decision of the A.F.P.F.L. leaders to oppose the Japanese indicated, in his opinion, their belief that they would get a fairer deal from the British, and Mountbatten felt duty-bound to see that they should not have to revise their opinion concerning the sincerity of London's desire to help them govern themselves. He also pointed out that the A.F.P.F.L. resistance movement arose before Allied rescue of Burma was in prospect and for ends of its own; but such ends and those of the United Kingdom were, in his opinion, not necessarily mutually exclusive.

The Supreme Allied Commander (SEA) had accordingly ruled as follows on June 2:

No person shall suffer on account of political opinions honestly held, whether now or in the past, even if they have been anti-British, but only on account of proven crimes. . . . It is not my policy that any section of the population shall be victimized for the political attitude they may have adopted at any time during the war or in the period immediately preceding it.

Any prosecution and sentence of Burmans on political grounds must be reported immediately to Mountbatten and any death sentence must

[64] Report from Colombo, July 20, 1945.   [65] Mountbatten, p. 200.

await his personal confirmation before being executed. Such a policy, he insisted, was supported by common sense, by the desire to promote good relations with the Burmans, and by regard for the views of the outside world.[66]

On June 16, Lord Mountbatten met General Aung San and Thakin Than Tun at Rangoon. He obtained their consent to have disorderly units of the B.N.A. who refused to obey the orders of local British commanders treated as mere bandits. He also told the A.F.P.F.L. leaders of plans to include selected elements of the B.N.A. in the reconstituted Burma army and acceded to U Aung San's request to give disbanded veterans back pay in order to keep them out of mischief. General Rance arrived on June 17.[67]

One can acknowledge the practical wisdom of Lord Mountbatten's common-sense approach and still be obliged to concede that the considerations behind his decisions of June, 1945, exceeded the bounds of his military prerogatives. Reading between the lines of his candid *Report to the Combined Chiefs of Staff,* it is fairly clear that he admired the daring of the A.F.P.F.L. nationalist leaders and respected their integrity. One of the grounds on which Governor Dorman-Smith insisted on taking over from the CAS(B) as early as possible was the allegation that the sympathetic policy of the Supreme Allied Commander (SEA) for revolutionary Burmese nationalism was prejudicing the execution of the official British policy for postwar Burma—as indeed it was.

The other controversy between the governor and Lord Mountbatten relative to the character and duration of the role of the army in reoccupied Burma dated from 1944. Lord Mountbatten suggested that since two years would be needed to rehabilitate ports, public utilities, and internal transportation, to forestall threats of epidemics and famine, and to alleviate physical suffering contributory to unrest such objectives should therefore constitute the basis for procurement requests for American lend-lease aid covering the full period. This proposal was overruled at Simla's insistence in favor of limiting the army's civil affairs responsibility to a maximum of six months. This decision had the effect of severely restricting the availability of lend-lease supplies, which would be needed for purposes of civilian rehabilitation. Until declared surplus by the army and turned back to American authorities for disposition, such lend-lease materials as motor transport, fuel, and road repair equipment and even arms and ammuni-

[66] *Ibid.,* Appendix F, pp. 230–231.   [67] *Ibid.,* pp. 203–205.

tion for the police would not be accessible for the use of the returned civilian government.[68]

The question of when CAS(B) should be terminated was reopened in the early summer of 1945. Lord Mountbatten wanted to delay Simla's taking over at least until the whole of Burma had been cleared of Japanese troops and the transportation system restored to proper working order. He asked also that the port of Rangoon and vicinity be reserved indefinitely as a military base for further operations which, it was then believed, would have to be extended eastward into other parts of Southeast Asia. The governor, by this time thoroughly alarmed over Mountbatten's allegedly undue leniency toward the A.F.P.F.L., protested vigorously and on July 17 got London's reaffirmation of previous decisions that the transfer of Burma to civilian control must take place before the end of 1945.[69] The unexpectedly early Japanese surrender in August increased the pressure from all quarters outside the army to make the change as soon as possible.[70]

Lord Mountbatten and General Rance made a final effort at Kandy in September to delay the shift until the end of 1945 on the ground that the civilian authorities would lack transportation and that it would be difficult to disband the Burmese forces as long as Japanese soldiers remained at large. But Governor Dorman-Smith was adamant. Since compelling military reasons to justify refusal of the governor's demand for early return were absent, London, on October 1, authorized the transfer. The governor and his staff arrived on October 16 to take over all areas except the Tenasserim peninsula and the mountainous region along the Sittang-Salween watershed from Thaton northward to Karenni, which remained for the time being under army control.[71]

The rivalry between the army and the civilian authorities unfortunately carried over into the succeeding period. Lord Mountbatten insisted on dismissing at the termination of his control the Indian

[68] *Ibid.*, pp. 191–194. [69] *Ibid.*, pp. 203–205.

[70] On August 23, Undersecretary Henderson, speaking for the new Labour government, reported that consultations were in progress to expedite the transfer of control to civilian agencies in Burma. He also assured inquirers that upon the governor's return he would immediately form an executive council including nonofficial members and that selection of a legislative council would follow at an early date. See *PD,C*, vol. 413 (Aug. 23, 1945), pp. 777–778. A similar Burmese demand was included in a series of resolutions passed by the A.F.P.F.L. on August 15, 1945. See Hinners, p. 213.

[71] Mountbatten, pp. 205–207. Military administration was formally withdrawn on January 1, 1946, and General Rance stepped out of CAS(B) on February 1.

laborers brought in by the army under contract. He explained that he refused to aggravate racial and political tensions by making the re-occupation synonymous with the resumption of large-scale Indian immigration. He argued that, since the government was able neither to ration goods nor to control prices, any attempt to control wages was equally untenable. The Indian coolie force was accordingly released from the terms of its contract and permitted either to return to India or to sell its services locally at the current wage rate.[72] To the civil government's lack of reconstruction materials and transport facilities was thus added the denial of the cheap and disciplined labor force which the army theretofore had used. Particularly serious also was the lack of willing co-operation between the military police and the intimidated and virtually demoralized civil police force, this in the face of widespread lawlessness and increasing political disaffection. Thakin Aung San had refused to accept a permanent major general's commission in the British army following his final conference with Lord Mountbatten at Kandy in early September,[73] so that the troublesome problem of reorganizing the P.B.F. and disarming its unacceptable elements had to be undertaken if at all without Burmese co-operation.

Strained Relations between Dorman-Smith and the A.F.P.F.L.

Governor Dorman-Smith found, upon his return to Burma, that the plenary character of his legal authority under Article 139 of the Burma constitution was qualified in many respects by *de facto* political considerations. For example, the Labour Government's authors of the king's message delivered in October, 1945, at the time of the return of civilian authority, acknowledged the assistance of Burmese forces in defeating the Japanese and promised rapid progress in expanding Burma's prosperity and political freedom. The message declared that Burma would be accorded, as early as possible, complete self-government within the British Commonwealth. The governor's rule, with the aid of a widely representative executive council, would last only until orderly elections could be arranged for a new House of Representatives, after which the new government responsible to the House would be empowered to plan for a new constitution. The king's message added that special arrangements would be made to protect

[72] *Ibid.*, pp. 192–194.

[73] Hinners, p. 214. Thakin Aung San on September 4 had asked that the Patriotic Burmese Forces be retained in the army with component units intact, whereas the Supreme Allied Commander (SEA) had agreed only to accept volunteers individually, with English-speaking persons as officers.

517

the welfare and indigenous institutions of the peripheral hill peoples. The governor's own proclamation was commendable, if apologetic, in tone. He renounced any feeling of bitterness or revenge and again boldly proclaimed that Burma's battle for freedom was over since the country's right to it was fully conceded. His only concern was that freedom be accomplished in a gradual and orderly way allowing full opportunity for all shades of opinion to find expression without fear.[74]

In point of fact, the battle between nationalist sentiment and the governor had already begun. The plans formulated at Simla for rehabilitating Burma's economic life by means of the various administrative "projects," utilizing the noninterest-bearing loan provided by London, committed the governor to a program which precluded the enlistment of Burmese nationalist support. The plan also filled his administration with personnel from prewar British business firms notoriously inimical to Burma's political aspirations. The government's further policy of honoring Chettyar land titles and mortgages and of utilizing immigrant Indian labor made doubly sure that the "gradual and orderly" processes contemplated by him would be resisted.

What was at stake in October, 1945, was whether the paramount consideration was industrial recovery and financial solvency as contemplated in the White Paper or whether the verifiable will of the Burmese people and their preparation for self-government should take precedence. If the issue came to a crisis and the governor should decide that the ill-disguised defiance of his authority by the A.F.P.F.L. council must be put down by force, he probably could not count on vigorous backing from London for such a venture or for that matter from Admiral Mountbatten himself who had repeatedly recognized the *de facto* political position of the nationalist leadership of the A.F.P.F.L. Even in the elemental task of establishing a minimal measure of police control, the governor lacked arms, transportation, and communication facilities. Burmese governmental administrative officials throughout the country were vulnerable to lawless intimidation, for both the disaffected nationalists and the dacoits were usually better armed than the police and both were infinitely superior in morale.

The political resources of the A.F.P.F.L. were on close examination considerable and expanding. By the fall of 1945, the league coalition included representatives from virtually every indigenous political

[74] Maung Pye, pp. 87–93.

group in Burma, including the minority peoples. At its center was a closely knit cadre of Thakins, long united by personal acquaintance and by experiences gained in a common struggle, sharing each other's confidence. The top A.F.P.F.L. leaders (Aung San, Than Tun, Mya, Nu) were men of recognized integrity and devotion to the cause of Burma's freedom, whose personalities and daring had captured the imagination and devotion of the people generally.

Of more tangible importance were the Patriotic Burmese Forces, in process of being demobilized. They numbered some 25,000 men with actual fighting experience who acknowledged unswerving allegiance to General Aung San, also head of the A.F.P.F.L. Dispersed to their respective towns and villages, the veterans were being reorganized as the People's Volunteer Organization, dedicated ostensibly to keeping order and to aiding rehabilitation. For the time being and in the presence of the overwhelming superiority of the imperial armies in Burma, the P.V.O. and Thakin Aung San abjured the use of force, but the veterans were available to the A.F.P.F.L. if occasion should arise for them again to go underground as a guerrilla resistance force. The All Burma Youth League, as a constituent element of the A.F.P.F.L., was closely affiliated in both its leadership and in its spirit to the somewhat older P.V.O. veterans' group.

A third major element constituting the mass support of the A.F.P.F.L. was the peasant and worker organizations sponsored by the affiliated Communist and Socialist parties. The Communists advocated revolutionary methods and employed approved Soviet techniques calculated to exploit nationalist sentiment for partisan ends.[75] Thakins Than Tun and Thein Pe, respectively chairman of the Politburo and secretary of the Communist Party, were actively enlisting peasant support on the basis of the "no rent, no taxes" revolutionary slogan and the outright expropriation of Chettyar and other rented lands for the occupying cultivators. Their agitation was not confined to the delta area, where real peasant hardship existed; it was pushed also in such regions of diversified agriculture as Pyinmana where in 1945–1946 the cultivators were prosperous and fully able to meet their obligations to landlord and government.[76] In the labor field, Communist

[75] Virginia Thompson, "Burma's Communists," *Far Eastern Survey*, XVII (1948), 103–104.

[76] Communist leaders at Pyinmana in early 1946 acknowledged allegiance to Thakin Thein Pe rather than to Than Tun. They refused to say that prosperous peasants would be permitted to pay rents due the landlords.

Thakin Ba Hein in July, 1945, formed the All Burma Trade Union Congress (A.B.T.U.C.), which was immediately affiliated with the A.F.P.F.L. Five specific unions were organized by Communist and Socialist agents within the ensuing year for transport, dock, railway, mines, and clerical workers.[77]

The Socialist program at first lagged behind that of the Communists even though several trade union organizers from Britain assisted the Socialists in development of their labor program. The Socialist-sponsored mass organizations were at a disadvantage partly because of greater effort and zeal displayed by the Communists and partly because Thakin Mya, head of the Socialists, refused to resort to the irresponsible "no rent, no taxes," land expropriation tactics of his Communist rivals. Thakins Chit and Tin assisted Thakin Mya in organizing the Socialist Peasant's Organization, and Socialist leaders Thakins Kyaw Nyein and Ba Swe were active in the labor field.

As a final source of strength, the A.F.P.F.L. council could count on sympathetic consideration on the part of various British sources in the matter of nationalist political agitation. The attitude of Admiral Mountbatten was obviously friendly, while that of the Labour Government at London [78] was certain to be far more understanding than the predecessor regime of Mr. Churchill. Burmans were particularly reassured by the friendly sentiments of a Labour Party member of Parliament, Mr. Tom Driberg, who visited the A.F.P.F.L. leaders in September and October, 1945, both at Kandy and in Rangoon. Driberg returned to London to champion the cause of nationalist Burma in Parliament. Before the end of October, 1945, he was pressing Undersecretary Henderson for information concerning amendment of Burma's electoral law, the date for a general election, and the enactment of changes in the 1935 act looking toward dominion status.[79] It did not require extraordinary insight to perceive as of early 1946 that if the A.F.P.F.L. could avoid serious defections and could keep the contest on a nonviolent political basis the final advantage would be all in favor of the league. In addition, British decisions regarding India would inevitably set a pattern for Burma policy, a situation all the more compelling because almost the only armed forces available

[77] Hinners, pp. 232–235. Thakin Ba Hein might have played a substantial political role except for his untimely death from natural causes in 1946.

[78] Lord Pethick-Lawrence became the new Secretary for India and Burma, and Arthur Henderson, as Undersecretary, was his spokesman in the House of Commons.

[79] PD,C, vol. 415 (Oct. 29, 1945), pp. 26–27.

for suppressing any Burmese insurrection would be those drawn from India.[80]

The principal points of difference between the governor's policies and the expectations of the A.F.P.F.L. can be summarized briefly. The cardinal political question at issue was Governor Dorman-Smith's determination not to accept the presumptuous claim of the league's council to speak for the people of Burma. In the economic field the official policy was geared to assist in re-establishing the prewar British firms and the Chettyar moneylenders, with the primary objective being to restore a taxation base and a favorable trade balance. What the Burmese cultivator needed, by contrast, was the importation and effective distribution of cattle and clothing, plus credits to finance a new crop, and continuation of Lord Mountbatten's policy of leaving occupants undisturbed on the land until some comprehensive new land policy could be devised. The paddy output for the 1945 season was only 42 per cent of prewar amounts. The British-manned "project" for marketing rice paid the peasant only 150 rupees per 100 baskets, or 50 per cent above the low 1941 price, whereas the cost of consumer goods and cattle had risen meanwhile more than four times. Burmans objected also to back pay for all civil servants with alleged favoritism shown to those who had evacuated to India. Finally, there was the policy of importing coolie labor from India, as well as London's plans for continued control over the hill peoples even after giving freedom to Burma proper.

The absence of any co-operative arrangement to provide livelihood and constructive outlet for the energies of the discharged veterans and the student group was an essential defect in the efforts to allay political disaffection and to restore order. Instead of a bold move on the part of the governor to capture public imagination and to utilize the widespread determination to fashion a new Burma in line with popular needs and aspirations, the Burmese could see only an attempt to turn back the clock and to restore a prewar type of prosperity which, in Mr. Furnivall's words, had passed the Burmese by and had operated to aggravate the decay of Burma's social organization and controls. Instead of bringing Burmans more actively into the economic sphere and thus correcting the fatal dichotomy of the prewar system, which put political power increasingly in Burman hands but left business operations a monopoly of the foreigners, Simla's plan actually put

[80] The African troops were the first to be evacuated from Rangoon, beginning in early 1946. British troops were not sufficiently numerous to quell rebellion.

representatives of European firms in control of the really functioning aspects of government, while denying to Burmans a legitimate outlet for their political sentiments.[81] The basic underlying problem was mutual distrust between the governor and Burmese nationalist spokesmen.

Dorman-Smith's Second Governorship, 1945–1946

Burmese efforts to come to an understanding with the returning governor began in September, 1945, a month prior to his arrival. An ably written communication, dated September 22, sent to him under A.F.P.F.L. authorization, indicated the conditions under which a co-operative program, which he professed to desire, could be worked out. It asked that all executive council portfolios except defense and foreign affairs be entrusted to Burmese hands in what, in effect, would be a provisional government. It proposed also that the higher judiciary be exclusively Burmese and that a Burmese adviser be posted to the London office of the Secretary of State for Burma. It requested finally that the governor make no long-term commitments, prior to the selection of the new executive council, covering immigration, trade, forestry leases, and oil and mineral concessions.[82] The governor no doubt regarded the communication as highly presumptuous and did not deign to reply.

The friction became sharper following the governor's arrival at Rangoon on October 16, at which time he addressed a general meeting at the Town Hall. Burmese spokesmen felt particularly that the governor's implied charges of Burmese fascism were unnecessarily provocative, as were his expressed concern about minority rights and his assertion that foreigners thought that Burmans wanted to move too fast. The governor's concept of the character and role of the prospective executive council in particular fell far short of Burmese desires for a provisional government. On October 19, the governor received a delegation from the A.F.P.F.L. consisting of Thakins Aung San and Than Tun and U Ba Pe, all of whom repeated earlier demands concerning the council and requested the governor to seek from London the necessary authorization to make possible a semblance of responsibility of the council to the people. The delegation accepted the gov-

---

[81] See J. S. Furnivall, "Twilight in Burma: Independence and After," *Pacific Affairs*, XXII (1949), 8–16, and "Burma, Past and Present," *Far Eastern Survey*, XXII (1953), 22–24.

[82] A.F.P.F.L. *From Facist Bondage to New Democracy*, pp. 63–68, 80.

ernor's invitation to submit eleven names for his consideration in selecting a fifteen-man council.[83] When the league submitted its eleven nominees on October 24,[84] it added two provisos: (1) that one of its nominees be assigned the post of home minister (a place already reserved for Sir Paw Tun) and (2) that its members be permitted to report to the league, to receive instructions from the league, and to resign en masse if such instructions were not carried out.

On none of the three points of basic disagreement, namely the A.F.P.F.L. request for London's modification of the White Paper with respect to council responsibility, its rejection of Sir Paw Tun as home minister, and the proposed collective responsibility of league councilors to their own group, was the governor willing to compromise. His task was to carry out, not to repudiate, the White Paper policy as fixed by Parliament; he could not jettison his loyal Burmese aides; and the advisory council must be responsible to him alone. His apparent conclusion that the A.F.P.F.L. was deliberately creating a deadlock by posing impossible demands was not clearly tenable.[85] The White Paper approach was not sacrosanct. It had already been modified by Mr. Amery and even by the governor, and the London government itself took the initiative in revising it some six months later. Sir Paw Tun was the inveterate political enemy of the Thakins, for as home minister in 1940–1941 he had jailed many of them. He was destined again to demand Thakin Aung San's arrest in early 1946. Finally, the league had no intention of seeing its leadership lured away in prewar fashion by the attractions and perquisites of councilor authority. No one could have prevented in any case the reporting of executive council proceedings to the league. Recognition of the league by the governor as a legitimate political party capable of responsible dealings would not have constituted acceptance of its full pretensions as a provisional government. One cannot be sure that further negotiations would have failed.

In this situation in which conference would seem to have been called for, the governor instead gave vent to his impatience. He refused to be dictated to and bluntly challenged the league's claim to represent the whole of Burma. He also flatly refused on moral grounds

[83] *Ibid.*, pp. 73–76.

[84] *Ibid.*, pp. 82–87. The eleven A.F.P.F.L. nominees included five older leaders, U Ba Pe, U Ba On, U Aye, U Razak (Mandalay Muslim), and Pyawbwe U Mya. The six others were Thakins Aung San, Mya, Thein Pe, and Nyo Tun (Arakanese) and two Karens, Mahn Ba Khaing and Saw Ba U Gyi.

[85] Collis, *Last and First in Burma*, pp. 248–252, 255–257.

to accept Thakin Thein Pe as a member of his council. The governor offered to include seven of the eleven A.F.P.F.L. nominees in the council, while reserving home affairs, frontier affairs, defense, and foreign relations for members of his official entourage. The councilors would be asked to carry out as executive ministers the program of reconstruction as approved by London. If they disliked it, they could either protest or resign. The league rejected this arrangement, and negotiations were accordingly broken off on November 1. They were never formally resumed. The governor subsequently declared that the door was still open for A.F.P.F.L. participation, but the matter had by that time become a matter of personalities and of "face." [86] In December, 1945, U Aung San denounced Dorman-Smith as unworthy to represent democratic Britain and flatly refused to join an appointive legislative council as leader of the Opposition. Admittedly he had no rival in the political field.[87]

As finally selected, the council included two *Myochit* Party members affiliated with the A.F.P.F.L. (U Aye and U Ba On), both of whom subsequently were forced to resign by the party leader U Saw, after he returned from Africa, in February, 1946. The council also included Sir Paw Tun, Sir Htoon Aung Gyaw, U Pu, U Tharrawaddy Maung Maung, Mahn Ba Khaing (a Karen), U Lun (a *Myochit* stand-in for U Saw), and two Europeans. Other A.F.P.F.L. nominees rejected the invitation of the governor, and the league embarked officially upon a vigorous program of opposition. It demanded appointment of a truly representative council, early elections for a Constituent Assembly, and publication of the governor's plans for economic reconstruction with opportunity for public consideration of them. The A.F.P.F.L. nevertheless carefully avoided incitement to violence, and a peaceful solution was clearly its objective.[88]

Rather than provoke a political feud by selecting a council not representative of Burmese opinion and thus negativing the possibility of a co-operative approach, the governor's selection seemingly might well have been postponed for a time. That a compromise solution was possible was suggested by the action taken by an A.F.P.F.L. mass meeting held at the Shwe Dagon pagoda in Rangoon on November 18, 1945. It accepted the governor's four personal representatives on

[86] Hinners, pp. 219–223; Walter D. Sutton, "U Aung San of Burma," *South Atlantic Quarterly*, XLVII (1948), 5–7.

[87] Collis, *Last and First in Burma*, pp. 255–256, 263–265.

[88] A.F.P.F.L. *From Fascist Bondage to New Democracy*, pp. 88–91.

the council and proposed that eleven nationalist representatives be added. It also relaxed the originally rigid requirement that the A.F.P.F.L. representatives be reponsible in their actions to their own league council. The governor apparently rebuffed the effort and refused to make any counterproposal.[89] An offer made by U Aung San at the end of the year to direct his restless P.V.O. followers to assist in reconstruction activities was seized upon by the wishful-thinking entourage of the governor as a sign that the league was really divided, that the Burman leader was losing his popular appeal in favor of his many political rivals. U Paw Tun seemed convinced that the league's influence was waning. Prominent Indian civil service officers (Wise and Pearce) concurred in the view that the arrest of U Aung San would probably clear the road for a new political alignment behind an All Burma Front, which could include the returning U Saw.[90]

In early 1946, the governor accordingly brought back the dissident political leaders Thakins Ba Sein and Tun Oke from their Japanese-imposed exile in Malaya and installed them as ministers of commerce and planning respectively. The next move was to return the governor's prewar friend, U Saw, from Africa. As the political leader considered most likely to challenge the A.F.P.F.L. leadership Dorman-Smith tried in vain to interest him in accepting a council post. This fairly obvious use of "divide and rule" tactics challenged the basic concern of the Burman leaders for national unity and, when persisted in, made virtually impossible any reconciliation. The inevitable result was to sow suspicion with respect to the governor's objectives and to cool off even moderate nationalist support for his program. Before long, Whitehall itself apparently began to detect a measure of confusion and political ineptitude on the part of the governor, for London initiated a practice of curbing his powers of independent decision on political matters.[91]

The tactic adopted by the A.F.P.F.L. in December, 1945, was to attempt to by-pass the governor by taking their case directly to London and to the British people. They raised money by subscription to pur-

---

[89] Ibid., pp. 91–94.   [90] Collis, Last and First in Burma, pp. 267–268.

[91] Hinners, pp. 245–249; Collis, Last and First in Burma, pp. 260–265. Thakin Ba Sein was strongly anti-Communist and agreed to co-operate on the basis of a promise of eventual independence. U Saw objected to the fact that the councilors lacked real administrative authority. He stipulated nearly all of the A.F.P.F.L. demands (except an interim government and immediate election of a Constituent Assembly) as the price of his collaboration. The governor refused. Collis (p. 279) claimed that London vetoed the proposal to give U Saw a councilor post because it distrusted U Saw.

chase air transportation to send a five to seven-man delegation to England. They asked for permission on December 28. The governor, refusing to concede the representative character of the league and understandably jealous of his own constitutional prerogatives, agreed only that two persons might go to London in a private capacity by ship as soon as passage was available for them. The A.F.P.F.L. request was renewed on January 15 and again on February 2, asking that a delegation of five, going in a private capacity, be provided with air passage. The governor's unacceptable counteroffer was that two league members plus a secretary, accompanied by representatives of other political parties, could proceed to London for the purpose of making private contacts as soon as passage for the group could be obtained.[92] When the matter of Dorman-Smith's alleged refusal to expedite the proposed visit of the delegation to England was brought to the attention of Undersecretary Henderson in Parliament, he refused to intervene. Henderson denied Driberg's accompanying accusation that the governor was attempting to build up U Saw as a counterbalance to the A.F.P.F.L.[93]

In January, 1946, the A.F.P.F.L. convened its first nation-wide rally at the Shwe Dagon pagoda at Rangoon. The primary objective was to close the ranks of all nationalist political forces as a means of substantiating the league's claim to speak for the entire country. By making a studied effort to avoid any threat of violence, the rally succeeded rather well in lining up all indigenous political sentiment, even the most moderate, solidly against the governor. U Aung San in particular, on this occasion, demonstrated that he commanded a degree of popular loyalty and respect amounting almost to hero worship.[94] The resolutions passed by the rally were the usual ones challenging the projects rehabilitation scheme, which took no account of Burmese war losses, and demanding the early election of a Constituent Assembly, the nationalization of agricultural land with compensation to private owners, and the attainment of freedom through peaceful means.[95]

[92] PD,C, vol. 418 (Feb. 4, 1946), pp. 1345–1347, vol. 421 (April 5, 1946), pp. 1515–1583. Collis (Last and First in Burma, p. 265) affirmed that London vetoed Dorman-Smith's proposal for favorable consideration of the request to send the delegation, but supporting evidence is not presented.

[93] PD,C, vol. 418 (Feb. 4, 1946), pp. 1345–1347, vol. 421 (March 25, 1946), p. 14. Driberg and Sorenson acted as spokesmen for the A.F.P.F.L. leaders, with whom they were obviously in close correspondence.

[94] See George Appleton in Asiatic Review, XLIV (1948), 242. Appleton gives high credit to U Aung San for integrity and for lack of dictatorial intentions.

[95] Hinners, p. 232; Sutton, pp. 6–7. As agriculture minister during the Japanese occupation, Thakin Than Tun had ruled that unclaimed land and that owned by

During the course of the rally a rift developed between extremist elements, right and left, to mar the effort of the A.F.P.F.L. to demonstrate its inclusive character. The clash occurred between the astute U Ba Pe and the aggressive youthful Communist Party leaders. The latter were making no secret of their intention to exploit the Popular Front approach to mobilize long-term mass support for peculiarly Communist ends. They nevertheless overreached themselves at the rally by exhibiting Communist insignia and propaganda slogans at every opportunity. As a means of challenging the aggressive Communist activities, U Ba Pe, in one of a number of simultaneous Rangoon public addresses sponsored by the rally, denounced all totalitarian governmental systems, including that of the U.S.S.R., as being inimical to Burma's aspirations for free political institutions. The speech goaded the fanatically Communist Thakin Soe into a public denunciation of U Ba Pe as "a tool of the imperialists," and the resulting furor threatened to disrupt the A.F.P.F.L. Because Thakins Than Tun and Thein Pe, the official Communist Party leaders, were determined at this critical juncture to avoid a rift in the national-unity front, they joined other A.F.P.F.L. leaders in criticizing Thakin Soe. Thakin Soe's Communist colleagues asked him to substantiate his accusation on pain of discipline by the party hierarchy.

The controversy within the Communist Party came to a showdown at the ensuing February, 1946, meeting of the Central Committee. Thakin Soe not only refused to accept criticism but countered by accusing his opponents of compromising with imperialists and opportunists. Attempts at conciliation were abandoned after Thakin Soe boldly undertook to take over the positions of both Secretary Thein Pe and Politburo Chairman Than Tun. Thakin Soe was accordingly read out of the party. He thereupon proceeded to form an independent "Red Flag" Communist Party of his own (as opposed to the official "White Flag" group) and resumed his wartime role as an underground guerrilla leader. The Red Flag Communists were officially outlawed in July, 1946. The followers of the colorful Thakin Soe were few in number but fanatically revolutionary, asking no quarter and giving none. The "Red Flags" enjoyed little mass backing and were more of a perennial nuisance than a serious political threat. Exclusion of the fanatical

---

"enemies of the state" should go to the resident cultivators (*BIB*, II, 182). As late as May, 1946, he refrained from demanding outright confiscation, although his antirent campaign implied it. See *The Burman*, May 29, 1946.

Communists from the A.F.P.F.L. undoubtedly strengthened the league's authority as a national-front coalition.[96]

It was following the rally of January, 1946, that Governor Dorman-Smith made his abortive effort to build up a political counterbalance to the A.F.P.F.L. by enlisting the backing of the returned exiles, Thakins Ba Sein, Tun Oke, and U Saw. Thakin Ba Sein made a futile attempt to revive the outmoded *Dobama Asiayone,* while U Saw, with more success, assembled the remnants of his prewar *Myochit* following. After U Saw was unable to enter the council on his own terms, he went so far as to force two of his followers to resign. Thakin Tun Oke had virtually no political following.[97] By March, 1946, it had become clear that the governor's endeavor to build up a rival organization to the A.F.P.F.L. had failed.

Serious consideration was given during March to the long-advocated proposal of Home Minister Sir Paw Tun to force a showdown by arresting U Aung San on a criminal charge. A plausible excuse was afforded at the initial meeting of the newly appointed legislative council on February 28, when U Tun Oke openly accused Thakin Aung San of responsibility for the murder of a village headman, following a court-martial trial, during the fighting of early 1942. The charge was turned over to the police for routine examination, and authorization was sought from London to arrest the accused if the alleged crime were authenticated. The move was opposed by British army leaders, including Lord Mountbatten, on the ground that such action was likely to provoke open rebellion at a time when conditions in India would rule out the use of Indian troops against the nationalist Burmese. Advisers of the governor, on the other hand, thought that rebellion would probably come eventually in any case and that the case against U Aung San was a valid one. Since the accused admitted freely his role in the court-martial proceedings in question, the evidence as finally assembled was sent to London on March 27. Some two weeks later, Rangoon received authorization to proceed with the arrest. This action was halted just in time by a countermanding wire from London. Since the essential facts of the incident were widely known, the move acted as a boomerang against the governor. Nationalist anger directed toward Dorman-Smith and his advisers thereafter ruled out any further possibility of

[96] Thompson, *Far Eastern Survey,* XVII (1948), 103–104; Hinners, pp. 232–235; Union of Burma, *Burma and the Insurrections* (Rangoon, 1949), pp. 2–6.

[97] Nu, *Burma under the Japanese,* p. 127; Hinners, pp. 245–249. When Dr. Ba Maw eventually returned from Japan in the summer of 1946, he refused membership in the A.F.P.F.L. and temporarily withdrew from politics.

reconciliation. The position and standing of U Aung San were enhanced materially when it became apparent that British army influence coupled with opinion within the United Kingdom and abroad made him immune from arrest.[98]

Before leaving the second governorship of Dorman-Smith, it is appropriate to describe some of the positive efforts toward economic rehabilitation made by his harried administration. Four important categories of the "projects" scheme were got under way, those for agriculture (rice and cotton), timber, road transport, and civilian supplies. The Burmah Oil Company and the Irrawaddy Flotilla Company utilized their own funds for the most part and were therefore not regular projects agencies. The regular projects drew on allocations from the multimillion-pound credit furnished by London. Government officials functioned as chairmen and as financial officers of the several projects and in some instances acted as technical advisers also. But the operating agents employed by the boards were members of prewar business firms. As a rule they retained the viewpoint of their several firms, so that Burmese political representation was nowhere represented in the setup. Nevertheless, governmental control was pushed so far that some projects officials resigned in protest. Such was the case of the head of the rice-marketing program. Some substantial economic gains were realized, and it was difficult to conceive at the time an alternative method of recovery. Undersecretary Henderson in London flatly denied charges that the Labour Government was facilitating the re-establishment of monopoly capitalism in Burma, pointing out that British Government funds were being used and that essential business experience and organizations-in-being could be provided only by private firms.[99] The Labour Department minister meanwhile sent out a trade union adviser to Burma.

Burman opposition to the return of prewar business firms was probably motivated more by political than by economic considerations. Few Burmese people had an urgent desire to get into business, a type of activity in which they had had no experience. It was nevertheless widely resented that before the war foreigners had exploited Burma's wealth to the alleged impoverishment of the people. This sentiment was buttressed by fear that political independence could never be real if the prewar economic system were revived.[100]

[98] Collis, *Last and First in Burma*, pp. 262, 274–275.
[99] Hinners, pp. 224–228; *PD,C*, vol. 421 (April 5, 1946), pp. 1529–1583.
[100] Appleton, *Asiatic Review*, XLIV (1948), 237.

Another constructive achievement of Dorman-Smith's second and brief governorship was the reviving and reducing to workable form of various aspects of the prewar agrarian reform measures. The governor's initial ruling in favor of immediate legalization of Chettyar titles was qualified by his urging the people for the time being to continue paddy cultivation without regard for rental contracts. A Land Disputes Act promulgated in May, 1946, assigned to special land commissioners summary jurisdiction over claims advanced by dispossessed landlords. Their decisions were to be based on presentation of legal records of title, but the penalties for wrongful occupancy were mild. A plaintiff could be accorded rental payments only up to twice the amount of the tax assessment. An occupant could also forestall eviction by payment of the land tax plus a small compensatory fee. In July, 1946, a Tenancy Act was issued covering cultivated holdings of 50 acres or less. It provided three-year tenures on the basis of "fair rentals" as set by district revenue officers and calculated on the basis of a fraction of the normal gross outturn. Evicted tenants would be compensated for improvements. Another measure provided that the government advance funds to local credit and marketing co-operatives and that a subsidy of 12 rupees should be paid for every new acre brought under cultivation. The price of paddy was kept at 150 rupees per 100 baskets, and the land taxes for 1946 were declared payable.[101]

The agrarian program was a tribute to the able civil servants who plotted it. Granted orderly conditions and the staff to administer the agricultural program, plus the needed draft cattle, this revised land policy constituted the basis for a constructive approach. As it happened, political events overtook it before it could be applied.

Denouement for Dorman-Smith

The total situation within Burma deteriorated rapidly after March, 1946. Political disaffection and lawlessness tended to coalesce because both stemmed from spreading defiance of governmental authority. As in similar situations in old Burma prior to political revolution, the countryside was "in a state of turmoil." [102] The disorderly situation hampered not only industry and trade but agriculture as well. The Irrawaddy Flotilla Company discontinued boat service in the delta in April because of dacoit depredations. Armed guards had to be assigned

[101] Hinners, pp. 224–231.

[102] Crime statistics for March, 1946, not including Rangoon, indicated 785 ordinary robberies, 558 robberies with intent to kill, and 265 murders.

to all trains, busses, boats, officials on tour, and projects groups. On April 22, the governor himself suggested, as a possible means to relieve the growing tension, the planning of new elections to set up a Constituent Assembly without returning to the 1935 constitutional system at all or perhaps the appointment of a new governor. The mission of the Secretary of State for India and Burma (Lord Pethick-Lawrence) to India from March to May 1, 1946, helped not at all because he was unable to visit Burma. Negotiations around May 1 to reconstitute the executive council by dividing the seats evenly between followers of Sir Paw Tun, U Saw, and U Aung San came to nought. On May 8, Prime Minister Attlee asked the governor to come to London for consultations. While preparations for the trip were proceeding, the governor became seriously ill with dysentery, which made necessary his making the trip by sea, June 14 to July 13.[103]

Meanwhile, on May 16, the governor had been obliged to solicit military assistance because of the complete inadequacy of the regular police to cope with the growing disorders.[104] In late May, the governor openly denounced U Aung San's P.V.O. as a private army which was resisting the authority of the government. The Burman leader pledged in rejoinder that the P.V.O. would not break the peace and declared that it was ready to assist in maintaining order and in rehabilitation. But he warned that wholesale strife would ensue if repressive measures were begun. A New York *Times* report from Rangoon, dated June 8, 1946, predicted that revolution was imminent.[105] The governor's parting report to Acting Governor Knight admitted that the A.F.P.F.L. was in fact the only nation-wide organization and that U Aung San was not only popular but apparently sincere and desirous of a peaceful settlement.[106] Eight months was a long time to take to learn the basic facts.

The deteriorating situation in Burma was twice debated by the British Parliament in the spring of 1946. The first debate was occasioned by the government's motion of April 5 to extend the extraordinary powers of the Burma governor under Article 139. Undersecretary Henderson accompanied his motion by the suggestion that regular elections preparatory to setting up a constitution-making body might come as early as June, 1947. He pointed out, nevertheless, that enor-

---

[103] Collis, *Last and First in Burma*, pp. 277–279.
[104] Hinners, pp. 249–250; *PD,C*, vol. 423 (June 3, 1946), pp. 1602–1607.
[105] Sutton, pp. 6–7; Hinners, pp. 249–250.
[106] Collis, *Last and First in Burma*, pp. 280–282.

mous problems of disorder, impaired transportation, and economic paralysis stood in the way, as well as need for franchise reform and the preparation of election rolls. The Undersecretary declared that the transfer must be orderly and peaceful and that any attempt to resolve the constitutional question by force would be resisted. He professed ignorance at the time of the current proposal of the governor and Sir Paw Tun to arrest U Aung San and declared that any such drastic move would require express approval by His Majesty's Government. In response to some Conservative Party prodding, Mr. Henderson reaffirmed that Burma's hill peoples would be permitted to decide their own political future apart from Burma proper.

The attack on Governor Dorman-Smith was led by Tom Driberg, who was obviously in possession of more detailed information from Burma than was the Undersecretary himself. He declared that the existing unrepresentative executive council and London's refusal to receive a Burman delegation augured no good. The political question could not await the achievement of economic recovery, for the A.F.P.F.L. enjoyed solid popular backing, and the deadlock was becoming increasingly serious. Driberg insisted that the only way to avert chaos was to strengthen the hands of the moderate and responsible Burmese elements to be found in the league. The more grudging and reluctant London seemed in approaching the grant of dominion status to Burma, the more would be the pull to a complete break away. He concluded by demanding the recall of Governor Dorman-Smith and the sending of a ministerial and parliamentary delegation to Burma. Conservative spokesmen had little to say in reply. They deplored Driberg's attack on the governor and insisted that private capital (but not the Chettyars) had an essential role to play in Burma's economic recovery, but they approved Driberg's demand for a delegation to visit Burma and tacitly accepted the idea of speeding up the reforms timetable. Approval of the motion to extend the governor's powers was not contested.[107]

The much longer debate on June 7 was preceded by the submission of questions from no fewer than a dozen members. The parliamentary queries and replies indicated that Burmese dacoits had the police on the run and that Rangoon was not keeping the London government properly informed.[108] The reports were that the governor's authority was badly shaken, that he was returning to England on sick leave, and

[107] PD,C, vol. 421 (April 5, 1946), pp. 1529–1583.
[108] PD,C, vol. 423 (June 3, 1946), pp. 1602–1607.

that he had appointed a senior civil service officer from India to serve as acting governor. Economic recovery efforts had run completely aground; anti-British feeling was growing, without effective rejoinder being made.[109]

The principal attack was again led by Tom Driberg. He attached the blame for the situation in Burma not to London's policies or even to the good-intentioned Dorman-Smith, but rather to the coterie of advisers at Government House, Rangoon, who were incapable by background and training of understanding the new political forces rising everywhere in Southeast Asia. He pointed out that even *The Times* correspondent had reported that the current policy had alienated the most patriotic and responsible portion of the population. Since Britain's rule was about to end in India and would surely end in Burma too, talks must be initiated in a nonpatronizing way with responsible national leaders, especially with U Aung San, in an effort to enlist the co-operation of the P.V.O. to put down spreading lawlessness. Driberg believed that the A.F.P.F.L. suggestion (on the India model) of an interim government pending the holding of elections was a good one.[110]

The principal Conservative spokesman, Captain Gammans, was just back from a hurried visit to Rangoon, where he had apparently picked up the views current in Government House. He confirmed Driberg's allegations that the situation was much worse than the published news indicated. He complained, however, that the governor lacked the men he needed and also the power to act as the situation demanded without reference to Whitehall. The original mistake, according to Gammans, had been to negotiate with U Aung San in 1945, for he was a traitor and a murderer. Since U Saw held out no promise as an alternative Burma leader, and no Burmese government servant under the circumstances dared risk opposing U Aung San's followers, the government had no alternative but to start governing, treating treason and murder for what they were and thus restoring confidence in British justice and fair dealing.[111]

In the absence of any newly formulated policy for Burma, Under-

[109] *PD,C*, vol. 423 (June 7, 1946), pp. 2308–2314, by Sir Basil Neven-Spence.

[110] *Ibid.*, pp. 2314–2318. Driberg was here supported in his high estimate of U Aung San as a responsible Burmese patriot by Mrs. Leah Manning and Major Niall MacPherson.

[111] *Ibid.*, pp. 2318–2323. Captain Gammans was supported by R. A. Butler, who attacked the projects scheme as an unwarranted bureaucratic restriction on private enterprise. Firm government to restore order was needed instead of anti-imperialist slogans. Butler declared that if Britain cleared out, someone else would go into Burma (pp. 2323–2331).

secretary Henderson could do no more than express the hope that elections could be held in April, 1947, and that a ministry could be installed the following June. He hoped that the A.F.P.F.L. would reconsider its stand and enter the executive council, which had been assuming increasing responsibility for administrative direction of affairs. He reserved the right to review any police action involving U Aung San but flatly refused to consider accepting the P.V.O. as an arm of the government. He ended by expressing thanks to Governor Dorman-Smith and his staff for all they had done.[112]

It was nevertheless clear that the governor's usefulness had come to an end. The Conservative proposal of military repression was unacceptable, and London could not ask Dorman-Smith to implement the alternative policy of enlisting the co-operation of the A.F.P.F.L. The appointment of a new governor was made tentatively prior to Dorman-Smith's arrival in England.[113] On August 4, Sir Reginald resigned, allegedly because of ill-health, and the former head of CAS(B) under Lord Mountbatten, the now Sir Hubert Rance, departed shortly thereafter for Rangoon to be the new governor. Sir Hubert was accorded full authorization to reconstitute the executive council on a broader and more representative basis.[114] Friends of Burma in Parliament had meanwhile moved to establish suffrage in Burma on an age basis of twenty-one years in preparation for the proposed election.[115] The new pattern of development was already indicated by the establishment in India of an interim national government in August, 1946, under Pandit Nehru's chairmanship.

One final important political development within the A.F.P.F.L., looking toward the exclusion of its Communist element, preceded Governor Rance's arrival. U Ba Pe, Thakin Mya and other anti-Communists began in May, 1946, to challenge the irresponsible "no rents, no taxes" campaign of the Communist agitators as leaving an ominous legacy for any future government. The action was spurred on by the so-called Tantabin Incident on May 18, 1948, across the river from Insein, where irresponsible Communist *provocateurs* waving hammer and sickle flags organized a popular demonstration and eventually attacked the police. Three persons were killed by the police in putting

[112] *Ibid.*, pp. 2331–2341.

[113] Collis, *Last and First in Burma*, p. 282. Dorman-Smith complained that he was treated shabbily by London.

[114] *PD,C*, vol. 426 (Oct. 21, 1946), p. 298.

[115] *PD,C*, vol. 425 (July 17, 1946), pp. 743, 1298–1299.

down the uprising.[116] In June, the league ruled that thereafter "party activities" carried on behind the A.F.P.F.L. façade (as at Tantabin) were outlawed and that only individual members of mass organizations could be members of the league. U Aung San's enforcement of this ruling in July, associated with the government's outlawing of Thakin Soe's Red Flag Communist group, forced Thakin Than Tun's resignation as general secretary of the A.F.P.F.L. In August came the flat prohibition of Communist activities within the rural branches of the league. Elections for the new general secretary of the A.F.P.F.L. in early September saw the Socialist Thakin Kyaw Nyein defeat by the narrowest of margins (53 to 52) the Communist candidate, Thakin Thein Pe. The latter participated briefly in U Aung San's first executive council formed in late September, 1946, but in October the trouble-making Communists, including both the Than Tun and the Thein Pe factions, were completely and finally excluded from the council of the A.F.P.F.L., amid widespread recriminations.[117]

This disciplinary action by the league not only strengthened the hands of more moderate elements who wanted to avoid armed strife, but also provided a much-needed lull in the revolutionary crescendo which had threatened to erupt in early June. Burman nationalist leaders who were in touch with parliamentarians like Tom Driberg and who saw certain hopeful signs on the horizon both in London and in New Delhi became aware that disruptive Communist Party objectives differed from their own. The Communists obviously intended to transform the impending nationalist struggle into full-scale social upheaval, during which the party's mass organization support could be utilized to capture political power. The two-way correspondence between Tom Driberg and the A.F.P.F.L. leaders undoubtedly contributed much to the confidence of the Burmese leaders in the possibility of a peaceful settlement. It was the task of Governor Sir Hubert Rance and Prime Minister Attlee to carry through, with the help of U Aung San and U Nu, the difficult assignment of a friendly and peaceful separation.

[116] Burma, *Report of the Tantabin Incident Enquiry Committee* (Rangoon, 1947), pp. 1–10. U Aung San co-operated with the governor in quieting the troublesome Tantabin situation.

[117] Hinners, pp. 251–256; Sutton, pp. 9–10; Thompson, *Far Eastern Survey*, XVII (1948), pp. 103–104.

XVI

Recovery of Independence

LONDON'S decision of August, 1946, to send Sir Hubert Rance to deal with the recognized nationalist leaders of Burma in accordance with the pattern already adopted in India prepared the way for a negotiated settlement. But the course was by no means clear sailing. At various points the political controversy threatened to erupt into violence, and except for the steadying personal influence of Thakins Aung San and Nu, president and vice-president respectively of the A.F.P.F.L., with aid from Rance, the outcome might have been different.

The first crisis occurred in conjuction with a general strike precipitated in September, 1946, shortly after Governor Rance arrived. A second occurred in early 1947 in connection with the negotiations of the Burmese delegation at London. A third developed following the tragic murder on July 19 of Thakin Aung San and six of his cabinet colleagues. The final Nu-Attlee agreement in October, 1947, was rejected by the White Flag Communists, distrustful of the concessions made to Britain and piqued over being denied the revolutionary explosion which they had expected to exploit for sectarian ends.

The armed nationalist struggle, which the conciliatory British policy had forestalled, eventually took the form of multisided civil strife to overthrow the government which had fashioned the new constitution and had negotiated independence. The outbreak of fratricidal strife among the Burmans encouraged the reckless leaders of the nationalist-

536

minded Karens in 1949 to undertake to set up a state of their own comprising much of Lower Burma. Only the inability of the insurgent factions to co-ordinate their efforts and the steadfast leadership of Prime Minister Nu, with timely assistance from Britain, enabled the fledgling government to survive.

General Strike and the New Executive Council

Soon after the arrival of Governor Rance at Rangoon and on the very day, September 2, when Pandit Nehru's provisional government in India took over control in India, a police strike began at the Burma capital. By September 6, some 3,000 police strikers were camped on the slopes of the Shwe Dagon pagoda following the customary pattern. It was not clear how much the strike was attributable to the genuine economic grievances of the police (base pay was only 18 rupees per month, or $6.50) and how much to political instigation. The timing indicated that the leader of the strike, U Win Maung, intended to confront the newly arrived governor with a challenge he could not ignore. Whether instigator or not, the A.F.P.F.L. from the outset supported the strikers by sponsoring efforts to provide them with food and shelter. At the same time the league offered to provide the government with P.V.O. volunteers to help keep order while the police were out. They even solicited, during the emergency, restraint on the part of patriotic dacoits in the interest of the national struggle.

The police strike was on the verge of folding on September 16, as a result of the police commissioner's offer of generous cost-of-living allowances, reportedly up to 250 rupees per month, when other groups entered the picture. On September 17, postal and government printing press workers went on strike, and the fever spread to all government employees on the following day. The commissioner's abrupt dismissal of 3,000 nonreturning policemen only aggravated the unrest. The collapse of the government services forced the resignation of the original executive council. On the appeal of the newly elected general secretary of the A.F.P.F.L., U Kyaw Nyein, the strike became virtually a general one on September 24, when railway and oil workers' unions joined. A mammoth striker-A.F.P.F.L. procession protesting the White Paper was staged at Rangoon on September 29.[1]

A disturbing side development at the time of the resignation of the

[1] *Daily Herald,* Sept. 7, 1946; *The Times,* Sept. 13, 1946; Manchester *Guardian,* Sept. 17 and 18, 1946; *Scotsman,* Sept. 19, 1946; *Daily Express,* Sept. 30, 1946; Hinners, pp. 251–256.

old council came as a result of the vigorous bid of ex-Premier U Saw to head up the new prospective council. He openly challenged the A.F.P.F.L. claim to represent the majority of the Burmese people and initiated feverish party organizational activities to support his claim. On September 21, as he was returning from a *Myochit* Party meeting, an unknown gunman made a nearly successful attempt on his life. He was shot while riding in his car, it was assumed, by a political enemy. U Saw's hurried trip to London for surgical treatment to save his eye did not prevent his selection as the sole *Myochit* member of the new council, but the incident started an ominous feud.[2]

Governor Rance acted promptly to enlist the aid of Burmese nationalist leaders in ending the dangerous situation. He met them for the first time on September 21 and within the ensuing five days completed the selection of a new council. As announced on September 27, the nationalist council was widely representative. General Aung San, deputy chairman of the council under Rance himself, was put in charge of the Departments of Defense and External Affairs. U Kyaw Nyein, as home member, and Thakin Mya led the Socialist Party contingent. Thakin Thein Pe was the sole Communist member. Saw Ba U Gyi replaced Mahn Ba Khaing for the Karens. Thakin Ba Sein represented the revived *Dobama Asiayone*, and U Saw the *Myochit* Party. U Ba Pe was also included. One of the significant compromise moves was the appointment of U Tin Tut, the senior Burman civil service official, as minister without portfolio. The governor's announced intention, made with London's approval, that the revised council would exercise, in practice, all the authority and power enjoyed by the Burma ministers from 1937 to 1942 won the confidence of the group.[3] Except for the Communist leader, Thein Pe, who was himself soon forced to resign because of his party's disapproval of the suppression of the strike, the new council was moderate and antirevolutionary. Within a week after it took over, the general strike was ended, on October 4. Because the Communist Party refused to accept the council's authority and because it was desirable to repudiate methods of violence, the party was finally and irrevocably excluded from the A.F.P.F.L. in late October. This latter action occasioned at the time surprisingly little protest from Thakin Than Tun,

[2] *The Times*, Sept. 19, 22, and 27, 1946; Manchester *Guardian*, Sept. 18, 1946; *Observer*, Sept. 22, 1946.

[3] *PD,C*, vol. 426 (Oct. 21, 1946), p. 298. Maung Pye (*Burma in the Crucible*, pp. 99–100) pays the following tribute to Governor Rance: "He was straight and sincere in speech. . . . He had no tricks to play, no axe of his own to grind, and did not care for subterfuges."

who made no secret of his intention to continue his revolutionary preparations in anticipation of the probable eventual failure of the A.F.P.F.L. to reach an agreement with London. To soften the blow, Thakin Soe was temporarily removed from his outlawed status.[4]

The A.F.P.F.L. made the most of its seizure of the political initiative. On November 10 came Thakin Aung San's four-part executive council–A.F.P.F.L. demand that London (1) agree to the election of a Constituent Assembly in April, 1947, (2) include representatives of the frontier peoples in such an assembly, (3) proclaim before January 31, 1947, that Burma would be accorded full independence within a year from that date, and (4) agree to a re-examination of the "projects" schemes within the same time period. Immediately following the issuance of these demands, Thakin Aung San made a tour of the Frontier Areas to persuade the Shan, Kachin, and Chin leaders to join independent Burma. He promised the frontier peoples separate status with full autonomy within the Burma Union, active participation at the center in a kind of states' Senate, protection of minority rights, and the privilege of secession. The Kachin leaders at Myitkyina were also assured that Burman and Shan inhabitants of the fingerlike river valleys within the prospective Kachin State of northern Burma could be incorporated in the new Kachin State provided fair treatment were accorded to such minorities.[5]

The Parliamentary Debate of December 20, 1946

London's consent to the holding of elections for a Burma Constitutent Assembly in April, 1947, was apparently accorded prior to Thakin Aung San's virtual ultimatum of November 10.[6] The Prime Minister's subsequent announcement to Parliament on December 20 was much more far-reaching. He proposed to invite to London a representative group of Burmans from the executive council to reconsider the provisions of the White Paper of 1945 and to discuss the implementation of constitutional pledges given to Burma by successive governments going back to 1931.

[4] Union of Burma, *Burma and the Insurrections* (Rangoon, 1949), pp. 2–6; *Daily Worker,* Oct. 23, 1946. The Soviet press interpretated the break between the A.F.P.F.L. and the Communists as the work of the British in supporting Dr. Ba Maw and other rightist politicians. See *Soviet Press Translations,* II (Seattle, 1947), 141–142.

[5] Hinners, pp. 259–266; *RFACE,* pt. ii, pp. 69–71.

[6] The king's previously prepared speech at the opening of Parliament on November 12 indicated that "steps are being taken to hold elections in Burma early next year, as the necessary preliminary to further constitutional progress." See *PD,C,* vol. 430 (Nov. 12, 1946), p. 6.

He coupled this proposal with recent developments in India, which, he declared, had stimulated Burmese desires to expedite their own advance to self-government. In connection with his affirmation that self-government should come to Burma by the quickest and most convenient path, Mr. Attlee commented as follows:

We do not desire to retain within the Commonwealth and Empire any unwilling peoples. It is for the people of Burma to decide their own future. . . . The day to day administration . . . is now in the hands of Burmese members of the Governor's Executive [Council]. . . . For the sake of the Burmese people, it is of the utmost importance that this should be an orderly—though rapid—progress.[7]

Replying for the Conservative Opposition, Mr. Churchill deprecated "the steady and remorseless process of divesting ourselves of what has been gained by so many generations of toil . . . and sacrifice . . . . [and] this undue haste that we should get out of Burma finally and forever." The only appropriate term for such a policy, he averred, was "scuttle." He denounced as gratuitous Mr. Attlee's placing Burma in the same category with developments in India prior to any Burma election or formulation of settled views. Delay, he declared, would have afforded time for the friends of Britain to rally and to state their case. Instead, loyalty was being repulsed and friendship abandoned while London's responsibility to primitive peoples for whom British justice and administration had guaranteed peaceful livelihood was being repudiated.[8]

The Prime Minister's reply was fairly conclusive. He reminded Mr. Churchill that he himself had sent the Cripps mission to India and that both India and Ireland were examples of Britain's doing the right thing too late. He added: "It is much more dangerous to lag behind than to keep up with movements of public opinion. . . . The country has not been too fast but too slow [in Burma]." Supporting speakers declared that the nationalist ferment in Asia could not be ignored and that the restoration of order and any economic advance were conditioned on obtaining the co-operation of the Burmese people.[9]

Approval by Parliament of Mr. Attlee's proposed invitation consti-

---

[7] *PD,C*, vol. 431 (Dec. 20, 1946), pp. 2341–2343.

[8] *Ibid.*, pp. 2343–2346, 2348–2350. Mr. Churchill's concluding reference was undoubtedly to the Karens, whose good-will mission had visited London in the summer and fall of 1946.

[9] *Ibid.*, pp. 2350–2361. Mr. Reid, Tom Driberg, and Lieutenant Colonel Hamilton supported Prime Minister Attlee.

tuted irrevocable acceptance of basic Burman nationalist demands. It could be argued that a Conservative government would, like Labour, have been obliged eventually to face political realities in Burma, but the timing and hence the circumstances would certainly have varied. As events proved, the Labour government's action was taken barely in time to avert armed rebellion.

The London Agreement of January, 1947

Mr. Attlee's invitation of December 20 was accepted by the A.F.P.F.L. leaders on December 26 after prolonged discussion. In order to convince U Aung San of Prime Minister Attlee's sincerity, the permanent Undersecretary of State for Burma visited Rangoon. On January 1, a six-member delegation consisting of Thakins Aung San, Mya, and Ba Sein, U Tin Tut, U Ba Pe, and U Saw departed for London, to arrive on January 9.[10] Arrangements for the London meeting were nevertheless accompanied within Burma by vigorous preparations for rebellion in the seemingly not unlikely contingency that Britain's concessions should prove inadequate. The well-armed P.V.O. militia organized under experienced officers awaited the signal to rise. By mid-January, a situation approximating general strike had developed, accompanied by a rising crescendo of political demonstrations by university students, veterans' groups, and Marxist mass organizations. A mob of 500 Communist partisans attempted to invade the Rangoon secretariat. At Yamethin, a Marxist stronghold, a local Communist administration was set up in defiance of the police. A league manifesto repeated the demand for a nationalist interim government, the early election of a Constituent Assembly, and complete independence. U Aung San declared that a peaceful settlement was preferred but that the country must be prepared to struggle if necessary.[11]

Fortunately the negotiations at London were concluded expeditiously and in an atmosphere of complete understanding. Among the list of "conclusions" drawn up on January 27, Prime Minister Attlee conceded that Burma's interim government would be regarded as that of a dominion, exercising full ministerial authority, and that, as soon as Allied armies were withdrawn, Burmese military forces would themselves come under the control of the Burma Government. To expedite

[10] Maung Pye, p. 102; Collis, *Last and First in Burma*, p. 284.

[11] J. S. Furnivall, "Twilight in Burma: Independence and After," *Pacific Affairs*, XXII (1949), 161–163; *The Times*, Dec. 23, 27, and 29, Jan. 14 and 15, 1947; Manchester *Guardian*, Jan. 8 and 21, 1947.

matters, it was agreed that the Constitutent Assembly would be elected not by adult suffrage but under the machinery of the 1935 act, including communal electorates. The eventual constitutional document, when framed, would be promptly presented to the British Parliament for approval. A selected portion of the Constituent Assembly, functioning as an interim national assembly, would meanwhile prepare for Burma's independence, whether within or outside the Commonwealth. London also agreed to contribute to Burma's current deficit and to grant an additional loan of £7.5 million. The settlement of financial obligations and arrangements for British military aid would be matters for future negotiation. Burma could be represented at London by a high commissioner and would be competent when fully independent to exchange diplomatic representatives and to join the United Nations.[12]

Paragraph 8 of the "Conclusions," touching the delicate question of the Frontier Area peoples, indicated, as an agreed objective, joint efforts "to achieve the early unification of the Frontier Areas and Ministerial Burma, with free consent of the inhabitants of these areas." It provided further that the executive council (after consultation with the non-Burman peoples) would nominate a Frontier Areas Committee composed of an equal number of members from Ministerial Burma and from the Areas "to investigate the best method of associating the Frontier Peoples with the working out of the new constitution for Burma." Burman political groups meanwhile were guaranteed free contacts with the peoples of the Frontier.[13]

The Burmese delegation upon its return to Rangoon faced considerable difficulty in obtaining approval of the London Agreement. Britain's concessions fell short of previous Burman demands, and many Communist partisans and P.V.O. guerrillas were thoroughly aroused and not quite ready to be denied their fight. Mingled dacoity and rebellion, much of it Communist supported, raged throughout February in the Pyinmana-Yamethin, Shwegyin, and Myingyan areas particularly.[14] Trouble also flared up in the Arakan region, where Thakin Soe, again underground, joined hands with malcontent members of an Arakanese

[12] Hinners, pp. 261–266; *PD,C*, vol. 432 (Jan. 29, 1947), pp. 777–780.

[13] *RFACE*, pt. I, pp. 1–2. Mr. Churchill in Parliament denounced the affair as another "dismal transaction," but Mr. Attlee recalled that Churchill's reason for exempting the application of the Atlantic Charter to Burma was that Britain herself was carrying out the principles of the Charter. See *PD,C*, vol. 432 (Jan. 28, 1947), pp. 780–782.

[14] Reported statistics on crime from January through March of 1947 numbered 773 murders and 5,743 dacoities. See George Appleton, "Burma Two Years after Liberation," *International Affairs*, XXIII (1947), 510–520.

separatist movement led by the anti-Japanese guerrilla partisan, the *pongyi* U Sein Da.[15] Not even Thakin Aung San's personal intervention on the occasion of the All Arakan Conference on April 1 prevented its approval of resolutions demanding open rebellion against British rule, nonpayment of taxes, and cancellation of agricultural debt.[16] Trouble in the Arakan division persisted into 1948 despite military repression.

In the political sphere, U Saw and Thakin Ba Sein, hoping to make political capital out of the seething unrest, refused to sign the London Agreement and eventually resigned from the council on March 5. They joined with Dr. Ba Maw in February to form the so-called "Democratic Nationalist Opposition Front." The important decision of the Communist secretary, Thakin Than Tun, at this junction to check the irregular violence of striking Communist workers and peasant partisans and to reject collaboration with rightist defectors helped materially to calm the situation. Nevertheless all of Thakin Aung San's enormous personal prestige among nationalist guerrilla elements was needed to obtain general acquiescence in the decision, registered on February 5 by the A.F.P.F.L. and by the governor's executive council, to approve the London Agreement. U Aung San was able to fill the council vacancies with two stanch supporters, U Ba Choe and U Razak.[17]

The most urgent item of business which claimed the attention of Thakin Aung San following the formal approval of the London Agreement was to work out some arrangement for associating the Frontier Area peoples with his interim government. Accompanied by Mr. A. G. Bottomley, British Undersecretary of State for Dominion Affairs, he proceeded on February 7 to Panglong in the Shan States to confer for a second time with the Shan *Sawbwa* princes and with representatives of the Shan, Kachin, and Chin peoples, all of whom he had met earlier in November, 1946. The Panglong Conference reached unanimous agreement that the political freedom of all peoples there represented

[15] Hinners, p. 288. U Sein Da and sixty-seven of his followers had accepted the government's amnesty offer in December, 1946, but trouble started again in January and more seriously in May, 1947.

[16] *PD,C*, vol. 438 (June 12, 1947), Supplement, pp. 147–148. Documents seized at the time of U Sein Da's arrest in May, 1947, linked him with Thakin Soe in an elaborate plan to seize power in the Arakan aided by Mujahid (Muslim) Partisans.

[17] *PD,C*, vol. 432 (Feb. 3, 1947), p. 1367; Hinners, p. 266; Furnivall, *Pacific Affairs*, XXII (1949), 219–220; *Statesman*, Feb. 22, 1947. The relation of the P.V.O. to General Aung San approximated a revival of the pre-British *ahmudan* allegiance to a personal leader, but it reflected little loyalty to the government as such. U Aye and other *Myochit* leaders refused to follow U Saw in his opposition.

would be hastened by immediate co-operation with the interim government.

It was further agreed at Panglong that co-operation should be implemented by the governor's appointment of an additional councilor, to be nominated by the newly formed supreme council of United Hill Peoples. The councilor would assume executive responsibility for the Frontier Areas. Two deputy councilors, one from each of the other two peoples, would assist the full councilor in carrying out their joint responsibility over the three areas. Each of the three councilors would deal with the affairs of his respective people and the deputy councilors would attend meetings of the executive council whenever Frontier Areas questions were under consideration. Other agreements at Panglong provided for the enjoyment of democratic rights by all citizens, for continued interim financial aid by the center to the Frontier Areas, for local autonomy, and for immediate consultations looking toward the demarcation of a Kachin State. The Mongpawn *Sawbwa,* Sao Sam Htun, became the first Frontier Areas councilor, while Sima Hsinwa Nawng became deputy for the Kachins and U Vum Ko Hau for the Chins.[18] The personality of Thakin Aung San and the skillful negotiations of U Tin Tut were reflected in these arrangements. Mr. Bottomley's report of the conference satisfied Governor Rance that the agreement was acceptable to the parties represented.[19]

The Frontier Areas Problem

Because the question of the future relationship between Burma proper and the Frontier Area peoples, including the Karens, was destined to become one of the abiding problems of the emerging Burma Union, the political situation of these regions, hitherto not considered, must at this juncture be brought into perspective. The two score or more hereditary Shan chiefs, formerly in vassal relationship to the Burmese kings, were obliged to accept British *sanads,* or authorizations, during the late 1880's which required among other things that they accede to the guidance of a British superintendent and his assistants. A *Sawbwa* was first made a member of the governor's advisory council in 1897. The first step looking toward the organic union of the several Shan states came in 1922, when a federal council of Shan chiefs was set up under the presidency of a British commissioner.

---

[18] *RFACE,* pt. i, pp. 16–18. Three Karenni observers were present at Panglong, but no representatives of the Karens proper or of the Was, Nagas, Arakan Chins, or the numerous other non-Shan inhabitants of the Shan States attended.

[19] *PD,C,* vol. 435 (April 1, 1947), Supplement, p. 298.

A six-member standing committee of this council, enjoying direct relations with the governor, was set up in 1935, by which date the number of states had been reduced by amalgamation from 43 to 35. The federal council received the revenue income from forests and mines and also some 40 per cent to 50 per cent of the ordinary revenues of member states. These funds were used for public works, education, medical administration, forest control, agriculture, and police purposes.

The British administrative staff for the Shan States in 1936 included, besides the commissioner, two superintendents and fifteen assistant superintendents. The more advanced areas (designated as Part II Areas), especially those contiguous to Burma proper, were gradually being assimilated before the war to participation in the central legislature, but most of the Shan plateau was governmentally and politically quite distinct from Burma. The various peoples of the extensive backward tracts (Part I) were administered, if at all, under the general supervision and control of the governor.[20]

Most of the hill areas inhabited by Kachin tribes in Bhamo and Myitkyina districts in the north and by the Chins along the western boundaries were also Part I segments of the so-called Scheduled Areas, administered on the governor's authority apart from the Rangoon government. The Kachin hill country included many fingerlike valley areas, previously mentioned, and was inhabited by politically more advanced Shans and Burmans. The three Karenni states lying to the east of the Sittang Valley in the latitude of Toungoo and Pyinmana were almost entirely autonomous and completely lacking in experience with representative institutions. Except for the location of the profitable wolfram mines at Mawchi, neither the British nor the Burmans would have been greatly interested in the rugged Karenni hills. The Frontier Areas also included the Karen-inhabited Salween District (to the south of Karenni), much of which was also classified as a backward (Part I) tract. It was not surprising under the circumstances that British officials familiar with the situation assumed that the political advance of the Shan plateau areas as well as that of the still more backward Kachin, Chin, and Karen hill areas might well take a different direction from that of the enfranchised people of the Burma plains.[21]

[20] *RFACE*, pt. I, pp. 12–14; Clarence Hendershot, "The Conquest, Pacification, and Administration of the Shan States by the British, 1886–1897" (University of Chicago thesis, 1936), pp. 283–284.

[21] Harvey, *British Rule*, pp. 84–86.

As in the case of Burma proper, the experiences of World War II changed the political attitudes of the Frontier Area peoples more than any outsider could have imagined. A considerable number of the Shans in particular caught from Burma the contagious desire for a greater measure of self-government free of British control. They also wanted representative institutions to modify the heretofore arbitrary personal rule of the *Sawbwas*. The *Sawbwas* themselves entertained some new ideas. When the postwar British director of the Frontier Areas Administration attempted to revert to the pre-1922 status, the *Sawbwas* formed their own executive council, apparently without asking authorization from Rangoon.

Shan contacts with Burmese political leaders in 1945–1946 were not uniformly friendly. The *Sawbwas* resented outside efforts to promote such organizations as the Shan States People's Freedom Congress, which was a direct projection of the A.F.P.F.L.[22] Thakin Aung San's visits in November, 1946, and again at the Panglong Conference of February, 1947, created a more friendly atmosphere. He offered, in effect, to allow the *Sawbwas* freedom to write their own terms of co-operation and also pledged continued financial assistance from Burma revenues. The Burman leaders were obviously prepared to pay a fairly high price to exclude British control and to include within the new Burma the mining, timber, and other resources of the Shan country.[23] The Shan States People's Freedom Congress was itself revived and reorganized in March, 1947, to assist Burman efforts to bring Shan representation into the Constituent Assembly and eventually into the Burma federation.[24]

Thakin Aung San and other A.F.P.F.L. propagandists apparently encountered little resistance in the Kachin and Chin areas, where the hereditary village and tribal chiefs (prototypes of the old Burman *myothugyis*) were unorganized and less able than the Shan *Sawbwas* to resist outside influence. The active Jinghpaw (Kachin) National Modern Civilization Development Association and its twin, the Kachin Youth League, drew heavily on Burmese nationalist inspiration. Their objective was to end the backwardness of the Kachin country. At Thakin Aung San's encouragement, these groups influenced the Kachin elders to ask for a Kachin State including Bhamo and Myitkyina districts and extending as far south as the borders of Katha District. On

[22] Many of the Burman political agitators were imprisoned by the *Sawbwas* at this time.

[23] The Bawdwin mines and the Namtu refinery, located in the Northern Shan States, were very large operations producing silver, lead, and zinc.

[24] *RFACE*, pt. I, p. 16, pt. II, pp. 14–15.

the basis of allegations that sixty years of British rule had accomplished no improvement in Kachin affairs, the elders were persuaded to leave the decision concerning their future British relations to the Constituent Assembly.

Aside from the general objective of leaving the British no foot-in-the-door opening, the Burman nationalists wanted Kachin support as a security factor on the China border and elsewhere. The Kachins as well as the Chins made excellent soldiers.[25] Chin leaders were similarly attracted by promises of rights and privileges equal to those of the Burmese, to be accomplished through central government aid in health and education, representation at Rangoon, and the chance to send Chins abroad as state scholars, plus the right of secession.[26]

As a means of counteracting the assumption advanced officially at Simla and at London that the non-Burmese races would prefer to continue under British control, the Panglong Conference promised the frontier peoples a wide measure of political freedom in association with an independent Burma. The task of recommending a positive policy regarding the former Scheduled Areas was assigned by the London Agreement to the Frontier Areas Committee of Enquiry.

The Frontier Areas Committee of Enquiry

This committee consisted of nine persons, four of them from ministerial Burma and four from the Frontier Areas, with a British chairman, Mr. Rees-Williams. The committee was by composition committed in favor of frontier participation in the Constituent Assembly, not only by the inclusion of a very strong Burman contingent headed by U Tin Tut together with U Kyaw Nyein, U Khin Maung Gale, and Thakin Nu, but also by the assignment to it of the three Frontier Areas councilors previously selected at Panglong. The Karen National Union was represented by Saw Sankey.[27] After making an eleven-day preliminary tour extending southward from Myitkyina to Loikaw, the committee held hearings at Rangoon (March 19 to 26) and at Maymyo (March 27 to April 21). The report was completed and signed on April 24, after the elections for the Constituent Assembly had taken place. It was approved by London on May 22,[28] prior to the actual convening of the newly elected assembly.

---

[25] *RFACE*, pt. ii, 54–57.   [26] *Ibid.*, pp. 71–72.
[27] *RFACE*, pt. i, pp. 18–21. During the final weeks of the Committee of Enquiry sessions at Maymyo, Saw Myint Thein substituted for U Kyaw Nyein.
[28] *PD,C*, vol. 437 (May 22, 1947), Supplement, p. 298; published also as Cmd. Paper 7138 (*PPC*, vol. X for 1946–1947) in June, 1947.

The Committee of Enquiry report contained four general recommendations: (1) that the interim councilors selected after Panglong should continue to co-operate with the executive council; (2) that Frontier Area peoples be allotted 45 seats in the Constituent Assembly, all members to participate fully in its operations (27 Shan, 7 Kachin, 6 Chin, and 5 others); (3) that any constitutional provisions affecting the federal principle or the Frontier Areas themselves must have the support of the representatives of the Areas; (4) that governmentally advanced (Part II) areas contiguous to Burma, especially in the Chin area and in the Karen-inhabited Salween District, be progressively amalgamated with Ministerial Burma. The Shans and Kachins wanted to set up autonomous states within a federated Burma, limiting central control to such matters as foreign relations, communications, money, and customs. The position taken by the Chins was equivocal, while the Karens apparently wanted no part whatever in a Burman state.

A special problem developed during the hearings on the proposed Kachin State when a Burman delegation from Bhamo objected strenuously to the inclusion of plains areas inhabited by Shans and Burmans. This was despite Thakin Aung San's earlier promise to Kachin leaders that the matter could be arranged provided the minority groups were fairly treated. A similar commitment had apparently also been made to the Kachins in February, 1946, by the regular commissioner of Sagaing, who had then suggested that a Kachin State including the plains areas could be set up under British or Burmese rule. Thakin Nu proposed holding a plebiscite to define the bounds of the Kachin State, but no agreement was obtained in April, 1947.[29]

The testimony of the Chin representatives was confused. They were obviously not prepared to assume the responsibilities of separate statehood and equally unwilling to become a regular district of Burma. They asked that Chins be represented in the executive council and ministry, in the Defense Department, and in the Public Service Commission and that Burma continue to assist the Chin area in the expenses of health, education, and local government services. At the same time they insisted on complete local autonomy and the preservation of ancient Chin customs. They clearly preferred to remain within the British Commonwealth and asked specifically that the British Government witness the Burman promises to all minority

[29] RFACE, pt. II, pp. 64–70.

groups, and especially to the Chins, to ensure their faithful observance.[30]

The attitude taken by spokesmen for the three Karenni states reflected unconcealed distrust of Burman intentions. They wanted to participate in the Constituent Assembly but declined to commit themselves to membership in a federated Burma until it had been demonstrated to their satisfaction that the Burmans would live up to their promises. They indicated also their particular concern to keep control of the valuable Mawchi wolfram mines which, they alleged, could make the Karenni people financially independent of Burma, even though mining operations would admittedly have to be done by outsiders. The Karenni wanted to be associated directly only with the United Hill Peoples' council and with the Frontier Administration. If developments in Burma proved satisfactory, the Karenni states might later be willing to join on condition that they have a councilor of full rank on the executive council and enjoy financial aid from Burma, along with full local autonomy and the option to secede at any time. With these demands was associated the adjacent state of Mongpai, where a Padaung chief had recently displaced the hereditary Shan *Sawbwa*. U Tin Tut and Thakin Nu became sharply impatient with the distrustful attitude and the sweeping demands of the Karenni representatives.

An even more serious problem came to light when the Karen representatives of Salween District testified before the Frontier Areas Committee. The prepared statement presented by nine representative Karen elders, reflecting decisions reached at a recent meeting at Shwegyin, opposed entering into any constitutional relations with an independent Burma. This viewpoint accorded with an earlier February decision made by the Karen National Union favoring the establishment of a separate British Karen colony with a seaboard along Burma's Tenasserim coast. The Salween District Karens would agree to federate with the Shans, Chins, and Kachins, but entirely outside Ministerial Burma.

Karen spokesmen attributed their distrust of Burman rule to historical factors but more immediately to the bitterness arising from Burma Independence Army excesses in the Salween District area perpetrated in April and May of 1942 (alleged killing, looting, and other acts of barbarism and religious intolerance). These had been followed

[30] *Ibid.*, pp. 71–72, 97–98. Only the fledgling Arakan Hills A.F.P.F.L. group favored direct union with Burma.

by repressive measures inflicted by Japanese-Burman agencies (village burning and thievery). On two occasions during the war, the Salween Karen volunteers had clashed openly with the Burmans.[31] The delegation expressed the conviction that the Karen population was certain to suffer if the British tie were cut, especially since neither one of the mutually hostile Karen and Burman elements was susceptible of control. Hence the only recourse was complete separation from Burma. The statement concluded on the following ominous note in accordance with the formal decision of the Karen National Union as a whole, previously formulated in February, 1947:

The Karens of this area firmly claim that their right of self-determination be recognized by the concession of a separate Colony for the Karens. If the British fail to honor this great responsibility of theirs, the Karens should not be blamed if they think of other alternatives to achieve their legitimate objectives.[32]

This intransigent statement of the Karen elders from Shwegyin was challenged later in the hearings by a youthful Karen delegation from Papun, but under somewhat dubious circumstances. This second group advocated full incorporation of the Salween District as a regular administrative unit of Burma. Subsequent questioning revealed that the ambitious Papun spokesman had become disgruntled over the ineffective efforts of the secretary of the Karen National Union to obtain for them desired forestry leases and agencies of supply. They had accordingly repudiated the demand for a separate Karen State, following the political intervention of the A.F.P.F.L. with the government, in order to satisfy their personal desires. U Tin Tut did not admit or deny that special consideration had been accorded to the Papun malcontents. He attempted nevertheless to justify the government's policy of assigning economic favors to the indigenous business elements in preference to Indian and British firms.[33]

---

[31] This friction was aggravated by Salween Karen assistance to Major H. P. Seagrim and other British guerrilla agents operating in the area. See Ian Morrison, *Grandfather Longlegs* (London, 1947).

[32] *RFACE*, pt. II, pp. 121–134, 175–178. The Karen National Union spokesman, Thra Tha Htoo explained later that delta and Bassein Karens need not be part of the proposed Karen State.

[33] *Ibid.*, pp. 147–158. Thakin Nu on this occasion attempted to blame the Anglican Bishop West for dictating general Karen policy. The Papun group advanced the even more preposterous allegation that the Karen decision reached at Shwegyin had been unduly influenced by the casual presence of a French Catholic priest.

The apparent Burmese policy of dispensing economic and political favors to break the unity of the Karen National Union was measurably effective, but it was not calculated to dispel Karen distrust, which was itself the basis of the obdurate and, from the Burman point of view, unreasonable Karen demands for independence. One tangible evidence of Burman good faith at this time was their declared intention to appoint the senior Karen military officer, General Smith Dun, as head of the new Burma army. The A.F.P.F.L. position was also somewhat strengthened, but not materially so, by the testimony of the president of its Karen Youth Organization affiliate, Saw San Po Thin, who had precipitated the Myaungmya strife in 1942 but had later, in 1945, led the anti-Japanese resistance movement in the delta. As president of the Karen Youth Organization, he favored the union of Salween District with Burma, but stipulated that it be governed exclusively by Karen officials. He admitted, under questioning, that the Karen Youth Organization had no unit in the district under consideration.[34]

The attitude of the Karenni representatives and of Salween District Karens plus that of the Karen National Union leadership generally was easily the most disquieting aspect revealed by the report of the Frontier Areas Committee of Enquiry. The hearings disclosed a big chasm of disagreement and distrust which subsequent efforts of the A.F.P.F.L. leadership failed to bridge and which led to the formidable Karen rebellion of 1949.

The Assembly Elections and the Karen Problem

The outcome of the April, 1947, elections for the Constituent Assembly was an overwhelming popular endorsement of Thakin Aung San and his London Agreement. A.F.P.F.L. candidates, many of them P.V.O. followers of Aung San, won more than 170 of the noncommunal seats compared to 10 for the opposition. The Communists elected only 7 of their 29 candidates, principally in Pyinmana and Akyab constituencies. The so-called Independence-First Alliance of Dr. Ba Maw, U Saw, and Thakin Ba Sein boycotted the elections, condemning the "appeasement of the imperialists" at London and charging violence and intimidation in the election campaign. Because the Karen National Union also refused to enter candidates, 19 of the 24 Karen seats fell uncontested to Karen Youth Organization representatives, and the remainder went to independent Karen candidates backing the A.F.P.F.L. The A.F.P.F.L. victory reflected also the suc-

[34] *Ibid.*, pp. 135–145.

cessful contesting of the rural vote by the Socialist Party led by Thakins Mya, Kyaw Nyein, and Tin, who along with U Aung San accused their Communist rivals of following instructions from India, of stealing the peasants' rice, and of consorting with dacoits.[35]

The seriousness of the absence from the assembly of spokesmen for the now thoroughly angry and alarmed Karen National Union needs further explanation. The considerable wartime efforts of the founders of the A.F.P.F.L. anti-Japanese coalition to placate the delta Karens, who had suffered admitted abuse during the war at Burman hands, had been only partly successful. The Karen Youth Organization was affiliated with the league, and the co-operation of the redoubtable Saw San Po Thin was enlisted. When the break with the Japanese came in late March, 1945, General Aung San assigned to the sensitive western delta area a Karen B.N.A. contingent led by Saw San Po Thin. This force effectively eliminated Japanese control, raised the British flag at Bassein, and was generally successful in preventing a recurrence of communal violence in areas under its control. But the wounds opened by wartime feuding were by no means healed, and the increasing prospect of the displacement of British control by that of the Burman majority conjured up dire forebodings among the Karen population generally. Saw Ba U Gyi, a well-to-do Cambridge-educated Karen of Bassein, who represented the Karen Youth Organization in the executive council of the A.F.P.F.L., was concerned among other things with watching council proceedings.

Meanwhile a demand was initiated in October, 1945, by a Karen mass meeting at Rangoon in favor of establishing a separate Karen State including the Tenasserim Division, along the same lines proposed by Dr. Sam C. Po in 1928.[36] The suggestion in the British White Paper of 1945 that the Karen-inhabited portions of the Scheduled Areas (the Salween District) be made into a Karen State was so unsatisfactory that a Karen delegation, including Saw Ba U Gyi, proceeded to London in August, 1946, to lay their cause before the British. During its stay (August to December) the delegation established wide

---

[35] Hinners, pp. 282–285. The meager extent to which developments in Burma were understood in Moscow at this time was indicated by *Izvestia's* completely erroneous statement of January 31, 1947 (*Soviet Press Translations*, II, no. 6 [March, 1947], 1–3), that Governor Rance had encouraged Dr. Ba Maw to reorganize his party in an effort to create a rift in Burmese nationalist ranks and to exclude Communists from the A.F.P.F.L. London had allegedly made no real concessions to U Aung San in January, 1947.

[36] See pages 370–371.

contacts in England and Scotland including unofficial conferences with Lord Pethick-Lawrence and other members of the Labour government.[37] But despite favorable press reaction, the time was inauspicious, for Mr. Attlee had already determined to send Governor Rance to make terms with the Burman nationalists.

In its booklet entitled *The Case for the Karens*,[38] the delegation stated its case. It declared that the long history of Karen mistreatment at Burman hands had been revived during World War II. The Burmese administration at the time had made little attempt to curb communal violence especially in the western delta and in Salween District, allegedly looking toward the extermination of the Karen race. Since the proposed Scheduled Areas Karen State lacked access to the sea, adequate ricelands, and communication facilities, the delegation presented two alternative requests to London: (1) that a special act of Parliament establish from Burma territory a Karen State equipped with a liberal constitution, operating under British protection, and having a seaboard or (2) that the same Karen State be permitted to join a Federation of Frontier Area States separate from Burma and enjoying dominion status within the Commonwealth. The delegation received a respectful hearing and some sympathy in Conservative political circles, but it returned to Burma empty-handed. As has already been indicated, Saw Ba U Gyi continued to co-operate with the A.F.P.F.L. nationalists after October, 1946, by accepting a post in Thakin Aung San's executive council. He eventually resigned in March, 1947, and was replaced by Mahn Ba Khaing.

The London Agreement of January, 1947, had forced the central organization of the Karen National Union (made up of affiliated district Karen organizations) to decide whether to participate in the Constituent Assembly elections and thus to acquiesce in the prospective amalgamation of Karen-inhabited areas with Burma proper. At a meeting at Rangoon in February, 1947, the Karen National Union divided over the issue. Saw San Po Thin and the opportunist Mahn Ba Khaing decided to go along with the A.F.P.F.L. and to accept the decision of the assembly-appointed boundary commission in demarcating the eventual Karen State. The majority group, led by Saw

[37] *RFACE*, pt. II, p. 169; *The Times,* Aug. 4, Dec. 6, 1946; *Scotsman*, Oct. 8, 1946; *Yorkshire Post*, Dec. 10, 1946. Other members of the delegation were Saw Sidney Loo Nee, Saw Po Chit, and Saw Tha Din. Saw Ba U Gyi came late and left early. Upon his return to Rangoon, he accepted a proffered post in U Aung San's new council.

[38] Published in London, 1946.

Ba U Gyi, voted to boycott the elections unless the A.F.P.F.L. indicated prior acceptance of seven stated demands, the most important of which (no. 5) specified "that the question of the creation of a Karen State with a seaboard in the United Burma be accepted in principle." Other demands included a 25 per cent Karen representation in the governor's council and in the prospective legislative council, separate Karen army units, a new population census, and Karen representation in the government services in proportion to population. The government allotted to the Karens some twenty-four seats in the assembly but flatly refused to concede demand no. 5.

The break between the A.F.P.F.L. and the Karen National Union was signalized not only by the election boycott, but more importantly by the decision of the Karen Union to organize its own paramilitary Karen National Defense Organization to parallel the Burman People's Volunteer Organization.[39] As already indicated, the hearings of the Frontier Areas Committee of Enquiry and the outcome of the elections did little to quiet Karen misgivings concerning their future safety and welfare under Burman rule. A tragic clash was in the making.

Preparations for Independence

The two most important political figures responsible for preparing for Burma's independence during the spring of 1947 were Thakins Aung San and Mya. Thakin Nu, although not a member of the council, ranked third, considerably behind the other two.[40] Thakin Aung San was the government's public relations man par excellence, vigorous and forthright in his leadership and possessing a personality capable of commanding the respect and allegiance of virtually the entire population, especially the potentially turbulent elements of the P.V.O. Thakin Mya, an older and abler man, was the responsible and level-headed negotiator, planner, and administrator. It was he who negotiated with Mr. J. I. C. Crombie of His Majesty's Government the financial agreement of April 30, 1947, and who, in May, acted as chairman of the special committee to draft a trial constitution. During June and early July, Thakin Mya played a leading role in the Constitutional Assembly and also headed the New Economic Planning Board to prepare a substitute for the discredited "projects" scheme.

[39] RFACE, pt. II, pp. 154–159, 179–180.
[40] Thakin Nu's participation in the Frontier Areas Committee Enquiry has already been mentioned. His role as president of the Constituent Assembly and as negotiator with London in June, 1947, will be considered later.

Thakin Mya's April 30 financial agreement with London represented a generous gesture on Britain's part, doubtless intended to demonstrate the tangible advantages which Burma could enjoy by continued association with the Commonwealth. London agreed to contribute substantially to meet Burma's current operating budget and to make additional advances during the ensuing year up to a ceiling of £18 million for capital expenditures under the various "projects." [41] The eventual sale of the capital assets of the liquidated projects, after deducting the costs of liquidation, would be applied to the reduction of the British Government loans outstanding. London left open for later discussion Thakin Mya's proposal that the interest-free loan be converted into an outright grant. On the Burmese side, the government agreed to take immediate steps to increase its revenues, to reduce its administrative expenses, and to stimulate savings. Burma also acknowledged as an appropriate charge against its revenues the cost of maintaining troops in Burma, the maximum amount being subject to negotiation. Burma also agreed to turn over to London the proceeds from the sale of those CAS(B) stores which were not lend-lease surpluses.

It was the hope of all Britons familiar with Burma's needs, and the expectation of some of them, that London's generous political and financial agreements would constitute a basis for Burma's decision, once given a free choice, in favor of dominion status within the Commonwealth. Some responsible Burman leaders, aware of the difficulties and risks of independence, apparently would have preferred some such solution, but the political realities of the situation forbade it. Even as late as February, 1947, Burma Chamber of Commerce spokesmen had revived distrust by protesting overvigorously the Socialist and prolabor tendencies of the emerging Burmese regime.[42] The unconcealed anxiety of even the pro-Burman British leaders at Rangoon that Burma must not forego the advantages of dominion status tended to make such a policy suspect, just as British advocacy of separation from India had done fifteen years before. The presence within the

[41] The promised sums were £12 million for Burma's 1945–1946 deficit plus the unspent balance of the earlier grant of £2.5 million to the Frontier Areas.

[42] Burma Chamber of Commerce, *Minutes of the Proceedings of the Annual General Meeting, February 27, 1947* (Rangoon, 1947), pp. 13–15. On this occasion Sir Arthur Bruce clashed with the Chamber's Burman guest, Thakin Aung San. The latter admitted Burma's need for outside capital until plans could be realized for ultimate nationalization of all important industry, but he denounced the "projects" boards for failing to take popular welfare into account and insisted that capital would never again be given free rein in Burma.

newly elected assembly of large numbers of ultranationalist P.V.O. representatives, heedless of the risks of independence, made a compromise political arrangement by the Assembly wholly out of the question. Another factor was that the Socialist-A.F.P.F.L. competition with Communist agitators for peasant support forbade the government's making any pro-British concession which could provide a club to their political opponents. As was demonstrated by the forced resignation of U Ba Pe from the executive council in May, 1947, the immediate political trend was toward the left and therefore away from any possible compromise.[43]

The virtual inevitability of Burma's separation from Britain became clear in the course of a five-day session of the general convention of the A.F.P.F.L., which began at Rangoon on May 18 to review the draft constitution prepared by Thakin Mya's committee. The convention numbered 800 delegates including all of the elected pro-A.F.P.F.L. members of the Constitutional Assembly (some 190), plus the party's executive and district officers.[44] Thakin Aung San's keynote address, stressing patriotic effort and subordination of rival "isms" to the essential task of developing a flexible, common-sense, practical, and progressive program for economic and political development, was sane and constructive. He denounced in particular, as a waste of time and energy, the debating of the Communist-sponsored question of whether "imperialism" would ever surrender its power willingly and peacefully, since time alone could and would answer that question. But the delegates were taking no chances. Their most important action was to approve a resolution proclaiming complete independence for Burma and its people.[45]

Acting in the same ultranationalist spirit, the Constituent Assembly itself, soon after it convened on June 10, unanimously (including the Frontier Areas delegates) approved a resolution cutting all ties with the British Empire. Only wishful thinking could have imagined a different outcome.[46]

[43] Virginia Thompson, "Burma's Communists," *Far Eastern Survey*, XVII (1948), 103–106; *The Times*, May 12, 1947. U Ba Pe was also detected accepting bribes as minister of commerce and supplies.

[44] Maung Pye, pp. 111–119; *The Times*, May 20, 1947. The A.F.P.F.L. delegates included representatives of the Karen Youth Organization.

[45] Maung Pye, pp. 119–141. Thakin Aung San challenged in particular those Burmese who insisted that all must "think alike, act alike, speak alike."

[46] Mr. Furnivall has suggested (*Pacific Affairs*, XXII [1949], 219–220) that a better psychological tactic from London's point of view would have been to advocate Burma's exclusion from the empire with the option of readmission.

London's disappointment over the brusque anti-British decision of the assembly was reflected in the strong Conservative pressure brought to bear on Undersecretary Henderson in Parliament, successfully resisted, to cancel Britain's promised contributions to Burma's governmental deficit.[47] Instead, the Labour government negotiated in the customary cordial spirit with the new Burman delegation, headed by U Tin Tut, who arrived in London on June 16 to arrange various important matters relating to the transfer of power. He was later joined by Thakin Nu and others. It was then agreed that joint missions would begin immediately to formulate provisional agreements covering such problems as defense, finances, nationality definition, commercial relations, and contractual obligations, so that they would be ready when the constitution was drafted.

Britain's announced policy was to maintain cordial relations even if Burma's decision was separation from the Commonwealth. London would recognize the existing interim government until the transfer of power took place and then would give legal effect to the new Burma constitution at the autumn session of Parliament.[48] The opportunity afforded Thakin Nu during his London visit for personal contact with the leaders of the Labour government was to prove most fortunate in the light of the unforeseen contingency of his taking over as Burma's Prime Minister following the death of Thakins Aung San and Mya and of several of their colleagues on July 19, 1947.

The tragic assassinations of July 19 were planned and executed at the instigation of U Saw. Two gunmen, using automatic weapons, forced their way into the secretariat room where the cabinet was in full session and attempted to kill them all. Besides Thakins Aung San and Mya, they murdered the highly respected Deedok U Ba Choe, Fabian Socialist and patron of literature and fine arts; Abdul Razak of Mandalay; U Ba Win, able and dependable ex-schoolteacher, older brother of Thakin Aung San; the Karen representative, Mahn Ba Khaing; the Sawbwa of Mongpawn; and U Ohn Maung, secretary to the government in the Department of Transport and Communications. U Saw's motivation was apparently a combination of frustrated ambition, anger, and vengeance. He had himself as already indicated,

[47] PD,C, vol. 439 (June 30, 1947), p. 927.

[48] PD,C, vol. 440 (July 24, 1947), pp. 1605–1607; The Times, June 18, 1947; Statesman, June 29, 1947. Also included in the delegation were Thakins Kyaw Nyein, Ko Ko Gyi, and Bo Khin Maung Gale. Britain's press hoped that India's contemporary decision to remain in the Commonwealth would influence Burma to do the same.

survived an attempted assassination by an unknown assailant, an act which he attributed to political enemies. U Saw's objective was apparently to destroy the existing nationalist government, to blame the crime on the British, and thus to precipitate a general revolution, which his own unscrupulous followers would seek to exploit to their own political advantage.

That U Saw's plot failed to succeed was due in large measure to the prompt action of Governor Rance in calling upon Thakin Nu, vice-president of the A.F.P.F.L. and president of the Constituent Assembly, to form a new government. U Nu's regime took over on July 20. During the two critical months following the assassination, Prime Minister Nu enjoyed the vigorous support of his long-time Communist friend, Thakin Than Tun, who accepted Nu's assurances that the British were in no way responsible for the crime and co-operated to thwart the threatened rightist coup by U Saw's partisans.[49]

While the June negotiations were being conducted in London, Burma's nationalist leaders were encountering the first evidences of sectional unrest. The first was a rebellion in Arakan which began in May and grew steadily worse with the passing months despite the government's capture of the *pongyi* rebel, U Sien Da. Thakin Soe's Red Flag Communists were doing their utmost to fan the flames, but popular unrest drew much of its support from provincial dislike of the prospect of returning Burman rule. Following the decision for independence, in mid-June, a group of Kachin leaders, apparently concerned over boundary and other questions, undertook to arrange private consultations with Governor Rance. U Aung San was reported to have declared bluntly that the Kachins must decide "whether they wanted to remain with their own kin or align themselves with British imperialism." He reportedly added: "If you frontier people side with the British and go against us, then it will go hard with you."[50] The unification of Burma would not be easy even with the best of leadership.

The tragedy of July 19 dealt a grievous blow to Burma's political future. The affable, intelligent, trustworthy, and politically capable Thakin Mya would be sorely missed, for he had been for many months the central figure in the planning for independence. Almost as serious would be the loss of U Ba Choe, a senior friend of the Thakins with

[49] Maung Pye, pp. 145–153; Sutton, pp. 11–13.

[50] *The Times*, June 17 and 22, 1947; Manchester *Guardian*, June 7, 1947; *Statesman*, June 18, July 4, 1947; *Daily Express*, May 20, 1947.

a wise head, whose selfless dedication to his country's well-being was above question. Completely irreplaceable was the beloved Bogyoke Aung San. At thirty-two, his unquestioned integrity, singleness of purpose, and demonstrated capacity for leadership made him the unrivaled hero of Burma's independence struggle.[51] In a situation where the idea of establishing national solidarity on the basis of the sovereign will of all the people was completely alien, Thakin Aung San's death removed the indispensable personality. The politically powerful, but utterly inexperienced P.V.O. was left with no one whose authority and discipline it would accept. The leadership of the P.V.O. faction, so prominent in the Constituent Assembly and so determined to maintain its momentary glory, degenerated rapidly during the closing months of 1947. The self-styled soldier-hero (*Yebaw*) organization attracted many undesirables to its ranks, lost sight entirely of its social uplift objectives, and split into quarreling camps.[52]

It developed during U Saw's prolonged trial, from October 8 to December 30, 1947, that the coup had been planned by a few *Myochit* leaders months before. Individuals impersonating the civil police and carrying forged documents had obtained consignments of arms from the Base Arms Depot in June and early July; the final decision concerning the assassination was reached on July 15. Both the arms and the vehicles used by the assassins were traced to U Saw's residence, where many of the stolen weapons were also found. U Saw was convicted of murder and hanged.[53]

The Constitution of the Union of Burma

In spite of the interruption occasioned by the crisis of late July, the Constituent Assembly under Premier Nu's leadership completed its work by mid-September. The document was formally adopted and

[51] Sutton, pp. 14–15; *PD,C*, vol. 440 (July 21, 1947), pp. 866–867. Undersecretary Henderson here indicated his high personal opinion of both Thakins Aung San and Mya as "men of great intelligence, courage, and public spirit." A Burman friend characterized Bogyoke Aung San as a battleground of paradoxes, simple and practical yet puzzlingly complex and mystical, blunt and outspoken to the point of rudeness and yet essentially courteous, humble and unassuming and yet proud and self-assertive in relation to political ends. As a student he was an intense devotee of history and politics. Above all he demonstrated a single-minded sincerity of purpose and an ability to command a following. He valued action above thought and coined the Thakin slogan, "We want fools to fight for Burma's freedom." See Maung Maung, *Burma's Teething Times* (Rangoon, 1949), p. 43.

[52] Union of Burma, *Burma and the Insurrections*, pp. 7–9.

[53] Hinners, p. 289; *PD,C*, vol. 440 (July 30, 1947), pp. 459–462; *The Times*, Oct. 16, 17, and 18, 1947.

enacted on September 24, 1947 (tenth day of Thadingyut waxing). It borrowed from a number of sources. From the French system came the provision for a President as titular head of the state, to be elected by vote of the combined houses of Parliament for a five-year term. From American practice came the idea of promulgating a formal constitutional document based on the principle of popular sovereignty. Other borrowings from the United States included a statement of fundamental rights (with certain variations), the establishment of an independent judiciary capable of determining the constitutionality of legislative enactments, and a federal system under which the component states of the Burma Union were severally represented in an upper house of the Parliament called the Chamber of Nationalities. The latter name was of Communist origin. The collective responsibility of the executive organs of the government to an elected Parliament was a direct adaptation of British practice found in Burma's previous constitutions. Furthermore, the entire body of legal principles and court procedure (including even the permissive use of the English language in Parliament and in court) was carried over from the British period. The constitution itself was printed in English and Burmese. Finally, those parts of the constitution (Chapters III and IV) relating to its socialist aspects borrowed substantially from the constitution of Yugoslavia.

The preamble to the constitution espoused the following objectives in the name of the sovereign people of Burma:

To maintain social order on the basis of the eternal principles of Justice, Liberty, and Equality and to guarantee and secure to all citizens Justice, social, economic, and political; Liberty of thought, expression, belief, faith, worship, vocation, association and action; Equality of status, of opportunity, and before the law. . . .

With the exception of the constitutional guarantee of freedom of religion to all persons resident in the Union of Burma, the general provisions of the bill of rights were reserved for citizens only. Citizenship status was limited to those born of indigenous parents, to those with one grandparent of an indigenous race, and to British subjects who had resided in Burma for eight of the ten years preceding January 1, 1942, or preceding the coming into force of the constitution and who elected permanent residency and citizenship. Such citizens were expressly guaranteed equality before the law, equal opportunity for employment and choice of trade or vocation, inviolability of person, dwelling, and property save by'actions taken in accordance with law. Citizens also enjoyed freedom of speech, of peaceful assembly, and of association and freedom to reside, to acquire property, and to follow one's chosen vocation anywhere in the Union. Buddhism was accorded a special (but undefined) position as the faith of the majority of Burma's citizens, but religious and linguistic minorities were to suffer no discrimination in admission to state educational institutions or to have any type of religious instruction imposed on them.[54]

The ownership of private property and the exercise of private initiative in the economic sphere were guaranteed, but within limits which conformed to the public interest and which prohibited monopolies and price dictation. Laws expropriating private property in the public interest should "prescribe in which cases and to what extent the owner shall be compensated." Single enterprises and entire branches of the economy could be nationalized or acquired by the state if the public interest so required.[55]

The constitution expressed solicitude for the welfare of peasants and workers. Large landholding was expressly prohibited. The state, as ultimate owner, was expressly empowered to regulate, alter, or abolish existing land tenures as well as to resume possession and redistribute land for use of individual tenants or for purposes of collective or co-operative farming. The state could assist workers to organize for protection against economic exploitation and for improving conditions of work. It could also legislate to provide housing needs and social insurance. Chapter IV, entitled "Directive Principles of State Policy," was intended for general guidance only and was not to be enforceable in any court. The key section (no. 41) declared flatly "that economic life of the Union shall be planned with the aim of increasing public wealth, of improving the material conditions of the people and raising their cultural level." Citizens possessed the right to work, to enjoy old-age and incapacity care as well as opportunity for education and leisure. Special concern was indicated for the economically weak, for children and nursing mothers, for orphans of servicemen, for disabled veterans, and for economic organizations not working for private profit. The operation of public utilities and the exploitation of natural resources were to be reserved for public bodies,

[54] Union of Burma, *The Constitution of the Union of Burma* (Rangoon, 1954), secs. 10, 13–17, 20–24. The abuse of religion for political purposes or to promote hatred, enmity, or discord between communities was forbidden.

[55] *Ibid.*, sec. 23.

to people's co-operatives or to companies 60 per cent of whose stock was owned by citizens.[56]

The Union Parliament was bicameral, consisting of a Chamber of Deputies and a Chamber of Nationalities, the former to be approximately twice the size of the latter. With the exception of 20 seats reserved for the Karens, in proportion to their numbers, all deputies were elected for four-year terms from general constituencies as fixed by law. Candidates must be citizens twenty-one years old, and voters eighteen. Religious orders (*pongyis*) could be debarred from voting and from membership in the Parliament. Members of Parliament were privileged in not being liable for court action by reason of any statement or vote made in the chambers. Membership in the Chamber of Nationalities was allocated arbitrarily between the various component peoples of the Union, with 72 seats of the 125 going to non-Burman elements.[57] Both chambers were to be elected simultaneously and were also to suffer dissolution at the same time. The Prime Minister and cabinet were collectively responsible, as in the British tradition, to the Chamber of Deputies, which also enjoyed special authority over the initiation and passage of money bills. In case the two chambers failed to reach agreement on a nonmoney bill, the deadlock was to be resolved by a joint vote of the members of the two bodies. Except for defense in case of invasion, the Parliament must assent to a declaration of war.[58]

Residual powers were vested in the Union Parliament, which could legislate for the whole or any part of the Union except in such matters as were assigned to the exclusive authority of the component states.[59] Any legislation authorizing the exploitation and development of forests, minerals, or oil fields located in subordinate member states could be passed only after consultation with the minister of the state concerned. The State Legislative List covered all aspects of local administration (agriculture, land ownership and revenue, police, markets and fairs, excise and property taxes, roads, education, health, poor relief), but state laws which trespassed Union authority, as determined by the Supreme Court, were to be inoperative. Only the Union Parlia-

[56] *Ibid.*, secs. 32–44, 218.

[57] The allocations were 25 Shan State representatives, 12 from the Kachin State, 8 Chins, 3 Karenni, and 24 Karens.

[58] Union of Burma, *The Constitution*, secs. 66–114. Emergency ordinances promulgated by the President were subject to subsequent approval of Parliament.

[59] The extensive "Union Legislative List" was intended to clarify rather than to restrict the jurisdiction of the Parliament.

ment could raise and maintain an armed establishment.[60] Until a regular Parliament could be elected and convened, the Constituent Assembly was authorized to function as a Parliament.

The councils for the three subordinate states (Shan, Kachin, Karenni) and for the two special districts (Chin and Karen) were severally composed of all the members of both chambers of Parliament from the respective geographical areas and constituencies.[61] A minister for each of the five areas would be nominated by the Prime Minister after consultation with the respective councils and would hold posts in the Union cabinet. The several ministers were empowered to summon or prorogue the respective councils which were entrusted with responsibility for governing the subordinate areas.[62]

The susceptibilities of Burman and Shan citizens resident within the Kachin State were taken into account by the requirement that half of the Kachin State seats in the Chamber of Nationalities and half of the cabinet posts should go to non-Kachins.[63] Within the Kachin State Council, furthermore, both groups were enabled to reject legislative measures prejudicially affecting any rights enjoyed immediately prior to the formation of the state. In addition, the general provision covering the right of secession after ten years (Chapter X) was made not applicable to the Kachin State.[64]

The constitution also made provision for the future establishment of a Karen State to be on a par with the Shan State and to include Karenni, the Salween District, and "such adjacent areas occupied by the Karens as may be determined by a Special Commission to be appointed by the President." The future action would be subject to the approval of a majority of the people of the three areas concerned and of the Burma Karens living outside, in a manner to be later prescribed by law. In the meantime a special region composed of the Salween District and adjacent areas, to be known as *Kawthulay*, would be administered under the authority of the Karen Council and the minister of Karen affairs. The jurisdiction of the proposed Karen

---

[60] Union of Burma, *The Constitution*, secs. 92–94, Third Schedule, pp. 68–76.

[61] Elected Shan *Sawbwas* exclusively made up that state's membership in the Chamber of Nationalities, but only non-*Sawbwas* were eligible for membership in the Chamber of Deputies.

[62] Union of Burma, *The Constitution*, secs. 154–165.

[63] India, Census Commissioner, *Census of India, 1931*, vol. XI, *Burma*, pt. I, map frontispiece. The Kachins constituted the largest single group in Bhamo District, but they were outnumbered by the Shans in Myitkyina District and by the Burmans in Katha.

[64] Union of Burma, *The Constitution*, secs. 166–178.

minister and council included also matters relating to Karen schools, cultural rights, and special constitutional guarantees.[65] Similarly pending the formation of the prospective Karen State, the three chiefs of the Karenni States and, if the population of Mongpai should approve, its chief also would represent their territories in the Chamber of Nationalities. The Karenni minister and a state council including all Karenni members of Parliament would constitute the government of that area, in the usual fashion.[66]

Several additional provisions completed the arrangements for the federal aspects of the Union. An area from the Chin Hills District and the Arakan Hill Tracts, to be designated by the Union President, should constitute the special division of the Chins. The minister of Chin affairs and his council would exercise control over the division in accordance with powers to be determined by legislative enactment.[67] The simple procedure for amending the constitution (by majority vote of both chambers and a two-thirds vote sitting jointly) included the provision that amendments affecting voting schedules and the representation of the several states in the Parliament must be approved by the states concerned. Similarly any bill to abridge special rights of the Chin or Kachin peoples must be approved by majorities of the parliamentary representation of these groups.

Finally, every state except the Kachin was accorded the right to secede from the Union after the expiration of a ten-year period from the date of the operation of the constitution. The procedure for secession required holding a popular plebiscite supervised by a joint commission from the Union and the state. Such a proposal should be initiated by the submission to the President of the Union of a formal resolution favoring secession and approved by a two-thirds vote of the state council concerned.[68]

In addition to giving to the state title over all agricultural land for purposes of redistribution to citizen cultivators,[69] the constitution gave to the Union Government a monopoly over the development and exploitation of timber and mineral lands, fisheries, underground

[65] *Ibid.*, secs. 180, 181. The Karen Affairs Council included Karen members of the Chamber of Deputies only, plus five or fewer Karens from the Chamber of Nationalities.

[66] *Ibid.*, secs. 182–195.

[67] With the consent of the council of the area affected, the Parliament was empowered to establish other such governmental units or to alter the boundaries of any existing unit.

[68] Union of Burma, *The Constitution*, secs. 196–204.   [69] *Ibid.*, sec. 30.

mineral, coal, and petroleum resources, and all potential sources of electrical energy. Only by special acts of Parliament could exceptions be made permitting private Burma citizens and firms if 60 per cent Burma-owned to invade the indicated government monopoly. Such exceptions could in no case be granted for longer than twenty-five years, and rights so accorded would be subject to amendment or repeal by act of Parliament at any time if required in the public interest. Authorizations for the operation of public utilities were similarly reserved to Union, state, or local governmental agencies and, by special consent, to citizens.[70] In keeping with this emphasis on state socialism was the provision that Burma's flag should be red with a cluster of six white stars grouped in the blue-colored corner canton.[71]

Planning the New State

How very far this liberal-socialist constitution departed from traditional Burma political institutions as described in Chapter I was the measure of the distance traveled since 1825 by Burma's political leaders. To define more clearly what was contemplated in the section entitled "Directive Principles of State Policy," a *Two-Year Plan of Economic Development* was hurriedly prepared and published in early 1948. It explained the general direction of development rather than set forth a precise program. The introductory statement prepared by Thakin Mya before his assassination explained that Burma's planned economy was intended to contrast with the laissez-faire system of British days, the chief objective of which had allegedly been the self-interest of foreign capitalists and entrepreneurs and complete lack of concern that Burman villagers share in the profits of rising production. The plan as proposed was designed to speed up the immediate recovery in production of the prewar industries and to lay the foundation for a balanced socialized economy for the long run, to the end that no individual or section of the population would be exploited for the benefit of another.[72] Increased production targets were

[70] *Ibid.*, secs. 218, 219. These provisions reflected not only socialistic principles, but also the overriding concern of the constitution makers to reserve all Burma's resources for indigenous development.

[71] *Ibid.*, sec. 215. Royalist agitation in October, 1947, attracted little attention, although some persons of princely lineage still wore their hair in topknots, and the frontier peoples may have preferred a king. See the *Christian Science Monitor*, Oct. 30, 1947.

[72] Union of Burma, Economic Planning Board, *Two-Year Plan for Economic Development for Burma* (Rangoon, 1948), pp. 1–3. The preparation of the plan

set for all established areas of the prewar economy in the light of available men, equipment, and resources.

In the primary field of agriculture, a threefold policy was outlined. Priority would be given to the early restoration of Burma to its prewar status of the world's largest exporter of rice and to achievement of self-sufficiency in widely diversified products. Cultivation would be developed on modern scientific lines, ensuring cultivators a fair return on their produce and protection against fluctuating world markets. Ultimately the land would be redistributed, eliminating landlordism, restoring alienated land, and preventing future alienation, but no coercion of cultivators was envisaged. For the ensuing paddy season the state would provide the necessary credits and would supervise the renting to cultivator tenants (at twice the rate of land revenue) of lands not rented by the present landlords. Eventually the state would acquire some two-thirds of the noncultivator-owned land in the delta area. A one-third increase of rice acreage (from 9 million acres to 12 million) was contemplated by 1951–1952, mainly through returning to cultivation some 2 million acres abandoned during the war. Self-sufficiency in cooking oils, sugar, peppers, and onions was promised by 1952.[73] Private moneylender operations would be regulated pending the launching of the Central State Agricultural Bank in 1949, which would give preference to co-operative society borrowers and to state colony units. The State Agricultural Marketing Board established as a British "project" would continue to purchase paddy from the cultivators at not more than twice the prewar price and would monopolize its export, thus siphoning off export profits and keeping the domestic price reasonably low and stable.[74]

The Two-Year Plan contemplated little alteration in the traditional operation of the Forestry Department except that all large leases which expired would not be renewed. The state would take over timber operations in one-third of the teak area during the first year and the re-

---

was interrupted by Thakin Mya's death in 1947; it was completed hurriedly in early 1948.

[73] *Ibid.*, pp. 4–10. Sugar prices would be fixed at twice the prewar figure, and cane would be processed in state-owned factories. Cotton production would be restored to the prewar surplus of 90,000 bales.

[74] *Ibid.*, pp. 10–17. The plan included marketing research, standardization of weights and measures, and experimentation in mechanized farming, plus establishment of the Institute of Agricultural Engineering and the Bureau of Agricultural Information.

mainder in subsequent years. The entire stand of teak trees was already state property. No expropriation of legal rights was contemplated, and foreign experts would be asked to aid in planning, administration, extraction, utilization, and export marketing. Notably absent was any proposal to give to the villagers free access to Burma's valuable timber resources.[75]

Plans for labor-employer relations were utopian (harmony, fair wages, improved conditions, conciliation machinery, elimination of unemployment, social insurance, etc.), but they did not call explicitly for forced mobilization and left open a wide field for private employment. Labor offices to be established in areas where large construction projects were contemplated would transport needed labor to the site, would "direct" employment of the force available to those spheres of work best suited, and would take responsibility for housing and welfare needs.[76] The order of precedence in the proposed nationalization program was: banking, utility industries, nonagricultural resources, large-scale manufacturing, and, coming last on the list, handicrafts and agriculture. The minister of national planning was to have a cabinet post, and his advisory board would be presided over by the Prime Minister himself.[77]

Plans for separating Burma from the British Commonwealth were completed by the negotiation of two final agreements with London. The first one, having to do with defense matters, was signed on August 29, 1947, by Bo Let Ya, Premier Nu's understudy at the time, and by John W. Freeman for the United Kingdom. It provided for the early evacuation of British military forces and the waiver of British claims previously advanced for payment covering the transfer of naval vessels, the initial equipment for the Burma army, and the fixed assets of the British army and Royal Air Force. The United Kingdom also agreed at Burma's request to educate officer personnel in England for the new Burma armed forces and to maintain in Burma for three years a naval, military, and air force mission for the purpose of training the new services locally.[78] Britain would also maintain and staff for one year the principal airport at Mingaladon and would contribute up to £40,000 annually to the

[75] *Ibid.*, pp. 18–19.   [76] *Ibid.*, pp. 39–42.

[77] *Ibid.*, pp. 10–17; R. M. Sparks, "The Nationalization Plans of Burma" (Temple University master's thesis, 1949), pp. 55–63.

[78] The functions, composition, and conditions of service of the British mission would be negotiated later, but Burma would pay only the cost of the actual instructional staff in Burma.

maintenance of the Akyab and Mergui airports. War materials would be made available in England for purchase by Burma on reasonable terms.

These generous terms on Britain's part were balanced by three Burma concessions: (1) that no armed forces mission would be received from outside the British Commonwealth; (2) that Commonwealth naval vessels and air force planes would be accorded entry into Burma at prescribed points upon notification from time to time; and (3) that any Commonwealth forces undertaking by agreement to participate in Burma's defense would be afforded "all reasonable assistance including facilities of access and entry." [79] The defense treaty was to run for three years and then be subject to cancellation thereafter by either party on twelve months' notice. Although the signing was widely publicized, the terms of this defense agreement were kept secret until publication, on October 27, of the terms of Burma's final treaty negotiated with the United Kingdom. [80]

The so-called Nu-Attlee Treaty signed on October 17, 1947, formally recognized Burma's independence and provided for exchange of diplomatic representatives. It incorporated the defense agreement of August 29 (Article 4) and provided that Burma should defray from its own revenues the pensions, provident fund payments, and leave salaries for service in Burma which were due British subjects not domiciled in India or Pakistan (Article 5). Burma's financial obligations also included CAS(B) costs from the time of the restoration of civilian rule. Britain canceled £15 million advanced to meet Burma's successive governmental deficits, but, beginning in April, 1952, Burma agreed to repay in twenty equal annual installments without interest the sums advanced by the United Kingdom on the various "projects" operations. In Article 7, the Burma Government agreed to execute contracts held by British persons or companies at the time of the transfer of power,[81] but this promise was qualified by an exchange of notes of the same

---

[79] Naval transfers included thirty-six motored harbor craft and one ocean-going vessel. Burma's naval and air forces would be accorded reciprocal rights in the United Kingdom.

[80] Maung Pye, pp. 164–169; *PP,C*, vol. XVI for 1947–1948 (Cmd. 7240), pp. 5–9.

[81] Great Britain, *Treaty between the Government of the United Kingdom and the Provisional Government of Burma* (London, 1947), pp. 1–11. The treaty was also published in *PP,C*, vol. XVI for 1947–1948, as Cmd. 7240. The remainder of the articles covered routine provisions concerning a commerce treaty, postal services, war cemeteries, civil aviation, double taxation, etc. U Tin Tut negotiated the financial aspects of the treaty.

date. Premier Nu explained that if the Burma Government should find it necessary in any particular case to take action prejudicial to United Kingdom interests in Burma, whether business or professional, it would consult with London in advance with a view to reaching a mutually satisfactory agreement. U Nu's statement concluded as follows:

I have, however, to explain that the undertaking given in the preceding paragraph must be read as subject to the provisions of the Constitution . . . as now adopted, and in particular to the policy of State Socialism therein contained to which my Government is committed. If, however, the implementation of . . . the Constitution should involve expropriation or acquisition . . . of existing United Kingdom interests in Burma, the provisional Government will provide equitable compensation to the parties affected.[82]

Parliamentary Approval of the Nu-Attlee Treaty

Within less than a week following the signing of the Nu-Attlee Treaty, a bill to provide immediate independence for Burma was introduced into Britain's House of Commons.[83] The measure came up for debate on November 5 at the time of the second reading. The debate afforded opportunity for a final Attlee-Churchill duel on Burma policy.

Mr. Attlee's defense of the independence proposal was very direct. He regretted Burma's failure to recognize the advantages inherent in Commonwealth membership, but took pride in the fact that in honoring repeated pledges to Burma going back to 1931 the British Commonwealth was demonstrating that it was indeed a free association of peoples, not a collection of subject nations. He pointed out that British representatives had participated at various stages in arranging for recognition of the rights and wishes of the minority peoples and that, barring one group of the Karens, the non-Burman peoples had accepted the new constitution. A Shan *Sawbwa* had recently been selected as the provisional President. The new constitution provided for a parliamentary government with special provision for minority representation in the Chamber of Nationalities. Mr. Attlee concluded by expressing the hope that the next chapter in Britain's relations with Burma would start, as planned, on January 4, 1948, with enduring ties of friendship established.[84]

[82] *Ibid.*, pp. 10–11.

[83] *PD,C*, vol. 443 (Oct. 23, 1947), pp. 235. The bill was introduced October 23, 1947, and the terms of the treaty were published in Parliamentary Cmd. 7240 on October 27.

[84] *PD,C*, vol. 443 (Nov. 5, 1947), pp. 1836–1845. A second Karen mission visited

Mr. Churchill argued in reply that the utilization in Burma of a fraction of the British troops assigned during the postwar period to Palestine would have sufficed to carry through the original White Paper policy. Such a program, he alleged, would have afforded opportunity for calm and deliberate consideration of Burma's future constitution in full appreciation of the values of Commonwealth membership. Mr. Churchill's own reluctant approval of Lord Mountbatten's acceptance of Thakin Aung San's offer of military co-operation in 1945 had involved no expectation that the leader of the quisling Burman army would later be regarded as the plenipotentiary of the Burma Government. Mr. Attlee must therefore bear full responsibility for a decision which might concern the future of the entire British Commonwealth. The Conservative Party leader prophesied that rebellion was brewing in Burma and that a bloody welter was in prospect. The reported consent of the hill tribes was of dubious genuineness. Britain, he concluded, was rebuffing the loyalty and faithful service (of the Karens) and was contributing ruin to many and a fearful retrogression of civilization in the East by thus abandoning its responsibilities in Burma.

Mr. Churchill's point of view was strongly supported, as on previous occasions, by Captain Gammons. He was pessimistic of the prospects of independent Burma on every count, security-wise, governmentally, economically, and in terms of internal order. He reaffirmed the argument of the White Paper of 1945 that restoration of economic processes and orderly conditions in Burma were prerequisite to the effective functioning of any democratic system. He charged that the negotiators at the Panglong Conference were for the most part the nominees of Thakin Aung San. The Karens and the Anglo-Indians in particular were much opposed to the new order. Captain Gammons prophesied that Burma was really being given "anarchy, a lower standard of living, and probably extinction of its independence within ten years." [85] A more temperate statement of Conservative Party views came from

---

London in 1947 headed by Saw Ba U Gyi, who resigned as head of the Ministry of Transport and Communication to lead it. An embittered Anglo-Burman protest against the constitution had also been forwarded to Conservative members of Parliament asking for a special hearing (*ibid.*, pp. 1074–1075).

[85] *PD,C*, vol. 443 (Nov. 5, 1947), pp. 1877–1897, 1902–1911. Earl Winterton (pp. 1930–1931) delivered a sarcastic attack on the Attlee proposal, impugning the respectability of Burma's political leaders and the intelligence of his own parliamentary hecklers. Mr. Baxter echoed the traditional jingoist praise of the glories of the empire, charging that the Socialists were ashamed of it.

Mr. Nicholson, who insisted that his party had no less good will for Burma than had Labour and was actually acting in more responsible fashion. Despite Burma's discourtesy in leaving the empire in the face of ample evidences of British good will, he insisted that there existed no choice but to go through with the independence program, a policy on which the British community in Burma was unanimously agreed. He urged his Conservative colleagues to abstain rather than oppose the motion.[86]

Labour Party spokesmen presented a vigorous rejoinder to the Churchill-Gammons argument. They pointed out that it did no good to enrage a nation by insulting its martyred hero and declared that the political awakening of the East was perhaps the greatest event of the times.[87] The reconquest of Burma by British troops based in the United Kingdom and without support from India was not an undertaking to be blithely contemplated, especially when such an attempt would close the door to any future reconciliation. There was no point in making Burma fight for its freedom as the United States and South Africa had to do.[88] Sir Stanley Reed, although highly pessimistic about Burma's future prospects and convinced that it had made a mistake, came to Labour's support in a note of sane realism. Said he:

We have to get rid, now and for always, of the idea that we know better what is good for every other people than they think they know themselves. . . . We are giving to Burma the fullest opportunity to work out her own freedom, and . . . that Burma should have this opportunity . . . I have not the shadow of doubt.

The Undersecretary of State Arthur Henderson concluded the debate with the following memorable and dignified affirmation of faith:

This Bill is in keeping with the highest traditions of this House. . . . This nation of ours, which stands in the van of freedom-loving peoples, is the better able to understand the aspirations towards freedom of another people. We have done much over past decades to aid and encourage Burmese progress in the art of self-government. Let us now bestow the priceless gift of full independence in a mood at once generous and hopeful and with our sincere wishes for Burma's future peace, prosperity, and social advancement. I hope and believe that . . . we shall create a new relationship between the peoples of the British Commonwealth of Nations and of Burma that will be based on the solid foundation of mutual friendship, trust, and

[86] *Ibid.*, pp. 1876–1877.   [87] *Ibid.*, pp. 1852–1858, by Wyatt and Davies.
[88] *Ibid.*, pp. 1869–1873, 1877–1884, 1911–1914, Lieutenant Colonel Hamilton, Mr. Reid, Lieutenant Colonel Sir Walter Smiles, and Leah Manning.

respect, and one which will have lasting strength because its roots are firmly implanted in the charter of freedom which we are considering to-night.[89]

Approval of the motion was by a vote of 228 ayes to 114 noes. At the third reading of the measure on November 14, a new theme appeared to the effect that the contemplated action concerning Burma would take away some of the anger of the severe critics of Britain's allegedly imperialistic policies, especially in the United States and in Russia.[90] Royal assent to the measure was reported December 10, 1947.

Burma at long last was free. The formal inauguration of the new state occurred on the early morning of January 4, 1948, a date and hour determined as most propitious by the best available astrologers. The *Sawbwa* of Yawng-hwe, Sao Shwe Taik, became the first President and Thakin Nu continued as Prime Minister. Premier Nu's statement on the occasion included the following memorable note:

We lost our independence without losing our self-respect; we clung to our culture and our traditions and these we now hold to cherish and to develop. . . . We part without rancour and in friendship from the Great British nation which held us in fee.[91]

Reception of the Nu-Attlee Treaty in Burma

The reception in Burma of the treaty of October 17, 1947, was considerably more disturbing than were the dignified expressions of disappointment in Britain. The two groups most directly antagonistic to the treaty, but for entirely different reasons, were the Karen National Union and the Communist Party. The Karen "nationalists" were probably more angry with the British than with the Burmans, for London's action was regarded by many of them as a betrayal of traditional Karen aid and friendship. Most of the Karens viewed with dire forebodings the assumed probability of Karen mistreatment under Burman rule, and for the militant minority intent on achieving by direct action a seaboard state of their own, the future was ominous with the prospect of civil conflict. Premier Nu achieved a measure of reconciliation with the Karens by leaving the door open for agreement on a future Karen state and by approving in September, 1947, a constitution for Karenni (called Kayah). But Saw Ba U Gyi and Mon

[89] *Ibid.*, pp. 1947–1958. Mr. Henderson also referred to Article 3 of the Atlantic Charter which had affirmed "respect [for] the right of all peoples to choose the form of government under which they live."

[90] *PD,C*, vol. 443 (Nov. 5, 1947), p. 1958, vol. 444 (Nov. 14, 1947), p. 683–771.

[91] Maung Pye, p. 211.

dissidents from Moulmein continued actively planning for secession.[92]

The Than Tun (White Flag) Communists challenged the Nu-Attlee treaty as a disgraceful sellout to the British imperialists. They objected particularly to the exclusive position accorded the British military training mission, including provision for the almost routine access of British ships and aircraft to Burma's ports and landing fields. Also objectionable were U Nu's pledges to pay pensions and provident funds to retired British personnel and compensation for expropriated British interests. The Communists would not heed U Nu's explanation that Burma must accept outside assistance for the creation of its security forces and that honorable dealings in matters of property rights and financial obligations were sound policy in the long run.

Objections to the treaty were not the only reasons for ending the six-month-old Communist effort to work out a *rapprochement* with the A.F.P.F.L. The Communists had already developed sharp differences with the Socialist Party over policy and organizational tactics. The coauthor of the Two-Year Plan, Socialist U Kyaw Nyein, preferred an experimental and orderly approach to the problem of transferring land to peasant cultivators, whereas Communist Than Tun advocated immediate expropriation from landlords without compensation by means of People's Courts and local agricultural committees. The two parties had also been engaged throughout 1947 in a vigorous political contest to enlist labor union and peasant backing.[93] Especially following the death of Thakin Mya in July, the Socialist organizational campaign led by Thakin Ba Swe, also secretary-general of the A.F.P.F.L., took advantage of Socialist connections within the league and the government, including allegedly manipulation of patronage and even bribery, to counter Communist intrigue with some intrigue of its own. The Socialists tended to defend the use of political pressures on the ground that the end of preserving a government dedicated to Burma's welfare justified using the necessary means.

The Nu-Attlee agreement apparently triggered the break which the embittered political contest between Socialists and Communists had made inevitable. The closing months of 1947 and January of 1948 witnessed a rising tide of Communist-instigated labor and peasant unrest. Such efforts at the time were quite ineffective politically in the

[92] *The Times*, Aug. 6, Sept. 24 and 25, 1947; *Statesman*, May 28, June 15 and 18, 1947; *Straits Times*, June 6, 1947. The Mon leader U Po Cho resigned from the A.F.P.F.L.

[93] E. M. Law Yone and D. G. Mandelbaum, "Pacification in Burma," *Far Eastern Survey*, XIX (1950), 183–184.

context of achieved independence. It apparently required a considerable push from the outside to persuade Thakin Than Tun to resort to the madness of armed rebellion which began in March, 1948. This story will be told in Chapter XVII.

The third potential source of trouble for the fledgling Burma Government was the already-mentioned youthful veterans' organization (People's Volunteer Organization), an inactive guerrilla force with units in nearly every locality. The P.V.O. had lost much of its political importance by A.F.P.F.L. acceptance of London's conciliatory policy of 1947, and its members were restive. Following the death of U Aung San, the creator and acknowledged leader of the organization, it had, as previously indicated, deteriorated in discipline, partly by reason of its accretion of disorderly elements not properly eligible for membership. The P.V.O. resented particularly the efforts made in November, 1947, by Socialist leaders of the A.F.P.F.L. allegedly to repudiate an agreement reached in the previous May, which had ruled that the Socialist Party would control the mass agencies of the league while the P.V.O. would constitute its only military organization. The Socialists attempted in November to amalgamate the veterans' group with their own apparatus of mass control. The P.V.O. rank and file did not want to be reduced to a political and military nullity, much less to be settled on ricelands in the role of cultivators, a vocation to them quite unfamiliar and entirely beneath the dignity of national heroes. Many seats in the Constituent Assembly were held by P.V.O. representatives, and yet these elected leaders were almost entirely lacking in the necessary educational qualifications and administrative talents for service in the government. The cabinet as reconstituted by Thakin Nu in August, 1947, contained not a single P.V.O. leader.[94]

The P.V.O. had relatively little objection to the Nu-Attlee Treaty per se and no substantial ideological quarrel with their Socialist rivals in the government. The veterans' group tended nevertheless to drift under Communist influence because the two groups had a common enemy in the Socialists as the dominant element within the A.F.P.F.L. government. The Communists, furthermore, advanced better-sounding and more articulate arguments to attack the official policy than the Cinderella lamentations of the P.V.O.[95] In addition, the Nu-Attlee agreement had deprived both the Communist and the militant P.V.O.

[94] *Ibid.*, p. 184; Furnivall, *Pacific Affairs*, XXII (1949), 160; *Statesman*, May 13, 1947.
[95] Thompson, *Far Eastern Survey*, XVII (1948), 105–108.

574

partisans of their expected participation in the armed nationalist struggle against the imperialists, a contest which both had planned to turn to political account.

Burma's independent government faced serious administrative difficulties and internal contradictions quite apart from the fact that armed insurrection threatened before it could develop a trained army of its own. The youthful political leaders of the A.F.P.F.L., intent on planned economic development, would make the government all pervasive. This was in contradiction to demands for local autonomy and in some degree to the views of the mature judges of the Supreme Court, who were committed in large measure to liberal principles of government guaranteeing a considerable measure of individual freedom and initiative. The people as a whole had no appreciation of popular sovereignty and election methods, but rather continued as heretofore instinctively to keep away as far as possible from a government which they had never learned to trust.

The almost immediate withdrawal from the administration of the non-Burmese officials, mainly British, who before the war had occupied nine-tenths of the responsible top positions, was itself enough to threaten governmental collapse. With notable exceptions, the highly educated Burmans lacked political influence, and the politically influential too often lacked training and experience. To the routine demands of governmental operations on a minimal basis were to be added the onerous duties connected with banking and exchange controls, the dispensing of agricultural credit, rice purchase and handling, regulation of foreign trade, and the activities of purchasing missions abroad, plus the actual creation and operation of many projected industrial enterprises. In this vast economic field, Burman experience was almost nil, while nationalist distrust of experienced prewar British and Indian banking and business firms was even greater than Burman dislike of the non-Burmese civil service.[96]

Premier Nu, the head of Burma's government, was in 1948 a leader of uncertain qualifications. He had been in the public eye since his student-days' strike of 1936, but he had not distinguished himself as an administrator or as a political leader of very solid convictions. He was personable, honest, patently sincere, but he was also very adaptable and his demonstrated interests and talents were oratorical and literary. He had tried his hand at writing a number of novels and plays during his student days and his prewar period of imprisonment.

[96] Furnivall, *Pacific Affairs* XXII (1949), 155–160.

One propagandist novel for the Thakins had attacked Burmans who copied the pretensions and vices of the Westerners, but it had raised dilemmas which the author could resolve only by suicide.[97] Another of U Nu's works had experimented with the Freudian view that sex was the dominant motivating force for human conduct. Other writings carried a distinct Marxist tinge, although Thakin Nu was apparently too much interested in personal human problems and in the tragic overtones of life itself to concentrate overlong on the narrowly economic Marxist approach. He was at the same time a religious man and a sincere Buddhist.

During the war, Thakin Nu, on occasion, had toured Burma speaking in behalf of Japan's Greater East Asia Co-Prosperity Sphere objectives, all with apparent sincerity, while at the same time he was privy to A.F.P.F.L. preparations for resisting the Japanese. At the end of the war, he accompanied *Adipadi* Dr. Ba Maw to Moulmein rather than join the Thakin-led attack on the Japanese. It was this element of indecision and lack of daring that left him devoid of influence over the veterans' group, which had idolized Bogyoke Aung San. Aside from Thakin Nu's role as U Aung San's successor in heading the A.F.P.F.L., he enlisted a considerable measure of popular respect for his sincerity and for his role as the nationalist leader who had actually negotiated the country's freedom. It helped also that he was clearly not a politically ambitious man. Thakin Nu enjoyed no organized mass following comparable to that of the Socialist or Communists. His eventual role as a convinced champion of liberal democracy and popular sovereignty could hardly have been anticipated in 1948. In the confused first half of 1948, the Premier apparently met recurring problems by common-sense improvisation, a policy which in the end afforded full scope to the essential sincerity and decency of his character.

Associated with Premier Nu as leaders of the most influential party within the A.F.P.F.L. were the Socialist twins Thakins Kyaw Nyein and Ba Swe. But they were by no means identical twins. U Kyaw Nyein was an honors graduate in English and in law. He was a convinced Marxist, intelligent and widely read, and coauthor of the Two-Year Plan. He had served as private secretary to Dr. Ba Maw during the war. Following the war he was closely associated with Thakin Mya and became the general secretary of the A.F.P.F.L. in 1946, following Thakin Than Tun's forced retirement from that post. He

[97] Thakin Nu, "Man the Wolf of Man," unpublished manuscript.

was at times daring to the point of rashness. In spite of his acknowledged abilities, which assured him a high place in the political
hierarchy, he was not uniformly popular with his political colleagues,
whose personal sensibilities he was inclined occasionally to disregard.

Thakin Ba Swe was a man of action rather than a student and
thinker. He never completed his university course. He had first
emerged politically in the late 1930's when imprisoned as the leader
of the oil workers' strike. He was, therefore, from the outset a labor
leader and organizer, the head of the Trade Union Congress. In 1947
and 1948 he played a leading role along with Thakin Tin in developing the Socialist Party's All Burma Peasants' Organization, of which
Tin became the perennial president. U Ba Swe enjoyed a reputation
for honesty and was a leader of impressive presence and personality
as well as a levelheaded and discreet man. He was also approachable
and widely popular. His indigenous brand of Marxism was of uncertain character, but he was capable of employing all the Communist
clichés when addressing his idolizing "comrades" of the Trade Union
Congress with their red hammer and sickle flag.[98]

The only A.F.P.F.L. political leaders who approached the influence
of the top three in 1948 were Thakin Tin of the All Burma Peasants'
Organization, and after 1947 minister of agriculture, and Bo Let Ya,
second in command of the Burma resistance army under Bogyoke
Aung San. He was minister of home affairs and defense and Deputy
Premier in 1948. Thakin Lun Baw, who had been elected to the House
of Representatives in 1936, served as head of the Public Service Commission. Another person of potential leadership was the dependable
Bo Khin Maung Gale, who later, as home minister, recruited the
paramilitary, Socialist-sponsored Union of Burma police. The only
senior civil servant who shared administrative responsibility with
the youthful Thakin leaders was U Tin Tut, who served as finance
minister after August, 1947, and was Burma's commissioner-designate
to London.[99]

[98] Ba Swe, "The Pattern of the Burmese Revolution," *Burma*, II (1952), 1–12.
[99] Thakin Nu, *Burma under the Japanese* (London, 1954), pp. 126–128.

XVII

Rebellion and Recovery

THE launching of the newly independent state of Burma was the prelude to the outbreak of a series of rebellions, which narrowly missed destroying the government of Premier Nu within little more than a year. For a variety of reasons a number of dissident groups were reluctant to accept the authority of the new regime, and with firearms at their disposal, they proceeded to challenge the legal authority. The movements were for the most part politically motivated, but they were also in part the actions of criminal elements collaborating in the traditional Burmese fashion with political disaffection.

Behind the turmoil were the two generations of prewar lawlessness and social demoralization, greatly aggravated by the wartime displacement of several million uprooted persons. Many Burmans utilized the successive interregna of the war period to embark on an orgy of looting and stealing. Such activities along with the fighting itself had gone far to undermine popular respect for property rights and even for life itself. The war also, for the first time in history, had put arms in the hands of a multitude of unauthorized persons, who found reason to use them for illegal and nefarious ends. The spectacle of Burmans locked in fratricidal strife tempted Karens trained in the use of military weapons to undertake to set up a Lower Burma state of their own at Burman expense. It was the action of the Than Tun Communists, largely under outside instigation, that precipitated the orgy of violence, but it was the determined effort of the Karen rebels which came nearest to wrecking the government.

The rebellions failed in large measure because they could not be co-ordinated. Some of the Burman rebels returned to the fold to fight the Karens. Another factor favoring the government was that control of the capital of Rangoon gave it access to foreign military and diplomatic support, especially from British Commonwealth countries, and at least a modicum of income from a monopoly of rice sales overseas. Another consideration was the facility with which government was able to maintain contact by air with regions distant from the capital and otherwise completely isolated. The crisis eventually brought to light in Premier Nu qualities of leadership and clarity of vision exceeding by a considerable margin capabilities previously shown as a politician and as a statesman. He emerged from the ordeal with enhanced stature as leader of a political triumverate, of which the other two were the Socialist leaders, U Ba Swe and U Kyaw Nyein. It was these three who subsequently came to grapple with the manifold problems of the postrebellion period, political, economic, educational, and particularist.

The Communist Rebellion of 1948

The recognized leader of the majority (White Flag as distinguished from the underground Red Flag) Communist Party in Burma was Thakin Than Tun. He had earned an enviable reputation during the war as an administrator, as one sincerely concerned for the welfare of the people of Burma, and also as a daring champion of nationalist liberation from colonial rule. In addition to being the prime organizer of the A.F.P.F.L., he had sponsored the Communist All Burma Peasants' Union (aided by Thakins Thein Pe and Ba Hein [1]) and the All Burma Trade Union Congress (A.B.T.U.C.), which was the more immediate concern of his Indian associate H. M. Goshal. In early 1946, when his popularity as a nationalist was exceeded only by that of Thakin Aung San, Thakin Than Tun was searching for new ideas and for aid from any quarter which promised benefit for the new Burma. He was less doctrinaire as a Marxist than Thakin Soe, less pro-Russian than Thakin Thein Pe, and remarkable as a person of integrity, dedication, and tireless industry.

Thakin Soe (Red Flag Communist leader) was a colorful agitator and guerrilla fighter, violently partisan and incapable of political compromise, one who made a religion of his Marxist ideology. Thakin

[1] Ba Hein's death in November, 1946, removed one of the ablest Communist organizers.

579

Soe, in 1946–1947, commanded a relatively small fanatical following, which was making a nuisance of itself as an ally of local insurgents in the Arakan area and in the delta but which never constituted a serious threat to governmental authority.

The third Communist leader, Thakin Thein Pe, was the better educated of the three, more articulate and sophisticated and highly Russophile. He was better at intrigue than at organization, but possessed no stomach for the hardships and hazards which were the lot of the underground fighter.[2] His eventual role as an active Communist was to prod the government, the P.V.O., and the university students in a Marxist direction. He was particularly influential as of 1945–1946 in promoting the irresponsible "no rent, no taxes" campaign in the pro-Communist Pyinmana area. His talents for intrigue were limited only by a penchant for venturing into blind alleys. Only Thakin Than Tun headed a real Communist movement.[3]

The Communist cause in Burma suffered loss of influence as a result of the abrupt defection of Thakin Soe's faction from the A.F.P.F.L. in early 1946 and the exclusion of the Communist Party as a whole from the league in October, 1946. By 1947 the less radical government-backed Socialist Party program of mass organization, led by Thakins Mya and Kyaw Nyein, had eclipsed that of the Communists in the delta and was competing strongly under Thakin Ba Swe's leadership in the labor field. The Communists entered candidates for the Constituent Assembly elections of April, 1947, only in their areas of strongest influence, in Sandoway (on the Arakan coast) and in the far more important Toungoo, Pyinmana, and Yamethin railway corridor leading to Upper Burma. Even then only seven of their twenty-five candidates were elected. The situation was even more adverse for the Communists at the close of 1947. Nationalism was easily the paramount political issue, and in this field the A.F.P.F.L. had won the honors.[4] Even after

---

[2] See Law Yone and Mandelbaum, "Pacification in Burma," *Far Eastern Survey*, XIX (1950), 83; Thompson, "Burma's Communists," *Far Eastern Survey*, XVII (1948), 105; Union of Burma, *Burma and the Insurrections* (Rangoon, 1949), pp. 2–6. Neither Thakin Soe nor Thakin Thein Pe could approach Thakin Than Tun's reputation for integrity and for accepting responsibility.

[3] Soviet commentators in 1947 expressed no preference as between Soe and Than Tun, but the latter emerged as the only mass leader.

[4] The Communist "no rent, no taxes" campaign in the Pyinmana area in 1946–1947 was an appeal not to peasant need but to avarice, for the area was very prosperous. The author, in an interview with Pyinmana Communist leaders (followers of Thein Pe) in early 1946, received no reply to his query whether the party would prevent a cultivator who had earned a good return on his sugar-cane crop

Thakin Than Tun's break over the terms of the Nu-Attlee Treaty, the objections to it were made more on nationalist than on Communist lines. The dismal showing of the Communist-fomented strike effort of January, 1948, was due to the fact that the Nu-led A.F.P.F.L. government had clearly achieved far more than what the Communists denounced as "sham independence."

Thakin Than Tun's personal commitment to nationalist as well as to Communist ends and his complete lack of accord with contemporary interpretations in the Moscow press concerning what was happening in Burma [5] suggest strongly that, apart from the generally accepted strategy of popular-front collaboration with nationalist liberation efforts, the White Flag Communists were not operating under direct Soviet or Cominform control. Thakin Than Tun's only apparent European contact was with Yugoslavia, and his relations with the Communist Party in India were tenuous prior to 1948. Moscow's propaganda apparently cared little about what was happening in Burma, but was concerned mainly with besmirching the sincerity of the intentions of the Attlee government. The London authorities acted contrary to Marxist dogma by surrendering colonial control without a fight. Thakin Than Tun was preparing throughout 1946 and 1947 to exploit for Communist ends the expected Burmese struggle for national liberation, but until the publication of the final treaty terms he conceded, as Moscow did not, the sincerity of both the British and the A.F.P.F.L. negotiators. It is clear that Thakin Than Tun's break with U Nu was partly because of genuine dissatisfaction over the terms of the treaty. Nevertheless, a major consideration behind his decision to rebel related to the fact that continuation of his policy of collaboration on a nationalist basis afforded no opportunity for waging a successful Communist revolutionary struggle. It was on this latter

---

for the previous year (as many had done) from honoring his rental agreement with the landlord.

[5] Despite Thakin Than Tun's exclusion from the A.F.P.F.L. in 1946, he accepted the London Agreement of January, 1947, participated in assembly elections, kept on friendly terms with Thakin Aung San, and co-operated with Premier Nu following the assassinations. The Soviet press meanwhile had been denouncing (1) Aung San as a British agent hired to crush the general strike and the Communist Party, (2) the London Agreement as a fraud, (3) Aung San's murder as having been instigated by Machiavellian British intrigue against its own alleged agent, and (4) Thakin Nu as a stooge of London unable to make a move without permission of the British authorities and the prewar British firms. All of this was quite unknown in Burma and lacked any relevance to the facts. See Virginia Thompson and Richard Adloff, *The Left Wing in Southeast Asia* (New York, 1950), pp. 110–120.

point, in any case, that Moscow's new directive of late 1947 in favor
of launching violent struggles in all colonial areas came to coincide
with Than Tun's apparently reluctant decision to break the peace.

The change in Communist world-wide tactics that developed in
the fall of 1947 stemmed primarily from the impact of Marshall Plan
aid to Western Europe, which bid fair to end the theretofore likely
prospect of Europe's economic collapse and the establishment of People's Democracies in France, Italy, and possibly Germany. The Soviet
signal to shift in the South Asian colonial area from popular-front
tactics to overt revolution as a means of sabotaging the Marshall
Plan was announced by Zhadonov in the early fall of 1947 and was
carried to India by the first Soviet ambassador, Novikov, who reached
New Delhi in late November. The new Cominform directive precipitated an immediate crisis within the Indian Communist Party, driving
P. C. Joshi from his posts as party secretary and editor of *People's Age*,
and eventually from his membership in the Politbureau, while elevating Ranadive as the new leader. In February, 1948, the Communist
World Federation of Trade Unions carried the directive further by
sponsoring the convening in Calcutta of the first Congress of the South-
east Asia Democratic Youth.[6]

The sessions of the youth congress were largely dominated by Yugoslav spokesmen for the Cominform. The Burma youth delegation included both A.F.P.F.L. and Communist representatives. But the
A.F.P.F.L. group along with Indian Congress Party delegates withdrew in angry protest over the authoritative affirmation of the leaders
that both countries had achieved only sham independence and that it
was time for workers and peasants to turn on the imperialist collaborators in the interest of full liberation. The Burma Communist representatives, including Thakin Than Tun and H. M. Goshal, also attended the late February session of the Indian Communist Party
Congress, where complete triumph of the new secretary, Ranadive,
over Joshi was registered. The return of Than Tun and Goshal to Burma
in early March, accompanied by two Yugoslav Communist leaders,
set the stage for the overt break which occurred on March 27 and 28.[7]
Whether or not it was true, as alleged by the Burma Government, that
Goshal brought back a twenty-seven-page booklet entitled "Chances

---

[6] For a fuller discussion of postwar Soviet policy in South Asia, see the author's
chapter (no. 19) in George B. de Huszar, *Soviet Power and Policy* (New York,
1954).

[7] Law Yone and Mandelbaum, *Far Eastern Survey*, XIX (1950), 183.

of a Revolution in Burma in 1948"[8] which contained the official Cominform indictment of U Nu's "sham-independence" government and an appeal for a people's uprising to wreck it, there can be little doubt that the party sessions in India played a large part in precipitating the rebellion in Burma.

Immediately following the return of the Communist leaders to Burma they made an initial abortive attempt to rekindle the trade union strike of January. But the clinching argument in favor of overt struggle was the apparent enthusiasm demonstrated at the conference of the All Burma Peasants' Union held at Pyinmana in mid-March and attended by an estimated 75,000 people. Goshal there promised to all free land and no taxes and presented the call for immediate struggle. The two Yugoslav visitors added their considered opinions that Burma was indeed ripe for a people's revolution. In a final attempt to bring the workers into the act, Thakin Than Tun staged an openly subversive "resistance rally" of the A.B.T.U.C. at Bandoola Square in Rangoon on March 27. Three-fourths of the 3,000 workers in attendance were Indians, and the meeting therefore failed to ignite any serious Burman explosion.[9] When the police moved tardily to arrest the leaders responsible for the subversive meeting, they discovered on March 28 that Than Tun and Goshal had already departed for Pyinmana and that the revolution had begun.

In Lower Burma, the White Flag Communist rising was limited largely to guerrilla operations from peripheral jungle areas and foothills, but in the main railway corridor running northward from Toungoo to Yamethin they took over complete control. Thence they spread eastward to the oil-fields area along the Irrawaddy River. To the west of the river they maintained control for the next eight years. The party could raise an estimated 25,000 armed partisans. The situation presented a serious problem, but it would not have become critical had it not been for the disaffection which developed in the P.V.O.[10]

[8] Union of Burma, Ministry of Information, *Is It a People's Liberation?* (Rangoon, 1952), pp. 7–11. The allegation cannot be authenticated.

[9] Union of Burma, *Burma and the Insurrections*, pp. 15–19. The A.B.T.U.C. represented mainly the dock workers, the sawmill workers, and employees of the Burmah Oil Company.

[10] *Ibid.*, pp. 15–19; *Soviet Press Translations*, III, no. 19 (Seattle, 1947), 586–588. In an article entitled "The Situation in Burma" appearing in *Izvestia*, Sept. 12, 1948, I. Plyshevsky explained that the Burma Communist rebellion of March, 1948, grew out of a strike of 25,000 oil workers in four British concerns as a political protest against Burma's sham freedom and that the peasants later backed the

The Problem of the P.V.O. Rebellion

The disaffection in the P.V.O. group was in many respects a more formidable political problem for Premier Nu's government than the Communist rebellion. The P.V.O. was an integral part of the A.F.P.F.L. and was prominently represented in the elected assembly, where it could influence legislation and policy. It was also a veterans' organization, officered and partly armed. Cadres were located in virtually every locality of Burma, so that it was far more widespread than the Communist cells. The P.V.O. leaders also maintained close personal connections with members of the five Burman battalions of the regular army, which had been recruited in 1945–1946 from the parent Patriotic Burmese Forces. As political rivals both of Premier Nu, whose authority and whose Marxist League unity proposal (first suggested in late 1947) a majority of the veterans disdained, and of the Socialist Party, which had tried in vain to absorb their organization, the P.V.O. as a body was conditioned favorably to the acceptance of Communist propaganda hostile to Premier Nu. Their basic demand to be allowed a substantial role in running a coalition government, which would also include the Communists, was inadmissible on both political and administrative grounds. Following U Nu's futile efforts to come to terms with the P.V.O. in November and December, 1947, the Premier, faced by more pressing matters, pushed the problem aside for several months. He was eventually obliged to cope with it in a more virulent form following the outbreak of the Communist rebellion.

If the new Burma Government displayed during the spring of 1948 evidences of instability and confusion, the reasons are not far to seek. The ruling A.F.P.F.L. coalition deserved the thanks of the people for delivering Burma from colonial rule, but it lacked, in 1948, not only administrative capacity but also the substance and the credentials of authority. The league was hopelessly divided in a power struggle between the quarreling Socialist and P.V.O. factions, both vying for control now that the unifying influence of the independence struggle was gone. Premier Nu had neither a mass following of his own nor sufficient time to generate popular understanding and appreciation of the value of orderly constitutional procedures for achieving Burma's social and economic objectives. The idea of popular sovereignty was itself incomprehensible to most Burmans. Thakin Nu

---

strike. Nu's bourgeois government was pro-British and was, according to Plyshevsky, setting the stage for Britain and the United States to send in troops.

could not qualify as a new king, for he lacked authentic hereditary claims, a fortified palace capital, and a strong dependable army.[11] He lacked the influence which General Aung San could have wielded within the P.V.O. and also the latter's capacity for knocking heads together in a situation where persuasion and compromise could not avail. There was in the spring of 1948 no escaping the fact that political power in Burma was being contested and that the new regime must face the demand to establish its right to rule in a test of strength.

The tactic adopted by Premier Nu was apparently influenced by his tendency to take overseriously the irresponsible charges of his critics that he had betrayed the nationalist cause and the socialist principles of the constitution. He undertook to answer such attacks by making overt moves in the direction of nationalization and at the same time attempting to arrive at a basis of co-operation with the P.V.O. on purely ideological grounds. He accompanied this effort by the politically debilitative announcement that he intended to retire from politics in June, 1948, to a monastery and to turn over affairs of state to his heir apparent, Bo Let Ya. He also admitted publicly that the A.F.P.F.L. had itself become corrupt and privilege-seeking and that this fact accounted for the demand of the masses for freedom from its control.[12] During the crucial two months of May and June, 1948, U Nu was denied the advice of his most articulate Socialist Party supporter, U Kyaw Nyein, who was obliged to retire for a time from public affairs because of health reasons.[13] This led to the questionable expedient of accepting the assistance of the aboveground Communist Thein Pe in devising a so-called Leftist Unity Program as a basis for accommodation with the dissident and pro-Communist faction of the P.V.O.

In May, 1948, came the government's publication of the *Two-Year Plan of Economic Development* as already described,[14] except for the change that the priority for land redistribution was raised from last to near the top to meet Communist competition. On May 31 followed

[11] The Premier's secretary, U Thant, on April 8, 1948, presented by radio an able defense of orderly constitutional government, stressing the advantages of democratic processes over revolutionary violence as a method for the progressive realization of the socialist state, the welfare of the nation generally, and the protection of basic human liberties. Such considerations were unfortunately irrelevant to the actual political struggle. See Union of Burma, *Burma Speaks* (Rangoon, 1950), pp. 32–34.

[12] *The Burman*, May 28, 1948; Thompson, *Far Eastern Survey*, XVII (1948), 105–106.

[13] Thompson and Adloff, pp. 101–106.   [14] See above, pp. 565–567.

the abrupt official declaration that the Irrawaddy Flotilla Company and also a major segment of the British-operated teak concessions were being nationalized on June 1. The law to nationalize the Flotilla Company by June 1 had been hurriedly passed by the Burma Parliament on the previous April 9, but without specifying precisely what assets would be taken over, the circumstances of the transfer, or the terms of compensation. A special committee to determine the basis, representing both the government and the company and presided over by a judge of the High Court, was far from reaching agreement at the time of the May 31 pronouncement.[15]

Equally disturbing to anti-Communist Burmans and to London was the subsequent release of the fifteen-point Communist-oriented Leftist Unity Program, which came in early June. Point one affirmed Burma's desire to enter into political and economic relations with the U.S.S.R. and Communist Europe, and point 15 (later abandoned) proposed setting up a Marxist League, presumably government-sponsored, to propagate Marxist doctrines and the study of leftist writers generally. Some of the fifteen items merely reaffirmed the socialist provisions of the constitution, such as abolition of private ownership of land, state control of foreign trade, the nationalization of "monopoly industries" to be run by government and the workers, guarantee of labor's rights, promotion of co-operatives, and the like. New emphases included the proposal to transform the Burma army into a People's Democratic Force, the establishment of Popular (Soviet-type) Governments in the Frontier Areas, reduction of rents and taxes, reform of the bureaucracy and local administration on a "democratic" basis, with elected village committees (People's Courts) to be vested with police and judicial and fiscal powers, and refusal of all outside aid which might compromise Burma's economic or military independence.[16]

This Leftist Unity Program, permeated as it was with Communist ideology and terminology, aroused a sense of consternation within anti-Communist circles in Burma and also abroad. It was the price in terms of ideological surrender which U Nu was prepared to pay in order to get the P.V.O. to help him against the Communist rebels. But since the Program itself had no relevance to the basic power struggle,

[15] The government was offering £200,000, while the company was holding out for seven and a half times that amount. See *PD,C*, vol. 447 (Feb. 8, 1948), pp. 2425, vol. 459 (Dec. 8, 1948), pp. 474–483; Thompson and Adloff, pp. 98–105. Burma offered compensation on May 31, but only in nonconvertible bonds.

[16] Thompson and Adloff, pp. 98–105. The Program as finally issued was a revision of an original draft prepared by Communist Thein Pe.

it operated contrary-wise to encourage the radical leaders of the P.V.O. to intensify their impossible demands that rebellious Communist elements be themselves included in a round table unity conference. The minority-group "Yellow Band" P.V.O. (as distinguished from the Communist "White Band" majority) eventually participated in A.F.P.F.L. approval on July 2, 1948, of the Leftist Unity Program after dropping point 15 about Marxist indoctrination.[17]

Burma's Leftist Unity Program became the subject of British diplomatic inquiries both at Rangoon and at London especially with regard to its bearing on relations with the United Kingdom. Rangoon's halting explanation was that the Premier's intentions had been exaggerated. He had in mind only a privately sponsored Marxist indoctrination program rather than the unqualified official acceptance of a pro-Communist orientation. Item 15 would be dropped out of the Program in any case. The British Government was also decidedly unhappy about the abrupt fashion in which the nationalization decisions had been implemented on May 31 in the absence of any acceptable prior agreement as to the amount or the kind of compensation.[18] Mr. Bevin indicated to Parliament that he was not satisfied that the degree of consultation agreeable to Burma fulfilled the spirit and the letter of their treaty. He proposed to seek to preserve good relations with Burma and would consider altering that policy only if events should prove that his confidence in Burma's readiness to carry out her treaty obligations was misplaced.[19]

Relations between the two governments deteriorated further when, early in July, the Burma Committee entrusted with the compensation negotiations was reorganized with the Flotilla Company representative left out entirely. In December came the announcement from Rangoon that payment, if and when made, would have to be in non-negotiable bonds. But by the end of 1948, the financial stringency of the Burma Government was so severe because of the spreading insurrection that London regarded the essential need to be the strength-

[17] Union of Burma, *Burma and the Insurrections*, pp. 19–23. Thakin Thein Pe returned repeatedly to this Marxist indoctrination proposal with reference to the university curriculum.

[18] *PD,C*, vol. 449 (April 7, 1948), pp. 140–141. Mr. Bevin on April 7 acknowledged Burma's right to nationalize basic industries but only if fair compensation were given.

[19] *PD,C*, vol. 452 (June 17 and 21, 1948), pp. 655, 932; Manchester *Guardian*, June 18, 1948. London wanted legitimate claims for expropriated British property met in acceptable currency. Dorman-Smith in the *Daily Express* (June 15) blasted Mountbatten for having established Communist rule in Burma.

ening of its position. Political pressure was then adjudged more likely to retard than to accelerate eventual payment to the British companies.[20]

The Burma Government underwent a serious internal crisis during and following the crucial sessions of the supreme council of the A.F.P.F.L. held from July 1 to 5, 1948. The immediate issues were the prospective resignation of Thakin Nu as Premier scheduled for July 20 and what to do about the imminent P.V.O. rebellion. The opposition to Thakin Nu was led by the majority-faction P.V.O. leader Bo La Yaung, who was opposed by U Tin Tut and by the Deputy Premier Bo Let Ya, destined presumably to succeed Thakin Nu. The formal decisions of the council were all on the moderate side. It voted to drop point 15 of the Leftist Unity Program, to reject a resolution seeking accord with the insurgent Communists of Upper Burma, and to censure the P.V.O. malcontents for staging outside public demonstrations, during the course of the conference, in support of its Communist-appeasement program. But the atmosphere was violently partisan, especially following the final ruling that the P.V.O. must restore, on penalty of being itself excluded from the A.F.P.F.L., members expelled for co-operating with the government. Civil war was inescapable.

A cabinet crisis immediately ensued. The minister of commerce and chairman of the Socialist Party, U Ko Ko Gyi, resigned on July 5. He was followed on July 10 by U Tin Tut and Bo Let Ya, both of whom joined the army. When, on July 16, the entire cabinet resigned, Thakin Nu finally agreed to carry on as head of a caretaker regime until Parliament met on August 15. After Dr. Ba Maw and Thakin Ba Sein in late July began their joint political campaign, including press appeals, for the people to unite behind their leadership to save the country, Premier Nu eventually agreed to stay on until the scheduled date for the general elections in April, 1949. The cabinet crisis was finally resolved when U Nu was formally selected as Premier on September 14 along with a new cabinet of twenty-one members.[21]

While political confusion raged within the ranks of the A.F.P.F.L., conditions of disorder and rebellion throughout the country steadily worsened. In July, the "White Band" P.V.O. led by Bo Po Kun and

---

[20] *PD,C*, vol. 459 (Dec. 8, 1948), pp. 474–483. Sterling reserves held in England were backing Burma's currency, as a segment of the sterling area.

[21] *The Times,* July 3, 6, 12–17, Aug. 2, 1948; *Daily Telegraph,* July 5 and 7, 1948; *Observer,* July 11, 1948; *North China Herald,* July 18, 1948.

Bo La Yaung rebelled. In August followed the mutiny of two of the five fully equipped Burman battalions of the Burma Rifles, one at Mingaladon (near Rangoon) and the other at Thayetmyo. The minority "Yellow Band" P.V.O. group led by Bo Hmu Aung alone remained loyal. The area infested by the P.V.O. rebels extended from Bassein and Maubin upriver as far as Prome. They were also active in Hanthawaddy and Pegu districts north of Rangoon. Except for the fact that the rebel P.V.O., the Communists, and the mutineers quarreled over jurisdictions and otherwise failed to co-operate, the situation of the government would have been extremely seriously. The regular army, commanded by General Smith-Dun, a Karen, and consisting now mainly of non-Burman Karen, Kachin, and Chin regiments, was able to prevent the mutinous Mingaladon and Thayetmyo battalions from joining hands for a march on Rangoon, a move which might have been fatal. The efforts made by a mediating peace mission headed by U Thwin from August to December failed to find any responsible group capable of speaking for the P.V.O. rebels as a whole.

On September 19, 1948, the assassination of Cabinet Minister U Tin Tut by a political opponent robbed the government of its most experienced leader.[22] Meanwhile the growing restiveness among the Karens, both within the Karen National Defense Organization and in the army, combined with the Karen National Union demand for a separate Karen state, presented an even more ominous threat to the harried government.

The Karen Rebellion

During the period of confusion following the assassination of U Aung San in July, 1947, local units of the Karen National Defense Organization (K.N.D.O.) acted on their own authority to protect Karen interests in various regions of Lower Burma. The most noteworthy instance was the quiet and bloodless occupation of Moulmein by Karen irregulars in July, 1947, done ostensibly to protect the city from threatened Communist-bandit seizure. The Karen unit was well behaved and withdrew voluntarily two months later under conditions of general amnesty and an understanding with the Karen commander of the Burma army, General Smith-Dun, that local K.N.D.O. units

---

[22] Law Yone and Mandelbaum, *Far Eastern Survey*, XIX (1950), 184; Union of Burma, *Burma and the Insurrections*, pp. 9–10, 23–25. The two mutinous P.V.O. leaders later demanded control over the key Defense and Home Department portfolios.

could continue to take responsibility for protecting certain Karen areas. The Karens were later authorized to guard the Twante canal leading from Rangoon port to the main Irrawaddy channel.[23] The Moulmein episode indicated how tenuous was the government's control over outlying areas and also that the K.N.D.O. consisted of something other than bandit-revolutionaries.

Karen dissatisfaction with Burma's new constitution, as approved in September, 1947, centered directly on the provision for the initial establishment of the "special region" of Kawthulay (Articles 180 and 181) and the eventual definition through legislative action by the Chamber of Deputies of a Karen State consisting mainly of the backward Salween District and adjacent Karen-majority areas. The Karen National Union (K.N.U.) denounced these provisions as wholly unsatisfactory and began none-too-secret preparations for the creation of an independent Karen-Mon state including all the Tenasserim Division. Eventually, especially following the loss of government control over much of Lower Burma in 1948 as a consequence of the multiple rebellions, the proposed Karen State was conceived by some proponents as destined to include much of the Irrawaddy delta also. The spectacle of internecine Burman strife, the obvious weakness of the government, and Karen army dissatisfaction over having to do so much of the fighting to maintain the legal authority—all combined to aggravate unrest and to stimulate the ambitions of the more reckless Karen partisans. The government was less worried than it might well have been because it had full confidence, and properly so, in the loyalty of General Smith-Dun, the Karen commander of the Burma army. In July, 1948, Premier Nu reportedly obtained a promise from Karen leaders not to seek a separate state except by peaceful democratic means.[24]

Events moved relentlessly toward a break during the latter half of 1948. One factor contributing to the deterioration of Karen-government relations was the authorized but hurried recruitment by Socialist Party agents of the Burman Auxiliary Union Military Police. This undisciplined bandit-ridden *Yebaw* (soldier-hero) army was placed under control of the home minister and not under General Smith-Dun's command. The Karen population distrusted the new police units and regarded them as an unofficial private Socialist Party army. The

[23] Hinners, "British Policy," pp. 327–331; Law Yone and Mandelbaum, "Pacification in Burma," *Far Eastern Survey*, XIX (1950), p. 184.
[24] Hinners, pp. 310–331; Glasgow *Herald*, July 2, 1948.

stage was set for another Burman-Karen clash. In September, 1948, a force of the K.N.D.O. seized Moulmein temporarily for a second time; similar units captured temporarily Shwegyin and Kyaukgyi in Toungoo District. Temporary Karen mutinies occurred in the Southern Shan States. Civil war also flared in Karenni, where efforts of K.N.U. agents to influence the Red Karens to join the proposed Karen State were resented by the leaders of the Catholic Karen faction. Increasing numbers of individual Karen desertions from the army to join the K.N.D.O. were disquieting, as was the growing friction between Karen regulars and the new *Yebaw* army. Thievery and banditry developed on both sides. Dissident Mon nationalist elements, equipped with their own Mon National Defense Organization also appeared, simultaneously with a revival of particularist disaffection in the Arakan. On September 18, Alexander Campbell, Burma correspondent of London's *Daily Mail*, was arrested in Rangoon for complicity in fomenting Karen rebellion.[25]

The traditional pattern of Burmese revolution was clearly developing. Burman intelligence knew months in advance that some of the Karens were planning rebellion, but the government believed that General Smith-Dun and other loyal Karen officers would be able to forestall the break. When the Home Ministry later attempted to use *Yebaw* forces in a preventive action against the Karens, fighting began.

It was against this ominous background of threatened territorial disintegration of the Burma state that the Rangoon authorities in October, 1948, set up the Regional Autonomy Enquiry Commission headed by Justice U Ba U and including the K.N.U. leader, Saw Ba U Gyi. Its assignment was to explore the possibility of satisfying the "legitimate aspirations of the Mons, Karens, and Arakanese nationals."[26] The government was obviously in a weak bargaining position and was apparently inclined to make reasonable concessions to avoid further political deterioration. But the activities of the commission did little to relieve the growing tension. Karen leaders professed

[25] *Daily Express*, Sept. 18, 1948; *The Times*, Sept. 20, 1948; *Daily Telegraph*, Sept. 20, 1948; New York *Times*, Oct. 6, 1948. One Colonel J. C. Tullock of Calcutta, who had served with the Karen underground during the war, was apparently co-operating with Alexander Campbell. A British Seventh-Day Adventist missionary, the Reverend J. W. Baldwin, who had learned to know the Karens as war chaplain, joined actively in the rebellion. Baldwin eventually escaped to Siam, only to be expelled by the Thai as politically undesirable. See the *Evening Standard*, Feb. 4, 1950, and the *Daily Telegraph*, Sept. 17, 1951.

[26] Union of Burma, *Regional Autonomy Enquiry Commission Records* (Rangoon, 1951), p. 26. This is hereafter cited as *RAECR*.

dissatisfaction because it failed to visit important centers and was acting too tardily. The commission's visits were sometimes, as at Tavoy, followed by anti-Karen demonstrations sponsored by the A.F.P.F.L. The formal report of the commission, as submitted in February, 1949, recommended limiting the Karen State, as previously planned, to the backward Salween District and adjacent Karen-majority areas. The rebellion had already begun in late January.

Instead of waiting for the decision of Justice U Ba U's commission, the K.N.U. leadership, on November 13, 1948, in association with two Mon nationalist groups, presented the government with a formal demand for an independent Karen-Mon State to include the entire Tenasserim and Irrawaddy divisions plus additional contiguous Lower Burma districts (thirteen all told), excepting only the capital city of Rangoon. This declaration of independence and secession was predicated on the dubious affirmation that the Karens of the area were not a minority but a large and compact population. Actually the 1931 census had indicated that they were a majority in only two of the thirteen districts (Salween and Thaton) and constituted together with the Mons a bare 60 per cent in a third district (Amherst).[27] This apparently impossible ultimatum was obviously dictated by Karen political ambitions as well as by fear, and it did much to dissipate the fairly widespread foreign sympathy for their cause. It drew most of its inspiration from the pattern of traditional hostility between the two peoples dating from the eighteenth century and especially attending the three British wars of conquest and World War II.[28]

The K.N.D.O. rebellion broke in late January, 1949, first at Bassein, in the western delta, and shortly thereafter at Toungoo and at Insein. Careful planning was in evidence except at Bassein. There followed the defection of most of the Karen regiments in the regular army. A daring, and successful, air-borne Karen raid on Maymyo, using planes commandered at Meiktila airfield, obtained the release of a Karen

[27] India, Census Commissioner, *Census of India, 1931*, vol. XI, *Burma*, pt. I, report by J. J. Bennison (Rangoon, 1933), map frontispiece, pp. 190–191. The Karens challenged the accuracy of the essentially linguistic census of 1931 on the ground that many Burmese-speaking Karens in the delta area had been tabulated as Burmans. The census itself, however, indicated that 61 per cent of the Mons living in their old home district of Pegu were Burmese speaking in 1937, but were counted in the census as Mons.

[28] *RAECR*, pp. 17–23, 26. A less presumptuous Karen demand was formulated at the same time by Saw Johnson D. Po Min, M.P., who called only for the separation of all Tenasserim Division except that part of Toungoo District west of the Sittang River.

army contingent stationed at the summer capital. The group returned southward via Mandalay and, with the co-operation of Communist insurgents in the Pyinmana-Yamethin sector, reached Toungoo. One Karen regiment attacked Mingaladon, cantonment adjacent to Insein, and obtained from it abundant arms and munitions. A third Karen unit stationed at Prome on the Irrawaddy River prepared to move southward in a motorized column toward Rangoon. K.N.U. efforts to suborn the Chin and Kachin contingents of the regular army failed, but a Karen rebel column operating in the Southern Shan States area in the fall of 1949 stirred the Pa-O, or Toungthus, to the point of rebellion. The Karen raiders also generated some assistance in the Kachin country to the far north.[29] A temporary Karen State administration was set up at Toungoo.

The general plan for all Karen forces to converge on the Rangoon capital, in the time-honored Burmese fashion, failed. The overconfident motorized column moving southward from Prome blundered into a trap and was cut to pieces by artillery fire and air strafing, while the main Karen drive from Toungoo was checked above Pegu by a regular Chin army battalion.[30] The Bassein effort collapsed quickly. If the well-armed Karen contingent at Insein had advanced immediately on Rangoon, only ten miles away, the capital might have fallen in early February, but the government was eventually able to interpose effective defenses. Some of the P.V.O. rebel units in the delta forgot their alleged grievances against the government and joined in the defense of the capital. Nevertheless for several months the harried Burmese Government hovered on the brink of disaster, dependent almost entirely on non-Burman and outside support. One of the most serious effects of the formidable Karen rising was that it afforded time for the other rebellious groups, Communist, P.V.O., and

[29] Pa-O relations in British times with the ruling Shan Sawbwas had never been friendly. Some of the Toungthus around Taunggyi, who numbered all told possibly 300,000, were already challenging Shan authority under covert A.F.P.F.L. instigation in 1949. But the Karens brought them arms and ammunition plus military leadership. Together they captured and held Taunggyi for a time. Since the Toungthus were incapable of setting up a formal state administration, the region tended to degenerate governmentally into the petty domains of rival and often feuding headmen, whom neither the Sawbwas nor the government could effectively control. The Kachin president of the United Hill Peoples' Congress, Sima Duwa Sinwa Nawng, turned down Karen overtures to join the insurrection, but Naw Seng, a kind of Kachin Robin Hood, collaborated with them. See Union of Burma, *Burma and the Insurrections*, pp. 14–15.

[30] Several fence-sitting military elements at Pegu were allegedly bribed to remain neutral while the Chins took over the fight.

army mutineers, to consolidate their hold over central Burma under a so-called "United Democratic Front." Rivalry between the several factions prevented effective co-ordination of action, however.[31]

The Karen military threat in 1949 was not the only cause of anxiety for the government. On February 4, 1949, began a strike of the Federation of Service Unions, including most of the civil service personnel. This followed a 15 per cent to 30 per cent cut imposed in January, 1949, on all government salaries. In some districts only scattered individuals maintained a semblance of administration, although the police for the most part were unaffected. This strike reflected the long-simmering feud between the somewhat better-educated bureaucracy and the inexperienced "political upstarts" dominating the A.F.P.F.L. government, who allegedly knew nothing about administration. The administration was prevented from falling apart largely through vigorous pressure by Premier Nu on the Rangoon secretariat and by his lightning visits by air to strategic district centers upcountry. Generally speaking, governmental authority survived only in little islands of control surrounding important district administrative centers. It is difficult to see how the government could have survived at all apart from the new air communication facilities available from Rangoon.[32]

Another seemingly heavy blow came on April 1, 1949, when five Socialist Party and "Yellow Band" P.V.O. members of the cabinet resigned their posts. The action suggested a desire to abandon the sinking ship, the only saving feature being that the two groups did not join the opposition. Other evidence indicates that the defection was made with Premier Nu's consent for the double end of releasing the Socialist leaders for political reorganization activities and of enlisting behind the government conservative elements to be jettisoned later. Chief Justice U E Maung took over for a time five vacant ministerships, and U Tun three others. Eventually a majority of the ministerial

---

[31] *Vernacular Press Translations* (Rangoon), Feb. 19, 1949. The so-called Democratic Front formed by Communists and the P.V.O. advocated co-operation with the Russian bloc, repudiation of the Nu-Attlee Treaty and expropriation of foreigner-owned land without compensation.

[32] Union of Burma, *Burma and the Insurrections*, pp. 10–11. Premier Nu's address to the secretariat chiefs in September, 1949, was a threatening and caustic attack against civil servants who were ambitious for political power. He invited his hearers to fall in line with the new order based on the constitution or to quit. They must, he insisted, forego recriminations and striving for personal interest, function only through proper channels, and exercise honesty and responsibility in office. See Thakin Nu, *From Peace to Stability* (Rangoon, 1951), pp. 27–36.

posts (seven of thirteen) were assigned to minority-group representatives. The Socialist and P.V.O. leaders apparently wanted to escape the virulent criticism from both rightists and leftists, to which they were being subjected as members of government. They withdrew to mend their party political fences and to enlist popular support.[33] Three Socialists eventually returned to the cabinet in January, 1950, but the party secretary, U Kyaw Nyein, did not return until 1951. The government repeatedly postponed the elections scheduled for 1949; they were not held until June, 1951.

Recovery from the Abyss

The multiple rebellions of 1948–1950 failed to destroy Premier Nu's government for a number of reasons. Except in scattered areas and on periodic occasions the dissident groups were unable to co-ordinate their efforts or their objectives. In the Toungoo-Pyinmana area, the Karens and the Communists co-operated in their common objective to deny the government the use of the Rangoon-Mandalay Railway line. The Communists also held open an escape route into the delta proper for Karen refugees fleeing from Bassein. But ideologically and in ultimate aims the two groups were very far removed. Rivalry and personal jealousies kept the other groups apart. A second factor was the strength which Premier Nu's government derived from its possession of the capital-seaport of Rangoon. It afforded direct diplomatic and commercial relations with the outside world and substantial emergency income from the government's monopoly of the export of rice. At the outset the Karen insurgents received encouragement from private British sources who were friendly to the Karen cause and were convinced that London had treated Britain's loyal friends most shabbily. But the politically ambitious demands of the K.N.U. and their resort to overt violence denied them the support expected from their many other friends. The prospect for outside assistance for the Karens dwindled as the months passed.[34]

---

[33] Union of Burma, *Burma and the Insurrections,* pp. 11–13; Thompson and Adloff, pp. 106–107.

[34] As a result of a tip from the British embassy at Rangoon, in September, 1948, the Burma Government intercepted the incriminating pro-Karen Tullock-Campbell correspondence between Rangoon and Calcutta. Twice in February and once in March, 1949, Captain Gammans and other Conservative members of Parliament urged that Britain's military mission be withdrawn from Burma rather than see it aligned against the Karen uprising. The Labour government spokesmen, in reply, refused to dictate to the Burma Government how it should use arms purchased from Britain and insisted that the military mission was advisory

Because the leaders of the rebellious K.N.U. were for the most part Baptist Christians and the outbreak started in three mission centers, the Burma Government tended to blame the American missionaries and to dub the uprising the "Baptist Rebellion." This allegation ignored many contradictory elements of the situation, for many Christian Karens opposed the rebellion. The uprising was, in fact, not religious, but broadly national including both Buddhist and animist Karens. The American missionaries deprecated the wartime feud from which the rebellion developed and were in no position in 1948–1949 to tell the K.N.U. political leadership what they could or could not do.[35] Once the bloodletting began, false rumors of a Burman-planned slaughter of all Karen military personnel and alleged Karen atrocities fanned the flames of partisan strife far beyond the bounds of control by any responsible party. Many persons who had no part in the plans for the rebellion became involved. Thakin Nu himself went so far in his endeavors to protect Karen noncombatants against lawless violence that Burman political enemies began calling him "Karen Nu."[36]

A major factor in defeating the rebellion was the steadfastness and personal influence of Premier Nu himself. He almost singlehandedly kept a semblance of civil administration alive in the face of unreasoning criticism and admitted corruption and also despite the strike of the civil servants and the seeming desertion of Socialist and P.V.O. leaders from his cabinet. Once the confusion of his misguided 1948 efforts at Marxist appeasement had been dissipated, he stood out foursquare in refusing to surrender to armed bandits the sovereign power entrusted to him by the people. He thus raised a democratic standard around which Burman liberals and all who favored orderly constitutional processes could rally. It was largely his influence also which kept the United Hill Peoples' Congress loyal, especially the militarily important Kachins and Chins. Premier Nu's leadership during the crisis

---

only and in a technical sense. See *PD,C*, vol. 461 (Feb. 14 and 23, 1949), pp. 764, 1854, vol. 462 (March 7, 1949), pp. 792–795. Many members of the European community at Rangoon disapproved the extreme nature of the Karen demands, but believed that they had been provoked into rebellion by *Yebaw* excesses especially within Rangoon itself.

[35] Efforts to forestall the break were made by the visiting treasurer of the American Baptist Foreign Mission Society in 1948, by ex-missionary members of the American embassy staff, and by Dr. E. Stanley Jones, who visited Rangoon on the eve of the rebellion. The settled policy of the American Baptist Mission in Burma was not to participate in political affairs in any way.

[36] Thakin Nu, *From Peace to Stability*, pp. 65–71.

elevated him for the first time to the rank of a bona fide national figure backed by a genuinely popular following, even though it was not organized as a mass movement in the Marxist sense. His subsequent espousal of a revival of the Buddhist faith added to the popular regard and confidence which he was able to command. He became the link between the Burmese people, whose religious faith he shared and whose folk tales he knew, and the sophisticated Westernized Socialists who dominated much of the thinking and planning within the A.F.P.F.L. government. He also maintained sufficient detachment from the gathering confusion of administration deficiencies and political chicanery to be able to criticize both the A.F.P.F.L. and the government.[37]

The Premier's natural sympathy for liberal democratic procedures was also demonstrated in 1949 in the field of foreign affairs. When his first request to the United Kingdom for financial aid and arms was considered in late February at a New Delhi meeting of Commonwealth representatives, they proposed unanimously that conciliation of Karen dissidence under Commonwealth mediation would be the surest means of restoring order and solvency in Burma. This proposal Rangoon rebuffed sharply, for the Burmans were not ready to allow outsiders to decide their internal affairs or to consider the possibility of Burma's rejoining the Commonwealth. All the while the London government was resisting Conservative pressure both in the press and in Parliament that Britain cease throwing good money after bad in Burma and that any future assistance be made conditional on Burma's agreement to provide equitable compensation for expropriated British properties.[38]

Relations between Rangoon and London improved considerably after Judge U E Maung took over the abandoned post of foreign minister in March, 1949. He not only stressed Burma's need for arms but talked also about seeking a just and amicable settlement of the capital investment claims of friendly nations. He even suggested that a defense pact with India and Pakistan might be considered.[39] The response of the London meeting of Commonwealth Prime Ministers, held in May, was a proposal that the United Kingdom, India, Pakistan, and Ceylon should set up a co-ordinating committee at Rangoon, functioning under the direction of the resident ambassadors, to propose measures for aid-

[37] See Tibore Mende, *South East Asia between Two Worlds* (London, 1955), pp. 170–171.

[38] New York *Herald Tribune*, March 4, 1949; *Statesman*, March 8, 1949; *Yorkshire Post*, March 21, 1949; *PD,C*, vol. 462 (March 7, 1949), pp. 792–795.

[39] Glasgow *Herald*, May 18, 1949.

ing U Nu's government in restoring order. The Labour government decided in June to provide Burma with 10,000 rifles to replace those taken by mutineers, and it continued to resist Conservative pressure to make such aid conditional on Burmese concessions to British interests or possible reaffiliation with the Commonwealth. The London press, although concerned about charges that Britain had deserted its Karen friends, hoped for positive results.[40]

The proposed program of Commonwealth assistance was shelved temporarily in late June, following the acceptance of invitations to visit London by Burma's General Ne Win and Foreign Minister U E Maung. The general arrived in July and the foreign minister in August. They also visited the United States briefly. The principal topics of conversation at London and in the United States concerned the need for military equipment and munitions, but the whole field of Burma's financial and security needs entered the discussions. Although U E Maung insisted that the threat to Burma as a result of the Communist victory in China was exaggerated in the West, he did not repudiate that factor as a basis for assistance. He even talked of encouraging private capital investment in Burma and the possibility of Burma's joining a Pacific Security Pact "sponsored by the right people at the right time." [41] The result of these and subsequent negotiations was renewal of the talks among the Commonwealth ambassadors at Rangoon on October 14, 1949, covering financial and military aid. The outcome was the negotiation of a Commonwealth loan of 350 million rupees as announced by Foreign Minister U E Maung from New Delhi in early December.

Accompanying the announcement of the Commonwealth loan in New Delhi and apparently without prior consultation with Rangoon, U E Maung indicated that Burma would in all probability be represented at the forthcoming Commonwealth Conference at Colombo in the person of Premier Nu himself. This was apparently the opening which political enemies of the foreign minister had been waiting for. In any case the statement was abruptly denied at Rangoon by the assertion that Burma, "not [being] a unit of the British Commonwealth

---

[40] *PD,C*, vol. 464 (May 6 and 11, 1949), pp. 1444–1446, 1828–1830, vol. 466 (June 24 and 27, 1949), pp. 43–44, 749–750; Manchester *Guardian*, May 13, 1949; *Statesman*, June 24, 1949; *The Times*, Aug. 9, 1949. The British Treasury, in June, 1949, decided to distribute to British firms the sum of £10 million for damages suffered in Burma during the course of the war. The Irrawaddy Flotilla Company was allocated £1 million under a special agreement dating from 1942.

[41] New York *Times*, Aug. 14 and 26, 1949; *Observer*, Aug. 28, 1949.

and having no intention of reëntering it, has not been invited to . . .
Colombo." Premier Nu explained rather lamely that he had planned
to visit Ceylon at the time, but not for the purpose of attending the
conference.[42] The differences went fairly deep. When U Nu, in June,
1949, had proposed enactment of a bill permitting foreign capital to
develop Burma's resources, the Socialist-controlled Parliament had
buried it. It was Premier Nu's expectation, and U E Maung's also, that
technical and other forms of needed assistance could be obtained for
Burma on a nonprofit basis from countries concerned to maintain Burma
as a bastion of democracy in Asia. The Socialists, on the other hand,
had tended to praise the successes of the Communist revolution in
China. In early December they had obtained U E Maung's consent
to the recognition of Red China, allegedly as a means of preventing
border raids. After the difference over the Colombo Conference announcement, the Socialists forced the resignation of the foreign minister.[43]

Following the departure of U E Maung, the Socialists began to re-
enter the cabinet. Three second-ranking party leaders were added in
January, and three more in March. An interesting interlude took place
at the time of the formal induction of the last three on April 4, 1950.
In conformity with the advice of learned astrologers consulted by the
government to the effect that current difficulties were allegedly attributable to the cabinet's having been constituted on an inauspicious day,
it was at first agreed that the entire cabinet would resign. Its reconstitution was scheduled for 9:15 to 9:20 on the morning of April 4 as being
the most suitable time. When the actual day arrived, a number of the
old members balked at going through with the plan, and only the three
new members obeyed the recommendations of the astrologers.[44]

Problems of Recovery

Even after the Burma Government, by the spring of 1950, had ex-
tricated itself from its previous position of dire peril, it still faced
baffling problems of disorder and economic disintegration. Masses of
refugee peasants, who had fled to Rangoon and other relatively secure

[42] *Statesman,* Oct. 15, Dec. 7 and 22, 1949.
[43] *Scotsman,* June 15, 1949; Manchester *Guardian,* June 16, 1949; *The Times,*
Dec. 11 and 19, 1949; *Hindu,* Dec. 8, 1949; *Daily Telegraph,* Dec. 21, 1949.
[44] *Hindu,* Jan. 4, 1950; *Statesman,* March 1 and 7, 1950; New York *Herald
Tribune,* April 2, 1950; New York *Times,* April 4, 1950. U Win, U Kyaw Myint,
and Bo Khin Maung Gale entered the cabinet in January, 1950, and U Tin, U
Khin Maung Lat (a Muslim), and Archibald Rivers (Anglo-Indian) in March, 1950.

urban centers, could not be persuaded to return to the disturbed countryside. The Land Nationalization Act, voted in October, 1948, was not
implemented because of the confusion caused by the rebellions. When
its application was attempted tentatively in 1950, vigorous protests of
dishonesty and favoritism were aroused.[45] Internal transportation by
river and especially by rail was virtually paralyzed partly as a result
of the widespread insurgency and partly from sheer lack of equipment
and efficient operating personnel. If Burma's basic prewar industries
in rice milling, timber, oil, and mining were to be revived and many
new economic operations added, capital requirements and technical
assistance had to come from outside. All this must be done in the face
of handicaps to foreign investment already incurred as a result of the
socialist provisions of Burma's constitution and the outright expropriation of assets of prewar firms.

Finally there was the urgent problem of developing an effective local
government which could function regularly and could merit popular
support in areas where insurgency had disappeared. The corrupt habits
of many of the officials and the traditional antipathy prevailing between
nationalist politicians and government civil servants aggravated the
problem. Nationalist leadership forgot with difficulty its indictment
of prewar administrative personnel as parasites living off the treasury,
as stooges of the foreign ruler, and as betrayers of the nation. In similar
fashion the usually more experienced civil servants resented the presence of "young fools" (seventh standard [grade] politicians) in high
governmental positions, often lacking as they were in education, experience, and capacity. Interference by local A.F.P.F.L. officials had in fact
gone very far to demoralize the routine operations of local government.
Premier Nu himself felt obliged in 1950 to exhort civil servants to
eschew politics, to accept defined governmental policies, and to perform their duties honestly. He also reminded politicians that agitators
had no monopoly on sincerity and patriotism, not to mention capacity.[46]

[45] The Land Nationalization Act of October, 1948, abolished landlordism and
limited an agriculturalist's holding to 50 acres as a maximum. It also required
recipients of such redistributed land to join government-sponsored agricultural
co-operatives which would supervise borrowing, repayment, and marketing operations. Elected village committees would control the co-operatives under the supervision of district land committees. Former owners were to be compensated in
nonconvertible bonds in proportion to the tax assessment on the land taken over.
State farms were to be set up by 1950. No serious attempt was made to apply
this act until April, 1950. See Union of Burma, *The Land Nationalization Act,
1948* (Rangoon, 1949); Hinners, pp. 337–340.

[46] Thakin Nu, *Translation of the . . . Prime Minister's Speech* (Rangoon, 1950),
pp. 1–13. Addressing a series of divisional conferences of government officials,

One of the factors aggravating this lack of co-operation between government servants and political leaders was the application of the Democratic Local Government Act, passed by unanimous vote of Parliament in February, 1949. It provided for popular election at all levels (village, township, subdivision, and district) of local government councils entrusted with directive powers. Council decisions, subject to approval at higher levels, must be respected and carried out by government officials. The authority of the village headman was superseded by locally elected councils consisting of eight village elders, who theoretically exercised court jurisdiction over both criminal and civil cases. This system of pyramiding councils virtually abolished the office of the township *myook* and the district deputy commissioner, in a fairly obvious imitation of the Soviet system of "democratic centralism," all to be dominated by pervading party direction.

The experiment failed for a number of reasons, not the least being the revival in aggravated form of evils which had beset the district councils under dyarchy. Local A.F.P.F.L. party leaders were too often undisciplined persons, partisan in spirit, who dictated both elections and council decisions, sometimes under the influence of bribery. Abuses of power by council members generated a strong counterdemand that electoral districts be empowered to recall councilors for misuse of their authority.[47] Generally speaking, the village *ludu* (masses) proved to be quite incapable of expressing articulate views regarding governmental objectives and needs, but they were not happy when outsiders intervened officiously. The Socialist Party local councils, like those of dyarchy, contributed little to the positive direction of governmental policy and nothing to training in self-government. The Rangoon municipality came under special criticism for its conspicuous and continuing failure to oust squatters, improve sanitation, regulate markets, and care for such basic needs as road repair, garbage and sewage disposal, and water and electric power supply.[48]

Some of the best government servants resigned rather than submit to continued political interference and intimidation, for they dared not offend local A.F.P.F.L. leaders, even those of dubious character. The local "peace guerrilla" remnants of the partially demobilized Burman Auxiliary Union Military Police, unpaid by government, cus-

U Nu warned ominously: "There is still hope if we call a halt to our evil practices and mend our ways. If not, the whole structure of our Union will collapse."

[47] *Bama Khit*, Sept. 9, 1950; *Tribune* (Rangoon), Sept. 20, 1950. See Tinker, *Foundations of Local Self-Government*, ch. viii and p. 243.

[48] *Guide Daily*, Sept. 29, 1950.

tomarily collected so-called "gate fees" from travelers and sometimes resorted to even more questionable measures of personal aggrandizement. The regular army operating on the fringes of insurgent-held territory was sometimes almost as destructively predatory as were the local bandits. The whole constituted, as of mid-1950, a far from pleasing picture, especially in view of the absence from Premier Nu's cabinet of leading Socialists, who represented the most substantial element of the A.F.P.F.L. The central authorities were frequently powerless to interfere in district affairs, which were actually being run semi-independently by party henchmen.[49]

Although the insurgent threat against the authority of the government was, according to Premier Nu's estimate of September, 1950, 95 per cent dissipated, major areas of the countryside were not under effective policing. Seldom did the army control more than four or five miles on either side of the leading trunk roads or river channels of nominally subdued areas. Organized dacoit bands, intermingled with rebels, operated up to the very edges of many government-occupied towns. Trade was stagnant, especially along the railway lines. Informed press comment suggested that not more than 35 per cent of the country was really under control.[50]

The task of developing a disciplined army with a trained corps of officers was far from complete, although morale was good and General Ne Win's leadership was effective in dissipating the rebel threat.[51] The main Communist group was dislodged from its Pyinmana-Yamethin stronghold astride the trunk railway to Mandalay and was pushed for the most part westward into jungle-desert terrain and beyond the right bank of the Irrawaddy River. Small Communist-bandit groups were widely dispersed. The K.N.D.O. exercised a semblance of administrative control over large consolidated sections of the Irrawaddy delta and

[49] *New Light of Burma,* Oct. 13 and 19, 1950; *Tribune Translation Service* (Rangoon), Oct. 23, 1950. U Kyaw Nyein, partly because of illness, remained aloof until early 1951; U Ba Swe functioned after February, 1949, as commissioner of Irrawaddy Division and exercised a wide measure of political as well as administrative authority. U Win had served similarly as commissioner for Upper Burma and Bo Hmu Aung (Yellow Band P.V.O.) for the area extending from Rangoon's environs northward to Toungoo. See *Vernacular Press Translations,* Feb. 22, 1949.

[50] *Voice of the Union,* Sept. 6, 1950; *Tribune Translation Service,* Sept. 19, 1950; *The Progress,* Sept. 9 and 26, 1950. Burma's railways incurred an operating deficit of 50 million rupees in 1949–1950.

[51] General Ne Win succeeded Smith-Dun as army chief when the Karen rebellion started. He also served for a time as minister of defense.

a considerable area of mountainous terrain along the left bank of the Sittang and southward through the Salween, Thaton, and Amherst districts. The Communist and Karen rebel elements were responsible for perhaps three-fourths of the reported antigovernment incidents occurring in the spring of 1950. U Nu's generous offer of amnesty of July, 1950, including all rebels except those guilty of serious crimes, had little effect on these hard-core resistance groups, who were destined to remain a problem for at least a half decade longer.

Economically, the gross-volume output for Burma in 1949–1950 recovered noticeably from the near collapse of the previous year, but it was still only some 62 per cent of the prewar (1938–1939) level and barely more than the level attained in the politically distraught year of 1946–1947. Capital formation savings were negligible in terms of the needs for recovery and new investment.[52] In June, 1950, the government was obliged to write off as uncollectible an accumulated 70 million kyats (Burmese rupees) of agricultural debt owed by cultivators and to start afresh with better lending and credit machinery and the offering of more generous per-acre assistance (28 kyats as compared with 7 kyats only). The government launched an agricultural bank, which would lend to local co-operatives at 6 per cent and they to cultivators at 12 per cent per annum. But the co-operatives were either nonexistent or irresponsibly run, and the habit of not repaying government-provided loans was not easily dispelled.

The government was heavily criticized for keeping the domestic price of rice at approximately one-half the export price available to the monopolistic State Agricultural Marketing Board. The government could point only to its agricultural reforms (land redistribution, lower rents and taxes, easier credits, etc.) and to social benefits in extenuation of its policies.[53] Particularly popular was the government's firm refusal, in June, 1950, to reconsider, at the request of spokesmen for visiting Chettyar landlords from Madras, the established land compen-

[52] Frank N. Trager, *Toward a Welfare State in Burma . . . 1948–1954* (New York, 1954), pp. 2–3.

[53] *Ibid.*, pp. 16, 17, 21, 23; *Sun*, Sept. 11, 1950. Legislative enactments for the benefit of the peasants included the Tenancy Standard Rent Act of 1947 (setting rents at twice the land revenue assessed), the Tenancy Disposal Act of 1948 (administered through local committees), and the Burma Agriculturalists Debt Relief Act of 1948, canceling all debts incurred prior to October 1, 1941, and outstanding on October 1, 1946, and exempting debts contracted after the latter date from the payment of interest. Included also were the Land Nationalization Act of 1948 and the Agricultural Bank Act of 1948. See Thakin Nu, *Forward with the People* (Rangoon, 1951), pp. 20–27.

sation rate of only 12 times the annual revenue (Chettyars wanted 30 to 40 times) payable in nonconvertible bonds.[54] But almost nothing was done to develop new employment and productive facilities in the field of industry, a situation which could not be allowed to continue indefinitely.

The crescendo of criticism presented by the traditionally outspoken vernacular press of Rangoon in the fall of 1950 had the Socialist Party, the A.F.P.F.L., and the government very much on the defensive. Editors alleged that there were too many "young fools" in places calling for experience. The Socialist Party, it was charged, controlled the army and its officer selection and training, as well as the village councils and the local redistribution of land, all in the interest of strengthening the party organization.[55] Premier Nu apparently was not considered so objectionable, but the co-operative enterprises which he advocated were declared to be no solution, because they too were being run dishonestly in the interest of friends and relatives, while the residue of the consumer goods was disposed of in the black market. Such abuses were obviously spoiling the good name of the co-operative principle. The A.F.P.F.L. as a whole was also declared to be devoid of democratic principles and to be losing the confidence of the people. It was charged that extreme leftists abused their power, imprisoning political enemies arbitrarily and making impossible the appearance of rival party organizations. Finally, the editors asked when the elections, now four times postponed, were going to be held.[56]

One need not conclude that such press criticisms were universal or even fully representative of public opinion to recognize that they were symptoms of the necessity for governmental initiative toward positive political and economic objectives designed to discount the disturbing trend toward social and administrative disintegration. Burmese social traditions (family solidarity, religious festivals and worship, community organization) were by no means entirely destroyed, but they persisted in far too many instances more from inertia than from any innate vitality. If they were to be revitalized as social controls in the service

[54] W. S. Desai, *India and Burma* (Bombay, 1954), pp. 100–104. Indian cultivators during the initial experiments with land distribution in the Syriam area were treated the same as were Burmans. All Indians in Burma were adversely affected by their inability to transfer their funds from Burma to India.

[55] *Oway*, Sept. 19, 1950; *The Progress*, Oct. 22, 1950; *Tribune Translation Service*, Oct. 31, 1950.

[56] *Sun*, Sept. 23, 1950; *The Progress*, Oct. 6 and 18, 1950; *Hanthawaddy*, Oct. 20 and 25, 1950.

of positive and constructive ends, it would have to be done in terms of affirmative nationalist objectives going beyond the purely negative hatred of colonialism, the Chettyar, and the Indian laborer, and also beyond advocacy of the negative Buddhist ideal of withdrawal. Since Burma's 18 million people, unlike the 2 million of 1800, could not possibly return to a primitive self-contained economy, planned development utilizing foreign capital and technical assistance to supplement state savings and investment must be devised to channel economic activities toward social ends. To the youthful leaders of Burma's government such an approach appeared to be the only answer if British and Indian economic masters were not to be allowed to return and if no new colonial risks were to be incurred.[57]

The Commonwealth Approach

The change in the Burmese attitude toward British economic aid was gradual. Premier Nu told the Burma Chamber of Commerce (British) in December, 1948, that a socialist state could not be created by fiat overnight and that the government would therefore welcome cooperation with foreign business groups if they would agree to give as much weight to improving mass living conditions as to profiting their investors.[58] In March, 1949, the Government Economic Council (sans the Socialists) recommended that in view of the government's inability to act at the time, private capital should be invited to participate in developing transportation and electric power facilities and the manufacture of iron, steel, paper, and sulphuric acid, as well as the old-line industries of milling, teak extraction, and mining. This move was followed in April, 1949, by Rangoon's extending a substantial measure of compensation to several expropriated British firms.[59] By August, 1949, private participation was being actively solicited for reviving both the teak industry and the faltering inland water transport system.

In October, 1949, as previously indicated, the Commonwealth ambassadors at Rangoon took up in a serious way plans for an intergovernmental loan as an investment in the stability of South Asia and the preservation of democracy. In an exchange of notes with London in December, 1949, Premier Nu extended and renewed previous assur-

[57] See Furnivall, "Twilight in Burma," *Pacific Affairs*, XXII (1949), 2–8.
[58] Thakin Nu, *Toward Peace and Democracy* (Rangoon, 1949), pp. 165–166.
[59] The Rangoon Telephone Company received £150,000; the Irrawaddy Flotilla was offered £307,500, which was later raised to above £400,000; the timber firms would be paid in teak logs delivered to their mills. See *PD,C*, vol. 472 (March 20, 1950), p. 86.

ances that Burma would accord fair treatment to United Kingdom business interests. A parliamentary delegation was invited to visit Burma in January, 1950, and U Nu made a return visit to London as guest of the British Government in May, 1950.[60] This policy survived, with some difficulty, the return of the Socialists to power.

One result of the friendly Commonwealth approach to Burma's requests for aid was the convening in Ceylon in early 1950 of representatives of the so-called Colombo Powers (Commonwealth and Burma) to determine the magnitude of emergency aid available for Burma and the contribution which each participating country could make. It was agreed that an interest-free loan of £6 million to run for two years would be made of which sum the United Kingdom would advance three-fifths, and India, Australia, Pakistan, and Ceylon lesser amounts. This loan was in addition to a short-term British grant of £500,000 to help Burma's State Agricultural Marketing Board buy up the new rice crop and prepare it for sale.[61] Labour Party sponsors of the policy insisted that the proposal was investment in the future stability of Southeast Asia, in the preservation of the Commonwealth principle of consultation, and in the promotion of freedom and democratic government. Foreign Minister Bevin declared that any implied qualification of Burma's independence would inevitably play into Communist hands and that British interests in Burma would be worth little unless internal order and friendly relations with Britain were established.[62] The generous motivation of the Commonwealth loan set an important precedent for subsequent policy even though the £6 million loan voted in June, 1950, was actually never drawn upon by Burma. This was partly because assistance in the form of an outright grant under the United States Technical Co-operation Administration (TCA) was in prospect. Mr. Philip Jessup of the Department of State visited Burma in April

[60] PD,C, vol. 470 (Dec. 15, 1949), pp. 331–332, vol. 472 (March 20, 1950), p. 1558, vol. 475 (May 8, 1850), pp. 233–243.

[61] The Labour Party and some of its Conservative opponents were in sharp disagreement at the time over whether or not to attach political or economic conditions to the proposed loans. Conservatives wanted to exact a *quid pro quo* in the form of preferred access to Burma's rice, more serious consideration of unsettled British claims, guarantees against future expropriations, Burma's adherence to a Pacific Security Pact, and some kind of settlement satisfactory to Britain's Karen friends.

[62] PD,C, vol. 472 (March 23, 1950), pp. 1953–1954, 2192–2214, vol. 473 (April 3, 1950), p. 96, vol. 475 (May 8, 1950), pp. 233–243. The Colombo Treaty terms can be found in Great Britain, Treaties, *Agreement between the Governments of the United Kingdom . . . Australia, India, Pakistan, Ceylon, and . . . Burma* (Rangoon, 1950), no. 41. The leading objector was Captain Gammons.

of 1950, and an agreement with the United States for technical aid was signed in September, 1950. Another factor was that the profits from the government's sale of rice abroad in 1950 earned some 130 million kyats,[63] and more profits were in prospect.

In two important areas of industrial activity the Burma Government reverted with noteworthy success to the postwar Simla proposition that firms with experience in given fields could best supervise recovery efforts. Taking advantage of the permissory clauses of the constitution, the government, in 1951, entered into an agreement with the old Burma Corporation, on a 50 per cent joint-venture basis, to revive the silver, lead, and zinc mining operations at Bawdwin and to reactivate the adjacent Namtu refinery in the Northern Shan States.[64] The arrangement eventually restored production on an increasingly profitable basis for both parties to the joint venture. A similar arrangement with three British oil firms providing for a one-third ownership by the government (with funds advanced on loan by the London government) was subsequently concluded in order to get oil production under way.[65] In this instance, the presence of continued Communist insurgency in the oil-fields area delayed the initiation of the joint enterprise, but substantial progress was nevertheless being made by 1956.

Orientation toward Democracy and the United Nations, 1950–1951

Burma's gradual shift of policy away from an extreme leftist orientation toward democracy was encouraged by the outbreak of the Korean War in June, 1950. When faced with a situation of obvious Communist aggression against the United Nations, Burma's representative at the UN Assembly voted unhesitatingly with the majority to condemn the North Korean action. As Premier Nu explained to his own Parliament in early September, the UN was Burma's only recourse in case she her-

[63] Mr. Attlee's government, in 1951, took favorable action on U Nu's request for a sterling loan to help Burma finance the purchase of one-third share in the Burmah Oil Company. See *PD,C*, vol. 491 (March 28, 1951), pp. 455–456; *Sun*, Sept. 11, 1950.

[64] Half the stock of the new Burma Corporation (1951) was to be government-owned and half of it owned by the new private British Mines Company, whose stock was exchanged share for share by holders of the old Burma Corporation stock. See Daniel Lloyd Spencer, "Foreign Participation in South Asian Enterprises," *Far Eastern Survey*, XXIV (1955), 42.

[65] *Ibid.* British oil firms put up the sum of £750,000, an amount in excess of their obligation, as a gesture of good will. Government had the option of increasing the proportion of its own capital holding at any time to any level desired, but it was under no obligation to do so.

self should suffer a similar attack, and if Burma now tried to be over-clever and refused under the circumstances to take a clear-cut stand, it could lay no claim to aid in a possible future contingency. U Nu em-phasized that the Korean decision was pro-United Nations and that Burma would strive to remain on friendly terms with China; but the realignment was nonetheless clear.[66] A week later, on September 13, Burma signed the Technical Aid Agreement with the United States, calling for the expenditure during the current year of some $8 million. An announcement was also made concerning the impending visit to Burma of an American military mission.

Rangoon's conservative press hailed the new policy and subsequently cheered the Inchon-landing feat by UN forces in Korea. It openly blamed the U.S.S.R. for fomenting war while talking peace and for sabotaging the United Nations.[67] But this favorable reaction was far from unanimous. Strong opposition to Burma's new international align-ment with the UN and the anti-Communist West developed at lower levels of the Socialist Party leadership, especially within the Trade Union Congress (Burma) headed by Thakins Lwin and Hla Kywe. For almost a year prior to the Korean crisis, these men had advocated affiliation of their Socialist group of unions with the Communist-directed World Federation of Trade Unions (W.F.T.U.). They had also actively supported the Burma sessions of the Communist-sponsored World Peace Congress, in open defiance of the wishes of the Burma Government and the A.F.P.F.L. as a whole.[68] U Ba Swe had been obliged in May, 1950, to deny Socialist Party approval to the pro-Communist proposals of Thakin Lwin, who was nevertheless strongly supported by the official Socialist Party paper, *Voice of the Union*. Whereas the top Socialist leaders, U Ba Swe and U Kyaw Nyein, wel-comed the visit to Rangoon by representatives of the International Con-federation of Free Trade Unions, Thakin Lwin absented himself.[69]

The rift within Socialist ranks was in part the accomplishment of the

---

[66] *Tribune Translation Service*, Sept. 6, 1950; *New Times of Burma*, Sept. 5, 1950.

[67] *Sun*, Sept. 14 and 19, 1950; *Tribune Translation Service*, Sept. 18 and 19, 1950; *Bama Khit*, Sept. 21, 1950.

[68] Thakin Lwin's advocacy of the W.F.T.U. affiliation began in August, 1949. He was prevented only by travel difficulties from sending observers to the Peking meeting of the W.F.T.U. in November, 1949, where Red China's role to "liberate" Southeast Asian countries was affirmed. Thakin Lwin's May Day address in 1950 had praised world Communist leaders and had told the cheering unionist followers, equipped as always with their red hammer and sickle flags, that his decision to join the W.F.T.U. was definite.

[69] *Oway*, Sept. 14, 1950.

articulate and persistent Communist propagandist, Thein Pe (Myint).[70] The Socialist organ, *Voice of the Union,* in July, 1950, had condemned United States intervention in Korea, and had denounced President Truman as a second Hitler and the New York *Times* as an organ of the "warmongers." Thakin Hla Kywe in the Parliament flatly denounced U Nu's policy of Korea in September, 1950.

The issue of the Trade Union Congress (Burma) defiance of both the A.F.P.F.L. and the heads of the Socialist Party, with which it was affiliated, was met squarely. Both Thakins Lwin and Hla Kywe were excluded from the A.F.P.F.L., and the T.U.C. (Burma) was disaffiliated until new officers could be elected. Eventually, on October 17, U Ba Swe, recently returned from Europe, headed a new executive committee of the T.U.C. (Burma), and ten days later it was reaffiliated with the A.F.P.F.L. In December, 1950, the excluded left wing Socialists formed the pro-W.F.T.U. "Burma T.U.C." and also the new Burma Workers' and Peasants' Party. The last-named group came in time to be recognized as an aboveground Communist Party, although it was apparently never fully identified with the White Flag rebels. The government's policy of permitting the Burma Workers' and Peasants' Party free outlet for political criticism in the press and on the platform as well as in Parliament not only prevented its coalescence with overt rebellion but also contributed materially toward strengthening the liberal democratic tradition. Except among the university students the aboveground Communists exerted little apparent influence.

U Ba Swe's refusal to go along with dissident Socialists and his support of Premier Nu's new international alignment were clearly important. Nevertheless, he still allowed his audiences to carry him away at times, when he would talk like a thoroughgoing Marxist revolutionary. The T.U.C.(Burma) kept its special red hammer and sickle flag.[71]

[70] Thakin Thein Pe eventually added "Myint" to his name. He had also sponsored the "Russia, China, Burma Good-Will Association," which included student representatives from the Rangoon University Student Union. He continued to urge the use of Marxist books for university classes.

[71] *Voice of the Union,* Sept. 9, 11, and 12, 1950. U Ba Swe ostensibly espoused Marxism without qualification, but he refused to make the program in Burma a carbon copy of the U.S.S.R. or China. He obviously preferred peaceful methods to violence, but did not hesitate to threaten direct action to curb obstructionist counterrevolutionaries of the right or deviationists of the left. He reconciled Buddhism and Marxism simply by affirming that the first dealt with spiritual aspects of life ignored by Marx and the second with mundane affairs negated by Gautama. U Ba Swe in 1950 exhorted university students to get into politics, to sabotage colonial-type education, and to avoid becoming "puppets of the imperialists."

Pro-Communist leaders of the All Burma Peasants' Organization (Thakins Lwin, Chit Maung, Tin) were also replaced by loyal supporters of the A.F.P.F.L. Thakin Tin later returned to the party fold. The *Voice of the Union* itself was a victim of the rift and ceased publication in December, 1950.[72]

Most of the pro-A.F.P.F.L. press gave qualified support to the United States aid program. Even the Socialist paper conceded that the offer was worth examining. Some regarded it as paltry in size, a sesamum seed in an elephant's mouth. The official A.F.P.F.L. organ explained that the aid program meant closer economic relations with the United States but that it carried no real political significance.[73] Only the conservative *Bama Khit* declared that Burma's future depended on grasping the friendly hand of the Anglo-Americans, suppressing the pro-Russian elements behind the government, and halting abruptly the nationalization program.[74] The proposed visit of the United States military mission to Burma was actually canceled in late September in the face of the objection of General Ne Win. Distrust of American military policy in Asia and the fear that the United States might possibly bring pressure to bear on behalf of the rebellious Karen nationalists, plus the 1947 agreement with Britain to invite only Commonwealth military advisers—all stood in the way.[75] The American aid program was approved in early October with but a single dissenting vote in Parliament.

Two other events during the period from June to October, 1950,

[72] *Voice of the Union*, Dec. 1, 1950.

[73] *New Light of Burma*, Sept. 16, 1950.

[74] *Bama Khit*, Oct. 10, 18, 25, and 1950. The *Guide Daily* (Sept. 14, 1950) looked for traps and suggested that the Economic Co-operation Administration (ECA) gift horse might be diseased and germ laden. The *Voice of the Union* (Nov. 16, Dec. 1, 1950) warned that the crumbs of American economic aid to Burma were a prelude to the overthrow of its leftist government and the transformation of Burma into a U.S. military base. The UN, it affirmed, was, in reality, only a department of the United States Government.

[75] At this juncture, General Ne Win surrendered his cabinet posts (Home and Defense Departments) in favor of the more politically active ex-commissioner of Upper Burma, U Win. The alleged and probably the principal reason for shifting General Ne Win was that he needed to give his full time to developing the army. Behind the decision was also the earlier refusal of General Ne Win to comply with orders to use the army in Tennasserim Division to check illicit tin and rubber operations after his demand was refused that such industries be declared nationalized. Relatives of high Socialist Party leaders stood to lose by nationalization of tin especially, and the outspoken General Ne Win was accordingly *persona non grata*. The general did not wear political harness gracefully, but he remained the firm supporter of Premier Nu.

signalized Burma's shift away from a Marxian orientation. One was the refusal of the council of Rangoon University and of the students themselves to approve the proposal advanced by Thakin Thein Pe Myint within the council in June, 1950, that the university curriculum be Communized by prescribing for most degree examinations books written by Marxist authors and in English translation.[76] Thakin Thein Pe's argument was that the constitutional objective to make Burma a socialist state required positive preparation within the schools. His original motion failed for lack of a seconder, but a substitute motion advanced by U Kyaw Nyein established a special committee, including him and Thakin Thein Pe, to re-examine the entire university curriculum. The university students in September not only vetoed the Marxist curriculum but voted also to ban political parties from the campus. These issues nevertheless returned later to plague the University Student Union and council.[77]

As part of the government's shift to a moderate approach, Premier Nu also sponsored and obtained unanimous parliamentary approval in early October, 1950, for three bills designed to promote religious revival and reform. The *Dhamma Chariya* Act established two government-sponsored ecclesiastical courts, one at Rangoon and one at Mandalay, whose function it would be to restore order within the Buddhist *Sangha,* or monastic order. The need for such action was obvious, but the proposed religious courts faced an appallingly difficult problem. The second *Vinissaya* Act established a Pali University system which would regularize accreditation standards for teaching and examination in the Buddhist scriptures by the qualifying monastery *Sayadaws.* Monasteries with ten or more full-time students in Pali could apply for accreditation, while teachers qualifying under a preceptor's examination administered by the Pali University would be supported by state funds. A representative from each affiliated monastery college would serve on the large Pali University governing body, from which a smaller executive group would be selected. A third legislative enactment established a *Buddha Sasana* Organization to promote religious objectives throughout the entire country. It was intended to sponsor

---

[76] Such textbooks as Lenin's *Imperialism,* Plekhanov's *Materialist Concept of History,* Stalin's *The State,* and Mao Tse-tung's *Peoples' Democracy* were proposed by Thakin Thein Pe.

[77] *Tribune Press Translations,* June 10, 1950; *Sun,* June 11, 1950; *Daily Telegraph,* Jan. 10, 1951. By January, 1951, a majority of the student union had reverted, under Burma Workers' and Peasants' Party instigation, to a pro-Communist position.

translations of the scriptures in simple Burmese, graded for instructional purposes, to the end that Buddhist ethical teachings would be directly inculcated in the schools. The *Sasana* Organization, with active government support, would also undertake to propagate the faith within Burma and abroad. Premier Nu's contemporaneous denunciation as propagandist effrontery the Communist allegation that Marx was wiser than the Lord Buddha marked his seeming complete repudiation of his celebrated pro-Marxist Leftist Unity Program of June, 1948. U Nu now based his pacification appeal on the word of the Lord Buddha that enmity could not be overcome by enmity.[78]

Although no member of the Parliament opposed Premier Nu's religious reform proposals, many political leaders were considerably less than enthusiastic about them. The moves were, of course, anathema to Communists and fellow travelers. Others saw in the new policy a repudiation of U Aung San's constitutional principle of the secular state, a possible revival of the influence of the obscurantist *pongyi* politicians, and a probable squandering of funds and effort on objectives irrelevant to Burma's crying economic needs.[79] Such misgivings gained additional point two years later when Premier Nu announced his intention to convene in Burma, in the pattern set by King Mindon some eighty years before, the Sixth Historic Buddhist Council to recite and transcribe a corrected version of the *Tri-pitaka* scriptures. The initial cost to the treasury for the construction of an artificial-cave assembly hall and a new pagoda to house relics was an allocated 5.5 million kyats.

Nor were the members of the *Sangha* themselves entirely happy about the reform aspects of the scheme and the conduct of the Pali University examinations.[80] Disgruntled *pongyis* who were omitted from the governing body proceeded to organize, in June, 1951, the "Burma Sangha Party." This body denounced Premier Nu as a Communist for sowing dissension among the clergy and for advocating the nationalization of pagoda lands. The new party flatly condemned the A.F.P.F.L. as the enemy of Buddhism and exhorted voters to support any opposition candidate in the ensuing election. At least two overt political demonstrations involving several hundred monks at a time were staged

[78] John F. Cady, "Religion and Politics in Modern Burma," *Far Eastern Quarterly*, XIV (1953), 158–161; *Statesman*, Jan. 4, 1951.

[79] The obtaining of allegedly sacred relics from India, Ceylon, and China (a Buddha tooth) supported these charges of obscurantism.

[80] The results of the first two preceptor examinations, held in 1950 and 1951, had to be thrown out because the questions were prematurely distributed on both occasions.

in September, 1951, demanding the repeal of religious legislation, explicit recognition of Buddhism as the state religion, and removal of the officials of the Ministry of Religious Affairs.[81]

Despite the negative aspects of U Nu's religious reform program the gains were considerable. Premier Nu here reassociated the authority of the Burma state and the cause of Burmese nationalism as well with an appreciation of the Buddhist faith which was deeply ingrained in the popular consciousness. This move clearly challenged the spread of an alien Marxist cult of materialism and revolutionary violence by reaffirming the ethical and social values of Burma's own culture. Even though many probably agreed with U Kyaw Nyein's estimate that Buddhism alone as a religion of withdrawal could never halt Communism apart from a frontal attack on poverty,[82] it seemed equally obvious to observers that if Burmese society was to recover its sense of ethical direction some indigenous antidote to an amoral secularism would be required. Most Burmans sensed that Premier Nu's religious instincts were politically and socially valid.[83]

The final move which the government took in the direction of a democratic orientation was the calling of the first general election under the constitution, beginning in June, 1951. The salutary effects were numerous. The election test forced the governing A.F.P.F.L. to repudiate many of its own irregularities and to espouse some positive principles and objectives: (1) the socialist state to be realized in a peaceful, orderly fashion; (2) rejection of antireligious ideologies; (3) neutrality in the cold war but opposition to aggression; (4) fair treatment of minority peoples; (5) land nationalization, agricultural credits and lower rents for peasants; and (6) a planned program of economic development in the people's interest. The A.F.P.F.L. could also boast that it had won independence for Burma and had rescued the infant Union from disaster. The political campaign afforded Premier Nu in particular an effective opportunity to dramatize the principle of the people's sovereignty which he allegedly held in trust and which he refused to surrender to dacoit-rebels with guns. If the rebel factions represented

[81] Cady, *Far Eastern Quarterly*, XIV (1953), 159–162.

[82] Mende, pp. 172–174.

[83] For a thoughtful critique of the shortcomings of nationalism as an integrative factor in new Burma, see James McAuley, "Paradoxes of Development in the South Pacific," *Pacific Affairs*, XXVII (1954), 144–149. Western technical and financial assistance, lacking any relevant philosophy defining objectives and principles, can lead, McAuley insists, only to popular frustration and political confusion. He suggests that both Burma and the liberal West must search their souls if they are to outdo the dogmatic Marxist faith.

the people's interests, as alleged, let them submit that claim to the people's free decision.[84] Prior to the election campaign, the government restored salary cuts made to civil servants in 1949. Official apologists also stressed that educational expenditures in the new budget were increased by 70 per cent and medical services for the people were up 350 per cent, despite the fact that 40 per cent of the budget still had to go for the suppression of rebellion.[85]

The opposition parties could do little to match the claims of the A.F.P.F.L. and were hopelessly at odds among themselves. The dissident pro-Communist Burma Workers' and Peasants' Party and "Burma T.U.C." combined to form the People's Democratic Front, which proclaimed the rights of the workers. It denounced American aggression in Korea, Burma's accepting aid from "imperialists," and racial friction. The group set up their headquarters, interestingly enough, in Shwebo, home of the Konbaung dynasty. Two other quasi-Communist groups, the amnestied White Band P.V.O., which campaigned as the People's Party, and the so-called "People's Peace United Front" of U Aung Than (older brother of U Aung San, who resigned from the A.F.P.F.L. in February, 1951) refused to co-operate with the Burma Workers' and Peasants' Party although they were very similar ideologically. The rightist parties of Thakin Ba Sein (Burma Democratic Front) backed a settlement with the Karens, catered to *pongyi* backing, and talked of peace. Dr. Ba Maw's *Mahabama* faction posed as leftist, but for a time backed the Anglo-American aid program, while U Ba Pe's Burma Union League made a rather forlorn case for the landlords and the employer group. The Arakanese nationalist organization fought with more success than most on a straight platform of regional autonomy. The divided opposition parties could not match the strong A.F.P.F.L. organization, which resolved local frictions and presented a strong slate of candidates effectively supported.

The voting began in some 30 per cent of the 250 constituencies on June 12, 1951, and the election was virtually completed by the end of the year. In disaffected areas the elections were either suspended or confined to a fraction of the full constituency. The vigilance of the Election Supervision Commission, headed by Justices U E Maung and U Ba U, did much to ensure that the elections were fairly conducted

[84] *New Times of Burma*, Oct. 25, 1951, from Nu's broadcasts of Jan. 11 and 13, 1951. U Nu declared that Burma's "stepfather," whom leftists preferred to their parents, had aided Burma neither economically nor politically.

[85] *Tribune Translation Service, Editorials*, Sept.–Oct., 1950.

and free, although disorderly conditions prevented many from voting. Radio time was allocated equitably to all parties in the contest. What violence occurred was attributable in large measure to the still un-disciplined *Yebaw* "peace guerrillas," but this was minor. Some 40 per cent of the eligible voters participated, and the outcome was an over-whelming 95 per cent victory for the A.F.P.F.L. candidates. The magni-tude of the victory was due in part to the generous role permitted by the A.F.P.F.L. to affiliated non-Socialist, non-Burman groups, such as the All Burma Muslim Congress, the Union Karen League, and the Chinese Chambers of Commerce. The government's only real defeat was sustained in the Arakan area, where local autonomy candidates won out, 6 to 1.[86] The outcome was as much a triumph for the moderate Socialists as for Premier Nu, and it made possible the formation of a strong Socialist-controlled cabinet in March, 1952. U Ba Swe was in a particularly strong position, while U Kyaw Nyein relieved him of the post of secretary-general of the A.F.P.F.L. The two joined U Nu to become the three dominant political personalities.[87]

Economic Development Plans

While the elections were being completed, the planning for Burma's future economic development got under way. The ambitious character of the resulting blueprint, designed to lift Burma from the status of a producer of raw materials and cash food crops to that of a diversified and more nearly self-sufficient industrial economy, was clearly not a decision forced by public demand rooted in distress or unemployment. It stemmed in part from the painful experiences of the war, which had seen Burma nearly destitute of cloth and many other essentials for living.[88] In still larger measure it was due to the determination of youthful Socialist leaders to end the stigma of colonial economic status and to have Burma blossom as a modernized state. This urge to modern-ize industrial-wise was responsible for the general neglect of the vast and immediate advantage attainable through agricultural improve-ments, especially in drainage and irrigation, improved seeds and animal husbandry procedure, and the use of fertilizers. In agriculture the in-itiative was left largely to the cultivator. The character of the technical

[86] Election data is taken largely from a manuscript seminar paper prepared by David Werfel.

[87] United States Information Service, "Review of Burmese Press Comment," Feb. 29 to March 6, 1952.

[88] Japanese efforts to improvise in order to meet some of these needs suggested new avenues of economic activity.

assistance available from the outside aggravated the tendency toward plotting grandiose long-term industrial objectives, but foreign advisers did not create the tendency.[89]

The first year of the technical assistance program produced a plethora of surveys of economic problems and potentials at once glamorous and enticing and also confusing and deceptive. First came a survey of economic problems by fields, undertaken by a group of British economists. Then followed, on contract with the American ECA, the preparation of an economic and engineering survey of Burma by the Knappen, Tippetts, and Abbott (K.T.A.) Engineering Company and the Robert R. Nathan Associates. The first draft of the survey was completed by early 1952. Then came the efforts of the United States technical assistance specialists to co-ordinate and implement the multifarious economic objectives and to initiate practical assistance in such fields as health and sanitation, transportation, and housing. A United Nations Social Services Mission also entered the picture, focusing efforts on welfare needs, cottage industries, public administration, labor-management problems, and statistics. The plans as a whole crystallized in the comprehensive *Pyidawtha* welfare state program, which was projected by government leaders in August, 1952.[90]

The *Pyidawtha* Conference staged at Rangoon from August 4 to 17, 1952, set forth, in an introductory speech by the Premier and in a series of succeeding policy resolutions, a comprehensive program of action relating to all aspects of Burma's economy. It also attempted to promote popular interest and participation in the endeavor by permitting a large measure of local initiative and self-help. U Nu declared that a new existence for Burma could not be realized by folding one's arms, mocking each other, and playing at insurrection, but only by planning and by persistent effort of the people in co-operation with a well-intentioned government. The ten policy resolutions stressed the need for increased popular initiative in local welfare activities through assignment of substantial administrative authority to democratized local bodies. The sum of 50,000 kyats was assigned to each township unit to be expended for needs as determined locally, in the hope that additional local funds could be raised. The program included long-term and short-term plans for land nationalization plus plans for agricultural

[89] Trager, p. 7.

[90] *Ibid.*, pp. 11–13. *Pyidawtha* has been freely translated as "welfare state" but "co-operation between people and government for the happiness of the country" is probably nearer the true meaning.

expansion and diversification. Wherever feasible, these policies would be extended to the people of the hill areas as well. Other items covered public health provisions, public aid to housing, detailed plans for developing transportation and communications, vocational and teacher training, and free public education including adult education projects continuing up through the professional levels. But the crux of the program was the projection of an eight-year plan of capital investment in industry which would see some $1.5 billion spent by 1960, two-thirds of the amount to come from local savings, private or public.[91]

In the *Pyidawtha* program the government was giving expression to its hopes and to its pride by blessing officially the K.T.A. economic and engineering survey. It failed to take into account the fact that the K.T.A. report was based on optimum conditions incapable of immediate realization.[92] In the light of continued insurgency entailing large military expenses and disruption of transportation facilities, as well as widespread demoralization of governmental administrative services,[93] the welfare scheme was clearly overambitious and productive of frustration. Dissatisfaction was aggravated by the fact that two years of United States technical aid had produced so much in the way of plans and so little in the form of tangible achievement,[94] although Burman administrative inefficiencies and lack of management experience were largely responsible. To the governmental problem of restoring the minimal governmental essentials of policing, courts, tax collections, and postal service were now added innumerable additional functions attendant on planned economic development. These included, as indicated earlier, the operation of intricate exchange and trade controls, the functioning of purchasing missions abroad dispensing enormous sums of money, the problem of land redistribution, and the initiation of both business ventures and social welfare schemes of large magnitude.

Official awareness of the shortcomings of the old-type civil service machinery, cautiously routine in its traditions and incapable of assum-

[91] Union of Burma, Ministry of Information, *The Pyidawtha Conference, August 4–17, 1952, Resolutions and Speeches* (Rangoon, 1952).

[92] Trager, p. 57.

[93] During the five-week period from April 17 to May 21, 1952, the Rangoon press reported 167 overt incidents of insurgent and dacoit activity, a number probably only a fraction of the actual total. The government did move to set up a Karen state in 1952, including adjacent townships from Thaton and Amherst districts.

[94] The TCA program promoted some ninety projects all told, but very few of these were ever fully realized.

ing responsibility for executing high-level economic decisions, led to the creation by legislative action of a great number of corporations and boards to handle the development projects. These were headed as a rule by leading political personalities. Thus the Mineral Resources Corporation was at first headed by U Ba Swe, the Industries Corporation by U Kyaw Nyein, and the Agricultural and Water Resources Corporation by U Kyaw Dun. To these were added six top-level boards, to handle rice purchases and sales (the State Agricultural Marketing Board), timber utilization, inland water transport, railways, electrical supply, and national housing. Only a few of these corporations and boards were operated under any clearly defined relationship with the old-line departments of government, except that a number of the new bodies were headed by ministers of the cabinet. Over all was the general Economic and Social Board headed under explicit constitutional provision by the Prime Minister himself. The Ministry of National Planning was responsible for supervision, priorities, and general implementation. Neither at the top nor at intermediate levels were the personnel resources of the Burma Government equal to the demands technically and administratively which the program entailed.[95]

Other barriers to the achievement of the *Pyidawtha* welfare state were associated with some ingrained social and cultural habits not capable of easy adjustment. Burma's value judgments and incentives to conduct differed from those of the industrial West. Casualness in habits of industry, traditional distrust of each other in business ventures, and lack of experience in merchandising and trade were not attuned to business needs. The limited extent of the changes really desired by the people generally, whose co-operation in the new order could not easily be coerced, was another factor. In short, Burman folkways and mores, ideas of personal status and dignity, educational incentives in general and the expectations of graduates in particular, rudimentary experience in labor-management relations, and the absence of a tradition of thrift and savings for deferred ends—these did not fit into the needs of an industrial society. Finally, there were the lack of essential coal and iron resources and the vulnerability of the government's capital-accumulation activities, through the State Agricultural

[95] Trager, pp. 41, 58–59. The system of corporations and boards was in many respects strikingly similar to the postwar "projects schemes" of the British in that the units operated outside regular governmental channels. The Burmese counterparts were presumably more concerned with social welfare, but they were far less competent technically and business-wise than the "projects" boards, as planned in 1945, would have been.

Marketing Board, in taking advantage of the temporarily inflated prices obtainable for Burma's rice exports. Even in the relatively lush times of 1952–1953, few government agencies spent more than half their capital budgets because of administrative difficulties.[96]

A windfall in Burma's economic development program came from the country's reparations settlement with Japan. It included provision for the construction by Japanese engineers of a hydroelectric project in the Kayah State (Karenni) above Loikaw, where the stream draining Inle Lake below Taunggyi drops 1,200 feet in a short distance. The substantial electric current capable of being generated at the site was to be distributed by high-tension wires to users in the adjacent Sittang Valley highway-railway corridor. The project would require several years for completion; preparations for the utilization of electric power were well advanced by 1956.

The Discontinuance of United States Technical Aid

One of the results of the lack of notable accomplishment in economic development after two years of expert assistance was that an increasing number of Burmans began to question the efficacy and advisability of United States technical aid. They complained not only that it was too theoretical but also too officious, too secretive, too involved in endless meetings and discussions. As one articulate Burman put it, the material results were hardly sufficient to balance the burden of gratitude incurred as a result of substantial expenditures (up to 30 million annually) in American funds. Other superficial aspects of the aid program recalled unwelcome memories of the extravagant mode of living (palatial houses with air conditioning, servants, cars, lavish entertainment) formerly practiced by the prewar British mercantile community. Attitudes of patronage, a kind of self-righteous satisfaction with regard to American generosity, frequent lack of concern for Burman sensibilities, plus general refusal of the visiting experts to identify themselves with the people aggravated the sense of Burmese dissatisfaction.[97] This type of resentment was in addition to the fairly widespread suspicion that such largess as the United States was dispensing to Burma and elsewhere in the world must somehow be motivated by concerns other than interest in the progress and stability of the government as organized.

[96] Trager, p. 32. The price for exported rice was around £50 per ton; internally it was £30.

[97] *Nation*, April, 5 and 7, 1953.

A basic practical difficulty was that the American aid program operated on a year to year basis, whereas commitments needed to be made for a longer period of time. The foreign aid appropriation usually cleared isolationist obstructions in the Congress at Washington in an atmosphere of cold-war tension which often stressed American self-interest in establishing its own security with regard to the world Communist threat and had correspondingly little relevance to Burma's own concerns and desires. The change of names from the original Economic Co-operation Administration (ECA) to the eventual Mutual Security Administration (MSA) in 1952 was in itself sufficient to precipitate a serious debate in the Burma Parliament and to elicit from both opposition leaders and cabinet ministers allegations that the United States was trying by its aid program to drag Burma into World War III.[98] Even the majority who voted to continue the assistance program objected to its possible military implications. Many were on the alert to detect any possible ulterior motive which might indicate that the United States was using Burma as a pawn in the world power contest with the U.S.S.R.

Nevertheless and in spite of all these oftentimes petulantly expressed suspicions and objections to the presence of some 100 American experts plus smaller numbers from the United Nations, Colombo Plan participants, and British joint-venture personnel, the foreign aid program was making a tangible showing in the direction of economic progress by early 1953. Those in a position to appreciate how much slack there was to take up realized that real gains in health, education, and economic well-being were in prospect. As late as January, 1953, Premier Nu praised the American aid program for speeding up Burma's recovery and denied as fantastic and untrue the opposition charge that the United States was using Burma in an attempt to establish an economic monopoly and a military base in Burma.[99] Similarly at the ECA Far Eastern Conference held at Bandung in February, 1953, Burma's representative, U Kyaw Myint, said, in reply to Communist charges, that U.S. aid to Burma had been without political strings, had embodied no slavery as alleged, and was much appreciated by the Burmese people.[100] Many high government officials and a large

[98] *Manchester Guardian Weekly*, March 27, 1952, p. 7; U.S. Information Service, "Review of Burmese Press Comment," Jan. 18 to Feb. 14, 1952.

[99] *Ibid.*, Jan. 20, 1953, U Nu's broadcast.

[100] *New Times of Burma*, Feb. 11 and 12, 1953. The ECA Far Eastern Conference voted 12 to 0, the U.S.S.R. abstaining, to approve a resolution that American aid was not enslaving East Asia.

segment of the population were almost as stunned as was Washington at the sudden announcement in late March, 1953, that U.S. assistance was no longer acceptable after the close of the current year, on June 30. The pressing reason was found in the sharp disagreement which had developed since 1951 between Rangoon and Washington over the status of Chinese Nationalist refugee troops in Burma's easternmost Shan States. These differences were aggravated by America's implied encouragement of Chiang Kai-shek's Formosan regime in 1953 to renew the China civil war.

When the original two brigades of the Kuomintang 8th Army, plus camp followers, entered Burma's Kengtung state from Yunnan province in December, 1949, and early 1950, the Burma Government had been in no position to disarm them or otherwise to devote attention to them. During the ensuing year and a half the Kuomintang forces under General Li Mi developed a fortified headquarters near the Siamese border, built an airfield capable of receiving four-engine planes, and acquired from some quarter, presumably by purchase in Siam or by air from Formosa, arms, ammunition, and medical supplies. Serious trouble began in mid-1951, when the greater portion of General Li Mi's near-destitute forces began to move westward across the Salween River, where they preyed on the inhabitants. In 1952 addition Nationalist Chinese refugee troops crossed the unguarded border of Burma's northern frontier, at points some 300 miles distant from Kengtung. Other contingents of the Kuomintang forces made contact across the Southern Shan States with Karen insurgents to whom they sold recoilless rifles and other weapons of recent U.S. manufacture. The attempt of the two Chinese groups to join hands in late 1952 as well as their collusion with Karen rebels threatened to throw a vast area of northeastern Burma into turmoil at a time when all of the country's available military resources were sorely needed to restore order and transportation in the central valley region. River and railway transportation, pacification of the oil-field area, and resumption of teak extraction were all essential to economic recovery. The possible development, unmolested, of a center of Nationalist Chinese operations in northeastern Burma would also provide Peking's Mao Tse-tung with a ready-made excuse, whenever he needed it, to carry the Chinese armed struggle into Burma. The feuding between the two resident Chinese factions within Rangoon had already reached near violence.

During 1952, the Burma Government accepted repeated assurances

621

of the Department of State that the United States was not assisting General Li Mi and was in no way responsible for his activities. Only the Burma Workers' and Peasants' Party and other pro-Communist groups at the time attacked American policy as being directly responsible for the situation.[101] The growing seriousness of the Shan State crisis in late 1952, coupled with various statements and policy decisions on the part of the newly elected Republican administration at Washington in early 1953, caused the feeling of distrust and anger to grow in Burma. Many took offense at the suggestion made by America's newly elected President, interpreted out of context, that Asians should fight Asians. Even more ominous appeared the action to step up American military aid to the French in Indochina and, above all, the decision to "unleash" Chiang Kai-shek's forces in Formosa to renew their attacks on the Communist-held mainland while the American fleet protected the island from Red Chinese attack. It was against the background of such policy pronouncements that many Burmans professed to see in the Kuomintang problem a Machiavellian plot on the part of the United States, hiding behind its technical aid shield, to generate a situation of local tension with Red China which would drive Burma into an American-sponsored anti-Communist military alliance. The Burma Government was prevented with difficulty in December, 1952, from bringing the question of Kuomintang occupation of Burmese territory before the United Nations. It could not be dissuaded a few months later.

The break came in March, 1953, after official and unofficial Burmese appeals to Washington to control Formosa's tactical operations and the alleged distribution of arms to the Kuomintang forces brought negative results. The submission of simultaneous statements by both Formosa and Washington that they were not responsible for arming and supporting General Li Mi was denounced by the progovernment press in Burma as collusion in a barefaced falsehood and as proof that Washington, in unholy alliance with the Kuomintang, was making a stooge of Burma. The angry editorial comment ran as follows:

The sooner the KMT are taken out of Burmese territory by the Formosa Government to whose designs the American Government is privy, the better it will be for Burmese-American friendship. Let another Asian country

[101] The Burma Workers' and Peasants' Party in November, 1952, denounced the Kuomintang forces as stooges of American imperialism and offered to recruit volunteers to fight the Nationalist Chinese.

[Thailand] who has succumbed so easily to dollar domination provide the military footing which the Formosa Government . . . wants.[102]

Rangoon's decision of March 17, made public twelve days later, to the effect that further American aid would be declined after June 30, 1953, was accompanied by official expressions of appreciation for the technical assistance program itself. But Rangoon made clear that there could be no mixing of U.S. aid to Burma with Formosa's plans to renew the civil war in China. The government's paper declared that if, with the help of a powerful friend, the Kuomintang troops continued their provocative operations in the Shan States area the chance of Burma's becoming a second Korea was very great.[103]

The United States aid program was thus a casualty of America's Formosa policy and Washington's inability to control the use of military equipment provided to the island government. The Ford Foundation took up part of the assistance burden, the United Nations another share. More serious was the sowing of distrust and suspicion of American good faith, with the result that a multitude of Burmans who resented the Kuomintang affair began to credit as true all forms of anti-American propaganda.

The anti-American attitude generated in 1953 opened the door to more intimate Burmese relations with Communist China and the U.S.S.R. Diplomatic relations with the two leading Communist powers had been established in 1950 and 1951 following Burma's prompt recognition of the Peking regime in December, 1949. Subsequent developments included the attendance of a Burmese delegation, led by Cabinet Minister U Tun Pe, at an economic conference held in Moscow in April, 1952. This was followed by a prolonged visit in both China and Russia from September to October, 1952, of a four-man delegation headed by Thakin Tin, president of the All Burma Peasants' Organization and minister of land nationalization, for the study of collective agricultural methods.[104] Burma's relations with China were still

[102] New Times of Burma, March 3, 1953; see also Feb. 3 and 5, March 6, and 26, 1953.

[103] Ibid., March 27 and 29, 1953; Mende, pp. 153–154. A number of the American technical advisers were retained on special contract with the Burma Government after official aid ceased.

[104] U.S. Information Service, "Review of Burmese Press Comment," April–May, Sept.–Oct., 1952. The initial Burmese delegation to Moscow and China included two anti-Communists and two pro-Communists (see Nation, July 3–6, 1952). The Chinese were especially cordial to the delegation members.

clouded by the daily broadcasts from Peking by Communist Bo Aung Gyi in support of the Than Tun rebels and by the even more disturbing Chinese military "liberation" move into Tibet in October, 1952.[105]

The Chinese embassy at Rangoon meanwhile maintained correct political relations with the government and gave no discernible encouragement to the Communist rebel factions. The Chinese press in Rangoon tactfully condoned Burma's UN vote on the Korean issue, at the same time condemning alleged U.S. aggression in Korea, Formosa, and Vietnam. It praised Burma's support of Red China's entry into the United Nations.[106] It was Burma's continuing concern to afford no provocation for Chinese military or political penetration along the extended and undefended China border.[107] The unfortunate Kuomintang episode not only contributed a setback to Burma's economic program; it also gave a different direction to its foreign policy.

[105] Mende, p. 192; *New Times of Burma*, Oct. 29, 1952. Most of the Burmese press was seriously concerned over the Tibetan affair because it shattered the hope that China's influence would be peacefully exerted.

[106] *Oway*, Sept. 10, 1950; *New Times of Burma*, Nov. 2, 1950. Only one Chinese paper in Rangoon, the *Freedom Pao*, remained pro-Formosan. Communist Thein Pe Myint urged a nonaggression pact with China, backed the "liberation" of Tibet, and praised Peking's forbearance in not occupying Bhutan and Sikkim as well.

[107] *Guide Daily*, Nov. 23, 1950.

XVIII

Prospects and Problems

BECAUSE of the difficulty of achieving proper balance and perspective, a narrative account of political developments within Burma since 1953 is neither feasible nor desirable. It will perhaps suffice to define some of the basic characteristics and problems which appear likely to persist as factors of political significance and concern for the immediate future.

Political Leadership

Of primary importance is an understanding of the locus of political power and the fundamental problems of those who wield this power. The central postindependence figure was, of course, U Nu. He was until June, 1956, simultaneously Prime Minister of the government and the president of the A.F.P.F.L. He was the champion of democracy in Burma, the liaison between the sophisticated modernism of Burma's younger generation and the traditional cultural values of old Burma, and, finally, Burma's good-will salesman abroad par excellence. His personal rectitude and his reputation as an advocate of public welfare afforded him a vantage point from which he could denounce in measured terms the manifold shortcomings of both his government and his party. He became an enthusiastic lay defender of religious revival, which to him provided a kind of stabilizing reaffirmation of Burma's national culture. He was also a patron of indigenous literary efforts and the chief supporter of the Burma Translation So-

625

ciety, which undertook to make foreign books of merit available in Burmese translation. Although some of his countrymen apparently discounted the Premier's "surfeit of sincerity" and regarded his religious concern as little more than a propagandist's pose,[1] U Nu clearly possessed the confidence of the Burmese people to a marked degree, including that of the minority groups.

Premier Nu defended the government's revolutionary program as a necessary measure to uproot a colonial-type ideology and to set up a regime dedicated to human progress and well-being. Irresponsible power was, in his opinion, not revolutionary but reactionary; free elections were needed to hold political and military strength accountable to the people's will. Dictatorships, he declared, inevitably turned reactionary because, as the Lord Buddha said, man relishes evil more than good.[2] In his view, greediness and exploitation arose primarily from a failure to recognize the basic Buddhist truth that material things are impermanent and fleeting. The profit motive was wrong essentially because it led the strong to want more than they needed to have. The *Pyidawtha* effort, by contrast, was the attempt of a government, sharing the people's confidence, to carry out the people's will. The moderate and legal character of Burma's democratic regime, he affirmed, repudiated the maxim of the kings of old Burma that many innocent must suffer to ensure that no evil-intentioned person survived. U Nu also praised democracy domestically as a means of ending the forcible scramble for power, traditional to Burma, whenever a ruler died or a government changed. Democracy guaranteed for the people freedom to criticize the authorities, to form rival parties, and to worship freely. It also put an end to old Burma's traditional warfare with its neighbors, which historically had prepared the way for imperialist domination.[3] These were clearly not the utterances of a Marxist revolutionary.

But U Nu shared power with two Socialist Party leaders, U Ba Swe and U Kyaw Nyein, who took their socialism seriously and whose mass political following constituted by far the most influential element of the A.F.P.F.L. U Ba Swe was by reputation approachable and

---

[1] Tun Pe, *Sun over Burma*, pp. 7–12.

[2] Thakin Nu, *Forward with the People* (Rangoon, 1951), pp. 9–14, 62. On August 24, 1953, U Nu told representatives of the armed services that real soldiers were distinguished from gunmen by their avoidance of bullying the weak, of ill-treating the people, of looting and plundering. Soldiers guilty of such conduct were traitors to the Union, he declared.

[3] *Ibid.*, pp. 45–55.

forthright, neither devious nor intriguing, albeit committed in a thoroughgoing way to the relentless nationalization of all important aspects of Burma's economic life.[4] His formal education was meager, and his political authority derived from certain elemental traits of personality which attracted a wide following. He was from its organization closely identified with the All Burma Peasants' Organization, of which Thakin Tin, the minister of land nationalization, was the perennial president. This organization became the rural activating arm of the A.F.P.F.L., and had vast political influence and responsibility for administering the land nationalization program.[5]

As minister of labor and head of the T.U.C. (Burma), U Ba Swe was the idol of his working-class political followers, who proudly displayed their red hammer and sickle flag and cheered their leader's Burma-brand Marxism. As minister of defense, U Ba Swe was director of the anti-insurgent operations of the army as well as of irregular local defense forces. In co-operation with the minister of the interior, U Khin Maung Gale, the Socialist Party could command directly the services of the independently recruited Union military police and the undisciplined *Yebaw* "peace guerrilla" contingents. Finally, U Ba Swe acted as Deputy Premier and headed one of the principal government corporations. In June, 1956, he took over the Premiership temporarily. His authority was quite independent of U Nu.

The other outstanding Socialist leader was U Kyaw Nyein, an intelligent and well-informed person, who evaluated Marxist principles in operation with enough clarity to see why state ownership and collectivization frequently do not work as planned.[6] He was somewhat less doctrinaire than U Ba Swe and also differed from U Nu by attaching little faith to the assumption that Buddhism alone could interpose an effective barrier to the Communist impact on Burma. As previously indicated, he was convinced that a frontal attack on pov-

---

[4] As an example of the methods used, U Ba Swe as labor minister interdicted by police action, in 1955, the operation of a private bus line in Rangoon. He forced the bus owners to accept a fixed nominal fee for each round trip and installed his own T.U.C. (Burma) drivers organized as a pseudoco-operative bus organization. This was done as a policy decision without benefit of hearings or enabling legislation, subject only to the possibility of court redress for some of the bus owners who refused to go along. The court later denied any redress.

[5] Leaders of the All Burma Peasants' Organization frequently clashed with their A.F.P.F.L. urban counterparts and usually won out in the contest for power.

[6] A case in point was the splendidly equipped cotton textile factory at Insein, which operated at a heavy loss under inefficient state management, partly because the long-staple cotton required had to be imported.

erty as such was required. U Kyaw Nyein was at times a thorn in the side of faculty members in the university council because of his advocacy of the revamping of the curriculum along Socialist lines. As secretary of the A.F.P.F.L. and as minister of industries, U Kyaw Nyein directed the ambitious program of industrialization. His authority was, therefore, considerable, but he had sometimes been rash, and he lacked the mass personal following enjoyed by some of his colleagues. U Kyaw Nyein re-entered the cabinet in early 1953 and was a prime mover and a leading participant in the Asian Socialist Conference which convened at Rangoon in early 1953. The objective of the conference was to strengthen the ties between the various Asian Socialist parties and to relate them to the broader world Socialist program. Mr. Clement Attlee participated as an honored observer from England representing the British Labour Party.[7]

Many of the second- and third-level leaders of the A.F.P.F.L. serving as army officers, ambassadors, ministers, and board chairmen and as directors of the supporting Socialist mass organization groups were friends of the top three political figures or were associated with the prewar Thakin Party and especially with the university strikers of 1936. Especially noteworthy were Thakin Tin, older than most of his colleagues and the champion of land nationalization as president of the All Burma Peasants' Organization, and U Khin Maung Gale, the home minister. The latter directed not only the regular police but also the Bureau of Special Investigation and the Union military police, which some were inclined to regard as a Socialist Party army.[8] Bogyoke Ne Win, as head of the regular army, was a close friend and confidant of Premier Nu but kept somewhat aloof from active politics. The ranking Socialist Party leader in the army was Brigadier General Aung Gyi. As a nonpolitical agency under General Ne Win, the Burma army gradually developed into an enlarged, well-officered, and disciplined force. The leading prewar nationalist leader, U Ba Pe, was discredited, not merely because of his propensities toward corruption, but also by reason of alleged treasonable intrigue.[9]

The A.F.P.F.L. operated as a well-organized group, capable of disciplining defiant members and of settling local feuds, which fre-

[7] *Burma*, III (1953), 8–20, 34, 35.

[8] Some contingents of the Union military police, as at Taunggyi, contained hill-people recruits and were highly competent military units, not politically indoctrinated in any sense. The Bureau of Special Investigation functioned under Premier Nu's authority to ferret out corruption at all levels of government.

[9] For the story of U Ba Pe's final intrigue, see *Hindu*, Jan. 3, 1955.

628

quently arose between urban leaders and those of the All Burma Peasants' Organization. It seemed at times peculiarly susceptible to student pressure, which tended to follow the Communist line. Through its local units, persons elected to the various local council groups could be influenced in the use of their powers.[10] The party from top to bottom was more Western than traditionalist, more nationalist than Marxist. Collectivization was favored as a means of strengthening and modernizing Burma, allegedly in the interest of the people as a whole, rather than to the advantage of the prewar foreign moneylenders and investors and a favored few of the Burmans. Burma's sophisticated youthful leadership was on the whole fully committed to the adaptation and assimilation of the varied contributions of the outside world in terms of social objectives, philosophical evaluations, and technological skills including Western medicine and health procedures. Relatively few youth in high political position shared Premier Nu's concern to revive traditional ethical and religious values per se.[11]

Administrative Problems

The necessity for realizing a higher performance in terms of honesty and efficiency in governmental administration has been repeatedly stressed by Premier Nu and other observers. The situation had been far from satisfactory before the war, as the Bribery and Corruption Enquiry had demonstrated. The Burman regime would have been hardpressed to fill the gaps in the traditional departments of government following the withdrawal of efficient British and Indian personnel. The task became almost impossibly difficult with the proliferation of the bureaucratic structure consequent on the undertaking of a planned economy. The need for staffing expanded governmental services and the scores of minor economic projects produced the elevation of many unqualified but politically favored persons into posts demanding trustworthiness, technical competence, administrative experience, and capacity for accepting responsibility.

[10] The government's paper, *New Times of Burma* (March 13 and 14, 1953), exhorted local committees of the All Burma Peasants' Organization and the A.F.P.F.L. to see that men of requisite qualifications and character were elected to local self-government councils "without unreasonable discrimination on political grounds."

[11] Under government encouragement, the schools and segments of the university endeavored to revive the tradition of doing reverence to elders and to teachers. Most of the staff and the students of the university paid little heed to this effort and adopted a strictly secularist attitude which repudiated all religious tenets.

As the plans for state-sponsored economic development matured in 1952 and 1953, administrative standards apparently became worse instead of better. Virtually every high official in the secretariat reportedly tried to get control of some nationalized enterprise or industry, which meant a chance for enhancement of personal power and income. Cabinet jobs multiplied, as did chairmanships and member posts on the numerous project boards. It was not the modest salaries paid but rather the perquisites of government service that attracted incumbents—a residence, a car and driver, the prestige of high connections politically, and then the opportunity to dispense favors. Sheer incompetence and the lack of incentive for efficient performance added their heavy toll in failure to translate plans, appropriations, materials, and labor into tangible, productive facilities.[12]

The efforts of high-level leaders of government to correct such deficiencies have been largely ineffectual. As one editor pointed out, denunciation of bungling and corruption was of no avail so long as the state continued to embark on additional large-scale enterprises for the management of which competent men with experience were simply not available.[13] The establishment of the Bureau of Special Investigation under the Premier and the home minister with plenary authority to ferret out corruption tended to check flagrant abuses of power, but the problem of inefficiency was aggravated because it became more hazardous for officials to take responsibility for decisions. Premier Nu even felt obliged to caution officers within the Bureau of Special Investigation against the tendency to be puffed up with power, haughty, and swaggering in their relations with the people generally.[14]

The malfeasance and inefficiency in which the State Agricultural Marketing Board (S.A.M.B.) became involved were destined to cost Burma's economic development program dearly. The opportunities for

[12] Completed housing projects in Rangoon were often sadly deficient in water and sanitary facilities; road construction languished for lack of engineers numerous enough and experienced in the task; innumerable blocks and bottlenecks plagued the lives of foreign experts trying to see plans through to completion.

[13] *Nation*, June 4, 1953. The editorial called attention to the heavy losses being incurred in 1953 in the potentially profitable inland water transport operation as a result of its assignment to political operators. Eventually efficient Chittagonian crews were put back on the river steamers. The editor declared: "It is folly for the government to go into technical fields, of which the I.W.T. . . . was one, without filling this vital defect [by supplying competent management]."

[14] A routine notation that a particular university department was responsible for library books assigned to it frequently resulted in the locking up of books for safekeeping and their complete inaccessibility to students who should be reading them. See Thakin Nu, *Forward with the People*, pp. 65–66.

carelessness and graft were enormous in executing the vast responsibilities of the board for purchasing, transporting, processing, and marketing abroad Burma's annual rice crop.[15] As long as export prices remained abnormally high (£50 or more per ton), the board could and did realize enormous profits despite its admitted deficiencies.[16] Serious trouble loomed when, during the last quarter of 1953, Burma's rice output increased to 85 per cent of the prewar level, while both the price and the volume of overseas sales began to decline.[17] Unfortunately no adequate measures were taken to prepare storage facilities in anticipation of a buyers' market. The substantial carry-over of unmarketed rice from purchases made in the spring of 1954 was vastly increased a year later. Important barriers to increased sales were the efforts of Burma's S.A.M.B. to maintain a price above the world level combined with deterioration of the quality available for export. This was due to poor handling and storage facilities, including failure to prevent, through proper fumigation methods, infestation of granaries by insects and weevils. From every market came complaints that Burma's rice was not up to standard.

In a desperate effort to move the mounting surpluses for which storage was lacking, Burma's marketing agencies concluded a number of barter agreements, many of them involving Communist countries who were anxious to gain entrance into Burma for their own goods and technical services. Most of the large volume of expensive capital equipment on order called for payment in dollars or sterling exchange; the government was thus obliged in 1955, because of foreign exchange deficiencies, to curtail normal consumer-goods imports sharply in order to conserve its foreign currency while hoping that some of the materials in short supply might be obtained by barter. Thus the two most lucrative sources of government income, from rice exports and from import duties on goods purchased by rice profits, contracted drastically during 1955–1956. To these losses of revenue was added the spoilage of vast quantities of government-owned paddy for which

[15] Available to almost any clerk was the opportunity to misrepresent the amount of paddy purchased by getting the peasant seller to sign a blank receipt; this would be filled in at the discretion of the official who was to profit from the transaction. See the *Nation*, March 18, 1956.

[16] Thakin Nu, *Forward with the People*, p. 6. Premier Nu, in February, 1953, admitted that the S.A.M.B. had functioned imperfectly in the procurement and movement of rice, but he thought that conditions were improving.

[17] Frank Trager, *Toward a Welfare State in Burma* (New York, 1954), pp. 16, 23. Rice sales declined by 20 per cent in volume and by 23 per cent in price during the last quarter of 1953.

no storage was available during the rains. Moves on the part of the Bureau of Special Investigation to check the alleged contents of a number of storage premises produced repeated burnings of the go-downs under investigation. The eventual indictment and removal of high officers of the S.A.M.B. helped the situation but little. The assignment of the able M. A. Raschid to the post of minister of foreign trade was one of the few hopeful aspects of the situation.[18]

Burma's foreign economic advisers could still make out a plausible case that Burma's economic crisis of 1955–1956 was only temporary because increased production under the development program would eventually more than compensate for immediate sacrifices. But such a conclusion was clearly contingent upon the government's improved ability to make these numerous enterprises tangibly productive and profitable. In the meantime the value of the kyat steadily declined on the international exchange. If Burma failed to recover lost markets and if the world price of rice tumbled further, the government's unqualified commitment to purchase domestic paddy from cultivators at 280 kyats per 100 baskets might preclude any large future profits on rice sales abroad even if the business were more efficiently handled. Meanwhile Burma was becoming creditor on a state-to-state basis to numerous Communist countries from whom it was frequently impossible to purchase the goods needed at reasonable prices.[19]

Education and Religion

Aggravating Burma's lack of administrative talent were the deficiencies of the educational program supposed to meet the need for trained and responsible personnel. Selected individuals sent abroad for advanced study on state scholarships usually performed creditably, but the product of the public schools program in Burma designed to fill third- and fourth-level posts was discouraging. This was notwithstanding the government's considerable outlays for education and its adoption of a policy of free tuition through the university and professional schools. The lack of success was attributable in large

[18] On the occasion of the first arrests of S.A.M.B. leaders in 1955, the entire staff attempted to force their reinstatement by resigning en masse. When Minister Raschid moved to accept the resignations, the staff agreed to come back on his terms. Serious embarrassment for Raschid developed in May, 1956, over excessive purchases of cement on barter account in Communist Europe.

[19] Burma sent rice to Ceylon on China's credit account to pay for rubber shipments from Ceylon to China. Rice bartered to the U.S.S.R. was sent to food-short North Vietnam. Purchasing missions sent to Communist Europe found the prices high and types of available export goods limited.

measure to overrapid extension of the program of English instruction to all schools in grades above the fifth standard. This was coupled with a shortsighted reduction of the preparatory program from ten years to nine. Weaknesses arising from the scarcity of qualified teachers, especially in English, were aggravated by habits of student indiscipline and lack of industry, a problem which dated from the prewar period. The percentage of passes in the combined high school final and matriculation examinations in 1950 was only 17 per cent; by 1955, it fell to 11 per cent. Even so, attendance at Rangoon University increased from a prewar level of 2,000 students to 8,000 in 1955. Another negative aspect of the situation was that school training tended to destroy respect for elders and to widen the gap between youth and parents by the propagation of antitraditional views and ideologies.[20]

An investigating UNESCO Educational Mission, visiting Burma in 1951, reported that the teacher-training program was totally inadequate, that retirement of school administrators at the age of fifty-five robbed the schools of badly needed experience, and that motivation was artificial and divorced from an appreciation of the intrinsic value of the educational opportunity per se. The mission recommended that external examinations for high school graduation be abolished and that matriculation to the university be decided on other relevant grounds. Parents and teachers needed to develop a better degree of understanding and co-operation, and local education boards would have to accept greater responsibility for meeting the appalling need of equipment. It recommended also that English instruction should begin on a noncompulsory basis at the third grade level and that the full ten-year preparatory program be revived.[21] Meanwhile the government discontinued Judson College as part of the university system on the alleged grounds that it had caused disagreements and had given rise to problems of disciplinary control. Alternative contributions to higher education by missionaries were similarly discouraged.[22]

The crucial problem of educational indiscipline and disaffection centered on the campus of Rangoon University and particularly in the

[20] *Bama Khit*, Sept. 25, 1950.

[21] UNESCO Educational Mission, *Report of the Mission to Burma, May, 1951*, by R. M. Tisinger, C. L. Hernandez, and F. T. Fairey, pp. 16–45.

[22] See Burma, *Report of the Education Reconstruction Committee* (Rangoon, 1947), p. 12. The outbreak of the Karen rebellion was responsible in part for the government's vetoing a proposed American Baptist Mission technical school at Moulmein. Both the Karens and the Kachins were particularly enthusiastic about education. The Karens preferred English to Burmese as a second language. See UNESCO Educational Mission, *Report*, pp. 46–56.

activity of the University Student Union. Thakins Aung San and Nu and other leaders of government had themselves contributed much to the prewar tradition of political activity on the part of university students, especially in connection with their vigorous agitation of 1936 to 1939 for reform of the University Act. Now the Premier's homilies regarding concentration of student attention on religion and academic studies were notoriously ineffective. Politicians were still tempted to fan the flames of unrest,[23] while the predominant temper of the campus was one of disrespect toward teachers and authority. The standard of English fell so low that lectures in many departments slowed down to longhand dictation speed. Attendance at lectures became casual in the extreme. A student riot in October, 1953, occasioned by a protest against the council's shortening of the vacation period, required the intervention of police with rifles and tear-gas bombs to quell it.

Convocation addresses by the Premier, speaking as chancellor of the university, only dramatized the problem. He stressed the need for a Buddhist revival, for the erasure of greed, anger, and ignorance, and for a demonstration of diligence in the pursuit of training which would qualify students to serve their country. He denounced renegade students who were catering to politicians with special interests, who were interfering with educational activities, who were "ignoramuses, Mr. Zeroes, destructionists." All who wanted to play politics, he declared, should leave the campus.[24]

Immediately following the 1953 riots the Chancellor-Premier based his appeal for purity of mind, action, and speech and for the search for wisdom and knowledge directly on the four noble Truths of the Buddhist faith. On these, he declared, depended one's future plane of existence. For those students interested only in their mundane personal advancement, he pointed out that they would get nowhere by frittering away their time, by interfering with others, or by becoming dupes of outside manipulators. He attempted to demonstrate the theme that all outside powers acted in self-interest by citing the many vagaries of Soviet power politics since 1917. It was, he insisted, a

---

[23] In September, 1950, when the Student Union was trying to oust the slanderous and vindictive pro-Communist leader, Maung Maung Kyaw, in favor of new officers with a serious purpose as students, U Ba Swe slowed these efforts by blasting the existing education system as only another version of the colonial system and by urging students to enter politics in order to change the evil system. See *Voice of the Union,* Sept. 10, 1950.

[24] Thakin Nu, *From Peace to Stability* (Rangoon, 1951), pp. 180–188.

matter of elemental wisdom to avoid insulting great powers who could hurt you, and rather to be prepared to act in concert with them where mutual advantage could be served. Burma had no place in the future for political leaders who gaped in idle admiration of others and neglected their own training by playing politics. Students capable of corruption in elections and of persistent abuse of senior teachers could not be trusted as future leaders of the country. The country, he concluded, had had more than enough of rebellion, agitation, and lawlessness, of opportunism and corruption.[25]

The Premier's sane counsel was, for most, only the voice of one crying in the wilderness. Politics under direct Communist instigation continued to harass the educational program of the university. Attendance at lectures was lax and study habits lackadaisical. The basic temper of antireligious secularism influenced younger staff members as well as students, and political opportunism played a considerable role in administrative and instructional policies as well as in student activities. The students of the university were exposed, as was no other segment of Burma's population, to the full effect of the "acids of modernity" from the outside world, and they habitually blamed others for their frustrations. To many of them, religious inculcation was irrelevant to the achievement of personal advancement and to the attainment of the social and economic objectives of the modern state. Many believed that seriousness as a student had no positive correlation with economic or political success. It will probably take a long while to dislodge this debilitating tradition. Meanwhile the university provided as many problems as solutions in the matter of political and administrative responsibility.

A different aspect of Burma's problem of cultural reintegration, at the other end of the religious spectrum, was the persistence of animistic beliefs and practices coupled with a continuing regard for the wisdom of astrologers and numerologists and for the purveyors of charms and talismen. Newspapers in 1951 gave serious attention to the assertion of a leading astrologer that the government should have taken care to determine the propitious day for starting the elections and that it could ensure continuance in office and protection against evils by building within Rangoon suitable *nat* shrines where the spirits could be effectively propitiated.[26] Manipuri Brahman practi-

---

[25] Thakin Nu, *Forward with the People*, pp. 84–98.
[26] *The Burman*, March 5 and 30, 1951.

tioners around Mandalay enjoyed after the war a revival of popularity as soothsayers, astrologers, numerologists, and instructors in Hindu *Yoga* exercises.

Finally there remained the task of working out a satisfactory relationship between the Burma Government and the newly revived ecclesiastical authority within the *Sangha*. Six leading *Sayadaws* under the presidency of the Nyaungyan *Sayadaw* made up the *Sangha Weneiksaya* or high ecclesiastical court at Mandalay. Its jurisdiction was shared by a number of local *Vinissaya* courts. But within a Buddhist order always hypersensitive to any suggestion of governmental interference, disgruntled or indisciplined groups tended to bring their alleged grievances into the political arena.[27] The center of monastic indiscipline as well as of *pongyi* political activity remained, as before the war, in the capital city, Rangoon.[28]

The ultimate political results of U Nu's convening of the Sixth Buddhist Council are difficult to ascertain. Sophisticated critics of the Premier denounced him for satisfying his personal vanity by imitating King Mindon and also for acting unilaterally in the matter before obtaining approval of the move from his own cabinet members and from the executive council of the A.F.P.F.L. The expensive imitation-cave convention hall, the foundation of which was laid in February, 1954, was ridiculed by some as a traditionalist anachronism. The elaborate ceremonial recitation of the sacred Pali texts without any thoroughgoing effort at textual criticism was meaningless to many. The expenditure of 60 lakhs of kyats (6 million) on an allegedly useless and discredited Pali University and "peace pagoda" was similarly discounted as ill-advised.[29] Burma's assembling of alleged Buddhist relics from India, Ceylon, and China clearly looked to the past and not to the future.

In the Premier's apologia for convening the Buddist conference, he made a defensible case for the necessity of dispelling shameless and immoral monks from the *Sangha* and for determining and publishing

[27] *Nation*, June 10 and 22, 1953. In June, 1953, monks in Rangoon who had been ejected from their *kyaung* by the local *Vinissaya* court appealed for redress to the central ecclesiastical court and then to the civil court of Rangoon.

[28] *The Burman*, Sept. 21 and 24, 1951. In one instance, 150 demonstrating monks, apparently of the better sort, demanded the names of those responsible for leaking the Pali examination questions and called for the removal of self-seekers in yellow robes. On September 24, 1951, some 300 monks besieged a gate of the secretariat. They denied that legislative enactments were binding on the monks and demanded that police seize Sten guns hidden in *pongyi kyaungs* in Rangoon.

[29] Tun Pe, *Why I Resigned from the Cabinet* (Rangoon, 1953), pp. 1–7.

a corrected and annotated version of the scriptures, as recommended by the *Mahatheras* (great teachers). But why did this call for the cave and for relics? U Nu's recitation as history of the fabled visit of the Buddha himself to Mon Burma accompanied by some 20,000 *arahats* (monks) and the even more remarkable subsequent daily journeys by air for a week by the Buddha and 500 accompanying *arahats* between Upper Burma and the Jetvana monastery in India [30] strained the credulity of the most believing. And yet Premier Nu's policy of religious revival undoubtedly served to strengthen the hands and the influence of reputable *Sayadaws*, who now acted with greater confidence and assurance in the knowledge that in U Nu and in the judicial branch of the government particularly they had friends in high places. Whether the propitiation of the *nats* or revival of a religion of withdrawal from ephemeral mundane considerations could make any affirmative contribution to a socialist welfare state the Burmese alone would have to judge, but the country stood to gain immeasurably in its social cohesion and its moral fiber if the *Sangha* could be purged of impostors and the ethics of the Buddha restored to a position of respect.

Regionalism and the Minority Peoples

Contesting the basic commitment of Burma's political leaders to a planned welfare state was their equally adamant determination to fashion an effective instrument of government for the entire country which could assert its authority everywhere in behalf of governmental objectives. This nationalist ideal includes as an implied goal the eventual absorption of various ethnic components into a unified national social structure. Such a development calls for a negation of regionalism, linguistic division, and racial or religious communalism. Culturally, the sharpest tensions are probably found with the politically conscious religious groups such as the Muslims and the Christians. The All Burma Muslim Congress was refused in early 1956 continued affiliation with the A.F.P.F.L. as a communal political group. The Christianized Karens harbored their ingrained fear of Burman rule and treasured their considerable assimilation of American and European cultural contributions. Burma's Chinese community at its postwar size was assimilable and would probably constitute no serious problem unless Burma should become involved in another Far Eastern war. Marriage to Burmese women afforded a continuing means of

[30] Thakin Nu, *Forward with the People*, pp. 144–169.

637

assimilation. What would happen to the constitutional provision for religious freedom if Buddhism became the principal touchstone of cultural homogeneity and patriotism was nevertheless a matter of concern to all minority groups.

Regionally, the most critical issues arose in the Arakan, where the tradition of long-continued independence from Burmese control (prior to 1784 and after 1825) was still very much alive, and in the traditionally autonomous states of the Shan *Sawbwas* and the chiefs of Karenni. Elsewhere, the problem of political and cultural assimilation concerned the continued Burmanization of the Kachin and Chin peoples of the hill areas of the upper Irrawaddy Valley and the mountainous India-border areas. The special Ministry of Culture was created to promote the process of assimilation.[31] The Burman majority was quite prepared to acknowledged the political and cultural contributions of minority groups to national independence and welfare and took care to say nothing in disparagement of their customs and aspirations. But a homogeneous people was the inevitable goal.[32]

The immediate political aspect of the problem of maintaining the Union of Burma intact centered around the special right accorded to the several subordinate states (except the Kachin) under Chapter X of the constitution to secede from the Union after ten years' time. The ten-year period would expire in 1958. The problem was particularly urgent with respect to the Shan State, a large strategically important area containing valuable known mineral deposits and other potentialities for economic development. The hereditary Shan chiefs (*Sawbwas*) resisted firmly early postwar efforts at Burman political infiltration, but during the Kuomintang emergency of 1952 they had agreed to relinquish certain executive powers to the central authority. The Burman press, somewhat prematurely, hailed the event as a bloodless revolution marking a milestone in the political development of the Shan people and in the destruction of feudal fetishes

[31] Po Lat, "Union Culture: Its Sources and Contacts," *Burma*, vol. III (Oct., 1952). The official view was that a unity of culture existed among the peoples of the Union and that existing differences are only expressions of the same culture at different stages of development. The Burman and Pyu peoples had long since been amalgamated; the Mons had been almost absorbed, and Shan assimilation was in progress. The Karens, Kachins, and Chins were also mainly Tibeto-Burman, and all were allegedly suitable for becoming parts of a closely knit cultural organism.

[32] *New Times of Burma*, Feb. 12 and 13, 1953. U Tun Pe as minister of Union culture on the anniversary of Union Day (dating from the Panglong Conference of 1947) stressed the sovereign equality of all the peoples of Burma under the constitution and urged that racial and sectional rivalries be submerged in a common patriotism and a just and fair distribution of wealth.

carried over from British (and pre-British) times.[33] The politically sophisticated *Sawbwas,* fully cognizant of undercover efforts sponsored by elements of the A.F.P.F.L. to subvert their authority, drew closer together in their own United Hill Peoples' Congress. They also established temporary liaison, in 1955, with Toungthu (Pa-O) rebel elements who were at the time being hard pressed militarily by central government forces. Whether or not Shan State would opt for independence in 1958 became an important issue, but not a clear-cut one, in the 1956 elections. Much would depend on the kind of terms Rangoon would be prepared to offer the Shans, at the time of decision, for continued adherence to the Union of Burma.[34]

What happened in the Shan State would inevitably have wide repercussions elsewhere in Burma. The otherwise hopeless Karen-Mon rebellion active in parts of Salween, Thaton, and Amherst districts was apparently being kept alive in the forlorn expectation that upcoming events might facilitate the creation of an independent Karen State with a seaboard after all. Karenni (or Kayah) would also probably follow closely the pattern set by the Shan State. If concessions in favor of local autonomy were eventually made to peoples living east of the Sittang Valley, the demand for Arakan self-rule, quite vocal since 1951, would reach a fever pitch. Akyab realized little or no economic recovery from the leveling it suffered during the war, and the broad road under construction from Prome westward to the Arakan coast was not likely to improve Burman-Arakanese relations materially.

Dissident Chin leaders were kept in line after 1948 by "marrying" them to the government's bureaucracy (the modern substitute for the old king's harem). A.F.P.F.L. political control in the Kachin State was also tenuous,[35] but the Kachins enjoyed no option under the constitution to secede from the Union and also little political choice

---

[33] U.S. Information Service, "Review of Burmese Press Comment," Oct. 1 and 20, 1952.

[34] The triangular political contest in 1956 was between the United Hill Peoples' Congress, the United National Pa-O Association, and the All Shan States' Organization (part of the A.F.P.F.L.). Although the Pa-O disliked *Sawbwa* rule, now weak, they seemed to prefer it to stronger Burman control (see the *Nation,* March 14, 1956). The United Hill Peoples' Congress won fourteen seats and the All Shan States' Organization only one in 1956.

[35] *Nation,* June 1, 1953. The A.F.P.F.L.-sponsored Kachin minister, Sama Duwa Sinwa Nawng, fell into ill repute with the Burma Government in 1953 for sponsoring a grandiose scheme of industrial development. He was eventually displaced by a Kachin Christian leader, who was not subject to Rangoon's direct control. The rebel Kachin "Robin Hood," Naw Seng, operated for a number of years on both sides of the Burma-China border. Sama Duwa's group won the 1956 election.

but to continue in it. They were separated from Communist China only by an undemarcated boundary, with Kachin relatives living on both sides. The genuine tradition of Arakanese nationalism and Karen resentment over alleged discrimination plus the divide-and-rule tactics of the government in playing political favorites and pitting Karen against Karen appeared to be the most formidable barriers to realizing the objective of political and cultural homogeneity.[36] National unification problems will doubtless concern Burma's rulers for many decades.

As the party which accomplished Burma's independence and saw the Union through the dark days of the rebellions and as the sponsor of the *Pyidawtha* welfare state project, the A.F.P.F.L. with its political appeal and its superior organization was certain to be carried to victory in the general elections of 1956. Popular dissatisfaction with the performance of the ruling party prevailed on a considerable scale, but it covered the entire political gamut from left to right and could not, therefore, be effectively organized. The Nationalist Unity Front tended to play into the pro-Communist hands of the Burma Workers' and Peasants' Party, despite Justice U E Maung's active participation. The underground Communists, in process of liquidation by the army, were not in the political picture in 1956, and the Karens had lost all but seven of their twenty-four communal constituencies after the Karen State had been formed in 1953.

The outcome of the 1956 elections was nevertheless mildly surprising. The Nationalist Unity Front coalition, including mainly the Burma Workers' and Peasants' Party and assorted Communists such as Thakin Thein Pe Myint, captured 43 seats, more than the entire opposition had garnered in 1951. The Arakan nationalists again swept the polls except in one election district where their candidate was jailed. A clear majority of the Kachin State seats went to the party of a leader who had in 1953 broken with the A.F.P.F.L. The United Hill Peoples' Congress, allied temporarily but not identified with the A.F.P.F.L., won nearly all of the Shan seats in Parliament. Incomplete returns as of June 14 (some contests were postponed) indicated 138 seats for the straight A.F.P.F.L. candidates plus nearly 30 from allied groups in a total of 217.

The most noteworthy change in the new cabinet, which was formed in mid-June, was the elevation of U Ba Swe to the Premiership. U Nu

---

[36] For a discussion of Socialist Party policy within the Karen State, see articles in the *Nation*, Jan. 29 to Feb. 3, 1955.

resigned voluntarily, ostensibly to find time to reorganize and purify the A.F.P.F.L. and to generate, if possible, an improvement of public morale and of standards of public conduct.

As in 1949, when the Socialists withdrew temporarily from the cabinet, the shift was made without contest or rancor. The presumption was therefore strong that U Nu would continue active in political and governmental affairs.[37] He resumed the Premiership early in 1957.

The boast of the A.F.P.F.L. that it would rule Burma for the coming forty years continued to be an improbable claim. Most observers nevertheless conceded that the league would continue in power for another decade, long enough to see whether the leader's dreams of a strong, united, and progressive Burma were likely to be realized. Burma needed time, accumulated experience, and internal peace.

Internationally, independent Burma was convinced that she had no choice but to stay on good terms with Communist China and to give the Peking regime no provocation which could result in intervention. Thus may be explained the furor in 1952–1953 over the Kuomintang affair, Burma's support of Peking's entry into the United Nations, and Rangoon's repudiation of Formosa. Most Burmans believed that friendship with China was feasible as well as necessary, although border difficulties would inevitably arise. In collaboration with India and Indonesia in particular, Burma followed a strictly neutral course with respect to the world tension between the United States and the U.S.S.R. It opposed any move of the anti-Communist powers which seemed likely to make Southeast Asia a theater of operations in another world war. Burman opinion regarded the Ho Chi Minh regime in North Vietnam as more genuinely nationalist than that of Ngo Dinh Diem in the South. Any overt move by Chinese armies southward would probably drive the neutralists into the Western camp, but this contingency seemed unlikely from Rangoon's point of view as long as Southeast Asia did not itself constitute a base from which the security of the Chinese Communist regime could be threatened.

Although Burma moved to cancel her military treaty with the United Kingdom in January, 1953, relations with London continued friendly and respectful; a comprehensive debt settlement was signed in November, 1953. Of the United States, Burmans were somewhat prone to believe the evil rather than the good and were not quite convinced that America could be trusted to use its vast power wisely. Burma was more friendly with Yugoslavia than with any other Communist

[37] *Nation*, May 5–16, June 12–14, 1956.

country (Tito's independence was a factor), but they also watched achievements in China with interest and were fully prepared to accept help from any quarter provided it was free from political strings. The U.S.S.R., as an instigator of world revolution, was not trusted by many, but Moscow was also conveniently distant.[38] Friendly relations with Russia served conveniently to discredit further the threadbare canard of the Burma Communists that the country continued to be a preserve of the colonial imperialists.

Finally, Burma attributed high value to its membership in the United Nations, through which alone it could play a significant role in world affairs and to which it must look in the long run for its guarantee of survival as an independent state. Burma's future depends not only on its ability to deal with pressing internal problems but also on an improvement in the climate of world affairs.

[38] In June, 1954, U Kyaw Nyein characterized the Communist world revolution as more ruthless, more systematic, more inclusive and blatantly self-justified than the old-style imperialism (U.S. Information Service, "Review of Burmese Press Comment," for June, 1954).

GLOSSARY, BIBLIOGRAPHY, AND INDEX

Glossary

Adipadi, leader (Fuehrer), head of state (also spelled *Adhipati*)
Ahmudan, royal-service status
Akunwun, granary supervisor or revenue officer
Anashin Mingyi, lit. "dictator king," Ba Maw's assumed title
Aphwe, association
Arahat, monk
Aso, service corps group
Aso-ya-min, bureaucratic middle-class group
Asu, royal-service unit
Athi, nonroyal-service status
Athin, synonym for *asu*
Athintha, royal-service population
Athiwun, official in charge of *athi* population
Atwinwun, lit. "interior burden-bearer," palace privy councilor
Azat gaung, ward constable
Baho, central (also headquarters)
Bama, Burman or Burmese ("Burman," as used herein, refers to the majority
  ethnic group)
Batamabyan, Pali examination
Bo, colonel (commissioned officer in royal Burma army); title recently ap-
  propriated by any leader of armed band
Bogyoke, general
Byedaik, lit. "bachelor quarters," palace office of the *Atwinwuns*
Chaukri, riverine customs post
Crore, Hindustani for 10,000,000
Dacoit, armed brigand
Daing gaung, supervisor of a service unit
Dattaw, sacred-relic items
Daw, lit. "auntie," title for mature Burman lady; also pertaining to royalty or
  government
Dhamma, Buddhist law
Dhamma Chariya, Buddhist law court
Dobama, we Burmans

Dobama Asiayone, We Burmans Society

Einshemin, lit. "lord of the Eastern House," heir apparent to the throne

Gaing-gyok, district monastic "bishop"

Gale, small (the accent is on *le*)

Galon, mythical bird victorious over Naga serpent, which symbolized British imperial rule

Galon Raja, bird king; title assumed by Saya San

Gaung, head person; used for village constable

Gaung saung, political observer (of officials)

Gyi, big or great (often a suffix)

Heiho Tat, labor army (Japanese recruited)

Hkaing, township tax collector or the percentage of taxes allocated to the collector in a local administrative unit

Hlutdaw, lit. "place of release," royal council or council hall

Hpaungwun, officer in charge of royal barges

Jaghire, "fief" of royal official

Kala, color or caste; used opprobriously for Indians

Karma, the law of deed (Buddhist)

Kayaing, administrative district

Kayaingwun, district supervisor or commissioner

Kempetai, Japanese military police

Komin-Kochin Party, "One's Own King–One's Own Kind" Party (of the Thakins)

Konbaung, Burma's last dynasty

Konbo, court fees

Ko-yin, Buddhist novice monk

Kundaw, arbiter of dispute, government-authorized

Kutho, merit

Kuthodaw, royal merit memorial at Mandalay

Kwin, unit of surveyed (settlement) land

Kyat, Burmese coin theoretically worth 21 cents

Kyaung, monastery

Kyaung-serai, monastery clerk or secretary, royally appointed

Kyaungtha, monastery students

Kyedangyi, village official, largest taxpayer

Lakh, Hindustani for 100,000

Lewun, paddy land official

Ludu, mass population

Ma, title used for younger women

Maha, great

Mahabama Party, Great Burma Party (Ba Maw's)

Mahadan-wun, ecclesiastical censor

Mahagandi, Buddhist sect ("low church" group)

646

Maha Sangha, great monastic agency (Ba Maw's invention)

Mahathera, great Buddhist teacher (of 20 years' standing)

Maung, Mr., title used for younger men or in referring to one's self

Min, prince

Mingyi, great prince or king

Myanma Shwepyigyi, lit. "Burma Great Golden Country," Burma Free State

Myanma Wunthanu Aphwe, Burma (National) Service Association

Myetaing, land survey or survey for tax purposes

Myingaung, cavalry leader

Myo, town or domain

Myochit Party, Love of Country Party (U Saw's)

Myoma, principal city or part of city

Myook, British township officer

Myosa, lit. "eater of the town," princely fief holder

Myosade, sacrificial dedication of city gate or wall

Myothugyi, township headman

Myowun, royal Burmese governor

Myoyon, governor's hall or court

Nainggandaw Adipadi Anashin Mingyi, Ba Maw's full title as head of state

Nakan, messenger

Nat, spirit or devil

Nga, old synonym for *athi;* latterly applied to criminals

Ngabwinsaing, Five Groups Alliance

Okkata, chairman

Pongyi, lit. "great glory," Buddhist monk of full standing

Pwe, popular dramatic performance

Pyidawtha, lit. "pleasant royal country," freely translated as "welfare state"

Pymon, silversmith assayer-banker

Rahan, (Pali) holy man

Salut, term for nonroyal cultivated areas

Sanad, (Hindi) agreement exchanged with a Shan prince

Sangha, (Pali) assembly or order of monks

Sangha Sametggi, monks' political council

Sangha Weneiksaya, ecclesiastical court

Sasana, (Pali) religion, teaching

Sasana Takkathe, Buddhist University

Sawbwa, Shan prince

Saya, teacher

Sayadaw, royal title for abbot of Buddhist monastery

Saya-Wungyi, official palace tutor

Seridawgyi, court secretary

Shahbundar, port intendant

Shin pyu, monastic initiatory ceremony for youth

647

Shwe, gold

Shwedaik, gold house or treasury archives

Shwemyo, golden city (of Mandalay)

Sinyetha Party, "Poor Man's" Party (title of Ba Maw's party, 1936–1939)

Sitke, assistant administrative or military officer

Sittan, sworn evidence of revenue inquest

Sulagandi, Buddhist sect ("high church" group)

Swaraj, (Hindi) freedom

Taikthugyi, circle headman

Taing, administrative unit in provinces

Taing-dan, provincial or *athi* population

Tat, army

Tathmu, army lieutenant

Taungya, hill cultivation

Tawkegaung, forestry official

Taya-konbo, civil court fees

Tayathugyi, judge of civil court

Tayayon, civil law court or hall

Tha, people, son; also "pleasant"

Thakin, lord or master; title adopted by youthful members of *Dobama Asiayone*

Thamada, president

Thamadi, village tax assessor

Thathameda, Upper Burma tax on nonagricultural income

Thathanabaing, royally appointed head of Buddhist *Sangha* (the accent is on "baing")

Thenat, rifle or firearm

Thenatsaye, army captain

Thenat Wun, defense minister

Thugyi, headman

Thugyisa, plot of land alloted to the headman

Thutes, class of wealthy taxpayers

Thwethaukgyi, brotherhood (blood-mingling) leader, army sergeant

U, lit. "uncle," used to refer to respected elders, never for one's self

Upesin, qualifying examination for monk

Vinaya, (Pali) monastic discipline

Vinayathera, monk learned in discipline

Vinissaya Act, Pali University Act

Vinissaya Court, ecclesiastical court

Wa Tat, Circle Army

Windaw Hmu, palace brigade commander (there were four of them)

Wun, burden or burden-bearer, high government official

Wundauk, lit. "support (or prop) for the *Wun,*" *Hlutdaw* assistant to a *Wungyi* minister

Wungyi, great burden-bearer or royal minister of state

Wunsa, family food reserve

Wunthanu, protector of national interest; derived from *vamsa anurakkhita* (Pali)

Wunthanu athin, nationalist cell or group

Wutmye-wun, commissioner of ecclesiastical lands

Ye, water

Yebaw, soldier hero or comrade

Ye Bo Hmee, police superintendent

Yewun, lit. "water minister," officer in charge of war boats

Yoma, range of mountains

Yon, hall or shed

Ywa, village

Ywagaung, village head or constable

Zambudipa, great south island of Hindu cosmology

Zayat, resthouse

Bibliography

ABBREVIATIONS

ABFMS   American Baptist Foreign Mission Society
ABMFS   American Baptist Mission Field Secretary

Burma

BIB   Intelligence Bureau, *Burma during the Japanese Occupation*
BLCP   Legislative Council, *Proceedings*
BL,HRP   Legislature, House of Representatives, *Proceedings*
FRRIC   Home Dept., *Final Report of the Riot Inquiry Committee*
IRRIC   Home Dept., *Interim Report of the Riot Inquiry Committee*
RAB   *Report on the Administration of Burma*
RBCEC   *Report of the Bribery and Corruption Enquiry Committee*
RCII   *Report of the Committee to Ascertain . . . How the Imperial Idea May Be Inculcated*
RDC   *Review of the . . . Report . . . of District Councils and of Deputy Commissioners' Local Funds*
RFACE   *Report of the Frontier Areas Committee of Enquiry*
RLAC   *Report of the Land and Agricultural Committee*
RPA   Police Dept., *Report of the Police Administration*

Burma, Union of

RAECR   *Regional Autonomy Enquiry Commission Records*

Great Britain

BRCE   Burma Reforms Committee, *Record of Evidence*
BRCR   Burma Reforms Committee, *Report*
BRTCP   Burma Round Table Conference, *Plenary Sessions, Proceedings*
IRTC   India Round Table Conference, *Proceedings of Sub-Committees*
ISCR   India Office, *Report of the India Statutory Commission*
PD,C   Parliament, House of Commons, *Debates*
PP,C   Parliament, House of Commons, *Sessional Papers*

JBRS   *Journal of the Burma Research Society*

BIBLIOGRAPHY

I. BIBLIOGRAPHICAL GUIDES

Cordier, Henri. *Biblioteca Indosinica: Dictionnaire bibliographie des ouvrages relatifs à la Péninsule Indochinoise.* 4 vols. in 2. Paris, 1932.

Embree, John F., and Dotson, Lillian O. *Bibliography of the Peoples and Cultures of Mainland Southeast Asia.* (Yale University Southeast Asia Studies.) New Haven, 1950. Pages 150–317.

Hall, D. G. E. *A History of South-East Asia.* London, 1955. Pages 763–789.

Hobbs, Cecil C. *South-East Asia: An Annotated Bibliography of Selected Reference Sources.* Washington, 1952.

Lasker, Bruno. *Southeast Asia: A Select Bibliography.* New York, 1956.

Trager, Frank, ed. *Burma Bibliography.* (Human Relations Area Files.) New Haven, 1956.

II. PRIMARY SOURCES: ARCHIVAL MATERIALS AND GOVERNMENT PUBLICATIONS

Aitchison, C. U. *Collection of Treaties, Engagements, and Sanads.* 5th ed., vol. XII. Calcutta, 1931.

American Baptist Foreign Mission Society. *Annual Report* for 1921, 1922, 1923, 1933, 1938. New York, 1921–1938.

——. MS. Correspondence for the Burma Mission for 1921, 1923, 1924, 1925, 1931, 1938. New York headquarters.

American Baptist Mission Field Secretary. *Annual Report* for 1921, 1930, 1931. Rangoon, 1921, 1931, 1932.

Archives de Ministère des Affaires Etrangères, Chine. Vol. XVII (1855). In the Paris depository of the French Foreign Office.

Burma. *Interim Report of the Riot Inquiry Committee.* Rangoon, 1938.

——. *Report of the Agricultural Finance Committee.* Rangoon, 1929.

——. *Report of the Bribery and Corruption Inquiry Committee, 1924–1930.* Rangoon, 1930.

——. *Report of the Committee Appointed to Ascertain and Advise How the Imperial Idea May Be Inculcated and Fostered in Schools and Colleges in Burma.* Rangoon, 1917.

——. *Report of the Committee Appointed to Examine the Land Revenue System of Burma,* by J. S. Furnivall. 2 vols. Rangoon, 1922.

——. *Report of the Committee on Expenditure on the Public Services, 1939–1940.* Rangoon, 1940.

——. *Report of the Education Reconstruction Committee.* Rangoon, 1947.

——. *Report of the Frontier Areas Committee of Enquiry, 1947.* Rangoon, 1947. Pt. I, *Report;* pt. II, *Appendices.*

——. *Report of the Land and Agricultural Committee.* Rangoon, 1939, 1949. Pt. I. *Tenancy;* pt. II, *Land Alienation;* pt. III, *Agricultural Finance;* pt. IV, *Regulation of Money Lending.*

652

——. *Report of the Pali University Enquiry Committee.* Rangoon, 1941.

——. *Report of the Rangoon Town Police* for 1929, 1930, 1931, 1932, 1938. Rangoon, 1930–1939.

——. *Report of the Tantabin Incident Enquiry Committee.* Rangoon, 1947.

——. *Report of the Village Administration Committee.* Rangoon, 1941.

——. *Report on the Administration of Burma,* for 1913–1940. Rangoon, 1914–1941. Published annually.

——. *Review of the . . . Report on the Working of District Councils and of Deputy Commissioners' Local Funds in Burma* for 1923–1924, 1925–1926, 1927–1928. 5 vols. Rangoon, 1927–1929.

——. Anglo-Burmese Conference. *Towards a Greater Burma: Speeches on Burma Reconstruction.* Simla, 1944.

——. Education Department. *Annual Report on Public Instruction in Burma,* for 1922–1939. Rangoon, 1923–1940.

——. ——. *Ninth Quinquennial Report on Public Instruction in Burma for the Years 1932–1933 to 1936–1937.* Rangoon, 1938.

——. ——. *Report of the Vernacular Education and Vocational Reorganizational Committee, 1936,* by A. Campbell. Rangoon, 1936.

——. Fiscal Committee. *Interim Report on Local Taxation.* Rangoon, 1940.

——. Home Department. *Final Report of the Riot Inquiry Committee, 1939.* Rangoon, 1939.

——. ——. *Interim Report of the Riot Inquiry Committee.* Rangoon, 1938.

——. ——. *Report of the Bribery and Corruption Enquiry Committee, 1940.* Rangoon, 1941.

——. ——. *Report of the Secretariat Incident Enquiry Committee.* Rangoon, 1939.

——. ——. *Report of the Village Administration Committee, 1941.* Rangoon, 1941.

——. Income Tax Department. *Report on the Administration of the Income-Tax Act in Burma for 1921–1922.* Rangoon, 1923.

——. Intelligence Bureau. *Burma during the Japanese Occupation.* 2 vols. Simla, 1943–1944.

——. Labour Statistics Bureau. *Report of an Enquiry into the Standard of Living and Cost of Living of the Working Classes in Rangoon,* by J. J. Bennison, Rangoon, 1928.

——. Legislative Council. *Proceedings.* Vols. I–XXXII. Rangoon, 1923–1936.

——. Legislature. House of Representatives. *Proceedings.* Vols. I–IV. Rangoon, 1937–1940.

——. Police Department. *Report of the Committee to Advise on Murders and Dacoities.* Rangoon, 1927.

——. ——. *Report of the Police Administration* for 1875–1940. Rangoon, 1876–1941. Published annually.

——. Settlement Department. *Initial Report on the Second Revision Settle-*

ment in the Mandalay District, Season, 1922, by H. F. Searle. Rangoon, 1924.

——. ——. *Pegu District Settlement Report*, by B. O. Binns. Rangoon, 1934.

——. ——. *Report of the Third Revision of the Hanthawaddy District*, by U Tun Gyi. Rangoon, 1934.

——. ——. *Report on the First Regular Settlement Operations in the Myingyan District, Season, 1910–1911*, by John S. Furnivall. Rangoon, 1912.

——. ——. *Report on the Original Settlement Operations in Labutta Township, 1924–1925*, by U Tin Gyi. Rangoon, 1926. An extremely valuable report.

——. ——. *Report on the . . . Settlement of Kyaukpyu District of Arakan Division, Season 1914–1916*, by J. Claque. Rangoon, 1917.

——. ——. *Report on the . . . Settlement of Thaton District, Season, 1908–1911*, by T. Couper. Rangoon, 1911.

——. ——. *Report on the Summary Settlement of . . . Areas in the Pegu and Hanthawaddy Districts*, by Maung Dwe. Rangoon, 1921.

——. ——. *Report on the Third Settlement of the Pyinmana Subdivision of Yamethin District . . . Season 1931–1933*, by R. S. Wilkie. Rangoon, 1933.

Burma, Union of. *Burma and the Insurrections*. Rangoon, 1949. Includes maps.

——. *The Constitution of Burma*. Rangoon, 1947, 1954. In English and Burmese.

——. *Enquiry Commission for Regional Autonomy, Report, 1952*. Rangoon, 1955. In Burmese and English.

——. *The First Interim Report of the Administration Re-organization Committee*. Rangoon, 1949.

——. *Karen Race Special Enquiry Commission Report of 1950*. Rangoon, 1951.

——. *The National Income of Burma*. Rangoon, 1951, 1952.

——. Economic Planning Board. *Two-Year Plan for Economic Development for Burma*. Rangoon, 1948.

——. Ministry of Information. *Burma Speaks: A Collection of Broadcast Talks*. Rangoon, 1950.

——. ——. *Is It a People's Liberation? A Short Survey of Communist Insurrection in Burma*. Rangoon, 1952.

——. ——. *Kuomintang Aggression against Burma*. Rangoon, 1953.

——. ——. *The Pyidawtha Conference, August 4–17, 1952: Resolutions and Speeches*. Rangoon, 1952.

Burma Gazette. Pt. iv (1918), pp. 453–456, 1171–1176. Reflects the rise of national feeling during World War I.

Furnivall, John S. MS. Notes on the *Sambudipa U-Hsaung: Kyam,* or "The Garland of Zambudipa." This is a treatise on the regalia of the government of old Burma compiled around 1762, available in the Bernard Free Library of Rangoon.

Gazetteers. Vol. A of the following reports:

> *Bhamo District,* by Dawson. Rangoon, 1912.
>
> *British Burma.* 2 vols. Rangoon, 1880.
>
> *Insein District,* by Furnivall and Morrison. Rangoon, 1914.
>
> *Mandalay District,* by Searle. Rangoon, 1928.
>
> *Maubin District,* by Tin Gyi. Rangoon, 1931.
>
> *Pegu District,* by Page. Rangoon, 1917.
>
> *Shwebo District,* by Williamson. Rangoon, 1929.
>
> *Thaton District,* by Tin Gyi. Rangoon, 1931.
>
> *Toungoo District,* by ——. Rangoon, 1914.
>
> *Yamethin District,* by Wilkie. Rangoon, 1934.

Great Britain. *Burma: A Statement of Policy by His Majesty's Government, May, 1945.* London, 1945.

——. *British Foreign and State Papers.* Vol. 87. London, 1898.

——. *Burma Criminal Law Amendment Act.* London, 1931.

——. *Conclusions Reached in the Conversations between H.M.G. and the Delegation from the Executive Council of Burma. PP,C,* Cmd. 7029. London, 1947.

——. Burma Reforms Committee. *Record of Evidence.* 3 vols. London, 1922.

——. ——. *Report of the Committee . . . to Make Recommendations . . . in Connection with the Application to Burma of the Provisions of the Government of India Act as Amended in 1919,* Sir A. Frederick Whyte, Chairman. London, 1922.

——. Burma Round Table Conference. *Plenary Sessions, Proceedings.* London, 1932. Also published as *PP,C* (1932), vol. VI, Cmd. 4004.

——. ——. *Proceedings of the Committee of the Whole Conference.* London, 1932.

——. Central Office of Information. *The Campaign in Burma.* London, 1946.

——. India Office. *Government of Burma Act, October, 1935 . . . Memorandum on the Draft Orders and Views of Provincial Governments . . . and on Financial Inquiry of Sir Otto Niemeyer.* Cmd. 5181. London, 1936.

——. ——. *Government of Burma Act, October, 1935.* 26 George V, ch. 3. London, 1936.

——. ——. *Government of India Act, October, 1935.* 26 George V, ch. 3. London, 1936.

——. ——. *Letter from the Government of India to the Secretary of State and Enclosures.* Cmd. 123. London, 1919.

——. ——. *Report of the India Statutory Commission.* Cmd. 3568. London,

1930. Vol. I, *Survey;* vol. II, *Recommendations;* vol. XI, *Memorandum Submitted by the Government of Burma;* vols. XV–XVII, *Extracts from Memoranda and Oral Evidence by Non-officials.*

——. ——. *Report of the Rebellion in Burma Up to 3rd May, 1931, and Communiqué of 19th of May, 1931.* Cmd. 3900. London, 1931.

——. ——. *Report on Indian Constitutional Reforms.* Cmd. 9109. London, 1918. The Montagu-Chelmsford report. Also *PP,C,* (1918), vol. VIII.

——. ——. *Scheme of Constitutional Reform in Burma if Separated from India.* Rangoon, 1933.

——. ——. *Trade and Immigration Relations between India and Burma after the Separation of Burma.* Cmd. 4985. London, 1935.

——. India Office Archives. *Bengal Political Correspondence.* MSS. EUR., D106, "A Description of Hindustan and Adjacent Countries by Walter Hamilton." 2 vols. 1820.

——. ——. ——. MSS. EUR. E63, no. 155, "Deputation to Ava. Season, 1795–1796." Symes's mission in 1795.

——. ——. ——. "Extracts and Observations Respecting the Dominions of Ava Chiefly from a Journal Kept by Dr. Francis Buchanan (now Hamilton) . . . in 1795."

——. ——. *Home Department (Upper Burma) Series.* Vols. 2720 (for 1886), 2966 and 2967 (for 1887), 3203 (for 1888).

——. ——. *India Public Proceedings.* Vols. 1847–1849 (for 1882).

——. ——. *India Secret Proceedings.* Vols. 9 (for 1837), 14 (for 1838), 114 (for 1844), 180 (for 1852), 226 (for 1859).

——. ——. *List of Proceedings . . . for Northwest Provinces and Other Minor Administrations: Index for 1834–1899.* London, 1902. Much of the valuable material listed in this index has not been utilized.

——. ——. "Sketch of the Sinphos or the Kakhyens of Burma" in *Tracts,* vol. 266. Calcutta, 1847.

——. ——. *Views of Local Government on the Working of the Reforms.* London, 1927.

——. ——. Foreign Department. *External Political Proceedings.* Vols. 483 (for 1868), 1218 (for 1878), 1392 (for 1879), 1745 (for 1881), 1924 (for 1882), 2116 (for 1883), 2435 (for 1884). A score or more volumes of this series running from 1885 to 1899 await careful examination.

——. India Round Table Conference, London, 1930–1931. *Proceedings of the Committee of the Whole Conference.* London, 1932.

——. ——. *Proceedings of Sub-Committees.* London, 1931. Pt. ii.

——. ——. *Sub-Committee's Reports, Conference Resolutions, and Prime Minister's Statement.* Cmd. 3772. London, 1931.

——. Parliament. House of Commons. *Debates* for 1917–1938, 1943, 1945–1948.

——. ——. ——. *Sessional Papers.*

1919, vol. III: "Joint Select Committee Report on the Government of India Bill." London, 1919.

1922, vol. XVI, Cmd. 1671: "Correspondence Regarding . . . the Application to Burma of the Provisions of the Government of India Act as Amended in 1919." London, 1922.

1922, vol. XIV, Cmd. 1672: "Draft Rules under the Government of India Act . . . Constituting Burma a Governor's Province under the Act." London, 1922.

1930–1931, vol. XII, Cmd. 3883: "Report of the Royal Commission of Labor in India." London, 1931.

1931–1932, vol. XII, Cmd. 3900: "Report on the Rebellion in Burma up to 3rd May, 1931." London, 1931.

1931–1932, vol. XIX, Cmd. 3997: "Statement on the Moral and Material Progress and Condition of India for 1930–1931." London, 1932.

1932–1933, vol. VI, Cmd. 4004: "Burma Round Table Conference, Plenary Sessions Proceedings." London, 1932.

1932–1933, vol. IX: "Joint Committee on Indian Constitutional Reform: Memorandum by the Secretary of State for India on the Scheme of Constitutional Reform in Burma." London, 1934.

1932–1933, vol. XIX: "Report of the Joint Committee on Indian Constitutional Reform." London, 1934.

1933–1934, vol. I: "Proceedings of the Joint Committee on Indian Constitutional Reform." London, 1934. Pt. I, *Report;* and pt. II, *Proceedings.* A valuable condensation with a special Burma section.

1933–1934, vol. VI: "Joint Committee on Indian Constitutional Reform." London, 1934. Pt. I, *Report.* Contains a special Burma section.

1933–1934, vol. VII: "Records . . . of the Joint Committee on Indian Constitutional Reform." London, 1934. Pts. I and II.

1933–1934, vol. XVII: "Moral and Material Progress and Condition of India during the Year 1932–1933." London, 1934.

1934–1935, vol. IX, Cmd. 5101: "Report by Sir Laurie Hammond on the Delimitation of Constituencies in Burma." London, 1935.

1935–1936, vol. XIX: "The Burma Criminal Law Amendment Act, 1936." London, 1936.

1944–1945, vol. X, Cmd. 6635: "Burma: A Statement of Policy by His Majesty's Government, May, 1945." London, 1945.

1947–1948, vol. XVI, Cmd. 7240 and Cmd. 7360: "Treaty between the Government of Burma regarding the Recognition of Burmese Independence." London, 1948.

——. Treaties. "Agreement between the Governments of the United Kingdom . . . Australia, India, Pakistan, Ceylon, and the Government of the Union of Burma regarding a Loan to Burma." Rangoon, London, 1950.

India. Census Commissioner. *Census of India, 1931.* Vol. XI, *Burma.* Rangoon, 1933.

Richardson, D. *The Damathat; or The Laws of Menoo.* Trans. from the Burmese. 2nd ed. Rangoon, 1874.

United States. Information Service. "Review of Burmese Press Comment." Rangoon. A weekly.

——. Office of Strategic Services. *Japanese Administration of Burma.* Washington, 1944.

——. ——. *Japanese Development of Burma's Economy.* Washington, 1945.

——. ——. *The Problem of Law and Order in Burma under British Administration.* Washington, 1944.

——. ——. *The Structure of the Government of Burma.* Washington, 1944.

III. PRIMARY SOURCES: ACCOUNTS BY PARTICIPANTS

A.F.P.F.L. *From Fascist Bondage to New Democracy: The New Burma in the New World.* Rangoon, 1945.

Appleton, George. "The Burmese Viewpoint," *Asiatic Review,* XLIV (1946), 233–246.

Ba Gyan. "The All Burma Youth League," *Burma,* III (1953), 56–60.

Baldwin, J. W. "The Karens in Burma," *Journal of Royal Central Asiatic Society,* XXXVI (1949), 102–113.

Ba Maw. *Burma's New Order Plan.* Rangoon, 1944.

Ba Swe. *The Burmese Revolution.* Rangoon, 1952.

——. "The Pattern of the Burmese Revolution," *Burma,* II (1952), 1–12.

Bigandet, Father. *An Outline of the History of the Catholic Burmese Mission from the Year 1720 to 1887.* Rangoon, 1887.

Brown, George E. R. Grant. *Burma as I Saw It, 1889–1917, with a Chapter on Recent Events.* New York, 1925.

Browne, Horace Albert. *Reminiscences of the Court of Mandalay: Extracts from the Diary of General H. A. Brown, 1859–1879.* Woking, 1907.

Burchett, Wilfred. *Bombs over Burma.* Melbourne, 1944. A vivid, firsthand account.

Burma Chamber of Commerce. *Minutes of the Proceedings of the Annual General Meeting, February 27, 1947.* Rangoon, 1947.

Butler, Sir Spencer Harcourt. *Speeches.* Allabahad, 1923; Rangoon, 1927.

Collis, Maurice. *Trials in Burma,* London, 1945. Perceptive and pro-Burman.

Cox, Hiram. *Journal of a Residence in the Burmhan Empire and More Particularly at the Court of Amarapoorah.* London, 1821.

Craddock, Sir Reginald. *Speeches by Sir Reginald Craddock, 1917–1922.* Rangoon, 1924.

Crawford, J. *Journal of an Embassy from the Governor General of India to the Court of Ava in the Year 1827.* 2 vols. London, 1834.

Crosthwaite, Sir Charles. *The Pacification of Burma*. London, 1912.

Fitch, Ralph. *The Voyage of Mr. Ralph Fitch Merchant of London, to Ormuz and So to Goa in the East Indies, 1583 to 1591. In Pinkerton's Voyages*, vol. IX. London, 1811.

Fytche, Lieut. Gen. Albert. *Burma, Past and Present with Personal Reminiscences of the Country*. 2 vols. London, 1878. Vol. I is especially informative.

Geary, Grattan. *Burma, after the Conquest, Viewed in Its Political, Social, and Commercial Aspects, from Mandalay*. London, 1886.

Gouger, Henry. *Personal Narrative of Two Years' Imprisonment in Burmah*. London, 1860. This fortune hunter's memory is hazy sometimes.

Hamilton, Duke of. *A New Account of the East Indies . . . 1688 to 1723*. London, 1727. In Pinkerton's *Voyages*, vol. VIII. London, 1811.

Luther, Calista Vinton. *The Vintons and the Karens: Memorials of Rev. Justus H. Vinton and Calista Vinton*. Boston, 1880.

Malcom, Howard. *Travels in Southeastern Asia, Embracing Hindustan, Malaya, Siam, and China, and a Full Account of the Burman Empire*. 2 vols. Boston, 1839. Very useful descriptive account.

Marks, Dr. *Forty Years in Burma*. London, 1917.

Minto, Countess of. *India, Minto, and Morley, 1905–1910*. New York, London, 1934.

Mountbatten of Burma, Vice Admiral Earl. *Report to the Combined Chiefs of Staff by the Supreme Allied Commander S.E. Asia, 1943–1945*. New York, 1951. Excellent on the Burma campaign and on inter-Allied relations.

Nu, Thakin. *Burma under the Japanese, Pictures and Portraits*. London and New York, 1954. The most useful of Nu's contributions.

——. *Forward with the People*. Rangoon, 1951.

——. *From Peace to Stability*. Speeches from August, 1949 to April, 1951. Rangoon, 1951.

——. *Towards Peace and Democracy*. Rangoon, 1949.

——. *Translation of the . . . Prime Minister's Speech*. . . . Rangoon, 1950.

Phayre, Sir Arthur P. "Phayre's Private Journal of his Mission to Ava in 1855," *Journal of the Burma Research Society*, XXII (1932), 68–89.

Sangermano, Father Vincentius. *A Description of the Burmese Empire*. Trans. by William Tondy. Rome, 1833; Rangoon, 1885.

Seagrave, Gordon S. *Burma Surgeon*. New York, 1943.

Symes, Michael. *An Account of an Embassy to the Kingdom of Ava*. London, 1800.

Thein Pe, Thakin. *What Happened in Burma*. Allabahad, 1943.

Tun Pe. *Sun over Burma*. Rangoon, 1949.

——. *Why I Resigned from the Cabinet, Statement before Press Conference on August 13, 1953*. Rangoon, 1953.

Wheeler, J. Talboys. *Journal of a Voyage up the Irrawaddy to Mandalay and Bhamo*. Rangoon, 1871.

White, Sir Herbert Thirkell. *A Civil Servant in Burma*. London, 1913. One of the better accounts.

Williams, Clement. *Through Burma to Western China, Being Notes of a Journey in 1863*. London, 1868.

Yule, Sir Henry. *A Narrative of the Mission Sent by the Governor-General of India to the Court of Ava in 1855 with Notices of the Country, Government and People*. London, 1858. A classic description.

IV. NEWSPAPER SOURCES

British newspaper clippings covering 1919–1953, available in the Chatham House Archives, Dean's Court, Westminster, London: *Daily Express, Daily Herald, Daily News, Daily Telegraph, Daily Worker, Evening Standard, Financial News, Financial Times, Herald* (Glasgow), *The Hindu* (Madras), Manchester *Guardian, News Chronicle, Observer, Scotsman, Straits Times* (Singapore), *The Times* (London), *Yorkshire Post*.

Burman newspapers in English, available at Rangoon and Washington: *The Burman, Guide Daily, Nation, New Burma, New Light of Burma, New Times of Burma, Oway, The Progress, Sun, Tribune, Voice of the Union*.

United States newspapers: *Christian Science Monitor*, New York *Herald Tribune*, New York *Times*.

V. SECONDARY ACCOUNTS

Andrew, E. J. L. *Indian Labour in Rangoon*. London, 1933. A revealing close-up view of a deplorable situation.

Andrus, J. Russell. *Burmese Economic Life*. Stanford, 1948. A standard description of the economy of prewar Burma.

Appleton, George. "Burma Two Years after Liberation," *International Affairs*, XXIII (1947), 510–520.

Ba Han, Maung. *A Legal History of India and Burma*. Rangoon, 1952.

Baxter, James. *The Report on Indian Immigration*. Rangoon, 1941. An excellent study containing valuable statistical tables.

Bayfield, G. T. *Historical Review of the Political Relations between the British Government in India and the Empire of Ava*. Calcutta, 1835. A useful account, but highly partisan. The author was a member of the British Residency in Burma in the early 1830's.

Bell, Henry G. *An Account of the Burman Empire*. Calcutta, 1852.

Bigg-Wither, Col. F. "Cleaning Up Burma's Murder Zone," *Contemporary Review*, vol. 156 (1939), pp. 715–722.

Brown, D. Mackenzie. *The White Umbrella: Indian Political Thought from Manu to Ghandi*. Berkeley, Los Angeles, 1953. An excellent short treatise including excerpts from standard sources.

Brown, W. Norman. *The United States and India and Pakistan*. Cambridge, Mass., 1953.

Butler, Sir Spencer Harcourt. "Burma and Its Problems," *Foreign Affairs,* X (1932), 654 ff.

Cady, John F. "Conflicting Attitudes toward Burma," *Far Eastern Survey,* XV (1946), 27–31.

——. "Economic Development in Burma," *Far Eastern Survey,* XV (1946), 1–4.

——. "Religion and Politics in Modern Burma," *Far Eastern Quarterly,* XIV (1953), 149–162.

——. *The Roots of French Imperialism in Eastern Asia.* Ithaca, N.Y., 1954.

Cady, John F., Barnett, Patricia G., and Jenkins, Shirley. *The Development of Self-Rule and Independence in Burma, Malaya, and the Philippines.* New York, 1948.

Callis, Helmut G. *Foreign Capital in Southeast Asia.* New York, 1942.

Cambridge History of India, The. Cambridge, Eng., 1929. Vols. V and VI.

Carter, R. R. Langham. See Langham-Carter, R. R.

Chailley-Bert, Joseph. "Les Anglais en Birmanie" in *La Colonisation de l'Indo-Chine: L'experience anglaise.* Paris, 1892, pt. II, pp. 155–392.

Chatham House Paper no. IV. London, 1943.

Christian, John Leroy. *Modern Burma: A Survey of Political and Economic Development.* London, 1943. Pro-British in tone.

Coast, John. *Railroad of Death.* London, 1946.

Cochrane, Sir Archibald. "Burma in Wartime," *Asiatic Review,* XXXVII (1941), 691–694.

Collis, Maurice. *Last and First in Burma (1941–1948).* London, 1956.

——. *Into Hidden Burma.* London, 1953. The least valuable of Collis' books.

"Colonial Issue, The," *Economist,* vol. 148 (1945), pp. 401–403.

Craddock, Sir Reginald. *Dilemma in India.* London, 1929.

Crow, Sir Henry. "Burma," *Asiatic Review,* XXXVIII (1942), 260–262.

Dautremer, Joseph. *Burma under British Rule.* Trans. by Sir George Scott. n.d.

de Huszar, George B. *Soviet Power and Policy.* New York, 1954. Ch. XIX.

Desai, W. S. "Events at the Court of Ava during the First Anglo-Burmese War," *JBRS,* XXVII (1937), 1–14.

——. *History of the British Residency in Burma, 1826–1840.* Rangoon, 1939. A scholarly account based on British sources.

——. *India and Burma.* Bombay, Calcutta, 1954. Fair-minded and informed in its point of view.

——. "The Karens of Burma," *India Quarterly,* VI (1950), 276–282.

——. "The Rebellion of Prince Tharrawaddy and the Deposition of Bagyidaw, King of Burma, 1837," *JBRS,* XXV (1935), 109–120.

Donnison, F. S. V. *Public Administration in Burma.* London, 1953. A British-viewpoint description of the evolution of British administration in Burma.

Editorial. *Burma,* III (April, 1953).

Eldridge, Fred. *Wrath in Burma.* New York, 1946.

Elsbree, Willard. *Japan's Role in Southeast Asia, 1940–1945*. Cambridge, Mass., 1953.

Emerson, Rupert. *Government and Nationalism in Southeast Asia*. New York, 1942.

Enriquez, C. M. D. *Races of Burma*. Delhi, 1933. Comp. for the Government of India.

——. "Story of the Migrations," *JBRS*, XIII, pt. II (1923), 77–81.

Feiling, Keith. *A History of England*. London, 1949.

Ferrars, Max and Bertha. *Burma*. London, 1900.

Fielding-Hall, Harold. *A People at School*. London, 1906, 1913. A sympathetic and understanding book.

——. *The Soul of a People*. London, 1899.

Forbes, C. J. F. S. *British Burma and Its Peoples*. London, 1878.

Foucar, E. C. V. *They Reigned in Mandalay*. London, 1946. Contains valuable information, but account is marred by anti-Burmese prejudices.

Furnivall, John Sydenham. "Burma, Past and Present," *Far Eastern Survey*, XXII (1953), 21–26.

——. *Colonial Policy and Practice: A Comparative Study of Burma and Netherlands Indies*. New York, 1948, 1956. A good evaluation of colonialism.

——. "Communism and Nationalism in Burma," *Far Eastern Survey*, XVIII (1949), 193–197.

——. *Education and Social Progress in Southeast Asia*. New York, 1943.

——. "The Fashioning of Leviathan: The Beginnings of British Rule in Burma," *JBRS*, XXIX (1939), 1–137. Excellent and amusing.

——. *An Introduction to the Political Economy of Burma*. Rev. by J. R. Andrus. Rangoon, 1938.

——. *Progress and Welfare in Southeast Asia*. New York, 1941. Concerns the problem of reintegrating a plural society.

——. "Reconstruction in Burma," MS., 1943. Prepared for the Simla government's Reconstruction Committee.

——. "Twenty-five Years: A Retrospect and Prospect," *JBRS*, XXV (1935), 40–47.

——. "Twilight in Burma: Independence and After," *Pacific Affairs*, XXII (1949), 155–172.

——. "Twilight in Burma: Reconquest and Crisis," *Pacific Affairs*, XXII (1949), 3–20.

Great Britain and the East, Oct. 23, 1943. London.

Griffiths, Sir Percival. "Burma and Her Neighbors Today," *Asiatic Review*, n.s., XLVI (1950), 1063–1079.

Hackett, William Dunn. "The Pa-O People of the Shan State, Union of Burma." Cornell University thesis, 1953.

Hall, D. G. E. *Burma*. London, 1950. A brief account, good on the early history.

——. *Europe and Burma: A Study of European Relations with Burma to the Annexation of Thibaw's Kingdom, 1886.* London, New York, 1945, 1946.

——. *A History of South-East Asia.* London, New York, 1955. A basic study.

——. Introductory chapter to *Michael Symes: Journal of His Second Embassy to the Court of Ava in 1802.* London, 1955.

——. "New Light upon British Relations with King Mindon," *JBRS,* XVIII (1928), 1–11.

Hanks, L. M., Jr. "The Quest for Individual Autonomy in Burmese Personality," *Psychiatry,* XII (1949), 285 ff.

Harris, Edward Norman. "The Conservation of a Race as a Missionary By-product," *Biblioteca Sacra,* LXXVII (1920), 147–164.

Harvey, G. E. *British Rule in Burma, 1824–1942.* London, 1946.

——. *History of Burma from the Earliest Times to 10 March 1824, the Beginning of the English Conquest.* London, 1925.

——. *Outline of Burmese History.* Bombay, 1954.

Heine-Geldern, Robert. "Conceptions of State and Kingship in Southeast Asia." Cornell University Southeast Asia Data Paper, no. 18, 1956.

Hendershot, Clarence. "The Conquest, Pacification, and Administration of the Shan States by the British, 1886–1897." University of Chicago thesis, 1936.

Hinners, David G. "British Policy and the Development of Self-Government in Burma, 1935–1948." University of Chicago thesis, 1951. A very useful study.

Hla Baw. "Superstitions of Burmese Criminals," *JBRS,* XXX (1940), 376–383.

Htin Aung. "Customary Law in Burma" in *Southeast Asia in the Coming World.* Ed. by Philip Warren Thayer. Baltimore, 1953.

Hunter, W. *A Concise Account of the Kingdom of Pegu.* Calcutta, London, 1789. A rare and valuable book.

Innes, Charles. "The Separation of Burma," *Asiatic Review,* n.s., XXX (1934), 193–215.

Intow, E. Burke. "The Constitution of Burma," *Far Eastern Survey,* XVII (1948), 264–267.

Jesse, Fryniwyd Tennyson. *The Story of Burma.* London, 1946.

Jones, F. C. *Japan's New Order in East Asia: Its Rise and Fall, 1937–1945.* London, 1954. A useful book based on Japanese evidence.

Judson College. *Annual Report, 1921–1922.* Rangoon, 1922.

Kannampilly, K. M. "Parties and Politics in Burma," *India Quarterly,* III (1947), 238–244.

Klimov, A. "What Is Happening in Burma?" *Soviet Press Translations* (Seattle), II (1947), 140–142.

Knappen, Tippetts, and Abbott Engineering Company, associated with Pierce Management, Inc., and Robert Nathan Associates, Inc. *Preliminary Report on Economic and Engineering Survey of Burma.* Rangoon, 1952.

BIBLIOGRAPHY

Kyaw Min, *The Burma We Love*. Calcutta, 1945.

Kyaw Thet. Recorded lecture at Rangoon-Hopkins Center. Rangoon, 1954.

Langham-Carter, R. R. "The Burmese Army," *JBRS*, XXVII (1937), 254–276.

——. "Burmese Rule on the Toungoo Frontier," *JBRS*, XXVII (1937), 15–31.

——. "U Htaung Bo's Rebellion," *JBRS*, XXVI (1936), 33 ff.

Laurie, W. F. B. *Ashé Pyee, the Superior Country; or, The Great Attractions of Burma to British Enterprise and Commerce*. London, 1882.

——. *General A. Fytche's Administration of British Burma, with Notes on Opening Trade with South-West China*. London, 1873.

Law Yone, Edward, and Mandelbaum, David G. "The New Nation of Burma," *Far Eastern Survey*, XIX (1950), 189–194.

——. "Pacification in Burma," *Far Eastern Survey*, XIX (1950), 182–187.

Leach, E. R. *Political Systems of Highland Burma*. London, 1954.

Leach, F. Burton. *The Future of Burma*. Rangoon, 1936.

——. *The Problem of Burma*. London, 1945.

Lewis, James Lee. "Self-supporting Karen Churches in Burma." Central Baptist Seminary thesis, 1946.

Lloyd, John. "Planning a Welfare State in Burma," *International Labour Review*, LXX (Aug., 1954), 117–148.

Loo Nee, Sydney; Po Chit; Tha Din; and Ba U Gyi. *The Case for the Karens*. London, 1946.

McAuley, James. "Paradoxes of Development in the South Pacific," *Pacific Affairs*, XXVII (1954), 144–149.

McKelvie, Roy. *The War in Burma*. London, 1948. A labored British rebuttal of alleged U.S. claims concerning the importance of the Stilwell campaign.

MacKenzie, Kenneth R. H. *Burma and the Burmese*. London, 1853. Informative but anti-Burmese in tone.

McMahon, A. R. *The Karens of the Golden Chersonese*. London, 1876.

Marshall, Harry I. *The Karen Peoples of Burma*. Columbus, O., 1922. A detailed description of Karen traditions.

Maung Maung. *Burma in the Family of Nations*. Amsterdam, 1956.

——. "Burma Looks Ahead," *Pacific Affairs*, XXV (1952), 40–48.

——. *Burma's Teething Times*. Rangoon, 1949.

Maung Pye. *Burma in the Crucible*. Rangoon, 1951.

Mende, Tibore. *South East Asia between Two Worlds*. London, 1955.

Mi Mi Khaing. *The Burmese Family*. Bombay, 1946.

Mitton, G. E. *Scott of the Shan Hills*. London, 1936.

Mootham, Orby Howell. *Burmese Buddhist Law*. Oxford, 1939.

Morrison, Ian. *Grandfather Longlegs: The Life and Gallant Death of Major H. P. Seagrim*. London, 1947.

Moscotti, Albert D. "British Policy in Burma, 1917–1937: A Study in the Development of Colonial Self-Rule." Yale University dissertation, 1950. A useful survey.

664

Mya Sein, Ma. *Administration of Burma: Sir Charles Crosthwaite and the Consolidation of Burma*. Rangoon, 1938.

Nisbet, John. *Burmah under British Rule and Before*. 2 vols. London, 1901.

Nu, Thakin. "Man the Wolf of Man." Unpublished MS.

Owen, Frank. *The Campaign in Burma, Prepared for the South-East Asia Command by the Central Office of Information*. London, 1946.

Po, Sir San C. *Burma and the Karens*. London, 1928.

Po Lat. "Union Culture: Its Sources and Contacts," *Burma*, III (Oct., 1953).

Purser, W. C. B. *Christian Missions in Burma*. London, 1911, 1913.

Scott, Sir James George. *Burma as It Was, as It Is, and as It Will Be*. London, 1886.

——. *Burma from the Earliest Times to the Present Day*. London, 1924, 1925.

——. *The Burman: His Life and Notions*. By Shway Yoe. London, 1882, 1896, 1910. A standard treatise on Burmese traditions.

Scott, Sir James George, and Hardiman, J. P. *Gazetteer of Upper Burma and the Shan States*. 5 vols. Rangoon, 1900–1901. A mine of information on Upper Burma since the time of the kings.

Sen, N. C. *A Peep into Burma Politics (1917–1942)*. Allahabad, 1945.

Shway Yoe, pseud. *See* Scott, Sir James George, *The Burman*.

Singh, Ganga. *Burma Parliamentary Companion*. Rangoon, 1940. Contains useful miscellaneous information.

Smeaton, Donald Mackenzie. *The Loyal Karens of Burma*. London, 1887, 1920. Smeaton argues for Karen nationhood and their alliance with Britain.

Smith-Forbes, Capt. C. J. F. S. *British Burma and Its People*. London, 1878.

Sparks, Robert Merrill. "The Nationalization Plans of Burma." Temple University master's thesis, 1949.

Stuart, J. "Why Is Burma Sparsely Populated?" *JBRS*, IV (1914), 1–6.

Sutton, Walter D., Jr. "U Aung San of Burma," *South Atlantic Quarterly*, XLVII (1948), 1–16.

Swithinbank, B. W. "Responsible Government in Burma, 1937–1941: Summary and Discussion," *Asiatic Review*, XXXIX (1943), 153–160.

Thompson, Virginia. "Burma's Communists," *Far Eastern Survey*, XVII (1948), 103–105.

Thompson, Virginia, and Adloff, Richard. *The Left Wing in Southeast Asia*. New York, 1950.

Tinker, Hugh. *Foundations of Local Self-Government in India, Pakistan, and Burma*. London, 1954. A definitive work, crystal clear.

Trager, Frank N. *Toward a Welfare State in Burma: Economic Reconstruction and Development, 1948–1954*. New York, 1954.

UNESCO Educational Mission. *Report of the Mission to Burma, May, 1951*, by R. M. Tisinger C. L. Hernandez, and F. T. Fairey. Paris, 1952.

Warren, C. V. *Burmese Interlude*. London, 1937.

White, Sir Herbert Thirkell. *Burma*. Cambridge, Eng., 1923.

Windmiller, Marshall. "Linguistic Regionalism in India," *Pacific Affairs,* XXVII (1954), 291–318.

Wint, Guy. "The Aftermath of Imperialism," *Pacific Affairs,* XXII (1949), 63–69.

———. *The British in India.* London, 1947. A careful assessment of British rule in India.

Yaravoy, V. "The Situation in Burma," *Soviet Press Translations* (Seattle), II (1947), 1–3. From *Izvestia,* Jan. 31, 1947.

Zinkin, Maurice, *Asia and the West.* London, 1951. Zinkin follows Wint's lead.

Index

667